THE COMPLETE CANADIAN SMALL BUSINESS GUIDE

Fourth Edition

Bestselling Books by Douglas Gray

REAL ESTATE TITLES

- *The Canadian Landlord's Guide (Expert Advice to Become a Profitable Real Estate Investor)* (with Peter Mitham)
- *Making Money in Real Estate (The Canadian Guide to Profitable Investment in Residential Property)*
- *Real Estate Investing for Canadians for Dummies* (with Peter Mitham)
- *The Canadian Guide to Buying and Owning Recreational Property in Canada*
- *101 Street-Smart Condo-Buying Tips for Canadians*
- *Mortgages Made Easy (The All-Canadian Guide to Home Financing)*
- *Home Buying Made Easy (The Canadian Guide to Purchasing a Newly-Built or Pre-Owned Home)*
- *Condo Buying Made Easy (The Canadian Guide to Apartment and Townhouse Condos, Co-ops and Timeshares)*
- *Mortgage Payment Tables Made Easy (A Complete Canadian Guide)*
- *The Complete Canadian Home Inspection Guide* (with Ed Witzke)

SMALL BUSINESS TITLES

- *Start and Run a Profitable Consulting Business*
- *Start and Run a Profitable Business Using Your Computer*
- *Have You Got What It Takes? (The Entrepreneur's Complete Self-Assessment Guide)*
- *Marketing Your Product* (with Donald Cyr)
- *The Complete Canadian Small Business Guide* (with Diana Gray)
- *Home Inc. (The Canadian Home-Based Business Guide)* (with Diana Gray)
- *Raising Money (The Canadian Guide to Successful Business Financing)* (with Brian Nattress)
- *The Complete Canadian Franchise Guide* (with Norm Friend)
- *So You Want to Buy a Franchise?* (with Norm Friend)
- *Be Your Own Boss (The Ultimate Guide to Buying a Small Business or Franchise in Canada)* (with Norm Friend)
- *The Canadian Small Business Legal Advisor*

PERSONAL FINANCE/RETIREMENT PLANNING TITLES

- *Risk-Free Retirement (The Complete Canadian Planning Guide)* (with Tom Delaney, Graham Cunningham, Les Solomon, and Dr. Des Dwyer)
- *The Canadian Snowbird Guide (Everything You Need to Know about Living Part-time in the U.S.A. and Mexico)*
- *The Canadian Guide to Will and Estate Planning (What you Need to Know Today to Protect Your Wealth and your Family Tomorrow)* (with John Budd)

SOFTWARE PROGRAMS

- *Making Money in Real Estate* (jointly developed by Douglas Gray and Phoenix Accrual Corporation), along with instructional manual, and published by McGraw-Hill Ryerson

THE COMPLETE CANADIAN SMALL BUSINESS GUIDE

Fourth Edition

DOUGLAS GRAY and DIANA GRAY

New York   Chicago   San Francisco   Lisbon
London   Madrid   Mexico City   Milan   New Delhi
San Juan   Seoul   Singapore   Sydney   Toronto

The McGraw·Hill Companies

1 2 3 4 5 6 7 8 9 0   DOC/DOC   1 8 7 6 5 4 3 2

ISBN: 978-0-07-178471-9
MHID: 0-07-178471-3
e-ISBN: 978-0-07-178472-6
e-MHID: 0-07-178472-1

Care has been taken to trace ownership of copyright material contained in this text; however, the publisher will welcome any information that enables them to rectify any reference or credit for subsequent editions.

The material in this publication is provided for information purposes only. Laws, regulations and procedures are constantly changing, and the examples given are intended to be general guidelines only. This book is sold with the understanding that neither the authors nor the publisher is engaged in rendering professional advice. It is recommended that legal, accounting, tax, and other advice or assistance be obtained before acting on any information contained in this book. Personal services of a competent professional should be sought.

Library and Archives Canada Cataloguing in Publication

Gray, Douglas A.
The complete Canadian small business guide / Douglas Gray
& Diana Gray. — 4th ed.

Includes bibliographical references and index.
ISBN 978-0-07-178471-9

1. Small business — Canada. 2. New business enterprises — Canada.
3. Small business — Canada — Management. 4. New business enterprises —
Canada — Management. I. Gray, Diana Lynn II. Title. III. Title: Canadian
small business guide.

HD62.7.G73 2013   658.02'2   C2012-907971-5

Printed on acid-free paper.

To all those Canadian entrepreneurs, existing and potential, who have the desire to turn the dream of being self-employed into a reality

and

To all those counsellors, advisors, and instructors in the public, private, and educational sectors who encourage and nurture the entrepreneurial spirit in Canada

and

To all those thousands of business clients and seminar students throughout Canada, who have shared their insights and experiences with us.

Contents

Acknowledgments

We are indebted to the thousands of Canadian entrepreneurs and business clients who have shared their ideas and experiences with us over the years through our seminars, consulting practice, or business relationships.

We are also grateful for the assistance given us by many government and other representatives throughout Canada, who by their enthusiasm and dedication contribute to successful enterprise creation. These individuals come from diverse sectors, including federal and provincial government departments and agencies, the Business Development Bank of Canada, major chartered banks, colleges, universities, and the Canadian Federation of Independent Business.

Many thanks to Jonathan McNair of Wolridge Mahan in Vancouver for his input on Chapter 17 dealing with insolvency, bankruptcy, and receivership. Jonathan is a chartered accountant and trustee in bankruptcy. Thanks also to Ken Chong, chartered accountant, of DMCL, Chartered Accountants in Vancouver, for his review of Chapter 6 on tax considerations, and Matthew Gosden, chartered accountant of DMCL, for his review of Chapter 3 on understanding financial statements. We appreciate the kind assistance of Gary Arkin and Graham Honsa of Moffat and Company/Macera and Jarzyna, Barristers and Solicitors, and Patent and Trademark Agents in Ottawa. Gary and Graham are lawyers and intellectual property experts who kindly reviewed Chapter 18 on patent, trademark, copyright, and industrial design.

Thanks to Tony Wanless, freelance business writer and consultant, who reviewed and updated Chapters 12 (Business Communication Equipment), 13 (Marketing), and 19 (Using the Internet for Business Success). We thank the Canadian Franchise Association for kindly letting us use their excellent research on the current franchise legislation in Canada.

We acknowledge the kind permission given by Industry Canada and Public Works and Government Services Canada to use material from their excellent publications relating to patents, trademarks, copyright, and industrial design.

We would like to express our appreciation for the superb research skills exhibited by Charlotte Kates in the updating of the Appendix material.

Last, but not least, we would like to thank the staff at McGraw-Hill Ryerson for their patience, encouragement, and invaluable assistance.

Preface to the Fourth Edition

Over the 25 years since the original edition of *The Complete Canadian Small Business Guide* was published, we have been gratified at the positive and constructive feedback and suggestions we have received. We have attempted to incorporate as much feedback as possible in subsequent editions of the book.

In this new, revised, updated, and expanded fourth edition, we have made substantial changes to make the book relevant and current.

We wish all of you continuing success and satisfaction in your entrepreneurial journeys.

If you wish to provide us with your suggestions for improvements for the next edition, please refer to the "Reader Input" section under "About the Authors." Please check out our website at: smallbiz.ca. It is our hope that we may meet you at one of our seminars.

Preface to Previous Editions

This book was born out of a desire to encourage Canadians to consider the joys and challenge of entrepreneurship. It was written for those considering a new venture, and for those who have already embarked on the entrepreneurial adventure. There are very few practical small business books written *for* Canadians *by* Canadians. What makes this book unique is its comprehensive coverage of the key areas essential to small business success. The book is based on the authors' combined personal experience of over forty years as small business owners, and the authors' vicarious experience through consulting and speaking to thousands of entrepreneurs who have made the commitment to be their own boss. The book also includes the most current information available based on extensive research on all aspects of successful small business management.

Each chapter in this book is self-contained, although certain chapters naturally interconnect with others. As in any business operation, every decision has to be viewed in the context of the effect it will have on other areas of the operation.

It would be helpful for the reader to review the contents and the samples and checklists at the outset, to gain an overview of the benefits of the book. The book also includes a master checklist, action plan checklist, glossary, list of websites, list of key federal and provincial government departments, and sources of further information.

There are many definitions of an entrepreneur. *The Concise Oxford Dictionary* describes an entrepreneur as "a person in effective control of a commercial undertaking; one who undertakes a business or enterprise, with chance of profit or loss." A simple but accurate description.

Whether you intend to work at your business part-time or full-time or out of your home, office, store, or plant, this book will help guide you toward your personal and business profit goals.

We hope you enjoy reading this book and find the information and insights helpful and encouraging.

Douglas Gray and Diana Gray
Vancouver, B.C.
Web: smallbiz.ca

List of Samples and Checklists

Chapter 1

Starting a Small Business

Enthusiasm finds the opportunities, and energy makes the most of them.

— Henry S. Haskins

There are many reasons why you might be reading this book. Maybe you have always dreamed about having your own business, and the timing is now right for you to consider it more seriously. Possibly you have been recently laid off or have just retired. Friends of yours may have started up a business part-time or out of their home, and have been talking to you about it. It may be you are just frustrated at the insecurity, lack of challenge, or potential for advancement in working for a large institution. Possibly you already own your own business and want to be better informed in areas that are important to you.

The decision to go into your own business may be one of the most important career decisions you make, with implications affecting all aspects of your life. Many people are impeded from proceeding any further than the dream by fear of failure, risk, or uncertainty. Fear of failure is a legitimate concern, as studies indicate that over 75% of all new firms will fail within 3 years of start-up. One of the main reasons is lack of knowledge. This book will therefore provide you with that survival edge.

Small business in Canada is a vital part of the economy and fabric of our society. The small business sector accounts for a massive portion of the country's gross national product (GNP), and creates the majority of all new jobs. Approximately 85% of all employment is created by small business. On average, over 350,000 small businesses register for the first time every year. This number, of course, varies depending on the economy and other factors, and includes proprietorships, partnerships, and corporations. The estimate is based on statistics from provincial government proprietorship and partnership registrations, as well as provincial and federal new incorporations. In many cases, the small business person does not show up in provincial or federal statistics because he or she is self-employed and has no employees, or has not registered the business. At the same time, there are a substantial number of businesses that cease to operate every year, many of which do not show up in statistics.

The small business sector is a dynamic, innovative, and growing force that provides challenge, fulfillment, and financial security to over one million small business owners in Canada. Studies show that over 75% of these small businesses have fewer than five employees. There are many definitions of what constitutes a small business. The Canadian Federation of Independent Business (CFIB) generally uses the number of employees as a yardstick, with independently owned firms with up to twenty employees considered as small businesses.

This book has attempted to minimize the potential risk in starting up a small business. It will not only be a practical guide for you, but a reference source for future needs as your business grows. Not all the chapters may be appropriate for your needs at this stage, and the chapters do not have to be read in sequence. Other parts of the book are designed to provide you with further practical assistance, including the appendices, glossary, samples, and checklists. At the very back of the book, there is a section entitled "Reader Input." Our contact numbers, e-mail, and address are noted, as is our website. We would appreciate any feedback you have for improvement. You also might like more information about our seminars or consulting services.

This chapter will cover:

- the advantages and disadvantages of small business ownership
- the traits of successful entrepreneurs
- self-assessment
- recognizing consumer and business trends
- sources and types of business opportunities
- evaluating business opportunities
- choosing a business
- women in business
- home-based businesses
- dealing with growth and expansion of your business.

ADVANTAGES AND DISADVANTAGES OF SMALL BUSINESS OWNERSHIP

Many people have an idealized picture of the rewards of running your own business. There are benefits, of course, but there are also risks and frustrations. It is important to objectively look at both sides in order to make realistic decisions.

Advantages of Going into Business

You have the opportunity of making more money working for yourself than by being an employee. You have no ceiling on your potential income, as it is limited only by your energy, management skill, and good judgment. However, studies show that making money is not one of the main motivating factors of small business owners.

- You have the opportunity to satisfy your creative drive. Studies show that small businesses are more creative, productive, and responsive to changing conditions in the marketplace than are large corporations.
- You can't be laid off. In that sense, you have job security as long as your business is successful.
- You have definite tax advantages over people who are not self-employed.
- You set your own priorities as the decision-maker. You have control over your own destiny, as you are the only person responsible for the success of your company.
- Your workday will not be routine, as you are constantly faced with a variety of challenges.
- You have the opportunity to see your ideas through to completion.
- You have the opportunity to control the nature and direction of your own future.
- You have flexible work hours that can accommodate your personal and lifestyle needs.
- You can determine your own style of work environment.
- You will receive prestige, status, and recognition if your business is successful.

Disadvantages of Going into Business

- Your income may be irregular, depending on the nature of the business, the economy, competition, and other variables.
- Your involvement with the business is generally very time-consuming, especially during the early start-up years. This tends to have the effect of reducing time with friends or family, and recreation time.
- You will be under pressure to succeed from family, friends, investors, and creditors, because you have invested so much time, energy, and money.
- In most cases, you must commit considerable financial resources towards the operation of your business. This could vary, of course, depending on partnership or investor involvement or bank financing. Home-based businesses tend to require less start-up capital.
- You are faced with the risk of losing all your money in the business venture due to circumstances outside your control. Factors such as health, family, marital and partnership issues, and competition problems may not always be avoidable or predictable.
- You must be conversant and deal effectively with various management areas at the same time, in order to maintain proper control over the business, especially in the early stages.
- Considerable paperwork may be required by various levels of government, which represents non-revenue-generating time and expense.

TRAITS OF A SUCCESSFUL ENTREPRENEUR

What kind of person becomes an entrepreneur? What characteristics must a successful entrepreneur have? Whether people are born with these traits or learn them is material for good debate, but what we do know from numerous studies is that successful entrepreneurs tend to have several important personality characteristics in common. They are often strong individualists—optimistic and resourceful—and they usually have a high degree of problem-solving ability. There are many other traits that describe an entrepreneur, some of which are listed below.

- **Strong goal orientation.** Ability to set clear goals that are challenging but attainable; ability to continually re-evaluate and adjust goals to make sure they are consistent with one's interests, talents, and values, as well as personal or business needs. Rather than being content with the attainment of goals, successful entrepreneurs enjoy the challenge that setting new goals brings.
- **Persistence.** Steadfast pursuit of an aim; constant perseverance; continuing to strive for a goal despite obstacles; strong determination to reach goals regardless of personal sacrifice.
- **Ability to withstand business reversals without quitting.** Though perhaps disappointed, not discouraged by failure; ability to use failures as learning experiences so that similar problems can be avoided in the future; attitude that setbacks are only temporary barriers to goals; strong capacity to build on successes.
- **Business and product/service knowledge.** The entrepreneur must understand basic principles by which a business survives and prospers. That means comprehending the roles of management and responsibilities of employees to maintain a viable business. Although the entrepreneur must be in control of overall goals, he or she can't perform each task without help. Awareness of the functions of marketing, accounting, tax, financing, planning, and management, and how to deal with them, is therefore required. Must have a good level of understanding of the product or service.
- **Willingness to accept calculated risks.** Ability to identify risks and weigh their relative dangers; preference for taking calculated risks to achieve goals that are high but realistic. (Contrary to the stereotype that entrepreneurs are gamblers or high–risk-takers, the risks involved are often moderate, due to the amount of planning behind them.)
- **Strong desire for independence.** Genuine desire to be your own boss, free from external direction and control; sincere willingness and

proven ability to be self-disciplined in sometimes isolated working conditions; ability to organize activities to reach personal goals. Successful entrepreneurs are not usually joiners by nature. They often join only to network; that is, to make business contacts, further their ventures, or obtain useful information to solve problems. Studies have shown that reliance on social interaction and friendship may inhibit entrepreneurial behaviour.

- **Ability to handle uncertainty well.** An entrepreneur must have an ability to live with the uncertainty of job security. He or she must face many crises, take risks, and allow for temporary failures without panic. Successful entrepreneurs accept uncertainty as an integral part of being in business.
- **Self-confidence and self-reliance.** Strong but realistic belief in self and ability to achieve personal or business goals. Successful entrepreneurs have an enduring faith in themselves that gives them the capacity to recover from serious defeat or disappointment.
- **Versatility and resourcefulness.** Capable of dealing effectively with many subjects or tasks at the same time; can assume different roles and switch back and forth as required. During the early stages of the business, the entrepreneur will assume numerous and diverse business responsibilities, including marketing, sales, credit and collection, finances, employee selection, accounting, planning, and negotiating.
- **The habit of seeking and using feedback.** The skill to seek and use feedback from employees, the management team, and professional advisors on personal performance and goals for the business; the skill to take any remedial action required.
- **Physical health, with high degree of stamina and energy.** Staying healthy is essential to the intense demands and ongoing pressures of one's own business, especially during its early years. The long hours and pressures of business demand emotional and mental well-being. Also, a high level of stamina and energy is important to meet the intense demands of running a business. One needs the ability to work hard for long hours, often with less sleep than one is accustomed to. One must be prepared to make personal sacrifices. Because the pressures may be great, the success of a business may be determined by whether or not one's spouse, family, and friends can pull together and provide emotional support and understanding.
- **Self-determination.** Belief that one controls one's success or failure, and that it is not decided by luck, circumstance, or external events.
- **Objectivity and realism.** Ability to distinguish between oneself and the business, so that when a mistake occurs, one has the strength to admit

it and take corrective action; desire to deal with business decisions rationally and logically rather than emotionally and subjectively.

- **Openness to change.** Receptivity to change; ability to adjust perceptions, goals, or action on the basis of an assessment of new information.
- **Ability to apply ideas in creative ways.** Strong desire to originate an idea or product; to develop something new; to be innovative; to make something happen; to imprint personality, dreams, and ideas on a concept in a unique and different way; powers of both observation and imagination to foresee possible marketable ideas.
- **Sense of purpose.** A feeling of mission must motivate the person to go into business; the activity must have meaning. The mission may be to make an attractive profit, to sell some necessary and unique product or service, or to develop ideas or skills without the constraints of others' expectations.
- **Human relations ability.** Ability to understand and interact well with people of varying personalities and values. This is important when dealing with employees, bankers, investors, partners, suppliers, or customers, and is reflected in characteristics such as sociability, consideration, cheerfulness, cooperation, and tact.
- **Achievement orientation.** Desire to take on challenges and test abilities to the limit. Successful entrepreneurs are not ambivalent about success. They concentrate on ways to succeed, not on what will happen if they fail. Because they are objective, though, they build a "what if" scenario into the business plan, so that they anticipate problems and develop strategies to surmount obstacles in advance. Successful entrepreneurs adopt the attitude that if they do chance upon unexpected obstacles, they will find resourceful and effective ways to overcome them.

It is unrealistic to suggest that successful entrepreneurs possess all of the traits outlined. Many of the characteristics are interrelated, and not all are necessary for business success, so do not be overly concerned if you feel you do not possess every one of these qualities. The key question is how significant the missing traits are to your type of business and your business goals. Once you understand your personal strengths and weaknesses, you are then in a much better position to compensate for them by hiring employees, bringing in partners, or taking further training.

SELF-ASSESSMENT

Most people start a business without ever completing an honest, thorough personal assessment. Without this self-appraisal, your personal success in business could be limited. This section is intended to assist you in focusing on your strong points, identifying your weaknesses, and dealing with areas that need improvement. This will enable you to clarify your personal and business goals.

In the following categories, expand as fully as you like on your answers. To get the most out of your self-assessment, you should be free from distractions and take as much time as necessary. Rank your answers to indicate the degree of importance or impact on your future business.

- **Autobiography.** Summarize your own life history. Review and detail all aspects of your past, including credentials you have obtained, education, special projects, leisure time activities (including sports and hobbies), and travel experiences. List the work you have done, including all full-time, part-time, and summer jobs. Beside each job list all the roles you assumed or tasks you performed (e.g., coordinating, supervising, writing). Start with the most current time period and work backward.

- **Skills.** List all your skills. These are your developed or acquired abilities, such as researching, administering, instructing, problem-solving, selling, etc. Once you have identified your skills, rank them by frequency of use. This will give you a good indication of how important these are in your activities. Which skills do you believe will assist you in attaining your business goals? You may wish to refer to the book *What Color Is Your Parachute?* by Richard N. Bolles for a detailed list of skill areas to stimulate your awareness.

- **Personality attributes.** List all your personality attributes. Attributes are inherent characteristics, such as having an analytical, inquiring, or insightful mind, being compassionate or sociable, etc. Consider the common characteristics of entrepreneurs discussed earlier in this chapter.

- **Accomplishments.** List your most important job-related accomplishments. Examples may include negotiating a major contract for your employer, coordinating a major conference, or exceeding sales quotas. Then list your most significant non–job-related accomplishments: for instance, being elected as president of a club, organizing a fundraising event, or running a marathon. Rank your accomplishments from the most important to the least important. Then identify and write down all the skills used, talents demonstrated, and attributes shown which were needed to attain each accomplishment.

- **Personal and recreational interests.** Identify your personal interests (e.g., business, science, politics, health, environment, sports). List those activities (personal and business) that provide you with the greatest amount of personal enjoyment and satisfaction.

- **Community involvement.** List community or social activities you have participated in (e.g., church, hospital, clubs, volunteer organizations).
- **Hobbies.** List all your current and past hobbies (e.g., reading, painting, photography, gardening, cooking).
- **Things you like and dislike.** Think of the activities or circumstances that you like or dislike the most (work or personal). List the events that cause you the greatest amount of satisfaction and happiness and the events that cause you the greatest amount of anxiety, frustration, or unhappiness.
- **Strengths and weaknesses.** List your personal strengths and weaknesses. Rank them in order of intensity. Can you eliminate, reduce, or compensate for your weaknesses? Ask someone who knows you well (e.g., a relative, a friend, your spouse) to list what they perceive to be your strengths and weaknesses and to rank them. Do others see you as you see yourself?
- **The present.** Think about your present situation under various headings: social, career, family, marital, physical, emotional, financial. List the strong and weak points in each category. What impact will self-employment have on each of these categories? Ask your spouse the same questions. Is his or her assessment similar to yours?
- **The future.** List the personal goals that you wish to attain in 1, 3, 5, and 10 years. Will your business ambitions assist you in attaining these, and if so, in what manner?

By carefully focusing on your previous experiences and recognizing hidden talents and abilities, you will be better able to identify your personal and business needs. Any business or career you select should address and satisfy those needs. Know your strengths and capitalize on them. Identify your weaknesses and reflect upon how you can minimize their effect on your business activities. Be confident of your abilities, because in business when you are selling a service or product, you are selling yourself. If others believe in you and trust you, they will want to do business with you.

This self-assessment process will probably be an enlightening experience. A close match between your attributes and personality style, and the type of business you choose, will make a difference in the fulfillment you receive from the business and the degree of success you attain.

RECOGNIZING TRENDS

Trends are creating growth markets throughout Canada and the United States for certain types of businesses. Some of these trends are occurring nationally and internationally, while others are felt only on a provincial, regional, or local level.

A trend is an event which lasts a minimum of a decade. A fad, on the other hand, is short-lived and may last for only a few months.

There are several ways of learning what opportunities lie in future trends. One way is to read business-oriented newspapers and magazines in print or online. The national Canadian newspapers are *The Globe and Mail* (*Report on Business* magazine) and the *National Post*. Of course, read your local newspaper and magazines to keep current on local trends. National business-oriented magazines in Canada are *Profit, Canadian Business*, *ROB* (Report On Business), and *National Post*. There are also provincial and local business magazines at your local newsstand and public library and online.

In addition, you can become aware of many trends before they reach Canada by reading American business magazines and newspapers. Some of the recommended magazines include *Entrepreneur, Small Business Opportunities, Income Opportunities, Venture*, and *Inc*.

Other ways to anticipate or be aware of trends is to subscribe to trade magazines or newsletters in your field of interest and attend association or business networking meetings. Speak to suppliers and customers to find out which products and services are in greatest demand.

Another way of doing your research is to do a Google search—putting in keywords of interest to you for business opportunities or trends—to find articles and website information.

Some examples of current trends which could impact on the business you are considering include:

- **Rapid expansion of computer technology, Internet use, and e-commerce.** As you are well aware, the technology revolution has completely changed the way of doing business. No matter what type of business you are considering, you need to embrace technology in a way that maximizes your business opportunities and profit. You also need to understand how computer hardware and software can enhance your business image, give you a competitive edge, reduce stress, improve your management skills, and optimize efficiencies. Not only are most businesses using computer technology for their own operation, they are using their computer skills to actually create business opportunities. For more information, refer to the book by Douglas Gray, *Start and Run a Profitable Business Using Your Computer*, published by International Self-Counsel Press.
- **An increase in leisure time.** Due to shorter work weeks, flexible workdays, compressed work schedules, and people working at home (employed or self-employed), people have more time available for leisure activities.

This will result in increased travel, adult education and self-development courses, and an overall interest in recreation.

- **General aging of the population.** Studies show that by the year 2017, approximately 40% of the population will be over 50 years of age. This will create an interest in travel (especially group or package tours), products for the aged, retirement and investment planning, and assistance in home renovations and repairs. Downsizing from a home to a condominium or townhouse and an increase in the purchase or rental of retirement homes in a warmer climate will occur. We can expect to see an increase in sales of recreational vehicles (mobile homes) and any products to do with security (fire, medical, burglary, etc.).

- **Baby boomers.** Many baby boomers who have held off having a family (especially two-career couples) will now have their families. Therefore, products and services for children will be in demand, especially by parents who have a high disposable income, and therefore have higher expectations of quality and uniqueness in the products they buy. As the baby boomers buy older homes being sold by the senior population (for the reasons referred to in the previous point), there will be an increase in home renovations.

  - Baby boomers have an appreciation of and desire for nature and the outdoors, in terms of their adventure trips and leisure activities, perhaps as an antidote to the pressures of urban living. An increase in personalized services, such as investment and consulting advice will be in demand. In the case of two-income families, with or without children, demand for services and products (child care, housecleaning, etc.) which make life easier will increase.

- **An increase in health concerns.** The majority of the population is aging, and there is an increased interest in looking good, feeling good, and being healthy. This takes the form of participation in fitness and recreation, the purchase of cosmetics, and a desire to learn about the aging process through courses and publications. In addition, an increased awareness of the need for healthy eating habits is also occurring. This takes the form of better attention to diet and food preparation.

Especially with a product or service trend, being in the right place at the right time could result in huge financial rewards through uniqueness and volume sales. A word of caution, though: the trick to succeeding with business trends is much like the sport of surfing. You must get in at the start of the swell, ride through its buildup, and get out while riding at its peak. To stay in a trend beyond its lifespan may turn the business into a financial disaster.

FINDING BUSINESS IDEAS AND OPPORTUNITIES

There is a distinction between an idea and an opportunity. Many people have a good business idea, but the idea may not be a viable business opportunity with potential for success. Careful research, evaluation, and preparation of a business plan will separate the real opportunities from casual ideas. There are many innovative techniques for finding business ideas and opportunities, but before you start your search, make sure that you have completed the self-assessment (discussed earlier), which will help you to find opportunities suited to your lifestyle needs. Many of the sources below are also accessible on the Internet; for example, newspapers, public libraries, and the *Yellow Pages* and other online directories. Check out all the other sources for their Internet addresses at your public library, online, and through Google searches. The Internet makes all your preliminary research so much easier. However, be careful to check the accuracy of Internet sources. You need to apply more caution than with other sources of information, in terms of accuracy and objectivity. Here are some sources of information.

- **Internet.** As you are undoubtedly aware, this form of research is a veritable gold mine of information. By typing keywords into your search engine, you will find numerous Canadian and U.S. sites with information; for example: franchises, business opportunities, specific types of businesses, etc. Also refer to Appendix C for a list of popular small business websites.
- **Books.** There are numerous books available which detail business opportunities that can be started with minimal financing (i.e., about $500 to $10,000). Check with your public library and local bookstores.
- **Publications.** The key publications you should be aware of are referred to in Appendix B. National magazines which are oriented more towards the home-based business and small businesses are *Profit*, *Small Business Opportunities*, *Entrepreneur*, *Income Opportunities*, *Inc.*, and *Venture*.
- **Trade and business associations.** Almost every type of business has a professional or trade association which you may wish to check.
  - The association could be local, provincial, national, or international in scope. Look in the *Yellow Pages* print version or online, or do Google searches under "Associations." In addition, check your local library, as well as well as Google online, for directories that list associations in Canada and the United States. The main directories are *Directory of Associations in Canada* and *Encyclopedia of Associations*.

- **Trade publications and newsletters.** There are thousands of trade publications covering every type of business interest. Consult with the business resource librarian at your local library and ask to see the various directories of trade publications in Canada and the United States. Also, do a Google search online. The best-known directories are:
  - *Gale Directory of Publications and Broadcast Media*
  - *Business Periodicals Index*
  - *Canadian Advertising Rates & Data*
  - *Canadian Almanac & Directory*
  - *Canadian Business Periodicals Index*
  - Gale's *Encyclopedia of Business Information Sources*
  - Standard Rates and Data (http://next.srds.com)
  - *Ulrich's International Periodicals Directory.*
- **Foreign trade publications.** There are many foreign trade publications which list import and export opportunities. Check with your local library or provincial government small business resource centre.
- **The *Yellow Pages*.** These telephone directories list many products and services relating to small business. As you know, there is an online version, and most people do their research online using Google. If you have a print version, turn to the cross-referenced index and methodically work your way through the listings. Look for the types of businesses that supply products or services that interest you. For example, if you are interested in gardening, you would look up all the cross-referenced classifications associated with gardening. That would include florists, nurseries, and landscape architects.
- **Trade shows/conventions.** Trade shows can be an excellent way to examine the products and services of many of your potential competitors. You will meet distributors and sales representatives, learn of product and market trends, and identify potential products or services for your business venture. You will find trade show information in the trade magazines servicing your particular field. Also look at the annual directories that publish a listing of Canadian, the U.S., and international trade shows.
  - The main directories, can be found in your public library and/or provincial government resource centre as well as online through "keyword" Google searches.
  - Conventions also offer an excellent opportunity to stimulate creative thinking. At a convention you are exposed to speakers, panelists, films, and displays. You also have an opportunity to exchange ideas with other entrepreneurs.

- **Seminars/courses.** There are many seminars, workshops, and courses available on small business—including home-based business—offered through government agencies (the Business Development Bank of Canada and provincial government small business departments), school board and community college adult-education programs, and enterprise development centres. Contact these agencies or organizations and ask to be put on their mailing lists for upcoming programs. Seminars offer an excellent opportunity to meet other people with interests similar to yours.

- **Franchises/licences.** There are many business franchises and distributorships available. The range of types of product and service businesses include bookkeeping/accounting, interior decorating, housecleaning, lawn maintenance, restaurants, auto painting, and teaching. Statistically, the survival rate of franchises is high, because of the formalized and tested business plans and support systems offered by franchisers, including training, advertising and promotion, computer and/or other management and administrative systems, and ongoing monitoring of performance.

  - *Licensing* means having the right to distribute or manufacture a product within agreed-upon stipulations. The owner of the licence retains ownership of all product or service rights, then receives a royalty or fixed fee from the licensee.

  - There are good, bad, and mediocre franchises and licences, and any potential investor should be cautious. Obtain the advice of your banker, lawyer, and accountant before committing yourself to any contractual arrangement. Check the reputation of the franchiser through the Canadian Franchise Association (Toronto), provincial franchise associations, and the Better Business Bureau. You can obtain contact information about these franchise associations by referring to the "Sources of Further Information" section in Appendix B. For more information, refer to Chapter 8 on franchising. For a comprehensive coverage of franchising in Canada, read *So You Want To Buy a Franchise* (by Douglas Gray and Norm Friend), published by McGraw-Hill Ryerson, as well as *The Complete Canadian Franchise Guide*, written by the same authors.

- **Examination of existing products or services for improvement.** There are many excellent products, but few people know about them because of ineffective marketing. Investigate products you think have a possibility of success. Find out the marketing methods that were used. You might be able to obtain that product's distribution rights at a low price. There are innovative ways of modifying or repackaging an existing product to appeal to new markets. For example, there could be an industrial version of a consumer product, or vice versa. There could also be foreign-market possibilities that have never been explored. For example, if a product is seasonal, you could locate a country in the southern hemisphere which has opposite seasons. By exporting your product during your own off-season, you would be able to sell the product throughout the year.

- **Look for modifications to a product or service that would improve its marketability and profit.** Ask yourself the following questions: How can I:
  - make it safer, cleaner, slower, or faster?
  - make it at home and save overhead expense?
  - contract out to have other people make the product or perform the service in their homes?
  - make it more convenient or inexpensive?
  - cut costs of material and labour?
  - combine it with other products or services?
  - make it easier to package, store, or transport?
  - condense or enlarge its size?
  - make it easier to use?
  - make it less expensive to replace, repair, or reuse?
  - make it more attractive and appealing?
  - make it lighter, stronger, adjustable, thinner, or foldable?
  - make it quieter or louder? minimize its potential hazards? add new features?
  - improve its availability or distribution?
  - improve its production? improve its design? improve its marketing? improve it in other ways?

- **Distributors.** If you are interested in selling or distributing a product, contact the manufacturer to inquire if a sales territory is available in your area. There may be an opening, or possibly a dissatisfaction with one of the present distributors who may not be effectively performing in the territory. Distributors and wholesalers have an extensive knowledge of the strong and weak points of existing products, and the types of product improvements that are needed by their customers. Distributors can be located in the *Yellow Pages*, in the classified ad sections of business newspapers and magazines, as well as at business opportunity trade shows. Of course, do Google searches on the Internet using keywords of interest to you.

- **Travel and hobbies.** Whenever you travel, look for business ideas and opportunities. Many services and products may not have been introduced into Canada. You may be able to negotiate exclusive or non-exclusive Canadian distribution rights for a product. Alternatively, you may wish to duplicate, with modifications and improvements, the product or service. This is assuming that your efforts don't infringe upon any legal rights that the originator of the product or service might have. Think of the areas relating to your hobbies or leisure activities in which you believe a need exists. You might be able to devise creative ways of meeting those needs.

- In summary, when you are looking for potentially profitable opportunities, it is helpful to review some of the main categories of business opportunities:
  - providing an information or consulting service
  - identifying new opportunities arising from your current business
  - becoming an agent, supplier, or distributor for someone else's service or product
  - taking existing local products to new markets within Canada
  - transferring concepts from one industry to another
  - buying an existing business for franchise
  - imitating successful services or products
  - becoming an agent or distributor for a product imported into Canada
  - inventing a new product
  - capitalizing on a growth trend
  - solving someone else's problem
  - rebuilding, repairing, or adding to an existing product or service
  - identifying specific target groups and customizing services or products for their needs exporting Canadian products to other countries
  - finding productive uses for waste material.
  - catering to a market that is no longer being serviced
  - replacing imported products
  - targeting a small portion of a large market.

Creativity is an important attribute in successfully operating a business and will ensure that you are always alert for new opportunities, new products, new techniques, etc. Creativity is useful when you are at the idea-generating stage of selecting a business and at every other stage throughout the lifespan of your business. For example, you will need to be creative when searching out a suitable name for your business, sources of financing, potential customers, low-cost raw materials, etc.

Many people find "brainstorming" an effective means of generating creative ideas. A small group of people (usually from three to seven) meets in a round table discussion group format with an objective of identifying as many creative ideas as they can in the above categories. One person records on a flipchart or chalkboard all ideas suggested. Some ideas may sound impractical, zany, or impossible, but the task is to list as many as possible without being judgmental as to their appropriateness. In this way, inhibitions are removed and ideas are free-flowing. Relax and have fun with it!

Once the ideas have stopped flowing (you may have anywhere from thirty to eighty suggestions), you start the task of evaluating each of them for their merits. With the assistance of your group members, discuss each of the suggestions. You may find that parts of an idea may be workable in specific situations. Others may not work under any circumstances. Eliminate those ideas that would be impossible. Once you have identified the most workable solutions, attach a priority ranking to indicate which ones you should try first.

Brainstorming may assist you in shortlisting the businesses which have the most potential. The following section will help you to develop a list of factors to use in the evaluation process.

EVALUATING BUSINESS OPPORTUNITIES

Creativity goes hand in hand with evaluation. If you have a lot of creative ideas, but do not evaluate them, you could be destined for failure from the outset. Many business failures are the result of starting into business too quickly, without prior research, evaluation, and planning — usually because of excitement, enthusiasm, and over-optimism. On the other hand, if you only evaluate a few initial ideas, you may overlook untapped opportunities for true success and fulfillment in your business venture.

Reflect on the business ideas that have appealed to you at this point. Think about the personality traits required to succeed in that type of business. Do these match up with your own personal skills, talents, interests, and aptitudes, as discussed in other sections of this chapter?

Develop a set of criteria on which you can evaluate and rate each of your business ideas. Your criteria will be based upon many factors, including your lifestyle needs, financial status and needs, personal needs, business needs, background experience, etc. For instance, you may want to start up a part-time or full-time business out of your home. If your reason for going into a home-based business is that you want to supplement the family income while caring for your preschool children, factors that will influence your decision will include:

- Can the hours worked be modified to suit the children's schedule?

- Is the business still viable if only handled on a part-time basis until the children reach school age, when more time may be available?
- Will travel be necessary to pick up or deliver products?
- Will you be able to use a telephone answering service or machine to take calls when you are not available to the business?

You may find the following evaluation format useful. Start off by listing at the top of a sheet of paper your financial, lifestyle, personal, and business needs. List down the left-hand side of the page the various factors that will influence your decision. Once you have filled the page, make a sufficient number of photocopies of this form so that you can use one for each of the business ideas that you wish to evaluate. Then start to complete the centre column of the form with answers to each of your evaluation factors. Some responses may be considered to be favourable (pro), while others may present some difficulties for you (con). In the far right-hand column, indicate whether the factor has a pro, con, or neutral influence. You may need to do some preliminary research to fill in some of the answers. (If you are considering a home-based business and want to avoid various work-at-home schemes and scams, refer to our book, *Home Inc.: The Canadian Home-Based Business Guide*, Second Edition, published by McGraw-Hill Ryerson.)

Once you have completed this process for each of your business ideas, compare the businesses to identify which ones may be most profitable and appropriate for your specific needs. You will begin to see clearly how some business ideas may show great prospects, while others may involve a lot of hard work but little reward after your diligent efforts. You are now one step closer to making your final decision. Your final step is, of course, developing a full business plan, as discussed in Chapter 2 and as shown in Sample 4, "Business Plan Outline." Review your completed business plan(s) with your spouse, lawyer, accountant, advisors, business associates, and friends for their input and advice.

CHOOSING A BUSINESS

You may have an idea what business or industry sector you are interested in— manufacturing, wholesale, retail, or service. These sectors are each unique in their mode of operation, financing, management, and potential risk. Refer to Appendix C, "Website Resources." he next chapter, on "Business Planning," will assist you further in the selection process. There are many other issues you have to consider. Is your business to be a part-time or full-time business? Is your business to be operated out of the home, an office, or a plant? Another consideration is whether you are starting your business from scratch, buying a business, or buying a franchise.

The advantages of starting a business from scratch may include:

- the ability to start off the way you want
- personal ego satisfaction from the challenge of building your own business
- the ability to select a location of your own choice
- the ability to staff the business as you choose
- the ability to equip and decorate the premises to suit your own tastes and needs
- the ability to rent or build a business facility that meets your requirements exactly
- the ability to add on to the business in a graduated fashion
- the ability to access possible government financial incentives.

The disadvantages of starting from scratch may include the following:

- the inability to find a suitable site or business premises
- the inability to find and employ qualified personnel for your needs
- the longer time it will take to get the business ready to start, the longer time and additional expense it will take to become known by the public and establish a customer base
- the longer time it will take to gain momentum and obtain business growth and profit
- the difficulty in establishing the necessary cash flow.

The advantages and disadvantages of buying a business or franchise are covered in separate chapters.

HOME-BASED BUSINESS

Large numbers of people have chosen to market their skills and talents from home. Current studies estimate that more than 50% of new small business enterprises are operated out of the owner's home, and this trend is rapidly growing. The natural starting place for many of these businesses is the den, spare room, basement, or garage. Many home-based businesses are started on a part-time basis and expand into a full-time business at a later date. The significant majority of them are started by women. People are attracted to home enterprises for many different reasons and from many different groups, including homemakers, single parents, the disabled, the unemployed, hobbyists, and people interested in a second income. The same group of people could also be potential employees of a home-based business operation. Studies show that over 70% of the work force in North America is employed in service and information-related industries, and this percentage is increasing. Recent surveys have projected that more than two million Canadians have some form of home-based business.

Management of a home-based business is similar to any other business in most respects, in terms of the issues, options, and risks that have to be considered. There are special considerations, however, that are unique to a home-based business and require research and specific professional advice. Some of these considerations include managing a family business, marketing and selling techniques, and insurance, tax, legal, and employee matters. To obtain further information on these matters and others, you may wish to join an association for networking and educational benefits. Look in the *Yellow Pages* under "Associations" or contact your provincial small business department. There are numerous recently published books related to starting and running a successful home-based business. Also refer to Appendix C, "Website Resources," and do Google searches with keywords of interest to you. Our book, *Home Inc.*, will help you.

Advantages and Disadvantages

Running a home-based business is not for everyone. What may be an advantage to one person may be a disadvantage to another. Often, though, there are practical solutions for dealing with the disadvantages.

Advantages of a home-based business
- can be started on a part-time basis
- start-up costs and operating costs are much lower
- commuting time and expense are reduced or eliminated
- increased tax benefits and write-offs
- lifestyle can be flexible
- spouse and family members can be employed by the business
- flexible working hours
- more opportunities for the business to grow because of fewer financial constraints
- stress is reduced because of a more relaxed working environment.

Disadvantages of a home-based business
- isolation from the companionship and interaction with colleagues or fellow workers
- potential risk of working too hard because of a lack of separation from the work and home environments
- space may be cramped or inappropriate for ideal working environment or growth purposes

- discipline is required to establish and maintain productive work habits
- personal or family lifestyle patterns or priorities may be disrupted or set aside
- distractions and disruptions from family or friends may interfere with concentration
- business and family privacy may be impaired
- tensions and frustrations could potentially develop because of preoccupation with work blending into family relationship
- business may not be taken seriously by others due to lack of a professional business image
- it may be difficult to hire employees to work due to limited or inappropriate space
- business activity could create difficulties with neighbours.

Types of Home-Based Businesses

There are numerous types of home-based businesses that you may wish to consider. Here is a sampling of ideas to stimulate your imagination:

Service businesses
- agent (manufacturer's, distributor's, literary, sales, insurance)
- beautician, hairdresser, barber
- calligrapher
- catering, baking
- chimney cleaning
- clipping service (articles, ads, coupons)
- commercial graphics
- computer-related business (see section below)
- coordinator (projects, special events)
- consulting (management, financial, public relations)
- contracting—general, specialty (painting, carpentry)
- courier/messenger
- day care provider
- exporting/importing
- interior decorating
- instructor (music, art, dance lessons)
- janitorial/maintenance
- landscaping/gardening
- locksmith
- mover (furniture, equipment)
- photography (commercial, portrait, wedding)
- producer (shows, plays)

- professional services (accounting, bookkeeping, legal, dental, architectural, engineering)
- public speaker (seminars, workshops, keynote addresses)
- real estate
- repair work (auto, equipment, furniture, home)
- researcher
- sitter (house, pets, plants, elderly, disabled)
- tailoring/dressmaking
- telephone answering, wake-up calls
- translations
- tutoring
- videos (training, wedding, insurance, security)
- washing, ironing.

Computer-related businesses
- accounts payable and payroll system service
- annual report writing
- anonymous re-mailer service
- architectural and computer-aided design
- bid and grant proposal writing
- billing service
- bookkeeping
- bulletin board service
- business form, stationery, booklet, vanity publication, annual report and menu design and layout
- business plan writing
- client database service
- clip art service
- collection service
- computer accessory sales
- computer and online training for children
- computer cleaning, repair and maintenance, setup and training
- computer consulting for people with disabilities
- copywriting
- customized gift and promotional product creation
- data and archiving backup service
- data conversion
- data security consulting
- database creation, conversion, and management
- desktop video editing
- direct-mail marketing

- electronic clipping service
- electronic mail service
- electronic mailbox service
- employer online hiring training
- ergonomics consulting
- estate management
- expense analysis
- fax time rental
- fax-on-demand service
- financial planning and management
- foreign-language word processing
- freelance editing
- freelance writing
- garden and landscape design
- genealogy research
- graphic design
- home inventory cataloguing
- image and document scanning, enhancing and digitizing
- information broker
- interior design
- intranet administration
- inventory service
- investment analysis
- job hunting training
- junk e-mail filter service
- laser printer time rental
- mail-order sales
- mailing list service
- multimedia business presentation design
- multimedia genealogy publishing
- multimedia kiosk design and consulting
- network consulting
- newsletter, magazine, and catalogue design and layout
- occupational therapy
- online catalogue creation
- online form design
- online magazine writing and editing
- online research training
- online setup and training
- online teaching and tutoring
- people tracing

- print and pre-press consulting
- product and service tracing
- property management
- résumé writing
- sales and statistical analysis
- sign, banner, and poster design
- specialty magazine writing and editing
- system security consulting
- tax preparation
- technical editing
- technical writing
- telecommute consulting
- transcribing
- translating
- used PC sales
- utility bill auditing
- video conference consulting
- Web and business presentation clip art service
- Web sound and video clip service
- website design and administration
- word processing.

Common products and services made in and/or sold from the home

- artwork
- clothing
- cosmetics
- crafts
- door-to-door sales
- housewares
- insurance
- jewellery
- pottery
- toys
- woodwork.

One should be wary of advertisements for work-at-home schemes. While the media have an ethical responsibility to inquire about the legitimacy of the money-making offer before accepting the advertisement for publication, in practical terms this control procedure is not 100% successful. Some of the examples of the ads that frequently appear, primarily in the help wanted and business opportunities sections of newspapers and magazines, include "$1,500 weekly guaranteed," "Work two hours daily at home," "$590 for every 1,000 envelopes you mail, postage paid. Ask for free brochure; write...." If you have reason to be concerned about the credibility of the company, contact the Better Business Bureau and ask if any complaints have been made. Also do an online Google search for any complaints made against the company. You should be very skeptical and cautious in responding to any work-at-home schemes if:

- money is sought before a start can be made in the at-home business
- the promotional material says there is unlimited demand for the product or service
- there is no mention of the total cost involved
- promises are made that a lot of money can be made with very little work or on a part-time basis
- the promoter agrees to buy back the merchandise at higher than retail selling price—the catch may be "if the work is up to standard" which may be subject to very subjective and arbitrary criteria.

In short, be wary that a work-at-home scheme could be a scam.

WOMEN IN BUSINESS

In Canada, women are going into business at a greater rate than men, almost three to one. Studies show that twice as many female small business owners are still in business 5 years later, compared with male small business owners. In surveys conducted regionally and nationally, the same underlying factors are repeated on the success of women in business. They include the following:

Women Do Their Research

Before starting a business, a woman typically spends from 6 to 10 months researching the product or service, the best location for the business, and many other considerations. This compares with less than 4 months on average spent by her male counterpart.

Women Plan Ahead

While small business instructors extol the benefits of having a written business plan, women are the ones most often to heed this advice. As a follow-through on the research they have done, the preparation of the written business plan becomes an easier task. By the time this stage is completed, they have a fully developed concept and can see clearly the stepping stones they need to follow to lead them to their ultimate goal. A sample business plan is shown in Sample 4.

Even after the business has been launched, the need for planning continues. Events may occur outside your control that may cause you to periodically revise your plan. Women in general tend to have an ability to be in control of the global aspects of the business, yet at the same time continue to look ahead to tomorrow, next week, and next year.

Women Take Courses and Seek Advice

Women tend to readily accept the fact that they may not have all the necessary skills or business know-how. Consequently, they will enroll in courses that teach them how to read financial statements or prepare a marketing plan, for instance. Also, women tend to act more cautiously in an area in which they have little expertise, and seek the advice of others.

Women Have Realistic Expectations

In looking ahead to the profit potential, women tend to set conservative and realistic expectations. They tend to be less impulsive. Their practicality prevails, rather than their enthusiasm distorting their vision. They will write into their plan an anticipated slow period for the concept to catch on, for example. Women tend to be conservative in the decor and the spaciousness of their office or store facility—they will not overextend themselves financially with the hopes of making large sales tomorrow. This is a critical aspect of building a solid foundation from the outset, and gaining the trust and respect of your banker, suppliers, and staff. Women tend to take less money out of their businesses in the critical growth years. Studies show they take out less than half of the money taken by male entrepreneurs.

Women Are Committed to the Business

Because many women are not in business just for the money, they tend to persevere longer during hardships. Theirs is often a "lifestyle" business. At stake is their determination to succeed, which at times outlives the financial viability of the business. However, such determination is usually accompanied by an openness to new ideas and approaches. In leaving no stone unturned in their attempts to succeed, they usually do.

When it is stated that women tend to be more successful in business than men, it is most often the case that the word "success" refers to surviving in business longer. Because of her commitment and realistic expectations, a woman is more likely to "hang in there" during the slow growth of a business. While statistics are lacking in the area of overall profits made by men and women in business, it is perceived that men are far more successful than women. A man is likely to take greater risks, have greater access to finances, and therefore be able to generate larger amounts of money. These factors naturally relate to a higher "success" profile in the media and the business world.

DEALING WITH BUSINESS GROWTH

To grow or not to grow? The day may come when the owner of a healthy business thinks about expanding. Perhaps your business has grown so much that you are starting to feel cramped and disorganized. A decision must be made as to whether it is more financially viable to grow larger or to maintain the present size. It is a misperception to assume that expansion and more profit go hand in hand.

Growing larger will probably mean a longer workday, increased stress, additional expense, more debt, increased bookkeeping, higher inventory and supply costs, increased product or service line, the need to hire more employees, expansion into new markets, and more demands on your personal and family life. In addition, operating a larger enterprise requires greater management skills and operational systems. The changing dynamics of operating a larger business have to be considered seriously.

How will you know if and when it is time to expand? The answer is that you will clearly see the signs that it is time for a change; you will not be able to ignore them. At this stage you need to carefully review and rewrite your business plan. Consider it from two perspectives: (1) if you stayed the same size, and (2) if you expanded the business. Factors you should consider include:

- **Your personal and business goals.** Have they been met fully in your home enterprise? Have your goals changed? How will they be affected by moving?
- **Sales potential.** Have you reached your maximum potential sales for your existing form of operations? Will moving to a new location enable you to double or triple production? Compare your maximum sales potential in dollar figures.
- **Space.** Is lack of space limiting your growth? How much additional space is required for: working area, client visits, storage of materials, supplies, and inventory?
- **Time.** Do you at present do all the work yourself? Are there aspects that can be delegated to staff without risking the quality of service and personal attention to detail? Have you weighed the benefits of adding staff along with the cost of salaries and benefits, extra work space, hiring and training skills required, etc.?

- **Paperwork.** Is your present system of invoicing, receivables and payables, and bookkeeping well managed? Can it withstand the impact of expansion? Are you currently computerized? If not, computerization will be essential, in practical terms.
- **Changing roles.** With expansion, will you be more of a manager than a salesperson or a doer? Does this fit your talents and ambitions?
- **Additional financing.** How much additional financing will you need for the expansion and ongoing operating costs? Consider salaries, materials, renovations, rent, marketing, and advertising costs. Will you have easy access to such financing?

Expanding the Business

On the basis of your financial projections, you may have decided that expanding the business operation will increase your profitability. By hiring additional help for certain aspects of the business, you may be able to double your production while only marginally increasing your overhead costs. Perhaps increasing and improving your work space will enable you to work more efficiently and to achieve a greater degree of satisfaction. You may consider increasing staff and space, but this may increase your risk and borrowing and the amount of paperwork.

Adding to your home if you have a home office

There are many creative ways of modifying unused space in your existing house to convert it into additional space for your business. You may also want to make additions to your house or construct a separate structure on your property for your business needs, subject to existing municipal bylaws of course. (For more detail, refer to *Home Inc.*).

Moving to a bigger house if you have a home office

You may wish to build, buy, or lease a larger place to live to accommodate your growing business needs. This could provide you with the added or specialized space for your projected business requirements, and enable you to continue working from home.

Hiring employees to work from their homes

This is a very easy way of expanding as quickly as you need to, while keeping the costs to a minimum. Naturally, it depends on the nature of your business as to whether this is a viable option. For example, you could utilize services of the following types of employees: commissioned salespeople, software developers or programmers, data entry or research personnel, or telemarketers. You could also consider the use of temporary relief personnel.

Renting storage or warehouse space

Renting storage or warehouse space may be an option for you if you have an occasional or permanent need for more space. There are numerous mini-storage areas that you can rent month to month.

Contracting work to other businesses

Rather than having to rent additional office space or move your business to a warehouse, you may wish to subcontract out some of the extra work for temporary or occasional projects. This is commonly done by consultants.

Renting a packaged office

If your business is operated within an office environment, the most economical route is to rent office space in a shared office facility called a packaged office or executive suite or business suite centre. You can rent on a month-to-month basis or a longer term such as 6 months or 1 year. For a fixed monthly fee, the features of a packaged office include a fully furnished office; a central reception area and receptionist; a boardroom; a telephone answering service; access to support secretarial and word processing services; and use of fax, photocopier, and other office equipment. Besides the flexibility of short-term leases, you have no staff, furniture, or equipment costs, and no administrative or set-up time is required. Much time and money is therefore saved, as you do not need to shop around and select and purchase equipment that may only be minimally used.

Subletting space from another company

Many companies downsize to save on costs, depending on the economy, increased rent, etc., so there may be numerous opportunities available to sublet suitable office, retail, or warehouse space. The subletting company may also be willing to share staff, for example, the receptionist, who could answer your phone line for you. The main advantage to subletting is that most of the responsibility for the entire leased space lies with the person from whom you sublet. The main disadvantage, though, is that the person who holds the lease may decide not to continue at that location, and then you would be required to search for another location for your business.

Leasing space

When choosing suitable leased space, your options include office, warehouse, retail store, and shopping mall outlet. The deciding factors will be location, affordability, and risk. The lease may require a large deposit, personal guarantee, and long-term commitment. You should recognize, however, that lease clauses can be modified or removed in advance through astute negotiating techniques.

Refer to Chapter 9, "Location and Leases," for a detailed discussion. It is prudent never to sign a lease (or similar contract) without first having it reviewed by your lawyer.

In summary, your detailed revised business plan showing your key options will give you a clear picture of the financial viability of each option. While you will be able to generate increased sales, will the added costs result in increased profits? Will the additional time, risk, and stress be worth the effort? Review your revised plan with your professional advisors and get their input. Talk to others who have expanded in a similar way to hear their perspectives. Your decision will be founded on extensive financial calculations, research, and expert advice. This will enhance your chances for success.

Chapter 2

Business Planning

Long-range planning does not deal with future decisions, but with the future of present decisions.

— Peter F. Drucker

A business plan is a written summary of what you hope to accomplish by being in business, and how you intend to organize your resources to meet your goals. It is a road map of where you want to go in your business, the various routes you will take, stages along the way, and most importantly, where you will be when you have arrived at your destination. It helps eliminate the misunderstandings that can easily arise if you don't put your thoughts and research in writing. The plan outlines your organizational and management skills. It provides the basis for determining what further information you require. It is an outline of the company's availability and use of funds, management and employee personnel, products or services, marketing strategy, production techniques (if a manufacturing company), research and development program, and expansion or diversification program, as well as many other goals and objectives. It highlights the past, present, and future of the business.

WHY PREPARE A BUSINESS PLAN?

A business plan is one of the most effective management tools available. It can help you focus in a logical and organized manner on the future growth of your company. It helps you anticipate and meet the inevitable changes of the future in a pragmatic fashion. In the business plan you have a device for helping you control the business, allowing you to monitor and assess the progress of your objectives.

A well-prepared business plan provides the following benefits:

- It helps you identify your customers, your market area, your pricing strategy, and the competitive conditions under which you must operate
- to succeed. This process alone may lead you to discover a competitive advantage or new opportunity, as well as deficiencies in your plan.
- It helps to set the guidelines, such as the break-even point in profitability and cash flow, and the anticipated return on your investment (ROI).

- It encourages realism instead of over-optimism. When you have to put pen to paper to assess and quantify the various financial and logistical needs of your company, you have a much clearer picture of the next steps to take.
- Committing your plans to paper improves your overall ability to manage the business. You will be able to concentrate your efforts on correcting alterations from the plan before conditions become critical. It helps you avoid problems by anticipating them in advance.
- It exposes you to the methods and merits of the planning, budgeting, forecasting, and reporting processes that are so essential.
- It provides a budget that will help the lender or investor make an early assessment of your business feasibility and viability.
- It establishes the amount and timing of outside investment required. It helps reduce the time that it takes for a prospective lender or investor to assess and accept or reject your proposal.
- It creates an important first impression to a lender, investor, or potential partner in assessing you as a competent business manager.
- It identifies the number of employees needed, when they are needed, the skills they must have, and the salaries or wages they must be paid.
- It helps establish the size and location of plants and facilities for office space. It may very well show that you could do well with a "packaged office" service or could possibly operate out of your home with a telephone answering service.
- It helps identify the factors critical to the success of your business concept.
- It provides you with the opportunity on a dry-run basis to "operate" your business without financial outlay or risk.

Besides the detailed business plan, other factors that have to be taken into account include your personal goals, your business goals, and your financial projections. Part of planning is also being able to measure the results to ensure that your business plan is on target and accurate. You will therefore continue to use your plan to chart the progress and success of your business.

From the point of deciding to go into business, you have started your business plan. You probably already have a fair idea of the overall concept of the operation, the products you will sell, where you will locate the business, and an approximate time frame for start-up. Your mind will be overflowing with thoughts of how to set your pricing, how much money you will need, and how much time it will take to build your customer base. It is at this stage that you need to start mapping these thoughts on paper.

Many people do not venture out on their own because they become overwhelmed with the "what if" syndrome. A comprehensive business plan will enable you to anticipate "what if" problems and develop strategies to overcome them months before you start your business. This enables you to walk through each stage of your business plan on paper and to make many of your crucial decisions before you have invested any money. After working through your plan, you may come to the realization that there is little profit in the venture, or that it will require a large amount of start-up capital that you may be unable to raise, or that you will be tied to the business with little free time for yourself and your family. If this is the case, you may decide either to modify your business concept to build in these missing factors, to operate the business on a part-time basis, or to cancel your plan altogether. If the risk is too great, then your best business decision may be not to start the business.

Your goals, if not clear in your mind before you start your plan, will become more obvious as you go through the planning stages. Your personal as well as business goals will need to be considered thoroughly and discussed with your support network. Your network may include your spouse, children, parents, business associates, lawyer, accountant, friends, or relatives—those people who may be directly affected by your decision to go into business and whom you trust to give you honest, candid feedback and to assist you in realizing your goals.

DETERMINING YOUR GOALS

Before working on a plan for your business, it is important to establish your personal goals. These will largely dictate the type of business that you go into, whether it is a part-time or full-time business, whether you work out of your home or an office, whether you travel a lot or stay in one location.

When you are considering your personal goals, it is important to know your present financial net worth. For an example of a net worth statement, see Sample 1 at the back of this book. You should determine your existing as well as future financial needs. Sample 2 provides a personal cost-of-living budget form which you may find useful. Do you have sufficient financial resources to support yourself and your family during the initial stage of your business? Sample 3 provides a format for calculating your needs. Do you have available funds to inject into your business during the start-up phase? The sole wage-earner in the family may be faced with the additional stress of unmet family expectations in terms of time spent away from home, if these factors are not discussed openly beforehand. Other goals you may consider are minimizing taxes, having a home, and providing security for your dependents. Quality-of-life goals include your recreational activities, trips and vacations, challenge and fulfillment, and time spent with your family. Your personal goals may change from time to time throughout your life, and your business goals will have to be modified accordingly, based on changing circumstances.

An honest personal assessment of your skills, qualities, personality style, strengths and weaknesses, and likes and dislikes will help you further refine the type of business suited to your needs. For example, a person who enjoys meeting people and has natural sales ability can become easily frustrated and discouraged if most of his or her time is spent behind the scenes and processing paperwork. You may recognize certain weaknesses that you have and make a conscious decision how to deal with them. For instance, if careful record-keeping is an area you tend to neglect, the decision to hire a bookkeeper can alleviate possible frustrations.

Reviewing your personal goals and reasons for going into business will help you clarify specific goals for your business that parallel your personal needs. For example, if one of your reasons for choosing the entrepreneurial route was to make more money, then this will have a bearing on the type of business you go into. You may decide to start a business, build it to its optimum level of activity, and then sell it for a profit. On the other hand, if you are motivated by the idea of being your own boss, then this short-term goal of selling the business would not necessarily meet that personal need. When identifying your goals, you should be specific regarding that outcome, so that your degree of success can be measured. For instance, "making more money" should be rewritten to read "making at least $75,000 net profit before tax by the second year of operation, and $250,000 by the fourth year." It is important to do extensive research so that you can realistically project your goals, taking into account factors such as competition, suppliers, financing, personal resources, and personal commitment. Your goals should include short-term (first year) and long-term (years two to five) goals.

In reviewing your personal and business goals along with your personal profile of skills and attributes, you should be able to objectively assess if you are suited to the business you have chosen, and if it will meet your needs. Entrepreneurship is not for everyone. However, if you can identify with traits of successful entrepreneurs, and they are in line with your personal attributes and goals, then going into business for yourself may be the most satisfying career move that you can make.

HOW TO PREPARE AN EFFECTIVE BUSINESS PLAN

Not all business plans are alike, although they have many features in common. The content of your plan will vary depending on whether you have a service, retail, manufacturing, wholesale, high-tech, or research and development firm. A typical business plan outline is provided in Sample 4. Other business plans covering various industry sectors are available from provincial small business ministries, banks, speciality business plan companies, and major accounting firms. Almost all are available online, and many can be completed online as well (refer to Appendix B). You may wish to obtain free copies of the material available and decide which format is appropriate for your needs. As a useful guideline when preparing your business plan, the "Master Checklist," Appendix A, will require you to focus on the many issues to be considered when starting up a business.

The business plan should be typewritten, well-spaced, and organized with a table of contents. As you can see from the sample plan, it should have a summary that outlines your goals concisely, so that a potential investor, partner, or lender may have a capsule overview. This overview tends to be one to three pages in length, and hopefully convinces the reader to continue reviewing your plan. Although the brief summary occurs first, it should be the last part you write. The rest of the business plan covers such subjects as:

- market analysis and strategy
- products or services
- fixed assets—land, building, equipment
- staff and product operations
- management
- financial data
- risks and opportunities.

As noted, you can get excellent, professionally designed business plan software programs, and online interactive business plans that you can utilize and print off.

Government Regulations

There are certain government regulations and licences you will have to apply for, depending on the type of business you have chosen. Part of your planning process should include checking with the various municipal, provincial, and federal governments to become aware of the regulations that may affect your business. Sample 5 provides an extensive list of government regulations affecting small business.

Preparing Financial Projections

An integral part of your business plan is the preparation of financial projections. This is a critical component for a realistic assessment of the viability of your business. If you have not yet started your business, the projections will be based on various uncertain factors. You must identify your assumptions about the financial and operating characteristics of your business start-up. You must develop sales and budget projections. Then you must assemble these into an income projection (profit-and-loss statement projection). This information must then be translated into a cash flow projection. A cash flow projection is an analysis of when you expect the money to flow in and out of the business on a monthly basis. You need to know when you will be receiving money, how and when you will be able to make necessary payments to the landlord, suppliers, and staff. For instance, if you bill regular clients on the last day of the month, and 80% of your clients pay within 15 days of receiving their invoices, then you can expect to have a good cash flow around the twentieth day of the following month. If, however, your bank-loan payment comes due on the fifteenth of every month, then you may decide to close off sales a week before the actual month end, to accelerate the process by 1 week in order to meet your major financial commitment. In many cases, lenders rely very heavily on the capacity of your cash flow to service the debt, rather than on the equity base that you might have or collateral security that you may be prepared to give. See Sample 6, which is a cash flow projection with explanation of the component parts. You should work out your cash flow for the first year of the business.

After completing your cash flow projections, you must check your results by projecting your balance sheet. And finally, you have to do a thorough ratio analysis to compare your company's projected behaviour with that of similar companies. The next chapter, "Understanding Financial Statements," discusses in detail the use and type of ratios that will help you in this process, as well as the other financial statements mentioned.

As you go through the preceding steps, you will begin to see how decisions on such factors as advertising, marketing, production, distribution, and financing will have an effect on the viability, profitability, and liquidity of your company. You can readily see how important it is that you do a dry run on paper of all aspects of your business operation before committing yourself to the time, expense, and risk of a business venture.

Chapter 3

Understanding Financial Statements

Profitability is the sovereign criterion of the enterprise.

— Peter F. Drucker

Financial statements are often underutilized by small business owners who do not fully understand them. There is a perception that they are complex and can be interpreted only by professional accountants. On the contrary, once you become familiar with the overall concepts and the terms used, you will have an appreciation for the necessary valuable information they contain for the effective management of the business. It will enhance the quality and timing of your decision-making. You will be able to discuss the key factors and implications with your accountant and jointly plan your course of action.

Financial statements provide a picture of the financial health of the business at a given point. They primarily consist of a balance sheet and income statement. Most financial statements will also include a statement of cash flows that summarizes and classifies cash inflows and outflows during the reporting period. Financial statements will also include explanatory notes that provide more details about the account balances and the significant transactions of the entity. Financial statements are normally prepared as of the date of the business fiscal year-end, but can be prepared at any time, if necessary (e.g., for the sale of a business). Depending on variables such as timing of your fiscal year-end, how busy your accountant is, how well your records are kept, and the complexity of your business, the financial statements might take 2 to 3 months to prepare after the end of your fiscal year.

Canada Revenue Agency, banks, many creditors or suppliers, investors, and potential buyers of a business all require a company's financial statements for review and analysis.

This chapter will discuss the balance sheet and income statement, and the key business ratios that you can apply to financial information for analysis and comparison purposes. How to understand reports prepared by an accountant will also be covered.

WHAT ARE FINANCIAL STATEMENTS?

As mentioned earlier, financial statements consist primarily of the balance sheet and the income statement. An explanation follows.

Balance Sheet

The balance sheet is also known as the statement of financial position. A balance sheet is a statement showing what you own and what you owe. It consists of two sections: (1) the assets of the company, and (2) the liabilities and owner's equity. When the statement is properly completed, it is balanced, in that the assets are equal to the liabilities plus the equity (or capital). In other words, the amount of money you put into the business, plus the amount you borrow, must equal your assets (cash on hand, inventories, equipment). The balance sheet shown in Sample 7 at the back of this book is a typical format for a limited company. The shareholders' equity section is made up of share capital and retained earnings. For a proprietorship or partnership, this section is referred to as owner's equity or partner's equity, respectively.

While the balance sheet follows a standard format, it may contain additional items, depending on the circumstances relating to your type of business and the complexity of the business.

Income Statement

The income statement is also known as the statement of profit-or-loss or statement of operations. It presents a picture of the income generated (or loss suffered) by a business for a stated period. The cost of goods sold and the expenses of the business are deducted from the total sales to arrive at either the net profit or net loss for the period. Current figures can be compared to previous statements to see the changes that have taken place with the amount of sales, cost of goods sold, and expenses.

Sample 8 shows a typical income statement format. You will notice that there are two column for percentages on the right-hand side. This is not always found in income statements but is a very helpful reference point. The percentages of calculations are based on a ratio of the amount of the item in reference to the total sales or revenue. The total sales or revenue, of course, will represent 100%. The sample shown is for a corporation, but is a similar format for a proprietorship or partnership. The employment salary of the shareholder in a limited company would be shown as a pretax operating expense. In the case of a proprietorship or partnership, you would not be able to show the owner's salary or cash withdrawals as a pretax operating expense. Instead, there would be a heading called proprietor's or partners' drawings. This will be determined after the calculation of the net operating income (profit) of the business, and income tax would be based on profits of the business after consideration for personal exemptions and other allowable tax deductions.

UNDERSTANDING ACCOUNTING FRAMEWORKS

When accountants provide an assurance opinion (see below "Understanding Accounting Engagements") on financial statements they are giving an opinion on whether the financial statements were prepared in accordance with an accounting framework. Accounting frameworks provide guidelines for determining how to record an item (e.g., to show a particular expenditure as an acquisition of an asset or an expense), how to present an item (e.g., as a liability or as equity of the entity), and what other information must be disclosed in the financial statement notes. Starting in 2011, "for-profit" entities in Canada have been required to follow either Canadian Accounting Standards for Private Enterprises (ASPE) or International Financial Reporting Standards (IFRS). An explanation of these two accounting frameworks follows.

Canadian Accounting Standards for Private Enterprises

ASPE is a made-in-Canada accounting framework intended to meet the needs of the users of financial statements of private enterprises. This is a relatively straightforward accounting framework that gives the entity alternatives to help ensure that the cost of producing reliable financial statements does not outweigh the expected benefits. Disclosures required in the explanatory notes are much less detailed than under IFRS. ASPE would be the accounting framework most commonly used by private for-profit enterprises.

International Financial Reporting Standards

Unlike ASPE, IFRS is a set of standards set by an international accounting body. In Canada, publicly accountable enterprises (e.g., companies with shares listed on a stock exchange, credit unions, insurance companies, etc.) are generally required to prepare financial statements in accordance with IFRS. IFRS is designed for more complex entities and requires significantly more financial statement disclosure than does ASPE. Unless there is a plan on going public or other legal or contractual requirement to use IFRS, most private entities would elect to prepare their financial statements in accordance with ASPE rather than IFRS.

UNDERSTANDING ACCOUNTING ENGAGEMENTS AND REPORTS

It is important for you to have a general knowledge of the different types of reports prepared by professionally qualified accountants. Refer to Chapter 4,

"Selecting Professional Advisors," for information on selecting and utilizing an accountant. An awareness of the strengths and limitations of an accountant's report is necessary whether you are analyzing the financial condition of your own company or another company.

Reports are prepared under three main levels of assurance, referred to as *engagements*. These are audit, review, and compilation engagements. In Canada, the Canadian Institute of Chartered Accountants (CICA) sets the standards for the accounting profession in its CICA Handbook. An explanation of the types of accounting engagements follows.

Audit Engagement

The objective of an audit engagement is to enhance the degree of confidence of the users of the financial statements. The audit opinion is given in the form of a written report which normally consists of three sections. The first section discusses management's responsibility for preparing the financial statements. The second section outlines the auditor's responsibility to express an opinion on the financial statements, the nature of the work performed, and whether or not sufficient evidence was obtained to form an audit opinion. The third section provides the auditor's opinion as to whether the financial statements were prepared in accordance with the applicable accounting framework (see previous section on accounting frameworks). An auditor's standard report is appended to the financial statements.

EXAMPLE : AUDIT REPORT

To the shareholders of ABC Ltd

We have audited the accompanying financial statements of ABC Ltd, which comprise the balance sheet as at December 31, 20XX, and the statement of income, retained earnings and cash flows for the year then ended, and a summary of significant accounting policies and other explanatory information.

Management's Responsibility for the Financial Statements

Management is responsible for the preparation and fair presentation of these financial statements in accordance with Canadian accounting standards for private enterprises, and for such internal control as management determines is necessary to enable the preparation of financial statements that are free from material misstatement, whether due to fraud or error.

Auditor's Responsibility

Our responsibility is to express an opinion on these financial statements based on our audit. We conducted our audit in accordance with Canadian generally accepted auditing standards. Those standards require that we comply with ethical requirements and plan and perform the audit to obtain reasonable assurance about whether the financial statements are free from material misstatement.

An audit involves performing procedures to obtain audit evidence about the amounts and disclosures in the financial statements. The procedures selected depend on the auditor's judgment, including the assessment of the risks of material misstatement of the financial statements, whether due to fraud or error. In making those risk assessments, the auditor considers internal control relevant to the entity's preparation and fair presentation of the financial statements in order to design audit procedures that are appropriate in the circumstances, but not for the purpose of expressing an opinion on the effectiveness of the entity's internal control. An audit also includes evaluating the appropriateness of accounting policies used and the reasonableness of accounting estimates made by management, as well as evaluating the overall presentation of the financial statements.

We believe that the audit evidence we have obtained is sufficient and appropriate to provide a basis for our audit opinion.

Opinion

In our opinion, the financial statements present fairly, in all material respects, the financial position of ABC Ltd as at December 31, 20XX, and the results of its operations and its cash flows for the year then ended in accordance with Canadian accounting standards for private enterprises.

(signed)
Professionally Qualified Accountant
City, Canada
March 1, 20XX

Most limited companies are required by federal or provincial law to present annual financial statements to their shareholders. Unless the shareholders waive their right, these statements must be audited by a knowledgeable, independent, professionally qualified accountant who is appointed by the shareholders and is responsible for reporting to them.

Companies that have shares or debt securities listed on a stock exchange are required to have audited financial statements. Most small businesses waive that right, as audits are costly and not necessary in most cases in a small business.

The auditor will thoroughly examine the company's financial records and operations to verify that the information provided in the financial statements is reasonable during the period being audited. The procedures used by the auditor normally include: inspection of securities, cash counts, and other assets; confirmation of bank balances; examination of supporting documents, that is, invoices, paid cheques (to assure authenticity); evaluations of the company's internal control methods (to ensure that systems and procedures are in force to safeguard the company's assets and to assess financial statement risks); and making inquiries from within and outside the company.

If the auditor disagrees with the company on the accuracy or fairness of the financial information presented, he or she will qualify the report accordingly by making specific reference to the disagreement. Requests by the company for departures from the applicable accounting framework are usually the cause of the disagreement. The auditor is compelled to state the nature of such disagreement, quantify the amount, if possible, and explain the impact on the financial statements. Specific instances of such disagreements might include the valuation of assets or the method of recognizing revenue or providing for depreciation in the accounts. The accountant would also need to qualify his or her opinion if he or she is unable to obtain all necessary information to complete the audit work.

Review Engagement

A review engagement provides a substantially lower level of assurance than an audit. The objective of a review engagement is to assess whether the information being reported is plausible. A review engagement would again be providing assurance that the financial statements have been prepared in accordance with a particular accounting framework. Upon the completion of the engagement, the accountant will provide a report that is appended to the financial statements.

Review engagements may be prepared in instances in which the shareholders have waived their right to an audit. While an audit requires the public accountant to perform procedures to verify information provided by management, that

EXAMPLE: REVIEW ENGAGEMENT REPORT

To the Shareholders:

We have reviewed the balance sheet of ABC Ltd. as at December 31, 20XX and the statements of income, retained earnings and cash flows for the year then ended. Our review was made in accordance with Canadian generally accepted standards for review engagements and, accordingly, consisted primarily of inquiry, analytical procedures and discussion related to information supplied to us by the company.

A review does not constitute an audit and, consequently, we do not express an audit opinion on these financial statements.

Based on our review, nothing has come to our attention that causes us to believe that these financial statements are not, in all material respects, in accordance with Canadian accounting standards for private enterprises.

(signed)
Professionally Qualified Accountant
City, Canada
March 1, 20XX

is, correlating items to source documents and confirming balances with third parties, a review engagement consists of inquiry, analytical procedures, discussions with management, and potential additional procedures if the accountant's knowledge of the business and the results of other review procedures causes him or her to doubt the plausibility of the information. Plausibility is the main concern of the accountant in performing a review engagement, and the procedures performed will not be as thorough as an audit.

In performing a review, the accountant would acquire sufficient knowledge of the client's business to enable him or her to make intelligent inquiry and assessment of the information obtained. Due professional care must be exercised when performing a review of financial statements, and if anything comes to the accountant's attention that would cause him or her to believe that the financial statements were not prepared in accordance with the applicable accounting framework, this must disclosed in the review engagement report.

Compilation Engagement

A compilation engagement does not provide any assurance on the information presented in the financial statements. The financial statements would not necessarily be prepared in accordance with an accounting framework and are prepared for a specific purpose. The financial statements may be derived from estimated or even incomplete financial information. However, the information may be appropriate for the intended users of the financial statements, such as management, who are aware of possible limitations.

When used for other than the intended purpose, the statements may well be misleading. Hence, the "Notice to Reader" is a clear warning as to the limited use of such financial statements. Readers of statements prefaced by a "Notice to Readers" are well advised to be cautious and request additional financial information relating to the same period.

The following standard form of notice is appended to the financial statements.

EXAMPLE: COMPILATION REPORT

NOTICE TO READER

On the basis of information provided by management, I have compiled the balance sheet of ABC Ltd as at December 31, 20XX and the statements of income, retained earnings and cash flows for the year then ended.

I have not performed an audit or a review engagement in respect of these financial statements and, accordingly, I express no assurance thereon.

Readers are cautioned that these statements may not be appropriate for their purposes.

(signed)
Professionally Qualified Accountant
City, Canada
March 1, 20XX

As mentioned, accountants are frequently called upon to prepare unaudited financial statements for specific purposes.

These specific-purpose statements or summaries normally include monthly reports for management use, specific statements requested by auditors, or supplementary information required for purposes of a tax return. The statements are prepared for the specific purpose stated and will normally provide all reasonable disclosure so as not to be misleading for that particular purpose.

The accountant's scope in such an engagement is restricted to the preparation of the statement based solely on the information supplied by the client. While the professionally qualified accountant will normally ensure that the statements are not misleading for the purpose intended, there is no necessity for a review to determine plausibility or an investigation to assure accuracy of the overall statements.

The use of compilation engagements should generally be restricted to those situations in which the accountant has an understanding with his or her client, and believes that:

- the users are aware of the possible limitations of the financial statements;
- the user will not place undue reliance on the statements, because further information could be accessed if desired; and
- the statements will be used only for the intended purpose.

TYPES OF FINANCIAL STATEMENT ANALYSES

To properly understand your financial statements, you should understand and use three different types of calculations. These are referred to as *horizontal, vertical,* and *ratio analyses.*

Horizontal Analysis

This is a method of comparing revenues and expenses of the current financial year with figures from previous years, both in dollar amounts and percentages. For example, if you are a car dealer, sales can be compared to sales of previous years to determine if your sales have increased or decreased and whether this is on target with your business plan or represents an adequate return on the investment. The horizontal analysis will also be helpful in highlighting a good or bad trend which can be analyzed for serious decision-making. This could include maximizing a growth trend as it is occurring or improving the operational performance.

Vertical Analysis

This is a method of comparing each item of expense and cost of goods sold for services offered on the income statement, with the total sales or revenue within that same period. The purpose is to maximize your profits by thorough analysis of those expenses that can be considered to be major and to develop programs to improve your efficiency and cost savings in those areas.

Ratio Analysis

This is a comparison between two statistics. This is frequently used when comparing similar ratios for the total industry. These key business ratios reveal very specific information relating to the working capital (liquidity or cash flow), productivity, profitability, debt, and equity of your business. These ratios are most useful for new businesses that do not have previous trends. Published ratios may be used as a guide against which you can measure your overall progress. As a general rule of thumb, a variation for your business of 15% to 20% compared to published ratios could be considered acceptable. This will provide a proper degree of caution but still provide you with a helpful guide. Most ratios reflect a combination of balance sheet and income statement items.

BUSINESS RATIOS

There are many sources of ratios for industry or business sectors, most of which are available free of charge upon request. Most of the information is also available online. You can do a Google search under keywords such as "business ratios." You will see lots of options. You want to make sure that you obtain the most current ratios, and preferably ones based on the Canadian business context. American ratio information may also be helpful, as the base numbers are larger and the selection of businesses is more varied. Various sources of ratio information follow.

- Statistics Canada's Corporation Financial Statistics–Web: statcan.gc.ca
- Dun & Bradstreet's Key Business Ratios–Web: dnb.com
- The Risk Management Association–Key Business Ratios–Web: rmahq. org
- Small Business Ratio Calculators–Web: Bankrate.com
- Industry or trade associations

The following is a list of common business ratios that you can use for your small business. The description of the ratio outlines the purpose and how to interpret the information that you have obtained. As mentioned earlier, keep in mind that these ratios are only tools; the same ratio may vary widely for similar types of companies because of different sizes or locations of operations. Whether you have a retail, wholesale, manufacturing, or service business, these ratios will help you answer such critical questions as:

- Does the business have too much debt?
- Is the company slow in collecting receivables?
- Has the business overextended credit to the customers?

- Is the company carrying stale or excess inventory?
- Are operating expenses excessive?
- Is the owner obtaining a good return on his or her investment?

Although the relationship between any two comparative figures is commonly referred to as a ratio, it may also be shown as a percentage or a fraction. For example, if current assets are $100,000 and current liabilities are $50,000, the relationship of current assets to current liabilities ($100,000/$50,000) may be shown as 2 to 1 or 2:1 (ratio), 200% (percentage), or 2/1 (fraction). Some of the ratios also show as an average number of days. It is also helpful to keep in mind that there can be different names for the same ratio, although most of the common ones use the same terminology. For example, the quick ratio is also known as the acid test ratio and the current ratio is also known as the working capital ratio.

The following eighteen ratios are the most common ratios you might use. Not every ratio is necessarily applicable to every type of business. They are segmented under four categories of usage: working capital ratios, debt ratios, profitability ratios, and equity ratios. Remember to check out Canadian and American websites for their information. As noted previously, do a Google search under "business ratios."

Working Capital Ratios

Working capital ratios, also known as liquidity ratios or cash flow ratios, are clear indications of liquidity; in other words, how quickly a business can obtain cash. Liquidity is very important, because it reflects the ability of a business to pay its indebtedness. Various factors can reflect the liquidity of a business. Working capital ratios also measure the margin of financial safety a business has allowed against unforeseen circumstances. For example, if income from receivables or sales is slow and the company has obligations to meet, the liquidity of the business will make a difference in terms of whether those obligations are met on time.

Current ratio formula

$$\frac{\text{Total current assets}}{\text{Total current liabilities}} = \underline{\hspace{2cm}}$$

Interpretation: This relationship reflects how well the business is able to pay current debts and the quality and adequacy of current assets to meet current obligations as they become due. The current ratio can be taken from the balance sheet at any point in time. Normally, current assets should be at least equal to current liabilities. Any ratio less than 1:1 would imply that the business may soon have trouble paying its bills. "Current obligations" is normally deemed to mean payable within the 12-month period. The higher the ratio is, for example 2:1, the better the indication that the company is fairly liquid. The actual quality, composition, and management of those current assets is a critical factor in determining the real liquidity. If the ratio is high, for example greater than 2:1, it is possible that the company has excessive investment in inventory or ineffective use of cash. If the ratio is very low or less than 1:1, possibly the amount and term on the money that is owed by the business should be carefully analyzed. Restructuring of the debt or further investment may be required.

Quick ratio formula (also known as the acid test ratio)

$$\frac{\text{Liquid current assets}}{\text{Current liabilities}} = \underline{\hspace{2cm}}$$

Interpretation: This ratio is a refinement of the current ratio and is a more conservative measure of liquidity. The ratio expresses the degree to which a company's current liabilities are covered by the most liquid current assets. The rule of thumb is that this ratio should be 1:1 (or 100% or dollar to dollar). This ratio indicates the extent to which a company can pay current debt without relying on future sales. Quick assets are highly liquid assets, that is, assets that are immediately convertible to cash, such as inventory or marketable securities. Accounts receivable can also be included, although they are not as liquid as other forms of cash, because you are dependent upon payment from someone who may not be able to pay you immediately. If the ratio is on the high side, for example 2:1, a further analysis can show that there are excessive accounts receivable which may require a re-evaluation of the credit and collection policy of the business. It could also reflect an ineffective use of cash. If the ratio is on the low side (e.g., less than 1:1 because the company is undercapitalized), more investment may be necessary or business debt should be restructured to reduce the amount of monthly debt servicing.

Receivables turnover (sales/receivables) formula

$$\frac{\text{Net sales}}{\text{Average accounts receivable}} = \underline{\hspace{2cm}}$$

$$\text{Average accounts receivable} = \frac{\text{Opening receivables} + \text{Closing receivables}}{2}$$

Interpretation: The number of times accounts receivable are paid and re-established during the accounting period is measured by this ratio. The higher the turnover, the faster the business is at collecting its overdue accounts. This ratio is also used to measure the effectiveness of a firm's credit and collection policy. If the ratio is high, that can suggest the business is basically a cash-only business or the company has utilized a very effective credit and collection policy. If the ratio is low, it is important that the company reassess the credit and collection policy and pay more attention to receivables.

Average days receivable formula

$$\frac{365 \text{ days}}{\text{Receivable turnover ratio}} = \underline{\quad\quad}$$

Interpretation: This ratio shows the average number of days your customers take to pay their accounts. If the figure is low, that is good; it reflects an effective credit and collection policy. On the other hand, if the number of days is high, this amounts to interest-free loans to your customers and can seriously impair your ability to meet your payables. In this event, it is necessary to reassess the credit terms that you are offering and your overall credit and collection policy to reduce the number of days. Keep in mind that banks will frequently not extend a loan on a credit basis for receivables that are over a certain number of days (e.g., 60 days), as this tends to reflect a potential bad debt, poor credit management policy, and higher business risk.

Working capital turnover formula

$$\frac{\text{Net sales}}{\text{Working capital*}} = \underline{\quad\quad}$$

*Working capital is current assets – current liabilities.
Interpretation: This ratio shows how many dollars of sales a business makes for every dollar in working capital. It also reflects the company's ability to finance the current operation and measures how efficiently working capital is utilized. A low ratio may indicate an inefficient use of working capital in terms of generating sales. On the other hand, a high ratio may imply that working capital is not sufficient for maintaining high sales volume. From a creditor's viewpoint, of course, this could put a business in a very vulnerable position.

Payables turnover formula

$$\frac{\text{Purchases}}{\text{Accounts payable}} = \underline{\quad\quad} \text{days}$$

Interpretation: The number of days a business will take to pay for purchases made during an accounting period is measured by the relationship of purchases to existing accounts payable. This reflects on your credit rating, inasmuch as it reflects how consistent you are in paying your creditors on a regular basis. It also shows the effectiveness of your management in terms of collecting accounts receivable or possibly having a cash-only policy, therefore not being overextended in terms of your receivables.

Average days payable formula

$$\frac{\text{Average payables} \times 365 \text{ days}}{\text{Purchases}} = \underline{\hspace{1cm}} \text{days}$$

Average accounts payable

$$= \frac{\text{Opening accounts payable} + \text{Closing accounts payable}}{2}$$

Interpretation: The purpose of this ratio is to show the average number of days that you are taking to reimburse your suppliers.

Productivity and Debt Ratios

Productivity and debt ratios are an indication of small business management efficiency and effectiveness. They provide the basis for examining various aspects of the business by combining both balance sheet and income statement information.

Debt equity ratio formula

$$\frac{\text{Total amount of debt}}{\text{Total amount of equity}} = \underline{\hspace{1cm}}*$$

*Total amount of debt: current + long-term liabilities; total amount of equity: tangible net worth.

Interpretation: This ratio expresses a relationship between capital contributed by creditors and that contributed by owners. The ratio is an indication of leverage, reflecting your financial stability. The higher the ratio, the greater the risk being assumed by creditors. A ratio greater than one means the firm is using more debt than equity to finance investments. Borrowing funds, of course, is a way of gaining financial leverage for other aspects of your business. A firm with a low debt/worth ratio or a trend showing a decreasing ratio has greater flexibility to borrow in the future. A more leveraged, high-ratio company has a more limited debt-to-borrowing capacity.

If you compare published industry or trade ratios, it will give you an estimate of the degree of borrowing that the average firm in your sector considers safe. Credit-granting institutions will also be using similar ratios when they are analyzing your firm. If your ratio is higher than the norm, you could have considerable difficulty in borrowing additional funds from conventional lenders.

Collection period formula

$$\frac{\text{Accounts receivable}}{\text{Net sales} \times 365} = \underline{\hspace{2cm}} \text{ days}$$

Interpretation: This ratio is helpful in analyzing the collection ability of receivables and the efficiency of your credit and collection system. It should be looked at in relation to the allowable credit period you have established. For example, if you have extended credit for a period of 30 days, your ratio should be very close to that same number of days. As a rule of thumb, the collection period should not exceed 10 to 15 days longer than the maturity period of your credit deadline. For example, if your terms were net 30 days, the ratio should not exceed 40 to 45 days. This extra period of time allows for mail delays and processing time. When comparing the collection period of various industry ratios, it is important to keep in mind that allowances should be made for possible variations in selling terms.

The older an account receivable becomes, the greater the likelihood of your having a bad debt. If your collection-period ratio is decreasing, then it is a sign that you are becoming more efficient in your credit and collection policies. If it is less than the published collection period for the industry, it usually means that your collection policy is particularly effective. If your ratio is substantially below the industry average, it may mean that you are losing sales because of an overly stringent credit policy. On the other hand, if your ratio is particularly high relative to the industry norms, it could mean that you are in effect financing your customers and acting as their bank. This, of course, can have very negative effects on the management of your business and its profit potential. You could be paying high debt-servicing rates at the bank for the money that you are in effect lending your customers. It could also limit the volume discount purchases that you can make from suppliers to increase your profit line, because you are stretched in your line of credit at the bank.

Inventory turnover formula

$$\text{Average inventory} = \frac{\text{Opening inventory} + \text{Closing inventory}}{2} = \underline{\hspace{2cm}} \text{ times}$$

Interpretation: The purpose of this ratio is to show the number of times inventory is sold and replaced over a given period. It also assesses the quality of inventory. A high inventory turnover can indicate better liquidity or superior merchandising. Conversely, it can indicate a shortage of needed inventory for sales. Low inventory turnover can indicate poor liquidity, possible overstocking, obsolescence, or in contrast to these negative interpretations, a planned inventory buildup in the case of material shortages. A problem with this ratio is that it compares one day's inventory to cost of goods sold and does not take seasonal fluctuations into account. There are different ways to calculate inventory turnover. Some people prefer to use net sales, although that might be slightly misleading, because sales usually carry a markup over inventory cost. The important points to remember are that you use the same basis each time and that the comparison with industry ratios be the same. The main purpose of the ratio is to show how efficiently the inventory is being managed.

If inventory turnover is low, it could signal a number of factors: sales volume has declined; some of the inventory is damaged or dated and therefore difficult to sell; or if temporary, the firm has stocked up in anticipation of increased sales, say, just before Christmas. A high or increasing rate of inventory turnover generally means that inventory is well managed. A turnover rate that is too high may mean that the inventory is being kept too low, which could cause a crucial shortage of stock if there is an insufficient number of major items in inventory. In addition, insufficient stocking may not permit you to present an extensive enough or interesting enough assortment of products for your customers. If your ratio deviates considerably from industry standards, it may indicate poor marketing as well as poor management. If you are selling perishable goods, it is of course necessary that your inventory turnover rate be very high, or you will be suffering a high spoilage rate and consequent loss in profits.

Inventory supply formula

$$\frac{365 \text{ days}}{\text{Inventory turnover ratio}} = \underline{\hspace{1cm}}$$

Interpretation: The purpose of this ratio is to show the average day's supply in inventory. This will assist you in determining the actual number of days to sell and restock inventory. This ratio will act as a guide for you to improve your purchases, in addition to the cautions discussed in the preceding ratio on inventory turnover.

Operating expense/net sales formula

$$\frac{\text{Any operating expense}}{\text{Net sales}} \times 100 = \underline{\hspace{1cm}}\%$$

Interpretation: This ratio will assist you in telling how well you are controlling expenses. It will assist you in evaluating internal economic efficiency. For example, if you compare this ratio with a budgeted expense figure developed at the beginning of your year, you can see if your expenses compare with your projections. If so, there should be little discrepancy between the two figures. It also indicates the trend of your expenses.

You may have difficulty if your operating expense as a percentage of each sales dollar is increasing without a logical explanation. If your ratio is higher than the previous year, your profits will be eroded unless sales have increased. Even if sales have increased, the spread in terms of profit may not be parallel.

If you compare your ratio with the industry average and find it is below the industry average, this implies you are controlling expenses better than others in your industry. Conversely, if your ratio is much higher than the industry average, you should look at each of your expenses to see where your key expense dollars are being spent, so that you can focus on improving those areas of weakness.

Profitability Ratios

These ratios measure the overall ability of the firm to produce a profit. There are various ways the small business owner/operator can determine profitability. The information required to calculate the following ratios can be located on the balance sheet and income statement referred to earlier.

Gross profit margin formula

$$\frac{Grossprofit}{Net\ sales} \times 100 = \underline{\hspace{1cm}}\%$$

Interpretation: The purpose of this ratio is to determine the percentage of gross profit on each sales dollar. It reveals the actual percentage of sales revenue available to cover the operating and general expenses and taxes and to provide a profit. If you compare your gross profit with your average desired markup, you can see the effect of discounts and theft or spoilage on your business operation. If your ratio is different than your budgeted ratios, you will want to examine the reasons for this very carefully.

If your ratio is lower than the average for the industry or is decreasing, it may mean that your markup is too low or you are paying too much for your merchandise. The solution, among others, is to increase sales, decrease costs, and increase your markup.

Net profit margin formula

$$\frac{Net\ profit\ (after\ taxes)}{Net\ sales} \times 100 = \underline{\hspace{1cm}}\%$$

Interpretation: This ratio allows you to determine the percentage of net profit on each sales dollar. It is equal to the actual gross profit percentage, minus the percentage of each sales dollar required for expenses and taxes. Normally, an increase in the net profit ratio is a positive sign, while a decrease requires your attention in two areas—operating expenses and gross margin or markup. Compare with the industry norm. If your percentage is below, you should reconsider your cost of goods markup and expenses to account for the difference. This ratio is also helpful in reference to the management fee that you take from your business—whether it is a fair fee and whether you are taking too much or too little from the business.

Return On Investment (ROI) formula

$$\frac{\text{Net profit (after taxes)}}{\text{Total assets (tangible net worth)}} \times 100 = \underline{\hspace{1cm}}\%$$

Interpretation: This ratio determines the effective use of all financial resources. While it can serve as an indicator of management performance, you should use it in conjunction with other ratios to confirm that assessment. A high return, normally associated with effective management, could indicate an undercapitalized firm. Whereas a low return, usually an indicator of inefficient management performance, could reflect a highly capitalized, conservatively operated business. If you are lower than the industry average, it could mean that you have unwise investments or a poor product. It could also mean that you should analyze the assets for possible disposal and conversion to cash.

Return on owner's investment formula

$$\frac{\text{Annual net profit (after taxes)}}{\text{Total owner's equity}} \times 100 = \underline{\hspace{1cm}}\%$$

Interpretation: This ratio helps determine adequacy of owner's investment plus the effectiveness of its use. In other words, the return on investment (ROI) ratio measures the earning power of the capital that you have invested in your business. It is an overall indicator of the strength of your business. If the percentage is low, you have to ask yourself whether you are getting a sufficient return on your investment for it to be worthwhile. There could, of course, be other factors that you have to weigh, such as the potential investment risk involved, the various alternatives you have, the potential for long-term profit, or the potential for sale of the business at some future point (with a large capital gain in terms of the goodwill component). A substantial portion of the goodwill could be tax free. An increasing ROI is generally seen as a positive sign, since this ratio provides an overall barometer of the business. If the trend is decreasing, it could imply, unless there is a logical reason for it, that the firm has serious problems that need to be addressed.

Equity Ratios

These ratios measure the amount of financial investment of creditors or owners in the business.

Debt capital ratio formula

$$\frac{\text{Current liabilities + Long-term liabilities}}{\text{Total liabilities (including owner's equity)}} = \underline{\hspace{2cm}}$$

Interpretation: This ratio helps measure the level of creditors' support of your business. If the ratio is high, it means that the creditors have a large claim against your business. This could imply excessive debt requiring a serious reassessment of the borrowing policy of your company. If the ratio is low, it could indicate an ongoing commitment by the owner towards the business. This has to be viewed, though, in conjunction with other ratios, including the ROI ratio.

Owner's equity ratio formula

$$\frac{\text{Current liabilities + Long-term liabilities}}{\text{Owner's equity}} = \underline{\hspace{2cm}}$$

Interpretation: The purpose of this ratio is to measure the level of the owner's commitment to the business. This ratio should be looked at in reference to the debt capital ratio. A horizontal analysis will indicate if your investment is increasing or decreasing in value.

Sample 9 provides a summary of the ratios described, and may be helpful to use as a checklist when you are researching industry standards. The checklist will also be helpful if you are considering buying a business or franchise.

Now that you have completed this chapter, you should pause and applaud yourself. Trying to understand financial statements for the first time is hard work. Having come this far, you have certainly demonstrated one of the key characteristics of an entrepreneur: perseverance!

Chapter 4

Selecting Professional Advisors

A prudent man profits from personal experience, a wise one from the experience of others.

— Joseph Collins

GENERAL FACTORS TO CONSIDER

Professional advisors are essential to small business success. They can provide knowledge and expertise in areas in which you have little experience. They will round out your management team, so that your business is operating most efficiently, with minimal risks and good, sound management advice. It is important to recognize when it is necessary to call in an expert to assist you. Because of the costs associated with hiring a lawyer, accountant, or consultant, some business owners are inclined to try the do-it-yourself approach. This can be a shortsighted decision and detrimental to your business. For instance, the person who processes his or her own income tax return rather than hiring a tax accountant may miss out on small business tax exemptions that could save much more than the cost of the accountant's time. Or a person who signs a lease or a contract without having it reviewed beforehand by a lawyer may regret it for many years to come.

Lawyers, accountants, bankers, business consultants, and insurance brokers serve different functions, and you have to be very selective in your screening process. The right selection will enhance your prospects for profit and growth, while the wrong selection will be costly in terms of time, money, and stress.

There are many factors you should consider when selecting advisors, some more related to paid professional advisors than free advisors, but all are important. The person's professional qualifications, his or her experience in your specific area, and fees for services are factors you will want to consider. It is helpful to prepare a list of questions covering these areas, plus other questions relating to your specific needs, and pose these to each of the prospective advisors. Some people may feel awkward discussing fees and qualifications with a lawyer, for instance, but it is important to establish these matters before you make a decision to use that person's services. If you decide to hire the individual, it is also a good business practice to follow up the initial meeting with a letter confirming the fees agreed upon and other terms discussed, or request the professional advisor to do so. Some of the most common selection criteria are given below.

Qualifications

Before you entrust an advisor with your work, you will want to know that he or she has the appropriate qualifications to do the job. This may include a lawyer's or accountant's professional degree, university degree in the area of expertise, or other professional training relative to the area of work. The fact that the person is an active member of a professional association or institute usually means an ongoing interest in seminars and courses to keep his or her professional training current.

Experience

It is very important to take a look at the advisor's experience in the area in which you are needing assistance. The degree of expertise, the number of years' experience as an advisor, and percentage of time spent practising in that area are critically important. How much you will rely on their advice and insights is obviously related to the degree of experience they have in the area of your business concern. For example, the fact that a lawyer has been practising law for 10 years does not necessarily mean that he or she has a high degree of expertise in the area on which you are seeking advice. Perhaps only 10% of the practice has been spent in that specific area. An accountant who has had 15 years experience in small business accounting and tax advice will certainly provide you with in-depth expertise about small business in general. If that accountant also has specialized experience with your type of industry, that is an additional factor that could assist you. It cannot be overemphasized how important it is to inquire about the degree of expertise and length of experience in your specific area. If you don't ask the question, you won't be given the answer that may make a difference between satisfaction and dissatisfaction.

Compatible Personality

When deciding on an advisor, make certain that you feel comfortable with the individual's personality. If you are going to have an ongoing relationship with the advisor, it is important that you feel comfortable with the degree of communication, the attitude, the approach, the candour, and commitment to your business success. A healthy respect and rapport will increase your comfort level when discussing business matters and thereby enhance understanding of issues.

Confidence

You must have confidence in your advisor if you are going to rely on his or her advice to enhance the quality of your decision-making and minimize your risk. After considering the person's qualifications, experience, personality, and style, you may feel a strong degree of confidence in the individual. If you do not, don't use the person as an advisor; seek someone else as soon as possible. Otherwise, there is a very good chance that you will not use the person's services as extensively as you should or when you need to. This could have a serious negative impact on your decision-making.

Fees

It is important to feel comfortable with the fee being charged and the payment terms. Is the fee fair, competitive, and affordable? Does it match the person's qualifications and experience? The saying "You get what you pay for" can be true of fees charged by lawyers, accountants, and consultants. For instance, if you need a good tax accountant to advise you on minimizing taxes, you may have to pay a high hourly rate for the quality of advice that will save you several thousands of dollars. On the other hand, if you only require the preparation of annual financial statements, then perhaps a junior accountant can do the job competently at a more affordable rate. Be certain the rate is within your budget, or you may not use the advisor's services effectively because of the expense factor. Not using professional advice when you need it is poor management.

Comparison

It is important that you do not make a decision as to which advisor to use without first checking around. See a minimum of three advisors before deciding which advisor is right for you. The more exacting you are in your selection criteria, the more likely it will be that a good match is made, and the more beneficial that advisor will be to your business. It is a competitive market, and you can afford to be extremely selective when choosing advisors to complement your management team.

SELECTING A LAWYER

There are numerous ways that a lawyer can help you, from the time that you have the idea of going into business during the pre–start-up phase, right through to the start-up. You also will need a lawyer during phases of expanding, diversifying, selling, or winding down your business. Your lawyer can help you in deciding the proper legal structure of your business, drawing up a partnership or shareholder agreement, and negotiating a management contract and numerous other types of contracts. Advice can also be given about employee contracts, firing employees, suing creditors, Revenue Canada or provincial tax audits, negotiation, wills and estate planning, buying a business or a franchise, financial documents, leases, patents, copyright, and trademarks. There are few business decisions that do not involve some legal, financial, or tax implication. It is important to keep that thought in mind through the day-to-day operation of your business. Ask yourself, "What is the legal implication of the decision I am making?" Then contact your lawyer to get the appropriate advice.

Although your lawyer is trained to give legal advice as to your rights, remedies, and options, it is you who must decide on the action to be taken.

How to Find a Lawyer

Lawyers in Canada must have a Bachelor of Laws degree (LL.B.) from a recognized Canadian university. The lawyer in Canada is called both a barrister and a solicitor, but depending upon the preference of the lawyer, the lawyer may act as a barrister or solicitor or both. A barrister is a lawyer who practises courtroom law and deals in civil and/or criminal legal matters. A solicitor generally does not attend court and performs services such as drafting or reviewing legal agreements, including wills, leases, mortgages, and contracts.

Some methods for finding lawyers follow.

Lawyer referral services

Most provinces throughout Canada have a lawyer referral program which is usually coordinated through the Canadian Bar Association. Simply look in the telephone directory under "Lawyer Referral Service" or contact the Law Society or Canadian Bar Association. When you call, explain briefly the specific problem you have or the type of business law on which you want a lawyer's opinion; for example, small business, contract, tax, patent, trademark, or copyright law. The lawyer referral service will give you the name of a lawyer in your geographic area, and you can arrange to set up an appointment with the lawyer. A lawyer will give you an interview of up to 30 minutes, for free or at a nominal fee (generally around $50, which may vary depending upon the province or the location. At the end of the interview, the lawyer will tell you whether he or she thinks you have a legal problem, what is involved, how long it should take to solve the problem, and about how much it will cost. Then, if you and the lawyer agree to proceed, you may hire the lawyer to help you for a negotiated fee. If you decide not to hire the lawyer, and wish to consult someone else, or if you are satisfied that you do not require any further help, it won't cost you any more than the nominal fee.

Most lawyer referral services permit a lawyer's name to be listed on a maximum of three specialty areas. Small business, which is sometimes categorized as commercial law, could be just one of the three specialties listed. Do not assume, therefore, that the lawyer specializes 100% in small business or commercial law. The lawyer may only practise 10% in small business law. Deal with a lawyer who spends at least 50% of his or her time in small business law. The higher the percentage of time spent, the greater the chance that the quality of advice you are going to be receiving is based on extensive experience in a wide range of problems encountered when running a small business.

Referral by friends, relatives, business associates, banker, or accountant

Ask these reference sources if they can recommend a lawyer who would be appropriate for your needs within the business context. A friend or relative might suggest a lawyer, for example, whose law specialty has nothing to do with business law, and who would be impractical for you to use. If someone recommends a specific lawyer, or a number of lawyers, ask the reason why he or she feels the person would be helpful for your small business needs, and what his or her personal experience has been with that lawyer.

The Yellow Pages—print and online

In the *Yellow Pages* telephone directory print edition and online under the heading "Lawyers," you may note that some lawyers have a preferred interest or designated specialty. It is common to see an offer of a free initial consultation.

Newspaper ads

With the recent removal of restrictions on advertising in most provinces, some law firms are now using newspaper ads to market their services.

Many lawyers will offer the initial consultation without a fee, as this provides them with an opportunity to hear what is involved in your situation and to decide if they are interested in taking on the work. It is also an effective "loss leader" marketing technique. You should take advantage of this opportunity to pose the questions you have prepared, to see if the lawyer is well-suited to your needs. It is quite common to have more than one lawyer assist you in your business needs, either for a second opinion or for advice in a different area of expertise. Patent and trademark law, for instance, is a specialized area in which most lawyers may not have had experience.

Searching the internet

Lawyers are now using the Internet to market their services. Do a search for the area of law that interests you under the name of the city you live—put keywords in Google and see what comes up.

Preparing for the Meeting

Because you are buying your lawyer's time, the less you use, the less it will cost. On the other hand, it is important that you clearly understand the advice that is given and what options are available to you.

Before going to see your lawyer, make sure that you get all your papers and documents together and put them in order—assuming that you wish to get advice on existing facts. Then, write out all the issues that you want advice on, and all the questions you want to ask. Arrange the sequence of your questions so that the critical matters are dealt with first. It may be helpful to give a copy of your questions to the lawyer, who could use that as an agenda for covering the various issues. Thinking about your questions will force you to focus on the reasons for seeing the lawyer. You will be satisfied that the meeting was productive when all questions are answered by the end of the interview.

When you talk to the lawyer, stick to the facts and make sure you tell your lawyer all the facts, good and bad. Ask questions if you don't understand the advice and ask what you can do to minimize costs. Request that the lawyer keep you informed of developments if you are retaining the lawyer on an ongoing basis. It is quite common for people to be unfocused, emotional, or overly enthusiastic, depending on the stage of their small business venture. The lawyer, by training and discipline, is supposed to be objective, balanced, and unemotional. It is important to bear this in mind; do not feel that the lawyer is indifferent to your needs.

After you have talked to your lawyer, you can keep your legal fees down by not making unnecessary telephone calls to his or her office. If you must call on routine matters, you may prefer to talk to the lawyer's secretary. The response would not necessarily translate into a bill being rendered for the time. Be realistic about the matters in dispute or the action you are considering. For example, you don't want to spend $1,000 in legal fees to collect a $500 debt owing to you. The high legal costs involved in litigation matters are covered in more detail in Chapter 15, "Credit and Collection," and Chapter 16, "Understanding the Litigation Process."

Understanding Fees, Disbursements, and Costs

Some of the factors that a lawyer considers when setting fees are as follows:

- the degree of specialization the lawyer possesses in the specific area
- the number of years the lawyer has been practising law
- the time spent by the lawyer on your behalf
- the legal complexity of the matters dealt with
- the monetary value of the matters at issue
- the degree of responsibility assumed by the lawyer
- the importance of the matters to the client
- the degree of difficulty in dealing with the issue
- the degree of skill and competence demonstrated by the lawyer

- the results obtained by the lawyer on the client's behalf
- the ability of the client to pay.

In many cases the legal fee structure is based on what other lawyers are charging. Although competition in the legal profession is obviously a factor in keeping fees competitive, there are many circumstances in which two lawyers will charge a different fee for performing the same routine or specialized service.

Types of Fee Arrangements

Hourly rate

A lawyer bills out on a fixed rate per hour for all work done. The fee could range between $200 and $350 or up to $500 or more per hour for an experienced lawyer in a speciality area, for each service provided, including telephone calls, dictating correspondence, reviewing correspondence from other lawyers, reviewing documents, researching statute and case law, meeting with clients, and preparing documents. If your file involves a litigation matter (you are suing someone or someone is suing you), the lawyer would be charging for all time spent on your behalf preparing for an examination for discovery or trial, interviewing witnesses, reading transcripts, and any other matters. This is covered in more detail in Chapter 16, "Understanding the Litigation Process."

Contingency fee

Most provinces in Canada allow lawyers to charge on a contingency fee basis; that is, for a percentage of the total amount awarded if the case is won. For example, let's say that you have a fairly strong case, but do not have the funds to pay your lawyer at the outset or for ongoing work on the case. Your lawyer may agree to act for you and charge a percentage of the amount that you may eventually receive, either at trial or on a negotiated settlement prior to trial. If you win, the lawyer receives the fee; if you lose or the matter is not settled, the lawyer gets nothing. You would be responsible for paying the lawyer's disbursements (out-of-pocket expenses) and costs. The percentage contingency fee will vary depending upon the amount of your claim, the degree of risk involved, and the stage in the proceedings at which the case is resolved. The normal range is between 25% and 40%. All contingency fee agreements must be in writing.

Percentage fee

Sometimes fees are calculated as a percentage of the value of the subject matter. This approach is often used when probating an estate or collecting a debt.

Fixed fee

If you hire a lawyer to provide a routine service, such as a conveyance or an incorporation, the lawyer may be able to quote a flat fee, regardless of how much work might be involved. A lawyer may use this method when the time required can be calculated fairly accurately.

Retainer

This is an advance or down payment to show your commitment, and to ensure the availability of the funds to pay the lawyer. The money is put into the lawyer's trust account. This initial payment may or may not be the entire fee. When the lawyer performs a service, an invoice would be rendered and monies would be taken from the retainer fee in the trust account to pay for the invoice. A retainer fee may also be used as a fixed monthly "salary" paid by a client who wants or needs the lawyer on call for problems or questions that occur from time to time.

In addition to paying your lawyer fees for time spent, you may have to pay for the lawyer's disbursements. Disbursements incurred on your behalf by the lawyer would include such things as photocopies, courier costs, registry searches, registry agent fees, long-distance telephone calls, fax charges, provincial or federal filing fees, process-serving fees, transportation costs, expert witness fees, examination for discovery fees, costs of transcripts, and research costs. It is not customary for lawyers to charge out secretarial time spent on your file; however, costs associated with paralegal services may be included in the fees charged.

As in any other business relationship, in order to maintain an effective rapport with your legal advisor, good communication is essential. Be certain you and your lawyer keep each other informed of matters of importance, so neither is operating without complete information. If you are in doubt about the particular advice you are being given, you may prefer to get a second opinion. This is reassurance that you are following the best advice for your business. Misunderstandings on fees or other matters should be immediately clarified to avoid having them mount into serious problems. If the relationship does not appear to be a beneficial one, you may decide at any time to use the services of another lawyer and to have the working file transferred to the new lawyer. If you seriously question a lawyer's invoice, you can have it "taxed" (reviewed) by a Court registrar. This is an informal procedure and results in the fee being upheld or reduced. Your local court office will be able to provide further information on the procedure.

SELECTING AN ACCOUNTANT

An accountant's chief concern is to monitor the financial health of your business and reduce both subsequent risks and taxes paid. Along with your lawyer, your accountant will complement your management team to ensure your business decisions are based on sound advice and good planning. An accountant who is familiar with your type of business can provide much insight and assistance in reviewing your business plan. An accountant can help you to analyze your operations, decipher your break-even point, pinpoint problem areas, and assist you in developing solutions. After the situation is evaluated, recommendations should be made to reduce the operating costs and improve profitability. The timeliness of the decision to expand your operations or to introduce a new product line is crucial to your success, and an accountant can assist you in your strategic planning. Your accountant can develop information systems that can alert you to problems before they arise. They may be manual or computerized systems for accounting and management information and controls.

It is somewhat pointless to enlist the services of an accountant to prepare financial statements without also having them discussed with you and interpreted. What do the statements mean? And how should you use the information to modify your day-to-day operations? Your short- and long-term plans should be based on the activity to date, noted improvements or trends, and your sales and operating cost projections.

An accountant can help you from the pre–start-up phase through the ongoing operation to the eventual sale or closing down of the business. The services that can be provided are wide-ranging, and include:

- setting up a bookkeeping system that both the owner and accountant can work with efficiently
- setting up systems for the control of cash and the handling of funds
- obtaining government grants and other means of raising capital
- preparing or evaluating budgets, forecasts, and business plans
- assessing your break-even point and improving your profitability
- providing advice on issues such as buying or leasing equipment, compensation, and benefit plans
- preparing and interpreting financial statements
- providing tax advice and financial planning
- preparing corporate and individual tax returns
- assessing risk and insurance planning
- providing advice on expanding, buying, or selling a business or franchise.

Qualifications

In Canada, anyone can call himself or herself an accountant. One can also adopt the title "public accountant" without any qualifications, experience, regulations, or accountability to a professional association. That is why you have to be very careful when selecting the appropriate accountant for your needs. There are three main designations of qualified professional accountants in Canada: Chartered Accountant (CA), Certified General Accountant (CGA), and Certified Management Accountant (CMA).

Accountants with the above designations are governed by provincial statutes. These professional accountants are regulated by their respective institutes or associations in terms of their conduct, professional standards, training, qualifications, professional development, and discipline. Rely on the advice of an accountant, therefore, only after you have satisfied yourself that the accountant meets the professional qualifications that you require for your business needs.

There are differences in the educational requirements, training, experience, and nature of practice of the different accounting designations mentioned above. Some accountants pursue careers in public practice (e.g., serving the needs of the small business owner); others enter positions in industry, education, or government, or specialize in the areas of management, cost, financial, or tax accounting. For further information, contact the professional institute or association for the specific type of accounting designation, and request an explanatory brochure. You can obtain the contact phone number from the *Yellow Pages* print or online editions, or other directories under "Accountants," or find out the address in your province from your local library, if you are located in a smaller city. The professional governing bodies are referred to as the Institute of Chartered Accountants, Certified General Accountants' Association, and the Society of Management Accountants.

How to Find an Accountant

A referral by business associates, banker, or lawyer

Often a banker, lawyer, or other business associate will be pleased to recommend the name of an accountant who has expertise in small business. Such referrals are valuable, since these individuals are probably aware of your type of business and would recommend the name of an accountant only if they felt the individual was well qualified and had a good track record of assisting small businesses.

Professional associations

The professional institute or association which governs CAs, CGAS, and CMAs may be a source of leads. You can telephone or write the institute or association with a request for the names of three accountants who provide public accounting services to small businesses within your locale. It is not uncommon for any initial consultation to be free of charge. You can also do a Google search with the keywords for the association to get contact info.

The Yellow Pages or other online directory services

In the *Yellow Pages* print edition or online, under the heading "Accountants," you will find listings under the categories "chartered," "certified general," and "management."

Ads in newspapers

Occasionally you will see ads in newspapers from accounting firms that are offering services in your area of specialty or interest.

Online searches

You can do a Google search with the keywords for your area of interest to get contact info and then follow up with at least three accountants or accounting firms.

Preparing for the Meeting

Prior to a meeting with your accountant, make a list of your questions and concerns. Put them in writing and list them in order of priority. As noted earlier, you will want to know the person's qualifications, areas of expertise, and method of record-keeping (e.g., is a computerized system used or necessary for your needs?). Ask the accountant what his or her range of experience is in your type of business: tax, small business advice, accessing financing, and buying and selling a business. Ask about fees, how they are determined, how accounts are rendered, and what retainer may be required. Ask who will be working on your file—the accountant, an articling student or junior accountant, or a bookkeeper.

Understanding Fees and Costs

Accountants' fees vary depending upon experience, specialty, type of service provided, size of firm, and other considerations. The fee can range between $40 and $250 or more per hour. It is common practice for an accountant to have different charge-out rates for the various activities performed: bookkeeping, preparation of financial statements, or tax consultation and advice. For example, if an accountant is doing bookkeeping, it will be at a lower rate scale; complex tax advice is charged at the high end of the range. Accountants generally charge for their time and for additional costs, such as a bookkeeper, secretary, or articling student. The bill-out rates for these various staff members vary, and you should ask exactly what you will be charged.

Accountants have what is called an engagement letter. It is prepared after the interview, if you agree to proceed with the accountant's services. The engagement letter sets out the terms of the agreement between you and the accountant, the nature of services that will be provided, what the fee will be for the accountant's services for various tasks, and the bill-out rate for other staff members. A retainer is usually requested. When that retainer is exhausted, a further retainer may be expected for ongoing work. If you have an incorporated company, it is common for your personal guarantee to be required on the contract letter. This is a guarantee that you will be personally responsible for paying any outstanding fees incurred by the company.

As with your lawyer, a good level of rapport and communication with your accountant will enhance the quality of the advice you receive and the effectiveness of your use of that advice. Openly discuss your concerns and questions with your accountant. You may from time to time wish to seek a second opinion on advice you have been given. If you are not satisfied with your accountant for any reason, you should find another accountant who could better meet your needs. This is not uncommon. However, you may be requested by your new accountant to sign a letter to the previous accountant confirming that you no longer are using his or her services and have retained a new accountant.

SELECTING A BANKER

When deciding which bank to deal with for your business affairs, it is advisable to shop around, especially if you are in need of bank financing. You will find that services and rates vary among branches of the same bank. It is helpful to have a banker who has had experience in your industry sector. As a banker's loan approval limit will vary from branch to branch, you will want a banker who has a loan approval level greater than the amount of money that you need to borrow. It is much easier to sell one person on the merits of your loan application than to have it screened at a head office branch by people you have never met. Another advantage of dealing with a banker with extensive experience is that generally you can negotiate a better rate of interest. Consider the following options:

- One of the most effective ways of selecting a banker is through a referral from your accountant or lawyer. If they spend a high percentage of their time on small business matters, they may be aware of specific bankers who understand the needs of small business owners, or who have had experience in your industry sector.
- If you are a member of a trade or professional association, you could ask the members what bank they would recommend, what banker, and why. In this way, you are finding a banker who is familiar with your industry sector.
- Contact a commercial banking unit or equivalent of the major chartered banks in your area, and ask the manager which senior loans officer in

that branch has expertise in your industry sector. Then set up a meeting with that person.

- Banking with the branch that your family has been dealing with for many years could add credibility to your own business relationship and loan application in terms of track record and reputation.

When putting together a loan proposal, you should elicit the assistance of your accountant and lawyer to ensure that it is complete. Shop around for the bank and branch that will negotiate the most favourable loan package. Once you have negotiated a package and have it confirmed in writing by the bank, proceed to transfer your accounts to the new bank.

In the ideal situation, getting to know your banker should start before you need to request financing. Take the opportunity to introduce yourself the next time you are in the bank. A few casual comments about your new venture could be followed up with a request for a brief discussion at the banker's convenience. At that meeting you might provide a sample or brochure of your product and discuss in general your overall business plan. Keep the banker informed on a casual basis of your progress. By taking the initiative to develop a first-name relationship with your banker, you have paved the way for a future loan request. Most people approach a banker only when their businesses fall upon tough times or they are in need of money. Therefore, the banker has to decide whether they are a high risk without having the opportunity to know them personally. If you establish a favourable relationship with the banker, and the banker is then transferred to another branch, it may be prudent to move your account to that branch if it is within your geographic area.

It is possible at some point that your relationship with your banker may not be satisfactory. This could be because the person with whom you had an excellent relationship was transferred to another branch outside your business locale, and the replacement does not develop the same quality relationship with you. Possibly a new manager has come into the branch, has reassessed your file, and wants to have additional security or a higher interest rate or wants to reduce your line of credit. Another factor could be that the head office of your bank has looked at certain types of industry profiles and has seen that there is a high failure rate or other problems in the industry that could impact on your business. As a consequence of this, a policy could be made that no further loans are given to businesses within that industry sector. Still another reason could be that the service you have been getting is not sufficient for your needs, or the branch is not sophisticated enough to meet your expanding requirements. Whatever the reason, if you are not happy with your banker, explore other options.

A banker can assist you in numerous ways, but the effectiveness of that assistance is based on the experience that the banker has had in the lending business and the knowledge the banker has in your industry sector. Your banker can assist you in setting up the various loan arrangements for your business operation. (More detail in terms of loan structures is covered in Chapter 10, "Raising Financing.") Your bank can provide a wide range of other services that can assist you in all phases of your business and for special needs; for example:

- operating loans
- term loans for plant expansion or renovation, or purchase of machinery, equipment, land, or buildings
- interim financing
- term deposits
- current accounts
- retirement savings plans
- factoring services
- Visa or MasterCard merchant accounts
- Visa or MasterCard expense accounts
- money transfers
- credit information
- merger and acquisition services
- leasing services.

Banks also have international centres, normally in the head offices of major cities, which provide such services for your small business as: foreign exchange; letters of credit/guarantee; international tax guidance; foreign collections; mail and cable payments; export and import data, financing and professional advice; and foreign credit information. As you probably are very aware, the banking industry is really putting its emphasis on electronic banking, in an effort to move away from the more resource-intensive "brick-and-mortar" traditional type of banking. Although you probably will still have to visit a brick-and-mortar site to sign the contract, you should check out the Internet to see the wide range of options available to you, for example, handling many of your transactions online, monitoring your account, etc. Refer to Appendix C for the website addresses of the major Canadian banks.

SELECTING A BUSINESS CONSULTANT/ COUNSELLOR

Anyone in Canada can use the title "consultant." So if you are selecting a business consultant to advise you, make certain you check on his or her qualifications and background. Does the consultant have a Master of Business Administration (MBA) degree or other degree that is related to the field in which you require expertise? Is a degree necessary or simply experience or knowledge? Is the consultant an active member of his or her professional association? How many years has he or she spent as a consultant in the field of expertise? Can he or she provide you with references from satisfied clients? These factors, along with the person's specific background experience, will aide you in identifying the right person to assist you.

Private consultants' fees range widely, but average between $100 and $400 or more per hour, depending on expertise and experience. Or a flat fee may be charged for a specific service, for example, a simple marketing survey or a feasibility study. Private consultants tend to specialize in various areas, such as credit and collection, product or service marketing, business plans, inventory control, advertising, security, computer systems, hiring employees, pricing, and a wide range of other specialized areas. They also have contacts with other resource sources of information that could assist you.

A consultant may render a bill on an interim basis—either when the account reaches a certain level or a certain task is accomplished—and request that the client pay the amount of the interim account for fees and disbursements. The invoice is usually due and payable upon receipt, unless other arrangements are made in advance and confirmed in writing.

Government counselling programs can assist you in a wide range of areas that relate to your small business and are usually offered at no charge. Topics would include importing or exporting; selling to the federal, provincial, or municipal governments; accessing government grants; explanation of basic small business management strategies; assistance in researching data relating to different aspects of running a business; and assistance in preparing business plans.

The process for selecting a business consultant will vary, depending on whether it is a free service or not. When starting out in business, your needs may be more general in scope and your funds somewhat limited. Therefore, accessing the free or nominal fee services offered by the government and some universities and colleges can be beneficial for starting you in the right direction.

Private consultants, on the other hand, can take the process a step further and actually complete the task. For example, a private consultant will ascertain your computer needs, perform a search of available hardware and software, and proceed, if you wish, to purchase the various components, install the system, and train staff on how to operate it. When hiring a private consultant, you would use similar selection criteria as you would to select a lawyer or accountant, making certain you check the consultant's references in advance. You will find that many of the following organizations, government programs, and foundations now have information on their websites. The same with major universities. You should consider doing your research on the Internet, whether you are looking for grants or loans or consulting assistance.

BDC Consultant

This is a program, operated by the Business Development Bank of Canada (BDC). The consultants have a wide range of expertise in specific areas. Following an interview at your BDC office to ascertain your needs, a match is made with the appropriate consultant. That person will then work with you on a particular project or an ongoing basis as your needs dictate, and for an agreed-upon project price or hourly rate.

Provincial Government

The small business department of each provincial government in Canada employs counsellors who are available without charge to provide counselling assistance to you during the various stages of your small business enterprise. You may have a specific question to ask over the telephone or online, or you may need to set a 1-hour appointment for advice on developing a marketing plan, for instance. The small business counsellors have useful planning guides and "how to" publications available at no charge to assist you. Many provinces have branch offices throughout the province to provide free small business advice plus a toll-free information number.

Federal Government

Industry Canada has small business counsellors who will assist you with your small business needs free of charge, for an agreed-upon fee in advance, or for a nominal fee. In addition, other government departments, such as Statistics Canada, Foreign Affairs and International Trade Canada, and Public Works and Government Services Canada can assist you with free research information.

Universities/Community Colleges

Some universities, community colleges, and technology institutes have "enterprise development centres" which provide instructional seminars and training on small business management, as well as counselling assistance for a nominal fee or an agreed-upon fee This one-on-one mentoring relationship can help new business owners establish a sound foundation for their operations.

Private Consultants

There are many private business consultants available who specialize in a wide variety of assistance. Checking in the *Yellow Pages* print or online under "Business Consultants," you will find a listing of consultants along with their specialty. You will frequently see newspaper ads in the business section of your newspaper, as well as trade journal ads that have names of business consultants. Another source is, of course, by means of referral from business associates or friends who could recommend a consultant they have used, or by referral from your lawyer, accountant, or banker. Do a Google search with the keywords for your area of interest. You will find lot of information about prospective consultants.

SELECTING AN INSURANCE REPRESENTATIVE

A broker is not committed to any particular insurance company, and therefore can compare and contrast the different policies, coverages, and premiums from a wide range of companies that relate to the type of insurance coverage you are seeking. Also, insurance brokers can obtain a premium quotation for you and coverage availability from insurance company underwriters if the particular business you have is unique or difficult to cover with other existing policies. Insurance brokers generally have a wide range of types of business insurance available. It is important to have confidence in the broker in terms of expertise, qualifications, and objectivity. Ensure that he or she is affiliated with a reputable firm. When selecting an insurance broker, you should ask about the person's professional credentials, expertise, and experience. You can find an insurance broker by looking in the *Yellow Pages* print or online under "Insurance Brokers." You can also obtain names of insurance brokers from friends, business associates, or your accountant or lawyer.

Every small business owner needs insurance for financial protection. Insurance is frequently required by creditors such as banks or landlords. Ask the insurance broker for brochures describing the main types of insurance and an explanation of each. The main categories and types of insurance that you should consider and discuss with your insurance broker are discussed in Chapter 20, "Insuring Your Business's Future."

Remember, whenever you are selecting professional or business advisors, speak to at least three advisors in each area. This will provide you with an objective basis for comparison and selection.

Chapter 5

Legal Considerations

Everything is more complicated than it seems.

— Murphy's Law

In the world of business, every business decision involves a legal implication, directly or indirectly. Part of a prudent and necessary business approach is legal risk management.

This chapter discusses some of the main legal issues you should consider. One of your first considerations when starting a small business is the form of legal structure you should choose. This will be necessary before you set up a company bank account, apply for a business licence, or register your company name. Your main choices will include sole proprietorship, partnership, or corporation. A description of each of these follows, along with advantages and disadvantages of each.

As many owners follow the incorporation route, the second part of this chapter deals with the process of incorporating a business. It reviews choosing a name for your business, directors and shareholders, classes of shares, provincial and federal registrations, and other considerations with which you may be faced. If you are involved in a partnership or shareholder situation, it is essential to have a well-constructed agreement in writing. Sample agreement checklists (Samples 10 and 11) are given at the back of the book. These will assist you in drafting an agreement outline for your own use. However, the samples are intended as guidelines only, and you should seek competent legal assistance before signing any agreement. As you can see from the samples, the contents of these agreements can be complex, but the underlying issues are important to clarify before starting up your business, if at all possible.

The last part of this chapter discusses how to "creditor-proof" your business to legally minimize your business and personal risks, in the event your business runs into difficulties.

For additional reference, see Douglas Gray's *The Canadian Small Business Legal Advisor*, published by McGraw-Hill Ryerson.

TYPES OF LEGAL STRUCTURE

The type of legal structure you decide on for your business will depend upon the type of business you are in, your potential risk and liability, and the amount of money you need to start with and expect to earn. If your potential risk and liability are high, the incorporation process will provide protection from possible disasters. On the other hand, a person starting a home-based business with little or no risk should consider the advantages of having a sole proprietorship. Once you become familiar with the differences between each form of legal structure, you should consult a lawyer and tax accountant. Your decision in this area is an important one.

Sole Proprietorship and Partnership

A sole proprietorship refers to an individual who owns a business in his or her personal name or operates through a trade name. The business income and the owner's personal income are considered the same for tax purposes. Therefore, business profits are reported on the owner's personal income tax return, based on federal and provincial income tax schedules. Business expenses and losses are deductible. It is advisable, though, to keep personal and business bank accounts separate. For instance, you should pay yourself a salary from your business account and deposit it into your personal account for your personal needs (food, clothing, lodging, personal savings). A proprietor is personally responsible for all debts or liabilities of the business.

A partnership is a proprietorship with two or more owners. The owners may not necessarily be 50/50 partners; they may have whatever percentage properly reflects their investment and contribution to the partnership. Each partner shares profits and losses in proportion to his or her respective percentage interest. The partnership business itself does not pay any tax. Instead, the individual partners pay tax based on their portion of the net profit or loss, and this is shown on their personal tax returns. In a partnership, each partner is personally liable for the full amount of the debts and liabilities of the business. Each of the individuals is authorized to act on behalf of the company, and can bind the partnership legally, except if stated otherwise in a partnership agreement. It is sound business advice not to enter any partnership arrangement without a written agreement between the partners regarding responsibilities for financing the business, sharing the profits and losses, working in the business, specific duties, and other important considerations. A checklist of what to include in a partnership agreement is provided in Sample 10 at the back of this book.

In a proprietorship or partnership, the company continues until the owner ceases to carry on the business or dies. If the business uses a name different from the owner's personal name, the company name (called a "trade style" name) should be registered with the appropriate provincial registry. The Consumer and Corporate Affairs office of the provincial government will provide the necessary forms to be completed and, if you wish, a copy of the Partnership Act, which governs sole proprietorships and partnerships.

Advantages of a sole proprietorship or partnership

- Few government and legal formalities make sole proprietorships and partnerships easy to form. In most provinces, there is a nominal one-time fee for registering the company.
- The personal tax rate is lower than the rate for corporations in certain situations. Therefore, during the early phases of the business, it may be more tax advantageous to remain a sole proprietorship or partnership. Once the business is earning substantial sums, the company could be rolled over into a corporation.
- Business losses can be offset against the owner's other income, thereby reducing the owner's overall personal marginal tax rate. There are some exceptions, and you should check with your accountant regarding current tax legislation.

Disadvantages of a sole proprietorship or partnership

The owner is personally liable for all debts and obligations of the business.

It is frequently difficult to raise capital, apart from conventional loans, because of the potential liability and risk.

Customers and creditors may perceive the proprietorship as having a low level of business sophistication. It may be perceived to be in business for the short term rather than the long term.

Some government loan, subsidy, or guarantee programs are available only to limited companies (corporations).

Sale of the business could involve having to disclose the owner's personal tax return.

If the business fails, the owners are not eligible to collect Employment Insurance benefits unless they have accrued enough employment time elsewhere or before pursuing the business.

Corporation (Limited Company)

A corporation is a business which is a legal entity separate from the owner or owners of the business. It is a formal business structure which, after being incorporated with the provincial or federal registry, must file annual reports, submit regular tax returns, and pay tax on the profits of the business. The owners of the business are called shareholders and have no personal liability for the company's debts, unless they have signed a personal guarantee. The liability of the company is limited to the assets of the company. The shareholders elect directors who are responsible for managing the business affairs of the corporation. Directors are usually shareholders. The profits of the corporation may be retained for reinvestment or distributed to the shareholders in the form of dividends at the discretion of the directors.

It is advisable to obtain legal and tax advice to assist with the preparation of the incorporation documents and shareholders' agreements. A checklist of items to be included in a shareholders' agreement is shown in Sample 11.

Advantages of incorporation

- The shareholders are not personally responsible for any of the debts or obligations of the corporation, unless a shareholder has signed a personal guarantee.
- A corporation has more financing options available. It is eligible for government financing incentive programs that may be unavailable to unincorporated businesses. It can attract investors and provide better security to lenders in the form of debentures, common shares, convertible shares, and other structures.
- The corporation continues regardless of whether a shareholder dies or retires.
- In general terms, a corporation can imply a higher prestige, more stability, and greater resources in terms of capital and expertise.
- There is increased stability in that shareholders can come and go but the business continues uninterrupted and all contracts of the corporation remain valid.
- A corporation can convert itself to a public corporation by meeting the requirements of the Securities Commission and other government regulatory departments. It can thereby raise money on the stock exchange by going public.

The following are some other factors which can be advantageous in reducing or minimizing your personal or corporate tax. You should seek professional tax advice from your accountant that would be customized to your situation.

- small business corporate tax rate
- deferred tax on business income
- capital gains exemption
- allowable business investment losses
- bonuses
- estate planning
- splitting income.

Disadvantages of incorporation

- Directors could be held personally liable in certain limited circumstances. Prudent and skilled legal strategic planning can minimize or eliminate this risk.

- The costs of incorporating are higher. Legal costs are approximately $500 to $1,000 or more, depending on the complexity of the incorporation, plus the lawyer's disbursements, which are approximately $300 to $400. This monetary outlay should be kept in perspective. It is simply another cost of doing business if the reasons for incorporating a business for tax or liability benefits are appropriate.
- The operating losses and tax credits remain within the corporate entity; they are not available to individual shareholders if the corporation is unable to utilize them.

In the vast majority of cases, however, the advantages of a corporate entity are compelling.

STEPS TO INCORPORATION AND LEGAL RISK MANAGEMENT

The complexity of the incorporation process will depend on whether there is one or a number of shareholders, and whether it is strictly a provincial corporation or whether it must be federally or extraprovincially registered as well. You may decide to have a lawyer incorporate a company for you or you may do your own incorporation or hire an incorporation service to incorporate a company. Ideally, you should have a lawyer do your incorporation, so you can obtain important legal advice relating to the corporate structure, shareholder agreements, and other issues before you start your business. The legal fees for the incorporation could range between $500 and $1,000 or more, plus disbursements, as mentioned earlier. Disbursements include provincial filing fees, search and reservation fees for the business name, long-distance phone calls, costs of the corporate seal and minute book, and photocopies. If you are planning to have more than one shareholder in the corporation, you will require a lawyer to prepare a shareholders' agreement.

You may decide to do the incorporation yourself because you are going to be the only person in the company and you have limited financial resources. Books are available that will assist you in incorporating your company provincially or federally. You can also buy incorporation kits or obtain them free of charge from many provincial government departments of consumer and corporate affairs. You can also obtain a free federal incorporation kit by contacting Industry Canada. Most incorporations can be done online in almost real time, once you have the company name reserved.

Choosing a Name

There are three main parts to the corporate name: a distinctive word, a descriptive word, and the suffix or corporate label. For example, the distinctive word could be "Superior," the descriptive word could be "Investments," and the suffix could be "Ltd." Your choice for a suffix would include: "Ltd." or "Limited," "Corp." or "Corporation," "Inc." or "Incorporated," "Ltée" or "Limitée." Before selecting a name, you may wish to contact your provincial Ministry of Consumer and Corporate Affairs or the equivalent department in the case of a federal incorporation. You can obtain a brochure describing the government's guidelines for the approval of corporate names.

You will need to check to see if the name conflicts with a name already in existence. Telephone directories of the major cities in Canada and city directories located in most major public libraries are a starting point.

In certain provinces you can request a name search directly from the ministry that handles incorporations. They will do a search of their data bank and advise you if the name you are seeking conflicts with other corporate names, proprietorship names, or partnership names. This type of search will also indicate any extraprovincial registrations with a similar name. The fee for this search varies but is usually between $75 to $100, and it takes from 3 to 5 business days to obtain a response.

For other provinces and for federal incorporations, you will have to obtain a New Updated Automatic Name Search (NUANS), which employs a computerized database of most of the proprietorships, partnerships, and corporate names used throughout Canada, as well as provincial and federal corporations and registered trademarks. The NUANS database is current, generally excluding the last 2 or 3 days of registrations, or a longer time lag depending on timing for information delivered from other provinces. A NUANS report is usually five pages in length and provides listings of similar corporations with their names. The computer printout lists the names in descending order of similarity. It generally takes 24 to 48 hours to obtain a name search on the NUANS system and costs about $100 or more per name search.

The reason you must check your proposed name against existing business names is to prevent your company from knowingly or unknowingly using a name that is similar to or the same as an existing business name. Otherwise, it could be perceived that you are attempting to benefit from the goodwill and reputation that has been established by the other firm. This of course could be unfair competition. The law allows a business or person who feels they have suffered because of this to sue you in court. A court injunction could be obtained to prohibit you from using the name any further, as well as a claim for damages that have been suffered because of your improper use of the conflicting name.

Provinces that have a computerized database will either accept or reject the name that you are considering. Other provinces where a NUANS search is required generally just accept the request for registration and do not approve its accuracy. In the case of federal incorporations, for which the NUANS search is required, the corporation branch will either accept or reject the proposed corporate name. Names are reserved by the provincial or federal government for a period of between 45 and 90 days. When a federal or provincial incorporation is rejected, it is because there is a conflict with a similar name or the name is too general. It could lack a descriptive word to indicate the type of business or possibly it contains a prohibited word.

There are certain names that are prohibited by law and therefore would be rejected. Some of the guidelines used by most provinces and the federal government are as follows:

- cannot suggest a government connection
- cannot suggest connection with the Crown or royal family
- cannot be objectionable on public grounds
- cannot be a well-known or established name
- cannot be identical to or similar to other company names
- some statutes, both federal and provincial, restrict or prohibit the use of certain words, for example, bank, RCMP, architect, lawyer, Better Business Bureau, dentist, provincial, or federal.

There is some degree of discretion by name examiners within the guidelines. If you object to the decision to reject your proposed name, you can request to speak to the registrar or have your lawyer speak to the registrar.

Some businesses prefer to use a trade style name rather than the incorporated name. You may have a trade style name by which you are known to the public and which you use on your business cards, letterhead, and invoices as a division of the incorporated company. Normally this latter reference is in small print on your stationery, but it has the legal benefit of telling the public that you are an incorporated company behind the trade style name. All trade style names should be filed in the appropriate provincial registry. There is generally a one-time nominal fee for this registration.

A numbered company is a corporation that uses a number instead of a name; for example, 157894 Alberta Ltd. The number is assigned (it cannot be requested) by the ministry from a consecutive series utilized for corporation file purposes. Whereas a corporation with a name in it is assigned a corporation number, the numbered company simply uses the corporation number that has been assigned as the name.

People use numbered companies for various reasons, for example, when they cannot get their preferred name accepted by the Corporate Registry or they simply want a personal holding company. Some people incorporate a numbered company and operate under a trade style name, which they file in the appropriate federal or provincial registry. The company's letterhead and stationery would show the trade style name as a division of the numbered company.

Another reason why people use numbered companies is to have a company incorporated quickly. The numbered company can be obtained the same day, whereas there is normally a time lag for the approval and registration of the corporate name. At some future point you can then request a change of name to one that you would prefer. On the other hand, there are people who do not change from a numbered company, because they are not attempting to establish goodwill under the corporate name. For example, if you were buying various apartment buildings or other real estate properties for investment purposes, a numbered company could be quite sufficient for your needs.

Who Makes Up the Corporation?

The owners of the corporation are its shareholders. Shareholders elect or appoint the directors to direct and make corporate policies for the management of the corporation. In larger corporations, the directors have to be approved at the annual meeting of the company, and are either re-elected or not. In a small business, the same procedure is followed, except on an informal basis. It is frequently the case that meetings are not actually held, but decisions are made instead by resolutions. The directors elect or appoint the officers of the company, such as president, secretary, and treasurer. The responsibilities of those positions are governed by the provincial legislation affecting corporations. The officers can be hired or fired by the directors at any time. In practical terms, in a small business, frequently the same people are shareholders, directors, and officers.

Shareholder and Partnership Agreements

The casualty rate of business partnership or shareholder relationships is very high. It is not uncommon to have conflicts occur due to differences of priorities, personalities, or philosophies over a period of time. In addition, there could be differing expectations by each of the individuals in terms of the contribution of time, money, and talent. Other factors that tend to cause friction include the issues of ego and power, frequently the undoing of business relationships.

Business conflict usually results when extremes occur. For example, when the business is doing very well, some partners or shareholders become greedy and would like to own the entire business and get rid of the other partners. Conversely, when the business is doing poorly, it is human nature for recriminations to occur, in which one partner or shareholder blames the other for the difficulties the business is going through. Another factor is burnout or lifestyle changes. Many people get tired of the time, energy, and commitment involved in a business operation and want to do something else—go into another business or otherwise free up their invested money. Marital or health problems can also cause a person to lose interest in the business or create conflict within the business.

For these reasons and the serious implications and consequences that would result, you should have an agreement to protect your interests. The agreement should be prepared prior to the incorporation of the business, or in the case of a partnership, prior to commencing business. You should also consider a management contract, even if the manager is one of the shareholders and directors (see Sample 12).

The sample partnership and shareholder agreement checklists (Samples 10 and 11 at the back of this book) can save you time and money. Review the checklists in advance with your partners and draft your own version of the key factors that you would like included in an agreement. Then take your draft agreement to your lawyer to be reviewed and finalized. The legal costs involved will depend on the degree of complexity of the agreement, the number of shareholders or partners, the number of meetings that might be held going over and explaining the various terms of the agreement, and other factors.

Directors

Although it is accurate that shareholders are not personally liable for any debts or liabilities of the corporation unless the shareholder signed a personal guarantee, directors and officers could still be liable. It is common for small business owner-operators to have their spouses as directors of the company. This has a lot of potential disadvantages, especially relating to leverage when borrowing money. Lenders are more likely to request that all the directors of the company sign personal guarantees for loans, which would mean that your spouse would be asked to sign a personal guarantee. Be cautious, therefore, about directorships.

The liability that most directors are potentially exposed to is statutory liability under federal and provincial legislation. Directors can be individually and collectively liable for the full amount of the debt or liability under most of these statutory regulations. If you are a director of a company, you are deemed to know or should have known of the obligations of the company to meet its legislative commitments. Some of the common areas of potential director liability are as follows:

- **Employee deductions.** When deductions are taken off an employee's salary, they are to be remitted every month to Canada Revenue Agency (CRA). If the funds are not remitted, CRA could sue you for the amounts outstanding, in your capacity as director.
- **Sales tax.** If you are operating a business that is responsible for collecting and remitting provincial sales tax, and the company fails to do so, you could be held responsible as a director.
- **Corporate income tax and GST/HST. (Goods and Services Tax/ Harmonized Sales Tax).** If your company owes money to CRA (Canada Revenue Agency) and fails to pay it, you could be responsible as a director.

- **Employment standards.** If your company has not paid employees for past services rendered or for holiday pay, then employees can formally complain to the appropriate government department. That department could sue you as a director of the company for arrears of wages and salaries owing to all employees plus holiday pay.
- **Workers' Compensation Board.** In the event that your company fails to make Workers' Compensation Board (WCB) payments, the WCB could sue the company and, depending on the provincial legislation, could also make a claim against the directors. In addition, employees who might not otherwise be eligible for WCB protection in the event of injury could sue the company as well as the directors for negligence, and the WCB could charge to your company the full amount of the payments that were incurred due to the employee's disability.
- **Extraprovincial business activity.** If you are doing business in another province and have not extraprovincially registered your corporation in that province, you could be personally liable as a director if someone sues your company in that other province. The test for doing business in the other province usually means having all the features of a business, such as telephone number and listing, office address, business licence, and staff. Marketing products by mail order throughout Canada from a provincial address does not mean doing business in another province. Speak to your lawyer if you intend to provide services or products outside your province.
- **Environmental damage.** Both the federal and provincial governments have protection legislation making directors liable for environmental damage caused by their company.

To protect yourself as much as possible from personal liability exposure as a director, it is your responsibility to be duly diligent in terms of monitoring the company's operation. If you do not have the time or inclination to do so, or you are being frustrated by the inability to obtain the information that you need because of poorly managed systems or lack of cooperation from management, then you should consider resigning as a director and making sure that you protect yourself in writing in terms of spelling out clearly the reasons for the resignation. Always keep copies of any correspondences.

Shares

When an incorporation is formed there are various types of shares that can be used for investment purposes:

- **Common shares.** Owning common shares represents part ownership in a company and provides maximum potential return on the investment for the company's initial shareholders and other investors. If the corporation should fail, though, all other creditors and preferred shareholders are repaid before holders of common shares.

- **Preferred shares.** This is a class of shares with a claim on the company's earnings before payment can be made on the common shares, if the company liquidates. Preferred shares are usually entitled to dividends at a specified rate when declared by the board of directors, and before payment of a dividend on the common shares. Preferred shareholders generally do not have voting privileges. Because preferred shares offer a smaller potential return than common shares, convertible preferred shares may be used, so that shareholders can exchange preferred shares for common shares when the company's future looks more promising.

- **Convertible debentures.** This is a form of long-term debt in which all or a portion of the debenture may be converted into common shares instead of being repaid.

- **Debt with warrants.** This is similar to the convertible debenture, but allows a creditor/investor to purchase a specified number of shares at a set price, even after the business has paid the debt but before the expiration of the warrant (e.g., 1 year or 2 years afterward). Because debentures and debt with warrants are both debt, they must generally be repaid before holders of common and preferred shares are paid, or shareholders' loans are repaid.

The company offering shares can be a public or private one. A public company is listed on a stock exchange, whereas a private company is not.

Provincial or Federal Incorporations

Depending on your needs, there are advantages and disadvantages to incorporating federally or provincially. If in doubt, make sure that you obtain competent legal and tax advice on the relative benefits involved. As mentioned earlier, a federal incorporation has to be registered in the province in which it is actually doing business. The exceptions are Ontario and Quebec. A federal corporation has the right to register in any province, whereas a provincial corporation has the right to carry on business only in the province in which it is incorporated. The right to register in the province does not automatically mean the right to do business, whether it is a provincial or federal corporation, if the business does not conform with provincial or local government licensing requirements or if it conflicts with an existing business with the same name. A federal corporation is authorized to use the courts to enforce contracts or collect debts in any province without having to be registered extraprovincially or as a foreign corporation in that province. The foreign corporation, incidentally, is a designation meaning that a corporation from outside the province is registering in the province. A provincial corporation must be registered in the province concerned to have legal status to use the courts under its name.

A federal corporation has more reporting requirements and restrictions on meetings than most provincial corporations. If you extraprovincially register your federal corporation in another province, you can have two reporting requirements—one for your federal corporation and one for the province in which you have extraprovincially registered.

Depending on the type of business you are considering, you may be required to incorporate federally. For example, if you have a business that involves interprovincial transport, or you have a radio station, then you are required by law to federally incorporate.

In terms of the filing-of-registration system, in Canada there are eleven general companies acts, one for incorporation under federal law and one each for incorporation under provincial law. In certain provinces, as well as in the federal government, the system for incorporating your company is called a *letters patent system*. This is the method used in the provinces of Manitoba, Ontario, Quebec, New Brunswick, and Prince Edward Island. The requirements, provisions, and documents to be completed are largely similar to those under the federal Canadian Business Corporation Act. In the provinces of British Columbia, Alberta, Saskatchewan, Nova Scotia, and Newfoundland, the system is called the *registration system of incorporating companies*. The documents are different than in the letters patent system, and the requirements can vary between the provinces. The net effect is the same in terms of limited liability protection.

Regardless of where you incorporate your company, you may wish to obtain a copy of the Company Act for that province or in the case of federal corporation, the Canadian Business Corporation Act. The provincial act is available through the Queen's Printer of each province and the federal act is available from the federal Queen's Printer. These acts are complicated though, and you need to have legal advice before making a business decision.

Extraprovincial Companies

When you are deciding to incorporate, consider your long-range objectives. If it is your intention to do business in other provinces across Canada, you have two choices. You can either incorporate in your own province and register your provincial corporation in each of the provinces in which you are actively going to be doing business as an extraprovincial corporation, or you can incorporate federally. If you incorporate your company federally, you still have to extraprovincially register your federal corporation in each province in which you are doing business. In terms of legal fees, the costs of an extraprovincial corporation are at least as much as incorporating in the other province in the first place. In other words, the legal fees and out-of-pocket expenses will be at least as much as when you incorporated your provincial corporation or federal corporation. The Company Act in your province sets out the rules and regulations to do with extraprovincial corporation. As previously mentioned, the normal criterion is that you have the appearance of operating your business in that province, such as a business address, telephone number at that address, *Yellow Page* directory ad, employees, and advertising.

It is important to appreciate the distinction between doing business in that other province from within that province and doing business in the other province from outside that province. For example, if you have a corporation in Ontario and you wish to have offices in all the other provinces across Canada from your Ontario base, you would need to extraprovincially register your company. On the other hand, you could have an extensive direct mail, telephone, or letter campaign to prospects in the other provinces. You are clearly trying to solicit business from those provinces, but you are not doing business in those provinces. If you fail to extraprovincially register your company when you should have, you could be personally exposed as a director in the provinces where you failed to register, as discussed earlier.

CREDITOR-PROOFING YOUR BUSINESS

Introduction

This section will raise your awareness of the proactive steps you should consider to protect your business and financial interests. You want to minimize your risks, in case your business runs into difficulties. It will also give you a starting point for discussion with your legal and tax advisors. The options outlined in this section, if done properly and with professional advice, will give you peace of mind. This will help balance the predictable stresses and uncertainty that come with running your own business.

What Does Creditor-Proofing Mean?

Creditor-proofing refers to conducting your business affairs in a way that legally minimizes your personal and business risk in a doomsday scenario. The term is somewhat of a misnomer, as you may not be able to totally eliminate risk, but you can minimize it substantially.

The rationale behind a defensive creditor-proofing philosophy, in the context of this chapter, is very simple. You have a legitimate right and responsibility to minimize your business and personal risk exposure. As a small business person, you are embarking on a venture and adventure which is inherently high risk. Statistically, four out of five small business start-ups don't survive the first 5 years. There are many reasons for this high failure rate, both internal and external. After reading this book, following its cautions, and getting the right professional advice, you should fall into the 20% of businesses that succeed beyond 5 years.

Starting and managing a small business is a major life commitment. It is immensely consuming and stressful and will make heavy demands on your personal and business time, especially during the start-up years, but also on an ongoing basis. There are many personal sacrifices. At the same time, you are helping to stimulate the local economy, create employment, and increase the tax revenue to the government.

You do your best in good faith in your business dealings. However, if events occur which you can't anticipate or control, you want to maintain your core sense of security. That means those things that matter most to your sense of personal well-being—your partner, children, family, and friends, and your sense of financial security.

Sadly, many small business failures are avoidable. Many business failures result in personal bankruptcy and marital distress and divorce. By being focused and proactive about setting up protective strategies, you can minimize the downside personal risks.

Don't Try To Do It Yourself

Creditor-proofing involves many strategic, tactical, and legal issues. It would be foolish to try to accomplish these protections yourself. The paperwork has to be done correctly to be enforceable. Also, you need to know what you can and can't do and why. You want to make sure that legal and tax decisions you make can withstand retroactive scrutiny from attack. Timing is also an important issue, as you don't want to just start out your business with the appropriate protections. You want to monitor your business protections on an ongoing basis, as circumstances arise. You should have a risk assessment checkup at least once a year.

How to select the right lawyer and accountant for your needs was covered in Chapter 4, "Selecting Professional Advisors." You need to get customized advice specific to your situation.

Timing Is Everything

When it comes to protecting your assets, timing is essential. You don't want to be in a position in which the strategic decisions you have made can be overturned by a creditor. That would defeat the whole purpose of creditor-proofing. For example, a creditor could claim that you purposely moved personal or business assets around or set up various corporate structures to avoid paying creditors. The primary test is whether your corporation was insolvent at the time, for example, in arrears or unable to pay its creditors in a timely manner. There are particular retroactive time periods for a transaction to be challenged, overturned, or reversed under federal bankruptcy and insolvency legislation and provincial legislation relating to fraudulent conveyance of assets or fraudulent preference of creditors. As a general rule, transactions can be looked at for at least 1 year previous. Your lawyer can give you more information.

Do a Risk Assessment

Your business risks are not static. They are always in a state of flux, as that is the nature of business and business cycles. That is why a regular checkup with your lawyer is essential, to pre-empt problems before they occur. A few conversations with your lawyer will help you develop a general sense of when you need to discuss risk issues, so that you can recognize the warning signs.

In any business, you need to do a SWOT analysis regularly—an objective and detailed analysis of the business strengths, weaknesses, opportunities, and threats. Under the categories of potential threats, consider the impact on the business of the following. There may be no impact or it may be mild, major, serious, or fatal.

- Competition enters your market area, thereby eroding market share, and you don't have the resources to compete.
- Lender interest rates increase, due to market changes, changed lender criteria, or re-assessment of your business risks.
- Difficulties ensue with the lender or inability to get more funds; a change of lending officer results in a personality conflict with new lending officer.
- Lender calls in or reduces the line of credit or calls the demand loan.
- Location problems with office building or "empty" mall results in reduced customer traffic; building and general area deteriorating and becoming unattractive.
- Landlord refuses to renew a lease or increases the rent dramatically on renewal.
- Employee turnover problems ensue or problem employees disrupt your operation.
- Theft or shoplifting undermine your profits.
- Collection problems arise with major customers.
- Client or customer sues for breach of contract or product liability.
- Insurance company denies claim for loss.
- Conflict with investors arises.
- Health, injury, or disability problems occur.
- Marital or business partnership problems occur.

- Arrears are owing to the landlord, and the landlord is threatening to send in a bailiff and is locking the doors or seizing assets.
- Lender or other creditor garnishes money from company account.
- Business is failing due to internal management problems.
- Business is failing due to external management problems, such as a major supplier or customer experiencing business failure.
- New technologies make your business obsolete or unsustainable financially.
- Client alleges breach of contract for failure to meet the quality or time-line expected.
- You underestimate a fixed-price contract and then run out of money before completing it.
- Employee brings a lawsuit claiming wrongful dismissal.
- Customer claims negligence or misrepresentation.
- Motor vehicle accidents cause injury to yourself, your employees, or others.
- Claims are made against you for infringement of trademark or other rights of another business.
- Fines are levied by Workers Compensation Board for workplace injuries or noncompliance with regulations.
- Fines are levied by municipal, provincial, or federal government for non-compliance with regulations.
- Actions are brought by creditors for personal guarantees you signed or collateral security you pledged.
- Lawsuits are brought by creditors, investors, clients, customers, employees, or government departments.

As you can see, there is no shortage of business risk issues to reflect on and deal with proactively and protectively.

Types of Creditors

Different categories of creditors, such as statutory creditors, secured creditors or unsecured creditors, have different legal rights in terms of claims against your business assets. Refer to Chapter 17, "Insolvency, Bankruptcy, and Receivership," for more detail. Directors of corporations can also be exposed to personal liability in certain situations.

Statutory or Preferred Creditors

Various federal government departments, such as Canada Revenue Agency (CRA), are statutory or preferred creditors. This would include arrears of personal or business income tax owing or employee payroll tax deductions at source or EI (Unemployment Insurance) and CPP (Canada Pension Plan) deductions at source that were collected but not remitted, and GST/HST (Goods and Services Tax/Harmonized Sales Tax) collected and owing but not remitted.

Under federal bankruptcy legislation and provincial legislation, there could be protection to employees for arrears of salary and holiday pay, up to a limit. In some situations, under the federal Bankruptcy and Insolvency Act, landlords can have priority ahead of secured creditors for up to 3 months rent.

Under provincial legislation, there is preferred creditor status in most situations, for example, provincial sales tax collected and owing, claims under Workers Compensation legislation, and claims for employee salary arrears up to a certain limit.

Secured Creditors

These are creditors who have secured their credit by some form of registered security. For example, a bank could be secured by business inventory under a section of the Bank Act, a lender could also have security by means of a General Security Agreement, or a Specific Security Agreement, covering various specific or general assets. A lender could have a mortgage on the business property or a collateral mortgage on your home to secure a promissory note. Generally, creditors who are secured are paid off in full, in order of priority, which is based on when they filed the security. A leasing company is a secured creditor, as it keeps title to the car or equipment until it is paid for in full. A landlord could be a secured creditor for certain assets under the Rent Distress or Commercial Tenancy provincial legislation.

Refer to Chapter 17, "Insolvency, Bankruptcy, and Receivership," for a discussion of other types of security that creditors could have.

Unsecured Creditors

The most common type of creditor, sometimes referred to as general creditors, this category includes any creditors that do not have security. This includes lenders who are not secured for a personal line of credit, trade creditors, and suppliers. Utility companies for electricity, telephone, gas, and cable would also fall under this category. The same would apply to anyone holding a court judgment or having a legal claim for a breach of contract.

Creditors under this category get paid only after everyone under the previous two categories are paid off in full. What is left goes into a general pool and is paid to creditors on a pro rata basis. That is, a percentage of their claim relative to the total amount owing to all the general creditors. Frequently, there is nothing left for general creditors in practical terms, or maybe just 5 cents on the dollar, after all administrative and legal expenses are paid off. That is why you want to be a secured creditor if at all possible. Conversely, you don't want to give out security if you are a debtor if you can avoid it.

Limiting Your Business Liability Exposure

There are many ways of minimizing the risks to your business. Here are the key ones to discuss with your professional advisors.

- **Separate your personal and business assets and liabilities.** Make sure you have a separate bank account set up for your business activities. Whether you are operating a part-time business out of your home or a nonincorporated business, you want to demonstrate the separation between the business and personal aspects of your life. Have separate cheques and records. You don't want to cause confusion with your creditors.

- **Incorporate your business before you start.** The problem with a partnership and proprietorship type of business is that, in law, you and your business are deemed to be one and the same. This means a creditor can go after your personal assets. This is high risk, as all your personal assets could be seized and sold if there was a judgment against you.

  The alternative is to incorporate your business. As discussed in Chapter 2, in law you and your incorporated business are deemed to be separate legal entities. For maximum protection, incorporate before you start your business, as the potential risk starts the moment you provide the service or sell the product. Some accountants tell clients that they don't need to incorporate for tax reasons until a certain profit level is earned. However, the compelling legal reasons for incorporation at the outset are more critical than tax considerations in most cases.

  To get the maximum protection from your corporation, always sign all documents in the corporate name, as an "authorized signatory."

- **Never have oral agreements.** Always make sure all your business dealings are clear and put into writing to eliminate the risk of uncertainty. For example, if you died or were incapacitated, how would anyone know what the agreement was if it is not in writing? Over time, people can innocently and honestly forget details. Others could exploit the lack of paperwork for their own interests. If a lawsuit occurred, it would be almost impossible to reconstruct and prove the facts when differing and sometimes self-serving recollections of the bargain exist. This type of uncertainty puts your business in jeopardy; it also wastes a lot of time, energy, and money.

- **Limit the liability in your contracts.** You can include in your contracts that your potential liability is to the amount that you received under your contract, or a fixed amount (e.g., $5,000). Don't be exposed to open-ended liability for client financial damages or losses.
- **Obtain adequate insurance protection.** Refer to Chapter 20, which discusses insurance, for a discussion of the various types of insurance to consider as part of your risk assessment.
- **Have a tight credit and collection policy.** Refer to Chapter 15, "Credit and Collection." A few bad debts could wipe out your profit for the year. This could mean that you expended your time and energy for free. A sloppy credit and collection approach could result in the death of your business.
- **Be careful about pledging corporate security.** Don't pledge any of your corporate assets to a creditor without first discussing the matter with your legal and tax advisors. You want to know the implications and alternatives. Also, your lawyer might negotiate a better deal for you in certain situations.
- **Make sure you have a shareholder's agreement with a buy–sell clause.** If you go into business with other partners, make sure you have a shareholder's agreement at the outset—during the honeymoon phase of your relationship and before reality sets in. See Sample 11, "Shareholders' Agreement Checklist." This document deals with the formulas for you or your partner to get out of the business relationship.
- **Utilize a holding company to protect business profit.** This strategy involves setting up a separate corporation, called a *holding company*, that holds the shares of your active corporation business. From time to time, when your active business makes extra money, it can declare dividends. This money will go to the holding company, as it holds 100% of the shares of the active business. If your active business was ever sued, the money would be protected in the holding company, assuming the appropriate legal steps were taken. The holding company could lend money back to the active company in exchange for security on assets or other tangible security, just like any secured creditor. You could own 100% of the shares of the holding company, which in turn owns 100% of the shares of the active company. The purpose of this exercise is to insulate each company from the other.
- **Utilize a sister corporation to own and lease assets.** Utilizing a sister corporation involves incorporating a third company that buys all the necessary equipment, furniture, etc., that your active company needs. This company then leases the assets to your active company. In this scenario, your active company would not have any tangible assets of worth, as all

the key assets are leased. Your leasing company could have obtained a loan from the holding company that was secured by the assets. If your active company were sued, a creditor would not be able to seize any assets. The holding company and leasing company are separate entities in law, and are not owned by the active company, even if you personally are the sole shareholder of all three companies. Also, a creditor does not have any legal contractual relationship or rights relative to those other companies.

- **Make sure you have a will.** If you die and have a will, the shares in your company will become an asset of your estate. If your spouse is the beneficiary of your estate, then he or she can take over the shares of the company. This should facilitate a smooth transition. If you have partners, you want the shareholder's agreement to deal with what happens to the deceased's shares on death—who gets them and when and how. Refer to the latest edition of Douglas Gray's *The Canadian Guide to Will and Estate Planning*, published by McGraw-Hill Ryerson.

Limiting Your Personal Liability Exposure

In addition to protecting the company from creditors, you also want to protect yourself and your family. Here are some techniques to discuss with your lawyer.

Protecting the family assets

Jane had always wanted to operate her own construction business. She owned a house, had three children, and wanted to protect her hard-earned assets from business risk. After getting advice from a business lawyer and tax accountant, she decided to structure her business in a strategic way before she started. She transferred her home over to her husband's name, as he was not involved in the business or any business, and incorporated the company and acted as the sole director and officer of the company. The Family Relations Act in her province would have deemed the family home as a 50/50 asset regardless of whose name it was in, in the event of a divorce. Whatever happened to the business, she did not want to put the family home or assets at risk. She had a firm policy of never signing any personal guarantees for the company, or pledging her family assets, thereby insulating herself personally from exposure. As part of her strategic estate planning, she updated her will and ensured that her insurance policies and RRSPs (Registered Retirement Savings Plans), were left to the designated beneficiaries. Nearly all her money would thereby bypass her estate, leaving very little for any potential creditors.

- **Don't sign or limit personal guarantees.** There is no point in going to the effort of incorporating a company, if you nullify the personal protection by signing a personal guarantee of the corporate debts. Don't sign personal guarantees at all, for example, to suppliers, trade creditors, landlords, etc. Alternatively, only do so for a bank if absolutely necessary, and then limit the amount of liability. For example, if the company is borrowing $45,000, and there are three partners, agree to be liable for a maximum of one-third only. Get legal advice before you sign any personal guarantee to a lender. Remember that the marketplace is very competitive. Use that knowledge as leverage when paying one creditor over another.
- **Don't pledge personal security.** Adopt a policy of not pledging any personal security, for example, your personal car, your house or a life insurance policy, under any circumstances.
- **Transfer property and other assets to your spouse.** You can transfer the ownership of your home and other personal assets, such as your car, to your spouse. That way, the assets are not in your personal name. In the event of a marital breakup, the matrimonial home is deemed to be owned 50/50 in most situations anyway. Also, under the family relations legislation of most provinces, family assets are combined for calculation purposes and then divided in half. Speak to your lawyer about the laws in your province.
- **Be aware of director liability.** If you are a director of a corporation, you do have liability risk, particularly under government legislation. Therefore, if you are a director, consider not owning any personal assets of consequence, to limit the potential risk.
- **Don't have your spouse as a guarantor or a director.** To limit the family's risk, you don't want to ask your spouse to act as a director or a guarantor.
- **Don't have joint accounts with your spouse.** If you have a joint account, and a creditor garnishes your bank account, they will seize all the funds in that account. By having separate accounts, you separate that risk.
- **Consider spousal RRSPs.** If your spouse is earning less than you are, you may wish to contribute to his or her RRSP as a spousal RRSP. You get the RRSP tax deduction, but your spouse gets the money in his or her RRSP account. Therefore, if a creditor tries to collect on your RRSP with a court judgment, there will be less money available. If an RRSP is collapsed to pay the creditor, there will only be the amount left after federal tax is taken from the RRSP amount. This fact gives room for your lawyer to negotiate with the creditor for some creative compromise settlement—for example, a maximum of 50 cents on the dollar, with flexible payment terms over time, interest free. Your lawyer can negotiate on your behalf if you are too emotionally involved. Also, your business lawyer will have experience negotiating and will have more credibility in the eyes of the creditor.

- **Consider RRSPs with insurance companies.** If you have an RRSP, RRIF (Registered Retirement Income Fund) or nonregistered investments with an insurance company, under certain circumstances, creditors are not able to collect on the RRSP. Check with your financial and tax advisor.
- **Sign business documents as authorized signatory of corporation.** In order to get the full protection of your corporation, always make it clear that you are signing on behalf of the corporation. That way, no one can try to claim that you were signing in your personal capacity.
- **Consider allocating CPP(Canada Pension Plan) primarily in your spouse's name.** Another income-splitting option, which also has the effect of putting more money in your spouse's hands, is to apportion a certain percentage of your CPP to go into your spouse's name. You are entitled to start taking out your CPP at age 60, at a reduced amount. This approach means that there is less money available for creditors from your personal income. Get tax advice on the appropriateness of this option.
- **Lend money to your corporation and become a secured creditor.** You could lend money as a creditor to the company and take back security, like any other creditor could. This could be in the form of a General Security Agreement, a Specific Security Agreement, an Assignment of Receivables, a mortgage on the business property, etc.

If your company wants to borrow money from a lender, and the lender does not want to be secured behind your security, then you can subordinate or postpone your claim to that of the other secured creditor. However, your security document remains registered. In addition, you can also have umbrella security from the company that covers you for any future loans that you give the company, under the same security document that you have registered. You don't need to keep registering security each time you advance a loan.

- **Consider a personal management company for services.** Rather than drawing a salary as an employee of your own company, you may wish to have a management consulting agreement with your own company as an independent contractor. You might consider a separate corporation as your personal management corporation. There are various tax and other considerations for this approach.

Limiting Your Estate Liability Exposure

What if you are still running your business when you die? The business could cease to function, as you are the key person. The business goes under, and creditors start looking for assets. If you are liable under a personal guarantee or as a director, then the creditors could claim from your estate.

Here are some options to discuss with your professional advisors to minimize the risk to your estate.

- **Make sure you have a will.** A current will that has been drafted with your lawyer and accountant is the first step. Refer to the latest edition of Douglas Gray's *The Canadian Guide to Will and Estate Planning*, published by McGraw-Hill Ryerson.

- **Make sure you have a shareholder's agreement with a buy–sell clause.** The need for this protection was covered earlier in this chapter.

- **Designate beneficiaries in your insurance policies.** By designating beneficiaries in your insurance policies, you enable the money to bypass your will completely. It is therefore not part of your estate and goes directly to your designated beneficiaries tax free. Your personal creditors can only claim from assets in your estate.

- **Designate beneficiaries for your RRSPs and RRIFs.** By designating a beneficiary for registered retirement plans, you bypass your will and your estate. The money goes directly to the beneficiary and is unavailable to creditors. You can also designate beneficiaries for your nonregistered investments.

- **Consider the use of trusts.** If you set up a living trust while you are alive, it bypasses your will and therefore your estate, on your death. A testamentary trust is set up through your will, and takes effect after your death. Both types divert assets out of your estate, away from creditors of your estate.

Keeping Peace in the Family

In a worst case scenario, your business goes under. The following suggestions can help ensure that your relationships with your friends, family, and relatives survive the business ordeal.

- **Secure loans from family and friends.** If you borrow money from friends and family, consider securing them with registered security, such as a mortgage or a General Security Agreement or a Specific Security Agreement. This makes them secured creditors, just like any secured creditor.

- **Consider loans plus equity.** You could structure your loans from family and friends to include an equity (share) feature as a value-added incentive.

- **Consider a convertible option from loans to equity.** You could give your family or friends who are loaning money the option of converting those loans in part or in full to share equity if they wanted to do so later. That is, after the company has proven itself to be viable.

- **Don't ask family or friends to sign personal guarantees or co-sign.** If you ask family, friends, or your spouse to act as a guarantor or to co-sign a loan, and the loan is called, you will regret it. The relationship may not survive the financial loss, depending on the amount and related circumstances.
- **Don't ask family or friends to act as directors.** Being a director carries a lot of potential liability to a lot of different categories of creditors. Depending on the business, the risk could be very high. Directors don't generally consider being sued personally and having all their personal assets at risk. That process does not engender the continuation of a meaningful relationship.
- **Don't ask your spouse to consent to collateral mortgage.** No matter how immune you think you might be to the statistical reality of business failure, don't ask your spouse to agree to a collateral mortgage on your house. Ask yourself how the quality of your marital relationship will be affected in a business downside situation, when the bank starts action to foreclose on the house.
- **Don't assign life insurance proceeds.** If you assign your life insurance proceeds to secure a loan and you die, your creditor could get all the money, leaving nothing for your family. If a creditor insists on insurance, and you have tried all alternatives, most banks will offer special loan insurance. A monthly insurance premium is added to your loan, and if you die, the loan is paid off in full.

Document Everything

You want to make sure that you have all the documentation necessary to protect your strategic plans, in a timely manner. Your legal and tax advisors can assist you in ensuring that all the paperwork is in order. Never rely on verbal deals or assurances.

SUMMARY

This chapter covered a range of options to explore with your professional advisors. It also demonstrated the complexity involved in the total strategic and protective picture. You need this knowledge to make the right business decisions and to plan proactively. Timing is everything. Work in an integrated way with your experienced legal and tax advisors. Don't consider any of the options in insolation; they need to be considered in context.

Chapter 6

Tax Considerations

Why does a slight tax increase cost you two hundred dollars and a substantial tax cut save you thirty cents?

— Peg Bracken

Income taxation in Canada has become increasingly complex. Tax laws and regulations are constantly changing, making it difficult in many respects for the small business owner to keep current, let alone understand the relevant tax laws. Proper tax planning is critically important to the entrepreneur. In addition to personal taxes, the taxation of the business and the treatment of the relationship between the owner and the business must be thoroughly considered.

Taxation and record-keeping are closely related. If an audit is required by Revenue Canada (now Canada Revenue Agency [CRA]), you will need to produce thorough records for review. The following general overview covers some of the issues relating to basic record-keeping and taxation. Sources of further information on the subject of taxation are discussed at the end of the chapter.

It is recommended throughout this book that a small business owner have a professionally qualified accountant from the outset, and throughout the life of the business. Make sure your advisor has special expertise on the subject of small business taxation if you are going to rely on that advice.

ACCOUNTING METHODS

Businesses normally use the accrual method of accounting for tax purposes, but may qualify for the cash method. A combination of the two methods is not permitted. In addition, there are special accounting methods for certain types of businesses permitted by CRA. These types of businesses would include contracting and farming.

Under the accrual method, income is reported in the year in which it is earned, regardless of when payment is received. Available expenses are deductible in the year when incurred, whether paid or not. The accrual method must be used by business people and professionals when inventory, accounts receivable, and accounts payable are significant factors in determining income, costs, and expenses.

TAXATION YEAR

The taxation year for individuals is the calendar year. The income from a business or profession of an individual must generally be reported on the basis of a fiscal year period that coincides with the calendar year, but must not be longer than 12 months. However, the fiscal year-end of a corporation or partnership may generally be determined by your accountant to be the date that is the most beneficial to you. But once the fiscal year-end has been established, you must maintain the fiscal year-end unless a change is approved by the CRA. The fiscal year-end is normally determined by your accountant to be the date which is most beneficial to you in your first taxation year. A short fiscal period may occur in the first year of operation if, for example, you started on August 1 and the first fiscal year-end is December 31. If work in progress fluctuates, choosing a year-end when the work level is high may maximize the amount of taxes that can be deferred. Proper selection of a year-end is therefore a significant consideration in deferring taxes for businesses starting up; your accountant can probably advise you here.

TAX EFFECTS ON DIFFERENT LEGAL STRUCTURES OF A BUSINESS

As mentioned in the previous chapter on the advantages and disadvantages of proprietorship, partnership, and corporations, there are distinct tax considerations for each type of business structure. Briefly, if you are the sole proprietor of your business, your salary and the profits that you earn in your business constitute your personal income and are taxable as such. When you file your personal income tax return, you must complete the Business Statement of Income and Expenses. This form can be obtained on request from CRA. It outlines many of the basic sources of income and type of expenses and allowances.

If your business is a partnership, partners are taxed on their share of the profits, whether withdrawn or not. Most partnerships are required to file a partnership information return reporting information on the partnership, partnership revenues and expenses, and each partner's share of partnership income or loss. The partners report their share of partnership income and any related expenses incurred in earning partnership income on a similar Statement of Income and Expenses.

A corporation files a corporate tax return, which is separate and distinct from the individuals involved in the company. It is therefore not filed with the personal income tax return, as is the case with a proprietorship or partnership.

A corporation in Canada is entitled to a small business tax reduction, assuming various conditions are met, if it generates income from an active business carried on in Canada. This reduction, which is approximately one-half the regular tax rate, is designed to help Canadian-controlled private companies accumulate capital for business expansion. Many provinces also allow a provincial tax rate reduction, as well as other possible incentives. An active business, as the name implies, is one in which people are actively involved in generating income from a business rather than earning passive income from property or income from a business the principal purpose of which is to earn interest, dividends, rents, or royalties.

A personal services business is the term used to describe an incorporated employee; in other words, an individual who is providing his or her employment services for a company through a service corporation. These companies are taxed at full corporate tax, and therefore do not receive the benefit of the small business tax reduction and have limited deductions, so providing services through a service corporation is generally not recommended Naturally, all these provisions could change at any time, as could any other incentive programs for tax reduction or deferral. Federal and provincial tax legislation is always changing, so obtain a current opinion from your accountant.

TAX PLANNING STRATEGIES

There are many ways of reducing, eliminating, or delaying tax on your business income. Here are several strategies to discuss with your professional accountant:

- **RRSP (Registered Retirement Savings Plan)** You want to make sure that you claim your maximum contribution available each year, which requires you to have sufficient "earned income" in the year (such as salaries and bonuses, but not dividends from your corporation). In addition, obtain advice on using spousal RRSP. In that option, you obtain the deduction, but your spouse receives the money in his or her RRSP. That way, when you eventually retire, the RRSPs should be close to balanced, thereby reducing the aggregate marginal tax rate and tax payable.
- **Spousal trust.** In this option, a formal trust arrangement would be established whereby the trust would hold the shares of the corporation for the benefit of you and your family. For example, you could hold 65% of the shares personally and your spousal trust could hold the remaining 35% of the shares.

    If the trust is structured properly, it is possible that each person who is a beneficiary of the trust could take out up to approximately $47,000 a year in dividends declared by your company and passed through the trust, tax free. This is assuming that the beneficiaries do not have any other taxable income. The figure noted could vary based on your province and change over time.

- **$750,000 Capital Gains Exemption on Sale of Small Business Corporation Shares.** This is one of the few tax shelters available to small business. Although it is still around, it could be reduced or eliminated any year. How it works is that if you sell the shares of your business, you could be exempt from tax on all of your capital gains on sale. The maximum amount would be $750,000 of exemption, assuming you have not already used up the $100,000 personal tax exemption portion of that $750,000 in the past.

  In order for this strategy to work, it needs to be done properly. You don't need to actually sell the shares of the business to someone else. You could transfer the shares to a company you set up or to your spouse, thereby triggering or "crystallizing" the capital gains. However, no tax would have to be paid, if any, on the capital gains until the company was actually sold in the future. You need advice from your accountant before using this technique, as you may need to "purify" the company beforehand. (A key condition is making sure that not more than 10% of the assets of the company are assets not considered to be used in the business, such as excess cash).

- **Estate freeze.** This is a very attractive strategy if you have children. In this example, you would convert the common shares of your corporation into preferred shares at the deemed fair market value at that time. By doing so, you would "freeze" the value of your interest in the company at its current value, although you would not have to pay tax on it at the time, or possibly ever, depending on the circumstances. You then issue new common shares in your company to your children or to a family trust for the benefit of your family. The share value would be $1 for example. Any increase in thee value of your business and company would accrue to the common shares for the benefit of your family and not to you, eliminating the exposure to additional capital gains tax that would be triggered on your death in regards to shares of your company.

- **Operating through a corporation.** One of the best ways to save on taxes is to operate your business through a corporation. The corporation pays a reduced small business tax of 13.5% which can vary based on your province and change over time, and up to a maximum amount. You can defer personal tax on any income you retain in the company, taking out your basic minimum needs. There are many other attractive money-saving benefits of using a corporation.

How to Pay Yourself

With smart tax advice, you can take money out of your business in a mix of ways to minimize or delay the tax hit. Here are some common techniques:

- **Salary.** If you take money out as a salary, you are taxed according to your graduated marginal tax rate. Depending on your income, this could have a considerable tax impact, not necessarily in your best interests.
- **Dividends.** In this approach, you would receive money when your corporation declares dividends. This could be at any time throughout the year that your accountant feels is advantageous to you. You are taxed at a lower rate for dividend income than salaried income.
- **Draws.** In this approach, your accountant accrues your bonus at the end of the year, and the bonus must be taken out within 6 months of the company's fiscal year-end. However, you don't need to declare the bonus until the following tax year, effectively deferring tax for a year, because the tax takes the tax paid in the company into account.
- **Capital gains.** The value of your shares at the outset of your business operation and at the time of sale determines the capital gains. You are taxed on one-half of the gain. However, as discussed earlier, there is currently an exemption for this gain, up to a ceiling. You would not be receiving this type of tax-free financial benefit until you eventually sell the business.
- **Holding company.** You could hold the shares in your corporation through a personal holding corporation. The effect of this technique is that when dividends are declared, the money goes to your personal management company, rather than to you personally. In effect, your holding company is like a bank. You can take out whatever you want from your holding company, depending on your needs and optimal tax planning timing.
- **Management contract.** You could incorporate a company and have a contract to manage your operating company. That way, your management company is a revenue buffer between yourself, permitting you to avoid paying personal income tax on the income. You can take out the money from your company as your needs dictate and when it is advantageous to you from a tax standpoint.
- **Paying family members.** Employing family members to help you in the business is a classic way of income splitting. As the individual marginal tax rate for each person is lower than it would be if all the money were paid to one person, there are aggregate tax savings.

EXPENSES

An expense is deductible if its purpose is to earn income, it is not of a capital nature, and it is reasonable in the circumstances. A capital expense means an asset which is depreciated over a period of time according to the Capital Cost Allowance (CCA) class to which the asset belongs. The allowance must not exceed the maximum rate allowable in any year. The percentages range from 5% to 100% depreciation in a year. You can obtain a copy of these CCA categories from CRA upon request.

There are numerous categories of expenses that can be deducted depending on the nature of your business. Your accountant will advise you as to which ones are deductible and which are not. Also, if some of the expenses are related to personal use, you are supposed to deduct that portion from the business expense. Reasonable remuneration paid to spouses for services rendered to the business is also deductible. The CRA form entitled Statement of Income and Expenses outlines some of the expenses that you may wish to consider. Your accountant may suggest other expenses for which you could be eligible.

TIPS ON MAXIMIZING WRITE-OFFS

It's not what you make, but what you keep—after taxes. While some business expenses are fully deductible within the same year, others must be depreciated over time. CRA allows you to go back 3 years and carry forward up to 20 years any legitimate business losses you incur. You then offset those losses against income. Remember to get in the habit of keeping receipts for everything. Your accountant can advise you later as to what expenses can be used and in what portion or fashion. Review the key areas to make sure you are getting the maximum tax-deductible expense and/or depreciation benefit. Many obvious expenses have not been covered here, such as supplies, rent or lease payments, or bad debts. As the government can change the tax laws at any time, make sure you have the current guidelines.

- **Home/apartment.** If you are operating out of your home, CRA states that the area of your home designated as your "business location" must be used exclusively and regularly for business-related purposes. This could include a work area, an office area, and storage space. If you do have customers coming to your home, claim a separate reception area and washrooms for business use, if that is the case, or else a portion of "common area" (personal and business) usage for business purposes.

   There are various ways of calculating the percentage of home office use. You can divide the total house or apartment square footage by the overall square footage used for business-related purposes or calculate the number of rooms used of the total rooms in the house—use whichever formula works to your advantage. Don't forget to also take a portion of the "common area" used for business purposes (e.g., the hallways and stairs). Also, don't forget to include any remodelling and decorating costs involved in converting a room. These improvements are considered allowable expenses.

In addition, you can claim a portion of all the house-related expenses for your home office use: mortgage interest and property taxes—or rent—plus insurance, maintenance costs, and utilities (electricity, water, heating, telephone). If your total house expenses are $25,000 per year for all the above, for example, and 25% of the square footage of your house relates to your home office, the deductible expense against business income would be $6,250 per year.

- **Car.** If you have one car and use it 50% of the time for business, claim half of all your car-related expenses (e.g., gas, oil, maintenance, insurance, interest on car financing) as business expenses. You are supposed to maintain a mileage logbook to support your business usage claim. For a jointly used car (personal and business), you may want to consider charging a per-kilometre charge instead. If you have two cars and use one exclusively for business, you can claim 100% of that car's expenses. In addition, be sure to claim depreciation of 30% on your car and deduct the appropriate portion each year from income. If you lease your car, the maximum write-off is $800 per month. Whatever price you pay for your leased car, the maximum save for depreciation purposes is $30,000. The figures noted can change over time.

- **Furniture and equipment.** Your office furniture, computer hardware, printer, software, and other equipment must be depreciated over time, using the capital cost allowance formula, which allows for a portion (from 20% to 100% per year) to be deducted each year.

- **Salaries.** Salaries paid to your children, spouse, relatives, or others to perform work for your company are also deductible business expenses. However, the amount you pay them should be reasonable in the circumstances.

- **Entertainment.** Entertaining existing or potential customers/clients for promotion or prospecting purposes is another deductible expense. You can claim as an expense 50% of the cost of the entertainment or meals, including tips and taxes.

- **Education.** Your professional or business education, such as books, seminars, conventions, or conferences, provides other opportunities to claim deductions against your business.

- **Trade shows.** Any expenses relating to trade shows that you attend for your business purposes are deductible. To find out about forthcoming trade shows or conventions, check with your chamber of commerce or government small business centres.
- **Travel.** If you travel for business-related purposes, you can write off all or a portion of expenses such as airfare, transportation, car rental, hotel, and a portion (50%) of your meal costs.

Remember to obtain tax advice prior to starting your business and on an ongoing basis from a professionally qualified accountant, such as a Chartered Accountant or Certified General Accountant. Advice customized to your specific circumstances is essential. The rule of three—that is, having an initial consultation with at least three accountants before selecting your advisor—is important. In most cases, the initial consultation is free. Ask in advance before making an appointment. Put your questions in writing, so you don't forget them. Ask about income splitting, fiscal year-end, business structure options, and ways of maximizing deductions and minimizing taxes.

GOODS AND SERVICES TAX

The goods and services tax (GST) is a Federal sales tax on most supplies of goods and services, except supplies such as medical services, basic food, education, etc., and applies at a rate of 5%. Many provinces have also harmonized their sales taxes at rates ranging from 7% to 10% for a harmonized sales tax (HST) rate ranging from 12% to 15%. You are not obligated to apply for or use a GST registration number if your gross sales do not exceed $30,000 a year. However, you may wish to do so, if you are paying out GST/HST on your purchases and want to get a portion of it back. The basic premise of GST/HST is simple, although there are various unique provisions in certain situations. Basically, there is an input tax credit for GST/HST you pay that you can offset against GST/HST you collect. You either remit the difference, if you owe money to CRA, or request a refund from CRA, if there is an amount owing to you. For further information, contact your local CRA office and obtain their current explanatory publications for small business and GST/HST.

What Is a Business Number?

The business number (BN) is a numbering system that simplifies and streamlines the way businesses deal with government. It is based on the idea of one business, one number. The BN includes the four major business categories of dealing with CRA: corporate income tax, import/export, payroll deductions, and GST/HST.

You can register for a BN by contacting CRA and by phone, mail, and fax. Each sole proprietor, partnership, or corporation will get one BN. Sole proprietors will get one BN for all their businesses. If you change the legal basis under which you carry on business, for example, your unincorporated business becomes a corporation or your corporation merges with one or more other corporations to form a new corporation, you will need a new BN.

If you are a sole proprietor or a partner in a partnership, you will continue to use your SIN (Social Insurance Number – provided to you by the Government of Canada) to file your individual income tax return, even though you may have a BN (Business Number) for your GST/HST, payroll deductions, and import/export accounts.

Who Must Register for GST/HST?

There are three important factors to consider when determining whether you have to register for and charge GST/HST.

- the nature of the goods and services you will sell or otherwise provide
- whether your annual worldwide GST/HST taxable sales, including those of any associates, are more than $30,000 in the immediate preceding four consecutive calendar quarters or in a single calendar year
- who you provide goods and services to (e.g. most supplies to nonresidents of Canada are exempt from GST/HST).

For further information, contact your professional accountant or CRA.

TAX AVOIDANCE AND EVASION

CRA does not object to a taxpayer openly arranging financial affairs within the framework of the law so as to keep taxes to a minimum. There is a distinction, however, between legitimate tax planning and tax evasion. When attempting to avoid or reduce taxes, be certain to obtain professional tax advice to ensure that your approach is within the bounds of legitimate tax planning. If a taxpayer deliberately conceals income or attempts to evade the payment of taxes by misrepresentation, fraud, or some other means, this will be deemed to be the commitment of an offence and is liable to civil and/or criminal prosecution. This will result in severe penalties: heavy fines and in some cases, jail sentences. In a proprietorship or partnership, you would be personally liable; in a corporation, the directors of the corporation could be liable.

SOURCES OF TAX INFORMATION

There are numerous sources of information available to assist you in your decision-making on tax-related matters. Some of the main sources include:

Canada revenue agency

CRA has many publications available to assist you in your tax planning. For the office nearest you, look in the *Blue Pages* of your telephone directory under "Government of Canada—Income Tax" or at cra-arc.gc.ca. If you want to obtain guidelines and other information you can contact them in person, by mail, via the Internet, or by telephone.

You can obtain copies of publications upon request. Some of the categories and types of publications include:

- **Interpretation bulletins, Special Releases, and Technical News.** These cover specific areas of income tax law that have been determined by the courts in many cases. Examples include Income of Contractors, Inventory Evaluation, and Interest Deductibility.
- **Information circulars.** These provide a summary of practical tax filing and compliance information for the taxpayer. Titles include Tax Evasion and Avoidance and The Tax Audit
- **Tax guides.** These are designed to assist taxpayers in preparing statements necessary for income tax purposes. The purpose of the guide is to present a simplified, understandable, layperson's version of the technical and complex provisions of the Tax Act. The Business and Professional Income Tax Guide is designed for a proprietorship or partnership, and the Corporate Income Tax Guide is for corporations. Also, ask for the GST and Small Business Guide and other related publications.
- **Information booklets.** These booklets have an overview of information that tends to be more extensive than in the circulars. Titles include Income Tax and Small Business and Commission Earnings.
- **Forms.** There are many types of forms available from CRA, including Statement of Income and Expenses from a Business. This is designed for a proprietorship or partnership. Other forms include Statement of Income and Expenses from a Professional Practice, and Capital Cost Allowance Schedule (for depreciation purposes).

Public libraries

Your public library has many books relating to tax that could be helpful to you. Speak to the business resource librarian and ask for assistance.

Bookstores

There are many books published on tax in Canada relating to tax matters and financial planning for individuals. Many of these are available in bookstores and are updated annually to keep current with tax changes.

Major accounting firms

Most of the major chartered accounting firms have free publications available upon request relating to tax matters for the small business owner. The material is updated to reflect current tax changes. To obtain a list of available tax booklets on personal or business related matters, look in the *Yellow Pages* print and online under "Accountants—Chartered" or on the Internet, and do a Google search. Also refer to Appendix B, "Sources of Further Information."

Accountants

As mentioned earlier, speak to an accountant with tax expertise in small business. Remember to initially interview at least three accountants on appropriate tax planning for your business before selecting an accountant. You want to make sure that the advice you are receiving is consistent before finalizing your decisions.

Lawyers

Some lawyers are highly specialized in the area of tax law and litigation. A small business owner would not normally require advice from a tax lawyer, unless he or she was involved in litigation with CRA on the matter of a dispute or appeal. If you have any questions on various complex legal issues relating to tax, ask your accountant for the name of a tax lawyer, or contact the lawyer referral service in your area.

WHY RECORD-KEEPING IS NECESSARY

Records must be kept in any type or size of business regardless of how small your small business is. In business, records are continually generated including bank deposit books, delivery slips, invoices, receipts, sales slips, contracts, and numerous other documents. When operating a small business, it is critically important that systems be developed for recording and filing the various types of records in order that they can be retrieved and examined quickly and efficiently.

Examples of typical financial records include:

- sales journal
- cash receipts journal
- accounts receivable ledger
- accounts payable journal

- cash disbursements journal
- credit purchases journal
- credit sales journal
- payroll journal
- general synoptic ledger.

Some of the nonfinancial records include records relating to personnel, equipment, inventory, and production. There are federal, provincial, and municipal government departments and agencies that have set rules and regulations relating to the keeping of records for a small business. For example, Statistics Canada requires that information be supplied upon request. CRA requires the payment of income tax by the business, as well as deductions at source, by the business, of employee taxes and contributions to Employment Insurance and Canada Pension Plan. GST/HST documentation must be kept. More detail on employee records and government requirements is covered in Chapter 11, "Personnel."

Some other external reasons for keeping records are as follows:

- raising financing and attracting potential investors
- selling a business
- creditor and supplier requirements
- insurance company requirements for a loss claim.

Internal reasons for maintaining records include:

- keeping you better informed about the financial position of your business
- making it easier to complete accurate income tax returns with supporting receipts for expenses
- eliminating most of the problems that might be encountered if tax returns are audited
- providing the basis for evaluating the condition and effectiveness of equipment
- reminding you when creditor obligations are due
- demonstrating good management skills and effective time management
- providing an opportunity for comparing budget goals with historical records and future projections
- permitting an accurate basis for ratio analysis in comparison with industry averages
- providing the basis for preparation of financial statements and other documents required to obtain credit or financing.

The Income Tax Act requires that you keep your records and books in an orderly manner at your place of business or your residence, as this material may be requested at any time by CRA for review or audit purposes. You are required to maintain business records and supporting documents for at least 6 years from the end of the last taxation year to which they relate. If you filed your return late for any year, records and supporting documents must be kept for 6 years from the date you filed that return. The following books and records may not be destroyed for 2 years from the day an incorporated business is dissolved, and 6 years from the last day of the related taxation year in the case of the termination of an unincorporated business:

- general and private ledger sheets
- special contracts and agreements
- general journal, if essential for understanding the general ledger entries
- all corporate minute-book records.

Other books and records must be kept for 6 years unless CRA grants permission to destroy them earlier. This would apply to:

- original books of entry, such as cash, purchase, and sales books or journals (except the general journal), inventory and production records, and payroll and distribution sheets
- sales invoices and statements and purchase and expense vouchers
- payroll time and rate cards.

Many people prefer the convenience of e-filing their tax returns. This is a very easy method and saves you sending in attached documents, unless they are subsequently requested.

Record-Keeping Systems and Equipment

The equipment and systems that a small business uses for record-keeping can range from simple, inexpensive manual procedures to more efficient and versatile computer systems. You should request advice from your accountant as to the most efficient record-keeping system for your type of business. The reality is that most small businesses use their computer for record-keeping. Naturally, the type of equipment that you have will change as your business grows. For example, if you are just starting a one-person business, you may only require a one-write system for cheque writing, a general ledger, and a ledger system for receivables and payables. As your business expands, it may require more specialized ledgers. Finally, if your business requires a sophisticated record-keeping system, you may want to purchase a computerized bookkeeping system. Here are some of the common systems that you may wish to consider:

- **One-write systems.** This system allows a user to enter a business transaction onto several forms at the same time by using carbon paper. This type of system minimizes the amount of information required for each transaction, thereby saving time and reducing the risk of error.

For instance, the basic system might combine the business cheque-book with the cash disbursements journal and employee earnings record. When the cheque is written, the information is transferred automatically by the carbon paper onto the appropriate journal and record. The amount is then recorded a second time in the proper category column on the spreadsheet. There are many types of one-write systems, including ones for cash receipts. For further information, look in the *Yellow Pages* print and online under "Accounting and Bookkeeping Systems." Also, do a Google search using the keywords.

- **Specialized record-keeping systems.** You may wish to consider a ledgerless system for accounts receivable and accounts payable. This type of system is suitable for a type of business with a relatively low volume of sales transactions. It enables the business to keep track of its accounts receivable and accounts payable with a simple filing system rather than detailed subsidiary ledgers.

- **Ledgers and journals.** Stationery and office supply stores sell many of the standard ledger and journal record systems, as well as binders with preprinted column headings with up to twenty or more columns.

  There are various forms designed to meet the specific needs of small business. Specialized record-keeping systems are also available through manufacturers, wholesalers, and trade associations to record transactions that are common to businesses in the same trade.

- **Specialized cash registers.** These registers are computerized to record sales-distribution entries for the sales journal as well as details for inventory control. There are many sophisticated types of cash registers available that are customized for different types of business needs.

- **Accounting software.** The most popular accounting software programs are: QuickBooks, Quicken, and Simply Accounting.

Chapter 7

Buying a Business

If there were dreams to sell ... what would you buy?

As an alternative to starting a business, you may decide to buy an existing business. While there are obvious advantages, there are also drawbacks. Buying a small business is a complicated and potentially risky transaction. Carefully assess the advantages and disadvantages of buying a business, determine the type and size of business you prefer, search for available opportunities, evaluate the business, negotiate the purchase price, and then sign all the necessary legal documents. It is essential that you have a lawyer and accountant to protect your interests and advise you properly before you even start your search, and certainly before you sign an offer.

ADVANTAGES AND DISADVANTAGES OF BUYING A BUSINESS

Whether the advantages of buying an existing business outweigh the disadvantages depends of course on your financial situation and your business knowledge and experience. Following are some of the advantages and disadvantages of buying a business.

Advantages of Buying a Business

- It is a faster way of getting into business without the cost, energy, time, and risk involved in starting up your own business and going through the hazardous stage of the first year or two of growth.
- You can examine the track record of the business and analyze the financial statements showing its revenue, expenses, and cash flow. In this way you can determine whether the profits are increasing or decreasing, and if it's a viable business opportunity.
- It is easier to project the potential of the business in terms of revenue and profit, thereby minimizing the uncertainty and risk that would be involved in starting from scratch.
- After you have negotiated a purchase price, you know the fixed amount with which you are dealing. You also know the state of the business in terms of its income and cash flow and its potential for growth based on

its history and other factors. When starting a business from scratch, you would have no idea of how much money you might have to expend to bring the business up to the same financial state and potential as the one that you are buying.

- You may obtain a return on your investment much sooner than if you start from scratch.

- A distressed business may be purchased at a low price and then turned around under good management to result in attractive profits. The reason for distress may vary from partnership split, health or marital problems, to burnout or poor management. If you have the skill to take over such a situation, this could be a viable option.

- You may be able to obtain financing more easily, because the lender can assess the history of the company in terms of its financial statements and proven sales rather than on optimistic projections.

- You might be able to obtain seller-backed financing for a portion of the purchase price. The seller may agree to take security on the business or various assets of the business for a portion of the purchase price. Another example is that the purchaser may defer the payments on the purchase price of the business over a period of 2 to 3 years. There could be tax advantages to the seller for doing this, and the buyer can use the cash flow from the business to pay the seller.

- It could be easier to obtain supplier financing, because suppliers who have dealt with the business in the past are familiar with its potential and viability. A trade creditor would therefore be more likely to extend a larger amount of credit and more favourable terms than if you started from scratch without any track record.

- A buyer might be able to purchase leasehold improvements which are already in place, at a considerable savings compared to what it would have cost to have put them in the business in the first place.

- The buyer can usually draw on the knowledge of the seller regarding the business, the best merchandise to carry, and invaluable information about the community.

- When buying an existing business, you may also inherit various other beneficial, nontangible assets such as production techniques, inventory control, credit and collection or other administrative systems, licences that may be hard to get, secret formulas, and a noncompetition covenant from the seller.

- Trained personnel who were directly responsible for the success of the original business may stay with the new owner.

- You can assess the management and administrative systems within the business to determine their efficiency. If they are appropriate, you can operate the business without any substantial changes in the systems and procedures.

- A great deal of the time-consuming investigation and guesswork is eliminated. Such factors as store size, the location of the business, what type of leaseholds or equipment to install, how many employees to hire, and what training is required—all these questions may be answered when you buy an existing business.

- An existing business might have an excellent location with high traffic volume and public familiarity and acceptance. It could take a considerable time for somebody starting from scratch to either find a similar location or reach the same point in terms of sales volume, reputation, and customer loyalty.

Disadvantages of Buying a Business

- The existing location of the business may not be as attractive as it was originally. This may be due to changing traffic flow, competition nearby, declining population base, and other factors.

- You could be locked into the present physical layout and location of the business because the lease comes as part of the purchase price. This could present problems if you want to expand the business at some future point but still have a long-term lease, or if you want to make alterations to the premises but it is not financially feasible.

- The business location that you are buying or a lease that you are assuming could be an older building that could cost you more money in heating, maintenance, or improvements than you are prepared or able to pay.

- You may be required to pay for a goodwill factor which you otherwise would not have to pay if you start your own business from scratch. The present owner's goodwill (the value that is placed on the present established customer base, business reputation, and net profit) may be difficult to assess.

- The seller may have had a poor credit and collection system, and therefore the customers took advantage of it. It could take some considerable adjustment to retrain the customers into a more responsible approach. Customers may be lost in the process.

- Some of the equipment might be obsolete or defective and may therefore require early repair or replacement.

- The previous owner's employees may not be suitable for the type of business operation you intend to run. They may be accustomed to sloppy procedures or lack of systems, and could resent your desire to operate a "tight shop." Employees might quit quickly if they do not like your style as a new owner, and this could create difficulties or delay getting replacement employees and training them promptly.

- If the business you are considering buying has customer ill will for any reason, you will inherit that problem, which could impair your business growth and investment.
- You may be temporarily locked into the management or operation policies of the seller, as well as the pricing structure for the services or products. Although you should be able to change these over time, they could result in customer resistance and a decline in revenue.
- The business may already have merchandise lines which have been established in the public perception as being part of your business image. You may want to alter those lines and that could create customer resistance.
- You could buy a business which has inherently serious problems that you were unaware of before you purchased the business.
- If you are buying shares of a corporation, you could potentially be exposed to a lawsuit for actions or debts owing by the previous owner of the business. Although you may have protected yourself legally and have all the necessary documentation, it could still be frustrating and time-consuming to deal with litigation matters.

Many of these disadvantages can be avoided through careful research and investigation. The following sections will assist you in going through this process.

LOCATING A BUSINESS

Many of the same factors that affect a person's decision to start a business need to be considered to know the type of business that you may want to buy. These include your experience in the area, interest, skills, personality, and lifestyle needs. Financing is a critical consideration in the type of business that you are able to buy. Chapter 10, "Raising Financing," details the considerations you should be aware of and potential sources of financing. In addition, you want to determine what type of business sector interests you, whether you want or need partners, your personal annual income needs, whether the nature of the business involves indoor or outdoor work, and the amount of personal interaction that would be required with customers, employees, and others. Other issues you will have to deal with are the amount of management expertise you have or want to expend, whether you need to hire managers, whether you want to eventually phase out of the business and hire someone else to manage it for you or possibly sell it. You may want to keep the business at a relatively small size in terms of management, and that makes a difference when looking for a business. The amount of travelling that you might have to do or the hours you are going to be expending on the business, as well as commuting time, are also factors. You may want to involve family members in the business, which could be a factor in deciding on the type of business that you may want to buy.

It is important to understand yourself, your strengths and weaknesses, your motivations and personal suitability for the business, before embarking on buying an existing business. Your family, friends, business associates, accountant, lawyer, and banker are all sources of candid input and advice that will assist in your choice. You may wish to retain a consultant who is expert in the specific type of business you are considering to make a candid assessment in terms of the viability of the business. Refer to Appendix A, which outlines the various questions you should consider when buying a business. By the time you have completed this checklist, you will have a much better idea of what you are looking for and whether you have found it.

Searching for Available Opportunities

Once you have decided that you want to buy a business, the type of business that you want to buy, have established your objectives clearly, determined your financial resources and the geographic area that you want to be in, among other factors, you now have to seek out the sources of available opportunities. Following are some sources to consider.

- **Newspaper print and online ads.** Ads frequently appear in the business section and the business opportunities section of the classifieds in print or online. Check the classified sections of all the newspapers in your local newspapers and in national newspapers, such as *The Globe and Mail* and the *National Post*. You may decide to place an ad in the paper, either in the business opportunity section or as a classified ad in the business wanted section.
- **Magazine print and online ads.** Local, provincial, and national business magazines (e.g., *Profit, Canadian Business*) have a classified section which lists businesses for sale.
- **Trade sources.** Trade publications may advertise businesses for sale. Contact the trade association and ask if there are any businesses for sale or place an ad in the monthly trade publication stating business wanted and a description. Other trade sources include manufacturers, distributors, suppliers, wholesalers, and salespeople.
- **Business brokers.** Business brokers specialize in the buying and selling of businesses. Ask to be included on a mailing list to receive updated lists of businesses for sale. The broker can act as an intermediary in terms of the preliminary negotiating process on factors such as financing, terms,

price, takeover date, and other matters. Investigate the broker's reputation, services, and contacts.

- **Realtors.** Small businesses are frequently listed for sale through realtors on the multiple listing service. Search out realtors who specialize in commercial real estate and are sophisticated in the matter of negotiating leases, buildings, and businesses. Dealing with an experienced and established realtor with professional training in commercial real estate will minimize the risk for you.
- **Trustees and receivers.** You can find the names of trustees or receivers in the *Yellow Pages* print and online under "Trustees in Bankruptcy." Ask to be put on their list to be notified of businesses that are for sale.
- **Professional advisors.** Your lawyer and accountant may know of businesses for sale that could be of interest to you.
- **Chambers of commerce.** Become a member of the chamber of commerce to gain a better knowledge of the business in the geographic area in which you are interested. You might consider putting an ad in the chamber newsletter stating "business wanted" along with details.
- **Cold call prospecting.** You may decide to contact the owners of a business and ask them if they are currently interested, or might be at some point in the future, in selling their business. They may not be interested immediately, but you could encourage them to consider an idea they otherwise may not have considered.
- **Searching the Internet.** By using thorough Google search techniques, you should find many different sites offering business opportunities. However, one should exert caution in taking claims at face value. You need to follow up with due diligence before you invest any money or make any other financial commitment.

Risky Businesses

In searching for businesses, there are a number of classic warning signs that should alert you to potential problems. Buying the wrong business could result in a financial disaster for you. The following is a partial list of common warning signs that you should be aware of. Additional cautions are presented in the next section on evaluating a business.

High pressure to buy a business

If you are experiencing a situation in which the seller or an agent of the seller is putting high pressure on you to buy the business, resist and be wary. Possibly the seller is ready to go under or is desperate to sell for some other negative reason. Perhaps the agent is eager to make a commission or feels that the listing is going to run out. Never put yourself in a situation in which you have to make a quick decision on something as critical as buying a business.

Unfamiliar business

It would be a serious mistake for any buyer to invest in a business about which he or she knows nothing. The dangers in running the enterprise are accentuated by inexperience and unfamiliarity. You could be buying a business totally unsuited to your personality, talents, or interest. You would be at a considerable disadvantage trying to survive and compete with your similar businesses. Many magazines and newspaper ads attempt to attract the unwary buyer with promises of "get rich, easy money" claims. For obvious reasons, avoid any businesses that are overly hyped.

Partner-wanted business

Some business partnerships that are based on sound economic data can work out well and may be worthy of your consideration. On the other hand, many business partnerships do not survive in the long run. This could be because of conflicts of personality, philosophy, policy, priorities, or unequal contributions of money, time, or skill. Some unstable and undesirable business operations attempt to defraud the unwary investor by obtaining an injection of funds into the business and then using those funds in an inappropriate fashion without any controls. For example, investment funds could be used for paying past creditors' debts rather than as working capital for future need and growth. Be cautious of any business partnerships that promise a disproportionate return based on the investment of money or time.

Businesses requiring skills that the buyer lacks

If the buyer lacks the necessary skills, the existing customer base could drain away quickly and the business could fail. If a particular business requires one-on-one direct contact between the owner and the customers, and the owner does not communicate effectively in terms of language skills or does not feel comfortable interacting with the public, this would not be a good choice.

Buyback business

A seller may attempt to induce a prospective purchaser to buy by promising to buy back the business if the buyer is not satisfied. Once the money has been obtained, the seller could renege on the commitment or maybe use up all the funds and disappear. Although you would have recourse to sue, in practical terms you could be wasting further money.

Owner claims to be skimming

A business owner may try to induce a sale by claiming that the financial statements do not accurately record the amount of cash that has come into the business. For example, if the business is essentially a cash-only business such as a delicatessen, the seller could state that in fact 50% more revenue was made than the records show. In other words, the seller would be stating (discreetly and obviously not in writing) that half of the cash was pocketed without being recorded or having tax paid on it. Don't purchase such a business. The situation would mean that you cannot rely at all on the financial records, which places you at high risk. In addition, you cannot base your purchase price on the assurance of the seller that they evaded taxes. Obviously the seller is not credible, and consequently the business is not worth considering any further.

Businesses which use up all investment capital

If you are considering a business which would require all of your financial resources to pay the purchase price, you could be in a situation that you are starting off undercapitalized, without working capital or reserve for future needs. For example, if you take over a business and there is a decline in sales and profit during the transition phase, you would not have any resources to be able to buffer the financial crunch. Never buy a business without taking into account your working capital and contingency fund.

Personal service business

There are special concerns you should be aware of if you are considering buying a personal service business (e.g., an architectural, engineering, law, dental, or legal practice). The main concern relates to the bonding and goodwill which has occurred between clients and the professional. Once the business is purchased, a substantial portion or possibly most of the clientele could leave and go to other professionals because of differences in style and operation. For example, you may require retainers in advance and send bills promptly every 2 weeks for services that you render. The previous owner of the personal service business may have been very sloppy in credit and collection procedures, never asked for retainers, and frequently left accounts unbilled for months on end. If you do buy a personal service business, you should build in protections, because the goodwill may not necessarily stay when the other party leaves.

Declining neighbourhood

If you are considering a business that is in an area which is changing rapidly in terms of the population base, reconsider. For example, perhaps the location is becoming more commercialized and older residential buildings are being torn down for office buildings. If your target market is the homeowner, and there is a shrinking population base in that area, that could cause sufficient loss of income that your business would not survive.

Emotionally based interest

If you are considering a business that you have a very positive emotional feeling about, and that feeling, rather than the business aspects, tends to dominate the decisions you are making, don't proceed any further. Overenthusiasm, unrealistic expectations, overly inflated projections, and optimism can very quickly turn into financial disaster. A business that you buy has to make objective good business sense first, at a price you can afford.

Failing or distressed business

Don't proceed any further if you are considering a business which is going through serious financial problems. The exception would be if you are an expert in that type of business, have clearly identified the reasons for the financial difficulties, and know that you have the expertise and management resources to turn it around. There are people who buy businesses with a turnaround strategy in mind and skillfully negotiate a purchase package which is very attractive. This can be done effectively, of course, only if the buyer knows what he or she is doing and is sophisticated in this type of distress purchase.

Online business

If you are considering buying a business run totally or mostly online, be very careful. If it sounds too good to be true, it probably is. If you are interested in running your own business online, you might want to start from scratch. If so, refer to Douglas Gray's *Start and Run a Profitable Business Using Your Computer*, published by International Self-Counsel Press.

EVALUATION OF A BUSINESS

After you have completed all the preliminary steps and have decided on the specific business in which you are interested, the next issue is determining what the enterprise is worth. The buyer, of course, is hoping to buy the business with as little financial outlay as possible. The seller frequently is looking at it from an emotional viewpoint in terms of the many years of time, energy, and stress that went into the business, and the small return that was taken out of it in the first years of growth. In addition, most business owners have an inflated assessment of the value of goodwill, which may have little or no bearing on the value of the business. There could be a considerable difference between the proposed selling price and the eventual purchase price after a thorough evaluation is done and negotiations are completed.

It takes time, effort, and skill to properly evaluate a business. It is important that you minimize the potential risk through careful evaluation. Various parties may be involved in attempting to set a price for the business, including the seller, the buyer, the business broker, the realtor, a professional commercial business appraiser, and a professional accountant. Depending on the experts' points of view, experience, and vested interest, the assessment as to what you should pay for the business could vary considerably.

After taking into account all the factors and input, rely on your accountant's advice plus your own judgment. Ultimately, the price of the business is really determined by the buyer, not the seller.

Why the Business Is Being Sold

One of the first steps in the evaluation procedure is to determine why the business is being sold. Some of the reasons may not have any impact, while other reasons could have a serious impact and could cause you to lose your investment completely. Here are some of the common reasons why businesses are sold:

- The facilities are obsolete and it would be too expensive to upgrade or move to a new location.
- The lease is almost ready to expire, and the landlord does not want to renew the lease or wants to renew it at a much higher price.
- The product line is poor, and the owner is having difficulty getting a new product line.
- Sales are declining, possibly due to changing economic or market factors, poor location, or unmarketable services or products.
- Competition has just come into the area or will be coming soon, and the owner wants to sell before that factor makes the business unattractive.
- The owner is having partnership problems.
- The owner is having marital or health problems, or wants to retire.
- The owner has lost enthusiasm or commitment to the business after many years of frustration and hard work, and wants to do something different in life.
- The owner wants to sell so that the money can be used to buy another and more attractive business opportunity.
- Government regulations (federal, provincial, or municipal) have just come in or will be coming in which would require the business to expend monies to comply with regulations, and the enterprise cannot afford to make the changes and remain competitive.
- The location of the business is no longer attractive because of changing zoning bylaws, traffic patterns, or transportation services.
- The owner is concerned about potential lawsuits and wants to sell quickly before the lawsuits commence.
- Due to a poor credit and collection policy, the business is unable to collect receivables and is suffering serious cash flow problems, and is unable to obtain further financing.

- The business has lost one or more key employees, which will have a negative impact on the operation.
- The business has lost one or more major contracts, without which it is no longer financially viable.

Factors That Affect a Business Evaluation

There are many factors which determine the ultimate evaluation and pricing of the business. In fact, an appraisal is largely an estimate or opinion of value which can vary considerably. For example, the value placed on the business by the seller, which will determine his asking price, is in many cases unrealistic. This is because the seller frequently sees value in relationship to cost, but in reality cost is not necessarily one of the viable elements of value. The business that may have cost the owner $40,000 to equip 4 years ago may be worth anywhere from $10,000 to $100,000 today, depending on factors which bear on the business market value.

At the outset of your inquiry, obtain financial records, including income statements (profit-and-loss statements) and balance sheets for the past 3 years, tax returns for the past 3 years, lists of accounts payable and accounts receivable, all other liabilities of the company, and the books of the business. Get a copy of the current lease, any contracts the company has with employees, suppliers, or others, and other documentation that your lawyer and accountant may request.

Here are the most common factors considered in establishing a selling price for a business:

- **Accounts receivable.** If these are to be included in the purchase price, they should be examined closely. Accounts under 30 days have a higher incidence of reliability, while those between 30 and 60 days are a higher risk. Any receivables over 60 days may be uncollectable. Before purchasing any accounts receivable, contact the customers to make sure that they agree with the outstanding balances. You may want to make an arrangement with the seller that you will defer payment or partial payment to the seller until you have received the accounts receivable.
- **Fixed assets.** This includes such things as the building, fixtures, and leasehold improvements. Although the original owner may have put in a considerable amount of money in leasehold improvements, the improvements may not have maintained their market value. Perhaps the improvements stay with the landlord at the end of the lease.
- **Movable assets.** This would include such items as equipment, furniture, and furnishings. The value of the equipment may be based on its original value, its replacement value, its auction-sale value as used equipment, or depreciated value.

- **Inventory.** You may want to use an independent, qualified appraiser to determine the dollar value of the inventory. A manufacturer may have several different types of inventory, such as finished goods, work in process, and raw materials. The inventory should be examined for style, condition, saleability, quality, age, freshness, and balance. Personally inspect the inventory to know what you are buying. Some of the inventory might be outdated and would be difficult to sell. If possible, purchase inventory at a discounted price. Inventory is normally paid for separately from the purchase price of the business and after it has been accounted for as of the day that the business is taken over. Other considerations that you have to take into account when dealing with inventory include:
  - Is the inventory in character with your target market?
  - How much of the inventory would have to be cleared out at a loss and what would that loss be?
  - Does the inventory list contain items that have already been sold and paid for and not yet shipped?
  - How does the average industry ratio of inventory to sales compare with the business for sale?
  - Has the seller kept adequate records of inventory, and in what form, and for how long?
  - Are all the items in inventory owned by the business or are some of those on consignment?
  - Does a lender have any security documentation covering inventory, such as to a bank?
- **Customer lists, business and creditor records, mailing lists, both in print and in an** customer **electronic database.** These items could be valuable assets for you. Make sure they are included in the sales agreement and that the seller is not entitled to use these lists for the seller's own purpose in competition with you or to give the lists and records to any other party without your written consent.
- **Licences.** What licences that are necessary for the operation of the business (e.g., a liquor licence) are included in the sale price and are they transferable to you? Make sure that the completion of the purchase is conditional upon the licence being transferred. Have you checked all the licensing requirements and municipal bylaws (e.g., health, fire and safety regulations, zoning bylaws, and other matters)?
- **Leases.** A lease is an essential part of the purchase price of the business, unless of course you are buying the whole building. The length and terms of the lease are important considerations in establishing the value of a business. You will want to have answers to such questions as: Is the lease transferable to the buyer with or without the consent of the

landlord? Is the present lease negotiable with the landlord? Should you negotiate an entirely new lease? Are there restrictions in the lease? Are there options for renewal in the lease? What rent-escalation or demolition clauses are built into the lease? Apart from leases with the landlord, there could be leases for equipment, signs, furniture, telephone systems, and many other items. In some cases, these leases are assignable. Obtain the actual lease documents for your lawyer's review. Possibly you will not want to keep some of the items leased.

- **Non-competition clause.** When buying a business, it is important that you protect yourself from the owner opening up a competing business across the street and putting your investment at severe risk. To avoid this problem, include a clause in the sales agreement prohibiting the seller from establishing a business in competition with you. Built into that restriction should be a time limit and a specified geographic area. A skilled business lawyer will know the correct wording.

- **Accounts payable.** This factor is relevant in terms of potential litigation and credit history. For example, are all the accounts current or are some of them past due and how long past due? Do any of the creditors have liens or encumbrances against the assets of the business or have they made claims for monies owing?

- **Prepaid expenses.** Sometimes a business will have prepaid expenses, such as insurance or last month's rent, or if the building is owned, property taxes for the year may have been paid in advance. Check to make sure that the items which have been prepaid can be assigned to you without penalty.

- **Intangible rights.** Patents, copyrights, trademarks, industrial designs, and business names can have very real monetary benefit to your business. If you want them as part of your agreement, they should be specifically included in the sales agreement.

- **Domain name and website.** This could be a considerable asset for your business. Depending on its historical use, it could represent substantial goodwill, as well as an additional source of income for direct sales. All this could be quantified to enhance the sale price of your business.

- **Employees.** Ideally you would try to keep the key employees who are experienced in the business and know the customers, the product or service, and the suppliers. Try to find out how many of the key employees would be prepared to remain with the business after you buy it.

- **Income/earnings.** The net income after expenses and before taxes is an important factor that has to be taken in context. For example, the net income is relative to how the business operator keeps his or her books, how efficient he or she is in buying, how well labour costs are controlled, how competently the business is managed, how well it's marketed and promoted, how careful he or she is about overhead and expenses, and how committed he or she is to making the business financially successful. Some buyers or sellers put a high reliance on the gross sales figure and feel that this is the true value of the business because it reflects the volume of activity and cash flow.

- **Type of business.** Some businesses are more popular than others and therefore have a greater buyer appeal. The higher the appeal, the higher the demand, and therefore a generally higher price.

- **Competition.** The amount of competition in the trading area plays an important part in the potential profitability and gross volume of the business. Do your research thoroughly and look for the following warning signs:
  - nearby major shopping centres which offer more attractive one-stop facilities for shoppers
  - heavy competition by discounters
  - the presence of a large number of competing businesses engaged in the same type of business that you are considering
  - competitors who offer special features, such as cheque cashing, delivery service, credit, delayed payments, and other inducements to attract customers.
  - If these factors are present, you could be forced to try to meet the competition by offering the same features.

- **Customers.** A significant factor to many buyers is the type of existing customer base that the business currently enjoys. Does the business cater to a few customers that make up the majority of the purchase volume?

- **Warranties.** If the business that you are buying offers products which are covered by warranty, you would need to know what warranties have been extended and the lifetime of each warranty. Possibly they are renewal contracts in terms of extended coverage which generates a cash flow for the business. To maintain customer goodwill, you might be obligated to honour the warranties.

- **Accounting practices.** Make sure that the financial statements were prepared by a professional, qualified accountant and that the accounting opinion is a credible one. Obtain your professional accountant's advice in interpreting the financial information. Auditing can be an expensive procedure, but depending on the nature of the business that you are buying and the amount of the purchase price, that might be a condition that you require before you finalize the purchase. Other factors that you should be aware of include:
  - unusually high depreciation which can artificially alter the profit figures by increasing them

- financial statements that are unrealistically overstated or understated statements that reflect a lower than normal product cost or net profit percentage.
- **Management.** Assess the quality and nature of the current management of the company. This factor will make a difference in terms of continuity of the business when a new owner takes over. For example, if the management has shown disinterest or incompetence, you should be able to purchase a business at a reduced rate and hopefully turn around the operation, therefore building up a clientele base. However, if the reputation of the business is bad and has been for a long time, it may not be possible to substantially increase the customer base.
- **Financing.** Determine whether the seller is prepared to take a sizeable down payment and carry the balance of the purchase price over time with security. The security could be a debenture or a chattel mortgage on equipment and vehicles or assignment of accounts receivable. The lower the down payment, the more potential buyers there will be, and the seller can therefore ask a higher price for the business. The converse holds true in cases in which the seller demands all cash.
- **Geographic area.** A business situated in an affluent area where the population has a higher disposable income may be more attractive than one situated in a low-income or less travelled area.
- **Industry ratio comparison.** A factor in influencing the evaluation of a business and the eventual purchase price is the comparison with published industry standards. If the comparison shows that the business for sale is more efficiently and profitably run in comparison to key ratios, that could increase the purchase price. This is assuming, of course, that the financial records and the backup documentation supporting them are shown to be accurate and not artificially contrived. Business ratios were discussed in Chapter 3, " on Understanding Financial Statements."

A sophisticated buyer will be able to review all the factors discussed and, after analyzing all the data, make an evaluation of the worth of the enterprise. This would at least provide a basis for considering whether to buy the business, assuming that the asking price is realistic enough to commence negotiations. It is critical that the buyer obtain competent legal and accounting advice, possibly consulting advice as well, before making any decision to present an offer.

Evaluating Goodwill

The area of greatest divergence of opinion in the evaluation of the small business is the value of goodwill. There is no firm rule for computing goodwill. Some people define goodwill as simply the expectation of continued patronage. Others define it more precisely as the value of a business in excess of its suggested book value. Still others construe goodwill to be that amount which is the difference between the tangible net worth of the company and its fair market value. The price the buyer should be willing to pay for goodwill depends on the earning power and potential of the business. If the earning power is low, the buyer will probably resist paying any amount for goodwill.

Goodwill must result in profits, or it cannot have value. Profit in this context is a residue after operating costs, salaries, and return on the investment. The buyer looks at the business for its ability to earn a fair return on investment (ROI), and considers the present and future earning power of the business as being of prime importance. The seller adopts a position that goodwill relates to the lease benefits, location, customer base, sales and inventory records, exclusive lines, connections with suppliers, licences, patents, trademarks, and copyrights. In the opinion of the seller, all these factors contribute to the earning power of the business and therefore deserve compensation. Goodwill is an intangible, because it is an opinion of the person evaluating it. It is not concrete, like tangible assets, such as a building, equipment, and other items that can be more readily evaluated.

There are various factors to take into account when attempting to establish a value for goodwill, such as:

- business and business owner's reputation
- location
- stability of company and industry trends
- age of the business
- profitability
- transition period in ownership changeover for training purposes
- key personnel staying with the company under the new ownership
- a broad customer base
- a widely used trademark or trade name.

The buyer should be careful in apportioning the value to goodwill, because of the tax implications. The seller is able to use the amount paid for goodwill as a capital gain. For this reason, the seller may want to apportion as high a factor as possible for goodwill. On the other hand, the buyer should try to have the value for goodwill as low as possible for tax reasons, because the buyer cannot get the same tax advantages for the goodwill component. The other aspects of the purchase—for example, chattels, leasehold improvements, and inventory—also have values apportioned to them. Make sure that you receive tax advice before committing yourself in any way to the apportioning of the purchase price.

Methods of Evaluating the Value of a Business

There are numerous methods and techniques used for determining a value for the business. It depends on who is doing the appraising. In most cases, a small business is priced by the seller based on a set of values. The methods used by the seller do not necessarily reflect a realistic or actual value of the business, but for the purpose of disposing of it, some value has to be assigned. As mentioned earlier, the suggested sale price could differ considerably based on what a professional accountant would advise, what a banker would suggest, and what a business broker would recommend.

Many of the evaluation methods require a thorough understanding and analysis of the financial information from the business, including income statement (profit-and-loss statement) and balance sheet. Ratios should be compared (for example, Sample 9, "Summary of Ratio Analyses" should be completed). In many businesses, the price may not necessarily include accounts receivable, cash, and inventory. These items are frequently negotiated separately and are not included in the overall purchase price.

The market value of a business means the highest estimated price the buyer would be warranted in paying, and the seller would be justified in accepting, without any undue or outside influence involved.

Undue or outside influence would include factors such as foreclosure, bankruptcy, receivership, competition, marital or partnership disputes, or health problems. If any of these factors are present, it should cause the price to drop. As a buyer, you should look for these factors in order to apply leverage in your negotiations.

Some of the methods used to evaluate a business include book value, liquidation value, replacement value, and gross multiplier value. The capitalization of income value (CIV) is one of the more reliable methods. It also involves a determination of the rate of ROI. A brief description of the CIV method follows, plus an outline of a typical selling price formula.

CIV

This method is concerned with the present worth of future benefits from investment in the business. In other words, the business value is determined by capitalizing its earnings at a rate that reflects the risk associated with that firm. A high capitalization rate would be chosen if the buyer perceives a high degree of risk. The rate could vary from as little as 15% to as high as 100% or more, depending on the perceived risk of the business and the efficiency of the management. A capitalization rate of 20% is frequently the minimum amount for the purchase of a small business that shows reasonable prospects for continued success and growth and has relatively no risk. As you can see, the higher the capitalization rate used, the lower the valuation arrived at for the business.

The CIV is used frequently because the business value is based on income or profit before depreciation, interest, and income taxes, and by using an appropriate capitalization rate which is acceptable to the buyer, considering all the circumstances. There are three steps to this process:

1. Determine the level of future earnings of the company based on average net earnings over the past several years, together with an estimate of the increase in earnings expected. Average net earnings include owner's salary.
2. Select an appropriate capitalization rate based on the ROI which buyers would be expected to demand. This is based on a fair ROI, for example, 10% to 25%. The risk factor plays an important role at this stage.
3. Capitalize the income by dividing the income by the selected capitalization rate. The outcome would constitute the selling price.

For example, the buyer pays $60,000 cash or with borrowed money, and his projected net income from the business is $24,000; his ROI (capitalization rate) would be 40%. The CIV also reflects the ROI which the buyer wishes to recover from the business to meet specific needs. On a 40% ROI, it would take 2 1/2 years to recover the initial investment, in the example given.

Selling price formula
The formula given on the following worksheet is based on an evaluation of the business's existing earning power and profit potential. The selling price approach is given from the perspective of the buyer. Keep in mind that because each business and sales transaction is different, the formula that is shown should be used only as a guideline to indicate some of the major considerations in the pricing of a business.

EXAMPLE : PRICING FORMULA WORKSHEET

1. Tangible net worth $
2. Current earning power $
3. Reasonable annual salary $
4. Total earning capacity $
5. Average annual net profit $
6. Extra earning power (line 5 minus line 4) $
7. Value of intangibles (line 6 × multiplier figure) $
8. Final price (a total of lines 1 and 7) $

Here is an explanation of each step in the worksheet:

1. Determine the tangible net worth of the business. This consists of the total market value of the tangible assets (excluding goodwill), including all current and long-term assets less total current and long-term liabilities.

2. Estimate the current earning power of the tangible net worth of the business; in other words, if the buyer is going to invest this amount elsewhere, such as stocks, bonds, term deposits, and other investments, what the return would be on an annual basis. Naturally this is calculated based on current interest rates, and the earning power would fluctuate based on economic trends and other factors. When determining the interest rate, try to make the comparison realistic in terms of investing in a comparable risk investment or business.

3. Determine a normal annual salary that the buyer would anticipate earning if employed elsewhere. For the purpose of this calculation, this would be the same salary that an owner-operator would take out of the business. When making a salary calculation, take into account that if employed elsewhere, the salary would also include fringe benefits which may be equivalent to 15% to 20% extra in value over the base salary. Take into consideration that if a buyer is employed by his or her own business, he or she could also receive benefits like Canada Pension contribution, medical and dental coverage, and use of an automobile.

4. Calculate a total earning capacity of the buyer by adding lines 2 and 3; in other words, if the buyer were going to invest the equivalent of tangible net worth outside the business plus an income from employment outside the business, what that total earning capacity would be. For the purpose of comparisons, don't take taxes into account.

5. Determine the average annual net profit of the business over a minimum of the past 3 years. Ideally, 5 years would provide a more accurate result. This average will be the total of all profit as obtained from the financial statements, and before any management salaries are taken out for the owners or taxes are paid. The average is determined by dividing the total profit over the time period used by the number of years used in the analysis. The reason that income taxes are not taken out is to make the calculations comparable with earnings from other sources or by individuals in different tax brackets. Admittedly, when comparing with other investments, there could be tax benefits that are not available from employment in a small business. When calculating the earnings, take a look at the trends. Possibly the earnings have been increasing or decreasing steadily, or fluctuating widely or remaining constant. Take these factors and trends into account in terms of adjusting the earnings figure as might be required.

6. Calculate the extra earning power of the business by subtracting the figure in line 4 from the figure in line 5. This figure represents the additional benefit in terms of extra earning income if you buy the business, rather than if you obtained outside employment and invested the equivalent of the tangible net worth. In other words, this figure might make the difference in terms of any incentive to buy the business that would justify the risk.

7. Calculate the value of intangibles by multiplying the extra earning power outlined in step 6 times the factor that is referred to as the years-of-profit figure. This multiplier figure is based on various factors. The questions to which you would have to obtain answers to determine the multiplier factor include: What expenses and risks would be involved in setting up a similar business? How long would it take to set up a similar business and bring it to a similar stage of development? What would be the price of goodwill in similar firms? Are the intangibles offered by the firm unique (trade name, trademarks, patents, location)? Will the seller sign a covenant agreeing not to compete? After evaluating the above factors, if you determine that the business is successful and well established, you may use a multiplier factor of five or more. You may use a multiplier of three for a moderately seasoned firm in terms of growth and length of time in business. A profitable but younger business may only rate a factor of one. To a certain extent, the multiplier factor is related to the number of years in business, but that is just one of the factors when trying to determine the correct multiplier factor for your needs.

8. Calculate the final price, which is obtained by adding the tangible net worth of the business (outlined in step 1) to the value of intangibles (outlined in step 7). This final price figure gives an estimated guideline only when determining a potential price for a business. As discussed in other parts of this chapter, there are many other variables which have to be taken into account.

METHODS OF BUYING A BUSINESS

There are two common methods of buying a business. One way is to buy the assets, which include a goodwill component, and the other way is to buy the shares, assuming it is a corporation. If you have the alternative of buying either assets or shares, there are various considerations that have to be taken into account which you should discuss with your accountant and lawyer before committing yourself. Here are some points to consider:

- company financing
- potential liability

- company credit rating
- leases and contracts held by the company
- tax implications (i.e., depreciation of fixed assets, sales tax payable).

Purchase of Assets

If the seller of the business is a sole proprietorship or a partnership, the sale must be conducted as a transfer of assets, as there is no corporation in which shares can be purchased. When purchasing assets of a corporation, the buyer typically sets up his or her own corporation and transfers all the assets and the lease into the new corporate name.

If a buyer is buying the assets of the company and therefore has a new corporation without any track record, the lack of a credit history could impair the amount of credit that would be extended to the company in the initial stages of operation. You will want to allocate as low a price as possible for goodwill, because the tax write-off benefits are not as attractive to you as they are for the seller. Conversely, you want to allocate as much of the purchase price as possible to equipment, fixtures, and other depreciable capital assets, so that you have as high a depreciation deduction as possible.

If the assets of the company are secured by a creditor's lien, mortgage, or other form of encumbrance, the transfer of assets cannot occur without the approval of the creditor. The creditor may not release the seller from the security, and may insist on having personal covenants of the buyer as well. Or, the creditor may consent to an asset transfer conditional on a renegotiation of the terms of the security. Protections can be built in to make sure that the assets are free and clear of any liabilities. Your lawyer should check the appropriate registries to see if there are any encumbrances or liens against the assets.

Purchase of Shares

The buyer may purchase the shares of the company from the shareholders. At the time of the sale, the shareholders resign as directors and officers. The buyer elects his or her own directors and officers. A modification to this approach is for the existing shareholders to sell their shares back to the corporation. The corporation then sells new shares to the buyer. A buyer may be able to purchase the shares of the business if the company has a high amount of debt, by paying the owners the difference between the debt and the purchase price. For example, if the business assets were worth $200,000 and the debt was $175,000, the buyer could pay $25,000 to the owner and assume the shares of the business.

In many cases, it may be difficult to have leases, contracts, or licences assigned to a new company. If this is the case, then a purchase of shares in the corporation would permit the business to continue without others necessarily knowing that there has been a change in ownership. Another reason for buying the shares of a company is that a tax loss could be available that could benefit the buyer.

If you buy the shares of a business that enjoys a very good credit rating, you would be obtaining the ongoing benefit of the excellent credit rating. On the other hand, if the credit rating is poor, that could have an adverse effect in terms of obtaining future credit and overall goodwill.

If a buyer is making a share purchase, then any and all liabilities that the business might have from the past remain with the business. For example, there could be contingent liabilities in claims by Canada Revenue Agency (CRA) for back taxes or reassessment of taxes, creditors may sue for past debts, customers may sue for an injury that was sustained in the past on the premises of the business, customers may make a claim on an express or implied warranty on products that have been purchased, and product liability claims may be commenced due to injury from the product.

BUSINESS PURCHASE DOCUMENTATION

After you have decided on the structure of the purchase transaction, you will want to make sure that you are properly protected with legal documentation. The legal documents include the offer to purchase and the formal purchase and sale agreement. The purchase and sale agreement would be for either an asset or share transfer.

Offer to Purchase

This is a common first step in buying a business. Whether you are making the offer directly or through a realtor, business broker, or lawyer, the offer to purchase agreement must be in writing and specific. Never make an offer to purchase agreement without obtaining legal and accounting advice in advance. The terms of the offer to purchase normally include such matters as the apportioning of purchase price if you are buying the assets, employees, transition-phase clause (owner staying on to assist in training), noncompetition clause, financing considerations, and timing of completion and possession date. The offer to purchase agreement normally includes a provision that all the financial records of the company, such as financial statements, balance sheet, income statement (profit-and-loss statement), sales records, contracts, lease, and all other necessary documentation, have been or will be supplied to the prospective buyer for review before any offer is firm.

You want to make sure that you can back out of the contract and avoid liability if for any reason you change your mind. For example, you may find out hidden problems with the business that you did not know before. There could be many other factors not covered in the offer to purchase that you want to subsequently include once you become aware of the situation.

It is necessary in most situations to have a clause that states that a formal purchase and sale agreement will be negotiated and drawn up by the parties after all the subject conditions in the offer to purchase have been removed.

Here are several tips that will help you in minimizing your risk when making an offer to purchase.

Keep the purchase deposit to a minimum

As a general rule of thumb, a deposit of 5% to 10% of the purchase price is requested as a gesture of good faith and sincerity. In fact, the broker or realtor involved generally wants to have the amount of their commission (approximately 10%) as the amount of the deposit. As the amount of the deposit is negotiable, attempt to pay as little as possible. An alternative is to pay a small deposit, such as $100, $500, or $1,000, and then have a clause that states that the deposit will be increased to a larger amount, for example, 10% of the purchase price, once all the conditional (escape) clauses have been removed.

Use escape clauses

Escape clauses are conditions that have to be met before the offer to purchase becomes a binding contract. Some of the most common escape clause conditions to benefit the buyer of a business include review and approval of offer to purchase by the buyer's lawyer and accountant; verification of all records by the buyer's accountant to the satisfaction of the accountant and buyer; appraisal of the business by an independent appraiser of the buyer's choosing; inspection of the business by a third party (potential partners or associates of the buyer); and approval by the buyer's bank for financing. These clauses are often referred to as unilateral conditions, because it is totally up to the buyer in this example as to whether or not the escape clauses are removed.

Buy the business through a corporation

You will probably want to incorporate a company to purchase the assets of the business, so you should make sure that the offer to purchase is in a corporate name. This would also help you when the formal purchase and sale documentation is complete, because if you default on the final agreement, your company may be sued, but not you personally.

Do not sign personal guarantees

If you have incorporated a company and signed the offer to purchase in the corporate name, avoid signing a personal guarantee. Have all the risk assumed by your corporation and insist on that point.

Insert a liquidated damage clause

The buyer should make sure that in the event the contract is breached, the deposit shall be deemed to cover all damages. This is referred to as liquidating the damages or lease losses.

Purchase and Sale Agreements

If the escape clauses in the offer to purchase have been removed, then a purchase and sale agreement is normally prepared on behalf of and at the expense of the buyer by the buyer's lawyer. The document is sent to the seller's lawyer for review and approval. The contract is signed by all parties, and this is followed by the transfer of payment and possession. These contracts are formal and can therefore be lengthy, sometimes 25 to 100 pages, depending on the complexity of the business being purchased and other factors. Frequently there can be collateral agreements, in addition to the main agreement, that have to be signed by the parties, or one or the other of the parties. In addition, key documents are attached to the contract as exhibits. This would include such items as financial statements, lists of assets, lists of inventory and supplies, copies of leases and other major contracts, lists of creditors, lists of customers, and other documentation.

You can see now why there is generally a two-step documentation process before the business actually changes hands, the first step being the offer to purchase, which is relatively simple and shows an agreement in principle, and the second step, which sets out the binding agreement between the parties.

There are key terms that should be included in any contract involving a purchase of shares or assets. Each contract should cover these basic questions:

- What is the amount of the purchase price?
- How will the purchase price be paid?
- How will the purchase price be apportioned?
- What assets are to be sold?
- What assets will be retained by the seller?
- How will inventory adjustments be made?
- How will accounts receivable be handled?
- How will other adjustments be determined?
- What about the seller's liabilities?
- What protection does the seller have if the buyer does not pay the assumed liabilities?
- What other warranties should the seller make to the buyer?
- What are the rights of the seller to compete?
- What restrictions should be imposed on the seller in operating the business prior to closing?

- What performance conditions has the seller included as part of the agreement?
- What happens to the records and books for the business at the time of closing?
- How are any disputes under the agreement resolved?

Like any other legal document, the contract to buy a business must be designed to meet the specific needs of the transaction. No two documents are or should be identical. The agreement therefore may contain most, but not necessarily all, of the points mentioned here, as well as other provisions to fully protect the buyer.

Professional Assistance in Purchasing a Business

Obtaining qualified legal and accounting assistance at all stages of a business operation is particularly important when dealing with buying a business or a franchise. Buying a business is serious business, involving serious money and lots of potential risk. It is false economy and very unwise to attempt to save on legal fees by doing all the work yourself. If problems occur in the purchase transaction, which is likely to happen if you do it yourself, then you will certainly be retaining a lawyer at that time to initiate a lawsuit or protect you from one. Discuss your concerns and needs with your lawyer in the preliminary interest stage and before ever signing an offer to purchase or a formal agreement.

You need to utilize the services of an experienced and expert professional tax accountant and business lawyer, who interact with each other in an integrated fashion to protect your business and financial interests. How to select a professional advisor was discussed in Chapter 4.

Chapter 8

Buying a Franchise

The buyer needs a hundred eyes, the seller not one.

— George Herbert

One of the decisions you will need to make about obtaining an existing business is how you will acquire it. Other than inheriting one, your options include: buying an existing business or buying a franchise. The unique difference in the franchise option is that the franchisor provides support in getting the franchise started, and continues the support through the life of the business. You may also be able to buy an operating franchise location.

There are two forms of franchise: a product/trade name and a business format. A franchisor who owns an established product name, logo, and/or trademark and sells the right to use its name, logo, and trademark to another party is known as a *product/trade name franchisor*. The right is actually an exclusive or nonexclusive licence to market the product name to wholesalers and retailers. An example would be a company that has the rights by licence to manufacture and to use the name Coca-Cola. With a business format franchise, the franchisor provides not only a product, name, and logo, but also the management and marketing support to create a "turnkey" business operation. Examples of this type of franchise include McDonald's, Dairy Queen, and Century 21. This chapter is primarily concerned with the latter concept of the turnkey franchise operation, and its advantages and disadvantages to the entrepreneur.

The business format franchisor may assist with site selection, owner and staff training, product supply, trademarks and logos, advertising and marketing plans, management and accounting services, system controls, and possibly financing. Besides the initial purchase price of the franchise, there is usually a percentage of the sales which is paid to the franchisor for the ongoing support. Under the franchise agreement, the franchisee is given the right to sell the goods or services within a certain geographic area or territory. The franchise agreement details the legal and commercial relationship between the two parties. The franchisee may sell goods or services supplied by the franchisor, or it could sell goods or services that meet the franchisor's quality standards.

The guidelines and conditions established for the franchisee can be very comprehensive and can include sources of supplies, standards of cleanliness, pricing policy, hours of operation, staffing requirements, and many other factors. The franchisor requires strict adherence to the guidelines to maintain consistency of image, quality, and service, and to ensure the success of the franchise. Studies show that approximately 90% of new franchisees continue in business more than 3 years. Less than 25% of nonfranchise businesses survive over the same period.

THE FRANCHISE OPTION

Is Franchising for You?

When considering the franchise option, you need to review your personal and business goals. How will a franchise benefit you in attaining your goals, compared with starting a business from scratch? Are you motivated by the challenge of doing it all yourself? Or does that concept cause you more than a little worry and apprehension? Perhaps you have specialized skills which you would like to turn into a business operation, but all the peripheral aspects of starting a business are somewhat intimidating. If this is the case, then the franchise option may be well suited to your personal and business needs. Some entrepreneurs prefer to have the security and support provided by a large and experienced company. A franchisee has a greater chance of running a business successfully because of the training systems and ongoing support that the franchisor provides. The franchisor obviously has a vested interest in the financial well-being of the franchise, as the more money the franchisee makes, the more money the franchisor makes. However, if your intention is to establish your business and then diversify or expand your operation, you may be restricted from doing so in a franchise situation. Your ability to expand would be based on available territories within your geographic area. In this case, perhaps franchising is not the route you should take.

For more detailed information, refer to *The Complete Canadian Franchise Guide, So You Want to Buy a Franchise,* and *Be Your Own Boss (The Canadian Guide to Buying a Business or Franchise),* by Douglas Gray and Norm Friend, published by McGraw-Hill Ryerson.[1]

Advantages and Disadvantages

If you are a potential purchaser of a franchise, you have to clearly evaluate a prospective franchise relationship by looking at both sides of the issue clearly. If after assessing your personal and business needs you decide not to buy a franchise, you may decide at some future point to become a franchise owner. In other words, you may decide to start your business from scratch or buy an existing one, and over a period of time expand your business concepts by means of a franchise

---

[1] Norm Friend is a Canadian franchise consultant who has been in the industry for many years. His website is: franchise101.net.

system. Therefore, the following outline highlights the advantages and disadvantages of franchises from the perspective of the franchisee and the franchisor.

Advantages to the franchisee

- being associated with an established company
- having a proven and successful business system
- having a reduced risk of failure
- having an increased chance of profitability within the first few years
- easier to access financing (banks, suppliers, franchisor)
- having reduced costs of supplies and materials
- having access to extensive advertising (national, regional, local)
- having continuing managerial assistance
- possibility of buying an existing operation.

Disadvantages to the franchisee

- high degree of control on the part of the franchisor
- potential dispute of agreement terms
- franchisor might not fulfill promises
- services provided by franchisor could be more expensive
- franchise fee comes off the gross revenue
- franchisor in another jurisdiction could create contract enforcement problems
- profits less than represented or anticipated
- misleading statements by franchisor
- franchisor could oversaturate market.

Advantages to the franchisor

- franchisees motivated to be financially successful
- beating the competition to the marketplace
- spread business risk
- reduced management costs.

Disadvantages to the franchisor

- franchisee might not fulfill obligations
- franchisee might impair reputation of franchise system
- potential litigation by dissatisfied franchisee
- growth by franchisor too rapid, causing operational problems.

Government Regulation of Franchises

Although there are several federal and provincial laws that apply to franchising, only five provinces have introduced laws that specifically apply to franchising. These provinces are Alberta, Manitoba, Ontario, New Brunswick, and Prince Edward Island, and their respective acts are summarized below.

The primary purpose of provincial franchise legislation is to protect the franchisee and require full disclosure by the franchisor, so that the prospective franchisee has a due diligence advantage.

At the federal level, various laws can apply to franchising, such as income tax, competition, privacy, packaging and labeling, and intellectual property statutes. At the provincial level, there are a number of laws that apply to franchising, including consumer protection legislation, sales taxes, liquor licensing, and class action. Franchisors wishing to carry on business in Quebec must also comply with the Charter of the French Language of Quebec and the Quebec Civil Code.

Alberta Franchises Act

Under the Alberta Franchises Act, franchisors are required to deliver a disclosure document to franchisees at least 14 days before the prospective franchisee signs any agreement or pays any consideration relating to the franchise (unless the payment is fully refundable). The disclosure document must contain financial statements and all material facts, including: information about the franchisor; obligations of the franchisee; fees and initial investment levels; the franchisor's financial statements; and other information, such as territorial considerations, the franchisor's proximity policy, restrictions on products and supplies, rebates and discounts accruing to the franchisor, and a list of franchisees currently operating in Alberta.

The legislation provides for a right of action for damages for losses suffered because of a misrepresentation in the disclosure document and a right of cancellation if the franchisor fails to deliver the disclosure document within the 14-day time requirement. Also, the franchisor is required to compensate the franchisee for any net losses within 30 days of receiving the cancellation notice.

The franchisor must provide details of any earnings claims information they provide, including material assumptions underlying its preparation and presentation, whether it is based on actual results of existing outlets, and the percentage of outlets that meet or exceed each range of results. The earnings claim information must have a reasonable basis at the time it is prepared. The disclosure documents must also state the place where substantiating information is available for inspection by franchisees. If the information is given in respect of a franchisor-operated outlet, the franchisor must state that the information may differ in respect of a franchisee outlet. Earnings claims consist of information from which a specific level or range of actual or potential sales, costs, income, or profit from franchisee or franchisor outlets can be ascertained.

A franchisor is not allowed to prevent a franchisee from forming an organization of franchisees or from associating with other franchisees in any organization of franchisees.

The act imposes a duty of fair dealing on both parties, which includes the duty to act in good faith and in accordance with reasonable commercial standards.

The disclosure document must contain copies of all proposed franchise agreements, financial statements of the franchisor, and reports and other documents in accordance with the regulations. A certificate stating that the disclosure document contains no untrue statement of a material fact and does not omit to state a material fact must be signed by at least two officers or directors of the franchisor.

If a franchisee suffers a loss because of a misrepresentation contained in a disclosure document, the franchisee has a right of action for damages against the franchisor and every person who signed the disclosure document. If the franchisor fails to provide the disclosure document within the time requirements, the prospective franchisee may rescind the agreement by giving notice of cancellation no later than 60 days after receiving the disclosure documents, or no later than 2 years after the granting of the franchise. A franchisor must, within 30 days of receiving a notice of cancellation, compensate the franchisee for any net losses the franchisee has occurred in acquiring, setting up, or operating the franchised business.

Manitoba Franchise Act (2012)

Franchisors in Manitoba are required to comply with all of the requirements of the Act, which include new disclosure document obligations, as well as a variety of "relational" provisions that will be read into every franchise agreement. Out of the provinces that have franchise laws in place, the wording, structure and substance of the Manitoba Regulation is most similar to that of New Brunswick.

However, the Manitoba regulation has some unique features. The biggest innovation of the Act is that it allows, in certain circumstances, for disclosure documents to be delivered in parts. This can be contrasted with other provinces which require disclosure documents to be delivered all at once. The Regulation defines the specifics of this "piecemeal" disclosure. In order to deliver a disclosure document in parts:

- the required "risk warnings" must be provided to the franchisee first;
- certain subsets of information must be provided in groups (information about the franchisor, information about the franchise, and lists of franchisees);
- the franchisor must include a specifically worded statement at the beginning of every document which is intended to form part of the disclosure document; and
- the signed certificate of the franchisor must be included with the last part of the disclosure.

The 14-day cooling-off period will only begin once the last document has been delivered to the franchisee. However, prior to the end of the 14-day cooling-off period, franchisors may nevertheless accept a fully refundable deposit of up to 20% of the initial franchise fee, to a maximum of $100,000.

Ontario's Arthur Wishart Act (2000)

The Ontario act was introduced after the Alberta Franchises Act and is quite similar to the Alberta Franchises Act, except that unlike Alberta's legislation, there are no residency requirements for franchisees. Under the Ontario act, the franchisee is not allowed to make any payments within the 14-day time requirement, even if the payments are fully refundable.

A franchisee may rescind the franchise agreement if the franchisor fails to provide the disclosure document within the prescribed time requirements or if the contents do not meet the statutory requirements. The franchisee may rescind the franchise agreement without penalty or obligation within 2 years after entering into the agreement if the franchisor never provided a disclosure document.

The franchisor, within 60 days of rescission, must:

1. Refund any money received from or on behalf of the franchisee, other than money for inventory, supplies or equipment;
2. Purchase any inventory, supplies and equipment at a price equal to the purchase price paid by the franchisee; and
3. Compensate the franchisee for any losses incurred in acquiring and operating the franchise less amounts expended on the repurchase.

New Brunswick

New Brunswick has published two franchising regulations. The first regulation sets out disclosure requirements similar to the requirements found in the other provinces that regulate franchising. The second regulation sets out a mediation procedure.

The provisions of the Act are essentially similar to those contained in Ontario's Arthur Wishart Act; however, there are some important differences. For example, the Act explicitly states that the duty of good faith and fair dealing extends to the performance and enforcement of the franchise agreement, which includes the exercise of a right under the franchise; as opposed to the Ontario Act, which does not specifically state that the duty extends to the exercise of a right under the agreement. Similar to the legislation in Alberta and Prince Edward Island, but unlike the Ontario Act, the Act specifically states that a confidentiality agreement does not qualify as a "franchise agreement" for the purposes of the timing of the 14-day disclosure period. This permits franchisors to enter into limited confidentiality agreements with franchisees within this period. The Act also provides an expanded due diligence defence to directors, officers, brokers, and franchisor's associates in respect of misrepresentations within the disclosure document.

The most unique feature of the Act is the prescribed party-initiated dispute resolution process, which is the first of its kind among regulated provinces. The Act states that if there is a dispute, one party may notify the other of the nature of the dispute and the desired outcome. If such a notice is delivered, the parties must attempt to resolve the dispute within 15 days of receiving the notice. If the parties are unable to resolve the dispute, a notice to mediate may be delivered, and upon delivery of such notice, the parties must follow the rules relating to mediation as set out in the mediation regulation. However, the mediation regulation permits the party that received the notice of mediation to decline mediation by providing a notice declining mediation.

The disclosure regulation generally requires disclosure similar to that in other regulated provinces; however, there are some noteworthy differences, for example:

- Delivery by courier or electronic means is specifically permitted;
- Disclosure documents prepared for use in other jurisdictions can be used in New Brunswick provided additional disclosure is provided as required by the Act;
- The disclosure document must include the table of contents of any manual or a statement specifying where in New Brunswick the manual, if any, is available for inspection;
- A description of the franchisor's policies and practices regarding internet or distance sales must be provided; and
- In addition to a list of current franchisees, the franchisor must provide a list of current businesses of the same type as the franchise being offered that the franchisor currently operates in New Brunswick.

There are other differences which must be addressed in the disclosure document, or franchisors risk a claim for rescission or misrepresentation.

Franchisors must prepare documents specific to New Brunswick—either a wraparound or a stand-alone document—or risk being offside the legislation. Alternately, franchisors with a national disclosure document can modify that document to comply with New Brunswick's unique requirements.

Prince Edward Island's Franchises Act

The Prince Edward Island franchise legislation is substantially similar to Ontario's legislation; however, it is modeled after the Uniform Law Conference of Canada's Uniform Franchises Act and contains some additional provisions. The act extends the duty of fair dealing to apply to the exercise of a right under a franchise agreement and permits the use of confidentiality and territory reservation agreements prior to delivery of a disclosure document.

The information would give you a good basis for assessing the merits of the franchise operation. You can also obtain copies of the franchise legislation for each province, and a comparison chart of the provincial legislation, from the Canadian Franchise Association (CFA; cfa.ca).

An experienced franchise lawyer will know the reputation of a franchisor and can provide candid advice and cautions. Don't assume that the registration of a franchisor in a province implies the government has approved or recommends the franchise in any way. It simply means the franchise has conformed with the regulatory requirements of the government. It is essential that you verify the information disclosed by the franchisor, by speaking with existing franchisees, a franchise lawyer, and a tax accountant.

Where to Find Franchise Information

There are numerous sources of general information about franchising, as well as specific information on franchise opportunities. To improve the quality of your comparisons and decision-making, review as many as possible of these sources outlined below.

- **Books.** Refer to the books: *So You Want to Buy a Franchise, The Complete Canadian Franchise Guide*, and *Be Your Own Boss*.
- **Government agencies**
- **Bank and accounting firm publications**
- **Canadian Franchise Association (CFA).** A trade association representing firms in a wide variety of industries who use a franchising method of distribution. CFA has several excellent publications and an information kit for prospective franchisees online and in print. They also have an e-newsletter, magazine, and webinars, and sponsor trade shows throughout Canada. The informational material includes a list of members, as well as franchise lawyers and franchise consultants. For further information, contact CFA. Refer to website: cfa.ca.
- **International Franchise Association (IFA).** IFA has many products and services for its members, as well as publications and other material for the general public on franchising. For further information, check out their website at: franchise.org
- *Franchise Yearbook.* This is published by *Entrepreneur* magazine and is a complete directory of all franchises in the United States and Canada under various section headings.
- *Canadian Business Franchise.* This bi-monthly magazine includes articles on franchising, as well as a selected list of Canadian franchise

companies. They also publish the annual *Canadian Busieness Franchise Handbook*. Check out their website at: franchiseinfo.ca.

- **Franchise shows and expositions.** CFA sponsors franchising shows throughout Canada. Valuable information can be obtained and comparisons can be made on all aspects of franchising, such as financing, buying, contracts, advantages, and obligations. In addition, franchise shows offer seminars, discussion panels, and workshops.

You would also benefit from on-site consultations with franchise specialists, such as accountants, lawyers, bankers, and various provincial and national experts. Check out trade shows on cfa.ca and franchise.org.

- **Franchise consultants/brokers.** A franchise consultant generally advises a franchisor on how to franchise a business effectively and frequently assists in the marketing and sale of the franchises on behalf of the franchisor. A franchise consultant may also be a broker in terms of selling franchises and would therefore have a vested interest, so verify that issue, as that could be a potential conflict of interest. A franchise consultant can also help with buying a franchise by providing objective advice. Obtain names from the CFA and do a Google search for franchise consultants in Canada.
- **Franchise lawyers.** It is critical that you retain the services of a franchise lawyer. If you want to be a franchisor, you want to speak to a franchise lawyer who specializes in that area. If you want to buy a franchise, you want to speak to a franchise lawyer who frequently represents franchisees. To obtain lawyer names with franchise expertise, do a Google search with keywords in your area. You can also obtain names from the CFA and by contacting the local branch of the Canadian Bar Association in your province to find names of lawyers who specialize in that area. Many large law firms would have lawyers with that speciality expertise. As discussed in Chapter 4, "Selecting Professional Advisors," it is prudent to obtain an initial consultation from three specialty lawyers before deciding which lawyer is the right fit for your needs.
- **Business brokers and real estate brokers**

SELECTING A FRANCHISE

Selecting a franchise should be approached with the same care, preparation, and caution as starting or buying a business. It is important to do thorough research, investigation, and analysis of the market, the product or service, the competition, the risk, and the potential return on investment. In addition, when buying a franchise, one has to thoroughly explore the history of the franchisor, its present reputation in the industry, and the contents of the franchise agreement.

As mentioned in the chapter on buying a business, it is critical that you seek professional advice. When buying a business, you want to make sure the lawyer and accountant specialize in commercial law and tax aspects, respectively. If you are considering buying a franchise, it is particularly important that you seek professional advisors who specialize in dealing with franchise businesses. No documentation or financial commitment should be undertaken without consulting these expert advisors in advance. The risk is simply too great.

Before starting a thorough review of any franchise, there is a quick test that you can apply to save you time, money, and frustration. Simply answer the following questions: Did the franchise representative refuse to give specific answers or any answers to your questions? Refuse to give you a list of franchisee references? Promise you high profits in exchange for minimum effort? Put high pressure on you to make a deposit or sign a franchise agreement immediately? Appear to be less interested in your ability to be successful in the business and more interested in selling a franchise?

If the answer to any of these questions was yes, you should seriously reconsider pursuing that franchise company any further. The franchise company that is truly professional will allow an objective and thorough investigation of each party by the other, without adding the stress of time constraints. If you are favourably impressed with the initial attitude of the franchise company, you may wish to contact the owner of one of the franchise locations closest to you. Ask the franchisee if he or she is satisfied with the franchise owner and if not, why not? This should provide you with more insight as to whether you wish to pursue that franchise further.

What to Look for in a Franchise

There are many key points to look for when assessing the merits of a franchise. The following outline discusses some of the main points that you should address. Also refer to Checklist B at the back of the book. If you are seriously considering investing in a franchise, complete the "Master Checklist" in Appendix A and read Chapter 7, "Buying a Business," because you are buying the franchise business from either the franchise company or the existing owner. Alternatively, you could be starting the franchise operation from scratch.

The main areas to examine in evaluating a franchise include:

- **Background of franchise company.** This includes its financial condition, creditworthiness, relationship with suppliers, franchisees, and customers, and length of time in business.

- **Management.** Investigate experience, qualifications, reputation, and commitment.
- **Viability of product or service.** Check on whether it is a new, trendy, or well-established product, its suitability for your geographic area, and proven market demand.
- **Potential profit.** Determine the net profit that would be available as a return for your risk of investment and time. Check with other franchisees to satisfy yourself that the figures you have been supplied with in terms of projections are realistic. Are these comparisons based on communities that are similar to your geographic market and economic area? Has there been an allowance for a franchisee's salary separate from the profits? Will the projected net profit satisfy your economic and personal needs?
- **Location.** Location is obviously a very critical factor in the success of any business. Satisfy yourself that the location is a viable one for the type of business. The franchise owner may own the premises and lease them to the franchisee, or the franchisee could lease the premises from a third party or purchase the premises outright. The franchisor will have to approve the site.
- **Premises.** Examine strictness of requirements on matters such as appearance, design, layout, colours, fixtures, and furnishings.
- **Operational controls.** Check for standardization of character, uniformity and quality of product, value of trademarks, and strictness of operational controls manual.
- **Training and start-up systems.** Check on the duration, nature, and extent of training, on-site or at franchisor's site, costs, supplemental training, and start-up assistance.
- **Ongoing assistance.** Inquire as to the type of ongoing assistance provided: computer systems for inventory control, purchasing, invoicing and delivery, bookkeeping and accounting, financial management, selection of inventory, research and development, maintenance of equipment, and hiring, training, and firing of employees.
- **Advertising and promotion.** Franchisees are required to contribute to a fund for national or regional advertising, generally based on a percentage of the franchisee's gross sales. The money from all the franchisees is pooled and used to develop promotional and advertising programs and materials for the entire franchise system. Does the system-wide advertising justify the costs involved? Are franchisees required to advertise at a local level at their own expense? Does the franchisor supply professional, prepared advertising and promotional material?
- **Franchisor financing.** Can this be done directly through the franchisor or arranged in cooperation with a bank by the franchisor?
- **Sales or assignment restrictions or latitude.**

There are three areas that are particularly important for you to consider. They are territory, fees and costs, and renewal and termination.

Territory

Most franchisors provide some form of territorial protection to the franchisee. The area covered by the territory may be small, such as a few blocks, or as large as a province or number of provinces, depending on the situation. In theory, the exclusive sales territory means that the franchisee has the right to sell the franchisor's service or product exclusively within that area. "Area franchising" implies that the franchisee would have exclusivity to a large sales region. The term "master franchise" implies that the franchisee would not only have a large sales area, but would also be able to subfranchise to others within the allocated territory.

Problems can and frequently do arise on the interpretation of the concept of territory. In many cases, the franchisee does not fully understand the implications. The franchisee could possibly go out of business because the franchisor itself starts up a franchise within the territory (either under the same franchise name or indirectly through a subsidiary company) or sells a location to a new franchisee within the market territory.

Some of the types of problems encountered on the issue of territory include the following:

- The franchisor or other franchisees may sell products in, or ship products into, your territory from locations outside your territory. In other words, technically they do not have a location in your territory, but they are encroaching into your market share.
- The term "exclusive sales territory" frequently means that a franchisee merely has the right of first refusal to acquire any additional outlets within the territory before any second franchisee can accept. The company may wish to start up its own operation or sell it to a franchisee. The problem is that the size, cost, and timing of the location may not be at all attractive or financially feasible to you. Therefore, you technically have waived your right of first refusal, allowing someone else to establish a location that could erode your market share and impact your income and profit potential.
- Some exclusive agreements are tied to external factors, such as population size within the sales territory. Over time, if the population exceeds the specified number, the company would be able to start up or sell a franchise location in your territory.

Fees and costs

There is a wide variation in the structure of fees and costs that the franchisor receives from the franchisee. You should make sure that the contract specifically states the fees that are included in your initial franchise fee and royalty, and the fees that are paid separately, periodically, or optionally on the part of the franchisee. Some fees and costs may be reasonable compared with the normal expenses an independent business would incur for the same services. In other cases the, franchisor may be making a considerable profit on the fees and costs which could be unreasonable in the circumstances. Your professional advisors would obviously be able to provide you with more insight on that important issue.

It is very important to know in advance the exact amount of all costs that you will have to pay, including initial and ongoing costs, and what benefit you are receiving for your money. Make sure that you get specific details on all cost items, such as the amounts, financing arrangements, time of payment, and other considerations.

If you are a franchisee who is considering an entire business system, as opposed to just having a franchise that sells a specific product or service, there are numerous areas in which payments may be required. Here is an outline of the main areas of fees and costs:

- **Initial franchise fee.** This fee is usually paid at the time that the franchise agreement is signed. The amount varies, depending on the type and size of the franchise. The fee normally includes the franchisor's costs incurred in selling the franchise, such as promotion, screening, selecting, and training potential franchisees. It also includes the franchisee's right to use the operating procedures and system, as well as the trade name and trademark of the franchisor.
- **Training.** Training cost for franchisee or staff, either at the franchise location or at the franchisor's training centre. The cost could include room and board, transportation, meals, and tuition.
- **Management assistance.** Factor in the cost for ongoing training and management assistance.
- **Start-up assistance and promotion charges**
- **Periodic royalties or service fees.** Royalties are usually calculated as a percentage of the franchisee's gross sales, although they could be on a fixed-fee basis. The royalties may be required to be paid on a quarterly, monthly, or weekly basis, and the percentage can vary considerably depending on the type of franchise business. In general, retail operations have a higher royalty than service operations. The royalties may or may not cover the ongoing services provided to the franchisee.
- **Product pricing fees.** The franchisor builds a profit margin into the price of all the products sold to the franchisee. In order to make a guaranteed profit, the franchisor requires that the franchisee purchase all or most of the goods and supplies from the franchisor.

- **Average contribution to advertising.** This may be based on a specified percentage of the franchisee's gross sales and is usually payable on a weekly or monthly basis. This contribution is normally for the franchisor's advertising pool and is separate from local advertising that the franchisee pays for.
- **Local advertising.** Some franchisors require that the franchisee pay a certain minimum amount on advertising on a local basis, with the nature and form of advertising to be determined either by the franchisor or the franchisee.
- **Supplies.** Don't forget the cost of buying or leasing equipment supplies and opening inventory from the franchisor.
- **Lease cost.** Compare the costs of paying the monthly lease on the premises to that of the mortgage if the premises were purchased.
- **Bookkeeping.** Include the cost of paying for centralized bookkeeping, accounting, and data-processing services.
- **Cost of site selection and development.**

Some or all of the above may be included in the initial franchise or licence fee or ongoing royalty, or may have to be paid separately.

Renewal and termination

A franchise agreement has a specific term at which the agreement ends. The term is normally between 10 and 20 years, but it can vary considerably depending on the circumstances. The contract is automatically terminated at the end of that period, unless there are provisions in the contract for renewal. If there are no renewal provisions, then of course you would not be able to sell the franchise business to anyone else. This is why a renewal provision is very important from a resale and return on investment viewpoint. When a franchise agreement is renewed, the franchisor normally requires a new contract to be signed which may have different terms and conditions than the original one. For example, there could be an increase in advertising contributions or royalty payments, and a franchisee may be required to make substantial improvements and renovations to the franchise premises to conform with current standards.

Every franchise agreement has provisions that permit the franchisor and the franchisee to terminate the agreement in certain circumstances. It is common for the termination rights of franchisors to be far more extensive than those of franchisees. From the franchisor's perspective, it is important to be able to protect the reputation and credibility of the franchise system for the benefit of both other franchisees and the franchisor. Any franchisee who impairs the reputation of the system and its standards could cause serious damage to the reputation of the franchisor. If the default is a minor one, there may be a 30-day notice period in which the franchisee has the option to rectify the default. If the default is of a more serious nature, termination is normally given without notice.

Some of the common reasons outlined in franchise agreement termination clauses that the franchisor may invoke include the claim that the franchisee:

- made an assignment in bankruptcy
- was petitioned into bankruptcy by creditors
- ceased to do business on the premises
- became insolvent and could not pay creditors
- was placed in receivership
- submitted financial reports that were inaccurate or misleading by understating gross sales on which royalties were based
- sold unauthorized products or services
- refused to cease activities that might damage the reputation of the franchisor's name and trademark
- breached the terms of a lease or sublease relating to the franchise operation
- failed or refused to pay amounts owing to the franchisor
- constantly made late payments to the franchisor
- failed to comply with established franchise operating procedures and standards.

The franchisee may have rights to terminate the franchise agreement in certain circumstances. These may include:

- failure of the franchisor to acquire the location specified in the contract
- inability of the franchisor to develop the site for operation
- failure of the franchisor to meet his or her contractual obligations to the franchisee
- serious illness of the franchisee
- full payment by the franchisee of all its outstanding debts and other financial obligations to the franchisor.

The Franchise Agreement

The franchise agreement is an important legal document. There is no standard franchise agreement, as agreements can vary widely depending on the type of franchise operation, the size and sophistication of the franchise system, or whether a new location is being established or an existing franchise is being purchased.

Some franchise agreements are very one-sided in favour of the franchisor, whereas other agreements are more fair and balanced in terms of the rights of both the franchisor and franchisee. Be very careful with some clauses, because they can be particularly restrictive to franchisees. For example, there could be a noncompetition clause in an agreement which states that if the agreement is terminated, the franchisee cannot compete with the franchisor in the same type of business in the same geographic area for a specific period of time (e.g., 2 years). The clause might say that this provision exists whether the agreement is terminated by the franchisor or franchisee. Therefore, if you terminated the agreement because the franchisor breached the terms of the contract, you could technically be restricted from competing within the terms of the agreement.

Another example of a clause to be wary of is the limit on the amount of damages (financial losses) that the franchisee could claim from the franchisor for breach of contract by the franchisor. In some contracts, it is specifically stated that the franchisee's claim is limited to a specific amount. This could be totally unfair if the amount is unrealistically low.

A typical franchise agreement format which includes many of the common contract terms and conditions is provided in Sample 13. This may serve as a helpful checklist.

Chapter 9

Location and Leases

Bargains made in speed are commonly repented at leisure.

— George Pettie

The location of your business is as important to your success as having a good product to offer to your customers. This chapter will discuss the many factors that influence your choice of premises, whether you should lease space or buy a building, types of leases, and the legal aspects of negotiating and signing a lease.

TYPES OF LOCATIONS

In your business plan, you will have identified factors that will influence where you conduct your business. Whether it is a part-time or full-time business and whether it is a service, retail, or manufacturing operation will of course have a bearing on your decision. Various types of locations you may wish to consider are discussed below.

Home-Based Business

You may decide to operate a business out of your house or apartment on a part-time or full-time basis. You should first check into any city bylaws or potential neighbourhood problems that may prevent you from doing so. If you have an auto repair business, and it is your intention to repair cars in your garage, your neighbours could complain about the excessive noise or fumes. If you have a hairdressing salon that you are operating out of your basement, neighbours could complain because of traffic congestion or lack of residential parking spaces.

The zoning of your residential area may permit certain types of home-based business. If there are bylaw restrictions, and the neighbours or competition complain, the city inspectors could require you to close down your business. On the other hand, there are many types of home-based businesses that do not involve customer traffic in the neighbourhood, such as a consulting business or mail-order business. In the former example, consultants almost always go to the client's place of business. In the latter example, you are sending out merchandise to customers who have either phoned in or written requesting the merchandise.

In order to establish a professional business image, many home-based businesses contract with a service bureau that offers a professional or corporate identity package. See the discussion of packaged offices below. This service normally includes telephone answering, business address, and mail forwarding for approximately $100 to $300 per month. Look in the *Yellow Pages* print or online under "Telephone Answering Services" or "Offices for Rent." Refer to our book *Home Inc.: The Canadian Home-Based Business Guide*, Second Edition.

Packaged Office

You may want to rent office space in a packaged office complex., sometimes referred to as an executive suite centre or business centre This can be done on a month-to-month basis or for a longer term, such as 6 months or 1 year. For a fixed monthly fee, the features of a packaged office include a fully furnished office, a central receptionist, a waiting room, meeting rooms, a boardroom, high-speed Internet, telephone answering, use of secretarial support, data management services, and access to a fax, a photocopier, and other office equipment. An office rental package may include 5 to 10 hours per month free use of secretarial or word-processing time. In addition, a meeting room or boardroom may be available free or at a nominal cost, if required.

The main advantages of choosing a packaged office location include low start-up capital required, low risk, and an accelerated time frame. Because the services, equipment, and furniture are already in place, it is actually an instant office. Much time and money is therefore saved from having to shop around, select, and purchase equipment that may only be used minimally. There would be no staff hiring, training, or administration costs. It provides the business owner with the opportunity to test a business concept with low overhead costs and minimal risks. Most leases can be terminated with 60 or 90 days' notice. A packaged office enables a business to use it as a temporary location during the growth phase until more space is needed. In other cases, a tenant may want to remain in the packaged office on a permanent basis, without any need to relocate or expand. If you are interested in the packaged office concept, look in the *Yellow Pages* print or online under "Offices for Rent." Also, do a Google search of the same keywords for your city.

Some communities have an "incubator" office established by the city or region, and subsidized by various levels of government. This is a similar concept to the packaged office, except that it tends to restrict the tenants to a maximum period, such as 6 months or 1 year, and the tenants have to be "approved" for eligibility. There is usually a provision for counselling, or other types of business management assistance.

Shopping Centre

If your business caters to the shopping needs of the public, you may want to consider the benefits of a large or medium-sized shopping centre. If the shopping centre has several major or national anchor stores, this will attract a large volume of potential customers. Major tenants might include department stores, large supermarkets, and many national chain or franchise retail or service operations. A similar concept, of course, is a lower-level shopping mall in a high-rise office building. Whether it is an aboveground or underground shopping complex, the traffic volume can be immense.

To decide if a shopping mall is for you, you should compare all the malls and the types of tenants that would either draw traffic to you or compete with you. Shopping centre leases tend to be very complex and have stringent clauses in terms of the landlord's rights and requirements. It is also common for the landlord to request a percentage of the tenant's gross sales in addition to the base rent. Obviously, this disadvantage needs to be weighed against the benefit of a high volume of potential customers.

Major Thoroughfare in City

Many businesses prefer to locate on principal streets with high walk-by and drive-by traffic, as well as a concentration of adjoining stores that will also draw traffic. It is common to find bakeries, grocery stores, drugstores, gift shops, clothing boutiques, and other similar stores in these areas.

Secondary Street in City

These business-lined streets are not in the same class as major traffic arteries. The rental cost per square foot is less, and there may be larger areas of space available, if that is necessary for your business. The type of businesses frequently located on secondary streets include beauty parlours, TV repair shops, dry cleaners, and insurance agencies, and would draw their customers primarily from their geographic area.

Industrial Location

If you have a business in the area of research and development, manufacturing, or distribution, you may be less dependent on the need to be close to your customers or have drive-by visibility. Instead, it may be more important to have larger premises at a lower rental cost. You may wish to search for a location in an industrial park or other area zoned for industrial use. Industrial parks tend to be established in areas where there is good transportation accessibility by air, water, rail, or major freeway. The rent in industrial areas tends to be lower, because the cost of land is lower.

Highway Location

For certain types of businesses, a highway location is essential to the viability of the business. The types of businesses that are frequently located on a highway include motels, doughnut shops, gasoline service stations, and small family restaurants.

FACTORS THAT INFLUENCE CHOICE OF PREMISES

- **Type of business.** The type of business that you are considering has a fundamental influence on the type of location that you will be seeking. Considerations include whether yours is a part-time or a full-time business, or one that could be operated from your home or out of an office. The type of business sector is another factor: whether it is a retail, service, distribution, wholesale, manufacturing, or research and development business.
- **History of the location.** A location might appear to have all the necessary ingredients for your business to be a success, but upon further research, it may turn out to be a location where many businesses have failed. Look for such warning signs as too many vacant suites in the building, for-lease signs, or going out-of-business sales. Another factor could be buildings adjacent to the location. They could be drawing away traffic because of better promotions, nicer facilities, and more attractive leasing rates. Possibly the landlord is difficult to get along with, and that is why many tenants are not renewing their leases. Maybe there has been a turnover of landlords or property management companies that has caused an instability in the operation of the building.
- **Future trends.** Consider what the future trends are going to be in your industry sector, as well as the future trends in the location. Possibly you have a business that is based on selling a fad product, which will have a very short lifetime, but for which there is a high demand. If you project that you need a location for a 6-month period only, then that fact will play a large part in your decision. Also consider the future trends of the location. Does the landlord intend to expand or promote the building location? What impact will this have on your business if you are located there?
- **Changing patterns of neighbourhood.** Take a look at the surrounding area. Is there growth activity occurring in terms of buildings or houses that would show an increase in a potential market? On the other hand,

if there is a declining pattern, that could impair your plans? Contact the municipal office and make inquiries regarding the development in your geographic market area over the next few years.

- **Competition.** Thoroughly research the competition that is in your market area. Possibly there is very little competition, or the kind of competition that could be threatening to you. For example, a large national chain or franchise operation could spend a lot of money on advertising and promotion. Also look at the proximity of the competition and determine their strengths and weaknesses. Would you have a competitive edge?

- **Walk-by traffic.** Consider the type of people who work or live in the geographic area of the premises. Are they your target market? Do you require walk-by traffic to make your business successful? Is there a suburban community with young families, and therefore material needs for furnishings, children's clothing, construction supplies, or other spin-off activities? Signage and visibility are important factors when deciding on a lease location. Are there any signage restrictions imposed by the landlord or the city?

- **Drive-by traffic.** Are you relying on drive-by traffic? Is there adequate parking readily accessible to your business operation? Is the parking free, as in a shopping mall, or will your customers have to pay to park in an underground lot or in a coin-metered space? If you have a business that serves trade customers and delivers products to them (e.g., automobile parts), then parking for your customers may not be an important factor. Is there traffic congestion throughout the day or just at various peak times during the day, evening, or weekend? Will any of these traffic problems seriously affect a customer's access to your location?

- **Hours of operation.** Hours of operation may be a consideration. Your landlord may have stipulations in the lease that the building is open for operation only within specified hours. If you are in a shopping mall, you may be required to be open for business at all times that the mall is open. This may result in a longer workday and higher staff costs than you anticipated. If your municipal bylaws do not allow opening on Sunday, whereas an adjacent municipality does allow Sunday opening, your competition in the adjacent area could take away a substantial portion of your business.

- **Rent payment.** Obviously, the amount of rent you are going to pay is a critical factor in determining whether the location is attractive. Many small business bankruptcies are due to excessive rental payments.

Ask yourself how the proposed rent measures as a percentage of your anticipated sales. Is the rent within industry averages as a percentage of sales? Rent costs in excess of industry averages can be justified only if the location allows for higher-priced markups or other benefits that offset the higher cost. Later in this chapter there will be a discussion of rental payments and minimizing the risk factor.

ADVANTAGES AND DISADVANTAGES OF LEASING

Few small business owners have the financial resources to consider buying a building and property. Even if they do have the resources, the decision to buy rather than lease space should be made only after considerable discussion with an accountant and a lawyer. Leasing provides flexible options that minimize the risk. The following outline discusses some of the main advantages and disadvantages of leasing from the perspectives of both the tenant (lessee) and landlord (lessor). From a negotiating viewpoint, it is helpful to understand both parties' points of view.

Advantages of Leasing to the Tenant

- Capital is not required to purchase the property, thereby freeing up capital for other business purposes.
- The lease payments are generally 100% tax deductible as an expense.
- It is generally easier to sell the business if no land is involved.
- It may be possible to negotiate an option to purchase the building and land at the end of the lease. In this case the advantage is the chance to acquire the land and building when the tenant can afford it, assuming it would be a financial or business advantage to do so. In an option-to-buy situation, it is common to have a predetermined fixed price with a time limit within which to exercise the option. There may be an adjustment formula for inflation (cost-of-living index).
- It may be possible to negotiate a lease with a variable monthly lease payment based on seasonal cash flow income of the tenant. The total annual rent would be fixed.
- Protections can be built in to minimize personal and business financial risk, as discussed in the last section of this chapter.

Disadvantages of Leasing to the Tenant

- In some situations, the tenant cannot depreciate improvements made on the lease property in terms of tax deductions.
- When the lease expires, the value of the potential of the business (goodwill) will not be of financial benefit to the tenant unless the landlord

agrees to renew the lease. This can be offset by having a renewal option in the lease.

- The tenant does not reap the extra benefit of appreciation of the value of the property, even though the increased value may be directly related to the presence of the tenant. Any capital gain in the property value accrues to the benefit of the landlord.
- It may be more difficult for the tenant to borrow money with leased premises, if there are no assets to pledge as collateral other than the lease agreement.
- The total cash expended by the tenant in rental payments may be greater, over the term of the lease, than if payments were made for principal and interest on the purchase of the property.
- Improvements made to the property by the tenant at his or her own expense are totally lost to the tenant upon termination of the lease. The landlord automatically assumes legal title to all improvements done to the property, unless there was an agreement in the lease allowing the tenant to remove certain improvements upon termination of the lease. Improvement costs can sometimes be substantial, especially if the tenant is the first tenant in a new building.

Advantages of Leasing to the Landlord

- During the course of the lease, the tenant may pay more rent than would be paid if the property was purchased, and the landlord still owns the property at the end of the lease.
- The tenant improvements made to the premises become the landlord's property at the end of the lease, unless there is a written agreement to the contrary.
- The landlord is able to obtain the tax advantage of owning the property by deducting depreciation on the building.
- The tenant may be responsible for all maintenance and repairs on the space being rented, as well as all or part of the taxes. If this provision is stipulated in the lease document, it minimizes the financial outlay and therefore risk on the part of the landlord.

Disadvantages of Leasing to the Landlord

- It is sometimes difficult to find financially capable and responsible tenants willing to lease at the rental rate required or desired, or to debt service the expenses and provide a return on the investment to the landlord.

- Leases are only as reliable as the tenants who sign them. Some tenants will break the lease at the earliest opportunity if it appears that the business is not going to be viable. Statistically, the high failure rate of small business means the odds are that a percentage of tenants will go out of business before the end of the term of the lease.
- There is a risk of loss of continuity of cash flow if the tenant leaves, thereby creating debt servicing problems, as well as empty space. The empty space could possibly deter other tenants from coming into the building.
- Even a very creditworthy tenant may get into financial difficulties at some point during the term of the lease. This would leave the landlord with rent collection or eviction problems, as well as possible litigation to recover the balance outstanding under the lease.
- The landlord may incur sizeable expenses or difficulty in releasing the space at the termination of the lease. The tenant may have made specialized improvements to the rented space for the specific needs of the business, which are unsuitable to anyone else. The landlord may therefore have to incur expenses of extensive reconstruction on the premises to attract a new tenant.

TYPES OF LEASES

To obtain a leasing arrangement suitable to your business needs, you should be aware of the options available. The following types of leases are the most common ones. The name used to describe each lease may vary in your region, but the concept behind the description is the same.

- **Ground lease.** A buyer may purchase a building or business property without actually purchasing the land under it. The land may be leased separately on a long-term lease basis (e.g., 99 years). By purchasing a building and leasing the underlying land, the financial outlay of capital for the land is eliminated, and yet the benefit of its use can be obtained. The cost of leasing the land can also be written off as a tax-deductible expense.
- **Net lease.** In a net lease situation, the tenant pays a flat rate which is all-inclusive of heat, light, water, taxes, common area use, ground maintenance, building repairs, etc.
- **Net lease plus taxes.** This is similar to the net lease, except that there is an agreed-upon extra expense for taxes. Any taxes over and above the base tax rate are passed on to the tenant totally or partially, depending on what is negotiated. The extra cost for taxes would normally be passed

on once a year, once the tax assessment has been obtained and paid by the landlord.

- **Triple net lease.** In this type of lease situation, the base rent is a certain price (for example, $15 per square foot of area rented), but the tenant is responsible for paying his or her proportionate share of all the extra charges incurred by the landlord. These are normally outlined in the lease agreement. These extra costs or operating expenses could add up to the equivalent of another $10 per square foot, for example. The total monthly rental outlay in this scenario would therefore be approximately $25 per square foot. The operating costs may fluctuate each year based on taxes, maintenance, insurance, and administrative and management costs. When one refers to a cost per square foot for lease space, it is quoted on an annual basis; to calculate the monthly rent, you multiply the square footage of the premises by the cost per square foot and divide by 12.

- **Index lease.** This type of lease is one in which the rent varies based on a formula of costs incurred by the landlord. For instance, the lease may vary every year based on the cost-of-living index to account for inflation.

- **Variable lease.** A variable lease is one in which the annual rent is agreed upon in terms of how it is calculated, but the monthly rent may vary depending on the seasonal nature of the cash flow of the business. For example, there could be a very low or no-rent period of 3 or 4 months because business activity is slow. The rent for the remaining months of the year would be high, to compensate for the period when the business was unable to pay rent.

- **Graduated lease.** This type of lease requires an increase in rental payment every month for a specified period of time. This is usually done to assist a business in its first year of start-up, so that the monthly payments are related to the increase in cash flow and revenue of the business. At the end of the graduated period, the rental payments by the tenant would then be at a fixed rate, usually as in a net or triple net lease.

- **Percentage lease.** There are several types of percentage leases. In one type, the landlord obtains no minimum rent but simply a percentage of the total monthly sales of the business. The landlord attempts to determine the tenant's potential revenue and bases the percentage on that amount. The percentage for rent could vary depending on the volume of sales. For example, it could be set at a higher percentage for a lower volume of sales, and a lower percentage for a higher volume. The tenant would have to calculate whether or not the base percentage could be too difficult for the business to pay, assuming that the gross revenues are obtained.

The other variation is that the landlord calculates a minimum rent based on the tenant's potential revenues, but the rent paid is based upon actual revenues. In other words, it is a percentage of the gross monthly revenue of the business. In this example, the landlord is able to budget on a minimum guaranteed rent until such time as the tenant pays a higher rent because the revenues justify it. In this type of lease, the landlord requires very tight accounting and reporting controls.

Another type of arrangement is for the percentage to be based on net profit. This type of arrangement has to be defined very carefully in the lease. The most common way is for the profit to be calculated before depreciation and/or interest and income taxes. There is usually a limit on the owner's salary; otherwise, the owner could inflate the salary paid out as a management fee or to relatives in order to increase expenses, so that there is no net profit. The landlord also frequently requires that a minimum amount of money be spent on advertising by the tenant, so that sales and net profit are generated. Another provision frequently found is that the landlord requires a minimum amount spent for maintenance, so that the premises are kept in good repair and condition.

The percentage lease is commonly used in the renting of retail stores in shopping centres. The landlord therefore obtains the benefit that the tenant obtains in terms of the large traffic volume going through the shopping centre which the landlord has established.

When dealing with shopping centre leases, be extremely careful that you obtain competent professional advice from your lawyer and accountant before committing yourself. The relationship with the landlord in a percentage lease is almost that of a partner, because the landlord has very tight controls on reporting and expenditure of monies by the business and the systems for keeping track of cash and giving out receipts. As the success of the tenant's business may only be partially due to the location, it would be prudent to try to negotiate a fixed maximum dollar amount that the landlord would be entitled to receive under the lease.

LEGAL ASPECTS OF A LEASE

The lease document is a contract, and like any other contract, it is legally binding and enforceable. The terms of the lease contract and all the rights that you and the landlord have under that contract will affect your business profit, your business survival, and the ability to sell your business at some point in the future. For these reasons, it is important that you thoroughly search out the ideal location for your business, carefully review the terms of the lease, and then discuss the offer to lease or formal lease with your lawyer and accountant before signing any documents. Once you have committed yourself, it could be very difficult or impossible to get out of the lease without severe financial consequences and litigation.

As leases are prepared by landlords for landlords, they tend to be one-sided. In other words, the lease requires commitments and obligations on the part of the tenant and restricts the tenant in many ways, but does not have the equivalent balance in terms of responsibility on the part of the landlord. This is the reason you need to have your lawyer protect your interests by attempting to renegotiate the terms of the lease to be more equitable and balanced, and in accord with your budget and the degree of risk that you are prepared to accept.

Oral or Written

If you are intending to rent premises on a month-to-month basis, you may not need or be required to sign a lease. If you are operating a business with that degree of uncertainty in terms of your tenure at that location, you are probably not too concerned about your long-term rights or options at that location. On a month-to-month lease, normally, either party can give the other party 1 month's notice to vacate. The goodwill component may be minimal if you were to sell your business, unless you had an attractive long-term lease in place.

The landlord may prefer to sign a month-to-month lease because the property is due to be torn down or construction work is to be done which limits the appropriateness of a long-term lease. To protect yourself fully, you should insist upon a written lease. For the terms of the lease to be enforceable, it has to be in writing in most jurisdictions in Canada.

The landlord usually insists that a lease be in writing to fully protect his or her interests and to be sure of the duration of a cash flow income from the rental. The landlord's bank may require proof of lease documentation in order to finance the landlord. A further reason is that any potential purchaser of the landlord's building and land will want to take a look at the nature and quality of the leases and tenants in determining the purchase price.

Offer to Lease

The first step when you are considering a space to lease is to present an offer to lease. Most landlords have property management agents, real estate agents, or other sales personnel employed to solicit offers to lease. In other cases, you may be dealing directly with the landlord without an agent involved. When an agent is involved, there is generally a commission paid to the agent by the landlord, which can vary considerably. For example, the agent may receive 10% of the gross base rent in the first year of a 3-year lease or 15% in the first year of a 5-year lease or 10% on the first 2 years of a five-year lease. Keep in mind that the landlord's agent is acting for and on behalf of the interests of the landlord, and has an incentive to have you sign the offer to lease in terms of making a commission. As mentioned before, the longer the lease term that you sign, the higher the commission that the agent receives. For example, if you are proposing a 2-year lease with two renewable options of 2 years each for a total of a 6-year lease, you might meet some resistance from the agent, who would otherwise try to encourage you to sign a flat 5- or 6-year lease because the commission would be higher.

Offer to lease forms vary considerably in format and content. Make sure that your offer to lease has escape clauses. These are conditions that have to be met to your satisfaction before you have a binding and acceptable offer.

Be certain that you have a copy of the formal lease to review before you submit your offer to lease. The formal lease document should be attached to your offer to lease as a schedule. Be wary of an offer to lease that states that a "standard lease document" will be required to be signed without that document being given to you in advance. Leases vary widely in their content and terms, and very rarely are any two leases the same.

The offer to lease sets out the specific terms between the parties that are to be modified in the formal lease document, in other words, the length of the lease term, the rental terms, the use of the premises, the name of the parties, the description of the property involved, the frequency of rental payments, the renewal options if any, and any other special and unique terms or changes to the lease. Obviously your lawyer will need to review the formal lease in order to properly advise you and suggest modifications to be specified in the offer to lease. The offer to lease would include a reference to the formal lease and the modifications, including additions and deletions that have been noted on the lease document. Therefore, when the landlord is reviewing the offer to lease, the complete package of the offer is available for consideration. After it has been submitted, it may be difficult or impossible to negotiate further changes. If you find another location or terms that you prefer, it is important that your lawyer notify the agent immediately in writing that the offer has been withdrawn. This is assuming that it has not yet been accepted.

The offer to lease ideally should be in the name of a corporate entity rather than your personal name. If you have paid a low deposit at the time of the offer, that minimizes your financial risk if you need to get out of the contract. If you have included various subject conditions in the offer to lease that have to be met by the landlord or yourself, and the conditions are not met, then you get your deposit back. In this regard, you may put a provision in the offer to lease that if the offer is accepted, you will increase the deposit to the amount of the first and last month's rent, or other arrangements that you might negotiate. Ask for the deposit to be held in an account with interest accruing in your favour. The landlord may accept the offer as presented or may come back with a suggested compromise. You may prefer to have your lawyer or accountant act for you in negotiating the terms of the lease. Often a business owner is unable to remain objective when he or she is caught up in the enthusiasm and excitement of making such a major business decision.

Be particularly cautious if you are making an offer to lease on a building that is currently under construction. It is common for delays to occur in construction, and even though the lease you may sign has a specific date for occupancy, there is always a provision in the lease that gives the landlord an out in terms of legal liability if delays occur. A description of clauses to consider in your offer, some helpful negotiation techniques, and pitfalls to avoid follow this section.

Formal Lease

Once your offer to lease has been accepted, you need to sign a formal lease. As mentioned earlier, it is very rare to see any two leases that are exactly the same. Some leases are simple ones, prepared by the landlord, and may be only a few pages in length. For use as the formal lease, the landlord may have purchased from a stationery supplier a commercial lease document that has approximately four to six pages. On the other hand, the landlord may have a lawyer prepare a document which could be anywhere from ten pages to 100 pages in length. The shopping centre leases and leases prepared by major Canadian real estate companies or national property management companies tend to be over forty pages. Attached to the formal lease document would be various schedules, including a sketch or map of the exact location that is being leased, or construction plans if you are making changes to a location in the process of being built. There are other documents that might be attached to the lease, setting out the terms between the parties.

As mentioned, there are many different terms in a lease depending on the sophistication of the landlord and whether you are leasing from a shopping centre or not. A description of the key terms that might be found in a lease will be given later in the chapter.

Impact of Government Legislation

Even though you may have a written lease setting out the terms of your relationship, there is government legislation which affects a landlord–tenant relationship. You should be aware of the following legislation.

Municipal legislation

Each community will have municipal legislation dealing with businesses in the form of bylaws that affect zoning requirements. These bylaws regulate the type of businesses that can be operated in various areas throughout the city. Health and safety regulations could have a bearing on the type of business that you intend to operate.

Provincial legislation

The provinces may have different titles and content in the following legislation, but the underlying purpose is the same:

- **Commercial Tenancy Act.** This legislation governs the relationship between the landlord and tenant, whether a lease is signed or not. Certain provisions of this Act can be waived in the lease, but the Act provides rights and remedies to both the landlord and tenant.
- **Short Form of Leases Act.** Some leases that are very short (a few pages in length) refer to the fact that the lease is to be governed by the Short Form of Leases Act. This saves the landlord from drawing up a lengthy lease, because the essential terms of the landlord–tenant relationship would be governed by that Act.
- **Rent Distress Act.** In the event that a tenant fails to pay the rent when it is due, the landlord is entitled to restrain (in other words lock up the premises) until such time as the rent arrears are paid. There are other protections for both the landlord and tenant which are set out in the Act.
- **Real Estate Act.** This Act covers factors such as the registering of a lease by the tenant or landlord in the Land Titles Office or the equivalent, depending on the province.

Federal legislation

The federal Bankruptcy and Insolvency Act sets out provisions for when a landlord or tenant is petitioned into bankruptcy or voluntarily declares bankruptcy. Refer to Chapter 17, "Bankruptcy, Insolvency, and Receivership."

Key Terms of a Lease

There are many key terms or clauses in a lease that you should be aware of to avoid pitfalls in your negotiating. Not all are included, and the sequence may vary. Shopping centre leases or leases prepared by major property management companies tend to be very extensive, and have many more terms than outlined below.

Rent clause

The rent clause may appear to be an obvious one, but it has to be clear for your protection. It must detail exactly how the rent is calculated and when it is due and payable. The types of rent have been discussed in an earlier section. You will need to know when the rent has to be paid. For example, if you are responsible for taxes and maintenance costs, are they payable once a year, when the landlord calculates what their costs have been for that year? Or does the landlord forecast operational expenses on a monthly basis, and you have to make that payment every month? In this latter example, you could request the landlord put those funds in a separate account that is interest-bearing to your favour. If there is a deficiency, you would have to pay up the difference at that time; if there is an excess, it would either be returned to you or credited towards the running account for the next budget period.

There could also be provisions for extra charges that the landlord would have the right to change arbitrarily every year. For example, in a shopping centre complex, there could be a provision for an administrative fee and promotion fee that is paid to the landlord for administering and promoting the mall. A clause in the lease might say that the landlord is entitled to increase its administrative fees from time to time as the landlord so wishes. This would be an open-ended clause that could limit your ability to budget carefully in terms of trying to calculate the exact rent over the period of a year.

Commencement date clause

This is the date that you would be responsible for commencing your rent payments. It may not necessarily be the same date as your taking possession of the premises. In other words, the landlord may have allowed you a rent-free period.

If you are leasing premises which are being constructed, the occupancy date may not be specific or accurate because of possible delays in completing the premises. You could have expended a lot of money ordering inventory and equipment (e.g., if you are opening a clothing store), to find that you have to wait for 3 or 6 months longer before you can move in. The fine print of most leases states that if there is any delay in construction the landlord is not responsible. There could be many reasons, such as lack of proper financing, construction management problems, or just simply unrealistic projections on the part of the landlord, that could cause the delay. Because of the terms of the lease, you might be in a position in which you do not have any legal recourse against the landlord. Therefore, in terms of financial commitments that you make, be particularly cautious about relying on good faith that the landlord's proposed date of completion of the building and occupancy is accurate.

Use clause

This is the provision in the lease which sets out exactly what your business intends to use the premises for. It is to your advantage to have the use description as broad as possible, in case you may want to expand the range of products or services that you offer through your business. If the use clause is too restrictive, that could limit your profit and could even impair your business survival.

Once the use clause has been agreed upon, the landlord may not be prepared to modify that provision at some later point. If you ignore that clause and offer a service or product that is not included, then you could be deemed to be in breach of the lease, with all the legal and financial problems that could occur, depending on the terms of the lease.

Noncompetition clause

This is a clause that you would insert in the lease to protect you from a competitor coming into the premises and causing your business to suffer. For example, if you were a dentist, you might want to have a clause in the lease stating that no other dentist could rent office space in the building during the term of your lease. If your jewellery store had a noncompetition clause, and a gift store in the building started to sell jewellery to compete with you, you could ask the landlord to invoke the noncompetition clause. On the other hand, if the gift store's use was very broad, the gift store could argue that there was no restriction in its lease in the type of product that it sold as far as jewellery was concerned. You can see why the use clause issue and the noncompetition clause are interrelated and very important.

Demolition/construction clause

There could be a clause in the lease that allows the landlord to give short-term notice (for example, 6 months) to the tenant to leave the premises. This could happen even if you have a 10-year lease. The landlord could arbitrarily give this notice if there is a clause allowing it to do so to demolish the building or make substantial constructional changes. Be extremely cautious in signing any lease that has such a clause; in effect, you just have a short-term lease. You would have great difficulty selling your business to any other buyer because of the high risk. What buyer would be prepared to pay for leasehold improvements or goodwill that you have developed over many years if the lease could be terminated within 6 months? In practical terms, the landlord may never invoke the demolition/construction clause, but the risk is always there for yourself and any potential buyer.

Acceleration clause

The landlord may have a provision in the lease that in the event of your default on the terms of the lease, the full face amount of the lease could be accelerated, and you could be sued for that amount. In other words, if you had a 5-year lease at $1,000 per month, the face amount of the lease would be $60,000 over the term. If you are 1 year into the lease and breach the lease, in theory, the landlord could attempt to sue you for $48,000 under the terms of an acceleration clause. In reality, though, the landlord would have an obligation in law to mitigate (minimize) its damages (losses) by immediately attempting to re-rent the premises if you have breached the lease and departed.

Default clause

There are many provisions throughout the lease that set out the basis on which the landlord can deem you to be in default. One obvious ground for default would be failure on your part to pay rent. There could be other grounds, such as using the premises outside the terms of the lease, going into bankruptcy, failing to have the required insurance on the premises, failure to keep your business open during the hours required by a shopping mall, failing to maintain your premises, subletting without permission, and many other provisions.

If a default occurs, there generally is a time period within which you can remedy the default after you have been given notice (for example, 3 days or 1 week or 1 month). If you fail to remedy the default within the time required, other legal and financial actions could occur, including having you evicted from the premises.

Penalty clause

The penalty clause provision may or may not be in the lease. It generally sets out that if you are in default of any of the terms of the lease, a 3-month penalty is imposed on you in addition to the other rights and remedies that the landlord may have against you. If you are paying $1,000 per month, then you would have to pay the 3-month penalty of $3,000. This is built in as an incentive for the tenant not to breach the terms of the lease. A penalty clause can be broad in terms of what constitutes a penalty, or it can be limited to the terms specified.

Entry clause

The entry clause provision sets out the basis on which the landlord can enter your premises. Obvious situations, such as leaking water pipes causing water damage, fire, and other reasons relating to safety and limiting damage, would permit the landlord to enter. There could also be other reasons that would allow the landlord to enter the premises without entry being deemed to be termination of the lease on the part of the landlord. The subject of entry is a key one in terms of the legal rights of the tenant. For example, if the tenant had paid rent until the end of January but moved out on January 20, and the landlord entered the premises to show the premises to a prospective tenant on January 25, the tenant could claim that the landlord had terminated the lease. If there were 4 years left on the lease, this could be a substantial loss to the landlord if he was unable to re-rent the space for the next 4 years. This example shows why the landlord would want to make sure that the entry clause in the lease allows the landlord to enter in certain circumstances without limiting the landlord's future legal options against the tenant.

Assignment clause

The assignment clause is normally combined with the subletting clause. It may state that the tenant is unable to assign the lease under any circumstances, or that an assignment may be acceptable with the prior written consent of the landlord, such consent not to be unreasonably withheld. In this example, the landlord has the right to investigate the creditworthiness of any prospective assignee. If the landlord believes that the assignee is not a good risk, the landlord can refuse to approve the assignment. In that event, the tenant would have to either find a new purchaser of the business, continue operating, or breach the contract and leave the premises.

Another type of assignment clause to be wary of is one that states that if the tenant requests the landlord to assign (or sublet) the premises, the landlord has the right to immediately, or 30 days thereafter, deem the lease to be terminated. The reason that a landlord may want to insert this provision is to give the landlord the option, if rental rates have increased since the commencement of the lease, to attempt to renegotiate the terms of the lease. For example, assume that the tenant is 2 years into a 5-year lease and paying $10 per square foot. The prevailing rate due to market demand in the area is now $20 per square foot in the premises. The tenant could sell the business at a very attractive profit, because of the immense savings to the prospective buyer in terms of rental. On the other hand, the landlord may not be prepared to accept the assignment and could immediately declare the lease to be at an end unless the prevailing rate of $20 per square foot was renegotiated into the lease. Naturally, this would have a serious effect on the ability of the tenant to sell the business at all or at the price the tenant was anticipating.

Subletting clause

This clause relates to the tenant subletting a portion of the space to a third party. There could be an economic downturn or other circumstances that require the tenant to save on overhead and expenses. One way to do this would be to rent part of the leased space to another business to reduce expenses and increase cash flow. The normal provision in the lease is that the landlord would permit subletting but only with the prior written consent of the landlord. This enables the landlord to do a check of the prospective subtenant in terms of the type of business he or she intends to operate. It is possible the subtenant might be contravening various noncompetition clauses in the master lease between the landlord and other tenants. The sublease clause may be an important one to consider in relation to a potential purchaser of the business, or for the survival of the business if downsizing is required at some future point.

Improvement/fixture clause

This clause sets out the provision that all improvements and fixtures on the premises shall be deemed to belong to the landlord. Upon installation, they immediately become part of the building, and cannot be removed without the consent of the landlord in writing in advance. Depending on the type of business that you have, you could be putting in expensive fixtures and improvements that you would like to take away with you at the end of the lease term. If this is the situation, you should negotiate very toughly at the outset on this point and specify the exact fixtures and improvements that you want to take away at the end of the lease.

The landlord may be concerned about damage that could occur to the premises if a tenant tried to remove improvements and fixtures. The landlord may therefore require a provision in the lease that any structural or other cosmetic damage that may occur to the premises as a consequence of your removal of the specified fixtures or improvements shall be repaired at your cost. On balance, you may feel that this is a fair stipulation.

Utilities

The utility provision sets out the expenses for which the tenant is responsible, such as electricity, water, telephone, sewage, garbage removal, or any other matters under these categories. The tenant may be responsible for paying a portion of the cost or all of the cost, depending on the circumstances. You should find out from the landlord what the average rates will be, and then modify those rates based on your anticipated usage of utilities depending on the type of business that you have.

Insurance

Most leases have a clause stating that the tenant is responsible for maintaining various types of insurance and specified minimum amounts of coverage for each. For example, there could be a requirement for a minimum $1,000,000 general liability coverage. The landlord may ask to see proof of coverage and proof that the premium has been paid.

Maintenance/repairs

In some leases, the landlord is responsible for all maintenance and repairs to do with the building and surrounding area, such as parking and landscaping. In other leases, the landlord wants to pass on to the tenants virtually all the maintenance and repair costs. This is usually done on a percentage basis, proportional to the amount of square footage that the tenant occupies.

If the tenant is responsible for these extra costs, it is important that the tenant have an estimate of the past costs and projected costs over the next number of years. For example, possibly the landlord needs to completely reroof all the premises or repair the parking lot because of numerous potholes, or completely repaint the premises inside and outside. You might feel it is unfair for the landlord to pass on to the tenant all these costs that should otherwise be borne by the landlord. The time to negotiate the maintenance/repair costs to your liking is at the very outset, before anything is signed.

Security deposit

Depending on the length of the lease, the landlord may ask for the last 1, 2, or 3 months' rent as a security deposit for any damage caused by the tenant. When an offer to lease is made, it is also common to have the landlord request the first month's rent, although technically that is not a security deposit.

Make sure that you try to negotiate with the landlord a provision in the contract that interest is to run to the favour of the tenant for the security deposit monies. If your rent was $2,500 per month and you paid 2 months' rent as security deposit, that is $5,000. If the lease is a 5-year term and you negotiated a flat rate of 10% per year on the security deposit, you would have an additional $2,500 to your credit by the end of the lease term. If you negotiated that the security deposit monies bear interest at the bank prime rate, which is variable, then you could take advantage of the changing rate of interest. You could also attempt to negotiate with the landlord that the security deposit monies bear interest at the bank prime rate and that interest be compounded. This would earn you even more money by the end of the term of the lease. Many tenants overlook the interest provision on their deposit money.

Guarantees or indemnifier

If the lease is in the name of a proprietorship or a partnership, the owners are automatically liable personally for the full amount of debts or liabilities of that partnership, including any liabilities due to a breach of the lease. For this reason, many people incorporate a company before signing a lease with a landlord. A landlord may request a personal guarantee or a guarantee from another company for a corporate lease. However, you should always try to negotiate out any guarantee and indemnifier provisions, which are similar in impact and liability The other reason for trying to get out of a guarantee or indemnity of a corporate lease is that the contingent liability that you are personally exposing yourself to will fetter your ability to borrow more money in the future, as the lender will look at the actual and contingent liability of your company and you personally, when assessing risk. Some suggestions for doing this are covered in the next section.

Promotion and administrative cost clause

In shopping malls, it is common to have a provision, as mentioned before, that the tenant pays a portion of the landlord's administrative and promotional costs. The tenant should be aware of what these costs have been in the past and what they might be in the future by speaking with the landlord and other tenants. It could turn out that the extra costs incurred would be greater than the amount that the tenant was budgeting for, and therefore the location would not be a viable one. It could also turn out that the amount that the landlord wants is unfair in relative terms compared with other shopping centre landlords.

Renewal clause

You may want to negotiate an option to renew the lease for a further term or terms upon the expiry of the present lease. Some option to renew provisions include fixing a ceiling on the amount of the rent increase if the option were renewed; having the rent increase based on a cost-of-living index; and having the rent increase negotiated between the parties and if an agreement cannot be reached, utilizing an arbitrator under a provincial arbitration act to make a decision.

Holdover clause

There should be a clause in the lease that states the terms if the tenant stays on the premises beyond the termination date of the lease. Normally it states that the tenant shall remain on a month-to-month basis after the lease has terminated and on the same rental terms. On a month-to-month lease, either the landlord or tenant can give each other 1 month's notice.

Option to purchase

If it is the tenant's desire at some point to purchase the premises, then this provision should be negotiated at the outset and clearly stated in the lease. Do not rely on the landlord's oral promise that you would have an option on the property and the terms of that option. The purchase price should be specified, or a formula for calculating the purchase price, and a stipulated period of time during which the option will be held open. This clause also protects the tenant from someone else buying the property for the duration of the option period. The landlord may require an additional payment for this option, which could be a flat fee payment at the outset of the lease, or a nominal amount paid every month over the term of the lease. The extra charge may or may not be applied against the eventual property purchase. The tenant may also negotiate a provision which allows the tenant the option to apply a percentage of the monthly rent payments towards the down payment or purchase price of the property if the tenant elects to exercise the option.

Minimizing Personal and Business Risk

There is always a potentially high degree of personal and business risk in signing a lease. The location may turn out to be a poor one; competition may start to affect the business; or health, marital, or partnership problems may impair the business operation. For these reasons and many more, it is vital that precautions be built into the lease to minimize risk as much as possible.

Many small business owners are not aware of the wide range of protections that can be negotiated into a lease. You need street-smart experienced business lawyer and tax accountant advice to assist your negotiations with the landlord, and optimize your protections and legal and financial risk exposure, both corporately and personally.

Here are some common effective techniques to discuss with your lawyer when negotiating the offer to lease.

Incorporate

It is wise to incorporate in any business situation which involves high risk. A long-term lease obviously involves potential risk. Statistically, approximately 75% of small businesses fail within 3 years of start-up. For all these reasons, incorporating a company and signing the lease under the corporate name would be a prudent consideration.

Penalty clause

You may wish to negotiate a 3-month penalty as the total amount of damages that the landlord would expect from the tenant in the event that the lease is breached. The landlord may require that the 3-month penalty be paid in advance and represent the last 3 months of the term of the lease or the penalty, whichever comes first. Again, make sure that you ask that the funds go into an interest-bearing account with compound interest to the favour of the tenant.

The tenant could budget as part of the start-up costs the downside risk as being 3 months and have that money put aside by giving it to the landlord under the terms of the lease. In this example, no other security would be given to the landlord and the landlord would have no further recourse against the tenant if the tenant left before the term of the lease.

Alternatively, it may be negotiated that in the event the tenant breached the terms of the lease, a penalty of 3 months' rent would be paid by the tenant, and the penalty would represent the full amount for which the tenant would be responsible. No penalty deposit would be paid in advance.

Another form of penalty provision could be that the amount of the penalty be decreased based on the length of time that the tenant remained in the premises under the terms of the lease. For example, in a 5-year lease, the clause might state that if the lease is terminated with 4 or more years left on it, there would be a 5-month penalty; with 3 to 4 years left in the lease, it would be a 4-month penalty; with 2 to 3 years, a 3-month penalty; with 1 to 2 years, a 2-month penalty; and with under 1 year left on the lease, it would be a 1-month penalty.

Short-term lease with options to renew

To minimize the risk associated with signing a long-term lease, you may instead decide to have the initial lease period relatively short. By the end of the short-term lease, you would be in a better position to decide whether it is viable to remain in the leased premises for a longer period of time. For example, rather than signing a 5-year lease it might be prudent to negotiate a1-year lease with two renewable 2-year options. If you wanted a 7-year lease, you might negotiate a 2-year lease with two renewable options for 2 years and 3 years.

This type of structure would enable you to stay for the full period of time if desired, but with limited time-interval commitments. A provision could be negotiated that there would be no increase in rent at the time of the first option, but that there could be an increase in rent at the time of the second option, if the landlord so elects. The clause would then set out the amount of the increase or a formula under which it would be calculated, if any rent increase were to occur.

No personal guarantee

For a corporate lease, it is not uncommon for a landlord to request a personal guarantee or guarantees or indemnities by the directors. Sometimes landlords use the word "indemnifier" rather than "guarantor." It sounds like a more benign terminology, but it is not. While approximately 70% of landlords might request a personal guarantee, the majority of those could be persuaded to waive this request through effective negotiating techniques. The most direct approach is to state that unless the personal guarantee provision is removed, other premises will be leased elsewhere that do not require a personal guarantee. You should have short-listed other attractive options, so you can be firm on the issue.

Another approach is to limit the extent of the personal guarantees. You may negotiate a provision that the personal guarantee automatically expires at the end of the first year of the lease. This clause could state that in the event that the lease is terminated by the tenant before the end of the year, the personal guarantor shall be responsible for the balance of the first year's rent. From the perspective of the landlord, the first year is probably the highest risk with a new tenant. The landlord would be protected in that the tenant would remain or be responsible for at least 1 year's rent.

If a personal guarantee is given, it could be on condition that the guarantee be limited to a fixed amount, such as a maximum of 3 months' rent. Whenever a lease is terminated, the landlord is required in law to exert his or her best efforts to locate another tenant. If the landlord was unable to re-rent the premises immediately, the personal guarantor would only have to pay up to, but not more than, 3 months' rent.

If your attempts to avoid giving a personal guarantee have been unsuccessful, your next step would be to minimize the overall risk and exposure. Wherever possible, do not agree to provide more than one guarantor. In the case of default, the landlord would be entitled to sue both you and the second guarantor for the full amount outstanding on the lease.

Free or reduced rent

Often a landlord is willing to offer a free rent period or reduced rental payments as an incentive to rent the premises. This is often the case when the space has been vacant for some time. Try to structure the rent payments in the first year to limit the financial outlay as much as possible. Following are some suggestions:

- Request graduated or reduced rental payments. Have the rental payments start at a low rate and graduate upwards to the higher amount every month over a period of the first year or possibly 18 months or 2 years. The aggregate amount may be less than the normal annual aggregate rent for the subsequent years of the lease.
- Negotiate from 1 to 6 months rent free. The amount of free rent will depend on the length of the lease, the improvements for which the tenant is paying, the type of business (if it enhances the image of the building), and other factors.
- Try to have the landlord pay for all the costs of renovations up to an agreed maximum. It depends on the circumstances as to how much the landlord would be prepared to pay. For example, the landlord might be desperate to have a good tenant in the building to draw in other prospective tenants as well as customers. The tenant might agree to a 10-year lease on the basis that the landlord pay $50,000 for improvements. Everything depends on the circumstances and your negotiating leverage.
- Ask for a free rent period. In one example possibly the first, fourth, eighth, and twelfth months would be free. This would provide the landlord with some cash flow throughout the year but would also provide the tenant with a monthly rent saving on a quarterly basis in the first year.
- Request that the first year of maintenance be waived. In the case of a triple net lease, the operating expenses over and above the base rent could be considerable. In this example, request that the first year is a net lease with a flat rate, with the triple net lease feature commencing in the second year. There would be no carrying forward of the triple net extras from the first year to subsequent years.

Construction allowances

If the tenant is going into premises that are being newly constructed, provisions may be negotiated with the landlord to save the tenant renovation expenses. The provision may state that the landlord would pay to have all the leasehold improvements done that the tenant requires, as a condition of the tenant signing the lease. It would be less expensive for the landlord to pay for such costs if the improvements are being done at the same time that the landlord is paying for the overall construction of the building.

Lease assignment

You should be careful to remove your personal liability and risk before selling your business and assigning the lease to a buyer. Otherwise, in the event that the buyer defaults on the terms of the lease, the landlord has the right to sue not only the buyer as the assignee, but also your company as the assigner. Ask the landlord to remove your personal guarantee (assuming you gave one) at the time that the lease is assigned. Be certain this agreement is in writing and signed by the landlord. The landlord can obtain personal guarantees from the buyer of the business if he or she wants.

If the landlord will not release your company from the lease, then incorporate a new company for any future business purposes, and transfer any assets to the new company. If the landlord refuses to release the personal guarantee on your original lease, and therefore you have ongoing potential exposure if the new buyer defaults on the lease, then arrange with the buyer to negotiate a completely new lease with the landlord. This may involve the buyer having to pay more rent and you may have to reduce the purchase price accordingly. The key point is to have your personal name released from any future liability exposure.

Negotiating a lease

In most situations the tenant does not negotiate directly with the landlord. Normally a landlord hires staff or a sales agent in the form of a realtor or property management company to advertise and negotiate the rental of the business premises. Landlords and sales agents tend to be sophisticated in terms of the negotiating process as well as effective sales techniques. Therefore, the small business owner is often at a disadvantage in terms of this type of business experience.

When you are negotiating a lease there are various strategies and tactics that you should consider. As in any negotiation, it is important to understand the needs of the other side. The sales agent's motivations include earning a commission and satisfying the landlord so that ongoing business can be obtained. As the sales agent is acting for and on behalf of the landlord, it is prudent not to disclose to the sales agent any information that could impair your negotiating position. Being overly enthusiastic about the location may reduce your negotiating stance. In other words, try to keep the sales agent guessing as to whether or not you are planning to select that location.

In the case of a landlord, there are several needs the landlord could have that would provide incentive for a deal to be made along the lines that you are proposing. These needs may include the following:

- **The landlord wants occupancy to attract tenants.** The more tenants in the building, the easier it will be for the landlord to attract other tenants into the building. It implies stability and traffic flow, and these are important factors to any tenant, as well as the landlord. If a location is newly opened or soon to be open, that should provide you with better negotiating leverage in terms of being one of the first tenants to sign up for the building.
- **The landlord needs cash flow to debt service the bank loan.** A landlord has to account to the bank in terms of generating the cash flow to pay the mortgage. The more unrented space in the premises, the less cash flow, and therefore the more pressure the landlord is under from the bank. The landlord may be motivated to rent the space and therefore may be more flexible in negotiating the lease. It may take the immediate cash flow pressure off the landlord, even though there is a risk that the tenant may not be around a year later.
- **Full occupancy enhances the selling price of the building.** If the landlord intends to sell the building, a prospective buyer would find it far more attractive and the selling price would be accordingly higher if the tenancy of the building is at full occupancy. In other words, there is a direct financial benefit to the landlord to be flexible in negotiations with the prospective tenant if it helps fill up the building.
- **It is easier for the landlord to access bank financing.** If the landlord wishes to borrow money on the building to invest in other buildings or for other business reasons, the bank will lend money to the landlord based on the amount of cash flow being generated by the tenants in the building. Therefore, this may provide incentive for flexibility on the landlord's part.
- **The landlord needs to compete in the leasing market.** In order to maintain maximum occupancy and remain competitive in lease costs, a landlord has to be flexible in negotiating leases.

It is helpful therefore when negotiating to understand the context in which the landlord is operating. In many situations you are doing the landlord a favour by becoming a tenant, not the other way around. This philosophical and negotiating viewpoint will help to balance an otherwise one-sided lease arrangement.

Steps in Negotiating a Lease

- Thoroughly understand leasing terms and concepts. Speak to your accountant and lawyer for clarification of your questions or concerns.
- Determine your overall criteria regarding the ideal location, the amount of money you are prepared to spend, and other factors.
- Thoroughly research potential locations and short-list them to three locations, if at all possible. Any one of these locations should be acceptable to you. Prepare a list of your questions and concerns to be answered by the landlord or his or her representative.
- Obtain all documents required to assess the three locations. This includes a copy of the lease, building plans if the building is being constructed, and other information that your lawyer or accountant may request of you.
- Review the documentation yourself and determine your priority in terms of your preference of location.
- Set up a meeting with your lawyer and accountant and discuss the prospective premises.
- Decide on your negotiating position regarding terms after your consultation with your professional advisors.
- Decide whether you are going to do the negotiating or have your lawyer do the negotiating on your behalf. If it appears tactically advantageous for you to do the negotiating, then make sure your game plan is well thought out in advance. If you involve your lawyer, it is common for the other side to involve its lawyer in the negotiating stage, especially in the case of negotiating legal terms in the agreement.
- Submit your offer to lease in detail with the formal lease attached, with any suggested modifications.
- Advise the agent that you are seriously considering other premises and if they are not serious about agreeing with your terms, then you will have no alternative but to take your business elsewhere. If you say this, make sure that you mean it. It may be necessary to walk away from the deal.
- Put pressure on the agent and the landlord in terms of placing a deadline on acceptance of the offer to lease. The deadline could be 2 or 3 days, or longer, depending on the circumstances. A major Canadian property management company or landlord may require the documents to be approved at head office, and this could take a longer period of time. In

general, the offer should not be open for any longer than a week, the shorter the better. Placing a deadline implies to the landlord that you are serious about going elsewhere if they are not in agreement.

If the landlord does not accept the offer, or if a counteroffer is made to you and you are not in agreement with it, then try the next location on your priority list. This approach will eventually get you the location and lease terms that you want. It is critical and prudent to use your tax accountant and business lawyer to assist with lease negotiations. This money will be well spent, and you will have peace of mind knowing that your decision is based on expert advice that will limit your personal exposure and risk.

For more information on real estate topics that could relate to your business options or decisions, refer to my Canadian real estate books published by John Wiley & Sons – *Making Money in Real Estate, Real Estate Investing for Dummies for Canadians, The Canadian Landlord's Guide, 101 Streetsmart Condo Buying Tips for Canadians, The Complete Guide to Buying and Owning Recreational Property in Canada,* and *Mortgages Made Easy.*

Chapter 10

Raising Financing

... they all observe one rule,
which woe betides the banker who fails to heed it,
which is you must never lend any money
to anybody unless they don't need it.

— Ogden Nash

One of the basic needs of any small business is money. Where to get it, how much to get, and how to repay it are fundamental concerns when starting out, and at other stages in your business. You will need to consider factors such as conventional and creative sources of funds, types of security required, choosing a lender, and where to get further information.

ASSESSING YOUR FINANCIAL NEEDS

Understanding the Stages of a Business

When starting a business, you have to consider the financial needs from start-up to ongoing daily needs, to expansion or diversification, to getting through difficult economic periods. Managing your business effectively means understanding and anticipating the different stages and planning for them—especially in terms of financing.

Start-up needs

If you are starting your business from scratch, buying an existing business, or buying a franchise, this will be the period of time you will have to expend the largest amount of funds.

Funds may be required for purchasing equipment, buildings, property, or initial inventory. You may also have to pay for capital expenditures, such as leasehold improvements (plumbing, electrical, painting, decorating), fixtures (signs, sheltering, lighting, counters), furnishings (furniture, pictures), equipment (photocopy machines, cash registers, typewriters), and tools and machinery. There are many other costs in the preopening and opening phase of your business, including legal and accounting fees, insurance premiums, deposits for the landlord, business licences, stationery, advertising, and opening-day special expenses (food, advertising).

When preparing your start-up financing needs you must also provide for contingency and reserve funds. The contingency fund is set up to cover unexpected expenses. This may represent from 10% to 25% of planned expenses. A reserve fund is established to carry the new business through the initial period of operation, when there may be reduced revenue. You may be fortunate to have an immediate customer base and therefore will require only a modest reserve fund. Because this is a rare situation, you should set aside money to cover a minimum of 3 months for overhead costs and salaries. In many cases, sufficient funds for a period of 6 months or possibly up to 1 year should be set aside to carry the business until it can sustain itself.

Ongoing daily needs

After the start-up funds have been assessed, your secondary financing needs will be for your day-to-day operations, otherwise referred to as working capital. In Chapter 3, "Understanding Financial Statements," which includes a discussion of financial ratios, you will see the formula for determining the working capital needs of your business. It is defined as the amount by which your current assets, such as accounts receivable, cash, and inventory, exceed your current liabilities, such as a short-term bank credit or trade credit payables. Working capital should be sufficient to provide for a payment of your current liabilities and for the financing of your day-by-day operations, including inventory and payroll. Your working capital needs will depend on factors such as the amount and terms of your accounts receivable and accounts payable, your seasonal buying needs, and the size of inventory. You must have adequate working capital to take advantage of trade discounts or buying in bulk in order to keep your costs down and your prices competitive.

Expansion

Funds may be required for sustained growth, expansion, or diversification. Funds for growth capital may be required for the hiring of new employees, acquisition of additional stock, introduction of a new product line, research and development needs, or new equipment or buildings. Your business at this point should have a clear financial track record, so that projections can be based on reality and history. Because of this higher degree of certainty, and therefore reduced risk to a lender, your likelihood of accessing funding is enhanced. Your request for funding is based on a greater probability of cash flow than you would expect from a start-up operation.

Lean economic periods or special needs

In some cases, specific financial needs can be anticipated; in other cases, they cannot. For example, if competition opens up across the street, interest rates go up, and key employees quit, you may require financing to get you through a difficult period.

Lean or slack times may be projected because of the seasonal nature of your business. For example, you may need funds to cover your expenses until the season commences, or you may need to purchase a large inventory of new product line prior to the season commencing. A lender may provide temporary financing on the basis of funds being paid back from profits earned during the peak periods of the season.

If your needs for financing during lean times are not for seasonal or normal reasons, then the bank may seriously look at the underlying reasons for your financial needs. The lender may not be prepared to provide any further financing. If you need financing because your service or product is not being accepted in the marketplace, or because of management difficulties, partnership disputes, marital or health difficulties, the lender may come to the conclusion that the business may not be able to reverse itself and cure the problems that are causing the financial difficulties. Your only recourse at that point is to inject further money into your business by means of personal loans or by finding other private investors who are prepared to take the risk.

Planning Your Financial Needs

Many small business people do not anticipate their financial needs until they are faced with an urgent problem. Or they are overly optimistic when preparing their projections. It is important to be conservative and realistic.

As part of your financing plan, you will have to complete various financial documents, such as a capital expenditure budget, a projected income statement, a balance sheet, and cash flow.

The following general guidelines should help you in preparing meaningful and reliable forecasts. Your financial forecasts should:

- reflect the most current and accurate information available
- include an explanation of your assumptions
- be realistic and reasonable
- provide documentation to support your forecasts (published industry ratios, etc.)
- provide an opportunity for input from management and professional advisors to increase the quality and accuracy of the forecast.

Your professional accountant may be able to assist you in preparing computerized financial forecasts based on various contingent scenarios with a higher degree of accuracy.

METHODS OF DEBT FINANCING A BUSINESS

Financing your business by means of borrowing money is called *debt financing*. There are numerous methods of debt financing your business, including accounts receivable financing, bridge loan, business improvement loan, leasing, and many other procedures. Most, if not all, of these financing methods will require you to fill out a bank application and may result in a proposal letter, such as in Sample 14.

Demand Loan

Demand loans are generally short term in nature and have no fixed repayment schedule. The funds are borrowed for many different purposes, and the interest rate is a floating rate that changes with the chartered bank prime rate. If your company is creditworthy and solvent, you may be able to negotiate a rate which is at the prime rate or 2% to 1% above the prime. Depending on the degree of risk and other factors, the bank may go up to 4%, 5%, or 6% above the prime rate for a demand loan. A demand loan means that the loans are payable on demand at any time that the creditor feels at risk.

Operating Loan (Line of Credit)

A line of credit is provided by banks to support day-to-day working capital needs of the business. The bank agrees to lend up to a maximum amount of money, as required, providing certain terms and conditions are met. This type of loan is normally of a revolving nature; in other words, it goes up and down depending on deposits and payables. Interest is paid only on the amount outstanding on a daily basis. It is prudent to avoid continuous operation at the upper end of a credit line, as in effect you are arbitrarily converting the line of credit to a term loan. A line of credit is normally secured by receivables, inventory, a debenture, and fixed or other assets.

Bridge/Interim Loan

This is a form of temporary financing used to bridge the commencement of a project until long-term funds or other government subsidies, loans, grants, or financing are received (e.g., if you are a contractor and need funds to complete a project because you do not get paid in full until the end of the project). Chartered banks are the normal source of interim financing, as is the Business Development Bank of Canada (BDC) a federal government Crown corporation.

Conditional Sales Purchases

Manufacturers of new equipment will frequently assist in financing the purchase of their equipment through the use of conditional sales purchases. The manufacturer may require a down payment of one-quarter to one-third of the purchase price and will carry the balance by means of a conditional sales contract. The purchaser has possession of the equipment or asset, and the vendor maintains ownership of the asset until the bill is paid in full, at which time the title of the asset transfers to the purchaser.

Floor Financing

With floor financing, the lender maintains legal ownership of the items "on the floor" while the retailer displays them for sale. In effect, it is a conditional sales contract arrangement that allows the title of the goods to transfer once the borrower has sold them and has received payment. This enables the business to have a high volume of product for sale without having to pay for it in advance. Floor financing is commonly used by large appliance, furniture, and car dealers to finance their floor stock.

Leasing

Leasing involves the use of vehicles, machinery, equipment, or space on a rental-fee basis, thus avoiding the need to invest capital in ownership. The ownership rests with the bank, leasing company, or landlord, while the business has the possession and use of the benefit. There are advantages and disadvantages to leasing, and each lease or purchase consideration must be looked at independently after receiving your accountant's advice.

Leasing is used in the following situations:

- when there are high capital requirements for new equipment, and there is little or no cash available
- when your cash is needed as working capital
- when the equipment will depreciate or need replacement within a 3- to 5-year period.

Further details on leasing were covered in Chapter 9, "Location and Leases," and are covered in Chapter 12, "Business Communication Equipment."

Letters of Credit

A letter of credit is a guarantee issued by a bank, on behalf of the client, to a supplier. It is a guarantee of payment in Canadian dollars (or whatever other currency is indicated), upon delivery of merchandise to the client in accordance with the terms and conditions specified in advance. Primarily used when importing or exporting goods, a letter of credit is usually irrevocable, and it is on that basis that shippers can rely on the letter of credit as security.

Accounts Receivable Financing

In accounts receivable financing, lenders pay cash advances to borrowers using accounts receivable as security. Accounts receivable financing allows the borrower to secure a continuous source of operating cash without entering into long-term financing arrangements. If the circumstances are optimal, the borrower can obtain up to 75% of the outstanding receivables under 60 days old. In exchange, the lender normally requires an assignment of book debts (accounts receivable), as well as a regular monthly listing of all the outstanding receivables. In the event that the borrower does not pay in accord with the agreement, the lender can advise the customers directly that all funds are to be remitted from that point on directly to the lender. Monies for this type of financing are available from banks, commercial finance companies, and factoring companies.

Another method is to assign the receivables to the lender, and the lender obtains the money directly from the customer. Car dealers frequently use this approach, as may mobile home dealers. The borrower is responsible for collecting the accounts receivable from customers and remits the funds to the lender.

Factoring

A factor is a business that purchases outright the accounts receivable of another business. If the factor purchases the receivables on a nonrecourse basis, it means that it cannot go after the business for any bad debt losses. Unlike accounts receivable financing, factoring is not a loan. The factor purchases accounts receivable for their value, usually advancing from 70% to 85% of approved receivables pending collection of those receivables. When the customer pays, the factor pays out the remainder due, less the factor fees and interest charges. Factors have traditionally been used in the garment industry but can be used for other purposes and business operations as well. It is possible that a factoring arrangement could have a "with recourse" provision, whereby you would be responsible for any bad debts. Naturally, interest and fee charges without recourse are higher than with recourse due to the greater risk to the factor company.

Factors are particularly useful for helping a business expand, financing an acquisition, filling seasonal inventory, or generating cash to buy out partners.

Many banks provide factoring services through association with factor companies. Factors do not require extensive loan documentation, because they are less concerned with debt to net worth ratios or business profitability. Their primary interests are:

- the credit reliability of their client's customers
- the basic honesty and integrity of the business owner
- the track record and history of the business owner and the company
- the ability and willingness of the client company to service merchandise, honour warranties, and handle customer complaints
- diversified receivables without a heavy concentration of debt in one or two accounts.

Inventory Financing

Inventory financing is used to either support a loan or obtain additional credit to increase inventory. The financing may be secured by a debenture or Bank Act security on the raw materials, work in progress, or finished goods that constitute the firm's inventory. Because inventory is not as easily liquidated as receivables, banks advance a lower percentage of the inventory's value than they would for receivables. Depending on the circumstances, the financing by banks or commercial finance companies can range from 50% to 75% of the value of the goods. Inventory financing may be combined with receivables financing to build inventory for peak selling seasons.

Trade Credit

Use of trade credit is a common form of business financing. Suppliers allow terms of credit such as 30, 60, or 90 days, or longer. This avoids the problem of having to pay in advance for the merchandise. In effect, the supplier is giving a small business a loan at no interest charge, as long as it complies with the payment terms. A discount may be offered for payment made within 10 days. Interest would run on any overdue charges over the agreed term. A further discussion of various types of trade credit is covered in Chapter 15, "Credit and Collection."

Credit Card Financing

A business may obtain a credit card, such as those offered by Visa, MasterCard, or American Express, to help pay its various expenses. Payment terms are generally either 5% of the declining balance monthly (Visa, MasterCard) or payment in full monthly (American Express).

Personal Loan

The owner may decide to borrow money personally and pledge personal assets as collateral for the loan. The money is then used for the business, either in terms of buying shares in the business (equity), or lending money to the business in the form of a shareholder's loan (for a corporation) or a personal loan, if it is a proprietorship or a partnership. Banks and consumer finance companies may provide personal loans.

There are many positive reasons to lend money to the business by means of a shareholder's loan. A short list follows.

- Interest on the shareholder's loan paid out to you by the company is a tax-deductible expense for the company.
- Lenders can consider the shareholder's loans as equity, as long as they are left in the company. Normally a bank will require a postponement of claim form to be signed by you, to the effect that you will not withdraw a shareholder's loan from the company until the bank loan is paid in full.
- You can take money out of the company without tax by having your investment structured as a shareholder's loan in part or in full. However, if you have signed a postponement of claim form, that could nullify the tax savings benefit.
- It is easier to repay a loan than to sell shares back to the company or to other investors.

GOVERNMENT ASSISTANCE

The amount of financial assistance available to small and medium-sized businesses through various levels of government amounts to billions of dollars a year. All levels of government have assistance programs. This would include federal and provincial governments and Crown corporations, as well as a few municipal governments.

Because all levels of government are aware of the vital importance of small and medium-sized business to the economic well-being of the country, governments maintain a comprehensive range of direct and indirect financial support programs to stimulate and foster entrepreneurial activity and success. New programs are always being added and existing ones discontinued or modified.

There are literally hundreds of different programs available, some specific to a certain industry, some specific to the type of expenditure involved, and others that are general business stimulation initiatives.

Government financing and assistance programs are available for all stages and needs of a business development, including developing your business management skills, financing your business, researching and developing the product, developing your employee skills, manufacturing your products, and marketing your products and service. Generally, government programs do not give you financing for existing debts—for obvious reasons—unless approval is given to consolidate debts and advance additional funds in a unique situation that meets their criteria. In addition, it is not common to receive government funding for working capital (ongoing monthly expenses). Of course, there are exceptions to this statement.

There are attractive benefits to considering government for financing assistance. In general terms, there are fewer requirements for collateral security compared with the private sector, and the amount of equity you are required to have in the business is less. This means less financial risk to you and, therefore, a reduced need to obtain funds from friends, family, or other investors. In addition, the cost of government loans is usually lower, and the government has equity financing, subsidy, cost-sharing, and grant programs that do not have to be repaid. Another benefit is that after you have obtained government financing, you are more credible and attractive to other potential lenders or investors.

Forms of Financial Assistance Programs

Financial assistance programs take various forms, as follows:

- **Loans at reduced interest rates.** These would be loans at rates of interest lower than conventional sources of financing. Loans from the BDC (bdc.ca) are an example. Another example is Industry Canada loans for small business (ig.gc.ca).
- **Loan guarantees.** The government will guarantee that a loan made to you by an approved conventional lender will be repaid. An example would be a business improvement loan (BIL) regulated under the Small Business Loans Act. The loan limits could vary over time. This federal government program is designed to assist small businesses in the purchase, installation, renovation, or improvement of equipment, usually fixed equipment. It also includes renovation of premises, leasehold improvements, purchase of land, construction, and purchase of premises. Funds are advanced by chartered banks and some trust companies and credit unions. In the event that you go out of business, the government guarantees the lender that they will be reimbursed for the debt outstanding, up to a certain amount (e.g., 90%). Part of this program currently requires the lender not to ask for a personal guarantee from you of more than 25% of the loan amount. Another example would be the Export Development Canada (edc.gc.ca). This federal Crown corporation, among other roles, issues guarantees to banks making export loans or issuing performance and bid guarantees.

- **Forgivable loans.** These are loans that are repayable in part or full, in certain situations, unless certain conditions are met or not met, in which event the loan is forgiven (not required to be repaid). One example is financing offered through Foreign Affairs and International Trade Canada (international.gc.ca) This program has various components. One initiative is to assist a Canadian company to export by paying for the company representative to attend trade shows outside Canada. If the company receives export orders within 2 years of the trip, for example, the money is repaid. If it doesn't, the loan is forgiven.

- **Loans with favourable repayment schedules.** In this situation, the repayment schedule of the loan is structured to be comfortable with the cash flow history of the company. This is common in businesses that are seasonal in nature or in which receivables come in at the end of a project or at various phases in the project. A BDC loan is an example of a loan for which a flexible repayment arrangement can be negotiated.

- **Grants.** This would consist of money paid by the government directly to the company or organization without any requirement that it need be repaid. Many federal and provincial governments have these types of programs to stimulate job creation or research and development. For example, if you were going to expand your business operation by building a much larger plant or some other facility, thereby creating more employment, you might qualify. Your effort would have the effect of saving the government money in Employment Insurance (EI) or welfare payments and creating a new tax revenue base from the increased business income and from additional employees paying income tax.

- **Cost sharing.** This form of assistance involves the government sharing the cost of the project.

- **Subsidies for wages.** The government may partially or completely pay for an employee's wages. Many of these programs are done through Human Resources and Skills Development Canada (hrsdc.gc.ca). Their purpose is to create new employment.

- **Subsidies for training and education.** There are many government programs to assist in training and education. For example, Human Resources Development and Skills Development Canada has programs that fund up to 75% of the cost of employee skill upgrading (e.g., computer training) or management training for business owners. Another example would be the New Exporters to Border States (NEBS) program conducted through the federal government services for entrepreneurs (canadabusiness.ca) and/or provincial governments. Financial assistance for up to 75% of the program cost is possible. In addition, easy payment plans are arranged in many cases. Also, the federal and provincial governments have prepared excellent booklets and other publications and material online on a wide range of topics. Most of this material is free or available at a nominal cost. Many government departments also have seminar programs to assist you in understanding the application process for funding, selling to government, exporting, or developing general business management or marketing skills. For example, Public Works and Government Services Canada (pwgsc.gc.ca), Industry, and Foreign Affairs and International Trade Canada are just a few of the federal government departments that offer seminar programs. Contact them and ask to be placed on a mailing list for upcoming seminars. You can also contact your provincial government departments in your areas of interest. As mentioned before, contact services for the main government departments are located in Appendix D.

- **Subsidies for consulting services.** The federal and provincial governments have consulting programs that are free or available at a reduced or nominal cost. Experts in various aspects of business provide a wide range of consulting advice through the BDC for a fee. Various provincial and federal government departments also provide researching, negotiating, and marketing assistance without charge, or at a reasonable cost, such as those services offered by Industry Canada and Foreign Affairs and International Trade Canada. In addition, Statistics Canada (statcan.gc.ca) has an excellent selection of research and other data that can be useful to you.

- **Insurance coverage.** The federal government and some provincial governments have insurance protection that you can obtain in the event a supplier does not pay you. This relates to exporting to other countries and minimizes the inherent risk.

- **Tax or other concessions.** The federal or provincial government departments may provide tax incentives for people to invest in your business or project. Examples would be the provincial incentive of providing provincial tax credits up to a certain percentage (e.g., 30%) to people who invest in a provincially approved venture capital program (VCP) or employee share ownership program (ESOP). See canadabusiness.ca and esop-canada.com. Another example would be the federal government immigrant investor program. In this case, the federal government will grant landed immigrant status to people from other countries who invest a certain amount of money in an approved investment for a certain period of time.

- **Equity financing.** The government, in this situation, would become a minority equity partner in your business by investing a certain amount of money. The BDC is an example of federal Crown corporation which has a program with this type of venture financing.

- **Government contracts.** This is an indirect form of government financing of your business. Federal and provincial governments and their Crown corporations buy billions of dollars of goods and services each year and have a mandate to purchase from Canadian suppliers first. For information on selling to the federal government, contact Public Works and Government Services Canada. See Appendix D for a reference address or the *Blue Pages* of your phone book, under "Federal Government." Speak with your provincial government purchasing department to get further information on doing business with them.

To contact them, look in the *Blue Pages* of your phone book, under your provincial government, or do an online Google search. Alternatively, to contact your provincial small business department, see also Appendix D.

Steps to Follow to Obtain Government Financing

Research sources of government funding

There are many sources of information in terms of government (federal and provincial) funding programs. It requires time and persistence, and you want to be thorough to make sure you have current information. The key sources are:

- **Directories of government financial programs.** You can obtain these from the business division of your public library or online or from the local business resource centre of your provincial business department.
- **Provincial government small business resource centres.** Look in the *Blue Pages* or online under provincial government. Refer to the provincial government listings in Appendix D. These resource centres can tell you about financing programs and refer you to other government departments for information on venture capital companies, ESOPs, the immigrant investor program, etc. The provincial government small business information services would also be aware of the availability of many of the federal government financing programs in your area of interest.
- **Specific federal/provincial and municipal government departments.** Once you have determined your needs and have done some preliminary research, contact specific government departments in your area of interest for current financing program information. For example, this would include the BDC; Foreign Affairs and International Trade Canada; Industry Canada; and Human Resources and Skills Development Canada. The contact information for these government departments is located in Appendix D, or check in the *Blue Pages* of your phone book for a local contact number, or do a Google search using appropriate keywords.

Determine specific program availability

Although a program may in theory be available, it could have been cancelled in the last budget process or possibly all the funds have been used up for that budget year. All government fiscal years run from April 30 to March 31, so there is a fresh infusion of funds in the early part of the fiscal year.

Become knowledgeable on program application procedures

Find out as much as you can about the program. Obtain the program information directly and read it thoroughly, speak to people providing information on the specific program, and who can assist in the approval process. Determine precisely what the eligibility criteria are. The government employees administering the program are invariably helpful. Their function is to assist you in attaining your funding objectives, if at all possible, assuming you meet the eligibility criteria.

Even if you don't meet some of the program's specific requirements, but meet its general requirements, don't hesitate to pursue the matter further. It could be that an exception would be permitted or that they can recommend some other program that would be a better fit for you.

Find out the reasons why the program is in existence

This is very important to determine. All government programs are designed with specific objectives in mind. In general, government programs are designed to enhance economic and social objectives in order to develop and ensure a vibrant society and a stable and growing economy. Your proposal should therefore conform to the government's objectives in order to be viewed favourably. In other words, what potential benefits will funding to you provide to their program? In providing these benefits, of course, you are attaining your own business financial and planning objectives.

Here are some of the benefits that you could provide to the government to meet their stated program objectives in exchange for funding. Attempt to identify other ones as well:

- developing new products
- researching and developing new technology
- replacing imported foods with those manufactured in Canada
- increasing the efficiency and productivity of your workforce or business
- creating new employment opportunities
- developing or increasing employee skills
- developing potential export markets
- stimulating employment in an area of slow growth or depressed economy
- conserving natural resources

- protecting the environment
- developing skills or opportunities in specific industries designated by the government as particularly important at that point in time.

Design your request to conform to government needs

As mentioned, it is important to understand the spirit and intent of the program and identify the benefits to the program if the government supports you financially. Customize your request to comply with their needs and within the context of their eligibility requirements. The emphasis should be on how you will meet their needs, not how you will benefit from their funding.

On the other hand, it is important to point out that to benefit their program, you do need their money and without it you could not benefit their program. The government also wants to be satisfied that your business has sound management and that the purpose of the funding is realistic and attainable.

Get assistance in preparing the proposal

If you have no experience writing proposals or don't feel comfortable expressing yourself persuasively in the written word, make sure you obtain professional assistance. There are lawyers, accountants, and consultants who are experienced in preparing and in many cases representing clients in the funding application process. You want to make sure you have everything going for you. If you decide to prepare your own proposal, it is highly recommended that you have it reviewed by more than one professional or expert to obtain their candid feedback.

Positive first impressions of your proposal are very important, for obvious reasons, in order to instill confidence in the viability and management of your business. If you have to re-submit the proposal because it was incomplete or poorly prepared, that fact alone could influence the final decision and result in your application being rejected.

Generally, there are more people applying for funds than there are funds available. The screening process for eligibility therefore has to be selective to enable the applicants with the greatest chance of fulfilling the objectives of the program to do so as a result of funding.

Look for additional funding programs

In the process of researching your government funding sources, you should see various programs for which you could be eligible. Depending on the needs of your business during the various stages of your business operation, you may decide to apply concurrently or sequentially for more than one program. Don't limit your potential funding opportunities by restricting your strategic financial planning to just one program.

Be patient and persistent

Most programs involve a lot of paperwork and approval can be a lengthy process. The more complex the proposal or the more money involved, the longer it will take. Also, be persistent and don't let any initial rejection deter you. Find out the reason for the rejection and see if you can modify the proposal to comply with government needs. If not, look for other program possibilities.

Remember to look for a range of potential government funding sources on an ongoing basis throughout the life of your business.

METHODS OF EQUITY FINANCING

Equity is the money that is put into the business in exchange for shares. A balanced debt-to-equity ratio is an integral part of a successful business operation. The greater the amount of debt, of course, the greater the risk. Circumstances that may require equity financing for your business include:

- when you have borrowed to your lending limit, or have used all available assets as collateral for other credit
- for buying out a retiring or deceased partner's share of the business
- when a company is expanding and its working capital needs have exceeded retained earnings
- for a major equipment purchase, plant expansion, or introduction of a new product line
- for research and development needs
- for turnaround purposes when purchasing an insolvent company
- for temporary refinancing purposes before going public on the stock exchange.

The primary source of equity financing is usually the owners of the company. The equity may come from personal savings, the sale of real estate, or other forms of assets or investments. There are other sources of equity capital available if your personal resources are insufficient. Some of these include:

- family and friends
- employees, private individuals, clients of professional advisors, suppliers, customers, and other parties
- major companies seeking vertical or horizontal integration of their operations
- foreign investors immigrating to Canada or foreign-controlled banks with branches in Canada

- federal or provincial government equity plans, either directly (e.g., through the BDC or provincial government development corporations) or indirectly (through incentive programs for the private sector to fund small business)
- venture capital firms—usually interested in high-risk businesses in which there is potential for a high return on investment. Where the size of investment is substantial, they may require a majority control position on the board of directors; not usually interested in daily business operations unless the business's survival is at stake
- pools of funds from individuals, pension plans, trust companies, insurance companies, private investment syndicates, corporate holding companies (usually arranged by a stockbroker or investment dealer).

METHODS OF INTERNAL FINANCING

Many business owners who are unable to access money in terms of debt or equity capital may be forced to reassess their needs, resources, and business management. For example, quick handling of accounts receivable, effective inventory control, customer prepayments, and cutting down on unnecessary expenses can free up funds not otherwise available. Operating in a more efficient fashion will lessen your need to look outside the business for financing.

Some of the various methods of internal financing are discussed below.

Customer Prepayments

A business can encourage customers to make a deposit, prepayment, or payment on delivery. This is a very common technique in the mail-order business and in service-type businesses.

Employees

Employees with access to capital may be willing to invest in the company because they understand its products and services and trust the management. A financial stake in the company's future could have a positive influence on the employee's work habits and commitment to the business. However, it could prove difficult to replace, remove, or retire the employee if the employee becomes unproductive or uncooperative. Therefore, any such form of investment should be written up in a contractual form through the assistance of your lawyer. Make sure that you have buyback or payback provisions built into the agreement as a precaution and to protect the business.

Inventory Control

Effective inventory control will ensure that there is the right amount of stock to satisfy customer demand. Determine guidelines for proper inventory purchases. Adjust your purchases to meet the peaks and valleys of your annual business sales. Too much money tied up in slow-moving inventory and debt servicing payments on inventory loans, and lost customer loyalty due to insufficient stock, is costly to your business.

Collecting Receivables

Receivables can be reduced by tighter credit-granting policies, better monitoring of accounts, and more effective collection policies. You may wish to consider credit cards or cash only as a means of sales. Further details are given in Chapter 15, "Credit and Collection."

Delayed Payables

Establishing a good working relationship with your suppliers can result in extended payment terms. Make certain they are aware of your loyalty to that firm and your repeat business. You may be able to negotiate a discount on volume or regular purchases.

Restructuring Payment Arrangements

There are times when a small business is not able to maintain monthly payments plus interest on loans or repayment to creditors. By using creative negotiating techniques, there are ways of getting around short-term problems. Some alternative repayment plans that you may consider include:

- a period of grace for principal loan payments during the start-up period of your business operation
- blended payments that feature a long amortization period resulting in low payments of principal in the early years
- graduated payments, that is, low payments on principal in the early years and higher ones later on
- payments of principal during the high season only, so that the business does not have a cash-tight period during the low-sales-volume season.

Selective Product Lines

Only handle product lines on which you get the most favourable terms from the supplier and which have the highest sales turnover and profit margin.

Fixed Assets

You may wish to sell your assets to a leasing company and lease them back, thereby freeing up cash for working capital purposes. On reviewing your assets, you may feel that some of them are not necessary to the business and may be sold to free up additional cash. By purchasing secondhand equipment and machinery, you can reduce financial outlay.

Renting or Subletting

You may decide to rent space for a store or factory rather than buying, to improve your leverage and your cash flow. By subleasing space, you can offset your monthly rent payments, thereby increasing your working capital.

Operating as a Subcontractor

You may wish to operate as a subcontractor, which could save overhead expense and risk for you. Conversely, you may also wish to subcontract your services to other companies, which saves on employees and overhead.

Stringent Management

By reviewing the points discussed above to determine how to conserve on capital and save on expenses, you can free up financial resources and minimize business risk. The business owner should analyze the financial condition of the business on an ongoing basis.

- Is the owner taking out too much from the company for personal earnings rather than keeping it in the company for working capital?
- How do the company's costs of goods and other expenses compare with other companies in the industry?
- Is the lease too expensive?
- Are supplies being wasted?
- How do actual expenses compare with budgeted expenses?

The business owner knows best where expenses can be trimmed from the operation. In addition to controlling expenses, the owner should always be looking for ways to increase profits, sell surplus inventory or assets, and maintain an effective receivables collection program. If the owner needs further help in improving profits and viability, a BDC counsellor or provincial government small business department may be able to provide management assistance. A private sector business management consultant may also be of assistance. For a detailed list of sources of financing, refer to Checklist C in the back of this book.

TYPES OF SECURITY REQUESTED BY LENDERS

When providing financing to a small business, lenders require security to ensure that they are repaid. Often the value of the security is considerably more than the amount of the loan. This is because if the lender has to "realize" on the security and convert it into money, only a portion of the value of the asset will be obtained after the sale. As well, costs of hiring a lawyer, accountant, receiver, or trustee may be involved.

Your business may be evaluated by three different methods:

1. **Going concern value.** This is the most optimistic method, which is an estimate of the business based on its capitalized earnings. This method assumes that the selling price, sufficient to cover the loan, will be obtained if the business is sold as a going concern. This method gives no indication, of course, of the value of the assets if the business is not sold in this manner. Lenders would be interested in a going concern value if they have a debenture on the company.

2. **En bloc.** This is an estimate of a price at which the assets could be sold, without removal or alteration, if the business ceased to operate. The en bloc value is based on the purchase of all the assets, not just some of the assets, and on using the same location for operation.

3. **Current liquidation value.** This is the most pessimistic method of evaluating the assets of the business. It is based on the estimate of what price the assets might be expected to realize in a forced sale or winding up of the business. Most lenders use this valuation in appraising the security for a loan, because they operate on the conservative premise that in a business problem situation, they cannot be assured of any higher value.

In Canada, we consider two basic types of property. The first is real estate. All the rest is known as "personal property." This includes goods and chattels; accounts, such as accounts receivable; money; securities; and intangibles, such as trade names, trademarks, and other forms of goodwill.

The types of security for loans follow the same general pattern. Personal property acts in provincial jurisdictions in Canada have become standardized for personal property security. The old forms of assignments of book accounts and chattel mortgages have disappeared and have been replaced with multipurpose Security Agreements. Debentures are generally replaced now by a General Security Agreement, but not always. It depends on the lender and which document is appropriate, in terms of priority of security claims and other rights.

General Security Agreements

Wherever a borrower owes money or any kind of obligation, it can grant a security interest in any personal property it owns. It is not necessary to set out the obligations in the security agreement. In fact, the obligations may be continual and may change from time to time. There will be a place to set out the nature of the personal property being secured. Personal property used as a security can include accounts, equipment, inventories, tangible personal property (documents of title and securities), intangibles (contracts, licences, goodwill, patents, trademarks, trade names, industrial designs, and intellectual property), and the proceeds of the sale of any personal property.

This type of document allows the lender to take continuing security over every facet of your business. In other words, the security is not fixed in time, but keeps adding new material or products as you acquire or produce them, as additional security. Consider the case of a manufacturing business. Everything from raw materials to inventory to the proceeds of the sale can be secured to the lender under this type of security. In the same manner, a financing company can factor its securities in order to raise more capital.

The security agreement will contain standard terms worth noting. You will covenant (promise) to protect the security, insure it, and keep it in good repair. You will also agree to provide the lender with timely financial information about your business. You will also agree to pay for the cost of preparing and registering the security and any costs of the lender if it is forced to realize on the security.

The document will describe events of default, in which case the lender will be at liberty to realize on the security. These typically include default in payment of any loan, the death or winding-up or bankruptcy of the borrower, the seizure of security by another creditor, and the impairment or destruction of some or all of the security.

In the event of default, the lender will have rights given to it by the security agreement. It may seize and sell the security or appoint a receiver of the business of the borrower, all at the cost of the borrower. The receiver may go in and take over and run the business of the borrower, and it may sell off the assets of the business or sell the business itself as a going concern in order to realize the monies necessary to pay off the debt.

Care should be taken if you are not incorporated. These documents do not distinguish between personal and business assets, and you could be pledging more assets than you intended.

Specific Security Agreements

These types of agreements are modelled on General Security Agreements; however, they secure only the assets listed. The rights given to the lender are not so wide as in the general document. These provide security more like the old chattel mortgages and assignment of book accounts. The General Security Agreement is more like the old form of document called a debenture, which is still used in certain circumstances, as noted earlier.

Registration

While these documents create rights and liabilities between you and the lender, it is necessary for the lenders to protect themselves from third parties who may loan you money on the strength of the same security or who may buy the security from you. For this reason, most provinces have developed a personal property registry system in which notice of the security is registered. The registration of this notice "perfects" the security and provides the lender with the added protection it requires relative to other lenders who may have some type of security document granted to them subsequently.

After negotiating with the bank, be certain to request that the bank will confirm in writing, by means of a loan confirmation letter (as in Sample 14), that it is prepared to advance funds, and under what circumstances, and with what security. Take the letter to your accountant and lawyer after receipt and discuss the implications of it before agreeing to the terms outlined. You may wish to have your lawyer or accountant attend the meeting in which you finalize the bargain and sign an security agreements. Once you have signed the security documentation, make sure that you obtain copies of it for your lawyer and your own files. Never agree to provide security without fully understanding the nature and purpose of the security documentation.

As mentioned, it is critical that you obtain advice from your lawyer and accountant regarding the implications of these various types of security from the legal, accounting, and tax viewpoint. Whether you are negotiating with a bank or other lenders, it is important that you agree to a package which is acceptable to you in terms of your risk, personal exposure, and leverage.

Other Security Your Lender Might Require

There are many other forms of security that a potential lender or creditor might ask of you. It depends on the lender's policy and the borrower's situation. Some of the most common types of security requested are as follows. Make sure you understand the nature and implication of this security and attempt to negotiate a security package you feel comfortable providing. Refer to Checklist D for a list of security documentation. If you give too much security away the first time, you have nothing left to give later if you require more funds from the same or a different lender.

Guarantor

A guarantor is a person who guarantees the payment of a note by signing a guarantee commitment. Both private and government lenders commonly require a personal guarantee from directors of a corporation as security for loans advanced to the corporation. If the corporation defaults in its financial obligations, the lender has a choice of suing the guarantor or the corporation or both for the monies outstanding. A guarantee is not requested of individual debtors, as they are automatically personally liable. However, a lender may require a co-guarantor.

Try to negotiate a limited guarantee to cover the shortfall in the security, if other securities have been pledged. Be very careful not to sign a personal guarantee for the full amount of the loan if at all possible, or an unlimited guarantee. Request a written release of your guarantee as soon as the business has paid off its obligation or can carry the debt on its own security. Resist having your spouse sign a personal guarantee of your debts. If your spouse is not an officer or director of the company, it makes this request more credible. It reduces the marital tension a notch if your spouse is not a personal guarantor, in the event your business fails. If you co-sign with others, remember each of you is liable for the full amount of the debt. Therefore, attempt to have the debt divided by the number of guarantors and then limit each of those guarantees to the reduced amount. Also attempt to avoid signing personal guarantees on your corporate obligations to the landlord, leasing companies, and general creditors. There are strategies to attempt to avoid giving personal guarantees to a landlord. For example, refer to Chapter 9, "Location and Leases." Your personal guarantee is often all you have left to negotiate on a future occasion, assuming you have any personal assets. Remember, the main purpose of using a corporation is to avoid personal liability. Small business people are frequently too naive and generous in giving out personal guarantees.

Indemnifier

This is similar to the concept of a guarantor, but different terminology. You are personally obligated to indemnity the creditor.

Promissory Note

A promissory note is a written promise to pay a specified sum of money to the lender, either on demand or at a specified time in the future.

Endorser

Borrowers often get other people to sign a note in order to increase their own credit. These endorsers are contingently liable for the note they sign. In other words, if the borrower fails to pay off the loan, the lender expects the endorser to make good on the note. Sometimes the endorser may be asked to pledge assets or securities as well, for example, a collateral mortgage on a home.

Demand Note

A demand note involves a written promise to pay the amount of monies outstanding to the lender upon demand.

Mortgages (Conventional, Collateral, or Chattel)

A lender may require a mortgage against your property for the advancement of funds. It could be a conventional first, second, or third mortgage against your property, or a collateral mortgage to a guarantee or demand note.

A chattel mortgage is on specific property other than land and buildings, such as a car or boat. The title of the chattel remains in the name of the borrower, but a lien against the chattel is placed in favour of the lender. The document you sign is generally called a specific security agreement; it itemizes the chattels pledged and is registered in your provincial registry.

Assignment of lease, rents, or mortgage

The assignment of a lease is fairly common security in franchises, so that the franchisor can assume the lease if the franchisee goes out of business or defaults on the franchise agreement. The franchisor could then resell the franchise with a lease in place.

If you have rental income, a lender may ask you to sign a document that would not be used by the lender unless you were in default of your loan obligations. In the event of your default, all rents that you had been previously collecting from tenants or subtenants would be diverted directly to the lender. The lender would notify the tenants and provide them with a copy of the assignment document.

You may have a mortgage that was given to you personally or corporately for security. In that event, the lender may want that mortgage assigned to them as security for your loan.

Assignment of life insurance

A lender may request that the borrower assign the proceeds of a life insurance policy to the lender up to the amount outstanding at the time of death of the borrower. Another form of assignment is against the cash surrender value of a life insurance policy, assuming you have that type of policy. Banks generally lend up to the cash surrender value of a life insurance policy.

Assignment of accounts receivable or contracts

A borrower may have to assign the business receivables or book debts to the lender to secure an operating line of credit or other loan. The borrower still collects the receivables; however, in a default, the lender will assume collection. The assignment is supported by submitting a list of the business receivables every month.

If you have any contracts with clients or the government for services performed, for example, you may be requested to assign those contracts to the lender.

Postponement of claim

If you have a limited company, and there are any loans from shareholders, the lender may ask for an agreement that the company will not repay the shareholders until the lender has been repaid in full. Be very careful about signing this document without accounting and tax advice. It is usually incorporated with the personal guarantee document, but it could be a separate page. The tax implications could be onerous. For example, you could be obliged to take out a salary, which is taxable, to meet your personal needs, rather than paying yourself back a part or all of the shareholder's loan, which of course is not taxable in your hands. You can see the tax planning implications.

Debenture

A debenture is a very powerful document to give as security, but can only be given by a corporation. If you are in default of the loan conditions, and the bank activates the debenture, it does so by appointing a receiver (usually a Chartered Accountant or Certified General Accountant). The receiver effectively takes over the corporation on behalf of the bank and sells either the corporation or its assets to pay the lender back its loan. Occasionally, you may have the ability to refinance the loan with funds from some other source, but once a receiver is appointed, your financial leverage to get funds elsewhere generally is reduced, for obvious reasons. Debentures are still requested by lenders in some situations; otherwise, the lender will request a General Security Agreement, which is similar in protection to a debenture.

General security agreement and specific security agreement

The two types of security documents have been discussed in detail earlier. As a reminder, the General Security Agreement is similar to the description given for a debenture. The Specific Security Document covers items that were previously referred to as chattel mortgages or assignment of accounts receivable. The concept is still similar; only the name of the documentation is changed, along with a different form of provincial registration of the documents.

Pledge of stocks or bonds

The possession of stocks and bonds may be transferred to the lender, but title remains with the borrower. These are sometimes referred to as "hypothecation agreements" and itemize the assets pledged. The security must be marketable. As a protection against market declines and possible expenses at liquidation, banks usually lend no more than 75% of the market value of blue chip stock. On government or municipal bonds, they may be willing to lend 90% or more of their market value. These percentages could vary depending on the perceived market value and the lender's policy, which could change from time to time.

The lender may ask the borrower for additional security or payment whenever the market value of the stocks or bonds drops below the lender's required safety margin.

Warehouse receipts
A warehouse receipt is frequently given to the lender as security and shows that the merchandise used as security either has been placed in a public warehouse or has been left on your premises under the control of one of your employees, who is bonded. The bank lends a percentage of the estimated value of only the goods that are readily marketable.

Floor plan contracts
In a "floor plan contract," either the manufacturer lends the items to the retailer, or the bank lends money for purchase of the merchandise on the condition that a trust receipt is signed showing the serial-numbered merchandise. This document requires that you acknowledge receipt of the merchandise, agree to keep it in trust for the manufacturer or bank, and promise to pay the manufacturer or bank as you sell the goods. This is often the only way that a small business could afford to have inventory displays, such as automobiles, appliances, or boats. In other words, the title to the merchandise is conditional on purchase.

Be very careful when negotiating your security package. Lenders will usually ask for a lot more security than they really need for the loan. They prefer to be oversecured. Your challenge is to find a lending institution that will accept a reasonable security package for your loan, appropriate for your overall circumstances and the realistic risks involved. This will allow you to retain unpledged assets that you may require at some future point. For example, the more personal guarantees you sign, the more contingent personal liability you have. You therefore have less personal negotiating leverage or bargaining ability with a future lender.

In summary, it is critical that you consult your lawyer and accountant before signing any security documentation. After your consultation, you may decide to renegotiate the security documentation for the loan, revise and reduce your loan needs, or apply to another lender. The market is very competitive. You may also want to attempt to diversify your loan sources, for example, exploring government financing programs or loans under the Small Business Loans Act.

Throughout this chapter reference is made to various types of security that lenders may require. See also Checklist D.

THE CREDIT-GRANTING PROCESS

Approximately 87% of small businesses in Canada utilize a chartered bank for financing purposes. This does not mean that a small business is using a bank exclusively, but for at least part of its financing needs. Therefore, it is important that you understand the process involved in the granting of loans. This will assist you in negotiating with the lender. There are specific questions that you should ask when selecting a lender.

Factors involved in the loan-granting process are: your meeting and request for money; the criteria used by the lender for approving funds; an agreement between the borrower and the lender regarding terms and amounts of money, security, and other factors; confirmation in writing as to the agreement between the parties; and signing of the necessary security required before the funds are advanced. The following is a discussion of the process.

Request by Borrower

It is best to set up an initial appointment to discuss the lender's policies without necessarily going into the details of your proposal. During the interview, you can discuss in general terms such questions as what type of collateral might be required, limitations that the bank might have on types of business loans that you are considering, the type of reporting information that you may be required to make, and any other information that the bank needs. This will prepare you for the type of information needed in your loan proposal. The loans officer may give you a loan application form to complete. (Refer to Sample 15 for a typical business loan application form.) At the preliminary meeting, the prospective lender may ask questions such as:

- How much money do you need?
- For how long do you need it?
- What do you plan to do with the money?
- How do you intend to repay the loan?
- What are the alternative sources of repayment if you have a problem?
- What types of security are you prepared to provide?

After the meeting, you should finalize your business plan and financial plan. Set up another meeting with the lender. Present your business plan and financial proposal along with a one-page outline of the essence of your application for funds. More detail on the preparation of a business plan and financial plan is discussed in Chapter 2, "Business Planning." A sample format for a financing proposal is shown as Sample 16.

Give the lender a reasonable time to assess your proposal. Depending on the complexity of the proposal, it may need to be referred to another level within the bank.

Lender's Approval Criteria

Prospective lenders want to know as much as possible about you and your business before making a decision to provide you with financing. The lender will be looking at various criteria, including character, capital, capacity, conditions, and collateral. Risks and bank policy are also considered. A brief description of these criteria follows:

- **Character.** The trustworthiness of a potential borrower will be considered. Your track record and integrity in terms of your business and financial history, such as personal credit history and management ability as demonstrated in your business plan, will weigh heavily in the lender's decision. Your level of commitment to the business, other than financial, is another perception that will be considered.
- **Capital.** This refers to the equity or financial investment that you are going to be putting in the business. Taken into account are such factors as the amount of investment, the quality of the assets that are purchased with your investment, the liquidity of the assets (ability to sell quickly for cash), and the overall liability of the firm. If you have a large financial investment in the business, this demonstrates to the lender a high degree of commitment on your part to ensure that the business succeeds. If you have very little invested, then in the eyes of the lender you could have very little to lose.
- **Capacity.** This refers to the capacity of the business to pay back the loan. The lender, of course, wants to get paid from the cash flow and profits of the business, and not from having to sell the security that you have pledged. The lender is interested in your cash flow projections and the basis on which you have made those projections.
- **Conditions.** The lender takes a look at the various economic conditions nationally and locally that are significant to your type of business. In addition, the trends in your industry are an important factor. Banks

compare your ratios with those of similar industries to see how realistic your projections are. In addition, banks monitor various types of industries that have a high failure or loan default rate.

- **Collateral.** Banks will frequently ask the owners of a corporation to sign personal guarantees or request other forms of collateral.
- **Risk.** The bank will look at the relative degree of risk involved in lending you money and the return that they are going to get in exchange.
- **Bank policy.** The lender assesses your application within the overall context of the bank policy. For example, the bank might have a policy against lending any money to someone in a speculative real estate development business at a time when the economy is poor and there are numerous foreclosures. The bank may have a policy that there is a 4:1 security-to-loan ratio required for new start-up businesses. Banks are not venture capitalists. If you are able to provide security which is only three times the value of the loan, then you would not technically comply with the bank policy. The bank may have a policy that all directors of the company have to sign guarantees for the loan. If there are three directors and two of them are not prepared to sign personal guarantees, then the loan can be turned down for that reason alone.

Agreement on Terms and Conditions

During this phase of the loan-granting process, both parties agree on the amount, type, and structure of the loan, the interest rate that is to be paid for the loan, and the security that is being pledged for it.

There are various factors taken into account in determining the interest rate:

- the cost of funds (prime rate, money market conditions)
- administration costs
- the degree of risk involved.

Sufficient lead time must be allowed when making a loan application. The length of the process may vary depending on the loan complexity from 1 day to 1 month or more from the commencement of the preliminary meeting to the finalization of the loan approval.

Confirmation of Loan Agreement and Signing of Security Documents

This is the final phase of the loan-granting process. The lender may provide you with a bank loan confirmation letter setting out the terms and conditions, or if the amount is small, the bank may confirm approval to you verbally. After the bank has accepted the loan application, the security documents will need to be signed before the funds are advanced to you. Make sure that you have spoken with your lawyer as well as your accountant before you agree to any final loan security documentation. Remember, you are trying to convince the lender of three important factors:

- Your loan application for funds is for a worthwhile purpose and those funds are sufficient to accomplish your business objectives.
- You have the credibility, integrity, and commitment to make your business a viable one, and the management skills or access to those skills to make it a profitable one.
- The loan can be repaid out of the normal operational activities of the business on a realistic cash flow basis, and the bank will not have to realize on their security.

MAINTAINING A RELATIONSHIP WITH THE LENDER

Although a bank's head office has basic lending rules and criteria, branch managers tend to have a considerable amount of discretion and flexibility over the loans they approve or reject. In addition, the terms and conditions of the bank loans may vary widely from branch to branch of the same bank, as well as between banks and between credit unions. There can also be a wide range of expertise and experience in evaluating and approving loan applications in certain business areas. A more experienced lender might make a favourable review of your proposal, whereas an inexperienced lender might reject it, or vice versa.

It is important to determine the lending limit of the loans officer you are dealing with. If the manager has a lending limit of, for example, $100,000, and your projected needs will never exceed $50,000, you only have to convince that one person on the merits of your application. On the other hand, if your needs exceed the lending limit, the manager will have to refer your request to a senior manager or to the head office for approval. In this latter example, someone would be making a decision on your loan proposal without ever having met you. If the manager has had success in managing the loan accounts, that reflects favourably on his or her judgment and will assist your loan approval.

In your selection process, you would therefore search for an experienced bank manager with excellent connections who has approval authority for a lending limit beyond your needs. You would also want expertise not only to judge the merits of your business application, but also to understand your type of business and industry sector. The lender has discretion on the interest rate, the amount of collateral, and the repayment terms of any loan approved. If you can, convince the lender that you have prepared yourself thoroughly, looked at the pros and cons in your business plan, and have prepared a well-documented proposal. This will greatly assist your negotiations. Refer to the section on selecting a banker in Chapter 4.

Once you have obtained your loan, your banking relationship does not end. It is an ongoing one until your loan is repaid. If you establish and nurture a good working relationship with the branch manager, it will assist you greatly in the long-term relationship. Some tips on maintaining a good relationship are as follows:

- if you run into unexpected problems, don't hide that fact from the lender. After you have determined reasonable solutions that may be available, inform the lender. If you cause the lender to have unpleasant surprises such as NSF (Not Sufficient Funds) cheques, stalling on loan payments, late loan payments, or unapproved overdrafts, this will certainly impair your relationship. It could very well cause your loan to be called.
- Establish a reputation for integrity by conducting your banking affairs in a consistent and realistic manner.
- Adhere to the policy set by the bank in regard to terms and conditions of the loan agreement.
- If your bank requests financial data, provide it without unreasonable delay.
- Invite the banker to visit your place of business, and explain your operating procedures and future plans.
- Be confident in your approach, and be prepared to negotiate the terms, by having done advanced planning after consultation with your professional advisors.
- Schedule regular meeting sessions with your banker to provide a progress report on your business plan. If you request these regular meetings as a courtesy, rather than a further attempt to get more money, it will increase confidence in you when you do need the money. Remember, if you are not satisfied with the initial negotiating terms proposed by the bank, or the relationship is unsatisfactory, consider other lenders. The lending process is highly competitive.
- For further insights on the financing aspects, refer to my books, *Mortgages Made Easy*, published by John Wiley & Sons, and *Raising Money – The Canadian Guide to Successful Business Financing*, published by McGraw-Hill Ryerson.

Chapter 11

Personnel

Leadership appears to be the art of getting others to want to do something you are convinced should be done.

— Vance Packard

In your business plan, you will have identified whether or not you will be needing the assistance of others to run your business. Besides the help you will be receiving from a partner, business advisor, or mentor, you may need to rely on paid staff to assist with the day-to-day operations. Your options include part-time or full-time workers, freelancers, or sales agents. The latter two refer to a subcontracting arrangement with another entrepreneur. In a subcontract arrangement, you can expect the individual to have proven experience, to be self-motivated and to be fully able to work independently. The compensation, therefore, is higher and sometimes supplemented with commission overrides or may be strictly based on commission payment for closed sales.

You may have decided to work on your own at first and hire staff to assist you only during peak seasons or after the initial start-up period, at which time you will be generating an income from sales to meet your payroll commitments. As there will be many demands on your time in running your own business, it is important to learn the art of delegation and recognize when it is timely to hire others to take on some of the routine functions of the business. Your time and talent will be required to ensure that your business progresses through the various stages of your business plan.

Of the multitude of problems cited by surveyed business owners, personnel has been identified as being the greatest concern, with financing as a secondary concern. The most commonly cited difficulty was in recruiting and managing good people. A business owner, caught up with his or her own enthusiasm for the business, often overlooks the fact that employees do not necessarily share the same interest, commitment, and loyalty. Care needs to be taken to ensure that the right people are sought, screened, hired, trained, groomed, and motivated to develop them into the type of personnel you want to represent your business. This chapter will cover hiring part- or full-time employees and the various stages of employee development, as well as the necessary government reporting requirements.

While the characteristics of a successful entrepreneur are many, having strong people skills will play a large role in creating a welcoming atmosphere that will be easily recognized by customers and staff alike. You should be a model for your employees so they can present a consistent and favourable style of personal interaction with customers when you are not in the office. If you are courteous, considerate, and fair to your employees, they will appreciate, respect, and be proud of their employer and will speak well of the company both on and off the job.

COMPLYING WITH GOVERNMENT REGULATIONS

Ministry of Labour

The first thing to do is to contact your provincial Ministry of Labour office and request a copy of the current Employment Standards Act and a guide to the Act. (The names of government departments and statutes can vary, depending on the province.) These booklets are free, and cover topics such as minimum wages, allowable deductions, hours of work, overtime, vacations and general holidays, severance pay, termination of employment, pay equity, etc. It is important that you are familiar with these regulations and follow them in your dealings with your staff. In so doing, you can protect yourself from any claims being made against you, such as wrongful dismissal.

CRA Canada Revenue Agency

Secondly, you will have to contact the local Canada Revenue Agency (CRA; cra-arc.gc.ca) office to request an Employer's Kit. At that time, you will be assigned an employer number which is to be used when submitting all records to CRA concerning your employees, wages paid, deductions taken, and so on. The kit will include:

- **Information for the employer.** An instruction booklet to help you get started.
- **Tax exemption forms.** To be completed by each employee, and then referred to when making income tax deductions and completing the annual CRA (Canada Revenue Agency) T4 summaries.
- **Current tables of income tax deduction at source.** This will be used at each pay period to calculate the amount of income tax to be deducted from each employee's wages earned during the previous work period.
- **Current tables for calculating Canada Pension Plan (CPP) contribution and Employment Insurance (EI).** Similar to the income tax tables, this will be used at each pay period to calculate the amount of CPP and EI premiums to deduct from each employee's wages.

- **Remittance form.** This will be used on a monthly basis to report to CRA the deductions made from employees' wages for income tax, CPP, EI, and the employer's contribution to CPP and EI must be filed along with your cheque by the deadline stipulated in order to avoid penalties. After submitting your first remittance, you will receive a computer-generated form on a monthly basis on which to file a report, even if it is a "nil" report.
- **Employer guide and information on completing the record of employment.** This will be needed when terminating employment, and covers the necessary forms and how they are to be completed, plus the deadline for submitting them.

Workers' Compensation Board

Some businesses are required to pay fees to the Workers' Compensation Board (WCB), while others are not. The fee is based on a percentage of annual wages paid. You should check first if your type of business is covered before completing any remittances. Usually businesses where there is a low risk of on-the-job personal injury (e.g., service businesses such as lawyer's office, consultant, typing service) are not required to pay.

Human Rights Legislation

You should check the provincial and federal human rights legislation that governs employers. The factors covered are similar for all provinces. The main basis on which discrimination is prohibited include:

- nationality, citizenship, race, colour
- age, sex, sexual orientation
- marital status, pregnancy/childbirth
- religious or political belief
- mental or physical handicap
- criminal conviction.

If it can be proven that you have been discriminatory in your hiring or firing or other disciplinary practices, you may be subject to court action which may include a heavy fine, as well as an order to reinstate the employee.

RECORD-KEEPING

Government and Payroll Records

Careful record-keeping is something which should not be overlooked, as you will have to be accountable to CRA as well as your employees for the exact hours worked, monies earned, and deductions taken. Following is a list of information which should be detailed in a payroll journal and open for inspection if an audit of your records is requested (see also Sample 17):

- employee's name, current address, birth date
- employee's social insurance number (SIN) and number of dependents
- employee's date of employment and termination
- employee's occupation
- number of hours worked each day
- wage rate and payment of wages
- deductions made from wages
- vacations and general holidays taken.

These records will be required on a weekly, biweekly, or monthly basis when calculating the amounts to be paid to your staff; on a monthly basis when submitting the employer remittance form to CRA, along with your cheque covering the deductions taken; and on an annual basis when completing T4 summaries for each of your employees. As well, on the termination of each employee, a Record of Employment form must be submitted to Human Resources and Skills Development Canada (hrsdc.gc.ca) for calculation of employment benefits. While this is the obligatory information that is required for government reporting, it is a good practice to keep a separate file on each of your employees to track his or her training, development, and performance.

Personnel Files

You should set up a confidential file on each employee. Initially, the file will contain a copy of the job posting or advertisement, along with the employee's application form, résumé, letters of reference, and test results (if any). Your notes from the personal interview, along with any comments from the references checked, should be kept in the file.

It is a recommended personnel practice to keep an ongoing record of the employee's performance. Admittedly, daily notes to the file may be too time-consuming and therefore discontinued after a short period. However, if you make a regular practice of documenting notable details on an employee's performance, your job will be made much easier when it is time to do a performance appraisal, approve a salary increment, or justify the termination of employment. For these records, a handwritten note to the file with the date of the incident or report is usually sufficient. Examples of items you may wish to include are:

- **Correspondence.** A copy of all correspondence of a personal or performance nature
- **Illness record.** Dates and hours missed and reason
- **Tardiness record.** Dates and hours missed and reason

- **Good performance.** Date and brief details of the achievement and benefits to the company
- **Poor performance.** Date and brief explanation of the incident and the cost to the company. Also note any details about how the employee dealt with the matter, if an apology or correction was offered, and any discussions about how the matter might be dealt with in the future.

Such careful documentation will be useful if a problem arises. You may become aware of recurring incidents and need to refer to specific situations and dates when reprimanding an employee. You will not know if tardiness is a problem, for example, unless there is a record of each occasion, perhaps showing a recurring pattern (Monday mornings, the day after payday, etc.). Similarly, other behaviour may be repeated, and your careful documentation will show a pattern and a reason for reprimand. You will avoid the trap of saying to an employee, "it seems your cash register till has been short rather frequently lately," without having any record of the amounts or the frequency. Only with a thorough "paper trail" will you have sufficient grounds for reprimanding the employee or terminating the employment.

It is equally, if not more, important for your staff to be aware that you recognize and keep a record of their accomplishments. This will be discussed further under employee motivation. Too often employers are thorough when keeping a record of the "needs improvement" items, and very sparse in their documentation of the achievements made.

Keeping an accurate and up-to-date file on each employee will simplify some of the more important tasks of personnel management. Files of previous employees should be kept for a minimum of 2 years, as you may need them for year-end income tax returns, inquiries from the former employee, or reference checks.

PERSONNEL POLICY

It is highly recommended that employers have a personnel policy manual. Personnel policy statements are a reflection of the owner's personal regard for his or her employees. Written policies on sick leave, vacations, holidays, travel expenses, security, and confidentiality can eliminate ambiguity and assist both you and your employees in resolving problems that might arise. But it isn't enough to state the policy. It must be adhered to by all personnel, including you, the manager. Each employee should be given a copy. Refer to Sample 18 for some ideas on what to include in your policy statements.

Procedures

Once you have outlined the company policies, it is helpful to identify the techniques that will be used or procedures that will be followed to carry out those policies. This could be handled by a few brief statements or sample forms that will be used. Sample procedures could include the items discussed below.

Performance appraisal

A brief written report will be prepared on each employee's work record once a year on the anniversary of the employment start date. A report will also be prepared for new employees after their first 6 months of employment. The report will be discussed with the employee for the purpose of commending good work and pointing out areas that require improvement.

Wage review

A review of each employee's wages will normally be carried out in conjunction with annual performance appraisals. The amount of the increase will be dependent upon external factors such as: inflation, cost of living, comparable wages in a similar industry position, as well as market demand for individuals with specialized skill sets. Internal factors that will be taken into consideration will include the individual's performance rating, merit increase for specific accomplishments, incentive for taking on additional responsibility beyond the scope of the position, and overall value to the productivity or profitability of the company.

In essence, keep in mind the economics of raising a person's salary, as opposed to having that person leave for a better paying job, and the subsequent costs to rehire and retrain someone new.

Job Descriptions

The job description is a list of duties to be performed. It should state clearly the tasks for which the individual has the responsibility and authority to act independently. While this list may change from time to time as your business expands, it is important to have a written job description for each position in your company. (Sample 19 is an example of a job description.) The job description will be referred to:

- when recruiting new staff
- when training new staff
- when reviewing employee performance
- when assigning pay increases
- when firing staff.

It is necessary for an employee to know the specific duties to be performed. This will eliminate misunderstandings regarding expectations that have not been clearly communicated. It will provide a means for discussing changes to the job requirements as your business expands, or reviewing the employee's performance. You will be in a difficult position with the Labour Board when firing an employee for not meeting all the requirements of his or her position if the specific duties have not been clearly outlined in writing in the first place.

WHERE TO FIND EMPLOYEES

A business is only as good as the people in it. Therefore, to effectively manage your business, you must take the time to find and hire the right employees. The smaller the business, the less you are able to afford the time and costs involved in hiring and then firing an ill-suited employee. Large companies employ people specifically trained in the selection of employees. However, as an owner-manager you will have to be concerned with all aspects of the personnel process, such as hiring, training, motivating, and disciplining staff.

The secret to finding the right person is recognizing the ideal personality traits as well as the skills and background experience required for the position. A review of the job description will help identify the skills required. More importantly, though, is the need to identify specific personality traits and attitudes. For instance, a relaxed, warm, confident personality will suit a customer service or administrative role, while a charismatic, energetic, fast-thinker will do well in a sales capacity. If in doubt, it is better to hire the right personality, than the person with just the skills. Keep in mind that it is easier to teach the skills than it is to teach an attitude!

Recruitment Firms

For the busy small business owner who may have little previous experience hiring staff, a personnel recruitment agency can provide a worthwhile service. Agency personnel have specialized training in placing well-worded newspaper advertisements, reviewing résumés, interviewing and testing prospective applicants, and checking references. You may prefer to deal with an agency that has expertise in placing personnel in businesses similar to your own. In this case, they may already have contact with qualified prospects, and therefore can provide a quick response to your request.

Within the last year or two a number of Internet-based recruitment agencies have started offering similar matchmaking services. They operate by charging a flat fee for posting your job opportunity on their Internet site. Candidates worldwide can post their résumés on the site (with no fee). The software then matches candidates' qualifications to your position and alerts the candidates, who then forward their résumés and cover letters to your e-mail address. This type of service can result in faster matches at a fraction of the cost of traditional placement agencies and draws upon a wider reach of candidates.

The role of the agency is not to hire staff for you, but to provide you with a selection of well-qualified prospects. It is your role to interview the prospects and make the final decision. Agency fees are the equivalent of 10% to 12% of the employee's annual earnings.

Internet-based recruitment firms charge a flat fee of approximately $500 to $1,000. In most cases, an agency will guarantee their placements for a certain time period. For example, if the person you hire turns out to be unsuitable for the position and leaves within a three-month period, the agency will continue to search for a suitable employee at no further expense to you.

Newspaper Print and Online Advertisements

The classified section of your local print or online newspaper is a good vehicle for finding applicants. If you are searching for a senior-level staff member, you may also consider the careers section of the print or online newspaper. By reviewing newspaper employment advertisements, you will become familiar with the wording of ads for similar positions. Staff in the classified ad department of the newspaper will be able to advise you which editions carry the most ads in the employment category. One must be careful with the wording of the ad, as human rights legislation prohibits discrimination against individuals based on sex, race, age, physical handicap, etc. Check with your provincial human rights departments to become aware of the requirements.

When you write an advertisement, specify the job title, qualification requirements, and salary range. By omitting to state that a minimum of 3 years' experience is required, for example, you may be flooded with unqualified applicants. The task of sorting through the stacks of applications is a time-consuming one. If, on the other hand, the ad is overly specific, you may need to run it for a longer period of time in order to get a sufficient number of applicants to review. To receive written applications, you would use your address or a confidential box number in the ad. If instead you include a telephone number, you should be prepared and available to prescreen applicants over the telephone and only invite résumés from qualified candidates. This will save time later.

Online Job Search Websites

There are numerous websites offering job opportunities online for free. For example, monster.ca, kijiji.ca, craigslist.com, etc. The more senior the position, the more important it is to use the services of a professional placement agency that will do a customized search and screening to best meet your needs and save you time and hassles.

Educational Institutions

Depending on the time of year, high schools and colleges may be a source of recruits. In the spring, graduating students are trying to arrange part-time or full-time employment. A student may be willing to work for you on a part-time basis while still attending school, and full-time during the sessional breaks. If little experience or training is required, this can be a very beneficial and inexpensive source of part-time staff. Some schools and colleges offer work-experience programs in which students work in your place of business for periods of 2 to 6 weeks or longer during their final school year. This provides them with additional training and provides you with no-cost assistance, although some time is required to work with these trainees. Some students may be interested in returning on a full-time basis after graduation.

Specialized Training Courses

Colleges, institutes, and private firms offer a wide variety of specialized training courses from which you can recruit employees. For instance, if you are looking for a computer operator, you may decide to contact an organization that offers such training. Typically, training courses are 3 to 4 months in duration; therefore, graduates may be available throughout the year. These graduates are often faced with the difficulty of landing their first job in the new field—they are trained, but inexperienced. If you have time to work with and coach an inexperienced individual, a long-term bond may develop that may be of mutual benefit.

Human Resources and Skills Development Canada

Your local HRSDC office will be pleased to assist in identifying suitable applicants. Much like a personnel agency, the HRSDC staff will find out from you the skills, attributes, qualifications, and background you are seeking, and will try to match them with the registrants in their files. There is no fee for this service. HRSDC does not place newspaper ads on your behalf but draws upon the people who have contacted the HRSDC branch for assistance in their job search.

Word of Mouth

By spreading the word to your business associates, employees, and past employees, some beneficial contacts may result. Networking groups such as the local Chamber of Commerce meetings and retail merchants' association meetings may provide an opportunity to announce that you have a position available in your company.

Help Wanted Sign on Store Window

A help wanted sign may produce interested people who live in your neighbourhood and are looking for work. However, a lot of unqualified applicants may inquire about the job, and you cannot interview an applicant and wait on a customer at the same time.

A combination of these methods may serve your needs best. The important thing is to find the right applicant with the correct skills for the job you want to fill. The next step, conducting well-planned interviews, will provide you with an opportunity to find out if the applicants are truly suitable to your business environment.

THE INTERVIEW

The objective of the job interview is to find out as much information as you can about the applicant's work background, especially work habits and skills. A well-constructed job application form will provide the factual information you will need to assist you in the screening process (see Sample 20). In addition, some thought should be given to the questions you will ask during the interview.

Planning the Interview

1. Decide on the qualities and background experience you are looking for, and list these in column format down the left-hand side of a blank page. Probably you will have already formulated some ideas when you were preparing the newspaper advertisement or discussing the position with others. In the centre of the page, draw three vertical columns with a rating of good, fair, and poor at the top of each column. On the right-hand side, you may leave a wide column for comments. For a suggested format, see Sample 21. You now have an interview form which can be photocopied and used, one per interview. This will ensure that each applicant is graded on the same factors.

2. Prepare the questions you plan to ask and arrange them in a sequence that will simulate a conversation, rather than merely being read from a checklist. Use this list of questions for each applicant. For instance, you may start off with general questions regarding where the person lives, and did he or she have any trouble finding the location. (This will tell you how close/far the person lives from your place of work, and if they feel the travelling aspect is going to be a problem for them.) Then move to the more specific questions relating to his or her work experiences. Proceed to a direct line of questioning that will test their self-confidence and maturity, such as, "How do you react to constructive criticism?" or "Can you identify what your major strengths and weaknesses are in a work setting?" Avoid asking questions that elicit a yes or no answer.

Instead, use open-ended questions that will allow the person to give a more complete answer and allow you to get to know his or her better. For instance, "Can you tell me about any previous supervisory experience you've had?" is more likely to elicit a thorough response than, "Have you had previous supervisory experience?" As you listen to the responses, you must evaluate the replies. Do they know what they are talking about? Are they evasive or unskilled in the job tasks? Do they appear insecure or lacking in confidence? Note your responses on the interview form.

3. Read the application and résumé and then reread it between the lines. What is your impression of the person? And what has the applicant neglected to tell you in the résumé? For instance, people who do not have a steady work history may have omitted to give the time period worked at each job. Does this mean the person has had several short-term assignments, gaps in between work history, or is ready for retirement and prefers not to show his or her age? While it would be a mistake for you to prejudge a person based on these questions, it is important for you to make marginal notes that will prompt you to ask specific questions in the interview. Don't forget that because of the many independent résumé writers in business, perhaps the person who wrote the résumé is not the one applying for the job. This reality should put less importance on the résumé itself and more weight on the interview.

4. Set well-spaced appointments with 5 to 10 minutes in between each in order to allow you time to review your impressions and make notes. Don't try to pack too many interviews into one day; rather, set a second period aside to conduct the rest of the interviews.

Testing and Assessment

Depending upon the nature of your business, you may wish the applicants to complete some tests to verify their skill level. For instance, a computer operator may be asked to prepare a simple spreadsheet to assess speed and accuracy skills; a sales clerk may be asked to perform a basic arithmetic test to assess a minimum standard of knowledge. These may be completed at the time the person attends the interview, and should be timed and supervised by a staff member.

Conducting the Interview

1. Be certain you are well-dressed and groomed. Remember, you set the standard for the dress code in your company. Try to avoid distractions and interruptions while you are interviewing. Do not answer the telephone. You will need your total concentration to listen with your eyes as

well as your ears. Have a clear desk and a tidy office so the interviewee is not distracted. Try to stay on schedule.

2. Be friendly and relaxed, and encourage the applicant to be relaxed as well. In this way he or she will open up more with responses and give you a better picture of the person under normal circumstances. Don't forget that most people are extremely nervous and stressed in an interview and testing situation—that tense personality you see may not be their normal personality. Be courteous and respectful. Allow an opportunity for the applicant to ask questions about the position or company.

3. If you feel the applicant is definitely not suited for the job, don't waste your time and his or hers—end the interview as quickly as possible and politely explain the reason (e.g., you are looking for a candidate with more experience or more knowledge of the product or customer base).

4. Ask the applicant to check back with you later, if you think you may be interested in that applicant. Never commit yourself until you have interviewed all likely candidates. You want to be sure that you select the right person for the job.

5. Write down any remarks for follow-up later. Review the skills checklist form and fill in a rating on each of the skill areas, along with specific comments. Remember, after several interviews it will be almost impossible to rely on your memory for the specific characteristics of each individual. Take a few moments to clear your mind of the previous interview and to reread the résumé of the person you will see next. Only call in that person when you feel in control of your agenda for the next interview.

Following Up after the Interview

1. Review your interview notes and test results for each applicant. Narrow the selection to the top two or three candidates.

2. Check references. Verify the dates given on the application form and the positions held with the previous employers. Ask questions such as: Why did the employee leave that position? Would you hire the person again if a position were available? Was his or her work poor, average, or excellent? Did he or she have a good attendance record? Did he or she get along well with peers, supervisors, customers? Did the person have any problem handling cash? Sample 22 provides a suggested format for reference checking.

3. With this added information, your decision may be clear. If, however, you are still unable to make a decision, you may wish to ask the top candidates to return for a second, third, or fourth interview. This time you may want to have your second-in-command conduct the interview,

or attend with you, to help in the decision-making. This is an important decision, as the right employee can help you make money. The wrong employee will cost you much wasted time and materials, and may even drive away your customers.

4. It is good manners and common courtesy to respond to the unsuccessful applicants to thank them for applying, and advise them the position has been filled. You may wish to keep your notes on these applicants in a file for a short time in case a second position becomes available, or if the top candidate does not work out.

WELCOMING THE NEW EMPLOYEE

Once a selection has been made, the successful applicant must be informed. This is usually done by telephone, at which time a starting date may be agreed upon. It is good business practice to send a letter of confirmation to the new employee outlining the terms of employment. Details such as the position title, starting salary, and start date and time should be noted. This may be a good opportunity to provide the new employee with a copy of the company policy and procedures handbook for review. As well, the probation period and company benefits should be specified. A probation period is the time period that you set for the new employee to learn the basic duties of the position. At the end of the probation period (generally 3 to 6 months), a review is usually done on the employee's performance and progress. At this point, a decision is made to put the person on permanent staff, to terminate the employment, or to extend the probation period until a certain level of performance is reached.

Introductions to other staff members are a first priority. You may assign another staff member to help the new person learn his or her way around the store or office. This buddy system will help the new employee feel welcome and will ease the natural nervousness of the first day on the job. The buddy will be able to answer routine questions and assist with introductions.

Answer any questions he or she may have regarding company benefits, policies, or procedures. Review the probation period. Identify who approves vacation time, and who the employee should call if he or she is sick and unable to report for work.

It is a good idea to take time to explain to the new employee such things as the overall business concept, objectives, standards, and main customer base. Some of this may be covered in the policy and procedures manual. Re-emphasizing key aspects of your business will start the employee off with a clearer understanding of the company. Provide copies of brochures on the company's products or services. If there are other staff members, a brief outline of the other staff members' responsibilities will clarify the pecking order. Be certain to identify other staff members with similar duties and responsibilities who may be able to assist and train the new employee.

Provide a copy of the job description. Review with the new employee your expectations during the first few days. Should he or she just observe the operations or assist someone else in a similar position? Who will be providing the training? What is involved in the training process? How long will it be? Following the training, who will supervise? What tasks should be performed immediately? How long will it be before the employee will be acting independently?

Second in importance to selecting the right staff is training new employees to work to your standards. Large corporate employers recognize this fact and spend thousands of training dollars each year. Much can be said, for example, for the success of McDonald's in the area of grooming staff to be punctual, follow procedures, smile, and keep the customer satisfied. The IBM sales-training program can be applauded as well. Employers who hire such previously trained employees can benefit from the willing, cooperative attitude and good work ethics they bring with them.

EMPLOYEE DEVELOPMENT

Some personnel work, such as keeping records, is of a routine nature. The more important aspects of personnel work deal with the development of employees to perform their work better and approach their full potential. Training falls under this category, as well as the subsequent stages of delegating, performance evaluation, morale building, and motivation.

The most effective method of training is on-the-job training; that is, hands-on training in the actual work environment, reinforced by explanations and demonstrations. Before getting started, you will need:

- a skills profile checklist (the skills or specific training needed to do the job)
- the job description (the list of duties to be performed and the frequency).

Both the trainer and the trainee will need a copy of each list so that the areas needing additional training can be identified.

Establish Your Starting Point

Use the skills checklist and the job description to review aspects of the job in which the employee has had previous experience or training. The employee may need training on how to operate certain pieces of equipment. Or perhaps the employee has operated similar equipment before. It is nonproductive to provide unnecessary training. However, you may want to double-check these skills to ensure they can be performed competently.

Plan the Sequence

Now that you know the areas that require training, arrange them in an appropriate sequence. Give a rough time frame for each skill to be learned, and the standard to be expected.

Explain

Explain to the trainee how a task is performed. Provide written instructions, if available, to supplement your explanation or for review later. Explain the care of equipment, what could go wrong, and preventive maintenance checks. A copy of the manufacturer's operations manual will also be useful.

Demonstrate

Show the trainee how the task is performed. Demonstrate slowly, and encourage questions. Repeat the demonstration. Provide an opportunity for the trainee to try the process. Watch carefully and give constructive feedback where necessary. Give positive feedback at every opportunity.

Practice Makes Perfect

Once the trainee has learned a new task or skill, allow as much practice as possible. Evaluate the trainee's ability, and reinforce the training in any weak areas. Provide positive feedback and encouragement.

MANAGING AND MOTIVATING EMPLOYEES

Effectively managing employees is a skill acquired through training and practice. Many books have been written on the subject, and courses are regularly offered through educational institutions. If you are hiring or managing staff, you should spend some time reading and taking courses on this topic. By applying some basic principles of respect and encouragement in the development of each staff member as an important individual, you will reap the rewards of loyal, trustworthy, and dependable staff. The following sums up the course on human relations (source: Anonymous):

The 6 most important words: "I admit I made a mistake."

The 5 most important words: "You did a good job."

The 4 most important words: "What is your opinion?"

The 3 most important words: "If you please."

The 2 most important words: "Thank you."

The 1 most important word: "We"

The least important word: "I"

Leadership Style

A leader is one who is in control, takes charge of a situation, and is decisive. A good leader or manager is fair, firm, and consistent, as well as flexible. Being flexible doesn't mean that you have to change your personality. You can be firm and still be friendly; you can be decisive and still be polite. You can give someone more freedom without giving away the company. The better you are at knowing how to treat your employees, the more effective you will be as a manager. And the employer–employee relationship will be more satisfying to both parties.

Hierarchy of Needs

Many theorists believe that people have different need levels in their work environment. They progress from one stage to the next, although some people "plateau" or stay at a certain stage for a period of time before advancing. Briefly, the stages are:

1. The basic or survival level is the starting point. In order to accept a position, a person needs to be assured that the wages offered are sufficient to meet his or her basic needs for survival (food, shelter).
2. A person's security needs relate to job, financial, and health security. These are most often addressed by an employer in a benefits package. Examples include: training and development, tuition fees for night courses, seniority systems, wage incentive plans, profit-sharing plans, insurance, pensions, medical/dental plans.
3. Having satisfied the basic and security needs, a person then seeks to satisfy his or her social needs. Having an opportunity to learn new skills, to make suggestions in his or her area or department, to interact with other staff, to attend staff meetings and be called upon for input are examples of how social needs may be met.
4. The self-esteem needs are satisfied by promotions, praise and recognition, added responsibility, and challenging work. At this final stage, the

employee is working independently, competently, productively, and has a sense of pride in performing at this level.

A manager's job is to recognize what stage the employee is at, and to assist him or her to progress along the ladder to his or her highest level of capability. Pushing too hard may discourage and frustrate staff who have a different learning pace. Effective use of a variety of motivation techniques will foster personal development for the employee, and in turn increase productivity and profits.

Motivation Techniques

You can reduce unwanted employee turnover and the high cost of recruiting, hiring, and training new staff by shifting these costs from hiring new employees to keeping and developing experienced ones. For example, you can motivate an employee to increase productivity by providing opportunities for career development. At the same time, you have improved the worker's skills and shown recognition of the worker's value and aspirations. Following are some additional motivational techniques.

Delegation

Delegation becomes a motivation technique when an employee is assigned an interesting and challenging task, and given the authority to see it through to completion. The person should be given some guidelines within which to perform the task, but left on his or her own to decide the method of accomplishing it. By assigning challenging tasks to an employee, you are addressing the person's need for self-development. You are providing an opportunity for the employee to demonstrate skills such as creativity, resourcefulness, and sales ability. This demonstration of confidence in the individual will most often result in his or her exerting an extra effort to meet your expectations, and perhaps surpass them. When this win–win situation occurs, it is a strong indication to you that the employee is capable and willing to handle greater responsibilities. If, however, this does not occur, do not assume the opposite. Perhaps the guidelines given were unclear, or you were not available to clarify the employee's questions. Or perhaps the task was too major and should have been divided into several stages, with the person reporting to you after each stage of the task.

Besides the obvious benefit of delegation (relieving you of an extra task), you will be encouraging staff to handle more senior responsibilities. Remember, many employees leave their jobs not because they are dissatisfied with the work, but because they are bored and the job no longer provides a challenge for them.

Shared decision-making

It is good management practice to encourage shared decision-making. This is a process whereby employees and management suggest ways to solve a problem, and the decision on which action to take is made by the group. When an employee has an opportunity to contribute ideas on a matter that affects his or her job, and the ideas are listened to and acted upon, the employee develops a sense of value and pride about the job. Often an employee will come up with a suggestion to make a task easier, less stressful, or less time-consuming. Improved job satisfaction and productivity are typically the result when employees are encouraged to personalize their own work space.

When an employee poses a problem and asks you how it should be handled, a suggested response is, "Do you have any suggestions?" Even if you are aware of a solution, encouraging employees to search for solutions will build a more reliable staff, who are prepared to resolve problems when you are not around. At first you will want the individual to report back to you with suggestions. At this point you could discuss the rationale and then jointly make a decision on how to proceed. As you develop confidence in the individual's ability, you should delegate the decision-making responsibility to the individual as well.

Another form is group decision-making. This technique is particularly useful when a problem arises affecting the staff, and the decision to be made may not be a favourable one for all employees. By involving the staff in a group discussion on the problem, and brainstorming possible solutions, everyone becomes aware of the difficulty at hand. As in any brainstorming session, all ideas should be listed (on a blackboard or flipchart, for example) without any value judgments being made. The group would then review the extensive list of suggestions, and highlight those ideas the group feels may be workable. Through this process of elimination, a few gems may emerge. Then the group's decision on the action to be taken is implemented. The benefit of the group discussion and decision-making is that now you have your entire staff working in a concerted effort to bring about a positive result to the problem situation.

Delegation and shared decision-making are only two of several techniques that can be used to erase the line between staff and management and have the two working as one. Increased productivity and profits will result. By monitoring closely the effectiveness of such techniques with various individuals, you soon will be able to identify natural leaders within your staff—those who should be considered for promotion, merit increases, or other forms of recognition.

Incentives

There are numerous incentives which an employer may use to satisfy a person's security needs. These may be earned by the employee after a certain length of time with the company or provided to all employees after the company has concluded a profitable year of business.

Pay increases

Perhaps the most obvious incentive for employees is a pay increase. This is a way to reward employees for their hard work and loyalty to the company. In a company with only one or two employees, the manner in which raises are handled may be less structured than in a company with numerous employees. In the latter situation it will be important to have an established system for reviewing employee performance and assigning pay increases.

A common system for pay increases is: (1) after the successful completion of the initial probation period—typically 3 to 6 months; and (2) annually on the anniversary of the employee's start date. Other companies may be less structured and award merit increases on a random basis. In this situation, it is recognized that each employee is an individual and learns at a different rate. Also, the responsibilities and complexities of the jobs may differ, one requiring a longer training period than another.

Factors that may affect your decision on the amount of the pay increase include:

- the ability of the company to pay more, based on the relative growth of your business over the past year
- the employee's work performance
- pay relationships within your business
- rates of pay for similar jobs in other organizations
- supply and demand for new employees
- cost of living.

Fringe benefits

While it is difficult to relate fringe benefits to employee productivity and job satisfaction, an attractive benefit package will contribute to the image that your organization is a good place to work. This image will attract prospective employees, reduce employee turnover, and favourably influence suppliers and customers.

Mandatory benefits include EI, CPP, Workers' Compensation, vacations, and statutory holidays. This may vary depending upon the province and the type of business (with regard to Workers' Compensation). As noted in an earlier section, an employer has a legal responsibility to provide these paid benefits to employees.

Other benefits will depend on you, your company, your employees, and even your community. The company's ability to pay for the benefits is an initial deciding factor to be considered. Next, you will want to know what incentives your employees would appreciate most. By making a special effort to satisfy individual employee needs, you reinforce the motivational value of the flexible benefit. Employees with young families often vote for good medical/dental plan coverage. If your business is located in a city centre, perhaps a paid parking space is an attractive feature. An employer who wishes to encourage continued staff training and development will frequently offer to pay the cost of courses, seminars, and workshops, and may even permit attendance on company time. Other benefits may include: membership in a professional association, profit sharing or bonuses, stock purchase plans, discounts on merchandise and services, subsidized coffee and meals, or extra vacation time.

Performance Reviews

On a periodic basis and prior to each increase, it is important to review the employee's level of performance in detail. This is an opportunity for you and your employee to objectively review past performance, discuss areas of difficulty, acknowledge positive achievements, and encourage growth and further development in specific areas. Each of these aspects is important to a properly handled performance review. Taking a positive approach in the interview will encourage openness. It will result in constructive feedback being given and received by both parties. Being respectful and sensitive towards the individual, particularly when giving constructive criticism, will also lead to positive results. It is important for you to become involved in helping the employee develop ways to improve, through extra training or backup support or by clarifying procedures. Often the person will have helpful feedback that explains why problems occur. Showing the employee that you are willing to take steps to correct such situations and make the person's job easier will improve morale, productivity, and loyalty.

You may learn that the employee is looking for increased responsibility or has an aptitude for working with equipment presently handled by another employee. Providing the individual with an opportunity to learn new skills will maintain his or her interest and enthusiasm and provide you with a more flexible staff member who is able to cover another area during a vacation or illness absence.

A written performance report should be completed and should provide the following information:

- whether the employee is performing at a satisfactory level
- areas that are handled in an above-average capacity
- areas that require improvement
- specific steps or suggestions for improvement.

Besides the specific aspects of the employee's job description that will need to be reviewed, you will want to consider other areas, such as: attitude (towards customers, peers, supervisors), punctuality (arrival times, days missed), and grooming (standard of dress, personal grooming). Refer to the sample performance review, Sample 23, which may vary depending on the position and your type of business. It is a good practice to give the employee a copy of the performance review and ask him or her to sign the form, verifying the report has been discussed. File the form in the employee's personnel file.

Exit Interview

When an employee resigns from a position in your company, it can be beneficial to meet with the employee and discuss openly his or her reasons for leaving. You could possibly learn straight from the shoulder what an employee really thinks. By listening carefully, you can pick up ideas to improve working conditions and morale and reduce staff turnover.

DISCIPLINING AND FIRING EMPLOYEES

An employer faced with having to fire a long-term employee is much like the disciplining parent who ponders whether it is more upsetting to the parent or the child. While there is certainly no pleasure in firing an employee, it is sometimes necessary in order to regain control of the efficient operation of your business. However, staff turnover is costly to any company. The time and costs involved in recruiting a replacement and retraining can be a major setback for a small company. As well, if the firing is not handled in an appropriate fashion, a very resentful employee may cause a considerable negative impact by speaking poorly of you to your customers and competition or perhaps initiate a wrongful dismissal claim against you.

A win–win situation may be the alternative if you practise constructive discipline techniques. A person whom you may perceive to be a problem employee may respond favourably to your consideration and respect and turn out to be a loyal, dependable employee. As noted under the section on employee motivation, fostering a positive working environment, will reduce staff turnover, and your business will have a much greater chance of success.

Before you undertake any of the following steps, you need to protect yourself by getting customized legal advice in advance from a lawyer who specializes in employment law representing the employer. You can get names from your lawyer referral service for an initial consultation or do a Google search for employment lawyers in your area and make sure you confirm that they specialize in advising employers, not employees. As mentioned in Chapter 4, "Selecting Professional Advisors," you want to have a minimum of three initial consultations to ensure the advice is consistent and to have a better basis for selection of the right lawyer to meet your needs. It is cheap money for peace of mind, and will accelerate your learning curve and confidence.

Constructive Discipline

Step 1: Evaluate the situation

When a performance problem first arises, you should give careful thought to the situation, check out the facts, and plan a course of action that will produce the most favourable results.

What not to do: A situation can be worsened by overreacting, so avoid the temptation of speaking or acting too quickly in a critical manner. Do not show heated emotion or anger. Blaming or chastising the employee in front of others, especially peers or customers, is a serious mistake. Not only will you lose respect in your staff and customers' eyes, but you could leave the door open for a labour relations claim to be filed against you.

What should be done: At the earliest opportunity after the situation has occurred and after you have ensured that your emotions are in check, ask to speak with the employee in private. When you are alone with the employee, make an "I" statement such as, "I feel disappointed about the manner in which that incident was handled." Ask for more information; don't forget, there are two sides to every story. Before you make a judgment, you need the other person's perspective. "Can you explain to me what happened there?" This is the employee's opportunity to speak in his or her own defence without being made to feel defensive. Listen for clues that will identify the root of the problem. Perhaps the employee has never been trained on certain parts of your operation, or has been misinformed about procedures, or has handled matters that way in the past at another company. Or perhaps the employee made a poor judgment in a stressful situation. Maybe he or she is preoccupied with family, financial, or health problems. All of these are forgivable—at least the first time.

If it appears that it was a lack of information or training that caused the problem, be certain to say so to your employee. Immediately plan a time when you can provide the necessary training. Include other staff in the in-service who may also benefit, even if for them it is merely a reminder. In this way, your staff will be able to pull together better as a team.

Before concluding the meeting, you should work out suggestions on how to handle a similar situation in future, so that the employee is left with a clear understanding of what is expected. It may be a good idea to document the correct course of action for your procedures manual.

In some situations, it may be poor judgment rather than lack of training that caused the incident. An example may be that the employee was under the influence of alcohol while on the job. Even in this type of situation, it is important to check out any information that you may be lacking. For example, it may be a special occasion, such as the employee's birthday, and alcohol was consumed at lunch. In any event, you should make the employee aware of the company policy in this regard and explain the negative impact it creates on customers and other staff. In a situation in which the employee's negative attitude has created a problem, a time limit should be established for the employee to work towards correcting the negative behaviour.

Following the meeting, you should document the situation that occurred, the date on which it occurred, the date and time of your discussion with the employee, major points discussed, and suggestions made for improvement. File your notes in the employee's personnel file. Many situations will end here, without any further discussion or discipline being required.

Step 2: Constructive discipline

Unfortunately, not all problems are dealt with as easily and quickly. Employee attitudinal problems tend to be the most difficult to correct, and sometimes where the employee does not demonstrate an effort to change, it is necessary to terminate the employment. It is for these occurrences that your consistency in following through these subsequent steps of constructive discipline is crucial.

A second meeting is necessary if the problem recurs, or a different situation arises based upon a similar attitudinal problem, or if the agreed-upon time frame for correcting the problem has not been met. At this meeting, you will want to refer back to the earlier discussions. Specifically referring to the suggestions for improvement made earlier, ask the employee if they have been practised, and if they proved helpful. Ask if the employee has any other suggestions to add. Stress the negative impact the behavioural trait has on the business, and the necessity for a change in behaviour to take place. State that you want to help the employee make the desired change. Agree upon a time frame that the employee feels is fair for the problem to be corrected.

This time you should document in a memo to the employee the discussions during your meeting, the agreed-upon suggestions for improvement, and the time frame. Have the individual sign a copy of the memo, acknowledging its receipt. Again, place the memo in the employee's personnel file and note on your day calendar the date that was agreed upon for the problem to be corrected.

It is helpful to make interim checkups on the employee, volunteering your assistance if required. Give positive feedback whenever appropriate, indicating to the employee that you are aware of his or her efforts to change.

Step 3: Resolution and positive feedback

Where an employee has made marked improvement and you are satisfied that he or she is performing at a standard acceptable to you, the matter may be concluded. It is helpful to have a brief meeting with the employee to relay your positive feedback and your appreciation for his or her efforts on the company's behalf.

Encourage the employee to come to you at any time with any problems, and suggest that together you can work out a solution. In this way you build loyalty with your employees. A manager should be firm, but also fair and consistent in dealings with staff. Staff need to know that you are consistent in the manner in which you treat problems and in the way you treat all staff members. Showing favouritism to one staff member can lead to the resentment and disloyalty of the others.

At times, human nature being what it is, an employee's performance may slide back to its previous unsatisfactory level. At any time you may need to reopen the matter, make the employee aware of your concerns, and set a new time frame for improvement. This time the period should be a shorter one, since you know the employee is capable of a satisfactory level of performance.

An alternative Step 3: Minimize the damage

If the problem persists beyond the agreed-upon time frame—whether the employee is unable or unwilling to change—you should plan to fire the employee at the earliest possible opportunity. Delay at this point will cause increased harm and disruption to the business and other staff. If you have taken all the appropriate steps, you can reassure yourself that you have acted responsibly as a manager to help the employee; however, you have a responsibility to your business and other staff.

Removing an Employee

While it isn't easy to fire someone, sometimes it must be done for the continuing health of the business. When firing an employee, you must take a number of considerations into account to determine the appropriate approach:

- Is the employee on probation?
- Has the employee been with the company a long time?
- Do you have an employment contract which has a termination clause?
- What impact do provincial or federal employment standards legislation have on the issue?
- What does your lawyer advise you to do in your particular situation?

Firing for just cause

You can dismiss an employee without notice if there is just cause. Depending upon the facts, you can argue that the employee is not entitled to receive severance pay. If the fired employee sues you for wrongful dismissal, you will want to be certain you have kept a thorough record of all incidents leading up to the dismissal. Some of the most common reasons for dismissal with just cause include:

- incompetence or insolent behaviour
- serious misconduct, willful disobedience, willful neglect of duty

- theft, dishonesty, fraud
- intoxication on the job
- cumulative effect: no one act would be sufficient, but when several acts are combined, could amount to just cause
- chronic absence from work and/or lateness.

When you are dealing with dismissal decisions, it may be prudent to first discuss the matter with your lawyer. If your lawyer is unfamiliar with labour law, seek the opinion of one with specific expertise. An informed legal opinion might cost $200–$400 for a 1-hour consultation, but could save you thousands of dollars that a bad decision might cost you, along with all the negative energy and wasted time.

Lay-off

When a staff lay-off is necessary, you are required to give reasonable notice or payment in lieu of notice, depending on your employee's length of service with the company. Your local employment standards office will be able to clarify what the legislation requires in your situation. For a long-term employee, the rough rule of thumb is from 1 week to 1 month's compensation for each year of service depending on responsibility. Examples of firing without cause include:

- corporate reorganization due to company merger or buy-out
- technological changes leading to redundancy
- downsizing of operation.

Delivering the news

The manner in which the firing or lay-off is done is an important consideration. It should be done in private and handled carefully, calmly, and unemotionally. The employee should be treated with respect and given an opportunity to provide an explanation, if appropriate. Don't beat around the bush. You should tell the employee that he or she is fired within the first few statements made. Again, it is important to make "I" statements such as, "I am disappointed things didn't work out here." "You" statements tend to be accusational and may have to be defended later. Never lose your temper. An abrupt, heat-of-the-moment dismissal seldom stands up to outside scrutiny and is usually noted with concern by other employees. The employee should be able to retain his or her dignity and gain a complete comprehension of the reasons for the employment termination.

You should be aware of the probation period as set out in your provincial labour standards legislation. For instance, in some provinces you will have to pay an employee who has worked more than 3 months the necessary severance pay and any outstanding vacation or holiday pay on his or her last day of work.

To avoid penalties, a Record of Employment form will have to be completed and sent to the HRSDC office within 1 week of termination.

Wrongful dismissal

The previous formula is, of course, the ideal. Unfortunately, too many managers are not committed to taking the time required to work with employees. Often the consequence is that they end up spending the time later defending their actions. If you fire for the wrong reasons, or without sufficient warnings, the situation can be turned against you by the fired employee, who may make a claim against you for an alleged:

- breach of provincial or federal human rights legislation
- breach of provincial or federal labour standards legislation
- defamation of character
- wrongful dismissal.

A damaging or negative assessment of a former employee—either written or spoken—may rebound in a lawsuit for defamation of character. It is important to think carefully before you speak or write in negative terms about past and present employees.

Your main protection is, as outlined earlier, careful record-keeping. Complete itemized documentation of the employee's incompetence, shortcomings, misdeeds, and failure to correct problems is what will be required to defend a wrongful dismissal suit.

Chapter 12

Business Communication Equipment

Never buy what you do not want because it is cheap; it will be costly to you.

— Thomas Jefferson

Business communication has gone through a massive transformation over the past three decades. If you wanted to talk to someone across town or across the country, you'd pick up the phone or write a letter. If the message was urgent, you might send a fax. Now it seems that office-to-office communication is always urgent. E-mail has become the primary and preferred means of communicating, although texting and social media such as Facebook or Twitter have been added to the mix and are beginning to rival e-mail for communication, especially among the younger generation.

The speed of getting the message to the other party has replaced the importance of overall presentation. E-mail has replaced the person-to-person contact of the telephone in many instances. Because people have such busy schedules, it often became a matter of "telephone tag" trying to connect. Instead, e-mail ensured that your message was received intact, was sent when you had the time and concentration, and was received and responded to when the recipient was available. That still holds true for the most part, but even that is now being impacted by smartphones and tablet computers that allow you to access the Web, send e-mails and texts rapidly, communicate instantly through social media, and essentially be "always on." While this may be a problem for some in terms of work–life balance, new communications technologies and online services have reduced the cost of operating a business by a large factor. With so much of business involving knowledge and information today, business communication equipment that used to cost more than $20,000 can now merely involve a laptop computer and a smartphone, for a total cost of a couple of thousand dollars.

Further, the plethora of software applications available today enables a small business owner to perform almost all the functions (financial management, strategy, marketing, human resources, and operations) required to manage the business. Specific but occasional needs, such as colour graphic presentations or shipping, can be served at business service centres such as Kinko's (now FedEx Office). Advancing technology also means that the business itself has been largely freed from traditional offices and equipment. This has given rise to the "Starbucks Start-up" phenomenon, in which business owners and employees generally work on computers and other devices at home and meet in coffee shops regularly to share information, strategize, and create and build a company. Many retailers no longer need large stores stocked with thousands of dollars worth of equipment; instead they can sell their wares online through a website. Even distribution can be performed largely through the Web, with only trucks and the postal service needed to physically ship products.

The speed with which the computer and communications industries are changing means that software and equipment you choose for your business today will likely need to be upgraded within a short 2 or 3 years. Therefore, when selecting a computer or other piece of equipment, it is less important to spend a lot of time searching for the ideal configuration. Within a matter of a couple of months new products will be available that will make that solution less than ideal. Prices are typically very competitive as well. Therefore, it is best to shop for what you need today. Opt for the fastest and most powerful computer and smartphone to meet your requirements for the present and foreseeable period of time. Trust that by the time your needs change, different software and hardware solutions will be available.

In addition to computers, some businesses may still require other equipment such as photocopiers, fax systems, telephone systems, etc. Each item, depending upon the cost and your usage, will require varying amounts of time and research.

TIPS ON SELECTING EQUIPMENT

The best advice that can be given is to do your research, know what equipment and features are available, and draw up a feature comparison chart before you shop. This process can be aided by the vast amount of information online about almost every product or service in existence. If you start talking to salespeople before you have done your homework, chances are you will spend a lot more time than necessary listening to enthusiastic sales pitches and become confused about the features you actually require.

Assessing Your Needs

If you are replacing a piece of equipment, what is your present volume or use? What problems or frustrations do you have with the equipment? What is your cost per usage? If you are searching out the equipment for the first time, what are your anticipated needs? What applications of use or special features do you think will enhance your efficiency and productivity? Are there business service centres or online services that can replace equipment used only occasionally? Is the equipment "must have" or "nice to have"?

List in priority order the features that are essential. Do you anticipate your needs increasing drastically over the next few years in volume or types of applications? In addition to equipment needs, you may have supplier needs. For instance, you may prefer to deal with an established and reputable company or directly with the manufacturer of the equipment. You may need a supplier that can provide initial and ongoing training support and equipment servicing. The amount of your equipment budget should also be listed with your needs.

Comparing What's Available

Once you are aware of your projected needs, identify at least three or four models of equipment or software applications that are designed to handle those needs. With the features and needs that you have prioritized listed down the left-hand side of a page, write the names of the three or four suppliers you have chosen and the respective model names across the top of the page in vertical column format, as shown in Sample 24. You may use this chart for note-taking when talking to suppliers about the specific equipment features. In this way, you will remain focused on your needs rather than being distracted by a salesperson's or marketer's emphasis on features that may be of minimal or no benefit to you.

Perhaps you made some initial inquiries and comparisons over the telephone. However, when buying software or a major piece of equipment, insist on a thorough demonstration to satisfy yourself that the equipment will do the job. Some suppliers, particularly of software, will allow you a free trial period in which you may use equipment at your place of business for a few days or a week. Photocopiers and colour printers fall into this category. More complex equipment like computers and telephone systems can require initial training and special installation before they can be operated. Much software has a "try-before-you-buy" feature that allows you to test the software and determine if it meets your needs. Many software packages offer "light," "medium," and "heavy" user options that provide a range of solutions to serve different requirement levels.

Once your chart has been filled in with the necessary comparative data, highlight those factors which most closely meet your needs. For example, if your business involves graphics, a colour printer would likely be essential. But they vary considerably in resolution and print quality. So you should highlight on your chart the model which demonstrated the quality feature you prefer. Perhaps you liked this feature equally well on another model; then highlight both. As well as highlighting the best-liked features, you should also draw an X through those items with which you were not impressed or which did not meet your needs. Be careful you are making "apple-to-apple" comparisons. Perhaps one supplier's feature is included in the price, while another's is considered an add-on feature which may then raise the price of the equipment beyond your budget. Don't hesitate to check back with the salesperson if you are unsure on any items. By the time you have completed this exercise, it should be easier for you to decide on the model or software that would best suit your needs.

Training, Service, and Supplies

Depending upon the type of equipment you are selecting, training and service support may have been listed with your essential needs. However, it is important to make specific reference to these factors before you make your final decision. Especially with more complex equipment, you will want to know the answers to these questions:

- If training is required, is it provided as part of the purchase price? At your place of business or theirs?
- Are training and operations manuals included?
- Will the vendor retrain new employees if you have staff turnover? Is assistance available, such as a toll-free help line or online support, during business hours or 24 hours a day, 7 days a week?
- If service is required, is it done at your office or theirs?

Many responsible suppliers will provide unlimited assistance to ensure that you are making effective use of their equipment. After all, this may lead to future purchases of other product lines or possibly word-of-mouth referrals to others regarding your satisfaction with their equipment and support.

For servicing the equipment, you will need to know the length of the warranty on the equipment, and how much a service contract will cost you after the warranty period has expired. What is their hourly service rate if you opt not to enter into a service contract? What is the company's response time to service calls? Emergency calls?

Some equipment suppliers are also in the business of selling expendable supplies needed to operate their equipment, such as photocopier toner and developer or laser printer cartridges. You should ask whether you are obliged to purchase your supplies from them, and at what cost. Some do insist on this for quality and performance control of the equipment.

Negotiating the Purchase Contract

You are now ready to make your final decision. Perhaps your comparison chart has helped you to narrow down your selection to two choices which are very close in features and price. Keep in mind that the office equipment business is extremely competitive, with many aggressive salespeople willing to put up a good fight to earn their sales commission. This being the case, a salesperson may be willing to reduce the price of the equipment in order to make the sale. Others who may have little flexibility on lowering the price may offer a free starter kit of supplies, a free training course for an additional staff member, free service on the equipment for a 1-year period, etc. Using good negotiating skills you may be able to strike a favourable bargain, while at the same time acquiring the equipment of your choice.

A word of caution in relation to price: it is not a good business decision to purchase equipment or software that fits your budget but doesn't fit your needs. This will only lead to increased costs and frustration. Perhaps an alternative may be to lease or rent for a monthly fee, rather than purchase, what you require, if it would otherwise be unaffordable. Following are some factors to know when leasing equipment, as well as other alternatives to buying equipment.

ALTERNATIVES TO BUYING EQUIPMENT

Rental Equipment

Some vendors have rental arrangements for their equipment. While the cost tends to be higher, it generally includes delivery, installation, initial training and ongoing support, instruction manuals, and servicing of the equipment. Because technology is rapidly changing, the rental option protects you from being left with obsolete or outdated equipment within a relatively short period of time. Things you should look for in the rental contract include flexibility of upgrading to a different model of equipment, duration of the rental agreement (if it can be cancelled prior to the end of the term, and what penalties would be levied), and whether you are required to carry insurance on the equipment for fire or theft. You may find, however, that some vendors are not prepared to rent their equipment. An obvious reason is that they do not have a market for the used rental equipment.

In today's Web-centric world, software is also being increasingly "rented" online. Called Software as a Service (SaaS), this option is often favoured by businesses that require very complex and expensive software but find the high fees difficult to justify. In the SaaS model, customers sign up at a website and gain access to accounting software, for example. Their unique data is stored on the company's servers and resides "in the cloud," as it is called, and so can be accessed by any computer anywhere. This also ensures that it is more secure. Rental software is always kept up to date, and so does not need replacing and is also more tax efficient, in that it is fully deductible, whereas owned software is treated as a depreciating asset. However, some businesses do not like to hand over their data to someone else, and so prefer to purchase and install software (some of which can be downloaded) onto their own computers.

Lease Equipment

The difficulty that many business owners have in finding sufficient financing has caused many to look at leasing as an alternative financing arrangement for acquiring telephone systems, photocopiers, office furniture, store fixtures, cars, trucks, and so on. Leasing provides 100% financing, which allows the growing company to conserve its capital. The realization that profits are earned through the use of the equipment, rather than ownership of the equipment, is turning more people to leasing. Before entering into a lease arrangement, however, you should be well aware of the advantages and disadvantages, and the different types of leases and lease options that are available.

Types of leases

The finance lease or conventional true lease is usually written for a term that does not exceed the economic life of the equipment. It usually provides for the following:

- periodic payments
- ownership of the equipment reverts to the lessor (the leasing company) at the end of the lease term
- the lease is noncancellable, and you have a legal obligation to continue payments to the end of the term
- the lessee (the person leasing) agrees to service the equipment.

If the lease has an option to purchase at the end of the lease term, it is in effect a conditional sales agreement. The purchase price is usually a percentage of the original price, or a dollar figure, and is negotiated at the time the lease is signed.

Leases are offered by commercial banks, insurance companies, finance companies, leasing companies, as well as equipment manufacturers.

Advantages of leasing

- The obvious advantage to leasing is acquiring the use of the equipment without making a large initial cash outlay.
- A lease requires no down payment, while a loan often requires that you contribute 25% or more of the purchase price.
- Leasing may help keep credit lines open for other business activity requiring financing, unlike a loan that may limit additional debts.
- A lease spreads payments over a longer period (which means they will be lower) than loans permit.

- A lease may provide a flexible payment schedule dependent upon your company's earnings, if your business is seasonal.
- A lease provides protections against the risk of equipment obsolescence, since you can get rid of the equipment at the end of the lease. However, with the speed of change in technology today, you may want to upgrade before the end of the lease: ask if this feature is included.
- There are tax benefits in leasing, since the lease payments are fully deductible as operating expenses. Check with your accountant on this point, as tax regulations are always changing.

Disadvantages of leasing

- Leasing usually costs more because of the high lease rates spread over a longer term.
- In a lease, there is no equity buildup in the equipment, since you don't own the asset. Some leases will provide a buy-out clause at the end of the term.
- A lease is a long-term legal obligation which is usually noncancellable, without you having to pay out the balance of the lease or incur a substantial penalty. Look at the fine print, and make sure your expectations and options are clarified in writing to protect yourself.

The lease agreement

A lease agreement is a legal document which carries a long-term obligation. You must be thoroughly informed of your obligations under the lease, and should consult your lawyer and/or accountant before you sign the agreement. Be reasonably sure that the lease arrangements are the best you can get, that the equipment is what you need, and that the term is what you want. Check into the lessor's financial condition and reputation. Once the agreement is struck, it's almost impossible to change.

Major provisions in a lease will include:

- the specific nature of the financing agreement
- the payment amount
- the term of the agreement
- disposition of the equipment at the end of the term
- schedule of the value of the equipment for insurance and settlement purposes in case of damage or destruction
- who is responsible for maintenance renewal options
- cancellation penalties
- buy-out option at end of the lease term special provisions.

Some of these factors may be negotiable, so do your research and compare lease rates, for example. The credit strength of your business will be a factor to the leasing company, who will grade you as a high, moderate, or low risk.

Business centres

For those who cannot justify the purchase of a piece of office equipment, due to minimal use, business centres can offer access to office equipment on a user-fee basis. A business centre (also known as a packaged office or executive suite) is a shared-office concept that caters to small businesses that do not require full-time use of a receptionist, boardroom, photocopier, fax machine, and so on. We discussed business centres in Chapter 9, so this is a brief overview. Typically, a business centre is equipped with a variety of state-of-the-art equipment and offers use of the facilities on a user-fee basis to in-house and outside clients. They are listed in the *Yellow Pages* print and online under the heading "Office and Desk Rental Space." Also, do a Google search. A business centre could become a one-stop shop for your business needs such as computer service, photocopying, printing, fax messages, and telephone answering and voice mail service. Descriptions of these services follow.

Computer services

Experienced computer operators will type your documents (mailing lists, business plan, promotional letters) using industry-standard software. Staff are trained and experienced in a variety of computer applications and proper business formats. You are paying not only for the typist's time, but also for use of the equipment and the quality and professional image of the work performed. You may decide to type your own in-house routine memos and to have a business centre create your important presentations and correspondence.

Fax service

Since faxing is so rare today, you might not require a fax machine, as you would normally scan documents or signed letters from your printer and send them as e-mail attachments. If you do have to send an occasional fax, go to a local business centre or subscribe to an online fax-to-e-mail service.

Photocopier

The combination of computers and scanners/printers means photocopiers are also rarer than they once were for most small offices, although companies involved in graphics may need them for comparative work. Of course, it all depends on your type of unique business needs. If you require bulk photocopying, you can use a business centre's machine for a small fee.

Corporate identity or virtual office

If you are working from home and prefer to have an official business address for the professional and stable image it creates, a business centre will permit you to use its address as your place of business. You would, therefore, receive mail and courier deliveries along with a telephone answering service for a fixed monthly fee. The rate may also include limited use of an office or boardroom where you could meet with your clients and conduct your business. This type of service is usually referred to as a corporate or virtual office identity package as it provides your business with a professional identity with all the appearances (staff and facilities) of a full-time office, but without the cost of one.

Full-time office

At a particular growth stage of your business, you may decide that a full-time office in a business centre will enhance your efficiency and productivity. The primary advantages include:

- no financial outlay required for furniture or equipment
- reduced risk, as a lease may be monthly, semi-annual, or annual
- experienced office staff without staff cost or administration (hiring, training, employee benefits)
- access to state-of-the-art office equipment, use of the boardroom and reception area
- more time available to conduct your business, as the centre is responsible for maintaining the premises, ordering supplies, servicing equipment, and so on.

Whether you require occasional or regular use of the facilities of a business centre, you should check around and compare not only rates, but also quality of staff performance and image of the centre. Remember, the image that you see when you first walk into a business centre is the same image that one of your clients will have of your own business. Business centres cater to different types of businesses, so you will want to be in an environment that is closely suited to your needs.

You are now aware of your equipment options: to purchase, rent, lease, or use the shared facilities of a business centre. Following is an overview of different types of equipment, their approximate costs, and how they can increase your efficiency.

COMPUTERS

Today, it's almost impossible to survive in business without computers. Certainly, you won't grow without one, because a computer performs most business functions. However, you must remember that a computer is just a tool — you need to know what jobs you want it to do before you decide what to buy or lease. You should list the jobs you want the computer to do for you, review the benefits that you will gain, and look at the costs involved and time that will be saved.

Computer Uses

A computer can be a valuable asset to the administration and management of your business. It will speed up basic administrative work and enable you to access more information on which to base management decisions. The following are the more common business computer applications:

- general information—storage and retrieval
- customer profiles
  - profiles on existing and potential suppliers and their products employee personnel records
- word-processing and graphics applications
- industry information
- communication
  - e-mail messaging
  - Internet faxing
  - no-charge long distance calling (through voice-over-Internet protocol)
- social media messaging
- online marketing
- operational manuals and business process guides
- accounting
  - sales invoices and purchase orders
  - accounts receivable and payable
  - general ledger
  - payroll
  - equipment depreciation
  - tax preparation
- management
  - monitoring movement of inventory in order to maximize turnover valuing inventory to assist in monitoring profitability
  - analyzing sales and profitability (which products or lines are the most profitable, which customers contribute most profit to the operation, which salespeople are the most effective)
  - preparing monthly financial statements and spreadsheets.
  - managing staff
- planning
  - preparing financial budgets
  - projecting cash flow analysis

- forecasting sales
- scheduling production runs
- strategic planning.

Once you have completed the list of jobs you want the computer to do for you, detail the information that is required for each application. You will need to quantify each application to know the size or capacity of the computer system you will need. For instance, how many customer accounts do you have? How many sales invoices are generated monthly? How many suppliers and creditors do you have? How many items in inventory?

The next step is to review your list of computer applications and place them in priority order: must have, should have, would like to have. When you are selecting computer hardware or software, start with your essential priority applications. Other nonimmediate needs, such as graphics and design, can be subcontracted to specialized companies . The benefits of using the Internet for doing business are covered in Chapter 19.

Hardware and Software

Selecting the right computer system is very important, so be prepared to devote time to your deliberations. Because this is a very technical subject, seek the advice of an independent computer consultant to make a recommendation on the appropriate hardware (the physical equipment) and software (the disks and programs) for your needs. The consultant may also assist with the initial training and start-up programming.

Today there are software packages available for almost every business function and every industry sector. Software packages are designed to suit many different businesses, and therefore are made as generic as possible, but function-specific software, usually in the form of online applications or mini-programs—"apps"—is becoming more popular.

Your software program selections will determine your hardware needs. You don't need a computer any bigger, faster, more sophisticated, or more expensive than is required to handle your software. It must, however, have the storage capacity to house the programming for each software program you intend to install and to allow for projected growth. Some questions to consider include:

- What operating system does the software run on? How much memory is required?
- Is there backup capability, such as backup drives, portable hard drives, or online backup and storage)? Without them, in the event of a computer problem, you could lose all your valuable business records.

- What type of printer do you require? If you expect to be producing high-quality reports and proposals, a laser printer is recommended. Will you require a colour printer? A quality ink-jet printer may meet your needs and budget over the cost of a colour laser printer.

Pitfalls to Avoid

Cost

One of the most common pitfalls is purchasing a computer system with inadequate capacity, or one which cannot grow with your business. To add additional storage capacity or new software programs after purchase can greatly add to the cost.

Inadequate software

There are numerous software packages available. Select the software that will handle your applications with ease, based on research, online reviews, and recommendations from those in your field.

Starting with complex applications

Selecting a difficult or complex application as your first computer application will cause frustration and much wasted time. You and your staff should learn by implementing more basic functions and attend courses to properly learn the software and its capabilities.

Poor documentation

Instruction manuals which are not "user friendly" will cause considerable delays for staff learning the software. An important consideration when you are selecting software is an instruction manual that is clear, concise, and easily understood without overuse of computer jargon. Section tabs, an extensive index, and a help section assist the operator to quickly find the necessary information.

FAX AND SCANNERS

Once it was impossible to function in business without a fax machine. Today, they are in some respects anachronisms, used primarily by some government agencies, health organizations, and legal firms. If you do require fax service, subscribe to an online service which faxes via e-mail. Ensure that it supplies you with a fax number for return faxes (which also go to your computer in the form of an e-mail). Since you'll probably be purchasing a scanner or scanner–printer combination for your business, you can scan in any documents and attach the resulting graphic to an e-mail which is then sent to the fax service. A Canadian service that operates internationally is MyFax (myfax.com).

PHONES

Special Features

Telephone companies are marketing an expanding range of invaluable and versatile telephone features that can make your business more efficient and profitable. The following is a brief guide to the features offered to small business and home business subscribers in three key areas. Inquire about continuing new advances.

Custom calling

- **Ident-A-Call.** Allows several different phone numbers, each with a distinctive ring, to be included on one phone line.
- **Call waiting.** Emits a beep when you are on the phone to tell you another caller is trying to reach you and, with a custom phone, allows you to put one call on hold, answer the second call, and switch back to the first caller.
- **Three-way calling.** Enables you to set up a three-party conference call without operator assistance.
- **Call forwarding.** Allows you to send your calls to another phone number, either automatically or if not answered within three rings, or if your line is busy because you are on the phone.
- **Speed calling.** Allows you to place a call with a short code.

Call management

- **Name display.** An added option to call display, which identifies the name of a caller.
- **Call return.** Advises you when a busy line is free and lets you return the last call placed or received at the touch of a button.
- **Call display.** Shows you an incoming caller's number on an electronic display screen before you answer the phone.
- **Call screen.** Allows you to block calls from those from whom you do not wish to receive calls. Callers from those numbers hear a recorded message that you are not currently accepting calls.
- **Call again.** Keeps trying a busy number for you for up to 30 minutes and rings you when the busy number is free.

TeleMessage

- **Call answer.** Automatically answers calls if you are on the phone or unavailable.
- **Family/extension call answer.** Provides personal answering service for up to four people who use the same line.

- **Voice mail.** Allows customers to send voice mail messages to you directly. It creates a better impression than a telephone answering machine and is far more versatile.

Cellular Telephones

Cellular telephones have become a standard communications tool in many businesses and have become a competitive necessity when people are on the road constantly and quick communications are needed. Small business owners are able to conduct business from their cars, remote locations, or just about anywhere. Most models offer call waiting, call forwarding, conference calls, as well as message-taking while you are away from the phone.

Increasingly, "smartphones" and their brethren, tablet computers, are taking over from traditional cellular phones and are adding a new dimension to business operations. Most smartphones or tablets have access to thousands of apps. Apps are available for communication and marketing, finance, strategy, inventory control, and many other business functions. Predictions are that a combination of smartphone and tablet computer will be the only computer people need in the near future.

To make computers or tablets truly mobile tools, cell phone companies also sell data-sticks, which link a device to their networks so that users can access the Internet through their smartphone plans. Data costs can accumulate rapidly, however, so these should be used sparingly.

Pagers

Once dominant in business as a communications device, pagers have largely been replaced by cellular phones. However, they are still used in health care and critical function situations, such as ambulance services and firefighting, where direct response is not required or cellular phone service is interrupted.

Automatic Answering Systems

In any business in which the telephone is a prime source of new business, careful attention should be paid to the manner in which the phone is answered during business hours. Thousands of dollars of advertising can be wasted if your business telephone is left unattended or answered inappropriately. In a one-person business, you must recognize that you will not be available to answer calls at all times. Therefore, you need an efficient backup system that will ensure that callers are greeted with courtesy, and an accurate message is taken. When you use an automatic answering system, the recorded message should be appropriate to your type of business and kept as brief as possible, so that callers don't become impatient and hang up. Most answering systems today are part of the telephone service package, but some businesses still prefer answering machines. Whichever, they can be a godsend for the busy business operator. The benefits of voice mail are discussed in Chapter 21, "Time and Stress Management."

ELECTRONIC CASH REGISTERS

Often referred to as point-of-sale electronics, this type of cash register is tied into a centralized computer for pricing, upgrading inventory control, reordering, and also handling credit checks. For operations with frequent sales, such as retail outlets, the cost advantages are clear: the reliability and accuracy of the record-keeping, the luxury of having daily sales reports automatically generated, and reduced staff time. Improved customer service is an added benefit. Electronic cash registers and the accompanying computer software and hardware have been customized by vendors for specific industries (e.g., the auto parts business). Such vendors also provide training and service support.

Chapter 13

Marketing

I didn't invent the hamburger. I just took it more seriously than anyone else.

— Ray Kroc (founder of McDonald's)

Marketing is an essential part of any business operation. Every business obviously needs customers in order to succeed. Marketing means understanding your customers and their needs. Marketing is also the process of selling what the market wants to buy, not what you want to sell. The function of marketing is comprehensive and includes such factors as researching, pricing, advertising, and selling. In addition, if you are a manufacturer or distributor, it would include such activities as product design, packaging, and labelling.

To be successful at marketing you must understand your potential market thoroughly. This includes understanding the demographic (age, income levels, employment, class) and psychographic (interests, attitudes, lifestyles, activities) aspects of the customers that you wish to attract to your business. You have to know your personal strengths and weaknesses, as well as those of your business and your competitors. You have to know how to buy and sell your product to make a profit from your specific market and how to communicate the benefits of your product or service to the market. You also need to know your overall business plan.

You will be able to help yourself by finding out as much information as you can about your markets on an ongoing basis and using that information to make decisions in the following areas.

- how to successfully introduce a new product, service, or business, or expand an existing business
- how to cope with changes that may occur, including those in the economy, people's tastes, preferences and attitudes, and population size and makeup
- how to determine your business potential in a realistic and objective fashion
- how to keep old customers and attract new ones
- how to increase the efficiency of the business by concentrating on what you do best, and thereby increase profits
- how to decide if you want to export your product or service. Refer to Chapter 14, "Export/Import."

THE MARKETING PLAN

The marketing plan is an action plan that you put in writing. It helps you determine the various factors and steps involved in performing the marketing function. The marketing plan must be coordinated with all the other business decisions outlined in the business plan and involved in the running of the business. These would include:

- financial decisions
- inventory decisions
- personnel and staffing decisions
- buying decisions
- decisions relating to bookkeeping and accounting systems
- production decisions, if you are a manufacturer
- distribution decisions
- location decisions
- pricing decisions
- decisions on how to deal with competitors and place the company in a unique position to attract customers
- layout and display decisions for retailers
- decisions on means of communicating to the public, including advertising and promotion
- decisions on personal selling.

From a marketing perspective, the successful small business owner achieves maximum profit with the right "marketing mix" providing the right product at the right price in the right place with the right amount of promotion. Marketing decisions are therefore centred around these four Ps, (some marketers now include a fifth P—people) among others. Poor decisions regarding any one of the four could easily lead to business failure.

The next section on components of marketing provides an overview of the key issues that one has to consider in preparing a marketing plan.

THE COMPONENTS OF MARKETING

Components of marketing that you have to consider include defining the type of business you are in, identifying your customers, researching your market, locating your business, pricing your service or product, communicating to your market, selecting your promotional mix, determining your market budget, and measuring your marketing success.

Defining Your Business

One of the first steps you have to take is to determine exactly what your business is going to be. For example, are you going to be a manufacturer, wholesaler, distributor, or retailer? Or are you going to offer a product or service? Do you intend to work part-time or full-time in your business? Do you intend to work out of your home or out of an office? These factors have a considerable bearing on your marketing plan.

The matter of selecting the right product is naturally a critical one. The term *product* could also include the concept of a service. Many service businesses refer to the packaging of their service as a product. When you define your product strategy, there are many considerations, such as design, brand name, packaging, and other factors. Service strategies have concerns, such as image, credibility, and consistency. Although there are similarities between product and service marketing, there are also differences.

Establishing a positive business image

A professional image and businesslike approach are important for any type of business. Ask yourself: How do I make my decision to patronize those businesses and services that I do? How are my impressions developed? How does my perception of the image of that business influence my continued patronage?

Think of your reaction to another question. Let's assume you see an ad for a business offering a product. The ad has a post office box as an address and a price for the product. You phone the number and a telephone answering machine responds and requests that you leave a message. What would be your initial impression of the business? One of stability, reliability, quality? Would you send money to the address for the product? Would you phone back again? Probably not. This is a good example of an "image" problem that could have been avoided by a different approach.

Some of the factors that make up the image your business conveys include:

- **Name.** The name of your business is particularly important. Keep it short and easy to spell, pronounce, and remember, and make sure it presents the image you want to convey.

  Be sure to check in the telephone listings or through an online search to see whether anyone else is using the same name, and check with the partnership and corporate registry in your province to make sure no one else has registered the name. See Chapter 5 for more information about the legal implications of your business name.
- **Type of legal structure.** The three types of legal structure (discussed in Chapter 5) are proprietorship, partnership, and incorporated company. Incorporated companies are identified by the word "Incorporated,"

"Limited," or "Corporation" (or the abbreviated form) at the end of the company name. If you are dealing with other corporations, you may be at an image disadvantage if you are not incorporated. For some, it may create the impression that you don't have much business depth or longevity, or it may divulge unnecessarily that your firm is in an early stage of business evolution.

- **Address.** Your address does create an image. It could be a positive or negative one, depending on your type of business. If you work in a metropolitan area, a Canada Post office box address may create a "transient image" (e.g., P.O. Box 12345, Station "A," Anytown, Canada). This is not recommended, as there are better options. Obviously this would not be the case in a rural area, where postal box numbers are the norm.

If it is important for you to project a business image to corporate clients, renting a mailing address service could be an option to consider. There are various types. One option is a packaged office company. Offices are rented out and "business ID" packages are provided for people who want to have a business image and address.

Essentially, you can present the business address, telephone number, and e-mail and website addresses on your stationery and business cards. You may also want to include a link to your LinkedIn profile to further establish your business image. Your mail would be either forwarded or picked up by you, according to the arrangements that you have made. It is common to use a telephone answering service at the same location to ensure that your business address is in all telephone listings and to consolidate your office needs. Look in the *Yellow Pages* print or online under "Offices for Rent." Do a Google search with the keywords.

Another option is to rent a box from a mailbox rental company. Many of these companies are franchises, with office locations throughout North America, in case you want to have a U.S. business presence. Mail Boxes Etc. is the primary example. These businesses are often located in business parks. They frequently offer other services as well, such as copying, desktop publishing, and sending and receiving courier parcels on your behalf. If you have a mailbox which you show as, for example, "#150–240 Front Street, Anytown, Canada," this will create the impression that it is a suite number. If you go to clients or customers, and not the other way around, this format could work well for you. Look for a location that is near you, and ideally one with a 24-hour/7-day access. You can find this type of business by doing a Google search for mailbox rentals in your city.

You may wish to consider the above options, in other words, an address other than your home address, for a variety of reasons. For example, for convenience (e.g., courier parcels if you are not home during the day);

for keeping your own address confidential; for image, privacy, or security reasons; or for business marketing reasons. Another reason could be for the purpose of your business licence.

- **Telephone.** For most businesses, the telephone is the most important means of communication. Your selection of telephone equipment and how you answer the phone will have a profound effect on your image. Some general telephone tips for people operating a business from home can be found in Chapter 12.
- **E-mail address.** You should have an e-mail address. Your customers or clients will expect it. Your e-mail address can be connected to your website. Alternatively, you can obtain an e-mail address from numerous sources: Google Canada, Yahoo Canada, Hotmail, and through Internet Service Providers (ISPs).However, generic e-mail addresses from online providers such as Yahoo and Hotmail can convey the impression of temporariness and of something to hide.
- **Website.** Unless your business is based almost solely on personal connection, your business must have its own website. For many businesses today, the website is the company's primary means of conducting business. For most other businesses, a website can be used for a wide variety of business reasons, for example, product sales, promotion, organization, or public relations. Refer to Chapter 19, " Using the Internet for Business Success." You can offer surveys to site visitors as a form of research feedback. You can also arrange to have your site linked from other related, noncompetitive sites. There are also other techniques to get interactive feedback, such as a newsletter that is e-mailed out to a database list.
- **Stationery, logo, and promotional materials.** The colour and quality of the letterhead and envelopes, as well as the size and type of printing, will create definite impressions. If it fits your business image, you may decide to use a unique and creative logo design or a colour of ink other than the standard black. The format and quality of the type on your letters also creates an image, so make sure you use a good quality printer.

A logo makes your business distinctive and memorable. You may either design your own or have one designed for you by designers who work through several online freelancer sites such as Elance or freelancer.com. "Clip art" logos can be purchased online and from commercial stationers and printers. It's generally a good practice to avoid cheap or free clip art. It can make your business look amateurish and small-time.

The logo should create a graphic image or representation of your business product or service. Use it to provide a coordinated image on all your printed and online material. Make sure your promotional material is professional in appearance. Again, if you have no design experience, enlist the help of someone who does, so you can avoid the "homemade" look. You may want to test the effectiveness of the message on different types of brochures and websites before committing to one design.

- **Dress.** Dress to reflect your business image when meeting people If you are a tradesman, for example, you would dress in practical, casual, and clean working clothes. If you are meeting with your banker, lawyer, accountant, or consultant, you should dress in appropriate attire. You want to look well-groomed, successful, and self-confident. If most of your business is online, dress can be more relaxed. However, it's a good idea to have different "work" and "off-work" dress styles. This helps to mentally separate the two parts of your life.
- **Workspace.** How much time, effort, and money you put into the appearance and contents of your workplace will, of course, depend on whether clients will be meeting you at an office or visiting your house, and the type of business you are running. At the very least, however, you will want your surroundings to be comfortable and conducive to the work you will be doing there. If you are going to have business visitors, be aware of such factors as washroom facilities, privacy, quietness, comfortable surroundings, pleasing furniture, plants, attractive and tasteful wall pictures, and a neat and orderly office. If you have a telephone answering service, have them take your calls while you are meeting with clients, so you are not interrupted. Look at your business premises through your client's eyes. What image is conveyed? Is that the image consistent with the one you want to convey?

Identifying your customers

By segmenting out the groups of people who will buy your products or services, you will be able to fine-tune how best to sell to that target group. Your target group will be people or businesses who have something in common. The group may be a very small, specialized segment or a very large one. Consumer markets may have similar characteristics, such as their educational level, type of occupation, income bracket, and lifestyle. Other factors, such as age, marital status, ethnic origin, and religious orientation, may also have a bearing.

Factors that may affect all markets include customers' buying patterns, their geographic location, and their priorities in terms of decision-making.

Depending on your goals and objectives, the preceding factors may or may not be relevant to your needs. You will have to determine other common areas of interest for the market that you are considering. One of the main purposes of defining your potential customer base is to find a market that might be underserviced. The more information that you have about your target market, the better you will be able to develop your marketing plan. There are several approaches in attempting to market to a target group.

Positioning
You want to position your business or your product or service in the minds of customers, so that they will perceive you to be different from and better than your competitors. Naturally, you have to direct your advertising and promotion specifically towards that segment in order for the benefit to be obtained.

Market segmentation
In this approach, you would have to find those segments of a large market that you feel that you can serve better than your competitors. This could be attributed to your special expertise or other factors. If a large market is dominated by major competitors, it may not be efficient or profitable for them to attempt to compete with you, if you are concentrating and specializing on one small segment of the market. Over a period of time, you could increase your market share substantially because you have established a niche in the market, and have focused your energies and resources on that one specific segment.

Creating new markets
This approach can be expensive, time-consuming, and potentially risky because of the long, involved process that might be required. On the other hand, if you have done your market research thoroughly and can estimate the size, nature, and potential purchasing power of that market in terms of unmet needs, it could be profitable for you.

Researching your market
Once you have determined your target market, you now have to obtain as much information as you can about it through research. Your advertising and promotion strategies, as well as many other business and marketing considerations, will be based on the outcome of your research. In doing your research, you should clearly define your research objectives; determine your time frame; estimate the amount of money that you should allocate for research; select the appropriate information sources; determine the methods of research that you are going to follow; and obtain the information, analyze it, and draw your conclusions. Most of your research will probably be done on the Internet, which is the greatest source of information in existence with it's billions of pages and focused search capability. However, searching effectively requires some skill, so taking a short course in Internet search techniques would be a good investment.

Many small business owners may feel that they already know the market well and no research is necessary, or they may feel that they have already done research and do not need to do any more. You may have a general idea about your customers, but the market is constantly in a process of change and evolution. Needs and priorities are always changing. These are influenced by factors such as age; changing a job; losing a job; retiring; having a family; moving; getting married; and developing different attitudes, tastes, and needs.

Businesses, as well as organizations and communities, are in a constant state of change. They are therefore going through various phases and stages which could influence your marketing approach. Factors involved would include changes in the national, regional, or local economy; changes in the population mix; or changes in municipal, provincial, or federal government regulations. These factors could impact on needs, priorities, and buying habits.

When doing your research, you should be aware of the many sources of market research information available. Statistics Canada offices or websites will be a good starting point for searching out data. The resource librarian at your public library will assist you in locating market surveys, trade journals, business directories, and other information. On the Internet, a good source might be online forums where people discuss a certain subject. The business social media site LinkedIn is also a good source, particularly its questions and answers service and specialized groups. Other sources may include:

- municipal and provincial (small businesses) government offices
- federal government offices of Industry Canada (ic.gc.ca) and the Business Development Bank of Canada (BDC; bdc.ca)
- trade associations
- chambers of commerce or boards of trade
- college and university business administration departments
- trade shows
- online telephone directories and industry lists
- wholesalers, distributors, retailers, customers, and employees
- commercial market research companies such as Dunn & Bradstreet

Professional researchers who have access to private databases

An effective way of identifying your market and its needs may be to hire a company that specializes in customer surveys and questionnaires. The surveys should be carefully designed to get as much specific information as possible. Once you have this information, you can decide which advertising or promotion vehicle will reach your customers and have the desired effect. The best way to get the right information, and as much as possible, is to keep your questionnaire or survey short and simple. This will encourage your customers to fill it out. A company which specializes in consumer surveys would be able to assist you in the type of interview or questionnaire that will obtain the most reliable results based on your type of business.

As mentioned earlier, your marketing decisions will be based on the four Ps of marketing success:

- providing the right **product** at the right *price*
- in the right **place**
- with the right amount of **promotion**.

Place or Location

The location of your business is based on many factors, including the type of business (retail, service, manufacturing, primarily Web-based, or brick-and-mortar), or a combination of one or two factors. In an offline, physical, service or retail business, you will need to deal with considerations such as potential growth of the area, traffic volume, other businesses in the area, suitability of the area, cost of premises, and accessibility. In a Web-based business, you will deal with considerations such as website domain availability, operating systems, servers and hosts, and other factors important to online business.

Further information on the importance of location and leasing considerations is provided in Chapter 9, "Location and Leases."

Pricing Your Service or Product

Pricing involves many factors, including what your costs are to produce or buy a product or produce a service, what the customer is prepared to pay, and what your competitors are charging. There has to be a balance among these factors. The other critical factor is to charge enough to make a profit.

Certain costs are common to all types of business, including direct and indirect costs.

In order to break even on the selling of a product or service, the price has to be set covering all costs and overhead. Once you have calculated the break-even point, a profit margin is then added to determine your final selling price. You also have to be flexible in determining your profit margin on certain products or services. Determining the best profit margin for a given product or service at a given time, taking all the competitive circumstances into account, is where marketing strategies come in.

Factors influencing the pricing strategy

Some of the factors which will influence your pricing strategy are as follows:

- **Stage of product life cycle.** Every product goes through a lifecycle. The main stages are generally start-up, growth, maturity, and decline. These stages are a function of not only product development, but also changing competitive conditions. Therefore, the price you charge this week may not necessarily be appropriate next week.

- **Sensitivity.** The sensitivity of your target market to changes in price is an important consideration. Depending on your market, an increase in price could cause a significant reduction in sales, or it may have very little effect. It all depends on the price sensitivity of your market. Therefore, the most profitable price is not necessarily the one which produces the highest volume of sales. The strategy is to determine the best combination of price and sales volumes which produces the best profits. Overpricing could cause a significant loss of volume, as buyer resistance turns customers to your competitors. Underpricing may result in no profits or a loss, or could damage your business image.

- **Discounts.** This is a common pricing strategy which could include discounts that are based on seasonal, introductory, quantity, or cash considerations, as well as promotions such as coupons. Another reason for discounts could be to sell excess or slow-moving inventory, match competitors' prices, or provide a loss leader to attract customers to the store. You may also wish to provide discounts in the form of absorbing freight costs.

- **Business image.** This is an important marketing consideration. How your business is perceived by your target group is definitely based on price, among other factors. If you want to create the image of a bargain store, then your prices should be consistent with that image. On the other hand, if you want to create the image of a luxury store, people are prepared to pay more. They may not be attracted to the cheaper product or service.

In summary, you need to match your pricing strategy to your overall marketing objectives. Your market objectives could include maintaining or increasing market share, maximizing long-term or short-term profits, stabilizing market prices, enhancing loyalty of distribution channels, or accelerating the exit of marginal competitors.

Types of pricing strategies

Once you have taken into account the various factors that influence price, there are numerous pricing strategies that you can adopt. Some of these strategies tend to be more appropriate for start-up businesses, others for businesses during the growth phase, and others for mature, stabilized businesses. Here are some examples:

- **Cost-plus pricing.** This approach involves adding a set percentage to the full cost of a product in order to establish an acceptable profit. One advantage of this approach is that it is simple. The disadvantage is that the business may not accrue the maximum profit it otherwise could, in terms of the customer being prepared to pay more.

- **Lowball pricing.** In this example, the price offered is below the actual cost. This technique is often used when bidding on a job. It is hoped that if the bid is accepted, future orders or spin-off work may result. This may be an effective strategy if the bids are sealed, so competitors do not know the price being offered. The obvious risk is that the business may not get the future work and could suffer financially because of the low bid.

- **Penetration pricing.** In this strategy, the producer attempts to seize a large market share by offering a low price in the hope that the savings of large volume production will drive unit costs down.

- **Price skimming.** This strategy seeks to maximize profits by targeting customers who place a high value on the product or service, and who are prepared to pay the highest price. This frequently relates to a new product or service and the business image that surrounds it. The disadvantage is that high prices may draw competitors into the market. They may prematurely drive the price down by targeting market segments that are more price-sensitive. Therefore, a price-skimming strategy has to be flexible enough to alter prices quickly to meet the competition if necessary.

- **Loss-leader pricing.** This approach is designed to attract additional customers by temporarily reducing the price of certain products to levels that fail to cover the full cost. Companies that do loss-leader pricing are generally established companies. They want to offer a full line of goods or services and maintain the price as constantly as possible.

- **Opportunistic pricing.** In this example, companies exploit the marketplace by increasing prices sharply during a decrease in supply of a product or service in demand. An example would be a shortage of food products because of a natural disaster or labour dispute. The customers may have no alternative but to pay the higher price. This approach could have long-term disadvantages to the company, because of customer resistance and negative feelings about being taken advantage of.

- **Price milking.** In this example, a company that has a large or loyal customer target group may price the product or service just above what competitive conditions or product costs might justify. Because the customer is conditioned to purchase from the company, there is very little, if any, change in purchasing habits.

- **Defensive pricing.** In this strategy, a business attempts to defend its market share of established products by the nature of its pricing. For example, a company that produces products at a low cost may maintain low prices in order to discourage potential competitors from entering the market. Alternatively, it may wait for the competition to enter the market and then retaliate with price cuts. In another example, a business may set a high price on a new product or service that competes with others offered by the company. The strategy is to make sure that sales of existing products or services are not impaired. In this way, the company protects its market share.

- **Competitive pricing.** A business sets its price to be exactly the same as its main competition.
- **Recessionary pricing.** Businesses that are suffering from an economic downturn may want to reduce prices below total cost in order to survive. For example, prices could be set at a level that would cover some of the fixed overhead costs and most of the direct costs of the product. Naturally, a company could not stay in business very long with this approach. Its main hope would be to outlast the competition.

Pricing for profit

Pricing a product or service is not an easy undertaking, and requires much thought, as well as computation. Its importance cannot be overemphasized, however, since incorrect pricing is a major cause of business failure. If all the costs of the business are not reflected in the product or service price, the business could lose money and fail. There is rarely an exact "right" price, but rather an acceptable price range within which you will want to work. Avoid the two common mistakes made by many new business owners: charging too much and charging too little. Use several approaches to arrive at a cost and "test" the price. If your ego is too much involved, your price may be too high.

Four main factors will help you decide what to charge for your product or service: (1) your direct and indirect costs; (2) the profit you want to make; (3) your market research data on competitors' prices; and (4) the urgency of the market demand. Below, a procedure is presented for setting a fair price for a product or service, but you may wish to modify it on the basis of your specific situation and other formulas that you have reviewed, including the pricing by the competition. These are very general guidelines only.

Typical product pricing formula

- **Material costs.** Figure the total cost of the raw materials you have to use to make up a single item. For some products (such as large furniture items), it may be easy to determine a per-item cost. However, with items produced in volume, it may be easier to obtain a per-item cost by dividing the material cost of a batch of items by the number of items eventually produced.
- **Labour costs.** Figure what you pay to employees to produce the item (whether or not you have employees now). You must assign a wage figure,

even if you are the only one producing the item. Take the weekly salary you pay someone to produce the weekly volume of items and divide it by the number of items. Add this figure to your material costs.

- **Overhead.** This refers to expenses such as rent, gas and electricity, business telephone calls, packaging and shipping supplies, delivery and freight charges, cleaning, insurance, office supplies, postage, repairs, and maintenance. The accuracy of your costing depends on you estimating logical amounts for all categories of expenses. If you work from home, figure in a portion of your total rent or mortgage payment (in proportion to your work space and storage areas), or assign a reasonable, competitive rent figure for the same amount and type of space. List all overhead expense items and total them. Divide the total overhead figure by the number of items per month (or time period you used above). This amount will be your overhead per item.

$$\frac{\text{Materials cost} + \text{Labour costs} + \text{Overhead expenses}}{\text{Number of items produced}} = \text{Cost per item}$$

- **Profit/competition/market demand.** Add an amount to the cost of each item so you won't end up just breaking even or making only a slight profit. Check your competition and see what they are charging. Retailers generally double the wholesale price, but this varies greatly, depending on the product, the competition, and the target market. If your product is a little better than that of the competition, charge a little more. If your product is comparable, price it similarly. Remember, you will receive the profit from each sale, in addition to the salary figure. Add the profit figure you have chosen to the total cost per item to get your total price per item.

$$\text{Cost per item} + \text{Profit} = \text{Total price per item}$$

Typical service pricing formula

- **Overhead expenses.** As detailed above, calculate all the costs related to operating your business from home to arrive at a total cost per month. Divide this by the average number of hours worked per month to arrive at your hourly expense.
- **Hourly wage.** Decide on a wage that you will pay yourself, taking into consideration your background, training, and special expertise in your field. Compare this with industry averages.

- **Hourly profit.** Add a factor to your hourly wage to provide a profit margin. Check your competition and the market demand.

Hourly overhead expense + Hourly wage + Profit = Total price per hour

If your small business is primarily Internet-based, then all the previously mentioned pricing strategies still hold, with a few exceptions. Studies have shown that while the Internet has driven down prices in some mass product areas, such as electronics, it has raised them in other areas, such as unique products or services. Also, some 80% of customers remain loyal to an online retail site such as Amazon and continue to buy from it, even if its prices are higher. Apparently, top service and ease of use usually triumph over lowest-price strategies and automated service.

Remember, the main purpose in operating a business is to make a profit. Don't undersell your product or service just because "I'd be knitting sweaters anyway" or "I'm just starting out" or "I work out of my home." If you have a new, rare, handmade product or personalized service, the demand may be so high that customers are willing to pay a little more.

It is important to note that pricing must be continually evaluated, as material costs will increase due to inflation. Your prices should reflect these increases.

Communicating with Your Market

Communication is to many people what marketing is all about. The process of letting your customers know what you are selling and convincing them to buy your product rather than your competitor's is the function of the communication process. The challenge is to communicate the right message to the right people at the least cost and obtain the maximum benefit. There are six basic types or channels of marketing communication. Some of the channels are more effective than others, depending on the type of business and the message that is being conveyed. The amount that each channel is used, and the nature of the combination of channels, is referred to as *promotional mix*. Different businesses may have different promotional mixes. The main communication channels are advertising, direct mail, sales promotion, publicity, packaging, and personal selling.

Selecting Your Promotional Mix

The basis on which you decide on your promotional mix is a very important part of the overall marketing plan. If you make the correct decision, it could have a dramatic impact on your sales and therefore on your profit. Conversely, if the promotional mix is not correct, you could lose a lot of money and possibly even go out of business. Here are some of the factors that influence the promotional mix:

- **Target market.** Defining your markets by effective market research is the first step. For example, if the products or services that you are offering are directed to the consumer market, then advertising might be the most important channel to reach as many people as possible. On the other hand, if your target markets are businesses, then personal selling will be the most important approach. In this latter example, direct contact with the company is necessary to convince them to give you ongoing business.

- **Size of market.** If your market is a large part of the population, or if it cannot be clearly defined, then communication channels that provide massive exposure could be effective. On the other hand, if your market is small and can be well defined as a group, then a specialized communication channel could be more effective.

- **Location of markets.** In order to save money, it is necessary to know precisely where your target markets are situated. If you have a market that is throughout Canada, a region of Canada, or a specific province, then you should use channels which will cover that geographic area. This could include national, regional, or provincial TV networks; radio stations with a broad listening network; magazines or newspapers that are distributed within the market area; direct mail; and, of course, the Internet. If your market is in a specific community, you could reach it in the same ways, even via the Internet, which in addition to connecting the world can also be hyper-local.

- **Timing.** This is an important factor. You should concentrate your promotional efforts around peak times for your type of industry. If you are a retailer, Christmas is one of the peak periods for sales. It is important to have knowledge of the production and timing requirements of different media in order to coordinate your marketing plans and needs. If you are advertising in a magazine that is published on a monthly basis, you may have to commit yourself to advertising space 45 to 60 days before the publication. Television ads, of course, could take several months of planning before they would be ready. Newspapers may only require 1 day's notice, or in the case of display ads, several days' notice, for commitment of space. Ads on the Internet, particularly Google AdWords, can be placed almost instantaneously, but to be safe, plan a couple of days in advance.

- **Stage of business cycle.** If you are just starting up your business, you may want to spend a high proportion of your budget to make the public aware that you exist. This would include what you are selling, and the benefits of buying from you. On the other hand, if you have an established business that has already positioned itself in the marketplace, the promotional mix may be more stabilized.

- **Coordination.** It is important that you have continuity and consistency in the method that is being used, to have the maximum impact. You may want to have people hear about your product on the radio, read about it in newspapers and magazines, see it displayed on TV and with Internet search engines within the same time period for maximum reinforcement purposes.

Channels of Communication

The main channels of communication that you should consider are advertising, direct mail, sales promotion, publicity, promotion strategies, packaging, and personal selling. All these channels are online but are often combined in some form (e.g., publicity, promotion, and personal selling) due to the conversational nature of the medium.

Advertising

The objective of any advertisement is to get the customer's attention, stimulate interest, create a desire, and encourage the customer to take action. As consumers are subjected to numerous messages from various types of media throughout the day, you must attract the consumer's attention in order to obtain the competitive edge.

It is important to develop an advertising plan to establish and control expenditures. The plan helps to make sure that advertising is consistent with the overall marketing objectives. It also accounts for competitors' activities, anticipates trends and special events, determines budgets, monitors expenses, and repeats the successful promotions. There are some excellent advertising and promotional planning guides available. They are published on an annual basis and are free or sold at a nominal fee. Some of the main ones include:

- marketing, advertising, and promotion calendar/workbook, available through the Retail Merchants Association of Canada (rmacanada.com)
- ad plan book, available through Newspapers Canada (newspaperscanada.ca)
- a comprehensive source of media information is a guide entitled *Canadian Advertising Rates & Data* (*CARD*). This guide includes advertising rates, technical specifications or requirements, size of audience reach, frequency, deadlines, and other information. Due to the cost of purchasing *CARD*, which is updated monthly and costs approximately

$600 plus taxes, many people prefer to view it at the public library. You can obtain more information about what is contained in *CARD* by viewing the website: cardonline.ca.

The following will provide you with a review of the main types of advertising media. A media checklist is provided in Checklist E at the back of this book.

- Newspapers are timely and convenient. The target market can be reached by specifying the section of the newspaper, such as sports, business, or entertainment.
- Radio advertising can pinpoint the target market and can reach a large audience. To be effective, radio should be used frequently and properly timed.
- Television is a very persuasive form of coverage targeting a large market. One of the drawbacks of TV is the expense to small business.
- Magazines are excellent for special interest groups or for mass readership
- Transit advertising (external) ensures that the message is relayed to drivers and pedestrians. If the advertising is internal, it directs the message to the passengers. This can be an effective means of directing your messages on a repetitive basis to the same audience.
- Signs are a relatively inexpensive form of advertising.
- Advertising on the Internet can take many forms, such as contextual ads on search engine results pages, banner ads, blogs, rich media ads, social network advertising, interstitial ads, online classified advertising, advertising networks, and e-mail marketing, including e-mail spam and digital promotion, used primarily by TV networks because of their expense, but expected to grow considerably as digital production costs fall. Online advertising allows for the customization of advertisements, including content and posted websites, For example, AdWords, Yahoo! Search Marketing, and Google AdSense enable ads to be shown on relevant web pages or alongside search results. Online advertising is extremely efficient in that costs are measured by "clicks" or views—results instead of intentions.

The most common ways in which online advertising is purchased are:

- CPM (cost per mille) or CPT (cost per thousand impressions) is when advertisers pay for exposure of their message to a specific audience. "Per mille" means per thousand impressions or loads of an advertisement. However, some impressions may not be counted, such as a reload or internal user action.
- CPV (cost per visitor) is when an advertiser pays for the delivery of a targeted visitor to the advertiser's website.

- CPV (cost per view) is when advertisers pay for each unique user view of an advertisement or website (usually used with pop-ups, pop-unders, and interstitial ads).
- CPC (cost per click) or PPC (pay per click) is when an advertiser pays each time a user clicks on the advertiser's listing and is redirected to the advertiser's website. The advertiser does not actually pay for a listing but only when the listing is clicked on.
- CPA (cost per action or cost per acquisition) or PPF (pay per performance) advertising is performance-based. In this payment scheme, the publisher takes all the risk of running the ad and the advertiser pays only for the number of users who complete a transaction, such as a purchase or sign-up

BDC provides a good guide to marketing online.

Methods of measuring the results and effectiveness of your advertising include:

- word-of-mouth reports from new or existing customers
- increase in in-store or Web traffic
- telephone or Web inquiries or orders
- increase in sales volume on items advertised
- increase in growth of the business over the long term
- formal or informal surveys or questionnaires.

There are a number of guidelines that you should keep in mind when dealing with print advertising such as magazines, newspapers, or direct mail. The principles that apply to print advertising are obviously applicable in many ways to other forms of advertising and marketing, such as online. Consider the following questions:

- Is your message clear and simple so that it can be easily understood, or is it packed with too much information that confuses the viewer or reader?
- Is your message relevant? Does it describe your service, product, or business in any meaningful fashion?
- Does your message offer a solution to your ideal customer's problem? Is it targeted to a specific situation?
- Does your message explain the benefits (not the features!) of your product or service to the customer so the customer will want to have his or her needs satisfied?
- Does your message distinguish itself in its uniqueness and approach, or is it very similar to your competitor's advertising?
- Does your advertising message stand out in terms of its headline to attract the readers' immediate attention, or could the readers miss the impact of your message?

Low-cost advertising techniques

Advertising makes potential buyers aware of your product or service, and hopefully induces them to buy. Another benefit of advertising is that it could expose you to retailers, wholesalers, or distributors who may approach you with bulk orders. Also, repeating ads in trade-related publications creates an impression of stability and credibility. You probably already know which publications target your market within your area. Otherwise, check with your newsstands and public library for further ideas. Here are some tips for low-cost (or no-cost) advertising strategies.

- **Word of mouth.** It is a cliché, but an accurate one: word of mouth, which includes recommendations and endorsements on social networking sites and blogs, is the best form of advertising. The more people who promote your product or service because they know you satisfy customers, the more sales you are going to make. Personal testimonials are very persuasive and credible Always remember , the customer is always right, even when the customer is wrong. Now that every business (and product or service) is reviewed online somewhere, a bad review from a dissatisfied customer can undermine your goodwill with many other people. You should, therefore, deal with any customer complaints in a prompt and efficient manner.
- **Business cards and stationery.** Creating a positive image with your business cards is very important. The initial impression should be a positive one. Your cards and stationery should also reflect the type of business you are in, and what you do. This could be reflected by your business name and/or a brief description below it; for example, "Search engine optimization (SEO) made easy."
- **Brochures and posters.** Brochures and posters have faded somewhat in the wake of the Internet's rise, but can still be very effective and relatively inexpensive Some of the advertising uses of a brochure are leaving it with a prospective client; distributing it at a seminar, presentation, or other distribution location; sending it as part of a direct mail campaign; mailing it after a written or phone request for further information, and attaching a cut-down version to your e-mails. Always obtain competitive quotes on brochure production and printing, because prices can vary considerably.
- **Flyers and tear-off ads.** Flyers and tear-off ads are a simple and inexpensive technique to use if your market is restricted to a certain locale. For a tear-off ad, the advertisement would be typed on a sheet of paper with tear-off tabs at the bottom of it, with your name and phone number on each tab. If you have a résumé service, for example, you could place an

ad on the bulletin boards in local universities, colleges, and institutes to elicit students who are looking for jobs. Or, if layoffs had recently been announced in your community, you could place flyers on all the cars in the employee parking lot announcing your résumé service.

- **Catalogues.** Catalogues tend to be more expensive to produce and distribute because of the cost of the photography, artwork, typesetting, paper, and postage. General catalogues are also fading in the face of the Internet because their main benefit—a menu of product selections—is more easily distributed (and for far less cost) through a website. However some companies that focus on a specialty, such as IKEA, still use catalogues effectively, usually as a supplement to their websites.

- **Trade and professional directories.** Many annually published directories accept paid printed display ads and online advertising. Some publications charge for a listing and others do not. If you carefully select your directory, you could accurately hit your target market. Check your library for directories related to your business. Most of these are also online and may have different price structures.

- **Classified and display ads.** You may want to consider advertising through display ads in newspapers and magazines. However, most display advertising, and particularly classified ads, are online, (where classifieds are often free). Craigslist and Kijiji are the dominant classified sites in Canada. See Chapter 19 for more details.

- **Cooperative advertising with suppliers.** Many manufacturers and suppliers will pay for a portion of your ad if you use their name or logo in some way in your ad or other marketing promotion. Do your research and talk to your suppliers and their suppliers.

- **Drop-shipping.** Publishers of online and offline magazines, catalogues, or newsletters are sometimes willing to act as distributors and sell your product by a drop-ship arrangement. In this situation, the publisher displays or lists your product, takes orders , and retains an agreed-upon percentage of the revenue plus the cost of distributing the publication. You are then sent the balance by cheque, along with the names and addresses of the people who ordered the product. It is then your responsibility to ship the product directly to the buyers, whose names can now be used for your mailing list. As with most business processes, drop-shipping has moved onto the Internet and has become popular with online retailers, because it increases sales and lowers costs. However, online drop-shipping has its problems, largely involving gathering product information, managing orders, providing good customer service, and removing poorly performing items. There are now online services that facilitate online drop-shipping.

- **Trade shows.** Trade shows can be an effective offline way to reach potential customers. A trade show is usually marketed to the consumer (end user) or the industry (retailers, wholesalers). At many of the trade shows, you can not only sell product but also generate potential customers or business contacts, such as retailers, wholesalers, distributors, manufacturers' representatives, and buying agents (e.g., for retail chains). Also, exhibiting is a good way to test a new product, do informal surveys, and build your mailing list by collecting business cards or names and e-mail addresses.
  - It is also common for booth exhibitors to conduct a seminar or speak at the trade show. This technique creates exposure for your product or service.
  - Attend some trade shows in your field before exhibiting. Afterward, ask exhibitors if the trade show has been successful, in terms of the number of sales, leads, or contacts, and the reputation and success of the promoter in advertising and marketing the trade show. Would they take a booth in that same trade show again? Also ask exhibitors if they would be interested in sharing booth space in the future, selling your product at their booth, or adding your product line to theirs.
  - Be careful in selecting trade shows. You could waste a lot of time and money exhibiting at a show that is poorly promoted or attended. Check out the reputation of the promotion company by making inquiries of people in the industry and the Better Business Bureau. To find out all trade shows scheduled across Canada, look online under "Canada Trade Fairs, Canada Trade Show Directory, Canada" or "trade show directories, United States" or contact your local public library.
- **Special Promotions.** You may wish to attract your target market by advertising such promotions as senior, student, or family discounts; free trial offers; "two for one" sales; and raffles.

Direct mail

Direct mail and direct e-mail are among the most effective types of promotion for a small business. They include circulars and flyers delivered by Canada Post or advertising distributors, mailers sent to prospective customers based on lists of names obtained from direct mail companies, letters and stuffers contained in monthly statements to existing customers, and e-mail sent to acquaintances, customer lists and, sometimes, purchased lists of e-mail addresses.

One of the main advantages of direct mail is that it allows you to determine exactly who will receive your message. Direct mail can be expensive, but the financial benefits can be justified if the targeting is precise. Direct mail is usually used for selling your product directly to the customer; announcing a new product, service, or business location; or reminding established customers to continue doing business with you.

Mailing lists are available from directories, commercial direct mail companies, associations, and internal records of your company. Also check with your library or online for a publication entitled *Direct Mail List Rates and Data*. Conduct an online search for direct e-mail lists by entering "online direct e-mail lists, Canada."

Sales promotion

Any activity which supports all your other advertising campaigns is called *sales promotion*. The main objective of a sales promotion is to encourage customers to make an impulse purchase while shopping, remind your customers about your business name by having it on various products, and demonstrate the benefits of your product or service. Sales promotions include a wide variety of products and techniques: calling cards; contests; coupons; free samples; prizes; giveaways, such as calendars and novelties; special events; point-of-purchase displays; demonstrations; Internet contests and campaigns; and trade show exhibits.

Some types of sales promotions are more effective than others, depending on whether you are in the service, retail, or manufacturing area. For maximum benefit, sales promotions should be coordinated with other aspects of your promotional mix and monitored regularly to make sure they are effective.

Publicity

Publicity is the process of obtaining free media coverage about your business or product. Good publicity could have a significant impact on the market in terms of your business credibility. Publicity tends to imply that the article or product, if well reviewed, has received critical and objective acceptance.

Since the Internet allows may people to be publishers in their own right, much of that media is now online, with new blogs, radio broadcasts, and video shows appearing constantly, many of them involving extremely specialized subjects or extremely local coverage. This variety allows you to target your messages more specifically to the market or markets you wish to serve.

Issuing a news release or article to the online or offline media is an effective means of getting free publicity. Your article may be used as a filler on a slow day. In order to get the attention of reporters and radio announcers, though, your message has to be newsworthy, interesting, and topical. If you are aiming at TV or online video news, it must also include strong visual material.

Some potential news stories:

- business or factory opening or expansion that could create employment opportunities and benefits to the community

- achievement of the athletic team that you have sponsored
- announcement of a new and unique service, product, or business.

Other techniques that a small business can use to obtain publicity are: contributing to the community through service club membership; sponsorship of athletic teams, charities, and public service; contribution or involvement in special community events. The more the public perceives your business image in a positive light, the more likely they will want to do business with you.

When using a publicity strategy, remember that it should not be about you or your business, but about the overall situation and narrative. Most news organizations are interested only in stories, almost always about individual people, that would be of interest to their particular group of readers, listeners, or viewers. They are not particularly interested in your business (unless it involves something very unique or of benefit to the general public) or what it does, but will mention it as part of the story. If you are planning a publicity strategy, there are many small public relations companies that can help. If you plan to do it on you own, study such techniques as "news values" before you begin.

Promotion strategies

For most small businesses, money for marketing is limited. You will be interested to learn, then, that some of the most effective marketing techniques are free or inexpensive and fall under the category of publicity or promotion. The following strategies are the most common ones, though not all of the examples would necessarily be appropriate for your type of business, or compatible with your style or personality.

Media releases and exposure

Media or news releases can be an extremely effective means of obtaining publicity—that is, if you do the release correctly. Most small business owners haven't the remotest idea how to prepare a release, and therefore do not use the technique or use it incorrectly. The secret is to create a media release which is newsworthy, interesting, and topical. Keep in mind that reporters, newscasters, and online information websites are constantly searching for material that could be of interest to their readers, listeners, viewers, or visitors. Some days they may have little material, while other days may be packed with late-breaking news. If your timing is right, your release could be used as a "filler" on an otherwise light news day. When submitting releases be certain to allow sufficient lead time in order to enhance the likelihood of your release being used.

The term "media" refers to the communication vehicles of print (newspapers, magazines, newsletters), radio, TV, and online news and specialty information operations, of which there are more every day. When deciding where to send a media release, do your research to target the correct persons within the medium in question—publishers, general editors, section editors, journalists, reporters, freelance writers, syndicated columnists, book reviewers, bloggers, news broadcasters, program directors, talk show hosts, or researchers.

The following resources may help you to locate the various media and the most suitable person for your release.

All media operations have websites, so look online under the search terms "Radio," "Newspapers," and "Magazines" in your area. Also look online for Internet bloggers in your area who may have an interest in your area of expertise.

Check online for *CARD*, a directory listing all the media in Canada. Also check directories which list various trade publications and online newsletters in Canada and the United States. Peruse the largest news websites, blogs, and specialty sites in your area of interest. On relevant blogs, you can post a rewritten (and relevant) version of your news in the comment section. Ensure it will relate to the specific blog post, however, or it will be marked as spam.

Contact the media concerned and inquire about the name of the editor, talk show host, program director, or news director, as well as the relevant e-mail address

Check the print and online media and gather names of reporters, writers, or columnists who write about subjects which could encompass your business area. And be aware of TV or radio news stories on which you could "piggyback."

You may want to send the release to several key people within the same newspaper, radio, TV, magazine, or local Internet-based organization such as the Huffington Post. For example, you may believe the subject matter of your media release would be relevant not only to a media outlet's business section, but also its lifestyles section and its seniors section. Usually each section has a separate editor, although a community newspaper or small website may just have a general editor.

Before you start preparing a release, there are a number of initial steps you have to take. You have to ask yourself what benefit you hope to get from the exercise. Do you want local, regional, provincial, national, or international publicity? It will obviously make a difference in terms of your media contacts and the content of the release. Set specific goals for your release, such as generating a telephone or e-mail response from prospective clients or customers; stimulating sales orders; attracting potential investors; or obtaining consulting contracts, freelance work, or speaking engagements. Do you just want to make the public aware of your product, so that they will look for it in specialty or general retail stores?

To prepare a good release you should follow these general recommendations:

- Make it clear and easy to read.
- Use short sentences and simple English.
- Make sure it is grammatically correct, with accurate spelling.

- Avoid flowery phrases, exaggerated or superlative statements, and other hype. Remember, this is an information release and not a sales letter.
- Write the release in a common computer writing format such as Microsoft Word, and then attach it to an e-mail to the reporters or editors you have identified. Put the headline in the subject line of your e-mail along with a notification that the attachment is a press release, and then put a (short) summary of the release in the body of the e-mail.
- If referring to yourself in the release, which is a common technique, use of the third person ("she" or "he" rather than "I") will make it sound like someone else has written about you, which is a desirable impression to create and makes it easier to quote yourself. Readers tend to believe what they read as being credible and accurate because it appeared in print, and publicity legitimizes information, but this is undermined if the first person is used.
- Keep the release to one page ideally, and not more than two pages, or it might not be read. Keep in mind that the reader of the release is time-pressured and has to select from many releases received every day. If the release goes on to a second page, write "more" in the lower right-hand corner of the first page, and create a second page.
- You may wish to attach a short, separate, biographical media release to your general release. The biography should read like an article and show why "the person being quoted" and your business are interesting. The more finished the appearance of your media release and/or biography, the more likely a busy reporter, writer, or editor will use it.
- You may also wish to consider attaching a photograph (ideally, professionally taken) to your release, depicting either yourself or the item being profiled. It should have good resolution.

There are several basic elements to a media release, as described below, concerning the format, layout, and content.

- **"MEDIA RELEASE" or "NEWS RELEASE."** Put these words in capitals at the very top and centred. Don't use the term "press release" if you intend to send it to media other than "the press" (newspapers).
- **Date.** Place the date of the release at the top left corner.
- **Contact person.** Put the name of the person who is the source of the release at the top left or right side of the page, so that they can be contacted for more information. Include the person's position/title, e-mail address, and phone number with area code.
- **Release date.** Put the date on which the media is to release the information. Generally, one states, "FOR IMMEDIATE RELEASE" in capital letters, unless the information is to be held or "embargoed" until a

certain date. This line should be placed on the right side of the page, just above the headline. Keep in mind that online news operations are very fast-paced; a release sent to one could be posted instantly.

- **Headline.** This is centred on the page and typed in capital letters. It summarizes the content of the media release so that the reader can quickly see what it is all about and decide if he or she wants to read further. It should, therefore, be an attention-grabber. Editors generally write their own headlines for actual publication, however.

- **Basic facts.** The first paragraph of your release should state some key facts and information you want the media to know, while at the same time indicating why the event or incident mentioned is important (if that isn't self-explanatory). It should cover the "who, what, when, why, where, and how" aspects of your story.

  It is important to have a "news peg" in this first paragraph, something to give the editors a reason to publish it, or the radio or TV broadcaster a reason to comment on it. If you can't cover all the basic facts in the first paragraph, finish in the second.

- **Important details.** You will want to add some details other than those covered in the "Basic Facts" section, in order to encourage the media to consider a feature story rather than just a brief announcement. You may cover the benefits of the product or service or why it is unique, pitfalls to avoid, tips to save money or make money, or quotes from yourself (in the third person, remember).

- **Supplementary information.** In this part of the release, which could be the third or fourth paragraph, you provide information which adds colour to a feature story. For example, simple questions consumers could ask themselves; discussion of the trends or implications involved; the impact on the community, such as increased employment or an export market created; or an award received.

- **Further information.** Many releases don't include this line, but it could be an appropriate one for your type of business operation, especially if the purpose of your release is to obtain a direct and quantifiable response from the public. The last line or short last paragraph should have your business name, your e-mail address and phone number, and a list of the free promotional material that is available upon request. Alternatively, the line may simply state that the product is now available (state where).

  Although this "Further Information" line is a form of advertising, editors will generally include it if they think it will benefit the readers or audience to have it noted.

- **Closing.** End the release by putting "End" or "-30-" centred after your last paragraph.

If you feel unsure about writing your own biography and media release, you might refer to a book on the topic or pay a freelance writer to prepare the material for you.

Media interviews

Your news releases, or discussions with decision-makers at local newspapers, magazines, radio, TV, or online news operations could result in interviews. You could have articles which profile you and your business, or appearances on TV, radio talk shows, or online radio and video websites. Over time, you could attempt to cultivate a relationship with the media, so that they perceive you to be an expert or credible authority. From time to time they may want to interview or quote you on matters relating to your area of "expertise."

If you have a specific event occurring, you should attempt to encourage media coverage of it. For example, an upcoming craft show could be considered newsworthy by the media in your local community. Television, radio, newspaper or video and/or blog coverage of the event would give you widespread publicity at no cost.

Online opportunities

The vast media universe that is the Internet has many other outlets and distribution centers for your release or a version of it. Many of them are better targeted to your specific market than general news supplied by the traditional media. Social media such as LinkedIn, Facebook, and Twitter allow you to post your "status," which is an opportunity to write and post a very truncated version of your release's main point. So does your e-mail list, particularly if it is a customer or prospect list. Similarly, the subject matter of your release can be posted on your blog (but written appropriately) to promote your business among subscribers. Lastly, the release makes good fodder for your e-mailed newsletter.

Cable TV opportunities

In addition to being interviewed on your local cable station, you may want to give a free gift of a product you sell or a service you provide to a local TV benefit auction. Obviously you have to weigh your actual cost against your perceived return, in terms of publicity value or increased clients, customers, or sales.

Another idea would be for you to produce your own local cable show in your specialty area. It could be an ongoing weekly half-hour show or a two-, four-, or eight-part series. For example, if you are a contractor, you may want to host a regular phone interview program on renovating old homes; if you are a doctor, physiotherapist, or chiropractor, you may want to host a regular series on health subjects or a specialty program on dealing with back pain; or if you are a craftsperson, you may want to host a program on painting or making pottery.

You will not get paid for producing a local cable program. It is a trade: you do the organization of the program, and the cable station provides the facilities and does the taping. But in addition to increasing your skills and self-confidence, such a program will provide your business with exposure and credibility.

Teaching courses and seminars

Teaching adult education classes is an effective way to make business contacts, meet prospective clients, obtain public exposure, and enhance your reputation as an expert. In addition to being paid, teaching also has the fringe benefit of keeping you current on your area of interest. There are many opportunities to teach a course or a 1- or 2-day seminar. Contact the continuing or adult education program coordinators of school boards, colleges, and universities in your area. Also consider YM/YWCAs, community recreational centres, seniors' organizations or centres, churches, and other groups that you perceive would be appropriate education vehicles for your program.

Speaking

Trade, professional, or community groups or associations regularly look for speakers for breakfast, lunch, or dinner meetings as well as conferences or conventions. In most cases you will not receive a fee, as these organizations normally obtain speakers for free. In the case of conferences or conventions, though, there are sometimes opportunities to get paid for your presentation. Check online under "Associations" in your city or region, or in one of various directories of associations available in your public library, and contact the program coordinators for the groups or associations that you think might be interested.

If you are in a personal services business, speaking on subjects related to your business is an effective marketing technique. This is particularly true for businesses such as consulting, counselling, real estate, child care, financial advising, and any of the "traditional" professions, such as law, medicine, or dentistry. People naturally want to have a relationship of confidence and trust with such professionals, and by giving speeches you have a chance to create that bonding, which may result in subsequent business.

Content marketing

Production of content—advisory, analytical, or "training" material and other information products—is an old technique that has been re-energized by the Internet, with its voracious appetite for material to fill websites, blogs, and other forms of web publishing. Content marketing involves the creation of commentary, articles, graphics, blog posts, case studies, white papers, and e-books. It aims to position the producer as a trusted expert who stands out in a landscape cluttered with advertising claims. Content marketing is often used by companies for targeted business-to-business marketing, but can also be used for marketing to consumers, if an impression of authority or expertise is required. This form of marketing usually follows a "how-to," case study, or industry analysis format.

Writing an article

Writing is a classic technique of content marketing that has been proven to help build credibility and exposure, and establish you as an expert in your field. Considering the large number of publications available, it should not be difficult to have an article published online, in a magazine or e-newsletter that potential customers would read.

You may already be aware of most of the publications in your area of interest or general publications that could be appropriate, but perform an Internet search nevertheless. Also consider writing a regular column or "guest post," perhaps monthly or more or less frequently, for a website that is relevant to your area of interest. Online forums are also good places to post smaller articles. Make the same offer to your community newspaper or other publication and to the local radio station. Most of these types of articles tend to be from 500 to 1500 words in length, although they are usually shorter online. After contacting the editor of the media outlet you have chosen, send your piece, along with a picture of yourself and brief biographical profile. Add your name, e-mail address, and telephone number to be included at the end of the article, if it is desired. In most cases you won't get paid, but you should get a byline, a little biography, and the opportunity to include contact information. In some cases you will be able to obtain free advertising space in exchange. At the least, you will convey your expertise on your subject of interest to the public, which will include your target customers.

Writing a book

Having a book, e-book, or workbook published is another marketing technique to establish yourself as an expert, as well as possibly producing ongoing income. You can either self-publish or find a publisher for your book. Self-publishing has become much easier on the Internet—there are many "publishing on demand" sites that will help you publish a book and will distribute it for you online, which has essentially become the main distribution channel for books (e.g., the book distribution channels of chapters.ca and amazon.ca). Attempt to evaluate the cost–benefit ratio of the exercise, in terms of your time, money, and resources, but recognize that today, many books are primarily marketing vehicles and not earners. This means you should look at the indirect benefit in terms of credibility; for example, you could use your books as promotional items, include them as incentives for people to buy your service or product, sell them at seminars or presentations, or use them as a tool to get appearances on TV or radio programs.

E-books have become more common than traditional books because they are shorter, easier to digest, and usually low-cost or free. E-books can range from full-length novels and business books to a few pages on a specific subject and are often offered for free download to bring a website visitor into the sponsoring company's business funnel. This is a system with several stages that attracts prospects and moves them along the stages of the funnel, where they are sold ever more relevant services or information products. It is a (very efficient) winnowing process in which only the most motivated prospects reach the end.

E-Newsletters

Newsletters have been around for as long as there has been marketing, but the Internet provided them with a much larger role. Today, everybody can be a media publisher by publishing e-newsletters, and some online newsletter writers have turned their e-newsletters into multimillion-dollar operations. If you know your business area well, have passion and enthusiasm for your subject, and can entertain readers and subscribers, you may also be able to amass a sizeable readership for your e-newsletter. Most e-newsletter subscriptions are free in that they act as marketing vehicles for a business—a second stage of the business funnel—but some are so informative that the publisher can both charge fees for them and use them as a marketing platform. For example, quickanddirtytips.com. Your e-newsletter could come out monthly, bi-monthly, quarterly, or semi-annually—although monthly seems to be the most common editorial schedule. Unless your subject matter is very complex, you should try to keep an e-newsletter to one or two written offline pages and concentrate on only one or two subjects—Internet users do not like long, rambling essays. Your e-newsletter could have tips, news, and ideas, some subtle promotion of your business, and possibly a question-and-answer column. Check other e-newsletters and see how they have done it and pick the techniques that work for you.

Contact Networks

A high percentage of the clientele of many small businesses is acquired through a contact network which can provide much referral business: relatives, friends, neighbours, business associates and acquaintances, past and present customers, employees, and your accountant, lawyer, and banker.

Selectively joining associations, clubs, or local online groups (some of which hold regular meet-ups) could also foster exposure and sources of new business. There are many types of clubs and associations: professional, trade, business, community, fraternal, religious, and charitable. There are also organizations set up which are specifically designed for networking. Developing a contact network is one of the most inexpensive and effective ways of increasing your business, LinkedIn being one such example.

Packaging

Packaging is an integral part of communication, because the manner in which a product is presented to customers will influence their buying decisions. The types of packaging used depend on the type of business. A service business could package the image of the service that it provides to the public by its layout, decor, overall appearance, and friendliness. This enhances the positive feelings of customers. That overall appearance can also be transferred to all its online material for the same purpose.

For retailers, it is important to have the name and address or logo printed on such materials as bags, boxes, wrapping paper, and containers and placed prominently on websites in order to develop and reinforce customer awareness. The more attractive or unusual the packaging, the more the customer will remember the retailer.

Personal selling

Personal selling involves a direct one-on-one relationship with the potential customer. It is important for the salesperson to have a clear understanding of the business and product and its benefits, and the potential target market and its needs. The goal of personal selling is to stimulate customer interest and desire to buy the product or service. The advantages of personal selling are that the message can be adapted to the needs, preferences, and unique situations of each individual customer; the approach can be varied; and customer response is received.

Sales representatives can be sources of current market information about competitors and customers. A reporting system can be established which facilitates daily recall of important observations.

There are five key steps that a sales rep will go through to close the sale:

1. **Approaching the customer properly.** The sales rep must project a friendly, positive, well-informed, well-groomed image.
2. **Understanding the customer's needs and preferences.** The sales rep must determine the customer's specific needs and motivations in order to choose the appropriate sales presentation. Not every presentation is going to work on every customer, as different customers have different personalities, motivations, needs, priorities, and financial resources. Obtain prospects through your website and direct e-mail. Several companies provide online surveying software but it is up to you to create the correct questions that will generate the best information. Don't include too many, because it will drive those being surveyed away. Customers will answer questions about their shopping experiences, but not if it takes too much time. Including a small reward, such as a free service or e-book, will probably help to create more responses
3. **Presenting the product or service.** In the process of presentation, the sales rep deals with the concerns and needs of the customer. These have already been determined to some degree in the previous step. The sales rep emphasizes the benefits and features of the product or service, its uniqueness, and how it will meet the customer's needs.

4. **Overcoming objections by the customer.** The sales rep may need to re-emphasize the key benefits and features of the product or service, and explain them in greater depth. The more the customer believes the sales rep to be sincere, objective, and well-informed, the more likely the customer will be to develop trust and confidence in the salesperson and the service or product. Dealing with objections in a respectful and patient fashion is essential.

5. **Closing the sale.** This is the final stage in the sales approach, and the one which is critical to the business profit line. There are various closing approaches, depending on the nature of the product or service, the style of operation of the business, and the type of target market customer. Many customers have to be convinced to make a decision right then and there. Factors such as unconditional guarantee of satisfaction, trying the product or service on a trial basis, promptness of delivery, and ease of credit card payment will help in the closing stage. Testimonials from credible people benefit the sale.

There are many training programs for salespeople to enhance skills. These programs are available through various associations such as Sales & Marketing Executives or the Retail Merchants Association of Canada. Many college and school boards offer continuing education classes on the subject of sales techniques.

For personal selling to be successful, it has to be coordinated with the overall promotional mix objectives. Advertising, direct mail, and publicity help to make the customers or potential customers aware of the service, product, or business, and motivated to have their needs met.

Many of the principles of personal selling also apply online, but they are, by the nature of the medium, applied in a different format. While online sales cannot mirror the offline sales process completely, it can apply these principles by designing the website to accomplish many of the same steps through the creation of a business funnel. Especially for information or educational products and services, the business funnel has become a standard method of bringing a personal component to what is essential an impersonal medium.

Getting Your Product to Your Customer

No matter how good your product is, it cannot benefit anyone unless it is available for the customer to purchase. The goal of any distribution system is to get your product to your target market in a timely and convenient fashion, so that it is easy for the customer to buy. But how you get it there says a great deal about how well you know your customers and their needs. There are four main methods of distributing your product: retailing, wholesaling, consigning, and agents or representatives. All are represented on the Internet; in fact, in some cases the Internet has made distribution easier, and so it has become the prime distribution method.

1. **Retailing.** This method involves personal selling: that is, face-to-face meetings with consumers or commercial or institutional buyers of your product. Retailing is the most direct means of selling your product and could create a higher gross profit for you, as it eliminates commissions or fees paid to wholesalers or agents. The drawback, of course, is that you have to do the selling yourself or hire salespeople. That involves time, expense, and, to some people, discomfort—discomfort in wearing the different hats of owner and salesperson.
   Here are some ways of selling directly to consumers:

   - retail shop or studio in your home
   - website or online "store" video on your website or on a video site
   - classified ad sites craigslist.ca and kijiji.ca
   - door-to-door sales and in-home demonstrations
   - eBay
   - street vending
   - public market home parties
   - trade shows, fairs, festivals, and flea markets.

   You could also consider selling directly to buyers for business, institutions, or government. Provincial and federal governments and their Crown corporations have a policy of buying from "Canadian or provincial suppliers of products or services first." In practical terms, though, you would have to have the production capacity to meet the large volume and consistency of quality requirements of large organizations. Most small businesses do not.

2. **Wholesaling.** Wholesaling is an ideal distribution method if you would prefer not to direct-sell. You would have the capacity to expand the volume of production and therefore the potential volume of sales. This is an indirect method of selling to the consumer and involves either selling directly to a retail outlet or through a wholesaler, who in turn sells to retailers. Some retailers will only deal with wholesalers and do not want to deal directly with the producers. Also, wholesalers will not generally buy unless a demand for the product has been demonstrated. This is because wholesalers expend the time and money to sell the product by means of sales calls, trade shows, trade advertising, special distribution programs, and direct mail promotions. The drawback of wholesaling, of course, is that you receive less money for your product than by selling it directly, as the wholesaler has to add a markup.

The main forms of wholesaling include:

- retail outlets (department stores, craft, hobby, gift shops, etc.) online and offline
- merchandise marts, premium sales
- online aggregator sites
- institutional buyers
- foreign markets

3. **Consigning.** This approach involves selling the goods through a retailer. It is frequently used by people who can't sell through a wholesaler, or who want to provide greater distribution and exposure of the product. If it is a new product without a track record, retailers may be reluctant to buy your products, but may be willing to display them on consignment.

   In a consignment situation, you remain the owner of all the consigned goods and only receive payment after they are sold. The retailer retains a percentage of the selling price as a commission or fee. However, this could tie up your funds and present cash flow problems. The retailer has no obligation to pay you until the goods are sold and can return the goods to you at any time. Another drawback to consignment is that you have no way of controlling or being reimbursed for damage to the product by shoppers. But despite these limitations, it is an option you may need to consider in order to get some exposure and create a product demand.

   Another variation of consignment is rack jobbing. In this approach, the retailer provides you with floor or shelf space to display your "rack" of goods free of charge. The "rack," or point-of-purchase display unit, is either supplied by you or by the retailer. You then pay the retailer a commission on sales.

4. **Agents, brokers, and manufacturers' representatives.** These people are independent, self-employed contractors working as commissioned salespersons. Their role is to act as liaisons between retailers or wholesalers and you, represent your interests, and promote the sale of your product. The advantages of using these services are that they save you money, since you do not have to hire employees; representatives only get paid if they perform; they free you up to spend more time on your other business matters, since customers are located for you; they provide you with the opportunity for business growth and increased sales; and they enable you to access new territories or obtain contacts because of their connections and experience in the industry.

   An agent is a person who acts for you in your business capacity. An example would be a booking agent who tries to book a professional speaker into trade shows or conventions. An agent for your product could have either an exclusive or a nonexclusive relationship with you. An exclusive agent could be more committed to expending time selling your product or service, but of course there is always a risk and limitation in "putting all your eggs in one basket."

A broker could act as an agent for both sides of the business, depending on the nature of the product or service. For example, a training broker could be retained by a speaker to sell corporate training programs. Conversely, a corporation could retain a training broker to search out, evaluate, and recommend training programs appropriate to the defined needs of the organization.

A manufacturers' representative is an agent who represents similar product lines from different businesses.

There are several ways of locating agents, brokers, or representatives: search online under "Brokers" or "Manufacturing Agents and Representatives"; look in online and offline trade magazines for ads; ask others in the industry whom they would recommend; go to a merchandise mart and speak to representatives or wholesalers; and attend trade shows.

Always make sure your business arrangement is covered in writing in advance, after you have concluded your negotiations. Don't forget to scan the market before deciding. You don't want to have any misunderstandings, with the stress or loss of goodwill and money which could result. According to the nature of the relationship, cover such matters (as applicable) as commission; each party's responsibilities; authority; exclusive or nonexclusive obligations; duration; sales territory; and policies concerning credit, down payment, retainer, discounts, billings, warranties, returns, shipping, packaging, and advertising. To be on the safe side and for peace of mind, if the agreement was supplied to you, have your lawyer look it over before you sign. Otherwise, develop your own agreement and show it to your lawyer for comment. Never base business relationships on a "handshake." The stakes are too high, and you will very likely regret it.

To be successful, you will probably have to initially become the marketing manager, along with your other business roles. The information and assistance you need is readily available, so take the time and be resourceful in seeking it. Read pertinent books and articles; attend an adult education class at your local college; access the information and help offered by BDC; contact your provincial small business centre or download information from your provincial small business ministry (search online under "small business counselling, Canada [or your province name, such as Ontario]"); access several private company websites that concentrate on small business, such as About.com's Small Business Centre, or canadaone.com; or hire a marketing consultant. Talk to other successful entrepreneurs whenever you have the opportunity. Effective marketing is an ongoing concern of every successful business. Be certain to repeat the techniques that work, and modify or discontinue those that no longer produce results. Continually test new markets.

Determining Your Marketing Budget

Factors such as your financial and personnel resources, place and size of business, target markets, and marketing goals and objectives will play a part in determining your total marketing budget.

Here are some of the common methods used in setting your budget:

Percentage of sales

The marketing budget is based on a percentage of past or projected sales or a combination of both. This is a more reliable method than basing it on profits. Profits in a particular period could be low or high for any number of reasons that have nothing to do with sales or advertising. The percentage of sales method is quick and easy. The exact percentage used will vary from business to business, and it may be helpful to check your industry average. Offline retail stores tend to budget in the range between 1% and 8% of total sales on advertising alone. Costs for small businesses advertising online through a pay-per-click system can vary widely and may not align with the business' profits.

Units of sales

In the units of sales method of determining your marketing budget, you would set aside a fixed sum for each unit of product to be sold. This sum is based on experience or knowledge of the trade. A budget is therefore based on unit of sale, rather than dollar amounts of sales. The units of sales method is not very appropriate for markets that are irregular, cyclic, or seasonal.

Matching competition

In the matching competition method, your marketing budget is based on what industry averages show your competition is spending. Keep in mind when checking industry averages that they relate only to advertising, rather than marketing, budgets. This technique does not take into account the special needs and advertising preferences of individual businesses and their market, such as pay-per-click (also called online paid search). Small businesses advertising online through Google AdWords' paid the search service (which has 80% of the market) an average $3.50 per click. However, there is much variation in this average. Businesses that use extremely targeted AdWords' paid search, such as "electric pet fence, Edmonton," may pay only a few cents; businesses that use broad and competitive search terms, such as "mortgage" may pay up to $80 per click. Opimum7, an American paid search consulting firm, suggests small businesses should budget for a minimum $1000 per month for paid search.

Goals and objectives

Another technique bases the marketing budget on an estimate of how much money is required to attain the company's marketing goals and objectives. In order for this method to be successful, you need to have a coordinated marketing program with specific objectives based on a survey of your markets and their potential.

The percentage of sales method determines how much will be spent without much consideration for what you want to accomplish. The goals and objectives method does the reverse. It establishes what you must do in order to meet your objectives. Only then are the costs calculated. The problem with this method is that it may be difficult to estimate with any high degree of accuracy. In addition, financial resources may not be sufficient to meet all the marketing objectives. It is important, therefore, to rank your objectives and allocate resources accordingly. Regardless of the method used, it is important to be flexible. You may need to change the budget plan based on reality and the resources available.

The budget period depends on the nature of your business. If shorter budget periods are used, this will enable your strategies to change based on immediate trends. It is important to allocate a contingency as part of your budget to deal with special circumstances. This would include special programs available in local media; introduction of a new product; cooperative advertising opportunities with manufacturers, wholesalers, or other noncompetitive businesses; and unexpected competitive situations. In this latter example, it is important to be aware of your competitor's activities at all times. Analyze how their approach might affect your business, and be prepared to act accordingly by advance planning.

Measuring Your Marketing Success

A necessary part of your marketing planning and strategy is having an ongoing system for testing its effectiveness. Tools to assist in that process include annual marketing, promotion, and advertising calendars or your own spreadsheet. In both, you record on a daily or weekly basis the sales and promotional expenditures and other variables that provide a basis for analysis. Another method, often used by consulting or information businesses that use spreadsheet prospecting lists, is to add sections that record revenue per client, time to sale, and other relevant costs, such as for websites, hosting, and direct advertising.

Many small business owners spend money on advertising without having means of tracking the effectiveness of that advertising. This makes for poor quality decision-making. If sales are up, there is a perception that the marketing plan is working properly. Sales, of course, are only one of the various components of the overall marketing program. Good business image, certainly another objective of marketing, may take much longer to turn into increased sales. Following are some of the marketing evaluation techniques available:

Point-of-contact market research

Add a question form to every online point of contact with every visitor, customer or prospect, such as an online order or query e-mail, etc. This form should include the question "How did you hear about us?" with a drop-down menu of options and a blank space marked "Other." To make this technique more effective, ensure that the person making the contact cannot move on until the form is completed (through a "Please answer this question" note). You could deepen this research by asking for suggestions on how their interaction experience with you could be improved. Be careful not to make the task too onerous, however, or your visitor may abandon the site.

This is an excellent way to track which parts of your marketing mix are optimal and which are a waste of time and money. It will also help add real information to your instinctual beliefs as to which marketing is working best.

Cost per sale

In this technique, marketing expenditures are divided by the total number of sales made to obtain an average cost per sale. This will give you another reference point to compare the effectiveness of your marketing over time

Coding

Because the Internet allows strong analysis or almost every move made by a visitor to a website or a special landing page, online coding has entered a new dimension. Pages can be examined regularly to track their popularity and can then be changed to maximize sales. How the page copy moved the visitor through the pitch and purchase process can be tracked. Names or number codes can be attached to all promotions and then asked for during client orders or queries as a tracking mechanism. This way, you can determine how a promotion is working. (If no code was entered, you then know that the visit likely resulted from an organic search and if your search engine optimization efforts are working.)

Testing

There are testing techniques in which you can isolate one element of your marketing mix to determine its effectiveness. For example, say you delete one part of your promotional mix for 1 month, and then the next month you add it in. There should be a clear increase in sales at the end of the second month if the added feature was effective. You can then assess the additional cost of the item being tested relative to the financial benefits. Website managers often perform "split testing," in which several landing pages are designed and then tested against one another to see which result in the most "conversions," or desired actions. Keep in mind that conversions may involve several actions that are not immediately sales-oriented. For example a desired action may be the downloading of a white paper or other informational product as part of the sales funnel.

LEGAL ASPECTS OF MARKETING

Before embarking on your marketing approaches, you should consider their possible legal implications. Your marketing, advertising, promotion, and selling techniques could be regulated by government. Your business could also have liability exposure from customers or the public due to a defective product or negligent service. Make sure that you check in advance the regulations that might affect you. Contact your provincial Department of Consumer and Corporate Affairs and Industry Canada. Your trade association may have information on common problems in your industry sector. After you have done your preliminary research, contact your lawyer and obtain specific advice to protect yourself.

The following overview will cover the main areas of which you should be aware, in terms of municipal, provincial, and federal legislation, and product liability.

Municipal Legislation

Most municipalities have legislation that regulates various business practices. If you have a storefront, there could be bylaws that restrict the size of signs above your building or prohibit sandwich boards on the sidewalk. The hours of business could be restricted in certain areas of the city, plus there could be a bylaw restricting the operation of retail businesses on a Sunday. None of these apply to the online aspect of a business, because it is "virtual" in that it has no physical assets. However, some municipalities have a "home office" licencing requirement depending on the nature of your home-based business. As covered in Chapter 20, if you have a home office, you need to have extra home insurance coverage to protect yourself in the event of a claim that relates to your home-based business operation or a location within your home.

Provincial Legislation

Most provinces have legislation to protect the consumer from illegal or unfair trade practices, defective goods, and other matters. The following general overview will discuss the Business Practices Act, Sale of Goods Act, and Consumer Protection Act. Although the titles and content of the following legislation may vary depending on the province, the overall purpose is still the same.

Business Practices Legislation (Federal or Provincial)

Business practices legislation applies to consumer transactions, not trade transactions. If a business operates in an unfair fashion in the process of inducing a consumer to sign an agreement, it could be contravening this Act. In addition, the consumer can sue the business for any financial loss. Any statement, offer, representation, proposal, or request made to the consumer by the business, with the intent to supply goods or services to the consumer, is covered by the Act.

This type of legislation also covers purchases, as long as the purchase is for personal, family, or household use. It does not cover transactions such as real estate, insurance, securities (stocks and bonds), and rental housing. When a business sells, leases, or even makes representations to a consumer, it would probably be considered a consumer transaction and fall within the Act. Naturally, this act is difficult to enforce in the case of some online businesses, because they cross provincial and national boundaries. In that case, use extra caution when dealing with Internet-only businesses.

Typical examples of illegal practices included in the legislation are quoted as follows:

False, misleading or deceptive practices:

- a representation that the goods or services have sponsorship, approval, performance characteristics, accessories, uses, ingredients, benefits, or quantities they do not have
- a representation that the goods are of a particular standard, quality, grade, style, or model, if they are not
- a representation that the goods are new, or unused, if they are not
- a representation that the goods or services are available to the consumer, when the person making the representation knows, or ought to know, they will not be supplied
- a representation that a service, part, replacement, or repair is needed, if it is not
- a representation using exaggeration, innuendo, or ambiguity as to material fact or failing to state a material fact if such use or failure deceives or tends to deceive
- failure to disclose important details which would affect a buying decision

Unfair practices that are made in respect of a particular transaction. In determining whether or not a consumer representation is unfair, it may be taken into account that the person making the representation, or his employer, knows or ought to know the following:

- that the price grossly exceeds the price at which similar goods or services are readily available to like consumers

- that there is no reasonable probability of payment of the obligation in full to the consumer
- that the proposed transaction is excessively one-sided in favour of someone other than the consumer
- that the business is making a misleading statement of opinion on which the consumer is likely to rely to his detriment
- that the business is subjecting the consumer to undue pressure to enter into the transaction.

Anti-Spam Legislation

In 2010, the federal government passed a law that aims to deter the most dangerous and deceptive forms of spam, such as identity theft, phishing, and spyware from occurring in Canada and to help drive out spammers.

The new act establishes a regulatory framework to protect electronic commerce in Canada. It:

- addresses unsolicited commercial electronic mail (spam) by prohibiting the sending of commercial electronic messages without consent;
- prohibits detrimental practices to electronic commerce, protects the integrity of transmission data and prohibit the installation of computer programs without consent in the course of commercial activity;
- prohibits false or misleading commercial representations online;
- prohibits the collection of personal information via unlawful access to computer systems and the unauthorized compiling or supplying of lists of electronic addresses;
- provides for a private right of action for businesses and consumers;
- provides for extended liability (follow the money);
- allows the Canadian Radio-Television and Telecommunications Commission (CRTC) and Competition Tribunal Canada to impose administrative monetary penalties on those who violate the respective Acts;
- allows for the international sharing of information and evidence to pursue spammers outside of Canada with our global partners.

Personal Information Protection and Electronic Documents Act (PIPEDA)

This legislation's purpose is to protect consumers from organizations that collect and store information that is not needed to manage their business. In a competitive atmosphere, businesses rely on personal information to identify and stay in touch with their customers. They use it to seek out new customers who might be interested in their products, or to determine what the market is looking for and what it will bear. They also want information about their employees, so they can administer benefits and ensure safe and productive workplaces.

The basic outline of PIPEDA looks like this:

- If your business wants to collect, use, or disclose personal information about people, you need their consent, except in a few specific and limited circumstances.
- You can use or disclose people's personal information only for the purpose for which they gave consent.
- Even with consent, you have to limit collection, use, and disclosure to purposes that a reasonable person would consider appropriate under the circumstances.
- Individuals have a right to see the personal information that your business holds about them and to correct any inaccuracies.

There's oversight, through the Privacy Commissioner of Canada, to ensure that the law is respected, and redress if people's rights are violated.

Sale of Goods Legislation (Provincial)

The sale of goods legislation in each province varies, and applies to a situation in which a seller agrees to transfer or transfers goods to a buyer for money. In order for a buyer to be protected by the legislation, there is a minimum amount of purchase required, generally over $50. The agreement between the parties must also be in writing. An exception is if the buyer has already accepted the goods or has made partial payment. Key issues include implied conditions and warranties, quality, quantity, and place of delivery of goods. The Act requires that all items sold be serviceable and reasonably free of defects. This implied warranty applies automatically to the retail sale of all new goods sold primarily for personal or household use. If there is a breach of the implied warranty, the buyer can only sue for damages. On the other hand, if there is a breach of an implied condition, the buyer can terminate the contract and/or sue for financial losses. The difference between a condition and warranty is that a condition is considered to be a major and fundamental ingredient to the contract. A warranty is usually considered to be a minor matter. If the consumer decides to commence an action for faulty goods, an action can be brought not only against the retailer but also against the manufacturer and possibly others in the distribution chain.

An implied warranty does not automatically give the buyer a right to return or reject the goods. Depending on the nature of the goods, the retailer may be entitled to repair or exchange the merchandise. Some retailers attempt to limit or negate the implied warranty. This is frequently done by a clause being inserted in the retail sales contract to the effect that the warranty revokes or limits all previous warranties expressed, implied or otherwise. The difficulty for the retailer in this example is that the implied warranty is governed by provincial legislation. In most cases, the law would consider void a waiver clause such as this.

Consumer Protection Legislation (Provincial)

The consumer protection legislation varies depending on the province, and applies only to consumer transactions and not to real estate transactions or to the purchase of insurance. Some of the provisions are discussed below.

The legislation covers a contract where the goods are not delivered at the time the contract is made or where the total amount of money is not paid at the time the contract is made. To be covered, the purchase price of the goods or services normally has to exceed $50, and a written contract is required. To be legally binding, the contract must contain various particulars, such as names and addresses of the parties; description of goods or services; itemized price of goods; statement of any security given, if credit is involved; full disclosure of the credit terms; statement of warranty or guarantee, if any; and signatures of both parties. Each party retains an original signed copy.

If a contract is made at a place other than the seller's permanent address (e.g., door-to-door sales), the buyer has a period of time (cooling-off period) in which to cancel the contract. This is done by letter delivered to the seller. This is called *rescission*, and generally applies to contracts of $50 or more. Upon receiving the consumer's request for rescission, the seller must return any money or other asset to the consumer.

If a consumer is buying on credit, the seller must provide the purchaser, before granting credit, with a clearly written statement showing the total finance charges and the annual percentage rate being charged. In addition, the seller must show in writing any additional fees to be charged to the consumer on default of payment. This disclosure provision applies to contracts for goods and services purchased on credit, monthly charge accounts, and all loans.

The legislation limits the consumer's liability in the area of unsolicited goods. Any unordered merchandise, either delivered or through the mail, may legally be kept by the consumer or can be thrown out.

The legislation allows the government to issue a cease and desist order, if it appears that an advertisement by a seller or lender is false, misleading, or deceptive.

Anyone found guilty of contravening any of the various Acts discussed is liable for a fine and/or imprisonment. A corporation committing the offence is liable for a fine.

Federal Legislation

The federal government has various legislation relating to misleading advertising and deceptive marketing practices, which of course apply throughout Canada. The main legislation is the Competition Act. In addition, there are other federal statutes which provide a degree of regulation over the content and style of an advertisement. In relation to certain classes or types of products, protective legislation is covered under the Food and Drugs Act, the Consumer Packaging and Labelling Act, and the Textile Labelling Act. In relation to specific situations, for example, radio or TV promises or testimonials, the advertisement would be regulated by the Broadcasting Act.

The following outlines the types of improper marketing or advertising practices, and how the Competition Act legislation is enforced.

Types of improper marketing or advertising practices

The most common misleading advertising and deceptive marketing practices causing complaints are as follows:

- **Higher price than advertised.** This is prohibited. The Act does not apply where the advertised price was an error, and has immediately been corrected.
- **Double ticketing.** If two or more prices are clearly shown on a product, its container or wrapper, the product must be supplied at the lower price.
- **Bait and switch selling.** This refers to a situation in which there is an advertisement of a product at a bargain price, and the advertiser does not have it for sale in a reasonable quantity. The seller attempts to convince the consumer to buy a higher-value product, or one of lesser quality, on the basis that there are no more products available at the bargain price. This type of deliberate attempt to mislead the public is prohibited.
- **Price fixing.** Under the Act, it is an offence for persons to conspire or arrange with another person to prevent or lessen competition unduly. In practical terms, this means that business people in the same market cannot agree to fix prices and thereby limit price competition.

There are other misleading advertising and deceptive marketing practices covered in the Act. These relate to performance claims, warranties, tests and testimonials, and pyramid selling schemes.

Enforcement of the legislation

Investigations under the Competition Act are undertaken as a result of complaints from the public, or independently by the government. Whenever there is a reason to believe any provisions of the Act have been violated, an inquiry is commenced. If the results of an investigation disclose evidence that provides the basis for a prosecution, the matter is then referred to the Attorney General of Canada. A decision is made whether to prosecute or not. All the misleading advertising and deceptive marketing practices offences under the Act are brought before the criminal courts, and each element of an offence must be proven beyond a reasonable doubt at trial.

The Marketing Practices Branch of Industry Canada publishes a quarterly report entitled *The Misleading Advertising Bulletin*. This bulletin provides information on convictions under the misleading advertising and deceptive marketing practices provisions of the Act, as well as other related matters of current or ongoing interest. Check: competitionbureau.gc.ca.and ic.gc.ca.

Legal Tips to Follow when Advertising

To minimize potential problems, the following advertising cautions should be understood and complied with by the business owner and any employees:

- Don't use illustrations that are different from a description of the product actually being sold.
- Don't use the term "regular price" in an advertisement unless it is the price at which the product is usually sold.
- Don't run a sale for a long period or repeated every week.
- Don't increase the price of the product to cover the cost of a free product or service.
- Don't use the words "sale" or "special" unless a significant price reduction has occurred.
- Don't confuse regular price with manufacturer's suggested list price, as they are often not the same.
- Don't overuse disclaimers.
- Don't make a performance claim before you can substantiate it, even if you think it is accurate.
- Don't forget that no one actually needs to be misled in order to convince the court that an advertisement is misleading.
- Don't sell a product above your advertised price.
- Don't forget that the legislation protecting the public covers the naive as well as the sophisticated consumer.
- Do avoid terms or phrases in an advertisement that are not meaningful or clear to the ordinary person.
- Do fully and clearly disclose all material that is important and relevant information in the advertisement.
- Do ensure that you have reasonable quantities of a product advertised at a bargain price.

- Do ensure that your sales force is familiar with the law in terms of representations, as advertisers may be held responsible for representations made by their employees.

Product Liability

Product liability simply means that if the consumer is injured or suffers financial losses because of a defective product, the consumer can sue for damages. The injured consumer can potentially sue anyone in the distribution chain for liability. This would include the manufacturer and the retailer, as well as the parties in between, such as wholesalers and distributors. A court would have to determine the relevant merits of the claim for damages.

The definition of consumer is very broad. It includes the original purchaser of a product, any person who received the product free, a subsequent purchaser from the original purchaser, or any members of the purchaser's family.

In Canada, the basic test to determine liability is whether a duty was owed to the consumer to take reasonable care that the product was safe. If such a duty existed, and it was not met, the grounds for liability could possibly be successfully asserted. It is up to the consumer to prove the claim.

In the United States, there is a legal doctrine called strict liability, which frequently is applied in the case of product liability. Strict liability means that the injured person does not have to prove negligence in order to succeed. Instead, the party being sued is deemed to be liable if the facts clearly show that injury occurred. It is up to the defendant to show why they should not be liable. For this reason, if you are a business owner selling, manufacturing, or distributing a product in the United States, be very cautious. The importer in the United States may require evidence that you have product liability insurance sufficient to protect the importer from any potential claims. The cost of product liability insurance might be extremely high, if it is available at all.

If you have any potential liability concerns about the product that you manufacture or distribute, obtain the advice of a lawyer who specializes in product liability law.

COMMON PITFALLS TO AVOID WHEN MARKETING

Now that you have a better understanding of the factors involved in marketing, you should know about some common pitfalls to avoid. Here are some of the frequent sources of frustration, and areas that create problems:

- unclear understanding of market due to failure to prepare, update, and follow a marketing plan

- unwillingness or inability to obtain, organize, and analyze marketing information
- ignoring or being unaware of what customers actually need and want
- developing a marketing approach based on the needs of the seller, rather than the buyer
- putting on sales promotions with terms and conditions based on product or business considerations, rather than market criteria
- being caught by surprise by changes in the market
- relying too heavily on market research data, instead of relying on or applying common sense
- failing to implement and consistently maintain a customer feedback system, and failing to review the content of the feedback and make changes accordingly
- having an inconsistent or inadequate sales coverage and market share across key market segments
- relying on market data automatically without analyzing it or looking for the implications behind the data
- lack of effective coordination with distribution channels, using an inefficient customer-ordering system, inadequate training and compensation of sales force, forgetting that the customer is always right
- failing to keep delivery promises
- failing to quickly and effectively deal with customer complaints
- pricing a major product too low and hoping that the volume will compensate for the discount
- being rigid rather than creative in thought, thereby missing potential innovative solutions and opportunities
- lack of repair service, shoddy workmanship on repairs, poor product quality, exaggerated product claims
- unsuitable or poor packaging, inadequate labelling or instructions.

Employees should be trained on matters dealing with customer satisfaction. Feedback should be elicited from employees on methods of improving the quality of service to customers.

SOURCES OF INFORMATION AND ASSISTANCE ON MARKETING

There are many excellent sources of advice and information that will help you perform your marketing function successfully. The following list will help you obtain specific information on the subject of marketing to assist you in the preparation and implementation of a marketing plan.

The Internet

There are millions of sources of marketing education online. If you are performing an online search, look past generic terms, such as "marketing," and be more specific. Pick individual aspects of marketing and use search term strings (three to five or more words) to zero in on relevant results. For example, for advertising, use a term like "the best advertising outlets for a business that sell shoes".

Provincial governments

Many of the provincial governments have booklets on marketing that are free of charge. These publications usually include a marketing plan guide, as well as various techniques of pricing, depending on whether the business relates to retail, service, or manufacturing.

You can also obtain free counselling advice from provincial small business counsellors on a wide range of areas relating to marketing within or outside Canada. Information can also be obtained on techniques for marketing to the provincial government purchasing department, as every provincial government buys services and products from the private sector. See Appendix D for a listing of provincial contact addresses.

Federal government

There are several federal government departments that can provide information and publications relating to the marketing functions, such as hazardous products, defective products, misleading advertising, or illegal marketing practices. Public Works and Government Services Canada provides an information kit with brochures for small businesses that are interested in selling goods or services to the federal government or Crown corporations. Foreign Affairs and International Trade Canada has comprehensive material and information available on marketing a product or service outside Canada. The subject of importing and exporting is covered in Chapter 14. Refer to Appendix D for contact addresses.

BDC

The BDC website is a source of much information related to operating a small business. Local BDC branches also offer consulting services to small businesses.

Colleges or universities

There are many marketing courses and seminars conducted through colleges and universities, as well as school board night school courses. These programs are noncredit programs for the general public and tend to be very practical. Contact the university, college, or school board continuing education department and ask to be put on the mailing list for any courses relating to marketing.

Libraries

There are many books available on the subject of marketing, relating not only to service and product marketing, but also to a specific industry sector. Many of these books are available through a public library or college or university library. In addition, the small business departments of many provincial governments have resource libraries available to the general public.

Trade associations

Trade associations can be of considerable assistance in providing information on effective marketing specific to the needs of that industry sector. The newsletter of the association plus seminars and workshops that are frequently offered provide an opportunity for ongoing marketing education. Trade associations can be located by searching for them online or by contacting the resource librarian in the business section of your public library and requesting a list of all associations in Canada.

Bank publications

Several chartered banks have publications on marketing for small business.

For more marketing tips and strategies, refer to my book, *Marketing Your Product*, published by International Self-Counsel Press.

Chapter 14

Export/Import

Small opportunities are often the beginnings of great enterprises.

— Demosthenes

Importing and exporting can be a profitable business. No business is too small to consider exporting or importing products or services. Like any business relationship involving another country, there are differences in law, style of business operation, language, culture, standards, tariffs, currency exchange controls, packaging and labelling requirements, payment terms, collection of accounts, and financing. All these areas and others require thorough research and understanding in order to minimize the potential risk. If you take the time to learn the procedures, tips, and strategies, you will not only have a challenging, fascinating, and educational experience, but could succeed in establishing a significant source of income.

This chapter provides an overview of the issues to consider when exporting or importing a product or service. Many businesses do both exporting and importing, whereas some just do one or the other. Some Canadian businesses prefer to start their experience by exporting to or importing from the United States. The geographic proximity, common language and customs, and established flow of trade across the border makes the market more convenient.

In addition, the Free Trade Agreement (FTA) between Canada and the United States, opened many opportunities. This has been replaced by the North American Free Trade Agreement (NAFTA) between Canada, the United States, and Mexico, and it, too, has greatly increased business export opportunities. The Canadian government from time to time negotiates free trade agreements with other countries or regions of the world, so check what opportunities are available. Other businesses may want to become established in a domestic market first, before venturing into the field of exporting or importing. Depending on the circumstances, an export or import business could be started part-time or full-time out of your own home to save overhead expenses, thereby minimizing the risk.

The final section in this chapter details the many sources of government advice and information, and other assistance available. You will find the resources available to you extensive and invaluable. By accessing the full range of free advice, you will minimize the potential business and financial risk involved in exporting or importing.

EXPORTING

Exporting is selling domestic products or services to international markets. Some of the material discussed here overlaps with the marketing information presented in Chapter 13, which discussed selling products domestically. This section covers the advantages and disadvantages of exporting, how to analyze market potential, and methods of financing.

Advantages and Disadvantages of Exporting

Anyone considering exporting should consider both the advantages and disadvantages of taking such an important step. Some firms that should not do any exporting do get involved, whereas other companies that should be involved are reluctant to do so because of lack of information or fear of failure. There is also the perception that only large companies can export. This is inaccurate, as studies have shown that many small businesses have done very well in the international marketplace. Not all the advantages and disadvantages listed below are applicable to every type of export situation, since it obviously depends on many factors, such as the nature of the product, shelf life of the product, and the amount of financing required.

Advantages of exporting

- additional markets and diversification of markets
- reduction of reliance on single domestic markets lowers unit cost of production
- increased efficiency by better utilization of personnel and equipment
- increased productivity
- offsets lack of domestic demand for seasonal products or cyclical downtrends
- increased sales—this is especially important when firms find their domestic sales stagnating due to strong competition, oversaturation of the market, or both
- increased profits, since fixed costs are already covered by existing domestic sales
- increase in number of customers
- potential high demand and low competition in foreign markets
- increased life cycle of existing product or service
- new knowledge and experience that can be applied to the domestic market
- chance of government financial and other assistance

- additional product or service lines
- tax advantages (e.g., tax-deductible travel expenses)
- source of needed growth capital
- can be operated part-time or full-time out of the home in many circumstances
- larger export transactions could create higher profit than many smaller domestic transactions
- smaller firms can take advantage of market niches not served by larger companies
- smaller firms are more flexible in reacting more quickly to changing market conditions or meeting specific customer needs.

Disadvantages of exporting

- requirement of additional and more complicated financing
- additional time, travel, and expense required to develop export market
- increase in shipping costs and paperwork
- possible product modifications (e.g., different colours or wattage to meet local needs)
- additional cost to redo brochures and informational material to account for different languages and literacy
- need to retrain or hire additional staff, as export sales staff would be required to look after selling, financing, packaging, documentation, advertising, and servicing
- lack of experience in the specialized area of marketing internationally
- lack of awareness in avoiding exporting pitfalls
- higher credit risks and for longer terms.

Methods of Building Export Sales

There are several methods of increasing your export sales: direct export, indirect export, licensing, and direct investment.

Direct export

With direct exporting, you are dealing directly with the foreign buyer. The products are shipped directly from the manufacturing plant to the buyer.

Many of the technical problems of the company wishing to export directly can be minimized or eliminated by using the services of experienced shipping agents and freight forwarders.

Indirect export

In indirect export, you would sell to a buyer in Canada for shipment to international markets. Your primary marketing role in developing sales indirectly involves sourcing out potential agents to represent your product. Following are several types of agent relationships.

- **Export broker.** This is a person who is employed as a specialist in specific product lines. The role of this broker is to bring a foreign buyer and domestic seller together. After a sales agreement has been signed, the broker receives a commission.
- **Resident buyer.** This person is a direct representative in Canada for large foreign firms who acts as a purchasing agent on a continuous basis.
- **Export commission house.** These are purchasing agents in Canada who are buying for specific projects abroad. The export commission house obtains the commission from the foreign purchaser if a sale is consummated. Usually it works closely with aid organizations, such as Canadian International Development Agency (CIDA; cida.gc.ca) or Export Development Canada (EDC; edc.ca).
- **Export merchant or trading company.** These companies purchase directly products that may or may not be competitive with existing product lines they handle.

As opposed to direct exporting, this method saves money on staff, advertising, travel, and paperwork. In addition, the credit risk is reduced, as is the expenditure of time and energy. The disadvantages include less profit than from direct exporting, lack of control over sales promotion used, lack of direct contact with the foreign buyer, and contract terms that may limit your flexibility.

Licensing

This technique of increasing export sales involves licensing a foreign firm to manufacture and sell your product under specific terms and conditions. The licensee is given the patents and production information, and may also be assigned other related copyright and trademarks owned by the Canadian company. The Canadian company receives a royalty on sales. In dealing with the licensing area, there are many potential pitfalls. Competent, specialized legal assistance is required. In addition, protections for patents, trademarks, copyright, or industrial design may have to be registered in the foreign country before any assignment would be valid. (Refer to Chapter 18, "Patent, Trademark, Copyright, and Industrial Design.")

Direct investment

This involves establishing a manufacturing operation in a foreign country. There are many government financial incentives in foreign countries to encourage construction of a manufacturing operation, as it creates employment and therefore helps the economy. The Canadian government also has funding for specific types of projects through CIDA. A common method of direct investment is a joint venture relationship with a foreign partner. One of the benefits of that type of relationship is reduced risk, because the partner would have an intimate familiarity with the unique business features of the foreign country. Naturally there is a lot less risk in selling a product to a foreign country than investing in that foreign country, particularly if there is political instability.

Selecting Your Product and Market

When you are sourcing a potential product for export, there are many techniques that you can use. Naturally, you would prefer to have a product which is not perishable and does not require a lot of servicing, as this would add additional risk, cost, and frustration. At the outset, it is prudent to be cautious in selecting a product. In addition, you may want to deal with just one product until you have developed the expertise to add additional product lines. If you do not have your own product that you are manufacturing, you could attempt to become an export agent for other manufacturers who want to have their product sold outside Canada.

Once you have determined the product or products you are interested in, you then have to look at the potential markets for those products. Advertising online or in print in a trade magazine, for example, in publications of the Canadian Chamber of Commerce (chamber.ca), the Canadian Manufacturers' and Exporters Association (cme-mec.ca), or the Canadian Association of Importers and Exporters (iecanada.com), is a way of eliciting the names of companies who may wish to export their products. You may also want to refer to the directory of Canadian manufacturers published by Dun & Bradstreet and to obtain membership lists from the Canadian Manufacturers' and Exporters Association and the Canadian Association of Importers and Exporters. Also, the federal government department Export Development Canada and Foreign Affairs and International Trade Canada (international.gc.ca) are excellent sources of assistance and information. Do specific Google searches under keywords to locate other sources of potential leads. Also check with your provincial government. Most provincial governments have departments to assist and encourage provincial businesses with export assistance, as it is to the vested interest of the province to export.

Before you decide to offer your services as an export agent and attempt to obtain an exclusive agreement for the specific market area, naturally you will have to educate yourself thoroughly in order to be credible as well as effective. The basic information that you need to obtain can be found in the federal and provincial government information sources referred to extensively later in this chapter, as well as in the next section, "Preparing a Market Analysis." These references will provide you with ideas on countries that need specific products, and products that need specific foreign markets. In addition, these publications provide you with tips on communicating effectively by means of e-mail, correspondence, or telephone; in face-to-face meetings; or through Skype or another VOIP option to personalize yourself when conducting export or import inquiries. Attending trade conferences is another obvious option to meeting firsthand with prospects.

Preparing a Market Analysis

Before doing a market analysis on the export potential for the product, you will have to consider doing an analysis of your existing company operation, if you are manufacturing in Canada. Look at your company in terms of sales, profits, prices, costs, product lines, production capacity, and inventories compared with the industry average. Determine if you can service the foreign market, and what additional financing might be required, as well as the additional production and personnel that may be required. As in any marketing assessment, you have to look at the product, the place it is going to be sold, its price, and the method of promotion.

When undertaking a market survey, you will need to obtain current trade statistics and information for each potential market.

You should be able to do most of your preliminary market research in Canada. Once you have selected a market, you should visit that country to confirm and supplement your knowledge of it. You will want to do this before committing yourself to exporting your product there. Before travelling to the country you wish to export to, it is important to consider the following:

- general background (geography, population, natural resources, industrial development, economics, present political situation, and cultural or religious considerations)
- market accessibility (restrictions, customs, currency, labelling and packaging, bilateral trade agreements, market policy, and attitude towards imports or products from Canada)
- market potential (current and potential demand, domestic production, existing exports from Canada, increase or decrease in imports, prices, market control, and acceptability of new products)
- market requirements or regulations (system of measurement, method of price quotation and payment, market preferences, and health safety and technical standards applicable)
- distribution channels (system of buying, normal distribution channels, agents or representatives required, amount of stock required, sales promotions available, exclusivity, servicing, transportation, and licensing or joint venture requirements).

Once you have assessed your market potential, you will have to consider, among other factors, the issue of pricing. There are two main methods of setting export prices.

Domestic price structure

In this method, you add the following export-related costs to your present domestic price: packaging, shipping, tariffs and customs, marine and export insurance, freight forwarder's fee, overseas agent's commission, financing, translation, and advertising and promotional literature.

Once you have determined the price by using this method, you may find that the price is too high to survive in the export marketplace.

Marginal cost

In this method, you take the direct costs of the product plus a share of the overhead that would relate to the export sales cost. You then add your expected profit plus all the additional costs referred to in the previous method (that is, the domestic price structure approach).

Whenever you are quoting prices to a customer overseas, it is important to be clear on their landed costs and what will be included in those costs. The currency of payment has to be specifically stated, as well as the method and terms of payment. As mentioned earlier, there are free publications available to help you cost out exactly the type of pricing that is suitable for your needs.

Export Financing

The financing aspects of export are different and have a higher risk than conventional domestic financing. You could find that the importer of your products has gone out of business or is defaulting on your payments for other reasons. These types of problems can naturally occur in a domestic marketplace. There are additional risks to exporting, such as refusal of a foreign buyer to accept goods, cancelled export or import permits, and critical problems in the foreign country, such as riots or war. Export Development Canada can provide insurance for many types of contingencies.

The main forms of financing are seller financing, that is, financing arranged by the seller (you as an exporter), and buyer financing. In this latter example, the buyer frequently obtains financing from Canadian government agencies. Most of the transactions and documentation is done electronically, of course.

Seller credits

- **Cash advance.** Import/export payments are seldom prepaid in full. Sometimes a percentage of the sale price is paid in advance as a good faith gesture, but in practical terms the importer of the product does not want to pay the money in full at the outset. From the exporter's point of view, if the total amount is received in advance, there are obviously no financing problems.

- **Letters of credit.** This is a form of promissory note in which the buyer promises to pay the exporter for the products as long as the instructions in the letter of credit are followed. Letters of credit should be guaranteed by a reputable bank and be irrevocable. A letter of credit must be accepted and confirmed by your bank and the buyer's bank in advance. Your bank guarantees payment as soon as your obligations under the agreement are met. There may be disadvantages in dealing with letters of credit, and you should obtain the advice of the international department of your chartered bank before manufacturing or shipping any goods.

- **Open account.** This method of payment is risky, and it should only be used where there is a high degree of confidence and a pre-established relationship, or between two branches of the same company. No bank financing is involved, nor is any responsibility placed on the bank to require fulfillment of any conditions relating to the shipment. The exporter ships the merchandise and sends an invoice directly to the buyer, who in turn is supposed to make payment at that time along the terms of the agreement between the parties.

- **Consignment.** In this example, the goods are shipped to the importer in another country without advance payment. If the goods are sold, you get paid for them. If the goods are not sold, they would normally be returned to the exporter. This type of arrangement normally occurs where there is a high degree of trust between the parties based on previous experience or to get rid of old stock that is no longer in demand domestically. There is a risk, of course, of the importer defaulting on his or her contractual obligations.

- **Drafts.** There are two main types of drafts—sight drafts and time drafts. Sight drafts are used when the exporter and importer have an established relationship. The exporter draws a draft on the buyer's bank, enclosing shipping and ownership documents for transfer of ownership of the exported goods to the buyer after payment of the amount of the draft. You are reimbursed directly by the buyer's bank or through your own bank. A time draft allows the buyer a period of grace between the taking of possession of the goods and payment through the buyer's bank. Under certain circumstances, an exporter may request bank financing upon receipt of the proceeds from the draft. In this type of situation, the exporter normally discounts the draft to obtain funds or pledges the draft to the bank as security for advances. Sight and time drafts are referred to as *documentary collections*.

- **Factoring.** In this type of financing, a factoring company purchases sales contracts at a discount and assumes the responsibility for the financial risk and collection. If the foreign buyer fails to pay, the factor takes a loss. Factoring normally occurs in industrialized nations rather than in underdeveloped countries. A factoring house acts on behalf of the seller, whereas a confirming house acts on behalf of the importer and guarantees that a buyer will pay when the payment is due.
- **Countertrade.** This method is primarily a barter method in which goods of equal value are exchanged, rather than money being exchanged. There are variations of countertrade, including an obligation by the exporter to buy products of equivalent value from the importer.
- **Bid and performance bonds.** When a Canadian exporter is bidding on a foreign contract, it is often required that a bid bond be arranged. If the contract is awarded, a performance bond would then be required. These types of financing arrangements are normally done through a chartered bank and/or the Export Development Canada.

Buyer credits

Buyer credits are a means of financing a foreign buyer to purchase the Canadian goods. The Canadian government normally provides the financing in order to encourage a contract to be made and provide working capital for the Canadian company. This would be done through the Export Development Canada or the Canadian International Development Agency (cida.ca) Whereas seller credit financing is nominally short term (under 1 year), buyer credits tend to be medium (1 to 5 years) or long-term (over 5 years). There is short-term buyer credit financing available, but it is based on the foreign buyer's ability to repay, and political and economic stability in that foreign country. Short-term buyer credits provide the exporter with cash flow to generate sales without increasing available operating lines of credit. Buyer credits are generally for large-purchase items, such as capital goods and services.

Obtaining financing

There are many forms of financing available for exporters. These include federal and provincial government financing, bank financing, or buyer or seller financing.

IMPORTING

Importing, like exporting, has the potential for very profitable returns. Also, the risk can be high, unless thorough research is done, and the target market is clearly understood. The freight forwarder, customs broker, and banker are the main experts to deal with when importing.

There is less risk in importing than exporting. When you start out, you have a much better understanding of your own market than you do a foreign market. You may already have a distribution company with existing products, and you want to add to your product line. You may want to be an exclusive distributor in Canada and advertise for local agents to market your product. You may be a manufacturer who wants to increase sales by adding products that complement existing product lines. Or you may be a manufacturer wanting to obtain cheaper component parts by importing directly, thereby cutting out the intermediary. Whatever your reasons, importing is an attractive business option to consider.

This section covers the methods of locating foreign products, pricing your product, dealing with Canada Border Services Agency (cbsa.gc.ca), and financing your imports.

Market Research

You should do thorough market research in Canada to determine the need for the product you have selected. Once you have determined there is a need, have priced your product accurately, and have obtained potential sources of financing, then you may want to take a trip to the foreign country to meet the manufacturer directly. Here are some of the factors to consider in your market research:

- Is there a similar product in Canada?
- What is the price and quality of the similar product?
- What does the foreign product sell for, and how much are you prepared to pay for it?
- Can you obtain financing from the exporter or the exporter's government?
- If the product is for human consumption, what Canadian government import restrictions are involved?
- What will be the actual cost to land the product in Canada, and what will be the total cost to have the product put on the shelf?
- Will you require a representative in the foreign country or a sales organization in Canada, and what will the costs for those be?
- At what point do you take possession in Canada, and at what point do you turn over the product in Canada?

Canada Border Services Agency

Once you have decided to import a product, you have to deal with Canada Customs and related government regulations. You can obtain detailed information by utilizing the following sources:

- **Canada Border Services Agency.** This department can provide information on duty, taxes, quotas, inspections, labelling, and documentation.

The have an online *Guide for Canadian Exporters* with excellent referral links.

- **Trade associations.** The Canadian Association of Importers and Exporters and the Canadian Manufacturers' and Exporters Association have information on rates of duty, value for duty, anti-dumping laws, new tariff items, foreign exchange, and other matters.
- **Customs brokers.** For a fee, these brokers will handle bringing goods into Canada, including carrying them through Customs. Do a Google search for customs brokers in the region of interest to you.
- **Publications.** Refer to publications available from Foreign Affairs and International Trade Canada.

Pricing Your Product

Be particularly careful when pricing a product that you are considering importing into Canada. Once you have done your market research, you will have a better idea of the associated costs. There are many costs between the time that the goods leave the manufacturer and the time that they arrive in Canada and are put on the shelf. Make sure that you build a healthy contingency and profit into the price and that the pricing will be competitive. If after your investigation you find the profit is marginal, it would be better to forget that product and look for another.

Here are some of the costs and considerations that go into the construction of your pricing:

- Cost of goods in Canadian dollars, because exchange rates fluctuate. Allow yourself a buffer in this calculation, as an underestimation will come directly from your profit.
- Freight costs could include inland freight to port of loading or loading area, terminal charges at the port of loading, ocean or air freight charges, terminal charges at the port of entry, and so on.
- Marine or air insurance
- Canadian government duty and excise tax
- Fees from customs brokers or freight forwarders
- Inland transportation to your warehouse
- Warehouse charges in Canada
- Final delivery costs or distribution costs
- Bank charges and rates
- Finders fees or foreign commissions
- Special inspections
- Your market development or advertising costs
- A portion of overhead costs.

Financing Imported Goods

Just as the Export Development Corporation in Canada provides direct support in making payments to foreign buyers of Canadian goods, many countries have similar or more extensive assistance programs to encourage exports. Prospective Canadian importers should thoroughly investigate all relevant opportunities.

SOURCES OF FURTHER INFORMATION

There are numerous sources of advice and information available on importing and exporting. Most of it is free for the asking. Here are the main sources you should consider.

Federal Government

Foreign Affairs and International Trade Canada (DFAIT; international.gc.ca) Foreign Affairs and International Trade Canada is one of the main government departments that assist in matters relating to exporting and importing. It has an incredible range of helpful export information. Here are some of the key departments:

- Info Export (infoexport.gc.ca). You can obtain complete information on all the export programs and services provided by the federal government. This office will also answer questions about importing. The type of services and publications available include:
  - export information kit
  - Canada Export section of the DFAIT website—current export market trends, successes, and opportunities
  - publications for exporters information on programs for export market development information on NAFTA and other free trade possibilities
  - referrals to other federal and provincial government departments and affiliated export organizations
  - a series of comprehensive booklets entitled *A Guide for Canadian Exporters* which contain geographic, cultural, climactic, economic, and market data for individual countries or market areas
  - contact with trade commissioners worldwide (tradecommissioner. gc.ca), as well as contacts with potential import/export business partners, and other sources of marketing information; trade commissioners are excellent sources of accurate and timely information "on the ground" in the geographic location of interest to you, whether for importing or exporting.

- *Directory of Canadian Representatives Abroad*, includes consular and trade representatives
- Special Trade Relations Division. For specific types of products that you may wish to export or import, there are bureaus set up to provide specific information or export controls in those areas.
- Trade Commissioner Service (tradecommissioner.gc.ca). This service maintains numerous trade offices throughout the world, located in the most strategic commercial centres. There are marketing experts in each of these offices. The role of the Trade Commissioner includes introducing Canadian exporters and importers to the appropriate business contacts in other countries, obtaining and forwarding inquiries for Canadian goods to Ottawa and Canadian exporters, and studying local conditions and needs. In addition, they can make direct inquiries or conduct preliminary surveys regarding potential market opportunities for a product. This would include determining the need for the product, competition, the methods of packaging and shipping, and tariff and trade regulations pertaining to the goods. The main emphasis of the Trade Commissioner is, of course, to encourage Canadian exports. Assistance to Canadian importers and manufacturers on supply of goods and materials in various countries is also available. A Canadian business can contact any one of the Trade Commissioners throughout the world for information on the potential target market. When contacting a Trade Commissioner for the first time, provide a brief history of your company, the type of products that you make or sell, copies of advertising material, your marketing plan, agency agreements, manufacture licence, direct sales, potential target markets, and previous export experience, if any.

Canadian commercial corporation (CCC; ccc.ca)

This is a Crown corporation which reports to the Ministry for International Trade. CCC acts as a prime contractor when foreign governments and international agencies wish to purchase goods and services from Canadian sources through the government. CCC attempts to identify Canadian sources, obtains good opportunities for suppliers, and certifies their capability to perform. The corporation helps to reduce the complexity of export sales for Canadian firms and encourages the use by foreign customers of smaller or less well-known Canadian suppliers. Foreign government buyers have the confidence that they can rely on the Canadian government for the reliability of the supplier. CCC assists in negotiations and monitors the contract management, inspection, shipping, and payment to suppliers. If there are any problems in payment, the corporation collects from the buyers.

EDC

EDC is a Crown corporation that provides financial services to Canadian exporters and foreign buyers to facilitate and develop export trade. The corporation provides credit insurance, surety, and performance guarantees for Canadian exporters. It also provides loans and loan guarantees for foreign purchasers of Canadian goods and services. For example, Canadian firms, regardless of size, can insure their export sales against nonpayment by foreign buyers. EDC normally assumes 90% of the commercial risk involving default or insolvency by the buyer, as well as risks associated with war or rebellion, blockage of funds, cancellation of import licences in a foreign country, or cancellation of export permits in Canada.

The corporation issues guarantees to banks making export loans or issuing performance or bid security. EDC has various types of export financing programs to assist foreign buyers to purchase the Canadian goods or services. The funds are paid directly to Canadian exporters by EDC on behalf of the exporters.

CIDA

CIDA operates Canada's program of official international development assistance in over 100 countries. The agency assists Canadian exporters to penetrate new markets in developing countries by supporting Canadian firms seeking opportunities for investment, joint ventures, and transfers of proven technology. CIDA programs offer financial incentives to Canadian firms in their efforts to develop long-term arrangements for business cooperation and to carry out project feasibility studies in developing countries. Additional assistance is available for identifying opportunities and establishing contacts through conferences and seminars.

Foreign affairs and international trade canada

This federal agency maintains a regional office in each of the ten provinces, and is an excellent resource for counselling advice and assistance in international export marketing opportunities. It can also provide helpful publications; Appendix B has a list of some of the material available. One should ask for the current list as well. Many documents are available for download at the agency's website. Educational programs, conferences, and workshops on various aspects of trade are provided. As Foreign Affairs and International Trade Canada is the main link between the trade promotion programs of the federal and provincial governments, it can direct you to the appropriate industry sector branch in Ottawa that has expertise relating to your product. Services provided include:

Canada Revenue Agency (CRA; cra-arc.gc.ca)

This government department regulates goods imported into Canada, in terms of duties and taxes, tariffs, prohibited and restricted goods, and other matters. If you are interested in importing, you should be aware of the requirements that will affect you. For further information and assistance, visit the extensive CRA website or contact the regional office closest to you. Some of the free publications available include *Thinking about Importing? What You Should Know*; *Value for Duty*; *Importing Goods into Canada? Documentation Simplified*; and *Customs Commercial System: Questions and Answers*.

Statistics Canada (statcan.gc.ca)

This department prepares and publishes a variety of statistical data on export and import matters in Canada. The Statistics Canada library has a comprehensive collection of foreign trade reports and other trade information published by sources overseas. Most of this information is available directly at the Statistics Canada website. This department will also prepare special tabulations of unpublished data to meet specific needs of a business inquiry. One of the many publications of Statistics Canada is called *Exports by Commodities*. This is published monthly, and provides the Canadian exporter with trade statistics classified by commodity and export market.

Public works and government programs Canada (tpsgc-pwgsc.gc.ca)

This government department deals with procurement for many Canadian government agencies, and provides many publications and resources, most available via its website.

BDC

The BDC has several programs that would assist anyone considering importing or exporting. These programs include:

- **Import/export seminars.** The BDC conducts seminars on exporting and importing on an ongoing basis throughout Canada.
- **Matchmaking program.** The BDC maintains a list of various parties who are looking for potential joint venture partners, licensing agreements, or investment opportunities. If you are interested in importing or exporting, this list of contact persons could be valuable to you. You may also want to be on the list yourself.
- **Free quarterly publication entitled Profits.** This publication lists export and import opportunities and has articles on exporting, importing, and marketing.

Provincial Governments

All provincial governments have trade promotion programs. In addition, some have trade offices in the United States, Europe, and Asia. Exports are vital to any provincial economy, and the range of government programs is designed to help you identify the most profitable export opportunities. Contact the clos-est branch of your provincial government small business or international trade department and request further information and publications to assist you in your inquiries.

Provincial government services to the exporter range from loans and insur-ance programs to incentive programs for participating in overseas trade missions and international trade fairs and exhibitions. In addition, the government can assist you in locating and meeting buyers, potential buyers, agents and distribu-tors, as well as provide skilled interpreters. Most provincial governments will pay to bring key agents and buyers from major world markets to the province to meet you personally if the circumstances favour it.

Municipal Governments

Some municipal or regional governments are set up to provide information, sup-port services, and financial incentives to encourage exports from the area. Contact your local community economic development department and make inquiries.

United States Commercial Service (USCS; trade.gov/cs)

This is a division of the United States Department of Commerce, Washington, D.C. Locations are listed on the USCS website. The purpose of this division is to counsel small to medium-sized Canadian companies on trade, investment, and other commercial matters involving the United States. The free services and publications in print and online available include:

- **Commercial library.** This library is accessible in the US & FCS offices throughout Canada. It features major U.S. trade and business directo-ries, information on trade shows, and major statistical yearbooks.
- **Commercial newsletter.** This is published at regular intervals and con-tains information on U.S. trade shows and trade and investment missions coming to Canada. It also highlights hundreds of new American products and services for which Canadian representation or partnerships are being sought. The newsletter is available free of charge.
- **Investment counselling.** The commercial service of the US & FCS provides information on programs and incentives available to Canadian firms interested in investing in the United States.
- **Agent distributor service.** This service helps U.S. businesses locate Canadian agents and distributors for U.S. products and services.
- **Trade missions.** By registering with the commercial section, you would be invited to meet any trade and investment mission representatives coming to Canada.

Seminars are frequently conducted in Canada on exporting to the United States. The commercial section will also assist Canadian business groups visiting the United States to identify sources of products and services. Assistance is also available to help Canadian buyers who wish to attend U.S. trade shows, in terms of arranging and facilitating the trips and arranging introductions to key people at the trade shows.

Foreign Trade Consulates

Every foreign consulate in Canada has a trade office whose job it is to sell goods to Canada. There are often offices in major Canadian cities. Look at consulates' websites—most will have sections or contact numbers specifically for trade departments.

Trade Associations

You may wish to search online to obtain the name of the trade association specific to your industry sector. In terms of importing and exporting, there are two main associations in Canada that can assist you. You may benefit by becoming a member of one or more of the following associations. Excellent newsletters, publications, seminars, and other services are available to guide you.

IE Canada: Canadian association of importers and exporters

Membership comprises companies that have a direct or indirect interest in importing into and exporting from Canada, as well as those that render professional services to importers and exporters. Services include seminars and conferences, as well as representation to various levels of government on matters affecting Canada's import/export community. Publications and other services include the following:

- **Daily news briefing.** This daily report of news about import/export matters and trade is delivered to all members.
- **Membership directory.** This lists all members of the association, including their contact information, addresses, telephone numbers, and product or service description.

Canadian manufacturers and exporters

The objectives of the association are to promote Canadian industries and to further the interests of Canadian manufacturers and exporters. There are a large number of services available to member companies interested in the export field. Some of these services are listed here:

- publications, including regular export and trade bulletins

- *Understanding Export*, a step-by-step comprehensive guide to selling in export markets; updated, revised, and based on the practical experience of successful exporters
- other books, surveys, and a wide range of publications on productivity, labour relations, export legislation, taxation, government grants and incentives, customs, and international affairs
- courses on export documentation and seminars on export marketing
- organization and escort of outgoing Canadian and incoming foreign trade missions.

Chambers of commerce (chamber.ca)

The Canadian Chamber of Commerce and local chambers of commerce and boards of trade in major centres across Canada provide a wide range of programs designed to promote Canadian trade. These programs include seminars and conferences providing information on specific markets, and programs designed to put Canadian companies in touch with foreign buyers. Documentation services required for exporting are also available, including the Carnet, which although not exactly an export document, permits exporters to take Canadian goods as samples or professional equipment into more than forty countries, without going through the normal detailed customs procedures. The Carnet is primarily used by salespeople carrying samples, exhibitors participating in foreign trade fairs, engineers and architects with valuable drawings, and musicians and film crews. A Carnet allows a business traveller to:

- use a single Carnet for goods that will pass through the customs of several countries on one trip
- make customs arrangements in advance for the countries to be visited, quickly and at a predetermined cost
- make a number of trips within the 1-year validity of the Carnet.

For further information, contact the Carnet Canada office closest to you. They can be reached through the Canadian Chamber of Commerce head office in Ottawa or division offices in Toronto, Montreal, and Vancouver.

Many local chambers of commerce and boards of trade across Canada also provide Certificates of Origin and other certification documents that are frequently required by importing countries.

International Chamber of Commerce has publications, including a worldwide chamber of commerce directory. Contact the Montreal office.

Also contact foreign chambers of commerce with branches (e.g., that of Hong Kong) operating in major Canadian cities. Obtain contact numbers from your local Chamber or Board of Trade.

Chartered Banks

The major chartered banks in Canada have large Canadian and foreign international divisions that can provide a range of services for potential importers and exporters. Through a worldwide network of representatives, subsidiaries, affiliates, and correspondents, the major chartered banks are continuously receiving inquiries on import and export opportunities. They can put you in touch with foreign companies interested in buying your products or with products to sell. Contact the International Trade Division of the bank. Obtain information about exporting and importing financing from the Canadian Bankers Association (cba.ca).

Freight Forwarders

A freight forwarder can provide a whole range of services dealing with the moving of freight from one point to another. This could include negotiating volume rates with carriers, using prebooked space, providing marine/air insurance coverage, and consolidating goods with other customers to save costs. Visit the Canadian International Freight Forwarders Association website (ciffa.ca) to browse their member directory of freight forwarders.

Customs Brokers

A customs broker prepares documents and pays duties and taxes on your behalf to Canada Customs on import shipments. Some customs brokers also engage in freight forwarding. Visit the Canadian Society of Customs Brokers (cscb.ca) for a directory of customs brokers throughout Canada.

Airline/Shipping Companies

You can obtain free information and material from any of the major airlines and shipping companies to assist you.

Libraries

Contact the business resource library of your local library and obtain information on the publications or databases they have relating to importing or exporting. Almost all of the information is available online. Some of the publications to look for are:

- *Guide to Canadian Manufacturers Directory*, published by Dun & Bradstreet
- Global Market Information Database

Other publications you may wish to obtain at your local library include:

- *Importing into the United States*, published by the U.S. Customs and Border Protection. It is also available online at cbp.gov. It covers customs organizations, clearance and duty, entry of goods, duty assessment, invoices, marketing, refund allowances, special laws, and foreign trade zones.
- *Guide to Incoterms.* This guide explains the terms and abbreviations that an exporter must decipher and use.

Colleges and Universities

Many colleges and universities have courses and seminars on exporting and importing and international marketing. Many school board continuing education courses on importing and exporting are also available.

Lawyers

If you are going to be involved in exporting or importing, it is important to retain a lawyer who has expertise in import or export law, including distributor agency or licensing agreements. The area is highly specialized, and you want to obtain the best-quality advice.

Chapter 15

Credit and Collection

Beware of little expenses; a small leak will sink a great ship.

— Benjamin Franklin

Most businesses rely on credit. Credit is either being extended to customers or being obtained from suppliers. In most businesses, credit flows in both directions.

This chapter provides an overview of the credit system and the factors to be considered before extending credit. Topics include practical suggestions on granting credit, establishing credit and collection policies and procedures, avoiding pitfalls, and collecting on debts.

GRANTING CREDIT

Advantages and Disadvantages of Extending Credit

For many businesses, extending credit is necessary to remain competitive and to grow. The small business owner who sells on credit will have a higher sales volume than one who sells on a cash-only basis. You will have to evaluate your own situation to determine whether the advantages of offering credit are greater than the disadvantages.

Briefly, here are some of the advantages:

- **Increased ability to compete with larger businesses.** It is a natural tendency for people to shop around for the best bargains. Many people limit their shopping to stores which give them credit. Regardless of the type of product you have, even though you sell at a lower price than a larger store, unless you grant credit or accept credit cards, you could lose out on potential sales.
- **Meeting or beating competitors.** If your credit terms are more attractive in terms of a lower interest rate, higher limits of credit, or easier access to credit than your competitors, these factors alone could provide you with the competitive edge.
- **Accessing a larger customer base.** Estimates show that between 65% and 75% of shoppers utilize credit to make purchases. Therefore, if you offer credit or accept credit cards, you are going to extend the size of your customer base. Otherwise, you will be limiting your sales to people who

are willing and can afford to pay cash. One benefit of people purchasing on the Internet is that only credit cards are accepted.

- **Larger amount of customer sales.** The offering of credit increases the size of the average sale. Customers with credit extended to them tend to purchase a greater amount per purchase, and are more responsive to sales and displays.
- **Orders by telephone.** It is easier and more convenient for customers to make purchases by phone.
- **Goodwill for your business.** Customers are more appreciative when they can buy goods with the convenience of credit. It builds customer loyalty.
- **Additional profit on financing.** Some businesses charge a financing charge that can range between 5% and 15% higher than the conventional financing charge that one would pay at a bank through a consumer loan or a consumer line of credit.
- **Utilization of credit information as a sales and promotion tool.** By analyzing the information stored in your customers' accounts, you would be able to obtain a profile of their purchase preferences, buying habits, times of purchase, and overall buying trends. This information could be utilized for sales promotions or advertising purposes, as well as direct mail.

Extending credit obviously involves disadvantages in additional expense and risk of a bad debt, as well as other indirect and direct costs. Some of the disadvantages are as follows:

- **Reduced working capital.** If your customers are slow in paying, then your working capital is reduced. Interest charges on your line of credit would reduce your overall profit.
- **Increased administration costs.** There can be considerable operating and overhead costs associated with extending credit, such as the cost of credit investigations, bookkeeping, and mailing out invoices and statements. Maintaining records with a computer system can be efficient but expensive in terms of the capital costs of the equipment (the hardware and software), as well as the training and salary of an operator.
- **Higher return of goods.** Studies show that there is a higher percentage of returns with credit sales than with goods sold on a cash basis.
  Frequently people buy first and decide later whether they really want to keep the items. If not, goods are returned, sometimes many months after they were purchased. This could result in a loss to you, as returned items may not be resaleable or could be out of season.
- **Bad debt loss.** Statistics show that despite the thoroughness of your credit application and your screening process, you are going to have a certain percentage of customers who are unable or unwilling to pay the amount that

they owe. Naturally, any bad debts that have to be written off will increase your operating expenses and in turn reduce your profitability. The following table gives you a graphic example of how many additional sales you would have to generate to compensate for a bad debt. These additional sales do not take into account other expenses in terms of additional staff time and costs involved in attempting to collect bad debt, which could be considerable.

Compensating for a Bad Debt

Additional sales required to cover the bad **debt** if your gross profit margin is:

Amount of bad debt	5%	10%	15%	20%	25%	30%
$100	$2,000	$1,000	$700	$500	$400	$330
300	6,000	3,000	2,100	1,500	1,200	990
500	10,000	5,000	3,300	2,500	2,000	1,650
700	14,000	7,000	4,700	3,500	2,800	2,330
1,000	20,000	10,000	6,600	5,000	4,000	3,300
2,000	40,000	20,000	13,300	10,000	8,000	6,600
5,000	100,000	50,000	33,000	25,000	20,000	16,500

Expenses would have to be deducted from any income that you receive from your customer and could include the cost of capital to finance the credit, personnel, equipment, supplies, professional advice, credit and collection agency fees or commissions, and, of course, bad debts.

Types of Credit Accounts

There are various types of consumer credit that you may wish to consider. Although the description of each type varies, they are all variations of the charge account.

- **Open account.** This is the most common form of account set up by a business owner for customers. The customer makes a purchase and must pay the account in full within a 30-day period of the statement date. As long as the customer pays within that time, there is no interest charged. The credit service is for a short term, with a credit limit established at the outset of the relationship. This limit could be increased due to a favourable credit history.
- **Installment account.** In this plan, the customer makes monthly payments on the purchase of a major expense item. The purchase could be by means of a conditional sales contract, which protects the seller by maintaining title in the seller's name until the purchaser has paid for the item in full. A

down payment of 10% to 20% of the item is usually required. The payment for the item may be spread over a period of 12 to 36 months and includes principal, interest, and service charges. Some business owners sell these conditional sales contracts to banks or finance companies in exchange for cash. The customer then pays the bank or finance company directly.

- **Budget account.** This type of account is generally for a shorter period (e.g., 3 months). The monthly payments are usually made without any interest or service charge incurred, as long as the terms of repayment are met. Sometimes a deposit is required.

- **Revolving account.** Within a 30-day period, the customer must pay the full amount or a minimum percentage of the outstanding amount on the monthly statement. The customer pays interest at whatever rate is established on the outstanding balance. This type of arrangement, as with other types of credit, allows the customer to purchase items on an ongoing basis, within the established credit limit.

- **Layaway plan.** The customer makes a deposit, generally 10% to 25% of the total purchase price, and the item is held by the retailer for a period of time, until the customer pays the balance owing. Once the customer has paid the balance owing, he or she is given possession of the merchandise.

Use of Credit Cards

In Canada, the three basic types of credit cards used are bank cards, membership cards, and single-firm cards. The credit cards issued by the major chartered banks include MasterCard and Visa. Membership cards include American Express and Diners Club. Single-firm cards are those issued by department stores and oil companies. Small business owners who wish to become authorized credit card merchants should contact the closest bank, membership card, or company representative. The credit card logos can be displayed by the business to inform customers that the business accepts those cards for payment.

The credit card company will establish the floor limit beyond which authorization must be obtained from the credit card company before a transaction is completed. Authorization is obtained by phone or by a computerized verification and authorization device. In the case of membership cards, the merchant slip is forwarded to the member office and a cheque, minus the commission fee, is sent back, generally within a 3-day turnaround.

Factors such as average dollar credit card sale and the annual volume of credit card sales will determine the commission rate you will be required to pay the credit card company. The higher the volume and sales, the lower the commission. You may wish to consider becoming a member of the Retail Merchants Association of your province, as one of the membership benefits is a reduced merchant commission. By using an automated authorization and deposit computer system, the retailer can enjoy a low commission (approximately 1–2%) regardless of the volume of sales. Check with your provincial branch of the Retail Merchants Association, as well as your local chamber of commerce or board of trade, to obtain further information.

Advantages of using credit cards

- **Access to a broader market.** As credit card systems have card owners in the millions, this provides an extremely large purchasing power.
- **Lower operating costs.** You do not need an internal credit and collection system.
- **Easy processing procedures.** The forms and procedures required to use a credit card system are easy to learn and administer.
- **Immediate payment.** It is equivalent to selling on a cash basis in that it provides you with instant working capital. In the case of the membership cards, there may be a slight delay of a week to 10 days before you receive payment in the mail.
- **Guaranteed payment.** As long as the merchant has complied with the verification and authorization requirements of the credit card company, the merchant slip will always be honoured in full, minus the amount of the commission discount. The credit card company honours the merchant slip regardless of whether a cardholder pays his or her bills or not.
- **Better competition with larger businesses.** In terms of attracting the credit card user, a small business which accepts major bank and membership credit cards can compete with larger businesses that have their own credit cards. Customers are generally conditioned to use credit cards before debit cards, due to the accumulation of points that could be used for travel, etc.
- **Instant credit.** There is no delay in checking on a person's credit or processing a credit application form.

Disadvantages of using credit cards

There are very compelling and positive reasons for accepting major credit cards. The disadvantages to using a credit card system are minor in relation to the alternative, which is having your own in-house credit and collection system. On the other hand, you may wish to establish your own in-house system because it is expected in your industry sector (e.g., providing trade credit).

- **Cost of credit card commission.** The commission for credit card merchant use ranges between 1% and 4%, depending on the volume of sales and the average cost of each purchase. These additional costs may have to be passed on to the customer in terms of the pricing of the product or service, or they may be absorbed by the business owner. The cost of paying the commission has to be looked at in relation to the cost of operating one's own in-house credit system.

- **Customer profiles.** A profile of customer purchases would not be on file, unless a separate means of recording this information was established.

Interac and Debit Cards

The money comes right out of the customer's account immediately, when the card is swiped through the electronic card system at the point of purchase or when the chip feature is used. Most cards are migrating to the chip system for security reasons.

The charges to the merchant are less than for a credit card. The key advantage is instant cash in your bank account and no bad debts.

Accepting Cheques

Many small businesses accept cheques from customers because they want to encourage impulse buying and repeat business. By accepting cheques, the business owner gambles that most of them will be good. Some retailers refuse to accept any cheques, because of the potential loss from a bad cheque and the related trouble of extra bookkeeping and administrative expenses. Other business owners accept cheques only from well-known customers, or ask to see the customer's credit card and driver's licence, the numbers of which they then write on the back of the cheque. Naturally, cheque users have more buying power than customers who only have cash.

Studies show that small businesses suffer heavier losses from bad cheques than do large businesses. This is probably because large businesses are more sophisticated and stringent in their cheque-cashing policies than many small businesses; also large businesses can afford to absorb the losses. Carelessness in adhering to a properly structured cheque-cashing policy results in more bad cheques and therefore higher bad debts.

Verification

It is important to closely examine a cheque before accepting it, to make sure that on the face of the cheque it appears to be valid. Here are some of the main items to be cautious of:

- cheque greater than the amount of purchase
- cheque from a nonlocal bank
- inaccurate date or amount on the cheque

- cheque that does not have customer's name and address on it
- cheque that is illegible
- cheques requiring two signatures
- no computer code on bottom of cheque.

Once you are satisfied that the cheque appears to be valid, you should obtain identification to verify that the person signing the cheque is the right person. You also want to have information about that person, sufficient to follow up if the cheque is not honoured. As long as you are exacting in your identification policies, the risk of forgery will be minimized. The following types of identification are frequently used, and the information written on the back of the cheque.

- **Current driver's licence.** If your province does not require a photograph on the licence, obtain additional identification that does have a photograph.
- **Credit cards.** This would include bank, membership, and department store credit cards. Oil credit cards can also be used, but they tend to have a low spending limit and can be fairly readily obtained.
- **Identification cards.** This would include corporate or government identification which normally includes a picture and signature.

Most businesses have a policy of requiring a valid driver's licence, plus one or two separate pieces of identification. Credit cards are the best ID, as they tend to imply that the customer is creditworthy. There are several types of cards and documents that are not good identification, and you should be wary about accepting them. Many documents were never intended for identification and can be easily forged. Examples are business cards, birth certificates, letters, library cards, bankbooks, work permits, club or organization cards, learner's permits, and unsigned credit cards.

An effective way of ensuring that proper verification is made on each cheque is to have a rubber stamp prepared for use on the back of each cheque. These rubber stamps can be made up at any stamp or stationery business for a small cost. The stamp may state, "For deposit only to the credit of (name of company)" plus a box with items listed. Following are several items usually included on the rubber stamp: type of goods or job; invoice and serial number; amount of sale; salesperson and authorization person; date; customer name, address, home and office phone numbers, and employer. Also included would be provincial driver's licence number; particulars of other types of identification including credit cards; and physical characteristics (sex, age, height, weight) of customer. You can readily see the time and hassle involved. Most credit-worthy people have a credit or bank card they can use. Encourage that protocol as your primary policy. Think twice about your logic and rationale of accepting cheques, given the considerable risk of a bad debt that is uncollectible.

Of course, if you are operating a business with regular customers or clients where personal or business cheques are the norm, that is a different matter. It is all to do with prudent financial business risk management.

Setting a cheque policy

You should establish a clear policy and have it written down and explained to your employees. For example, your policy might state that your approval or the credit manager's approval is required before any cheque can be accepted as payment. You may set a limit on the maximum amount of a cheque. You may have a policy that a cheque cannot be cashed for any amount more than the amount of the purchase. You should use a rubber stamp to maintain consistency of required information on the customer, as mentioned earlier.

You may want to verify a cheque through your bank if the amount is large. Your bank will usually provide this service to you. Have your bank contact the bank on which the cheque is drawn, to see if there are sufficient funds to cover the cheque. Have them inquire if the account is operating satisfactorily. You may wish to contract with a cheque verification service. Do an online Google search in your city using keywords such as "cheque cashing protection services" or "cheque protection equipment." Also check with your local chamber of commerce or board of trade or provincial branch of the Retail Merchants Association of Canada for services they can offer you.

It is unwise to accept any cheque that is postdated, unless of course you have an account arrangement where you know the customer well and you accept that means of payment on account. Do not discriminate when refusing a cheque. For instance, do not tell a customer that because they are a college student you will not accept their cheque. Make sure at all times that any refusal to accept a cheque is based on policy rather than personality.

A customer's cheque may be dishonoured because of intentional or unintentional error, insufficient funds, stop payment, no account or closed account, or forgery. You should immediately contact the person, politely explain the situation, and ask them to provide you with payment. Perhaps the error was an honest oversight, so be certain to use a positive approach. If all efforts to have the cheque replaced by the customer are unsuccessful, you have your rights in collection action. If you suspect fraud, you may report the matter to the police. However, police forces are generally understaffed and overworked in commercial crime matters, and usually will not prosecute a case for a small amount of money. Your other alternatives are to sue the person in small claims court or to refer the account to a collection agency.

ESTABLISHING CREDIT POLICY AND PROCEDURES

Setting a Policy

Once you have decided to extend credit, it is important to clearly establish your policy so that it is consistent and followed by your staff. The purpose of a credit policy is to make sure the credit that you extend will be paid to you in full without any or with minimal bad debt. A number of factors have to be considered when you are establishing your policy: your type of business; credit policies of competition; market factors; economic and industry conditions; working capital requirements; financial position; cost of credit; credit record system required; credit terms needed, and personnel required. (See Checklist F on credit and collection procedures.)

Credit policies that you may consider include:

- **Conservative policy.** In this example, you would require very detailed investigation of the applicant's application and creditworthiness before any credit is extended to them. You would be strict not only in the amount of risk you are prepared to accept, but the amount of credit that you would let each customer have outstanding at any particular time. Generally a small, safe amount is first granted, then increased as the customer's payment history becomes established.
- **Liberal policy.** In this approach, you would adopt a very lenient credit policy on the amount of credit that you are prepared to extend and the amount of credit that any particular customer would have. As part of this lenient policy, you may require a very minimal investigation of those customers who apply or very little investigation of customers you already know, or who have a very strong credit rating. In general, as long as the previous bill is paid, the customer dictates the ceiling on the credit limit based on their usage.
- **Prudent policy.** In this approach, you would set a credit limit based on the credit history of the customer, obtained from the Credit Bureau or Dun & Bradstreet or other investigative information.
- **Specific policy.** In this example, you would adopt the prudent approach in terms of determining the credit rating of the applicant plus a determination of the customer's specific needs, or a line of credit based on an examination of the customer's operation.

Characteristics of a Good Credit Manager

Once you have determined your credit policy, you will have a much better idea whether you need to employ full-time or part-time assistance to manage a credit and collection function. You may want to have the same people do both credit and collection, or possibly you may wish to do both roles yourself. Many small business owners feel uncomfortable performing the credit and collection function. Because of a lack of training or a mental block on the part of the business owner, credit and collection problems frequently go unattended, which causes the duration of accounts receivable to increase, as well as bad debts.

Credit management is an essential function that requires sound judgment, tact, and analytical and human relations abilities. The ability of a credit and collection person to interact positively but firmly with a prospective credit account customer or a collection problem is vital. Other traits such as courtesy, self-confidence, and initiative are also important qualities.

The ideal credit manager should be very familiar with all phases of the business operation and should:

- be aware of the sales and marketing characteristics of the competition
- keep well-informed on industry trends and economic conditions
- be familiar with the marketing objectives and sales policy of the company
- be familiar with the services and/or products of your company, so that they can better evaluate the benefits of those services or products to a potential trade customer
- have a background and knowledge of bookkeeping and accounting in order to accurately analyze and evaluate a customer's financial situation
- be convincing and demonstrate effective verbal communication skills
- show resourcefulness, adaptability, initiative, and sound judgment in dealing with difficult situations and circumstances
- have the capacity to analyze problem situations realistically and thoroughly, and deal with customer relations firmly and diplomatically, in an emotionally stable manner
- be able to obtain and protect confidential information, and show fairness in dealing with people and uncomfortable collection situations
- demonstrate by appearance and manner a positive and respectful attitude towards customers in order to establish and maintain goodwill
- have a sympathetic and understanding style in dealing with customers, and a flexible attitude and willingness to negotiate settlements, wherever possible, that are realistic in the circumstances.

Whether you are going to be performing the credit and/or collection function, or employ other people to do it, it is important to make sure that the person involved is properly trained for this important function. There are many educational seminars and courses that are offered on this topic.

The Credit Application

To avoid the risk of bad debts, it is important to have a credit application form which is thorough. The credit application form is the first step in the evaluation process of the applicant. You can obtain preprinted application forms from your credit bureau and commercial suppliers, and then modify them to suit your needs. You may have two forms, one for a consumer and another for a trade customer. See Sample 25 for a trade credit application.

It is essential to have current information on your credit applicant in order to make decisions in terms of granting credit and deciding on the terms and limit of that credit. This section deals with trade credit, as most small businesses would utilize an external credit card system, rather than an internal one, for consumer sales. The purpose of investigating credit information is to confirm the accuracy of the information provided on a credit application form. It also helps to make a better overall judgment of the soundness of extending credit to the applicant. Investigating the credit information on the applicant is done either by the business owner or credit manager, if there is one, or by external parties, such as Dun & Bradstreet or the Credit Bureau.

You may obtain credit information on an applicant through an interview of the applicant; the applicant's bank; trade creditors; sales staff feedback; credit bureau; or Dun & Bradstreet. The Better Business Bureau could inform you if there have been any complaints. The two main credit-reporting agencies in Canada are Equifax (Equifax.ca) and Transunion (Transunion.ca).

Evaluating the Credit Applicant

As discussed in the chapter on raising financing, there are various criteria for evaluating a credit risk, including an assessment of character, capital, and capacity. Refer to Chapter 10 for further review.

Once you have decided to accept or reject the application, you should confirm that in writing to the applicant. Your letter should confirm the credit limit that you have given to that customer, the penalties for late payment, and the selling terms with respect to when the payments are due. If you are rejecting a credit applicant, the letter could simply say, "Upon assessing credit information supplied from the customer and through other investigation, we find that the applicant does not conform to the policy requirements of the creditor at this point. However, the applicant's interest in applying for credit is appreciated."

MONITORING YOUR ACCOUNTS RECEIVABLE

Establishing Effective Records

Before you start extending credit, you must establish an efficient record-keeping system. A record-keeping system must accurately record and monitor all changes in the customer's account and indicate any arrears. Your system should track individual customer information, overall accounts receivable information, and aged accounts receivable analysis. Most small businesses maintain a computerized system to monitor customer accounts. For small business in Canada, some of the most popular software programs for accounting and credit and collection purposes are: Simply Accounting (sage.com), QuickBooks (quickbooks.ca), and AccountEdge (accountedge.com). Check with your local computer store for information on the latest accounting software and current versions, or you can download online Your need for time management, efficiency, and professionalism really dictate that you use software. It will also be expected by your bank and will save time and money when your accountant does your books and tax and goods and services tax /harmonized sales tax filings. It will also empower you with customized information in real time, 24/7, to meet your needs for analysis and reality-check reviews of your business management and financial operation, so you can pre-empt problems in a timely manner.

However, some still use the less efficient "old-fashioned" way. If you are still determined to resist progress, here are the two main types of records:

- **Individual customer ledger card.** This record sets out the essential details on the customer's account status. It will assist you in determining if you should extend further orders to the customer. You can obtain ledger cards from commercial stationers or design your own. The features that should be found in a customer ledger card include the account number, billing date, account limit, customer's name, address, business and residence phone numbers, authorized users of the account, any special restrictions or specialized requirements, the terms and conditions of sale, and a cumulative record of transactions. The record of transactions would show the date, the item, any debits (charges), any credits (payments), and the running balance. With this type of information, and as long as it is kept on a daily basis, you would have an accurate record on which you or your staff can base decisions.
- **Accounts receivable general ledger.** This ledger is a summary of the amount of money owed to your business. The ledger should be updated on a weekly, bi-weekly, or at least a monthly basis. In addition, you will

want to prepare an aged list of receivables (see Sample 26). Most banks require an aged list of receivables on a monthly basis to support an operating line of credit. You can obtain a ledger book for this purpose from any commercial stationery store.

Warning Signs

It is crucial to keep your accounts receivable as low as possible. Someone should be specifically designated to approve credit and to monitor accounts for warning signs. There may be one factor or a combination of factors that cause concerns. Here are some of the warning signs that can indicate problems and potential bad debt losses unless you take prompt action.

- Does your customer delay in giving you concrete information about his or her business that you may require from time to time to update your records?
- Is your customer's order much smaller or much larger than you would expect to receive in normal circumstances?
- Have you heard from reliable sources that your customer's business has been refused other trade credit?
- Does your customer fail to take advantage of cash discounts for prompt payment (for example, 2% to 5%)?
- Does your customer frequently or unexpectedly delay in paying the accounts on time?
- Has your customer sent you an NSF (Not Sufficient Funds) cheque without promptly notifying you, or a postdated cheque without obtaining your consent in advance, or a cheque with an error?
- Have you been requested to accept the return of merchandise for full credit?
- Have you seen any signs or reports from any sources that your customer is having financial difficulties or is laying off staff?
- Have you noticed from the cheques that you have received from your customer that they have changed their bank from the bank that shows on the credit application?
- Have you received a sudden or unexpected request from your customer for a very large order?
- Have you been receiving phone calls from other companies requesting information relating to the creditworthiness of your customer's account?
- When you have attempted to contact your customer by phone or letter, have these attempts been ignored?

If you have noticed any of the foregoing warning signs, it is essential that you take prompt action. You may wish to do an immediate credit check through the

Credit Bureau or Dun & Bradstreet or the Canadian credit-reporting agencies—Equifax or Transunion. In addition, you may wish to have your bank make an inquiry of your customer's bank as to the satisfactory operation of the customer's account. If there is a possible problem, you may wish to start collection procedures.

Analyzing Effectiveness of Credit Policy

Once you have established your credit policy and have the documentation updated regularly in your accounts receivable ledger or computer, you will have the basis for determining the effectiveness of your credit and collection policy. There are three main measurements: the average collection period, the aging of accounts receivable, and bad debt ratio.

- **Average collection period.** This calculation compares total accounts receivable with average daily credit sales. Take the credit sales within a short period of time (e.g., within the last month, but no longer than 3 months) and divide that figure by the number of business days during that period. If you have established your terms of credit at 30 days, then that is the figure to use. Your collection period should not exceed your normal selling terms, if you are running an efficient operation. The formula for calculating the average collection period is covered in the ratio section of Chapter 3, "Understanding Financial Statements." Once you have this figure, you can compare it with your previous history to see if that is normal for your business. You can also compare it with published industry averages.
- **Aging of accounts receivable.** This is a more accurate measure of the extent to which your accounts receivable are being paid in accord with the terms of your credit. When aging your accounts receivable, amounts outstanding are classified under various categories such as under 30 days, 31 to 60 days, 61 to 90 days, 91 to 120 days, and over 120 days. The aging process can be done on a weekly or monthly basis. The outcome will show the condition of your receivables as of that date.
- **Bad debt ratio.** Another method of determining the effectiveness of your credit and collection policy is to divide your bad debts by the total credit sales. This will give you a bad debt ratio. Once you have determined this ratio, compare it with previous periods and with published industry bad debt statistics.

COLLECTING OVERDUE ACCOUNTS

The credit and collection functions are, of course, interconnected. The more stringent that you are on your credit policy, the less stringent you will have to be on your collection policy. It would be prudent to decide to be stringent on both your credit and collection policies to minimize bad debts and keep your receivables at a current status.

Establishing Collection Policy and Procedures

In a small business operation, it is important to determine your policy and have it understood by your employees. Your collections policy should detail the steps that your firm will follow from the time that a customer account is first discovered to be delinquent or causing serious concern until the time that the account is collected internally or assigned to a third party for collection.

Although you want to treat your customers consistently in your collection procedures, you also have to take into account individual differences that will alter your particular technique for a specific customer situation; for example, such factors as how long the account has been past due, the amount of the account, and why the customer is not paying. Probably 95% of customers want to pay their debts to maintain their credit record and continue doing business with you. You want to maintain their goodwill so that they will refer their friends to you and continue doing business with you. There are two main categories of delinquent customers: those who are willing but unable to pay, and those who are able but unwilling to pay.

Following are the main reasons that customers become delinquent in their payments:

- **Overextended.** This customer may be overextended because of seasonal overbuying, receivable delays, excessive use of credit, or other factors. With this type of debtor, you may eventually receive all your money, but you should ascertain the problem immediately and monitor the account on a regular basis. For example, you may accept postdated cheques from the customer on a bimonthly basis so that you can ensure a workable repayment schedule. You may require that ongoing orders be paid for on a COD basis.
- **Personal misfortune.** Some customers may have some temporary difficulty because of personal illness or disaster of some nature. This type of customer should be dealt with on an individual basis, so that you can assist them in paying off their debt. You should attempt to be understanding and compassionate, but realistic in your expectations of regular repayments. You may require that ongoing business be done on a COD basis or by credit card only
- **Negligence or forgetfulness.** Some customers have the money to pay you but are inefficient in their administrative bookkeeping, and therefore do not handle their accounts properly. They may just deal with the

large bills first or the small bills first, and wait until they are pressed before they pay. This type of debtor needs to be reminded on a regular basis. If the collection procedures are consistent, they will continue to pay. You might decide it is too frustrating to monitor and administer the collection efforts with this customer, even though they have the ability and eventually do pay.

- **Intentionally slow.** Some businesses use trade credit for working capital, and extend their credit privileges to the extreme. They pay only when they are dealt with in a serious fashion, such as a threat to cancel credit. By looking at the profile of this customer on their accounts receivable ledger card, you will be able to see if there is a consistent pattern in this regard. As with the previous category, you will have to decide whether you want to do business with this type of customer.

- **Customer misunderstands terms of the credit agreement.** Possibly your customer did not fully understand when and how much they were supposed to pay.

- **Customer believes that bill is incorrect.** Your customer may feel that there is an error in the bill and, until it is corrected or explained, does not want to pay on the account. Naturally this could be a bluff to cause delay, but on the other hand it could be a legitimate and sincere concern.

- **Dishonesty.** There are customers who intend to abuse their credit privileges. Watch for signs such as threats to stop doing business with you, giving excuses for temporary setbacks which are not true, repeated broken promises to pay, consistent attempts to evade answering direct questions, and a tendency to complain that you are being too strict by referring to the liberal credit policies of other suppliers.

It is important to maintain positive and regular contact with your customers. Customers who are made to feel embarrassed because they are in arrears with your firm could cease doing business with you. If an account was not seriously overdue, this could be a greater loss to the business. If there is no regular contact, customers who abuse their credit with you could assume that it will be a long time before you are aware that the account is seriously overdue or before you attempt collection action.

Initial Stages of Collection

You will be using both telephone and letters to communicate with your customers in the collection process. Keep in mind that you not only want to recover the money owed to you, but you want to retain your customer's goodwill. Whenever you are communicating with the customer, therefore, you should reflect an attitude of fairness, as well as firmness. Various stages of collection involve distinct, graduated procedures with the content and timing of messages carefully calculated. Your style and tone of collection technique will reflect various factors, such as the customer's credit history with you, how important the customer is to you in terms of ongoing business, your assessment of the customer's viability and sincerity, the particular circumstances causing the customer's delay in payment, your standard industry approaches, and the type of company that you operate. Here are some examples of the stages of collection that may be appropriate for your type of business.

Reminder statement

Once the credit period has expired, you may send out a duplicate copy of the statement with a rubber-stamp message or a stick-on reminder. This could save you the expense of sending out letters. You can obtain from stationery stores preprinted reminder stamps, or you could have your own stamps prepared. If you are a member of your local Credit Bureau or Dun & Bradstreet, you can purchase adhesive reminder stickers that can be attached to the invoice. Check with commercial stationers and your trade association for other sample forms.

It is important to remember in the reminder stage that you should give your customer the benefit of the doubt concerning reasons for delay. Your customer may have been on holiday or sick, or there could be employee turnover in the payable department. Keep a friendly tone in the letter in terms of "please" and "thank you." It is important to send out the reminder promptly after the payment is overdue; for example, within a few days or at the most a week. If your customers perceive that you are well organized and carefully monitoring your accounts, they will take you more seriously.

Make sure you check with the ledger or accounting software records first to see if the payment is still outstanding. Possibly it has been paid but not yet fully recorded. If it is your policy to charge interest on overdue accounts, and this has been agreed to in writing previously, then the interest should be shown on the statement. The effectiveness and efficiency of your collection system will be enhanced by a computerized system with regular input on a daily basis of accounts receivable paid. See Sample 27 as an example of a reminder letter.

Inquiry stage

If you see that your customer has not responded to your reminder letter or invoice, you may wish to send out a follow-up letter. This letter could have a sticker attached stating that the account is now 30 days overdue (whereas the earlier reminder stated that the account was 15 days overdue). In this letter, which is part of the inquiry stage, you want to determine why payment is late, but the tone of your letter is friendly without any accusations and with a helpful attitude reflected. Address the letter to the appropriate individual. If it is a trade customer, the credit application form would show who is responsible for accounts payable. The letter should have a note of urgency. Sample 28 is an example of a follow-up letter. Other types of credit letters may be required if the follow-up is ignored. See Samples 29 and 30 for examples of a delinquent payment notice and a final request.

Planning Your Collection Calls

The telephone is the least expensive and most practical collection tool. You can make an unlimited number of local phone calls without adding to your phone bill, whereas each letter you write increases your out-of-pocket collection expense. In many cases it is far more practical to phone your customers than to send delinquency letters. As mentioned previously, it is important to maintain the customer's goodwill when trying to collect the debt. The three steps to the telephone collection process are the precall planning, the collection call, and the follow-up.

Step 1. Precall planning

In preparing for the telephone call, it is important to determine the problem, find the solution, and have the account returned to a current status as soon as possible. Ideally this will take just one phone call. By anticipating problems, you can maximize the productive outcome of the telephone call. Be certain you are familiar with the file, and ensure that it is accurate. Ask yourself:

- Was the account rendered to the customer on time and is the amount correct?
- Has the customer moved from the most recent address on your files and has the new address been noted?
- Was the merchandise returned and a proper credit made?
- Has the customer ever complained or inquired about the billing or the terms of the credit relationship?

Step 2. Collection call

While you may prepare for the telephone conversation, you cannot predict the outcome. You can do your best to control the tone of the call to ensure that it meets your objectives.

- Make sure that you speak to the correct person.
- Respect your customer's right to privacy and confidentiality, and do not discuss financial matters with unauthorized personnel.
- Once you are speaking to the correct party, identify yourself and your firm and state the reason for the phone call.

- If the customer doesn't offer a reason, ask the customer why the account has not been paid. Pause and wait for a response. Listen carefully to the answers that are being given by the customer and note them on your records.
- Ask the customer how and when he or she intends to repay you. This shows concern for the customer and that you wish to retain the customer's goodwill and business, assuming of course that you do.
- If you have conducted yourself with courtesy and sensitivity and have been firm and fair up to this point, the customer will likely want to cooperate. If a customer is angry at your approach, they may find various grounds for complaining, with or without merit, and look for excuses to avoid paying you.
- Make payment arrangements with the customer, if required. If the customer feels comfortable with and can meet the arrangements, obtain a commitment with the customer over the phone relating to future dates and amounts of payment. Record the outcome of this discussion in your notes. If possible, have the customer restate the accepted plan, including the date, amount, and method of payment.
- Thank the customer for his or her cooperation; this will reinforce the importance that you place on positive communication and an ongoing relationship. Tell the customer to forward the funds directly to the attention of a specific person in your firm—normally the person making the call.

Step 3. Follow-up

After you have completed the phone call to the customer, make sure that you record the exact date and amounts agreed upon. Outline the various problems, complaints, or excuses that you may have encountered in the phone call.

- In certain circumstances it is necessary to confirm in writing the verbal arrangement with the customer to ensure that the customer does not forget the terms of the bargain (see Sample 31 for a typical confirmation letter). If there is money owing to you by a trade creditor, it is particularly important to confirm it, as the amount and circumstances could warrant it. If it is a consumer credit matter with a small amount owing to you, then of course the letter of confirmation may not be necessary. Your policy and judgment on these matters will dictate your procedures.
- If a confirmation letter is received by the debtor within a few days after your phone call, it has the benefit of showing that you are organized in your record-keeping and seriousness. A confirmation letter restates the verbal agreement; reminds the debtor of his or her obligation to pay on the terms of the agreement; confirms the details of the agreement, such as the amounts to be paid and dates; and provides you with a written record of the outcome of the telephone conversation.

- In a confirmation letter, be certain that the tone is polite and the letter is short and factual. Keep in mind you want to assist your customer through any cash flow problems that he or she may be experiencing. This is assuming you want to maintain business in the future.
- If the customer does not comply with the terms of the new payment agreement, make sure that you follow up with a phone call immediately. Studies show that approximately 50% of customers who promise to pay require a follow-up stimulus before they meet their obligations. If the payment is substantial and comes from a trade customer, you may wish to call the customer and thank them for their cooperation after receipt of the payment and processing of it.

Research has shown that the most productive time for making collection calls to people's homes generally is between 8:00 and 10:00 a.m., and 4:00 and 8:00 p.m. This would relate to consumer rather than trade accounts, of course. Most people can be reached during those times. Keep in mind that if you make calls any earlier than 8:00 a.m. or any later than 8:00 p.m., it could be construed by the customer as harassment. The law is specific in not permitting anyone to threaten or harass debtors over the phone. Make sure that your staff are aware of provincial and federal regulations that affect the collection process. For example, most provinces have a Debt Collection Act which regulates debt collectors. In addition, most provinces have a Consumer Credit Reporting Act which sets out what information you can obtain about debtors. That is why you want any credit application to give you the authority signed by the applicant at the time, to undertake any credit information at any time from any credit-reporting agencies. The Orderly Payment of Debts Act, or equivalent legislation in many provinces, sets out the means by which a consumer creditor can restructure their creditor repayment obligations through a provincial government department. Have your lawyer advise you on the proper approach, to keep within the law. By being a member of the Credit Bureau and taking courses on credit and collection, you will obtain information to assist you in the collection function.

Using Outside Assistance

If after all your efforts you are unable to collect the amount owing to you by the customer, you have other options. You can write off the debt or turn it over to a collection agency or a lawyer. At this point, you have lost your profit. At best, you may only be able to recover a portion of the expenses that you have incurred.

Collection agents

In most cases, professional collection agencies make money only if they actually collect money from a customer. Their fee is a percentage of what is collected. Therefore, collection agencies tend to take whatever actions are required to secure the quickest response from the delinquent customer. Collection agencies charge different fees, depending on whether it is a consumer collection or a trade collection. The consumer collection rate is normally 50% of the amount collected. Collection agents charge the higher consumer rate for commercial collection if the debtor ceases to carry on business for any reason. This is obviously because of the greater efforts that will be required of the collection agency to try to collect from the business. The following terms are fairly standard in a collection agency agreement. The creditor is asked to agree to the following:

- The creditor assigns the account to the collection agency.
- The creditor agrees to advance actual court costs on all cases in which legal action is taken; court costs are usually refunded from the first monies collected on the account.
- The creditor agrees to report to the collection agent every payment made directly to the creditor by the debtor, on any of the accounts assigned to the collection agency; the creditor is to give full credit for such collection to the collection agent, when payment is made directly to the creditor,
- to pay all commission fees due to the collection agent no later than the tenth of the following month.
- The creditor agrees to leave the account in the hands of the collection agency for at least 12 months, after which all accounts not in the actual process of collection are returned upon request.
- The collection agent will not in any way be responsible for any account becoming barred by the Statute of Limitations while in the hands of the collection agent (if there is a 2-year deadline for commencing a lawsuit, and the collection agent fails to do so, it cannot be held liable).

The following scale of charges is an approximate amount for a collection agent to charge for collection of commercial debts. These can vary of course, but provide an approximate reference point.

- accounts less than $100: 50% commission
- accounts more than $100 but less than $500: 18% commission
- accounts more than $500 but less than $2000: 15% commission
- accounts over $2000: 10% commission.
- accounts forwarded to an out-of-town collection agent: 25% commission.
- In a case in which the creditor accepts returned goods in settlement of an account, the collection agent will receive approximately 15% of the value of those goods.

When you choose a collection agency, there are certain factors to consider. One factor is the image problem that your business will suffer if the agency uses improper collection tactics. Another factor is the policy of the collection agent. For example, some firms do not charge any fee for collecting an account if it can be collected within 10 days after a demand letter or phone call. Check with major credit-reporting companies and obtain information from them about their collection services. As mentioned earlier, the Credit Bureau in your community and Dun & Bradstreet have extensive collection resources that can be customized for your needs. Most of the major collection firms have automated collections. The collection agency should be able to continue to maintain a personalized and sensitive service using firmness and tact. The range of automated collection services include the following:

- **On-line computerized collection system.** Automatic and collection-directed procedures continually monitor and control the account through to recovery. Some specific features include automatic calculation of interest up to the date of collection at the rate you specify, automatic combination of multiple debtors, computer-generated trust accounting for prompt and accurate account remittance, and computer generation of progress and account status reports on request.
- **Computer-to-computer.** This system has the ability to accept accounts for collection directly from your computer.
- **Account control.** This computer system tracks account progress and presents your debtor files to actual collection agents for action on a controlled basis. An efficient paperless office means there are no misplaced files and therefore more effective collections.
- **Automatic forwarding.** While control of your accounts is always maintained locally, claims are promptly routed through other cities in Canada, the United States, and throughout the world as your debtor changes location.
- **Customized reports.** Status reports on your accounts are system-generated automatically or available with same-day delivery.
- **Accounts receivable program.** This type of service combines a precollection service with a regular collection service. At specific intervals— for example, 10-day intervals a collection letter printed on the collection agent's letterhead is system-generated. It is sent to your debtor instructing that payment be remitted to you directly. If this approach is successful, no recovery commission is generally charged.

If this approach is unsuccessful, the account is automatically placed as a consumer collection or commercial collection.

There are distinct benefits to using a credit bureau or Dun & Bradstreet. Debtors would realize that it could quickly show up on their personal or business credit record. This of course would affect one's credit reputation and ability to borrow funds the next time that a creditor or bank does a search. Most banks and major creditors will check with either the Credit Bureau or Dun & Bradstreet or credit-reporting agencies such as Equifax or Transunion for a profile before credit is extended. It is lot less stress, hassle, and expense to decline credit, than try to collect after you have extended credit.

Lawyers

Depending on the amount owing to you and whether or not you are dealing with a trade customer, you may decide to instruct your lawyer to attempt to collect the account. You may also wish to have all your credit accounts forwarded to a lawyer for collection. It depends on the nature of the outstanding debt and your individual business whether the lawyer will suggest a percentage of the amount collected (contingency fee) or an hourly bill-out rate. Lawyers will generally charge between 25% and 50% of the amount collected, plus any disbursements (out-of-pocket expenses) that the lawyer incurs on behalf of the client, on a collection contingency fee basis. The lawyer would draw up a contract that would be signed with the creditor or would confirm the arrangement in a letter of confirmation. Frequently, the legal implications of being contacted by a lawyer will persuade a customer to pay. The customer would know that litigation will result in legal fees. This normally is an incentive for negotiated settlement.

When you select a lawyer to do collection work for you, make sure that you retain one who is experienced in doing litigation work. As discussed in Chapter 4, on selecting professional business advisors, there are various approaches to finding a lawyer appropriate to your collection needs.

You may wish to sue in small claims court to save the expense of using a lawyer or a collection agent. Many provinces in Canada have a ceiling from $3,000 to $25,000 that can be claimed in small claims court. Small claims court is informal and is designed for laypeople to assert or defend the claim themselves. You can obtain further information on small claims courts by doing a Google search online under "provincial small claims courts." Free, downloadable publications that outline the procedures are generally available, as are print versions you can pick up from the court.

Suing in small claims court

If you are suing in small claims court, or if you are having your lawyer sue in a higher level of court, it is important to understand the litigation steps. Many people do not understand the procedures or tactical and strategic matters, involved with the litigation process. Other than small claims court, the procedures are technical and formal, and that is why you need a lawyer to represent you. Small claims court has very simplified procedures compared with higher levels of court. For further information on the litigation process, refer to Chapter 16, "Understanding the Litigation Process."

Chapter 16

Understanding the Litigation Process

A verbal contract isn't worth the paper it's written on.

—Samuel Goldwyn

At some point in your small business career, the odds are very great that either you will be suing someone or someone will be suing you. Litigation normally has a mystique to many people, and the process can be very frustrating and intimidating to the layperson. This chapter will discuss the various levels of court that you might be involved in, the actual litigation process in the major stages, the legal fees and expenses that might be incurred, and an explanation of common legal strategies and tactics. The overall benefit of this chapter should be to raise your level of awareness and insight into the litigation process. It is helpful to keep in mind that 95% of all litigation is settled before trial, either by a negotiated settlement, or because one side or the other discontinues the action.

For more information, refer to my book, *The Canadian Small Business Legal Advisor*, published by John Wiley & Sons.

THE VARIOUS LEVELS OF COURTS

Law is based on provincial and federal statutes, as well as the common law. Common law means previous court decisions primarily from Canada or England. In Quebec, the law is governed by the Civil Code, as well as other provincial legislation. There are some differences between the systems, but they are similar in their effect. This chapter will concentrate on discussing the typical legal trial process in Canada. The names of the courts or the various levels of courts, the pretrial steps, or the terminology in one province might vary from another province, but the concepts and procedures are similar.

In many provinces there are four levels of courts, which are governed by provincial legislation. (In some provinces there are three levels.) These are: small claims court, county court, supreme court, and Court of Appeal. The federal government has various levels of court, primarily the Federal Court of Canada and the Supreme Court of Canada.

Small Claims Court

Small claims court is designed for the layperson to present a claim without the necessity of hiring a lawyer. The monetary limit in small claims court ranges from about $3,000 to $25,000 or more, depending on the province A guide-book is generally available from the court which explains the step-by-step procedures to follow when making a claim. There are also books available online on small claims court procedures, as mentioned earlier. If you are suing someone in small claims court, you may find it helpful to attend the court beforehand as an observer to familiarize yourself with the process.

County Court

County court normally has a monetary ceiling of $25,000, although this can vary between provinces. The conduct of action in this court is formal and technical and requires representation by a lawyer.

Supreme Court

Supreme Court has unlimited monetary jurisdiction; it can hear any claim of any amount and of any nature. Again, the nature of the legal process at this level of court is formal and technical, and a lawyer is required.

Court of Appeal

If you believe the decision at the Supreme Court was legally flawed or handled unfairly, you can appeal the decision to the Court of Appeal. Approximately 30% of judgments appealed to the Court of Appeal are overturned.

Federal Court

The Federal Court hears matters relating to federal government legislation. An example, under the Income Tax Act, is your company being sued for arrears of taxes.

Supreme Court of Canada

This is Canada's court of last resort. It hears appeals from courts of appeal of the provinces. Appeals are heard from French- and English-speaking provinces, whether governed by the common law or by the Civil Code. The Supreme Court of Canada is selective in the cases it can handle, simply because of the workload involved. One criterion in the request for appeal is that the legal issues have a national implication or impact.

THE LITIGATION PROCESS

Although you may have very good grounds for suing someone, it may be far more pragmatic and expedient for you to resolve the dispute at the outset through personal negotiations with the individuals involved. In many cases, it may be far more financially beneficial to you to settle the matter out of court. You and/or your lawyer may wish to hold a "without prejudice" meeting with the other party in the dispute. The term "without prejudice" means that any information discussed or revealed in the meeting would not be permissible evidence in court. Therefore, both parties may participate in full and open discussions in an attempt to reach an amicable settlement. You may decide to have your accountant attend as well if there are various financial considerations involved.

After assessing the situation, you may come to the conclusion that it is not worth suing someone, because the other party has little or no assets, equity, or net worth. You may be suing a corporation with liability limited to the assets of the corporation. However, by the time the trial date arrives, the assets of the corporation may have been pledged as security to other creditors or to raise money to pay the lawyer to defend the lawsuit. Or you may decide not to sue when the amount in dispute is disproportionate to the costs and legal fees that would be incurred in the legal proceedings. Litigation can be extremely expensive, as will be discussed later in this chapter, in addition to being very time-consuming, full of potential risk of losing the case, and stressful. It can also involve expending a lot of negative emotion and energy.

If you are involved in litigation, whether you are suing or being sued, the following explanation of the major steps involved will be helpful in understanding the process. Small claims court involves a simplified version of these steps, or eliminates them, to expedite the process.

Writ of Summons and Statement of Claim

The writ is the document that initiates the formal legal process. The statement of claim is the document in which the plaintiff (the person suing) sets out all the particulars of the claim. It sets out the facts, allegations, and the nature and amount of claim.

The writ of summons is usually attached to the statement of claim and is filed in the appropriate level of court. After the claim is filed at the court office, copies are delivered to the defendants (the individuals or companies being sued). The process of serving the defendants with the documents may take several weeks, and is usually done by a private process server, or a provincial sheriff.

Appearance

An appearance is a short document filed in the court office by the defendant's lawyer. It simply acknowledges receipt of the writ and statement of claim, states that a defence will be filed, and is signed by the defendant, or a lawyer on behalf of the defendant. It is normally filed within 14 days of service of the writ and statement of claim. A copy of the appearance is served on the plaintiff's lawyer.

If no appearance is entered within the limited time, the plaintiff's lawyer can initiate steps to have a judgment entered in default of appearance. A judgment is an order by the court to the defendant to pay the plaintiff the amount of the claim. If this happens, the default judgment can be removed, but an application to the court has to be made and reasons given for failure to file the appearance on time.

Statement of Defence

The statement of defence is a document in which the defendant states the intention to defend the action, and replies to statements made in the claim. This is done by explaining the key issues, circumstances, and factual and legal defences. The statement of defence generally must be filed within 21 days of receipt of the statement of claim. If the statement of defence is not filed within the time required, a judgment in default of defence could be entered by the plaintiff. Again, this default judgment can usually be set aside by the court if an application is made to the court, and an affidavit is filed swearing that the defences that you have in the case have merit.

Where there is more than one defendant and there is no conflict between the defendants' stories and no conflict over liability, it may be prudent to present a joint statement of defence. This approach can result in substantial savings in legal fees.

Summary Judgment Application

After reviewing the defendant's statement of defence, a plaintiff may decide to make a summary judgment application to the courts. A judge will award a summary judgment when the facts and evidence clearly show that there are no merits to the defence. If the summary judgment application is successful, it terminates the legal proceedings, and the plaintiff is awarded a judgment against the defendant.

Counterclaim

Sometimes a defendant, in preparing a defence, may counterclaim against the plaintiff for monies allegedly owed by the plaintiff, or other reasons for set-off. A counterclaim is, in fact, a separate lawsuit against the plaintiff based on the same overall facts. For instance, if you have refused to make final payments on a piece of equipment that was delivered late, and the supplier files a lawsuit against you, you may enter a counterclaim on the supplier for damages due to the late delivery. Damages may include cancelled customer orders, missed promotion opportunities, or cost of wasted advertising. Your counterclaim may total the amount of the plaintiff's claim, and therefore one will offset the other. It could also exceed the plaintiff's claim.

Defence to Counterclaim

Where a counterclaim has been filed, the plaintiff has to prepare and file a defence to the allegations raised in the counterclaim.

Third-Party Claim

In some situations, a third party may be involved in the dispute and may be brought into the action by the defendant. This may be done by the defendant's lawyer filing and serving on the third party a document entitled *third-party notice*. The third party then has to prepare and file a defence and serve it on the plaintiff and the defendant.

Discovery of Documents

Discovery of documents means that one party gives to the other party in the litigation, through their lawyers, a list of the documents to be used as evidence. This is a list of relevant papers and other material, including letters, plans, diagrams, manuals, contracts, agreements, receipts, and any other matters relating to the case.

If a lawyer wishes to obtain a copy of items on the list, they can be supplied by the other lawyer or made available for photocopying. It is important for both sides to review these documents in order to prepare for the next stage, called the examination for discovery.

Examination for Discovery

An examination for discovery is an interview of the parties involved by their lawyers for the purpose of collecting the facts and evidence relevant to the case. A separate examination for discovery is held for each defendant and plaintiff. Each party is questioned by the lawyer of the other party, while under advisement of his or her own lawyer.

The examinations take place under oath and are reported verbatim, that is, word for word, by a court reporter. A copy of the transcript can be requested and later entered into court as evidence. The purpose of the examinations is to allow each party the opportunity to become familiar with the opposing side's case.

In addition, they serve the purpose of providing a better basis upon which to negotiate an out-of-court settlement. Examinations for discovery are an essential part of the pretrial process. Although the pleadings—that is, the initial stages of litigation including the statement of claim, defence, counterclaim, and defence to counterclaim allege various facts, they are not made under oath. The facts alleged could have substantial merit, very little merit, or no merit. The examination for discovery, conducted under oath, assists in clarifying how much merit may be involved in the pleadings.

Once the discoveries have been completed, both parties are in a position to assess the strengths or weaknesses of their respective cases. Approximately 75% to 80% of settlement negotiations that result in a compromise resolution before trial occur after the examinations for discovery.

Discovery by Interrogatories

There are occasions when a one-on-one examination for discovery is not practical, for example, if some of the parties live in remote areas or in another country. It saves costs in such situations to have the discoveries done by written examination. *Interrogatories* are a lists of typed questions posed by one party in the litigation to the other. Similar to the examination for discovery, they are usually done well before the trial and after the defence and other similar documents have been filed and served. The party who receives the questions must answer them in writing. These are called *answers to interrogatories*, and are usually in the form of a typed reply, sworn under oath.

As in examinations for discovery, the interrogatories are designed to discover more of the facts and issues of the case. Interrogatories are often helpful where there are no material documents to be disclosed. The answers to interrogatories can be used as evidence or for cross-examination at trial.

Trial Date Set

The trial date is set by the lawyer for the plaintiff based on an agreement between the lawyers as to the duration of the trial. If there is a disagreement between them, a trial date will be set based on the lawyer who suggests the longest duration of trial. Generally speaking, the longer the length of trial, the longer the wait before a trial date. The waiting time for a trial could be anywhere from 6 months to 3 years or longer.

Pretrial Conference

At any time after a trial date has been set, one or the other party can request of the court that a pretrial conference be held. The conference is attended by a judge and the lawyers for the parties, and considers such matters as the clarification of the legal issues and any other matters that might help in disposing of the action or settling the dispute.

Trial

The trial is held before a judge alone, unless the legislation in your province allows for a jury to be requested by one of the parties.

Each party presents its case, the plaintiff first, then the defendants all together or each in turn. Witnesses may be called or subpoenaed as well to give evidence on facts. Witnesses of the plaintiff give testimony to the plaintiff's lawyer, and are then cross-examined by the defence; and vice versa for witnesses of the defence. Expert witnesses may be called to venture professional opinions about some aspects of the evidence. For example, if a claim is being made for damages (financial losses), a professional accountant may be called to give expert testimony in the calculation of figures.

In the final stage of the trial, the lawyers present legal arguments in an attempt to persuade the judge and/or jury that the evidence and applicable laws call for a verdict in favour of their client. It is in these arguments that past cases which have a bearing on the present case are often brought forward. This is called referring to the common law or court case law. These cases generally come from any other court case in Canada, the United States, or England.

Judgment

The judge or jury has the responsibility to determine the extent that each party contributed to the overall problem and the amount to be paid. One or more of the defendants in whole or in part may be held responsible. Or, the plaintiff may have partly contributed to the problem. If the defendants have put in a counterclaim and the counterclaim is upheld by the courts, then a set-off will occur against any claim in favour of the plaintiff.

The judge will present an opinion on the case and state the amount of the judgment to be awarded and court costs, if any. The losing side is usually obliged to pay court costs to the other side, based on a specified tariff schedule. If the court awards party-party costs, this is a lower tariff schedule than solicitor-client costs. The court has the discretion to grant the higher level of costs if it is felt that the circumstances justify it. The highest level of court costs generally only represents between 15% and 35% of the actual amount of the winner's legal costs. Actual legal costs obviously vary, depending on the fee arrangement, the experience and efficiency of the lawyer, and the complexity of the case.

Appeal

After the judgment is rendered, one or more of the parties may decide to appeal either the finding of liability, or lack thereof, and/or the amount of the damages awarded or other judgment. A notice of appeal must be filed within a limited time after judgment. Appeals are heard before a panel of senior judges, and are concerned primarily with errors in the interpretation and application of law, as opposed to the interpretation of the facts and evidence. Like the trial process, the appeal process can be lengthy, expensive, unpredictable, and stressful.

Examination in Aid of Execution

Once a judgment has been obtained, the party who has been awarded the judgment is entitled to examine under oath the person or company on which the judgment was obtained. The purpose of this examination, which normally occurs in front of a court reporter, is to determine all the assets of the judgment debtor. Once all the assets are determined, then procedures can be commenced to collect the amount of the judgment.

Execution of Judgment

Once you are aware of the debtor's assets, there are various forms of execution of a judgment. These include garnisheeing bank accounts and accounts receivable; seizing assets such as cars, boats, and equipment; and commencing action on any real estate owned by the debtor. In many cases, the assets may be already pledged as security to other creditors, and very little equity, if any, may be remaining in them.

Settlement

It is frequently advisable that the parties attempt to reach a compromise rather than proceeding to trial. As mentioned earlier, civil litigation is very expensive, uncertain, and stressful. Negotiations can be conducted at all stages of the litigation process commencing from the service of the writ and the statement of claim. After the examination for discovery, negotiations usually occur in earnest as the bargaining positions become clear.

The courts encourage out-of-court settlements by providing a procedure whereby a party may make a formal offer to settle. If this is done within a limited time prior to the trial, and the outcome of the trial is at least as favourable to the offeror as the terms of the offer, the party who failed to accept the offer is penalized by the court by having to pay a high percentage of the offeror's legal expenses. The offer is open for acceptance until it is either formally withdrawn or the judgment is rendered.

METHODS OF ENCOURAGING A SETTLEMENT BEFORE A TRIAL

There are ways to encourage an settlement before a trial to save money and the risk and uncertainty of the outcome, along with the protracted time and stress. These options may not be available in all provincial or territorial jurisdictions in Canada.

Judicial Settlement Conference

In this process, any time after the initial formal pleadings have been completed (the legal claim, response, counterclaim, etc.), either party can apply to the court for a judge to view the pleadings in the form of an informal mediation meeting to obtain the judge's initial nonbinding candid feedback of the strengths and weaknesses of each side, based on the limited information before the court. For the hearing, the additional supplemental filings to support each side's claim are filed, and the lawyers provide oral argument to the judge to supplement each side's written submission position. The judge may defer his or her opinion until after all the documents are read and oral arguments considered, and a second day for a confidential hearing could be set to obtain the judge's feedback.

The primary purpose of this option is to attempt to accelerate a resolution, taking into account the initial feedback from the judge to provide some guidance, to favour a negotiated resolution. If the judge is able to encourage a resolution, the parties produce an agreed settlement document, which is signed by both parties, and the action is then dismissed. The requirement of this process is that both parties are attempting to see if a neutral third party (judge) can facilitate a resolution by both sides (lawyers and clients) and can appreciate that each side has strengths and weaknesses in the view of the court, which in itself is a positive catalyst to strike a deal and move on.

Mini-Trial

A mini-trial is an accelerated and truncated nonbinding short trial to obtain the judge's nonbinding feedback. It is more formal than the judicial settlement conference, which does not call witnesses. Again, this process can result in a judge giving his or her candid feedback of the relative strengths and weaknesses of each side's legal position and arguments. If a settlement does not result due to this tentative reality check, at least one has a basis for weighing the next steps of the litigation process preparation.

METHODS OF ENCOURAGING A RESOLUTION BEFORE LITIGATION

You want to avoid the litigation process if at all possible. One way is to build into any contracts you have that if there is any dispute, before any side commences litigation, that an alternate dispute resolution (ADR) process will be followed. An ADR process is a quicker, cheaper process to attempt to resolve a dispute.

Here are main stages of the ADR process:

Informal "Without Prejudice" Negotiations

This process involves good faith discussions in writing or in person between lawyers for the purpose of finding a resolution, where the written or oral exchange is confidential and cannot be used in any future litigation if discussions break down. Both sides confirm in writing that the process is "without prejudice" so it is clear and there is no misunderstanding. That way, both parties can be candid and forthright, but also pragmatic and constructive.

Mediation

In this process, an experienced, professional, trained and accredited mediator is utilized to attempt to facilitate a constructive dialogue to find a common point of resolution. The mediator does not recommend a solution, but attempts to use professional objective skill and training and various techniques to enable both sides to find their own positive accord, if such an outcome is possible. The mediator could be a lawyer or non-lawyer, and both sides have to agree in advance as to the choice of mediator. Names of professional business dispute mediators can be obtained by doing an online Google search with keywords in your city, and checking out reputation, credentials, and references. In the mediation option, each side agrees to pay half of the mediation costs.

Arbitration

This process involves the hiring of an experienced and trained arbitrator who can listen to both sides' written and oral arguments, and render a written and oral decision and recommendation of the assessment of both sides' respective strengths and weaknesses. The outcome can be a binding or nonbinding arbitration. Both sides have to agree in advance in writing as to which arbitrator will be used, and the parametres as to what will be covered in the arbitration. Each side pays half of the costs of arbitration.

Professional commercial arbitrators can be active or retired lawyers or judges, or non-lawyers. Names can be obtained by doing a Google search with keywords in your city, and checking on credentials, references, expertise, and experience.

LEGAL FEES, EXPENSES, AND COURT COSTS

To illustrate the potential high costs involved in litigation, an example will be given. Say you wanted to sue a debtor for $30,000 and retained a lawyer to represent you at an hourly bill-out rate of $250 per hour. This may be the average, but it can go up to $500 per hour or more, depending on the expertise and experience of the lawyer, the size of the law firm, and the complexity and monetary amount of the issue involved. It is generally rare for a lawyer to act on a contingency-fee basis for collection of debts, because of the risk that he or she may lose and therefore not be paid—but it all depends on the circumstances of the case. The defendant files a defence and a counterclaim against you for $30,000, claiming a set-off for sloppy workmanship, incomplete workmanship, and delays. You believe the defendant is bluffing and has no merits to the defence or counterclaim, so you proceed down the litigation road.

The pretrial procedures go on for a year and then there is a further 1- or 2-year wait before trial. At the trial you win on your claim, and the other side loses on the counterclaim. You are awarded court costs. The trial lasts a week, and there are many witnesses, and large quantities of documents. The legal issues are complex.

The following is an example, albeit extreme to make a point, of a breakdown of the type of legal fees and disbursements (out-of-pocket expenses) that you potentially could have incurred. Lawyers prefer to get paid retainers on an ongoing basis, and therefore you would have had to expend these monies from the commencement of the court action, up to and including trial. After reviewing this example, you can see why you need to have a very open and candid discussion with your lawyer about the downside of potential legals fees and costs, and have that in writing, and have comparative and competitive quotes. You can also see why you should work hard to find a reasonable and pragmatic settlement resolution.

Legal fees	$250/hour	Amount
The initial client meetings, obtaining instructions, and reviewing of documents	15 hours	$3,750
Drafting writ of summons and statement of claim, reviewing defence and counterclaim, drafting defence to counterclaim and other needed documentation	15 hours	$3,750

(Continued)

Legal fees	$250/hour	Amount
Demanding discovery of documents, preparing list of documents, reviewing lists from defendants, obtaining copies of documents from defendants, preparing and photocopying all plaintiffs documents to supply to defendants	10 hours	$2,500
Preparing for examination for discovery, including reviewing all documents, meeting with clients, preparing list of questions to ask or to anticipate	Approximately 1½ days' preparation (average for each day of discovery); therefore 8 days of discovery × 1½ = 12 days × an average of 8 hours per day = 96 hours	$24,000
Attending at examination for discovery	8 days of discovery × 8 hours per day = 64 hours	$16,000
Preparing for trial, including examining witnesses, reviewing documents, reviewing examination for discovery transcripts, reviewing the law that has been researched	Average 2 days' preparation for each day of trial 5-day trial × 2 = 10 days' preparation × 8 hours per day = 80 hours	$20,000
Researching all case law and statute law	25 hours	$6,250
Attending at trial for a 5-day trial	5-day trial × 8 hours per day = 40 hours	$10,000
Total of legal costs		**$86,250**
Disbursements		
Filing and serving of writ and statement of claim		$100
Photocopies		$1,000
Court reporter fees and transcripts of examinations for discovery		$2,000
Long-distance telephone calls, fax charges, etc.		$200

Legal fees	$250/hour	Amount
Miscellaneous		$200
Total of disbursements	–	$3,500
Total of fees and disbursements paid by plaintiff		**$89,750** Plus GST and provincial taxes if applicable, or HST
Financial Outcome of Trial		
Court costs by tariff schedule in favour of plaintiff based on party-party costs loser (defendant) has to pay (usually represents approximately 25–35% of actual legal expenses incurred)		$15,000
Judgment against defendant for amount of claim		$30,000
Plus interest as determined by the court from the date the money was owing (approximately 10%, but varies depending on prime rate of interest)	2-year period from date debt owing before trial = approximately $3,000 per year × 2 years = $6,000	$ 6,000
Total of judgment on debt owing plus interest and court costs	–	$51,000

Net Loss by Plaintiff

The plaintiff (the "winner") was awarded judgment on the $30,000 plus interest and court costs for a total of $51,000. When these amounts are subtracted from the total financial outlay by the plaintiff, there is a net loss of $38,750.

After looking at the preceding example, you might have considerable anxiety when contemplating suing or being sued. In the example given, even though the case was decided in the plaintiff's favour, the plaintiff was still out of pocket. As well, for a two-year period the plaintiff had to deal with the risk, uncertainty, anxiety, frustration, and negative energy of the litigation process. There are a number of questions that you should consider when looking at this example:

- Was the litigation exercise worth the aggravation and risk? What if the defendant succeeded in the counterclaim?
- What if the court did not award costs to either party in the event that both parties won on their respective claims or partially won on their claims?
- What if the defendant was a corporation, and by the time the trial commenced, it had no assets, and you had no personal guarantees?

- What if the defendant's assets were pledged as security to creditors or to the bank for a loan to pay the legal fees?
- What if the defendant corporation stopped doing business or went into bankruptcy just prior to or after the trial?
- What if just prior to trial your lawyer required another retainer to proceed any further, and you did not have sufficient cash flow or financial resources to pay the fee and therefore had no choice but to discontinue the case?
- What if the defendant's counterclaim against you showed up in a Dun & Bradstreet or Credit Bureau record and because of it, creditors, as well as your bank, would not advance further funds or credit to you?
- What if the nonpayment of the $30,000 debt plus the extensive legal fees caused your business to go under because you could not in the end collect on the debt? If you had signed personal guarantees for your corporate liabilities, you may have additional legal problems.

This litigation example demonstrates the potential perils of getting involved in a legal fight. Until or unless you received a judgment at trial, you would not be entitled to examine the debtor under oath as to the assets of the debtor. Therefore, you would have no idea if the company was pledging its assets, selling off its assets, or ready to go under prior to trial or shortly thereafter and before you can collect.

Some lawyers are more efficient and more expert than others in litigation matters. If you are involved in litigation, it is very important to make sure that the lawyer whom you have representing your interests is a skilled litigator. It is also advisable to ensure that your lawyer is a skilled negotiator and attempts at various appropriate stages in the litigation process to resolve the matter by out-of-court settlement, if at all possible.

LEGAL STRATEGIES AND TACTICS

When you are dealing with litigation matters, there are many tactical and strategic considerations that influence the outcome. It is common for settlements to be made not on what is fair, in the opinion of one or both parties, but on what is economically and pragmatically expedient in practical terms. It is helpful to understand these realities before getting involved in litigation.

The civil litigation process is adversarial in nature. That means that each side will exert their best efforts to convince the court on the merits of their respective positions, by accentuating the positive and rationalizing the negative as irrelevant or insignificant. At the same time, the goal is to try to diminish the merits of the other side's case. In other words, strongly argued positions at both ends of the spectrum frequently occur. The reality might be somewhere in the middle, or may be weighted on one side or the other.

The following factors or strategic approaches influence the outcome of the case or settlement. As you will see, they have very little to do with the facts or dispute at issue. They have a lot to do with tactics and strategies. In the examples given, it is assumed, of course, that all the approaches used fall within the guidelines of proper professional conduct. Keep in mind, though, that because it is an adversarial process, there is a wide range of approaches that can be used that are completely in keeping with that adversarial process. Some lawyers by nature or by client instructions are prone to try to find a point of settlement when the timing is right. Other lawyers by nature or by their client's instructions want to proceed and win regardless of the cost, without any desire or attempt to compromise or settle. Some of the strategies are listed here:

- A defendant may counterclaim, when in fact you may feel the allegations in the counterclaim to be totally without merit and simply a bluff. The practical effect, though, of a counterclaim is that it could affect your credit standing and reputation, because most litigation matters show up in Credit Bureau or Dun & Bradstreet records. In addition, it tends to confuse the issues in terms of your claim, and makes the overall litigation far more complicated than if a simple defence were filed.
- A defendant may attempt to delay the pretrial proceedings as much as possible by being slow in responding to the various stages, including production of documents or setting of examination-of-discovery dates. This could cause a lot of stress and expense, and lose the momentum of the conduct of the action. It is true in many cases that the longer the delay, the more likely that one side is prepared to settle. This is because the initial interest in asserting the person's rights has been replaced by an ongoing anxiety over the legal costs, the uncertainty of the outcome, and the need for money to compensate for the initial loss. People's priorities of a personal and business nature may change. In addition, being involved in litigation matters is very stressful to one's family life and business life.
- One party may attempt to frustrate the other by bringing on various motions (heard in front of the chambers judge) on procedural matters. This causes legal costs to escalate and can further complicate and delay the litigation process.
- One party may wish to delay the trial date as long as possible. The more complex the legal issues become, the more likely the trial date will be set further in the future. For example, one lawyer may state that it will be a 2-day trial, in anticipation of an early trial date. The other lawyer may disagree, and assert that the trial will take 5 days. A trial date

would therefore be set based on a 5-day duration, which could possibly be a 2-year wait. By the time the 2-year period is over, the person who wanted a shorter trial may have run out of financial resources or the will to continue, and therefore would be more receptive to an out-of-court settlement.

- One of the parties in the action may have financial resources which would enable them to continue all the pretrial procedures right up to and including trial, and then appeal the trial decision if it was not in their favour. If this is fully known and asserted at the early stage of litigation, that can have a very compelling impact on the other party to try to settle; otherwise, they may not have the financial resources to continue and could end up in a serious financial situation.

- If you are suing someone in another province, or in a different geographic area than where you reside, that could cause a lot of additional costs in terms of extra legal fees for the lawyer in your province and the lawyer retained in the other province, as well as extra costs for travelling for the examinations for discovery and the trial. In addition, if witnesses are going to be used at trial, there would be costs to pay for the witnesses' travel, accommodation, and other financial losses while they are at trial. These factors go a long way towards providing leverage to one or the other party to try to effect a settlement or have the action dropped.

- Another tactic is to garnishee the account of the party that you are suing, as soon as you commence an action. Some provinces permit garnisheeing before judgment, and others only allow garnishment after a judgment is obtained. You can garnishee only in specific situations, for example, if you have a fixed debt that is owing to you, as opposed to damages (financial losses) which may have to be determined and assessed at court.

  If you are suing a trade creditor and you have the address of the company's bank from the credit application form, you could garnishee the account for the amount of the debt. If you were successful in garnisheeing the full amount, that would provide very effective leverage on which to negotiate a settlement. It would mean that the defendant would not have those financial resources available to use for legal fees. It would also provide you with the peace of mind of knowing that there would be money available to you if you succeeded at the trial. (The funds garnisheed are paid into the court.) When garnisheeing a bank account, a bank is entitled to set off any monies owing to it by the customer. This means that if you garnishee for $10,000 and the bank is owed $10,000, then no amount of money would be captured and remitted to the court. If, on the other hand, the bank is owed $5,000 and the garnishee is for

$10,000 and there is at least $10,000 in the account, then $5,000 would be remitted to the court pending the outcome of the action.

AVOIDING THE PITFALLS OF LITIGATION

You have undoubtedly heard of the litigation process being referred to as a game, complete with strategic tactics, moves, ploys, and feints. As in any game, and litigation is inherently an adversarial process, if you don't know how to play it well or retain a lawyer who does, the odds of "winning" are not in your favour. A reality check would probably be helpful.

However, by avoiding the classic mistakes that many business owners make, you will be better able to deal with the litigation process from a position of perspective and insight. You could be suing someone for a debt owing, breach of contract, negligence, or for some other reason. No matter what catalyst is causing you to consider suing, keep the following pitfalls foremost in your mind.

Lawsuit Based on Emotion

You might feel that you have been wronged for whatever reason and you are naturally very upset. Your decision to sue, though, should be based on hard-nosed business realities. Maybe there is not much money involved, but it is a matter of principle. In that case, give yourself some time, maybe several months, to see if the intensity of your emotions has subsided. The litigation process itself has enough negative emotion and energy associated with it.

Unrealistic Expectations of Outcome

Many people assume that they are in the right and that they will "win" at the end of the day. However, the interpretation of the facts can vary, and very few issues in law are black and white. The litigation process is inherently unpredictable. In addition, when you factor in your legal fees from any judgment in your favour, maybe you won't be ahead of the game at all. If you win, the court costs you are awarded only amount to about 10% to 25% of your legal fees based on a provincial fixed-tariff schedule, so you still lose financially. And then you have the challenge of attempting to collect on the judgment.

Not Assessing the Defendants' Assets

You could "win" at trial, but still be a big time loser. The reason is that the personal or corporate defendant could have no assets in their name or have all their assets leveraged up with debt at the time you commence an action or by the time you get a judgment. In other words, the defendant could have mortgaged the remaining equity in their home, if being personally sued, to pay for business or legal expenses. If you are suing a corporate entity, the company could be a hollow shell without any net worth. If there are any business assets, they could be sold off or pledged as security for loans while your court case is proceeding.

Doing an objective risk assessment of the realistic potential of collecting on a judgment at the outset is key. You could be throwing good money after bad. You might conclude that the negative learning experience was a cost of business insight, not sue, and commit to changing your business policies and practices to pre-empt a recurrence.

Not Weighing Potential Gains versus Losses

In this situation, you need to realistically assess the relative pros and cons of litigation, in other words, the cost in money and lost productivity. Can you afford the fight to the end? Have you obtained various quotes in writing as to the cost of the complete pre-trial and trial process? Is the cost to pursue the matter going to be a lot more than the amount you are claiming? What if you lose? In the latter case, you will be out not only legal fees, but court costs as well. What if the defendant counterclaims against you and wins? You get the idea.

Not Considering a Settlement

The pragmatic and practical reality is that settlements occur all the time. Only about 5% to 10% of lawsuits ever end up at trial, with the exception of small claims court. Even small claims court has a settlement hearing process before trial, in many provinces. The purpose is to see if both sides could agree on striking a deal and getting on with life. Settlements save a lot of court time. You have heard of people settling the case on the courthouse steps? The reason is the uncertainty of the trial process outcome. Settling for 20%, 30%, 50%, or 70% of the original claim is better than the risk of getting nothing and being out legal fees as well.

Suing Too Early

In this situation, you commence your action before you have all the facts. Ideally, you want to have all the facts in your favour determined and included in your claim. It will show your opponent that you have done your homework.

Suing Too Late

If you wait too long, you could miss a statutory time limit to commence your action. Different types of actions and different provinces have different time limits.

Lack of Expert Legal Advice

Before you make any decisions, have a lawyer experienced in litigation matters review your case and give his or her opinion in writing as to the potential cost range. It is difficult for a lawyer to be precise, as it is still early in the legal fact-gathering process. Better still, have a minimum of three lawyers give you candid and objective feedback on your chances at trial, how long it will take, and how much it will cost. You need a benchmark for comparison. You also want to make sure that the advice is consistent, and if not, why not. If you contact the lawyer referral service in your province, most initial consultations are free or require a nominal fee. This will be time well spent. It will enhance your knowledge of the issues and risks and increase your confidence in your final decision. After following these steps, sleep on your dilemma for a few weeks or a month. See if you have the same opinion at the end of that time. Remember the axiom, "act in haste, repent at leisure."

Many potentially litigious situations may be avoided by effective business management and controls. A good level of communication between customers and suppliers, careful documentation of terms and conditions of verbal agreements, and timely follow-up on problem situations will reduce potential risks.

Chapter 17

Insolvency, Bankruptcy, and Receivership

People who try to do something and fail are infinitely better than those who try to do nothing and succeed

—Lloyd Jones

The terms *insolvency, bankruptcy*, and *receivership* are confusing to many business people. Considering the reality that approximately four out of five small businesses cease to operate within 3 to 5 years of start-up, the odds are very high that one of your suppliers or customers may fall upon such hardship. It is therefore helpful to have an understanding of the various concepts and stages of insolvency, bankruptcy, and receivership, and your rights and remedies, to make sure that you properly protect yourself. On the other hand, your business may suffer financial difficulties, causing you to try to arrange a settlement with your creditors. This chapter will provide an overview of the procedures involved, and advice on protecting your business and personal assets. Also, the reasons for business failure need to be reviewed, as forewarned is forearmed.

HISTORICAL CAUSES OF FINANCIAL DIFFICULTIES

There are various reasons why individuals and businesses have financial difficulties that may result in insolvency, bankruptcy, or, in the case of a business, receivership. Some of the reasons individuals have financial difficulties which may or may not impact on their small business include the following:

- employment problems, such as lack of work, irregular employment, or seasonal employment
- poor budgeting of income and expenses
- misuse or overuse of credit
- physical, emotional, or mental health problems
- loss of second income from spouse or from part-time employment
- partnership disputes
- marital problems
- dependence on alcohol or drugs

- family tragedy, such as loss of home, death, or disability
- personal guarantees of corporate debts called.

The main reasons for business difficulties include incompetence, lack of experience, neglect, fraud, and disaster. Dun & Bradstreet regularly does an analysis of business failures in Canada and prepares reports on the subject.

Inexperience and Poor Financial Stewardship

Inexperience and poor financial stewardship are a major factor in business failure. Resulting issues can be the difficult to detect and frustrating to correct. One or more of the following factors may be required before the business actually fails.

- **Excessive expenses.** The statistics show that it is very common for start-up businesses to spend more money than is really required, especially during the first few years. Careful cash flow management could avoid problems in this area.
- **Undercapitalization.** The business starts out with inadequate financial resources to meet reasonably projected needs and contingencies.
- **Receivables problems.** Firms in the first few years of operation tend to allow liberal credit and are careless with their collection procedures. This causes the receivables to increase in amount and age, thereby limiting use of those funds as working capital.
- **Excessive fixed assets.** A small business might invest too much money in fixed assets which are nonproductive capital allocations. It could be excessive to the minimum requirements of the business and therefore cause the business to be short of working capital or security leverage at the bank. For example, expensive furniture or equipment could cost two or three times as much as basic start-up items that the company could have purchased or leased.
- **Inventory problems.** When one is starting up a business, it is very common to be overly optimistic when trends and sales requirements have not yet been properly defined. This could result in too much money being tied up in surplus inventory which may not move as quickly as projected. On the other hand, not having enough stock of other items could cause loss of goodwill and customer loyalty. The time delay between the ordering and receipt of the inventory may be too long to maintain customer interest.
- **Low sales volume.** Many small business owners are overly optimistic during the initial start-up stages and delude themselves into thinking that they are going to generate far more sales or income than the facts or circumstances would indicate. Possibly cash flow projections were not done, or they were not based on realistic research.

- **Competitive weakness.** Due to insufficient planning and poor research of the competition and the needs of the marketplace, your business may not have the uniqueness necessary to attract a clientele base.
- **Poor location.** A poor location may cause a business to fail before potential customers know it exists. Careful market research could have helped the business owner to avoid this situation.
- **Lack of management experience.** Many small business owner-managers lack any managerial experience or training. Especially during the first few years of the business start-up, the owner may be wearing many different hats in terms of responsibilities of operating the business. Possibly the owner has little knowledge of or dislikes certain areas, for example, bookkeeping or sales, and therefore lets those important areas go unattended. A small business owner may feel that the expense for a part-time or full-time manager could not be justified at that stage of the business.
- **Unbalanced experience.** This occurs when the small business owner has excellent skills in certain areas and little or none in others, and fails to recognize the importance of those areas in which her or she is deficient. If the small business owner's managerial skills and weaknesses were assessed before business start-up, it could have become very apparent that there were deficiencies that had to be addressed. The deficiencies could be addressed by means of part-time staff, by retaining a professional advisor, or by taking courses.
- **Lack of specialized expertise in the business.** Some small business owners have no specific experience or background knowledge of the industry sector of their new business. It is essential to have at least a working knowledge of the service or product to be sold; otherwise, the judgment and decision-making that will be required will not be based on any realistic foundation. Also, it will be difficult to build customer and staff confidence.

Neglect

Sometimes, due to various factors, the business owner neglects to look after the needs of the business to the point of ignoring obvious signs of business problems. Neglect in business is frequently caused by bad habits, lack of confidence, marital or partnership difficulties, fatigue, or poor health. The first flaw can be cured by eliminating bad habits, assuming that the business owner is aware that they exist. Possibly outside consulting assistance would be able to identify bad habits of the management. The other factors are, of course, more difficult to resolve and could cause the owner's interest in the business to become lessened or to disappear altogether because of distractions or inability to concentrate and focus on the concerns of the business. In these latter situations, the solution may be to sell the business or to sell the interest of the owner to another partner or shareholder.

Fraud

Fraud accounts for a very small part of small business failures. Where bankruptcy is imminent, owners may defraud the business by taking assets and money out of it before it goes under, thereby defeating creditors' access to the company assets. False financial statements may be prepared in order to deceive Revenue Canada, the bank, or other creditors, or to convince suppliers to extend further credit. Or the inaccurate financial data may be used to sell the business for an inflated price. Premeditated overbuying occurs when a company intentionally overbuys on credit terms, then has a sale of the items to convert to cash before putting the business under. The suppliers would be left with a large debt which they would be unable to collect.

These examples involve a deliberate intention on the part of the small business owner to financially benefit at the expense of creditors in an illegal fashion; they do not refer to poor business management. If a creditor believes a criminal fraud has taken place, it can be reported to the police. In addition, under provincial legislation, a creditor could commence action alleging a civil fraud, in terms of the transfer of assets. Under the federal Bankruptcy and Insolvency Act (BIA or the Act), a creditor could also allege improper acts and request the trustee in bankruptcy to review them.

Disaster

This factor accounts for a very small portion of the reasons for business failure, and includes employee fraud, burglary, floods, and fire. Good insurance coverage may help to recuperate the financial losses incurred. However, unless you carry coverage for loss of income through business interruption, the time delay to rebuild the business may be too great to endure.

It is important for the business person to understand and be aware of the reasons businesses fail. The key point is that incompetence, which accounts for approximately two-thirds of business failures, can sometimes be corrected through candid personal and business assessment and planning before the business commences. One must have the desire and ability to recognize and compensate for deficiencies.

There are several other causes of financial difficulties in business which underlie many of the problems just discussed. These would include failure to realistically self-evaluate; establish, review and revise goals; anticipate obstacles; and learn from experience. A lack of sustained commitment is also a factor.

INSOLVENCY

Many businesses could be technically insolvent from time to time but not become bankrupt or suffer other business failure. The insolvency state could be a temporary one, for example, due to receivables and cash flow problems. With luck, or better still with improved management or professional advice, the business could turn itself around.

One of the definitions of insolvency found in the BIA could be paraphrased as follows: a person or company who is for any reason unable to meet financial obligations as they become due, or has ceased paying current obligations as they become due, or whose property or assets at a fair market value are insufficient to pay all financial obligations due or becoming due.

If one or more creditors want to petition an individual or company into bankruptcy, they need to establish that the debt or debts owing to the applicant creditor(s) amount to $1000 and the debtor has committed an act of bankruptcy within the 6 months preceding the filing of the application. The degree of insolvency must exceed $1000 in total to all creditors.

PROPOSALS

A proposal refers to an arrangement proposed by a debtor and negotiated with the creditors. There are three main categories of proposals—the informal proposal negotiated outside the BIA, a consumer proposal, and the formal proposal under this Act known as a Division I proposal.

Informal Proposal Outside the BIA

A debtor may make an informal proposal to creditors to negotiate either a reduction in the amount owed or a change in the terms of payment. In practical terms, it is common for creditors to agree to a settlement based on a percentage of the debt owing and with payment terms excluding interest. An informal proposal is usually only feasible when the creditors are few in number and believe there is no better financial alternative. If the debtor company has few assets that are not already pledged, then creditors might be inclined to accept a reduced dollar amount, because the alternative is to possibly get much less in a bankruptcy situation.

An informal proposal cannot be imposed upon a creditor who is not in agreement with it. In most instances, each creditor will have to be approached individually by the debtor. If the proposal is declined by the creditors, a bankruptcy will not automatically occur. However, the debtor must be cautious, because the approach itself is evidence of insolvency and can be used by the creditor as grounds to petition the debtor into bankruptcy. The advantage to a debtor of an informal proposal is that the debtor is not bound by the administrative procedures prescribed by the BIA and does not incur the costs of a trustee.

Following is the usual sequence of events in an informal proposal: the debtor presents the informal settlement alternatives to creditors. If the proposal is successful and the debtor complies with the terms agreed upon, the procedure ends here, and business will continue. If, however, the offer is unsuccessful, the debtor may attempt a formal proposal.

If a creditor has a personal guarantee of one of the principals of a corporation, then that could eliminate the desire to accept the informal proposal. As mentioned earlier, in partnerships and proprietorships, the owners behind those types of business structures are automatically individually and collectively responsible for the full debts and liabilities of the business. However, the personal guarantor may have sold all his or her personal assets or leveraged them up by pledging them as security, so there is no equity left.

Banks also settle for a percentage of a debt owing and terms without interest. It is not uncommon in the case of a personal guarantor for banks to settle for possibly 25 cents to 35 cents on the dollar, depending on the circumstances. Perhaps the individual who signed the personal guarantee has very little equity and is merely attempting to borrow money from relatives or friends in order to have a pool of funds to pay off creditors on a percentage basis. The payment terms could be over 2 or 3 years. For this reason many creditors are prepared to settle, because on balance it is better to receive 25 cents on the dollar in an informal proposal than 10 cents on the dollar from a formal proposal or 1 cent on the dollar from a bankruptcy. If you were thinking of making an informal proposal to a creditor or a number of creditors, it would be more effective to have a lawyer or trustee do it for you in terms of credibility, expertise, and impact. Most business owners are not skilled at negotiating out of their debts, because they are too emotionally involved with the situation.

Following are the main advantages and disadvantages of an informal proposal over a formal proposal.

Advantages of an informal proposal

- rejection of the informal proposal does not result in automatic bankruptcy
- cost is reduced
- same outcome could be achieved
- opportunity to have different settlement terms for different creditors
- avoid the stigma of action under the BIA.

Disadvantages of an informal proposal

- certain creditors may want to negotiate a better deal or hold out to be paid in full

- no stay of proceedings, in terms of collection, or other legal action by creditors during negotiations
- requires acceptance by all creditors, otherwise unsatisfied creditors could continue collection action.

CHART 1: SEQUENCE OF EVENTS IN A FORMAL PROPOSAL (DIVISION I PROPOSAL)

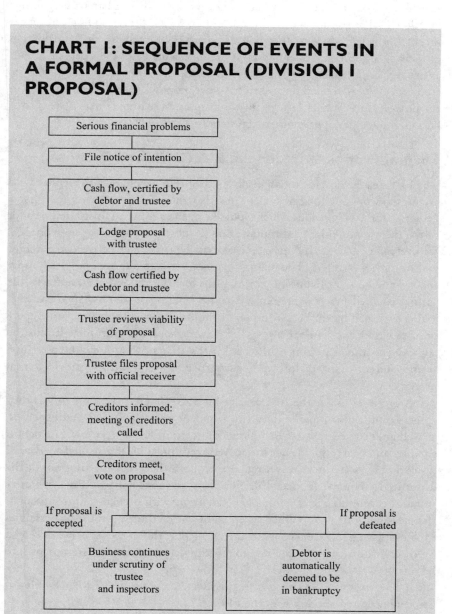

Consumer Proposal

For most people, the decision between filing a bankruptcy or a consumer proposal is a serious and confusing one. The provisions of the BIA dealing with consumer proposals are intended to help reduce the number of bankruptcy filings by allowing the consumers who owe less than $250,000 (excluding mortgages on their principal residences) to negotiate with their creditors for the reduction of their debt and/or extension of the time for payments of their debts. Certain executions on judgments, garnishees of income, and other collection actions by creditors may be stopped once the consumer proposal is filed. The first step in the process is to contact a trustee in bankruptcy. how to obtain a trustee is discussed in more detail in another section of this chapter.

Formal Proposals under the BIA (Division I Proposal)

The BIA creates the basis for an insolvent debtor to negotiate with creditors and attempt to work out an arrangement to satisfy them and yet remain in business. Otherwise, the only avenue which would be open to either an unsecured creditor or the debtor would be bankruptcy and the subsequent negative consequences for everyone concerned. A proposal is actually a contract between the debtor and his or her creditors. The main difference between a formal proposal under the Act and an informal proposal is that the formal proposal, if accepted by the appropriate percentage of creditors, becomes binding on all unsecured creditors and is governed by the Act. A proposal can be made either before bankruptcy or after bankruptcy. In the event that it is made after bankruptcy, it must be approved by the inspectors of the bankrupt's affairs before it can be presented to the creditors. Chart 1 provides a sequence of events with regard to formal proposals.

A proposal under the BIA cannot bind the secured creditors unless they agree. It must also provide for a full payment of trustee's fees and expenses, as well as specified preferred creditors and certain Crown claims. The debtor submits an offer to his or her unsecured creditors and, if accepted by special resolution at a creditors' meeting, the proposal becomes binding on all the unsecured creditors. A special resolution is one that is passed by a majority in number and 66.6% in value of the creditors with proven claims present at the meeting or by proxy. Once accepted by the creditors, it must be presented to and approved by the court. In the event that the proposal is not accepted by the creditors, it is treated as though the debtor made an assignment into bankruptcy.

There are several advantages and disadvantages to consider when looking at a formal proposal option under the BIA.

Advantages of a formal proposal

- Unsecured creditors are prevented from continuing lawsuits, which might result in the seizure of assets, without the court's consent.
- Debtor's cash flow can be used for current operating expenses without having to pay those funds to suppliers for past debts.
- All creditors are dealt with equitably, as set out in the priority fashion required by law.
- The debtor could attempt a temporary delay in payment (stay of proceedings) of his or her secured creditors. This opportunity is available under the Act. It is up to the discretion of the Court. During this interim, negotiations could take place for concessions or new investment funds sourced out. However, if the company is in a dire financial condition, with little hope for a turnaround or reorganization, the Court can refuse to provide a stay in that circumstance.
- Commercial leases are generally exempt.

Disadvantages of a formal proposal

- It may be difficult to obtain the required support from all classes of creditors.
- Depending on the degree of creditor involvement or control, the extra costs associated with trustee and related legal fees could be considerable.
- If the proposal is rejected, it will automatically lead to bankruptcy of the business. However, this potential risk should have the desired effect of encouraging a debtor to make a realistic proposal.

The Trustee should prepare a report to creditors which, among other items, provides the creditors with the Trustee's opinion as to whether the proposal has the potential to provide a greater return to creditors than a bankruptcy. Creditors should read this report and decide for themselves whether or not they wish to support the proposal.

Types of formal proposals

There is an unlimited variety of proposals under the BIA which might be presented. Some are:

- **Extension of time.** A proposal for an extension of time for payment to creditors will often contain other measures to decrease a debtor's obligations, for example, reducing the amount of the claim.
- **Percentage of profits.** The creditors agree to accept a percentage of the debtor's profits over time in satisfaction of their claims. The creditors' acceptance of this type of proposal and the court approval will depend

largely on whether the debtor's anticipated future profitability appears promising.

- **Basket proposal.** This is a request to the creditors to restrict their claims to particular assets, thereby enabling the debtor to carry on business with the remaining part of his or her assets. The debtor places specific assets in a "basket" held by the trustee, which is made available to the creditors who agree to accept those assets in full satisfaction of their claims. This procedure enables the debtor to carry out the proposal immediately by simply transferring the designated assets to the trustee. The trustee then determines the extent and priority of the claims to the assets.

- **Conversion of debt to equity or long-term debt.** The creditors agree to refinance the secured debt of a financially troubled debtor by accepting shares of the company instead of payment.

- **Lump sum.** The debtor offers a percentage on the dollar of the amount owing, excluding interest—for example, 10% on the dollar with payment 2 months after formal acceptance by all the creditors, or over two payments 6 months apart.

- **Liquidation proposal.** A debtor, who anticipates the eventual closing of the business but who wishes to avoid the consequences of bankruptcy, can submit a proposal to transfer all the assets to the trustee to sell and distribute the proceeds among the creditors. The rationale for a liquidation proposal is that if a company is permitted to be wound down in an orderly fashion, the assets will realize a higher value than if they were tainted with a receivership or bankruptcy.

Procedures involved in bankruptcy proposals

A business debtor wishing to make a formal proposal contacts a trustee and asks the trustee to supervise a proposal to be made to the creditors. The trustee assists the debtor in determining the terms of the proposal based on the circumstances. Other than the proposal itself, which must be completed and filed with the Superintendent of Bankruptcy, the forms are similar to those filed in a bankruptcy. When the trustee forwards the normal proof of claim forms sent to creditors, he or she also includes the proposal and a voting letter. The voting letter permits a creditor to vote on a proposal in writing without attending the creditors' meeting. The creditors' meeting is called by the trustee in order to discuss the terms outlined in the proposal. At the meeting, a creditor may suggest amendments to the proposal, and extensive bargaining can take place between the debtor and the creditors before the proposal is finally voted upon.

At the creditors' meeting, the debtor will attempt to have his or her proposal accepted, while the creditors will try to obtain the most beneficial arrangement possible. Each party knows, however, that if the proposal is not accepted, a bankruptcy will occur which usually will not benefit either party. Normally a representative of the office of the Superintendent of Bankruptcy attends the meeting of creditors. If the proposal is not approved, an immediate first meeting of creditors and bankruptcy is called.

Trustee's duties and fees

If the debtor is a business, the trustee will normally require guarantees of his or her fees and expenses from the principals of the company or from third parties, or will require an advance retainer to protect the trustee's fees. At the first meeting of the creditors, the trustee provides a report to the creditors on his or her investigation of the affairs of the debtor. The report indicates if there have been any possible preferences or transfers at undervalue. The report also indicates whether there have been any unreasonable payments to directors or improper payment of dividends, whether the proposal appears viable, and whether recovery for creditors will be enhanced by the proposal. The trustee may act as chair of the meeting and supervise the voting. If the proposal is accepted by the creditors, the trustee must apply to the court for approval. Normally the court will approve the proposal, although it may impose terms.

The trustee will be responsible, under the terms of the proposal, for collecting the amounts to be remitted to creditors. Once these funds have been remitted to creditors, the proposal obligations will have been completed, and a certificate of completion will be issued. The trustee will apply to the court for a discharge. In some instances, the trustee is given a responsibility under the proposal to completely supervise the affairs of the debtor until the proposal is completed. In other cases, the proposal calls for the election of inspectors by the group of creditors to supervise and control the affairs of the debtor until the proposal is completed.

A small business venture will normally proceed by way of an informal proposal, as trustee fees and expenses under a formal proposal can be substantial, thereby making it impractical.

BANKRUPTCY

The main purpose of the BIA is:

- control of distribution and equitable division of the insolvent debtor's assets to creditors; establishes a system of priorities for distribution of the debtor's assets and all creditors of the same class receive equal treatment

- rehabilitation of debtors, whether corporate or consumer; designed to provide the debtor a means of ending onerous financial obligations and attaining equilibrium and stability
- punishment of fraudulent debtors; provides a system for investigating and imposing sanctions for deliberate fraud
- regulation of receiverships, even though the debtor is not bankrupt
- encouragement of confidence in the credit system and overall economic and business viability.

In addition to knowing your rights and remedies under the BIA, as a creditor or debtor, you should be aware of other federal legislation, including but not limited to the Companies Creditors Arrangement Act (CCAA), the Wage Earner Protection Program Act (WEPPA), the Farm Debt Mediation Act, and the Winding-up and Restructuring Act (WURA), as well as various provincial statutes, including but not limited to the Commercial Tenancy Act and the Court Order Enforcement Act. For further information, speak to a lawyer who is an expert in these areas, in addition to a trustee in bankruptcy.

Canadian bankruptcy legislation provides for the administrative control of the debtor's financial affairs by the creditors. Although the trustee of the debtor's affairs personally attends to the role of turning the assets into money and other administrative matters, he or she is guided and instructed in these actions by the creditors and or inspectors.

Participants Involved in Bankruptcy Process

It would be helpful to understand the function of the parties involved in the bankruptcy process.

Bankrupt

This term refers to a person or company who has made a voluntary assignment into bankruptcy or was petitioned into bankruptcy by creditors.

Superintendent of bankruptcy

This person is an official of the federal ministry, Industry Canada. There are various representatives of the Superintendent across Canada who oversee the bankruptcy process and the administration by trustees who are appointed by the Superintendent. The Superintendent investigates allegations of offences in connection with a bankruptcy and intervenes, if necessary, in any matter or proceeding in court. He or she comments on the final statement of receipts and disbursements of the trustee.

Information on bankruptcy can be obtained from the Superintendent. More information on the Office of the Superintendent of Bankruptcy Canada can be found at ic.gc.ca/eic/site/bsf-osb.nsf.

The official receiver

The Official Receiver is an employee of the Superintendent of Bankruptcy whose principal functions are to appoint the trustee, examine the conduct of the bankrupt and the disposition of property, and preside at the first meeting of creditors. He or she participates in the overall administration of bankruptcies by receiving and investigating complaints and exercising surveillance over trustees. In the event that you have any information suggesting an irregularity in the bankruptcy, the Official Receiver should be contacted through Industry Canada.

The trustee

Generally, the trustee is a chartered accountant licensed by the Superintendent of Bankruptcy whose main responsibility is to take possession of the bankrupts assets, to liquidate those assets, and to distribute proceeds to the creditors according to the scheme of distribution outlined in the BIA. This is done under the direction of the creditors, who are usually represented by duly elected inspectors, and under the supervision of the Superintendent of Bankruptcy. If you would like to obtain the names of trustees for a bankruptcy, contact the Superintendent of Bankruptcy through Industry Canada.

The registrar

This person is a court official who settles unopposed bankruptcy matters coming before the court, such as petitions for receiving orders, discharges of bankrupts, and other routine matters. For example, the registrar may examine the bankrupt, or people who have knowledge of the bankrupt's affairs, in order to assist with the proper disposition of the assets. In addition, the registrar will settle matters regarding proof of claims, such as their validity and their disallowance or reduction, and approve the fees of a trustee and the trustee's statement of receipts and disbursements.

Inspectors

Creditors may appoint inspectors who have a fiduciary duty to the general body of creditors. They provide direction and assistance to the trustee and otherwise monitor the trustee's activities to ensure that the Trustee is acting in accordance with their duties and powers per the BIA. Generally the inspectors are familiar with the business of the bankrupt and can assist the trustee in obtaining the maximum realization (under distressed circumstances) from the bankrupts assets.

Priority creditor

There are creditors who are referred to as super-priority to the secured creditors, such as third-party property and 30-day goods creditors and trust and lien claims. Refer to BIA sections 81 through 81.6.

Secured creditor

This is a creditor whose loan or credit to the bankrupt is secured in whole or in part by a pledge of some specific property of the debtor by means of a General Security Agreement (GSA), mortgage, lien, or other charge on assets (e.g., a chattel mortgage against a car or a collateral mortgage against a house or property). There are other forms of security, including a pledge of stocks and bonds, debentures, assignment of accounts receivable, mechanics' liens, and various bank securities. The bankruptcy trustee cannot seize secured assets.

Preferred creditor

After the secured creditors have been satisfied, a preferred creditor (unsecured) is entitled to be paid ahead of claims by ordinary unsecured creditors. As funds permit, the claims of preferred creditors are paid out in the following sequential order, ahead of the general body of unsecured creditor. Here are some examples.

- reasonable funeral and testamentary expenses of a deceased bankrupt
- costs of administration of the bankruptcy
- 5% levy payable to the Superintendent of Bankruptcy
- wages earned up to 6 months prior to bankruptcy up to $2000, plus, for travelling salespersons, expenses of up to $1000
- municipal taxes that do not constitute a charge against real property
- rent up to 3 months prior to bankruptcy and 3 months of accelerated rent that shall not exceed the realization from the property on the premises under lease
- costs of the creditor who first attached the property of the bankrupt
- Workers' Compensation Board claims
- claims resulting from injuries to bankrupt's employees not covered by WCB, in certain circumstances.

Also refer to Scheme of Distribution in BIA, Section 136.

Unsecured creditors

Unsecured creditors are paid on a pro rata basis from the remaining net proceeds after the assets of the bankrupt are sold. In many cases, of course, there is nothing or very little available for the unsecured creditors. For example, if there are unsecured creditor claims of $100,000, and $5,000 is available in the debtor's estate after the preferred and secured creditors have been paid, as well as the trustee and the trustee's legal expenses, then the unsecured creditors would get 5 cents on the dollar.

It is imperative to note, however, that under the Act, an unsecured creditor may have the priority and right to reclaim the goods delivered to the debtor ahead of secured creditors if several conditions are met. These are known as 30-day goods claims. There are also special provisions for farmers and fishermen.

Acts of Bankruptcy

In order for a bankruptcy (voluntary or involuntary) to occur, an act of bankruptcy, as described below, must have taken place:

- where a person makes an assignment of his or her property to a trustee for the benefit of creditors, whether under the BIA or otherwise
- where a person leaves the country or remains out of Canada with the intent to defeat or delay creditors
- where a person permits an unsatisfied judgment execution to remain unpaid
- where a person exhibits a statement of affairs which shows he or she is insolvent at a meeting of creditors
- where a person disposes of property with intent to defraud or defeat creditors
- where a person gives notice to creditors that he or she has suspended payment of debts
- where a person defaults under the terms of a formal proposal made under the BIA
- where a person ceases to meet his or her liabilities generally as they become due, one of the most frequently alleged acts in bankruptcy petitions.

Voluntary assignment

An assignment in bankruptcy may be made by an insolvent person or company. A debtor assigns all of his or her property, or the company's property, to a trustee for distribution among the creditors. The assignment is accompanied by a statement of affairs listing the property owned by the bankrupt and details of liabilities. It is submitted to the local Official Receiver. The date the assignment is registered with the Official Receiver is the effective date of bankruptcy. The Official Receiver will appoint a trustee, who will then take possession of the bankrupt's property as expeditiously as possible, and commence administration of the affairs. If you are the debtor, you have the opportunity to select a trustee of your preference, who will be subject to affirmation by the creditors at the first meeting of creditors. Chart 2 shows the sequence of events in a voluntary assignment in bankruptcy, as well as a petition in bankruptcy.

Petition by creditors

Under the BIA, one or more creditors has the right to petition the court to issue a receiving order against the debtor declaring the debtor to be bankrupt. The grounds are:

- the debt or debts owing to the creditor or creditors amount to $1000 or more; and
- the debtor has committed an act of bankruptcy within the 6 months preceding the date the petition was filed.

The cost of petitioning the debtor, as allowed by the court, is payable under the bankrupt's estate as a preferred claim. A secured creditor cannot petition the debtor, unless the creditor either gives up the security it holds or devalues it by an amount that will make the creditor an unsecured creditor for $1000 or more.

A petition is appropriate for a creditor to consider when the debtor has ceased to pay his or her debts, but assets are still available for ordinary creditors; where it appears that shareholders, certain creditors, or others are being preferred, in terms of being paid off; where the financial position of the debtor is deteriorating rapidly to the detriment of creditors; or where fraud is suspected.

The Bankruptcy Process

The effective date of bankruptcy is the date the receiving order is granted. The petition is heard by the court approximately 10 days after it has been served on the debtor and the Superintendent of Bankruptcy. As soon as the court is satisfied that the debtor is insolvent, the debtor has committed an act of bankruptcy, and the petitioner is acting in good faith, a receiving order will be issued declaring the debtor to be bankrupt. During this 10-day period the trustee has no power to act and, given the financial problems in which the debtor finds himself, a number of things might occur which could be prejudicial to the creditors. The BIA therefore makes provision for the appointment of a licensed trustee as an interim receiver of the debtor's property. The interim receiver takes his direction from the appointing court order which may include the power to act immediately and take possession of the debtor's property. To obtain an interim receiving order, the petitioning creditor must demonstrate to the court that such an order is necessary for the protection of the debtor's estate. The creditor must also undertake the responsibility for any damages suffered by the debtor in the event the petition is ultimately dismissed.

Once appointed, the interim receiver assumes the status of a caretaker and cannot unduly interfere with the debtor's business, except as authorized by the court. If necessary, the court will grant the interim receiver power to dispose of property of the debtor that is perishable or likely to depreciate rapidly in value.

CHART 2: SEQUENCE OF EVENTS IN A BANKRUPTCY

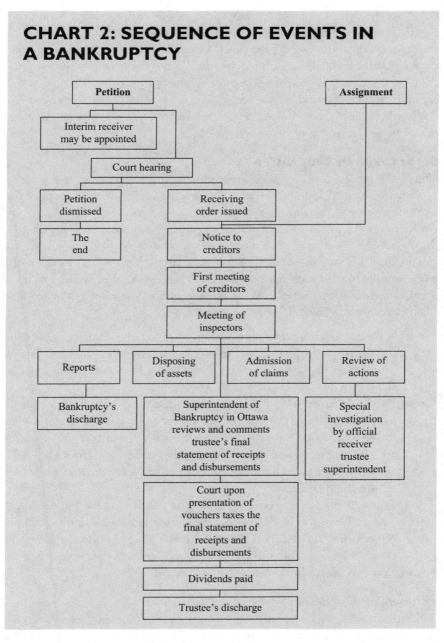

The interim receiver is in the awkward position of acting in the best interests of the creditors by ensuring that the assets of the business are not removed, while refraining from interfering in the ordinary course of business of the debtor.

After the date of bankruptcy, unsecured creditors are prevented from commencing or continuing legal action against the bankrupt for the recovery of the debt, unless authorized by the court. Unsecured creditors must make their claims through the trustee. Secured creditors' rights are generally restricted to the extent necessary to enable the trustee to satisfy himself or herself that the creditors' security is valid. There are some other possible restrictions however. Preferred creditors generally must await the orderly administration of the debtor's estate by the trustee before they are paid.

Steps taken by the trustee

The BIA imposes a duty on the bankrupt to make full disclosure to the trustee of his or her assets and liabilities, as well as details related to the disposal of any of the bankrupts property prior to the date of bankruptcy. Further, the BIA directs the trustee to investigate the conduct of the bankrupt prior to the date of bankruptcy for what are known as *preferences* and *transfers at undervalue* (TUVs). The Court can declare a TUV to be void as against a trustee in bankruptcy and order a party to the transfer to pay funds or otherwise return property to the bankrupt estate.

Correspondence that deserves prompt and careful attention will be sent out to all the creditors. These documents are:

- **Notice to creditors of first meeting.** This document informs the creditor of the bankruptcy, invites him or her to attend the first meeting of creditors on the date and at the place fixed, and advises that a proof of claim is to be filed.
- **Proof of claim.** This form asks the creditor to verify the amount of money which is owed and to substantiate the claim. Substantiation includes attaching some kind of record, such as an invoice, statement of account, or promissory note, to verify that the debt is owing. The creditor will also be asked to indicate his or her status as a secured, preferred, or unsecured creditor.
- **Proxy.** If the creditor is unable to attend the first meeting of creditors, a proxy form may be completed, appointing someone else to act on his or her behalf. It is fairly common for creditors to appoint the trustee as their proxy, especially if the creditors reside outside the geographic area in which the creditors' meeting would be held.

First meeting of creditors

The trustees will prepare a preliminary report on the affairs of the bankrupt for presentation to the first meeting of creditors. This preliminary report includes particulars of the value of all the property, the total liability, and the trustee's opinion of the types and validity of creditors' claims. In addition, the report contains the trustee's opinion as to whether the affairs of the bankrupt have been conducted properly. The Official Receiver or his or her nominee may examine the bankrupt under oath regarding the events that have occurred prior to the bankruptcy.

The first meeting of creditors is normally held within 3 weeks of the date of the trustee's appointment. The purpose of the meeting is to review the affairs of the bankrupt and either ratify the appointment of the trustee or appoint a new trustee. The creditors also decide whether to appoint inspectors to supervise the estate. A quorum at the creditors' meeting consists of just one creditor who has proven his or her claim. This creditor can be personally present, be represented, or be represented by proxy. Under summary administration (personal bankruptcy) a meeting of creditors is not usually called unless requested.

Rights of the creditor

A creditor who has a valid claim against the bankrupt, and who has supported his or her claim by lodging with the trustee a proof of claim that is accepted, may share in the distribution of the debtor's assets, providing there is enough money to pay the claims that are ranked before that creditor's. A creditor has additional rights, including the right to:

- examine the proof of claim of other creditors
- vote on any matters which may arise, such as selection, removal, or substitution of the trustee or inspectors
- object to the discharge of the bankrupt or the trustee
- appeal to the court if he or she is in disagreement with any act or decision of the trustee
- take independent action in the recovery of assets, with the permission of the court, if the trustee fails to do so.

In general, a creditor has the right to share, to vote, to examine, to appoint, to substitute, and to remove.

Duties of the bankrupt

Within 5 days after bankruptcy is filed, the bankrupt is instructed in writing to attend a meeting of creditors in order to supply more information about his or her pertinent financial situation. The bankrupt must be present at this meeting unless prevented by sickness or other sufficient cause. As required under the BIA, a bankrupt must act in an honest manner and cooperate fully with the trustee to facilitate the highest possible return from the disposal of the bankrupt's assets for the disposition to the creditors.

Following is a list of the bankrupt's duties. He or she must:

- reveal and turn over to the trustee all assets in his or her possession or control, including credit cards

- deliver to the trustee all records, books, and documents relating to his or her assets or affairs
- attend the office of the Official Receiver at the appointed time, to be examined under oath as to the facts relating to the bankruptcy
- submit to other examinations under oath when required
- provide a statement of affairs, normally prepared by the trustee, and including a complete list of all the assets and liabilities, including creditors' names, addresses, account numbers, invoices and amounts
- if any additional bills or legal documents are received by the bankrupt after the list is prepared, they must be forwarded to the trustee, or if any assets or debts have been accidentally omitted, the trustee must be informed promptly
- disclose to the trustee all property disposed of within 1 year preceding bankruptcy
- disclose to the trustee all gifts disposed of by the bankrupt during the 5 years prior to the bankruptcy, including how they were disposed, to whom, why, and for how much
- attend first meeting of creditors and other meetings when required, for examination
- not attempt to obtain new credit until discharged
- not make any payment to creditors without consulting with trustee help in the realization of his or her property and the distribution of proceeds among creditors
- execute such forms of other documents as may be required
- examine the correctness of all proofs of claim submitted to the trustee and disclose any false claims to the trustee by creditors
- remit to the trustee immediately upon receipt all money received from lotteries, inheritances, or any similar sources
- keep the trustee advised at all times of any change of address, employment, or salary.

The BIA outlines the penalties which can be imposed against the bankrupt who has not acted in an appropriate manner. If an interested party suspects that an offence under the Act has been committed, the information is relayed to the office of the Superintendent of Bankruptcy. If the Superintendent feels the circumstances warrant an investigation, the matter is referred to the RCMP. If found guilty, a bankrupt is liable under the BIA to imprisonment, a fine, or both, where the bankrupt:

- fails to perform his or her duties as previously described
- makes a fraudulent disposition of assets before or after bankruptcy

- refuses or neglects to answer fully and truthfully all questions when examined under oath
- makes a false declaration regarding assets or liabilities
- destroys, mutilates, conceals, or falsifies a document relating to the bankrupt's property after or within 12 months preceding the bankruptcy
- obtains credit or property by false representations after or within 12 months preceding the bankruptcy and until the date of discharge
- fraudulently conceals property of a value of $50 or more after or within 12 months preceding the bankruptcy
- pawns or pledges property on which credit has been obtained but not paid off within 12 months preceding the bankruptcy
- engages in a new business occupation or obtains credit in excess of $1000, without disclosure of undischarged bankrupt status.

Discharge of the bankrupt

A discharge by the court will generally provide final relief to the bankrupt. A first-time bankrupt with no surplus income (as defined by statute), is eligible for an automatic discharge 9 months after the date of bankruptcy, provided no opposition has arisen. A first-time bankrupt with surplus income will be eligible for an automatic discharge 21 months after the date of bankruptcy, provided no opposition. A second-time bankrupt may also be eligible for an automatic discharge; however, the time period is extended to 24 months (no surplus income) and 36 months (with surplus income), again providing no opposition arises. The trustee completes a report on the affairs of the bankrupt, cause of bankruptcy, and conduct of the bankrupt. The trustee advises the creditors that application will be made on a certain date for the bankrupt's discharge. Providing no opposition has arisen, the hearing of the application by the trustee for discharge of the bankrupt is held before the District Registrar of the court and is an informal procedure.

A creditor can oppose a discharge by appearing before the registrar, after giving written notice of his or her intention to do so. If a discharge is opposed before the registrar, the registrar may adjourn the discharge. The bankrupt should, in order to have further applications for discharge made, engage a lawyer who will arrange for the matter to be decided by a judge.

Once the matter is in front of the judge, the court may then make one of the following decisions relating to the matter of discharge:

- issue an order of absolute discharge, meaning that the debtor is no longer responsible for his or her debts, except for those listed by the court
- issue an order of conditional discharge, meaning that the bankrupt is required to pay a certain sum of money for distribution to creditors, and then obtain

absolute discharge; other terms may be imposed as well, for example, the court may state that $5000 has to be paid to the trustee to be distributed to the creditors, and once that sum is paid the discharge is given automatically

- issue an order of suspended discharge, essentially the same as an absolute discharge, except that the court orders a delay, and may also impose conditions, before the discharge is effective
- postpone the hearing to a later date
- refuse the discharge, a power rarely exercised by the court and only for serious reasons.

There are certain debts, however, that an order of discharge does not release the bankrupt from paying. These are:

- any fine, penalty, restitution order or other order similar in nature to a fine, penalty, or restitution order, imposed by a court in respect of an offence, or any debt arising out of a recognizance or bail
- any debt or liability for alimony
- any debt or liability under a maintenance or affiliation order or under an agreement for maintenance and support of a spouse or child living apart from the bankrupt
- any debt or liability arising out of fraud, embezzlement, or misappropriation while acting in a fiduciary capacity, that is, a position of trust
- any debt or liability for obtaining property by false pretences or fraudulent misrepresentation
- liability for the dividend that a creditor would have been entitled to receive on any provable claim not disclosed to the trustee, unless such creditor had notice or knowledge of the bankruptcy and failed to take reasonable action to prove his or her claim
- damage awards for bodily harm, sexual assault, or wrongful death

Also affected would be a debt arising from a loan made under the Canada Student Loans Act, the Canada Student Financial Assistance Act, or similar provincial legislation, where the date of bankruptcy occurred before the bankrupt ceased to be a full- or part-time student or within 7 years of the date on which the bankrupt ceased to be a full- or part-time student. However there is a further provision that, after 5 years since being a full- or part-time student, and given certain other conditions, the court may use its discretion and order that the debt is released.

RECEIVERSHIP

If a debenture or GSA is given by a corporation to a lender, and the terms of the document are not complied with by the debtor, then a receivership situation could occur. In this circumstance, a receiver or receiver-manager is appointed either by the terms of the document or by the court. Other forms of security in addition to debentures or GSAs, such as mortgages or assignments of inventory, could also involve the appointment of receivers. The debenture or GSA represent the most common ways that receiverships are triggered.

Debentures

A debenture or GSA is a form of security issued by the business borrower. The documents describe the nature of the security and specify the property it encumbers.

Appointment of Receiver

If the debtor defaults under the terms of the security document, the lender has the right to appoint a receiver or receiver-manager to take possession of the debtor's assets. The receiver then proceeds to take possession and deal with the assets.

If the directors of the company cannot reorganize the financial affairs of the corporation and pay out the security holder, the receiver takes control and indicates actions to be taken, such as sale of the assets or the company as a whole. This latter situation may occur when unsecured creditors are taking steps to collect unpaid accounts, such as garnisheeing, with the effect that the assets are being depleted to pay creditors who would otherwise rank behind the debenture or GSA holder.

In other instances, the business is managed by the receiver-manager to protect its value, including goodwill, so that it can be offered for sale as a going concern at the best possible price. This tends to occur when a business cannot be operated in such a fashion as to service its debt load and pay out creditors whose debts are due.

If you have any questions on the general topic of receivership or bankruptcy, you may wish to consult a trustee who specializes in these areas. Normally, an accountant who is a trustee in bankruptcy also acts as a receiver or receiver-manager. Look in the *Yellow Pages* print and online under "Trustees in Bankruptcy." If you are being asked to sign a debenture or GSA by the bank or some other lender as security on behalf of your company, make sure that you obtain competent legal advice from a business lawyer on negotiating the security document or negotiating out of it. In addition, make sure that you speak to your accountant regarding the implications of your business signing any security document before you do so.

Chapter 18

Patent, Trademark, Copyright, and Industrial Design

Anything that won't sell, I don't want to invent.

—Thomas A. Edison

Many small business owners are unsure of the meaning or significance of the area of law known as intellectual property. Intellectual property refers primarily to patents, trademarks, copyright, and industrial design. These terms and concepts are frequently confused. Whereas all of them are rights granted for intellectual creativity, they take different forms. Patents are for structure and function, whereas copyright is for literary, dramatic, artistic, or musical works, or computer software. Industrial designs are for the shape, pattern, or ornamentation applied to an industrially produced object. A trademark is a word, picture, or symbol or package design, or combination of these, used to distinguish goods or services by one person or organization from the goods or services of others in the marketplace.

These areas are governed by judge-made law as well as federal statutes, including the Patent Act, Copyright Act, Trade-marks Act, and the Industrial Design Act. Legislation is always in a state of flux, revised on an ongoing basis to reflect changing circumstances, including more efficient administration of the law and regulations. For this reason, if you are considering making an application under any of the above statutes, obtain the assistance from professionals. This is essential to save time, expense, and inconvenience, as well as to avoid potential pitfalls.

Legislation governing intellectual properties is administered and regulated primarily by Industry Canada. This department has branches in various cities throughout Canada. Industry Canada has an excellent series of free booklets on intellectual property available on request.

The federal government is also actively involved in encouraging and assisting the commercial application of technology in other ways. Further information on these programs is discussed later in this chapter.

The area of intellectual property is a fascinating but complex subject. As a business owner, you may want to protect your rights to your inventions. Alternatively, you may want to purchase or become a licensee of the inventions of others. Another option is to make a profit by manufacturing inventions of

393

others, without legally having to pay a fee to the inventor. In this latter example, the inventor lost or abandoned the patent rights or never registered them in Canada.

This chapter will provide an overview of the differences between the various types of intellectual property. It will also cover some of the considerations that you should be aware of to avoid potential problems caused by innocently infringing on the intellectual property rights of others. (Comments relate to the Canadian context; other countries have their own laws.)

PATENTS

On the average, under the new Act, a patent grants its owner a legal right to exclude others for 20 years from the date of filing, from making, selling, or using the invention to which the patent relates. Patents are granted for products, compositions, apparatuses, and processes, or methods that are novel, useful, and unobvious. Most patents are improvements over old technology. Only an inventor or assignee or other successor may obtain a patent for an invention. A patent is not extendable beyond its year term.

Patent Office

The Canadian Patent Office is situated in Hull, Quebec, and is part of Industry Canada. The Patent Office is part of a larger agency called the Canadian Intellectual Property Office, which is responsible not only for patent rights, but for most intellectual property rights. The exception is plant breeder protection, which is administered by Agriculture Canada.

One of the responsibilities of the Patent Office is of course to protect the inventor, but its other purpose is to promote economic activity and technological development by making patent and technical information available to the public.

The Patent Office provides a vast range of useful resource information. Here are just a few of its offerings.

- It provides access to millions of patents catalogued in the Canadian, American, and international systems. More than two-thirds of these patents are not registered in Canada and therefore can be used freely by Canadians. The best place to access international patents is through foreign intellectual property offices.
- Canadian patents have been classified into 70,000 different categories according to the international patent classification system, allowing for rapid retrieval of information on any given technology. It is possible to check whether technology similar to one's own exists, and how advanced it is.

- The Patent Office has expertise in a full range of technological and scientific activities. As a result, the office is well able to assess new developments in Canadian technology. It can also assist the public by directing them to the desired information and helping them interpret it.
- The Patent Office examines applications for patents and grants patents for inventions if, in law, the applicants are entitled to it. It also publishes and disseminates patent information, records assignments of patents, maintains search files of Canadian patents, and provides a search room for public use in researching issued patents and records. The Patent Office also has a computerized database available online.

Benefits of Patented Information

Knowledge of new technology often makes a difference between success and failure to a small business, for numerous reasons, including:

- launching new products into the market
- capturing or increasing a share of the market
- finding the best suppliers of new technology to meet the firm's needs
- reducing manufacturing and research costs to increase cost effectiveness
- increasing production and productivity
- anticipating, identifying, and challenging foreign competition
- avoiding the use of already patented inventions, thus avoiding legal problems.

It is impossible to keep current on technological innovations without using patent information. In comparison with other sources of commercially available technological information, patent information offers several key advantages:

- Highly selective search and retrieval is possible through the several patent classification systems, including access to patents from countries around the world.
- A patent search may identify trends and developments in a specialized field or technology.
- Not all inventions are protected in all markets around the world, so there is a significant amount of technology unprotected in Canada that is available for exploitation by Canadian firms.
- New product lines can be discovered and licensed from the patentee.
- Information is presented in a fairly uniform manner by the Patent Office and frequently is accompanied by explanatory drawings.
- Those involved in research and development can benefit from a search of patents, as information may be found that prevents duplication of research. Failure to check the information available at the Patent Office

could result in hundreds of thousands of dollars or more being spent on needless research, the methodology and results of which were already outlined and explained in considerable detail in Patent Office documents.

- In describing the novelty of an invention, a patent normally discloses information on what was previously known, thus providing a capsule survey of the state of the art. Unproductive avenues of inquiry may be identified after reading the description of the patent disclosure.
- Disclosed information is normally more complete than other documentary sources of information, such as technical periodicals.
- Those wishing to keep track of the work of a particular individual or company can see what patents they have been granted.
- A study of patents in a given field may very well generate additional ideas for research and development.
- The names and addresses of the patent owner and other principals are generally available through patent searches, including their interest in selling or licensing the patent. This assists contact between parties interested in exploiting the technology.
- Canadian firms can also take advantage of the manufacturing licences, called compulsory licences which the Patent Office has the power to grant. Under the Patents Act, the Commissioner of Patents may, subject to certain restrictions, grant a licence for the exploitation of a Canadian patent.

Criteria for Obtaining a Patent

Before you go to the expense and inconvenience of applying for a patent, you should ask yourself a number of questions. The minimum cost of preparing and filing one patent in Canada is typically around $6,000 to $10,000, if a patent agent is retained. If there is no possibility that the invention has any commercial feasibility, the money spent on the patent could be wasted. You should answer these questions:

- Is there an existing or potential market for the invention?
- Who are the potential purchasers of the invention and how much would they be prepared to pay for it?
- Where will the invention be sold or assigned, and who will negotiate the transaction?
- What would the cost be to manufacture the invention, and who would be prepared to manufacture it?
- Will you be able to obtain all the necessary financing to commercially exploit your invention, and where will you get the financing?
- Do you have the necessary business contacts and expertise required to market the invention in a commercially successful fashion?

Once you have decided that it is viable for you to proceed further, it is necessary to know the key criteria for an invention to be granted a patent. Three features of the invention have to be present:

1. **Novelty.** This means that the invention has to be new. Under the Patent Act, a patent will be granted to the inventor who is the first to file an application. Publication or public use of the invention by another person anywhere in the world before the patent application is filed is a bar to obtaining a patent in Canada. Patent Offices in Canada and the United States allow a 1-year "grace period" for the inventor to file the application if the invention has been publicly disclosed by the inventor or anyone who obtained disclosure directly or indirectly from the inventor, but not by anybody else.
2. **Utility.** The Patent Office will not issue a patent on something which doesn't work or which has no inherent or disclosed use. In other words, it has to have some practical benefit to it.
3. **Inventive ingenuity.** An invention must be a development or an improvement that would not have been obvious beforehand to people of average skill in the technology involved.

Registered Patent Agents

Although any Canadian can personally file a patent application within Canada, the preparation and successful acceptance of an application requires an extensive knowledge of patent law and Patent Office practice. It is therefore highly recommended that inventors consult a registered patent agent to handle such matters. If the inventor attempts to obtain the patent without the use of a patent agent, difficulties and delays could arise. If the patent is eventually obtained, it may not have been properly drafted to adequately protect the invention.

A registered patent agent must pass an examination in patent law and practice before being permitted to represent inventors before the Patent Office. The agent's associates will be well-versed on the intricacies of foreign law. Once the inventor has appointed a patent agent, the Patent Office corresponds only with the patent agent with respect to his or her application.

Patent agents may or may not also be patent lawyers. The list of registered patent agents is available from the Patent Office. You can also find the names of patent agents and patent lawyers on the websites of the Canadian Intellectual Property Office (cipo.ic.gc.ca) or the Intellectual Property Institute of Canada (ipic.ca). In the case of patent lawyers, you can obtain names of patent lawyers from the lawyer referral service in your area. It is always advisable to get at least three, if not more, professional opinions before making your selection.

Trade Secrets

Before you decide to patent, you may also want to consider the advantages of not patenting your technology. Some companies prefer to keep their inventions a trade secret. They believe that the advantages of nondisclosure outweigh the benefits of patent protection. An inventor who has not registered a patent, however, runs the risk of a competitor obtaining the product on the open market or through corporate espionage and copying it. The competitor could even apply for a patent on an improved and patentable version of the product, thereby inhibiting the inventor from marketing the invention. An invention that is kept a trade secret and sold openly in a manner that enables disclosure of the secret is immediately barred from being patented in most countries.

Publish and perish is the rule of thumb for patents. The only disclosure before your patent application is filed should be done in complete confidence. Nondisclosure/confidentiality agreements are a must. (See Sample 32 at the back of the book.)

Patent Registration Process

There are various steps and considerations to take into account when applying for a patent:

- **Preliminary search.** One of the first steps after obtaining professional advice is to do a preliminary patentability search in either the Canadian or U.S. Patent Office. The search may reveal that the invention cannot be patented, thus saving the cost of preparing and filing a patent application. The cost of conducting a worldwide search is prohibitive. The completed preliminary search is not necessarily conclusive evidence of the patentability of an invention. The Patent Office examiner may reject claims in an application on the basis of prior patents or literature not found in the preliminary search. If an inventor intends not only to patent the invention, but also to sell or use it in some fashion, an infringement search can be done to see if the invention conflicts with another patent. An infringement search is naturally more comprehensive and thorough than a preliminary patentability search, and therefore is considerably more expensive. This is because the inventor would have to have a high degree of certainty that there is not an infringement before committing a large capital investment to manufacturing.
- **Preparing and filing an application.** A patent application consists of an abstract, a description, one or more claims of ownership, and drawings. An abstract is a brief summary of the invention. The description gives complete and clear written details of the invention and the manner

in which it is useful. The claims define in a precise manner exactly what the applicant claims to own and the boundaries of the patent protection, and therefore fixes the amount of protection granted by the patent. This is why professional assistance is necessary. The challenge is to draft the claims in a fashion sufficient to identify the features that distinguish the invention from earlier ones, and then to specify those features in the claims so that the invention is defined broadly enough to provide maximum protection against potential infringers. At the same time, the claims have to be sufficiently specific to distinguish the invention from all prior inventions.

- **Acceptance or rejection.** If your application is accepted, you are given a notice of allowance, and upon payment of the final fee, the patent is officially issued to you. Your patent rights exclude others from making, using, and selling the invention, or importing the invention into Canada as of that date. It is not unusual for a period of 2 or 3 years to elapse from the initial date of application before a patent is granted. This is because the Patent Office receives thousands of applications for patents each year, and the applications are examined in the order received. Special orders can be given priority. If your application is rejected, you have an opportunity to overcome the rejection by providing the necessary clarifications. If the application is still rejected, you have a right to appeal.
- **Patent pending.** Sometimes an inventor or manufacturer will mark an article "patent pending" or "patent applied for." These phrases have no legal effect but give information that a patent application has been filed in a patent office. This serves to warn others that the patentee can enforce the exclusive right to manufacture the invention once and if a patent is granted. As mentioned earlier, the protection afforded by a patent does not start until the date the patent is issued.

Patent Protection Outside Canada

Obtaining a Canadian patent for a product or process does not provide any protection in other countries. As a result, a patent application must be made in each country where you intend to sell, assign, or manufacture the invention. Patent laws vary from one country to another, and some countries have no patent laws at all.

In most foreign countries, publication of the invention before the filing date of the application in those countries will bar the right to a patent. In other words, if you advertise or talk publicly to others about your product, display it at a trade show, or allow publication of its description anywhere in the world, you would be prevented from obtaining a patent within those countries. You would, therefore, not be able to prevent others from copying your product.

In the United States, an inventor has up to 1 year to file a patent application after publication of an invention. As mentioned earlier, the grace period in Canada is 1 year.

Assigning or Licensing a Patent

Once a patent has been obtained, the inventor has the exclusive right to sell or license the exclusive rights to others. The legal agreement to transfer rights to others takes the form of either an assignment (title transfer) or a licence.

An assignment occurs when all or part of the interest in the invention is transferred from the holder of the patent to another party, called the assignee. The assignee then assumes the ownership rights originally held by the patent holder. The arrangement must be in writing, and the Patent Office must be formally notified. Licensing differs from an assignment, in that the owner of the patent retains ownership, but temporarily allows the licensee to use the patent. This use is subject to the conditions or limitations set forth in the licensing agreement.

Before starting any discussions with domestic or foreign companies concerning assignment or licensing agreements, it may be necessary to openly discuss technology that has not been patented in either Canada or the foreign country. In such a situation, the parties should sign a confidentiality and nondisclosure agreement; otherwise, premature disclosure of unpatented technology could result in forfeiture of the right to protection (see Sample 32) Each agreement should be customized, of course, for your specific situation, and drawn up by your lawyer.

Another concern could be the disclosure of confidential patent information to employees. A person or company that holds the patent may require employees to sign a confidentiality agreement including a provision that any new innovations or intellectual property derived by an employee are deemed to belong exclusively to the employer. Sample 33 is a typical contract that an employer would require the employee to sign.

Have your lawyer customize it for you. If any of the above agreements were breached, the person asserting the intellectual property rights could sue in court. The claim would be for financial damages, as well as a request to the court for an injunction prohibiting the other party from using the intellectual property in any fashion. In practical terms, if the person who has breached the contract is outside Canada, it could be difficult to enforce the contract. In any event, it would be very expensive, and not necessarily a productive or successful exercise. The steps involved in a litigation action are covered in Chapter 16, "Understanding the Litigation Process."

Sources of Commercial Patent Opportunities and Ideas

Whether you are an inventor wanting to locate a potential purchaser or licensee for your patent, or whether you are looking for a patent to exploit for commercial gain, there are many sources of opportunities and ideas to pursue. Here are some ideas.

University research organizations

Contact the major university research organizations in your area, as well as throughout Canada. You can get the names of these research organizations from your public library. Request that you be put on a mailing list for any information that is distributed relating to inventions that have a commercial application, and specify the exact type of product that interests you. Inquire about their technology centres or research councils.

Canadian Industrial Innovation Centre

The Innovation Centre helps people evaluate their ideas and get commercially viable products on the market. To obtain a detailed brochure, contact the Centre in Waterloo, Ontario, at (519) 885–5870 or innovationcentre.ca.

Technology centres at technical institutes

Contact the technology divisions of institutes in your area; for example, British Columbia Institute of Technology (BCIT); Northern Alberta Institute of Technology (NAIT) in Edmonton; Southern Alberta Institute of Technology (SAIT) in Calgary; Ryerson Polytechnical University in Toronto; University of Ontario Institute of Technology in Oshawa.

Invention or trade shows

There are many trade shows offered throughout Canada, as well as the United States. This would provide an opportunity for inventors to display their product in the hope of finding a manufacturer or distributor to whom they can sell or assign rights. Conversely, you may want to attend the show to pick up ideas for your own benefit, as well as make contacts with potential inventors or manufacturers for purchase of their product. Major trade shows tend to be advertised in the national newspapers and in local newspapers in the area where a show is being held. There are annual directories that provide details on all the trade shows and exhibitions scheduled throughout Canada and the United States. Check with your local library and do online searches through Google for directories on trade shows, exhibitions, and conventions in Canada, the U.S., and internationally in the areas of interest to you.

Patent publications

Canadian and U.S. patent publications are available in many libraries throughout Canada, as well as online. The following directories are normally available and are updated weekly:

- *Canadian Patent Office Record.* This printed record comprises such information as the title of the invention and the name of the inventor. For some time periods, there are abstracts (short descriptions) and drawings available. The classification system is also available in some public libraries. Their website is: ic.gc.ca/cipo/patgazarc.nsf/cpor-eng?readForm.
- *U.S. Patent Office Official Gazette for Patents.* This publication is in printed form only. It provides information in a format similar to that of the Canadian material and is available in some public libraries. Their website is uspto.gov/news/og/patent_og/index.jsp.

Look for advertisements in both publications offering patents for sale or license. In addition, you may wish to place an ad to solicit a response from interested patent holders.

Newspapers

Look in the major national newspapers such as *The Globe and Mail* and the *National Post* for classified ads offering a patented or unpatented product for sale or license. You may also wish to place your own ad in the business opportunities section to solicit a response. Also look at the classified ads in major U.S. newspapers, in terms of seeking out potential patent opportunities. Look in your local newspaper as well.

Magazine and trade publications

There are numerous publications that could provide ideas of patent opportunities. The following directories are available in most public libraries, as well as online, to assist you in your search. You can also do a Google search using keywords such as patent opportunities, business opportunities, new products, etc., and the names of the product ideas of interest to you

- *Gale Directory of Publications and Broadcast Media* (United States and Canada)
- *The Standard Periodical Directory* (United States and Canada)
- *Ulrich's International Periodicals Directory.*

Names of Canadian manufacturers who might be interested in a new invention are available from a number of sources, including *The Canadian Trade Index,* published by the Canadian Manufacturers' Association, and *Frasers Canadian Trade Directory.*

Provincial governments

Many provincial governments keep a list for matchmaking purposes. The list includes names of inventors who have a product to sell, as well as investors who are seeking products with a commercial application. Contact the small business branch of your provincial government and ask to be put on the list.

Business Development Bank of Canada (BDC)

The BDC has a matchmaking service similar to the one described earlier under provincial governments. Contact the closest BDC office to your area and request to be put on the mailing list.

Patent lawyers and agents

Naturally, these professionals are dealing with inventors and prospective purchasers and assignees every day. Many are also members of the Licensing Executives Society International. Look for patent agents and intellectual property lawyers in the *Yellow Pages* print and online and via a Google search.

Personal curiosity

If you adopt the attitude and discipline of always looking for potential patent opportunities and ideas, there is a good chance you are going to find them. Many people are not clearly focused about their objectives in seeking commercial patent opportunities, and therefore are not consistently resourceful in obtaining them.

Research on the internet

You will find this technique very effective to find invention ideas or business opportunities. There are many inventor websites, as well as information from the Canadian Industrial Innovation Centre. This centre is a quasi-government organization which evaluates potential invention ideas. Check out its website at Canadianinnovation.ca.

TRADEMARKS

This section will cover the differences between a trademark and trade name, the advantages of registering a trademark, the criteria for registration eligibility, and the process involved. It will also cover such issues as registering a trademark outside Canada, assigning and licensing a trademark, and the use of registered trademark agents.

A trademark is registered for a period of 15 years from the date of registration. It is renewable every 15 years upon paying the required registration fees.

Differences between Trademarks and Trade Names

A trademark is a word, logo, symbol or design, or a combination of one or more of these features, that is displayed for identification purposes to the public. The display can be on commercial goods or their labels or containers, in association with the advertisement of services, or for the purpose of identifying the services or goods to purchasers. The purpose of the trademark is generally to indicate that the goods or services meet the same standard of quality as others associated with the same trademark, as well as their origin. It can also infer that the goods and services are approved or sponsored by the company or individual associated with the same trademark.

In general, the first person to use the trademark in Canada is entitled to register the mark and obtain exclusive rights. It is possible, though, to file an application to register in Canada, and thereby establish priority based on future intention to use the trademark. In practical terms, rights in a trademark are created through the use of a trademark on a product or in association with services. Although it is not required to register a trademark in order to use it, the advantages of registration will be discussed later in this section.

A trade name is a name under which a particular business is carried out by an individual, partnership, or company. It may also be the same as a corporate name of the company carrying on the business. A trade name can be registered under the Trade-marks Act as a trademark only if it is also used as a trademark. A trade name displayed in advertisements, in the provision of services, or on goods, labels, or containers may also function as a trademark.

Under the Trade-marks Act there are three main types of trademarks. These are referred to as certification marks, distinguishing guises, and ordinary trademarks.

1. **Certification mark.** A certification mark is a type of trademark used to distinguish goods or services that meet a defined standard. A good example is the Woolmark label used on clothing to indicate the presence of pure wool.

2. **Distinguishing guise.** A distinguishing guise means the shape or design of the product or packaging that effectively distinguishes the product from others. In order for a distinguishing guise to be registered, it must be proven that it has become distinctive through usage.

3. **Ordinary trademarks.** As mentioned before, a trademark can be a single word, a group of words, a slogan, a design or picture, or any combination of these. However, it must be used in association with goods or services to distinguish them in the marketplace. It must be distinctive enough that the public would not be deceived or confused as to the source of the product or service. A trademark often stands for

consistency of quality of the goods or services with which the trademark is used, and advertising is frequently used to reinforce this image to the public. A trademark can therefore become a very valuable asset to many companies and is a common distinguishing feature of franchise companies.

Differences between Registered and Unregistered Trademarks

It is not mandatory to register a trademark, but it is advisable to do so in many situations. If a trademark has not been registered, the holder of the trademark has what are called common law rights. In other words, rather than the Trademarks Act and cases relating to the Act providing protection, the owner of the unregistered trademark must rely on the courts to determine what is fair or appropriate in the circumstances.

The following is a list of the main advantages to registering a trademark, and the distinction from an unregistered trademark:

- A registered trademark would alert parties who might be contemplating adopting or using the same or a confusingly similar mark to the possibility of conflict with the mark. An unregistered trademark would not show up in the trademark registry, and therefore many people would be unaware of it.
- A registered trademark is national in its application, and therefore can usually be protected throughout Canada, whether it has established a reputation or goodwill in a particular area or not. An unregistered trademark can be protected only in the specific area in which it has established a reputation and goodwill.
- A registered trademark allows the owner to commence trademark infringement proceedings in the Federal Court of Canada, which has national jurisdiction, or a provincial superior court. The owner of an unregistered trademark would not have the same legal enforcement options available.
- A registered trademark, in certain cases, may provide legal protection against a noncompetitor. This would occur if it appears that the use by the noncompetitor might devalue the goodwill of the registered trademark owner. The owner of an unregistered trademark normally can commence an action only against a competitor.
- A registered trademark, after 5 years, can be deemed to be incontestable in some circumstances. The owner of an unregistered trademark, of course, would have no such automatic benefit or right.
- A registered trademark can be easier to register in other countries.

Eligibility for Obtaining a Registered Trademark

In general terms, a trademark is registerable unless:

- It is likely to be confused with a trademark already registered.
- It is a prohibited mark, for example, the Royal Arms, crest, flag, or emblems of a federal, provincial, or municipal governmental body, or the symbol of the Red Cross. In addition, scandalous or obscene materials or portraits or signatures of individuals who are alive or who died within the previous 30 years are also prohibited from registration.
- It is the name of an individual.
- It is clearly descriptive or deceptively misdescriptive.
- It is the name in any language of the goods or services with which it is used.

Although any individual can file a trademark application, it is prudent to obtain the services of professionals to do so on your behalf. A registered trademark agent has been trained and qualified by examination to represent applicants, and has been approved by the Trademark Office. You can obtain a list of registered trademark agents from the Trademark Office or look in the *Yellow Pages* print or online under "Trademark Agents—Registered." You may prefer to use a lawyer who is an expert in intellectual property, and who is also a registered trademark agent. Be very cautious about retaining anyone who is not a registered trademark agent or lawyer to make an application on your behalf. However, there are consultants available who can assist in trademark development and preparation. You can obtain the names of these consultants from a registered trademark agent or lawyer, or by looking in the *Yellow Pages* under "Trademark Development and Searching."

Trademark Registration Process

Prior to applying for trademark registration, it is usually advisable to conduct a registerability search in the Trademark Office. This is to determine whether there is an existing or pending registration of the same or similar marks relating to similar goods or services. If there is a conflict, it could prevent registration of your mark. The legal costs and search fees involved are reasonably low. This could help you avoid the expense of preparing and filing a formal trademark application. A search, of course, cannot assure that the trademark will be registered.

Preparing and filing an application

Once you have decided that there is a logical basis for making an application, the next step is to prepare it. In most countries outside Canada, separate applications have to be made for use with goods or use with services.

If the trademark has already been used commercially in Canada by the applicant, the date of first use in Canada for each of the goods or services associated with the mark is required. If the trademark has not yet been used in Canada for goods or services, and it is expected that the mark will be used within a period of approximately 3 years, it is possible to file a trademark application on the basis of proposed use in Canada. Once the mark has actually been used in Canada, a declaration to that effect is then filed with the Trademark Office before the trademark can be registered. The application should also include the logo insignia and drawing of the proposed trademark.

Acceptance or rejection of application

A trademark examiner will check the application and the availability of the trademark. If it appears that it is available, it will be published in the *Trademark Journal*, which is distributed to libraries and purchased by law firms and other parties which monitor trademark applications. If there is no opposition to the proposed trademark, the Trademark Office will issue a notice of allowance. The normal waiting time for obtaining registration, assuming that there is no objection, is approximately 18 months from the filing of the application.

If the application is rejected, there is a right to request a review and an appeal. If the application is opposed by a third party, the issue is resolved by the Opposition Board. If a registered trademark is not used by the registered owner after a period of 3 years from the date of registration, proceedings can be commenced to remove the trademark from the trademark registry.

Fees and filing costs

Fees will vary depending on whether you are using a lawyer or trademark agent, but for a simple trademark application the fees are very similar. The average fee for a lawyer, including filing costs, would be approximately $1000 if the application was not rejected or contested. Naturally, in the event of application difficulties, it would be important to ensure that you retain a lawyer to protect your interests and assert your rights. The legal fees in the event of an objection to the application could be considerable, depending on the circumstances. Filing costs vary from time to time, and a current list of Trademark Office filing fees can be obtained from the Trademark Office or Industry Canada.

Registering a Trademark Outside Canada

A registered trademark gives its owner the exclusive rights to its use in Canada *only*. If your products or services are sold in other countries, you should consider registration of your trademark in those countries where your products or services are used. Otherwise, you could lose your rights completely to the use of your trademark in those countries. If you intend to apply for a trademark in the United States and other countries, you would have a priority for your application in countries that are members of the Paris Convention for the Protection of Industrial Property. However, you are required to apply for registration within 6 months of the date of the filing of the Canadian trademark application.

Assigning or Licensing a Trademark

The rights to a trademark registration or pending application, with or without the goodwill of the business, can be assigned or licensed to another party. Any changes in the ownership or assignment of a registered trademark should be registered with the Trademark Office.

It is very common for trademark rights to be licensed to a third party. The agreement outlines the conditions and restrictions of the licence, including such issues as quality control, nature of use, duration of the licence, and associated fees. If the person using the licence breaches the terms of the agreement in any way, the licence can be cancelled and the licencee would not have any further rights to use the trademark. It is common for manufacturers to license companies to use a trademark. It is also very common in the franchise industry for the franchise company to license the franchisee to be a user. In many cases, the franchisor's trade name or trademark is a substantial part of its goodwill and distinguishes the wares or services of the franchise company. If the franchisor allows the franchisee to use a trademark without being licensed, the trademark protection could be lost and anyone could use the name. Therefore, it is very important that the owner of the trademark retain exclusive rights to it by ensuring that anyone using the trademark is subject to a proper licence agreement.

COPYRIGHT

Copyright means that the owner has the exclusive right to copy his or her work, or permit someone else to do so. It generally includes the sole right to publish, produce, reproduce, perform, translate, adapt, convert, publicly present, broadcast, or record the work, or any substantial part of it.

Copyright applies to all original literary, dramatic, artistic, and musical works, including books, writings, musical works, paintings, sculptures, photographs, motion picture films, encyclopedias, and dictionaries. Copyright also applies to material distributed on mechanical devices, such as CDs, records, cassettes, tapes, and computer software.

Copyright in most cases lasts for the lifetime of the author plus a period of 50 years after the end of the calendar year in which the author died. For photographs, records, tapes, and other manufactured devices that are protected by copyright, the right exists for 50 years from the making of the original device or master from which subsequent copies were directly or indirectly derived. If a photograph or its negative was authored by a corporation, then protection ends 50 years from the making of the photograph; however, if the photograph or its negative was created by an individual, then protection ends 50 years after the end of the calendar year in which the individual died. The author owns the copyright to his or her work, unless he or she was hired or employed by some other person to create the work, in which case the employer is the owner. However, freelance writers are not usually subject to this provision, as normally the writer retains all copyright to the article or book. Make sure that there is a contract in place expressly stating this is the case, in advance. Have an intellectual property lawyer review it. A copyright could also be sold or assigned to another person. This is covered later in this section. If the author of the copyright dies, the copyright will form part of the estate, and be passed on to the beneficiaries.

Differences between Copyright and Industrial Design

All literary, dramatic, musical, and artistic works are subject to copyright protection, regardless of the quantity in which they are reproduced. However, artistic works that are used as models to be applied to articles of manufacture, and are intended to be reproduced in numbers greater than 50, are protected only by the Industrial Design Act. Examples in this latter case would include dolls, toys, and pendants.

Acquiring Copyright

Copyright in Canada is automatically acquired upon creation of an original work by an author who was a Canadian citizen or a citizen of a qualifying foreign country at the time. Although voluntary registration is not required to obtain basic protection, it is advisable. On registration of the copyright, certification is issued providing evidence that the person registered is the copyright owner. This certificate can be used in court to establish ownership.

A lawyer specializing in intellectual property relating to video recording and software development could provide an expert opinion based on your circumstances, in terms of intellectual property protection.

Advantages of Copyright Registration

As mentioned earlier, one of the benefits of registration is that it provides legitimacy and legal credibility that the person registered is in fact the owner of the copyright. Of course, anybody could challenge the copyright if facts were presented to show that the owner was not the rightful one. There are also other practical and legal benefits to copyright registration, as follows:

- A registered copyright provides the owner with a basis for commencing a successful action for copyright infringement. The copyright owner could sue for an injunction restraining the copyright infringer for any further infringement, as well as claim for financial damages arising from the infringement. If the owner of the copyright did not have it registered at the time of the infringement, the defendants could claim that they were unaware of the copyright and had no reasonable basis for knowing that the copyright existed in the work. The copyright owner in this situation would only be entitled to obtain a court injunction to stop any further infringement.
- If the copyright is registered, it can provide very important negotiating leverage and credibility in the sale or licensing of the rights to the copyrighted work.

Copyright Registration Process

Anyone can register a copyright, and the procedures within Canada are fairly simple. Forms can be obtained from the Copyright Office or any branch of Industry Canada. There is a one-time registration fee to keep the copyright in force. You may wish to retain a lawyer or other qualified professional to prepare and file the documents for you, depending on the nature and complexity of the work. The processing time from the date of application until a certificate is received is approximately 5 to 7 business days.

Copies of the copyright work are not required and will not be accepted by the copyright office. However, if you have released a sound recording manufactured in Canada which has some Canadian content, or if you have published a new book in Canada, you are required to send one copy of the sound recording and two copies of the book to the National Library within 1 week of publication.

Copyright Protection Outside Canada

It is not necessary to make any indication on a book that it is copyrighted. If you want to ensure the protection of your copyright outside Canada, it is advisable to register your copyright in the other countries concerned, depending on the circumstances. You should obtain the advice of a lawyer specializing in copyright matters. In addition, a copyright infringement action in the United States may not commence or be successfully concluded unless the copyright has first been registered in that country. Make sure you receive expert legal advice.

Assigning or Licensing a Copyright

A copyright can be sold, assigned, or licensed in whole or in part. To be valid, however, any assignment must be in writing and signed by the owner. It is advisable to register the assignment or licence in the Copyright Registry in order to eliminate any confusion with the public. It also protects the rights of the original owner or assignee or licensee.

An assignment is a sale of rights or a particular right in a work to another party, and involves a transfer of ownership. A licence does not involve a transfer of ownership and is for a temporary period only. As mentioned in a previous section, a licence is usually based on a fee or royalty paid by the other party for the right to use a work, in a specified manner, and under certain conditions.

INDUSTRIAL DESIGN

An industrial design is any original shape, configuration, pattern, ornamentation, or any combination of these, applied to an article of manufacture, such as the shape of a table, decoration on the handle of a spoon, or the pattern of a fabric. The article must be made by an industrial process. Examples include furniture, jewellery, bottles, toys, wallpaper, electrical appliances, and office machines. The industrial design must be registered in the Industrial Design Registry within 1 year of first publication, public use, or sale anywhere of the design, or of articles bearing, embodying, or displaying it.

An industrial design should be registered in order to provide protection. The registration lasts for an initial period of 5 years, and may be renewed for up to 5 years. Once the registration has expired, anyone may use or sell the design in Canada.

Differences between Industrial Design, Copyright, and Patent

Protection provided by the Industrial Design Act is frequently confused with protection under the Copyright Act. Many designs, being works of art, are automatically protected under the Copyright Act. But once the original artistic work is used, or intended to be used, as a model or pattern to produce more than 50 single articles or sets of articles (such as prints), the artistic work then becomes an industrial design. This design can be protected only under the Industrial Design Act. Since the distinction is a fine one, it is advisable to seek specialized legal advice on this question.

Details or features of the construction, mode of operation, or functioning of an article may be able to be patented as an invention under the Patent Act, but it cannot be part of what is registered as an industrial design under the Industrial Design Act. An object can be protected by both patent and industrial design, though different attributes are protected by each.

Assistance from Patent Agent or Lawyer

Although you are entitled to apply on your own to register an industrial design, it would not be advisable. If you do not register the industrial design properly, potential legal problems and issues could impair your protection. There are lawyers who specialize in intellectual property, including industrial design, who are also patent agents. Or you could contact a patent agent, who may not also be a lawyer, to apply to the Industrial Design Registry on your behalf. Look in the *Yellow Pages* print or online under "Patent Attorneys and Agents—Registered." You can also obtain a list of registered patent agents from the Patent Office or one of the branch offices of Industry Canada. Fees vary, of course, but it would be prudent to obtain at least two and preferably three professional opinions before selecting your advisor.

You may also wish to obtain the advice of an industrial design consultant. You can obtain the name of a consultant from the patent lawyer or agent. You can also find these consultants listed in the *Yellow Pages* print or online under "Designers—Industrial."

Industrial Design Registration Process

The author of the design or the author's agent is the only person who may register it, unless it was created in the course of employment for someone else. In that event, the employer is the owner, and the only one authorized to request registration. The rights acquired by registration will become part of the author's estate and are passed on to the beneficiaries.

If you are an employer and there is the possibility that an employee may create a new design under your employment, you should consider a written contract to protect yourself. Refer to Sample 33 and seek your lawyer's advice.

A preliminary search in the Industrial Design Registry should be considered, especially if the owner is not generally knowledgeable about the state of the art relating to the design. Industrial designs tend to be inherently original, whereas inventions are more likely to be duplicated. In the latter case, therefore, there is more of a likelihood that someone else's invention could be inadvertently infringed upon, unless a preliminary search was undertaken. Once the application documents are filed, along with any drawings required, the Registry will process the application and will either accept it or reject it. If the application is accepted, the process from the filing of the application until the approval takes approximately 9½ months.

If the application is rejected, you have the opportunity to attempt to satisfy the problems and obtain the registration. If the matter cannot be solved satisfactorily, you have the right to appeal to the Patent Appeal Board to review the case, and if you are not satisfied with that review, you can appeal to the Federal Court of Canada. These various rights are also available for patent, trademark, and copyright matters.

The filing and registration fees relating to an industrial design application vary from time to time and can be obtained from the Industrial Design Office.

Any article displaying or embodying a registered industrial design may be marked in order that the design registration be protected and legally enforceable. The marking may be on the design article itself or on a label attached to it. Marks are no longer mandatory in Canada, but they can assist litigants in court.

Industrial Design Protection outside Canada

Registration of an industrial design in Canada does not provide any protection in countries outside Canada. Protection can only be obtained in foreign countries by filing for registration in each country. Most countries, under the Paris Convention for the Protection of Industrial Property, provide the applicant the benefit of using the filing date of application in Canada as the filing date, as long as the subsequent application in a foreign country is filed within 6 months of the application date in Canada.

Assigning or Licensing an Industrial Design

Once your design has been registered, you may assign or license a design to anyone else. The arrangement must be in writing, and the Industrial Design Office should be notified in writing.

An assignment means permanently giving up all or part of your interest in your design to someone else. In the case of a licence, you temporarily permit someone to make, use, and sell your design under very specific conditions and terms. In any matters of assignment or licensing, obtain the advice of your lawyer, as there are many potential pitfalls.

If you are considering registering an industrial design, you should read the other sections of this chapter relating to patent and copyright to familiarize yourself with the concepts and terms before speaking with your professional advisor.

AVOID INVENTION SCHEMES AND SCAMS

Have you had a creative idea that you think has market potential? That maybe with the right help and sufficient financial resources, you could make lots of money? Maybe you would also want to copyright the written content relating to your idea. You may also want to have a unique trade name for your idea. All these types of inventions are referred to legally as "intellectual property."

A lot of people have had dreams of making money from their creative ideas. For many, however, the dream turns out to be an expensive nightmare. There are lots of "creative" scams and schemes out there to take your money. So how do you explore the business potential of your idea and avoid the pitfalls? Here are some tips.

Pitches to Avoid

Most of the pitches that are aired on TV or the radio or printed in newspapers or magazines are from U.S. companies. That is why the hints below come from the U.S. Federal Trade Commission Consumer Alert Web posting, in conjunction with the U.S. Patent and Trademark Office. Check the site out yourself (ftc.gov) and look under the "Consumer Protection" category. Here are some lines that should raise your concern.

"We think your idea has great market potential."

Few ideas, however good, become commercially successful. If a company fails to disclose that investing in your idea is a high-risk venture, and that most companies never make money, beware.

"You need to hurry and patent your idea before someone else does."

Be wary of high-pressure sales tactics. Simply patenting your idea does NOT mean you will ever make any money from it.

"Our company has licensed a lot of invention ideas successfully."

Ask for a list of the company's successful clients and confirm that these clients have had commercial success. If the company refuses to give you a list of successful clients, it probably doesn't have any.

"Congratulations! We've done a patent search on your idea, and we have some great news. There's nothing like it out there."

Many invention promotion firms claim to perform patent searches on ideas. Patent searches by a fraudulent invention promotion firms usually are incomplete, conducted in the wrong category, or are unaccompanied by a legal opinion on the results of a search from a patent attorney. An unscrupulous firm promotes any idea or invention without regard to its patentability and may market an idea for which someone already has a valid, unexpired patent, exposing you to a patent infringement lawsuit.

"Our company has evaluated your idea, and now wants to prepare a more in-depth research report. It'll be several hundred or thousand dollars."

If the company's initial evaluation is "positive," ask why the company isn't willing to cover the cost of researching your idea further.

> "Our company makes most of its money from the royalties
> it gets from licensing its clients' ideas. Of course,
> we'll need some money before we get started."

If a firm tells you this, ask why they're not willing to help you on a contingency basis. Unscrupulous firms make almost all of their money from large, upfront fees.

> "Our research department, engineers, and patent attorneys have
> evaluated your idea. We definitely want to move forward."

This is the standard sales pitch. Many questionable firms do not perform any evaluation at all and don't even have the "professional" staff they claim.

Where to Turn for Objective Information and Advice

There are many options available to increase your learning curve. Here are some practical suggestions:

Canada Business Network

Contact or visit your provincial Canada Business Network office for information and advice. They are listed in the *Blue Pages* of your telephone directory under "Provincial and Federal Governments." You can also reach them at their website: canadabusiness.ca.

Canadian Innovation Centre

This organization is partly sponsored by government and has an excellent reputation. They will candidly assess the market potential of your idea. Contact them at (519) 885-5870 or through their website at: innovationcentre.ca.

SOURCES OF INFORMATION AND ASSISTANCE

The following list is a summary of the main sources of information and assistance on intellectual property.

Industry Canada

The head office is in Ottawa, but there are branches throughout Canada. To find the address closest to you, look in the *Blue Pages* of your telephone directory under "Government of Canada." Their website address is ic.gc.ca.

Canadian Intellectual Property Office

There are numerous publications available online at the Canadian Intellectual Property Office (CIPO) website (cipo.ic.gc.ca). Five publications in particular are especially helpful in explaining, in simple language, the most common questions asked by the public:

- *A Guide to Patents*
- *Guide to Trade-Marks*
- *Guide to Copyrights*
- *Guide to Industrial Design*
- *Intellectual Property at Your Fingertips*

After you have reviewed these booklets, if you have any further inquiries, contact the Patent, Trademark, or Copyright and Industrial Design offices of the Canadian Intellectual Property Office(CIPO) in Ottawa.

This federal department is very involved in encouraging, educating, and counselling entrepreneurs. One of its main mandates is the development of industrial, scientific, and technological success in Canada. It has various financial incentive programs for viable products, as well as other forms of guidance and opportunity creation.

Public Libraries

The public library is a veritable gold mine of free information. Contact the business resource librarian and explain your needs. Most major libraries will have the following information:

- general books on intellectual property
- Canadian and U.S. patent records
- directories of magazines, trade publications, and trade shows
- federal government statutes, rules and regulations relating to intellectual property
- publications of Industry Canada.

Provincial Small Business Ministries

Contact the office closest to you and speak to a small business counsellor to discuss your needs. They can be very helpful as a referral source to other contacts and information, as well as assisting you in focusing on the various steps that you need to follow in your overall business objectives.

Patent Agents and Lawyers

The vital role of lawyers and patent and trademark agents, has been discussed throughout this chapter. If your needs involve any or all aspects of intellectual property, or if your situation is complex or unclear, or if a legal opinion is required, then you should see a lawyer specializing in intellectual property.

Chapter 19

Using the Internet for Business Success

Technology is dominated by two types of people: those who understand what they do not manage, and those who manage what they do not understand.

—David Putt

Let's begin by assuming you are hungry. You see a restaurant. What would make you eat there? For most of us, price alone is not enough. We look for a clean and appealing location (and usually choose locations convenient or nearby) and, of course, we seek out the type of food that appeals to us and meets any dietary requirements. For each of us, these criteria weigh differently, but generally, our decision-making process is based on some combination of these factors. And, by the time our bill has arrived, we know whether we would eat there again, don't we? We use the restaurant as a metaphor for the sales process, because even a corner coffee shop can provide a level of service that keeps you coming back. For the price of a cup of coffee, you might be lucky enough to get a story and a smile, in addition to your order. And they deserve a tip, don't they?

At better restaurants, the experience has subtle refinements. You enter and a host greets you at the desk. When space permits, you are led to a table. A watchful waiter catches your eye to let you know that he or she is aware of you and subtle signals are sent indicating that they will soon attend to you. Often, they bring a glass of water or bread without even being asked, and between trips to other customers' tables, answer your questions and attend to your needs.

It might be worth thinking in a metaphorical sense, what kind of food service your Internet business would most resemble. Would you be a caterer, a fast-food outlet, or a cafeteria? If you applied the hungry customer principle to your Internet business model, where do they get the personal contact, the table service, the candy with the bill? Now, while there are obvious differences between the nature of serving food and serving an Internet-based customer's needs, the basic principle stands: the quality of the initial contact with the customer is an important part of the transaction, some would say the most important part. Your customers like to be acknowledged without undue delay, they need to be presented with a clear set of choices, and their orders need to be dealt with quickly and efficiently. The key to these last items is the website operator's ability to accept and effectively deal with customer queries and feedback.

What else is important to you when you are sitting in a restaurant? How do your potential customers decide where to shop and what to buy? In the next section, we'll take a look at a type of customer that I call the savvy shopper. Until then, consider other ways the restaurant metaphor might apply to your business's online presence. It's food for thought.

THE IMPACT OF TECHNOLOGY ON SMALL BUSINESS

The growth of the Web into the dominant vehicle for commerce has created what we call the savvy online shopper effect. These are the consumers who won't even set foot in a place where commission-driven salespersons push and pull with hard-sell tactics, and endlessly harass them with questions like "Would you like the extended warranty with that?"

It's not just the hard sell that turns them off. It's the fact that they feel they are not being listened to; they are looking for someone they can trust. And they look for signs of expertise. As a result, increasing numbers of consumers have become their own experts, using the power of the Web to educate themselves to an extent that no consumer in history has been able to do before. Web-based product information, multitudinous reviews of just about every product, and social networking conversations and peer reviews have provided the individual shopper with more knowledge than even an expert had a few decades ago.

Just about every consumer today has become an online shopper to some extent. Some still follow some old habits and shop in favorite stores personally; some, particularly younger shoppers, don't make a purchase anywhere without going online first to search for options, compare prices, and educate themselves about the product or service they're buying; the majority of shoppers in the Internet age judiciously mix methods, often researching a particular buy online and then choosing whether to purchase it online or from a favorite store. Some shoppers live online and rarely venture out from the Internet to physically buy a product: The may even buy their groceries or order food online and have the items delivered. The good news, I think, is that these savvy shoppers are usually willing to pay a bit more for products to have the luxury of not being subjected to the old-fashioned superstore super-sell.

The bad news is that even the savvy shopper is sometimes confused by all the noise on the Internet. And, although many things have changed in the new marketplace, one thing will never change: a confused customer never buys.

What Might Confuse Your Customer?

Your customers might be thrown off by any of the following:

- not understanding the product
- not understanding your jargon or terminology
- ineffective or misdirected communication.

Think of other ways that your customer might be confused. And keep in mind, explaining is always more powerful than describing.

The issue of ineffective communication is always a challenge. Sometimes, there is a language barrier, sometimes it is a game of telephone or e-mail tag. Fortunately, most people now have a tremendous range of communications and organizational tools at their disposal. Finding out how your customers prefer to be contacted and working to establish a pattern of effective communications is the easiest first step to achieving a positive seller–customer relationship.

Although the savvy shopper is armed with much information, he or she is probably at least as busy as you are and is either wise enough to realize—or too busy to take the time to learn—what it would take to learn all the required details. Whether they know it or not, what they need is a consultant who is an expert in the field. Analysis of Internet searching shows that many searchers never go beyond the first couple of result pages. This is because, despite their predilection for conducting research, savvy shoppers don't have the time to learn all the jargon and technical issues that differentiate today's products from one another. They need to cut to the chase, or at least focus on the big picture. So they trust recommendations much more than advertising.

How, Then, to Spot a Savvy Shopper?

Obviously, there is no single category of customer that you are likely to be dealing with, unless you are in an ultra-specialized niche or have the luxury of hand-picking your clientele. With that said, the savvy shopper looks for evidence of expertise, in order to feel safe about doing business.

The typical modern consumer is not in love with technology. Applications drive their decisions. Just as auto manufacturers have discovered, the love affair with technology for its own sake is over. Buyers are interested in solutions and productivity. Consumers look for the best mix of price/performance, name brand/quality, and service/support. Traditionally, corporate buyers have sought the latter items, while the clone buyers and value systems customers have focused on obtaining the first two factors from their local vendors. The savvy consumers are more likely to respond positively to the buzzwords that signify performance and quality than the "traditional" buyer, who was both relatively uninformed and relentlessly price-driven.

Which Works Best for Your Business?

Just as in technology and Web page design, where borrowing from other designs is practically standard fare, it is worth thinking about your closest competitors. You can be sure your customers do.

Keep in mind that almost everybody is a mixture of more than one personality type. Although there will always be consumers who are naive and easily "sold," we think that the new breed of shopper is savvy enough to recognize sales ploys to extract information or push an inappropriate product. The savvy consumer now goes right to the heart of the matter.

Why Is the Consumer Growing More Sophisticated?

Mainstream media coverage and the wide library of information on the Internet all contribute to increased consumer awareness, and many shoppers have been told to watch for certain key buzzwords while shopping.

HOW TO USE THE WEB EFFECTIVELY

To make your business's Web presence compelling, it is important to effectively match it to your "brick-and-mortar" marketing message, if you still have a brick-and-mortar presence. In this section, we'll examine some common categories of "traditional" businesses, and look at how online presence can leverage and strengthen other selling models.

One of the biggest sectors of e-commerce (electronic-commerce or business conducted via the Internet) is the so-called "business-to-business" model, often called "B2B" for short. Here, businesses provide products and/or services to other businesses, establishing long-term contracts over one-off retail sales. The emergence of B2B companies includes companies which began by focusing on hard goods, but grew to offer targeted business products, services, tools, and expert advice from a single point of purchase. Another example is an asset management firm that has grown from selling through trade magazine listings to selling B2B solutions via the Internet. In addition to selling physical goods, such companies can offer a wide variety of services, including temporary employment/recruiting, long distance and cellular services, Website hosting, e-commerce stores, and other business-centric services.

The Internet retailer typically moves through many phases of the market until the business finds its "niche." In today's Web-centric economy, many Web retailers find their focus in the business- and education-oriented customer. As the Web forced a re-examination of the traditional "channel" paradigms of wholesale versus retail, one of the great challenges in this category has become how to provide exceptional service while remaining competitive. This has resulted in innovative new business models created just for the Web. Amazon, which began as an online bookseller but is now a full-scale global department store and e-book publisher, is a very good example.

Keep these five points in mind when creating your online business:

- Just as in the online world, value-adding resellers often can't compete on price with megastores, nor should they have to. Customers can buy products more cheaply at a superstore, unless you give them a good reason to do otherwise.

- Customers often don't trust salespeople, and usually for good reason. Therefore, online businesses usually let the customer choose from several options.

- Desperation ploys have become more common as growing numbers of online dealers resort to the gray market, reboxing returns and other dubious activities that often end up damaging customer relations as warranty and service issues backfire. In turn, customers have become more skeptical.

- While many vendors are still trying to make websites pay, not all have struck upon the right mix of form and function to see their Web-based sales efforts pay off.

Those who can put the right pieces together stand to reap the rewards.

Focus on Service

Services now account for more than 50% of many Web-oriented companies' business. This trend—and the technical challenge of building a compelling Internet presence—means that in most cases your company needs many more people working to support the site than the traditional services operation.

A strong Web-based presence can also help deliver the support documentation needed for some "long sells," such as are often encountered when dealing with education or government accounts. Such accounts represent a significant revenue source for many businesses. But beware the temptation to pass people off to a "self-serve" website, if they are better served by a sales force. The Web, whether it is a customer needs–driven information source or an employee-centric intranet repository of data, is best mined by skilled hands.

A decade ago, few Web-based businesses were moneymakers, despite the successes of major online vendors such as Amazon.com, Chapters.ca, and Dell.com, largely because they concentrated on sales of goods, but lacked a strong service component, which the Web enables, and indeed, demands. However, e-commerce has advanced at such a pace that today most businesses consider the Web-based aspects of business first before considering the physical requirements. In fact, it could be said that in some categories, all new businesses are

Web-based service operations. Today, for small retailers and value-added resellers (VARs) to remain competitive, service must drives sales. Unless you make it easy for visitors to buy, they likely won't.

Successful Internet companies build value by providing opportunities for ongoing services. The "mass market" customer that now dominates online commerce is a new kind of customer who expects more—good products and quick, excellent, service. Today's customers, infused with knowledge also gleaned from the Web, expect more and will leave in a second if they don't get it.

It is up to you to ensure that your business model is flexible enough—and your communications systems and product lines friendly enough—to be able to meet the needs of today's—and tomorrow's—consumers.

Keep these tenets of e-business in mind:

Your customers want solutions, not technologies.

They are communications-driven.

They favour mainstream standards.

They favour systems with reduced total cost of ownership.

The Aggregator

Another category that has emerged online is that of the aggregator—the super-retailer who seems to stock millions of items, but draws from a number of sources: direct, wholesale, and through liquidation discounters. Like retail box pushers, these vendors are not usually service champions, but their prices are hard to beat.

A version of this aggregator model involves the online category superstore, such as Amazon, that has disrupted entire industries. By selling books online, Amazon offered buyers a choice of millions of books at seemingly low prices, putting many bookstores that couldn't adapt out of business. Amazon has now moved on to be a giant online version of the department store, selling clothes, appliances and items from many other retail categories and disrupting the traditional department store industry (and vastly bolstering the delivery industry). The only way a small business can survive against a powerful retailer like Amazon is to thoroughly understand its customers and provide better and more intimate service to them.

The Product-Focused Superstore

This category of online retailer focuses on name brands, and doesn't do much service beyond that which occurs at the time of the sale. They are likely to offer, as their brick-and-mortar counterparts often do, an extended warranty.

The average buyer at these vendors falls into one of two categories. First, we find the person with the money who is funding the knowledgeable buyer. This might be a parent paying for a product selected by a know-it-all kid, or a corporate purchasing department signing the cheques for an IT staff head. In either case, the savvy shopper picks the product, while the other signs the cheque—and, in the case of the corporate buyers, it's often a big one.

The second category is the price-sensitive shopper who has a shopping list in hand and is destined to come back more than once before the deal is closed.

Mail Order

A third category of vendors that are making hay on the Web are those that were, are, or pattern themselves after, mail-order vendors.

It's probably safe to say there aren't too many computer, smartphone, and peripherals resellers out there who haven't benefited from the surge of the Internet, wired and wireless, over the last few years. Indeed, the Net is widely attributed as the major force that drove the home computer boom and is driving the current version—cellular phones, smartphones, and tablet computers. Even those consumers who aren't very computer literate have a basic idea of the wealth of resources "out there" and are aware that the Net can provide a wide array of business, education or entertainment benefits. As well, millions of people use the Web daily to search out the caveats and gotchas of their intended purchases before dropping their bucks on the table.

LEVERAGE THE INTERNET

Almost every business today uses the Internet routinely. But many small businesses do not use its full power. Here's how you can benefit from this remarkable business tool.

- Search for information relevant to your clientele. No one person can possess all knowledge, so provide answers to common client questions. You may also want to have an intake system, even if it's by phone, for questions that can't be answered by the database. There's nothing that will bond your clients more to you than the fact that a human being will solve their problem by e-mailing an answer to them right away.
- Reinforce online presence. Reinforce your company's online presence with the kind of information that helps your clients make informed purchases. If you can show them this information on your company's website, you not only demonstrate that you have the answers but also the technical expertise to fulfill their needs.

- Another key piece of your online presence is the creation of a customer database. Encouraging your customers to interact with you via various channels has several potential benefits: most notably, you can track customers' specific likes and desires in a database. This information will allow you to refine your offerings and better serve—and keep—customers.

Everyone's Doing It—So You'll Have to Compete

As well, the Web has probably become more commercial than it was in the worst nightmares of the Internet old-timers. There are very few companies who don't fancy seeing their products or services listed somewhere on the Web—but it is fair to say that few who do post pages on the Web do so in a way that is truly effective. Nevertheless, almost every business must be on the Web today—it's where their customers are.

Educate Your Consumers

The general principle of something earning more than it costs is, of course, the fundamental principle behind effective marketing efforts. Virtually all businesses could benefit from a few hours spent with a good consultant on the subject of effective marketing. Even small companies can afford to bring in a design firm to help improve their image. To find them, conduct a search under the categories of "graphic design" or "small business marketing."

Take a cold look at the advertisements you are running right now, from your business cards and letterhead right on up to the media ads, online presence, or whatever else the company is doing. If they weren't designed by a full-time graphics professional, they almost certainly aren't as effective as they could be. Invest in your public image. It not only brings you more business; it brings you the right kind of business.

In these days, when so many of your customers routinely plug into the Net, they often have up-to-the-minute information on the latest issues with the products you sell. Clearly, a little time online researching these issues is time well spent. As the personal computer or Web-enabled device becomes ever-present, the logical evolutionary step is the emergence of more sophisticated consumers. They're increasingly not first- or second-time buyers, but older and wiser, fifth- or sixth-time buyers. These people need more sophisticated solutions than the hand-holding that beginners demand, and the seasoned consumer is less likely to window-shop and more likely to order via a website, or at least based on price point.

"Prosumer" is, of course, a term that emerged as professional quality results started to become available at the high end of the consumer price points. It happened in stereos, it's happening in digital video camcorders and editing decks and—surprise, surprise—it's happening with digital audio and video on computers and mobile devices.

These days, a growing number of progressive companies put experts online to demonstrate the vendor's expertise and knowledge and, for want of a better word, to evangelize their specialties. In fact, product evangelism, or "expertise marketing" as it is sometimes called, has become one of the most powerful ways to market a business. At the mimimum today, most websites should offer a Frequently Asked Questions (FAQ) page. Many others are also supporting this evangelism through blogs and other social media, such as Facebook pages and Twitter feeds If you aren't familiar with the techniques of business evangelism, there are several books on the subject available. The book *Selling the Dream* by longtime former Apple evangelist Guy Kawasaki is a good place to start.

Key Tips when Developing Your Online Business

Here are some proven techniques that work.

- **Elegant solutions.** Generally speaking, Apple's Mac OS–based systems haven't been faster at completing day-to-day tasks or less expensive than their Intel- or Unix-based cousins, nor is the Mac OS technically more sophisticated. Why are Mac users so devoted? The short answer is "because it works—elegantly." Best of all, users of all Apple devices have historically demonstrated a remarkable willingness to pay extra for that perceived elegance.
- **Capitalize on trends.** Apple didn't invent the WIMP (windows/icons/mouse/pointer) interface, nor did it invent the coding language that drove the first smartphone. But Apple is very good at seeing emerging technology trends and quickly capitalizing on them.
- **The right tool.** Typically, product "A" handles some tasks better than product "B" and vice versa. If your customers are coming in asking for Product A and you're spending effort trying to convert them to the Product B religion (or vice versa), you're working too hard. Offer both of the best alternatives—and know when to recommend a switch.
- **Overcome objections.** Provide services or systems that integrate more or less seamlessly into existing work environments. The message is obvious: eliminate the reasons people use to justify why they should not choose your product.
- **Focus.** Your core customer base might vary, but it is essential that you stay focused on who they are and what they want.
- **Upgrades and consumables.** For many businesses, it costs about five times as much to acquire a new customer as it does to keep an existing

one. Keep that maxim in mind when determining your product line and services.

- **Stop selling bad products.** Damage takes time—and much money—to undo. Some users jump ship. In most cases, they won't be back.
- **Lose the "not invented here" mentality.** Start borrowing good ideas from your competitors.
- **Capitalize on the solutions you sell—it's the best possible product demonstration.** Think about how Internet services could be incorporated into a customer- or employee-focused solution.
- **Admit mistakes.** When one occurs, turn on a dime and be quick to rectify any damage.
- **Hire your own marketing whiz.** There are a number of books and websites that provide guidance on online marketing. They are worthwhile reading for salespeople and CEOs alike. Of course, keep the following tenets in mind:
  - Think again. Don't be afraid to challenge your deeply held beliefs. Things change quickly. Is this product still the best solution? What markets are we competitive in? Who are our competitors?
  - Understand your audience. Listen to your customers, understand the values that drive their buying decision and then market products accordingly.
  - Security. The need for—or at least your ability to sell to the perception of—security grows stronger in today's Web-centric society. Security issues are strong motivators.

OBTAINING A DOMAIN NAME

One of the most important decisions you'll have to make regarding your Internet presence is your domain name.

Unfortunately, most of the best names are already taken (as you'll see when you do a search at any one of many websites operated by domain registration companies. At this point, most businesses that want a "generic" name will have to settle for multiple-word names (e.g., smartbuyersguide.com and so on). If your business name has a truly unique spelling, you may find that it is still available, but be prepared to consider alternatives—you'll probably need to, unless the name you choose is quite obscure. Many businesses today are becoming quite creative in picking a domain name that cleverly alludes to what the business does. For example, Involver (involver.com) is a company that helps large companies market through social media, primarily Facebook: it has developed a platform in which companies can become "involved" with their customers. Mint.com is an American website that provides personal finance tracking services and has benefited by strong name branding: It couldn't use mint.ca in Canada, because that belonged to the Canadian Mint. So it uses the domain mint.com/canada. You can test different names at almost any domain registry website for free.

How to Register a .com, .net, or .org Domain Name

You can register and pay for a "dot com" domain name (or several other less-popular variants, such as .org, .net, and the government and education-only .gov and .edu suffixes) through networksolutions.com or many other companies and their resellers, such as Net Nation, that offer the service. The domain registration field is very competitive and fees are as low as $10 per year. Commonly,

- .com is generally for commercial enterprises
- .net is mainly for networking or Internet companies
- .org is generally used by non-profit organizations or societies.

A number of specific specialty domain extensions have recently been released by ICANN (Internet Corporation for Assigned Names and Numbers), the international authority which oversees domain names, but they are very expensive and will likely be used exclusively by large organizations.

Domain name registration is sometimes offered for free by companies as part of the purchase of a website-hosting package.

How to Register a .ca Domain Name

In countries other than the U.S., other domain suffixes are available, denoting the country of origin. In Canada, for example, a company can register a .ca domain with the Canadian Internet Registration Authority (cira.ca), although that is usually done by the company you choose to register the name. Approval for top-level domain names like .ca domains take only seconds to complete. Other top-level domain names include .com, .net, .org, .biz, .info, .name, and a new one, .mobi, for websites that are aimed at mobile devices such as smartphones. At one time you could also register a name based on the province in which you operated (e.g., company.ab.ca), but that domain is rarely seen today.

Updating Records Yourself or Using an Internet Service Provider

Once registered and assigned to a specific Net address, you're not out of luck if you decide to change your Internet service provider (ISP). You can alter registration details for free at networksolutions.com or, for a nominal fee, your new

ISP can do it for you. Most ISPs (and competent in-house Web administrators) can save you money in other ways, too. Additional services are available from all good ISPs; contact them to find out about other possibilities.

Web Hosting

Web-hosting services (the managerial/maintenance aspect of your website) offered by ISPs vary widely. Ask prospective ISPs whether they support the following and, if so, what conditions are attached.

- Can you supply your own server (the technical equipment)? What is the charge? Do extra IP addresses or multiple domain names cost extra?
- How much does bandwidth (megabytes, gigabytes, etc) cost? Is the cost of usage tiered (the more you use, the more it costs)? Most Web-hosting companies offer a certain amount of "space" on their servers for a set annual or monthly amount, and then charge when this limit is surpassed. Be careful when managing a Web-hosting account: failing to trigger automatic deletions of some material from the server after a period of time can mean your space fills up and your account is suspended. Worse, it may just continue, but at a much higher rate. You won't discover this until you receive a much higher bill. Does the ISP or the larger service it resells "throttle" bandwidth or limit the streaming of information? Does it "block" access to certain websites of which it disapproves? You may believe that none of these issues matter or that you can do anything about them. But it's good to know about them in case you are caught in the rules by mistake.
- Is there more than one Web-hosting plan? What are the details of each one? (Typically, more expensive Web-hosting options provide more server space and more e-mail addresses. Some may also provide advanced features, such as e-commerce options or database-driven functions.)
- Do you have to pay extra for any services? Which ones and how much?
- Does your Internet service provider have a "heavy traffic charge" that could penalize you if your website becomes popular?
- Should you consider setting up your own Web server (and/or e-mail server, etc.) and what are the pros and cons?

Handheld devices such as smartphones and tablets use different systems, largely supplied by telephone companies, and have a different set of rules. If you plan to target the mobile market, be aware that users must pay much more for bandwidth and access than desktop computer users. In this case, your website should be kept relatively simple.

The offerings of Canadian ISPs can be compared at www.canadianisp.ca.

YOU'VE GOT A WEB SERVER—NOW WHAT?

Designing pages for a website is not entirely unlike creating pages for print-based publications, but there are some important differences. Designers already familiar with print-based design principles will be able to leverage existing skills, but may have to forgive click-happy Web users their relative impatience, and indeed, forgive the Web its immaturity, as they discover that typography on the Web is decidedly less sophisticated than that which has evolved over hundreds of years in the print domain.

Still, the Web's support of multimedia and interactivity presents exciting opportunities for innovative Internet-based content creation. This section is, first and foremost, about helping you design exciting pages.

Purpose of Your Site

This section assumes that you are interested in creating a business-oriented website, with pages that are both highly functional and compelling. We will, for this section, assume that you have access to either a Windows PC or a Mac. However, with different tools, there is nothing mentioned here that could not be accomplished on a machine running Linux, OS/2, or some other operating system. Mobile sites typically involve different design principles, but if you are at the level where you want a mobile site, you are likely also willing to have a professional designer create it. It is also assumed that your goal is to get the job done quickly and efficiently, rather than hack away at things the hard way. In short, we'll be focusing on designing a great site, not so much on the details or codes that comprise the individual pages.

The primary objective of your Web presence should be to effectively communicate your business's mission statement. It should serve your customers and/or your employees; it should further your long-term goals.

Your website can assist your business with:

- product and service sales
- promotion
- corganization
- public relations
- generating revenue through creative options.

Beyond that, it should incorporate principles of good design, and communicate its messages concisely and consistently. It's fine to add multimedia, video, and interactive elements, but don't let them get in the way of doing business effectively.

DESIGNING A WEBSITE

Website design has changed considerably in the two decades the Internet has been popularized. At first, as technical issues ruled, a website may have been blunt and cluttered with type, which was the easiest design to use. However, as increasing numbers of tools appeared on the scene (following the herd that moved on to the Web), website design became more sophisticated and also featured pictures, video, and complex graphics. Today, website designs tend to be simple, so as not to get in the way of the content on them, and often follow their unique purposes. Sales sites often feature lists of product pictures and information if they are goods-oriented; sophisticated and persuasive copywriting if they are more service-oriented. Information sites act much like newspapers did in another era, organizing that information into "data chunks" and making them easier to read, and mixing in pictures and other visual components to catch the eye.

The appearance of blogging platform software such as WordPress launched an era in which professional "themes," or low-cost, purchasable, pre-designed sites, could be downloaded easily. This allowed even the most design-challenged person to plug basic information, visuals, and feedback mechanisms into pages in a paint-by-numbers fashion that had surprisingly impressive results.

While do-it-yourself website design may be adequate and popular, any business intending to operate on the Internet, solely or in tandem with an offline component, will benefit from the advice of a professional website designer. Platforms like WordPress supply the basics, but only a professional can make a website attractive and compelling, with a distinct identity. Just as a business would hire a professional to design its distinct business cards, logo, and letterhead to create an identity, prudently investing in professional Web page design pays off in the long run.

Online publishing is no different than any other publishing, in that principles of classic form and clear communication are still the hallmarks of an elegant and effective page. Its only difference is that it allows (indeed, invites) interactivity.

Content and Audience

People use the Web for many different reasons. They could be seeking entertainment, might be information hounds, or may simply want to find useful and relevant information about products or services in which they are interested. Web pages also serve to reveal our personalities. Are you process-oriented or goal-oriented? In Web pages, if you are process-oriented, you probably tend to focus on the content; goal-oriented individuals tend to think about their audience. Is the latter strategy right or wrong? In fact, the "right" method might be to approach the matter as holistically as possible, developing your pages with both in mind.

What Is the Message/Who Is the Audience?

As with any design (or writing, or speaking or any other form of communication), two questions dominate all other considerations. Simply, they are "What do you want to say?" and "Who do you want to say it to?" Even if you employ the Field of Dreams principle ("if you build it, they will come")—and many website creators have, to their detriment—you will quickly realize that these two questions are more important than any other. They ultimately supply the feedback that best reveals the nature of your creation.

True, there may be many reasons to create a website. But there are only two that bring your target customers to that site—your website says the right things to the right people.

Those right things are your message, which could be low prices, superb selection, service that goes beyond the extra mile, or a strong personality that compels them to follow up in person, or, better yet, buy immediately. The right people are, of course, your audience—those who you believe you can best serve and who want your particular kind of product or service. The farther you stray from these two messages, the more the rule of diminishing returns comes into play. Essentially, communicating with everybody else is a waste of time.

Using Templates

As we said previously, there are now hundreds of website designs, or themes, available online that can guide you when creating your website design. If you're the do-it-yourself type, you could probably learn how to use them quickly and create a moderately professional-looking website. However, it would more likely be simple "brochureware"—a static, online brochure that involves no interactivity or personality. Scrimping on the cost of a website by buying a cheap template fits the old theme of "penny wise, pound foolish," in that it will not answer some of the more important questions. These include:

What do you want a visitor to do?

Why do you want them to do it?

How are you going to get them to do it? What is your persuasion technique?

How are you going to get them to come back (it's called customer engagement)?

Answering these questions requires more sophisticated knowledge that probably isn't in your skill set and can best be supplied by an experienced designer and copywriter. If you open a store, you're going to design the display cases, aisles, and overall look and feel to optimize the shopping experience and make customers comfortable, aren't you? So shouldn't you do the same with your online "store"?

Develop a Site Map

All projects begin with the development of an overall plan that acts as a guide before work on the details begins. Developing a website is no different. It is best to develop a website on paper first, starting with a conceptual "site map" overview of what information should go on each page, and how the pages should be linked together. Strive to make your pages consistent, with important information, such as how to contact the company, placed on each page. Study other sites that you like to determine what it is about them that makes them successful.

Think carefully about two things: the nature of the medium and your audience. If you are designing a website (or evaluating a competitor's site), you should consider the following points:

- Who are the readers?
- Why would they visit the site?
- Do they have common questions, needs, or concerns?
- How can you best communicate with them?
- What would make them come back?

As an exercise, it might be useful to write down an answer to each of the above questions and to keep your responses in mind when evaluating your own site.

PITFALLS TO AVOID

Of course, you must also consider what would make them not come back. This suggests that we ought to contemplate some of the problems that could be encountered. What would make you not return to a website? Would you revisit a site where:

- the page crashed your browser or took forever to load
- the screen was difficult or impossible to read
- the design or content was ugly or offensive
- the information was useless, inappropriate, or wildly self-serving
- the content was stale or obsolete

Without a doubt, what annoys you tells a lot about you. Did your own list of objections focus on page elements that annoy you: blinking text, too many advertisements, distracting animations, or whatever? Or, did you concentrate on the nuts and bolts of Net-based content delivery including the following:

- bandwidth limitations and performance issues
- compatibility problems with plug-ins, helper apps, or other software issues.

There are a few other general principles that can help steer visitors to your site in the direction(s) you want them to go.

- Online visitors are an easily distracted lot. They will abandon a site in seconds if it doesn't give them what they want or otherwise attracts them. Estimates vary, but generally, you have about 10 seconds before a visitor decides whether to stay or go. So copy and design are important. Catchy headlines are especially important, because many people base their decision on them alone.

- Many people have trouble dealing with pages that rely on "helper applications." A link to a help page doesn't seem to help much.

- Very, very few people are willing to "sign up" to gain access to a page that requires some form of registration, no matter how interesting the content.

- Visual appeal and simple navigation matters. Too many words, a cluttered design, and an "ugly" website turn people off.

- You may want to be experimental in your use of text, colour, etc., but few of your visitors will appreciate it. They're looking for information and perhaps a little entertainment, but not art. Stick to black text on a white background, and judicious use of spot colour (e.g., in ads or pictures).

- Be sure to test your website to make sure it works with all browsers, not just the one you use: browsers don't all act alike. Although this problem isn't as prevalent as it once was, it still exists.

- Speed of website loading is still a problem. Not everyone uses ultra-high-speed connections. Keep your website as simple as possible to increase loading speed. Opinion seems divided on how often you should change your website's design. Some advocate changing design substantially once or twice a year, to keep the look "fresh" and current. However, even if you never redesign your site, it is imperative that you update your site often—preferably daily, or at least weekly—if only for search engine optimization purposes. If you never change your site, you'll be completely ignored by the Web-crawling search engines. Fresh content is the best way to optimize a site for search engines (getting your site closer to a high ranking) and will also encourage visitors to bookmark your page for later visits.

Continually test different methods. Few visitors will tell you what they think of your site: If they hate it, they simply won't return! Continually experiment with different looks, navigation routes, and website copy to find which works best. But be careful to keep the tests small, lest you look chaotic and indecisive.

Keeping the Website Interesting

On business-oriented websites, there are a couple of categories of content that are consistently popular:

- fresh news
- timely coverage and in-depth analysis of almost any topic
- answers to frequently asked questions—FAQs.

Weblogs in which a business representative provides helpful and friendly tips and advice create loyalty among visitors.

For example, your site might provide details of new products or services, a few thought-provoking editorials (both your own and from trade journals or popular media), and a FAQ section related to your field.

Welcome to HTML Hell

Here are the five common pitfalls of amateur Web pages:

1. The page causes problems or error messages on the reader's computer.
2. The site contains plagiarized content.
3. The screen is difficult to read or navigate.
4. The site is ugly or contains offensive design or content.
5. The site features stale or obsolete content.

Virtually everything in this chapter relates to these five items in one way or another. Just because you can do something, doesn't mean you should. As we shall explore in the next section, a good design should be top priority.

PAGE LAYOUT AND DESIGN

While the process of designing a page layout is a unique creative act and may be approached in a myriad of ways, having a plan in mind before you start is likely to save you time and wasted effort. Such plans can materialize as rough thumbnail sketches on a restaurant placemat or in your favorite graphics program but, without a doubt, you are likely to come up with a better-looking page if you and/or your designer start with a conceptual sketch.

In paper-based publishing, designers focus on how to best communicate the message. This requires decisions on how many columns the layout will comprise, the position of headlines, graphic elements, appropriate typefaces, and so on. Because of the many limitations of HTML (Hypertext Markup Language) and the tools that were being used to code it, the majority of Web pages that appeared during the first few years of the Web's existence were built by adding some headlines and paragraph tags to text, throwing in a few graphics, and linking to one or more other pages. Voilà—a basic home page.

Fortunately, recent advances in WG Web-authoring tools and the advent of simple website creation tools, such as WordPress, Google Pages, and others have made manual HTML coding largely unnecessary. These will often suffice if your goal is to "just do it." However, if the website is important to your business (and most are), you would likely prefer to have it professionally designed. Nothing screams amateur like a website created by yourself or a friend's son or daughter.

Let us, for a moment, examine some principles of design from a traditional designer's perspective.

A good design should exist without question, and the message it carries should be consistent with that of your company's other endeavors. Here are a few online publishing traps:

- too many fonts
- the wrong message
- bad clip art (i.e., art images available on software or on the Web) and/or poorly scanned images
- phony-looking drop shadows
- not enough white space
- "eye assault"—low-contrast or other hard-to-handle colour combinations
- the "effect du jour."

The Wrong Message

The best rule is to ask: "Does the page communicate the right message?" Of course, before you can ask that question, you must determine it yourself. It's very common for business owners to try to cram too many messages together: pick one overriding message. Typefaces, graphic elements, and other design components must all work together in support of the message you are presenting. A number of issues must be considered in order for this to happen, all of which boil down to one thing: Who is the reader?

A page that would seem appropriate for a financial institution obviously needs to convey a sense of reliability, professionalism, and long-term stability. A design for a beer company, however, is probably most effective when it reflects the lifestyles—or at least the fantasies—of the twenty-something generation that is the primary target audience.

How to Design an Effective Web Page

Keep it short. You only have a few seconds to catch a reader's eye. Colour helps. A short list of your top attractions or newest products is better than a long list of everything under the sun.

- **Short headlines.** Keep headlines to six words or fewer. Keep lists to 10 items or fewer.
- **Make it interesting—involve the reader.** A description of a product's benefits is always more effective than a list of its features. Remember: explain, don't just describe. Make them think. Invite action and always avoid passive-tense phrases.
- **Great pictures.** Most are available on the Web at various picture sites. If you download one for use from a free site, be sure to credit the poster or the photographer. Top-quality pictures can also be purchased online from many picture distributors. Avoid badly scanned flyers or printed artwork.
- **The big picture.** Don't fall prey to "clip art syndrome," where amateur designers litter their pages with several small images. In design work, the secret is to be bold. Make the design stand out and take command of the reader's attention.
- **Focus attention.** When designing a logo or headline, pick the most important word and emphasize it. Make it bigger, bolder, and cleaner. According to colour psychologists, red stands out; blue recedes. Thus, blue makes a better background for a sidebar, red makes a better attention-grabber for a logo. Some combinations are effective, but have been corrupted by overuse or their negative connotations. Black text on a yellow background has great contrast, but reminds many people of those cheap, quick-printed flyers on canary yellow paper.
- **Simple typefaces.** Limit the use of exotic typefaces or, in the case of Web pages, graphics that look like typefaces. If angled, warped, stretched, shadowed, or italicized text isn't essential to the message you are trying to convey, resist the urge. Never use an exotic typeface as body text. Don't use more than three or four typefaces in a single page.
- **Contrast is the key to a successful design.** All emphasis is no emphasis. As a general rule, use a bold or extra-bold sans serif typeface (Arial, Helvetica, Verdana, etc.) for headlines, prices, and phone numbers. Body text (the small lettering that comprises the "body" of your message) should be a serif face (Times New Roman, Georgia, etc.). Typeface design is an area that has become high art in the print world over time; Web typefaces are now catching up. Never use all capitals in body text. It's okay for short headlines but quickly becomes tiring to read. Never use all caps in a cursive script font.
- **White space helps.** One of the biggest mistake amateur designers make is to try to jam too much on a page, which tends to tire out and agitate a viewer. Don't crowd every inch of your page with text and pictures. Put in lots of "air" and let it breathe. Leave plenty of white space around

all sides of your page—the latest trend in design and copywriting is to leave more white space than text and pictures. White space on edges and between text creates an elegant and intimate look; some adventurous designers have adopted the magazine technique of using only one or a few words on a page.

Common Grammatical Errors and the Web

While you are shaping up your page's content, be sure to avoid the most common grammatical errors:

- **Use "e.g." and "i.e." correctly.** The former is correctly used in place of the words "for example" the latter means "in other words." In both cases, be sure to follow the second period with a comma.
- **Proper use of punctuation.** Single quotes are often used where double quotes should be. Always use double quotes, unless you are using quotes-within-quotes, as you might if you are quoting someone who is, in turn, quoting a third party. In general, always put periods, commas, question marks, and exclamation points inside the quotation marks. The only exception to this rule is if the word or phrase in quotes contains its own punctuation.

  Beware of source material containing typographer's quotes "like these" instead of plain quotes "like these." While such smart quotes and smart apostrophes are very desirable on a printed page, they do not display correctly in all Web browsers. Other special characters, such as accented letters, and special symbols, such as ™, can cause problems. Be sure to test your pages with a variety of browsers!
- **Apostrophes denotes ownership.** Another mistake many people make is to put apostrophes after pluralized words. ("We sell IBM's" is wrong.) Note that the "s" in "the '91900s" is not preceded by an apostrophe. Remember that if a word ending with an "s" requires an apostrophe, it is correct to put the apostrophe after the "s" (e.g., Mr. Jones' car). Also, "it's" is a contraction of "it is" or "it has"— it's not the plural of "it" (which is "its") nor does it indicate belonging to it.
- **Use hyphens and dashes correctly.** A hyphen is correctly used to hyphenate. It is also commonly used in telephone numbers. Don't hyphenate word-pairs in which the first word ends with "ly" (e.g., highly-toxic is wrong.) An "en dash" (so called because it is the width of the letter "n") is slightly wider than a hyphen. An en dash is correctly used between two numbers, dates, or times. Wider still is the "em dash." It is traditionally used for in-sentence emphasis. Unfortunately, en and

em dashes suffer from cross-platform compatibility problems with some browsers. Don't use them on the Web.

- **Use bullets.** It is better to use a bullet (a dot like the one at the beginning of this sentence) than a dash or an asterisk to illustrate a point. HTML has several standard LIST types, allowing you to specify specific bullet types. If none of these is suitable, you can, of course, use small graphics as bullets instead.

- **Proper use of italics.** Italics are properly used to highlight publication or book names, editorial comments, foreign language quotations, or occasional words of emphasis. You should also use italics when a product name is used in a headline (e.g., "Will the new version of *Acme Software* work?"). Never use underlines, as these obviously look like links.

- **One period.** Don't use two spaces after a period. One will do.

- **Capitalization.** Using all capital italic letters is only appropriate for acronyms (e.g., SCSI, IBM, DOS). Do not use all caps for emphasis. Use italics instead. Do not capitalize words unless they are proper nouns (names, titles, business names, etc.)—even when spelling out acronyms. Small caps can be interesting, in moderation.

- **Check your spelling.** The number one grammatical error? Spelling mistakes. Even one typographical error in a document is one too many. Remember, your word processor's spelling checker cannot tell if the word "now" is misspelled as "not." Let the computer check the spelling first, then read your text over and look up any suspect words in a good paper dictionary. Be especially careful with names, which won't be in the dictionary.

  Canada versus the United States. No, it's not a Olympic hockey game. It's spelling. Many words are spelled differently in Canada than they are in the U.S. (e.g., honour vs. honor, centre vs. center, etc.) and your word-processing program won't save you from making mistakes. It is likely standardized to American English, and you have to key in Canadian spell-checking. If you have a website, be patriotic and use Canadian spelling. Your customers will quietly thank you.

  Remember, publishing—whether online or otherwise—is all about communication. An error in your grammar or spelling will sabotage all the effort you put into design and layout. These grammatical conventions are only the tip of the iceberg. There are dozens—hundreds—of other common grammatical errors. Strunk and White's *Elements of Style*, *The Chicago Manual of Style*, and Fowler's *Modern English Usage* are good books on the subject. It is worth picking up one if you are interested in creating documents that work.

Web Design Tips

Naturally, any notion of "good" design is very subjective, but here are some more general recommendations:

- Avoid centreing everything, especially body text.
- Avoid gratuitous use of italics and headlines for body text.
- Establish a clear hierarchy of information which is pleasingly situated on the page. Avoid pages that have a lot of small text above a large graphic or headline. This looks unbalanced.
- Fix broken or out-of-date links in a timely fashion.
- Check your existing pages for HTML problems, which can manifest as pages with missing information or improperly interpreted HTML.
- Be consistent with design elements.
- It is helpful to list an e-mail address. This is often put at the bottom of a Web page, along with a note that says when the page was last updated.
- Focus more on information and less on the marketing angle.
- Information is what will keep them coming back to your site. Provide a summary of "What's New."
- Keep load times down, especially on introductory pages or warn users in advance. If you, or the person doing the graphics for your site, are not grammatically and/or graphically inclined, have the pages examined and made over by a proofreader and a graphic artist.

MARKETING ON THE INTERNET AND GATHERING CUSTOMER INTELLIGENCE

Are you trying to figure out how to make your website pay? Do you wish you could read your customers' minds? Maybe you can. The Internet is a hugely popular source of online information; look how most buyers now routinely use the Web to shop for and compare products.

Doing Your Research

Gathering and making sense of the behaviour of visitors to your website will help you focus your online services to better meet their needs. Trading patterns can reveal something of how people shop, what they are interested in, and what they are thinking about. This will also help you in your advertising efforts.

Advertising

Considering advertising on someone else's site on the Web? A little research can help your investment pay off. The old real estate adage is right: it's location, location, and location. Search for the high-traffic or top-rated sites.

To find out how effective your website or online advertising is, tracking software is a must. Some organizations rely on their own programmers and devise a proprietary system. However, off-the-shelf solutions are available to track "hits." Some of these tools are discussed below.

Tracking Number of Visitors and Page Popularity of Your Site

There are several methods to track the popularity of your site.

Web server logfile analysis

Web servers record some of their transactions in a logfile, which can then be read to determine the popularity of a website. Statistics are recorded as:

- The number of client requests (or hits) made to a Web server. This is a very raw statistic because it does not indicate anything other than someone visited.
- The number of page views and visits or sessions. A page view is a request made to the server for a page, as opposed to a graphic. A visit is a sequence of requests from a uniquely identified client. Usually the server visited places a "cookie," or piece of tracking coding, on the visitor's browser.

Page tagging

Page tagging involves the use of counters that show the number of times an image has been requested, which allows an estimate of the number of visitors to a page. The resulting data is usually gathered remotely by a Web analytics company.

Hybrids

Hybrids combine both methods and add a few more options to overcome the problems endemic in each method. Most Web analytics companies use this method.

Online usage logs are a standard or optional feature of virtually every Web server. In the absence of the more sophisticated tools listed below, this information can help you determine where a visit originated from, its time and duration, and, of course, what the visitors were viewing.

Typically, these Web analytics software logs record every page view and hence, every visitor to the site. Those with advanced knowledge of spreadsheets or statistical analysis tools may be able to make sense of this mountain of data. But for the rest of us, a Web statistics analysis program would be more useful. Google Analytics—a free and by far the most-used analysis program—is an easier solution. This analysis will also indicate the most popular paid keywords and their usage rates so you can write your Web copy to maximize search engine optimization.

Web statistics analysis programs provide charts, summaries, and other facts that can help you make sense of the usage patterns at your website. Typically, they'll also highlight problems, for example, broken links or attempts to "hack in" to your server, should these occur.

Obviously, the reading pattern of online visitors to any particular website doesn't tell the whole story. There is much to be said for asking visitors outright how they feel about the service and products they obtain from you. Find out what products they are thinking of purchasing in the coming months, and what part of your operations could be improved upon. People like to know you care about their opinion.

No matter what trend analysis solution you favor, a tool that allows you to examine the most popular items and figure out the patterns is a valuable addition to your Internet business strategy.

Web-tracking software can help you prove how well a promotion or advertising campaign is working. With a spreadsheet or the built-in tools of some Web-tracking programs, you can easily prepare charts that show month-to-month growth. With effective tracking and a cohesive marketing campaign that points users to your website, you'll find that the number of visitors will increase predictably, with the greatest numbers of hits occurring on days when advertising occurs.

Using "cookies"

It is possible, with custom-coded Web pages or commercial offerings from a number of vendors, to gather persistent data known as a "cookie" when a visitor arrives at your website. These cookies can tell you if a user has been to the site before. Most cookies are used for legitimate reasons, such as when your browser takes you to a "run once only" welcome page after upgrading to a new version of its Internet Explorer Web browser. However, some sites can—and do—collect other information without your knowledge when you visit their site. Thus, many users are rightfully concerned about cookies that are surreptitiously collected while they browse the Web. By the way, you cannot obtain a user's e-mail address with a cookie. If that is your goal, you'll have to entice them to leave it, possibly in exchange for access to a subscribers-only area or by providing something else of value.

There are many ways you can improve customer feedback for your own business, but the Internet can play a role. In order to better serve your customers' needs, you have to gather intelligence. Nothing beats a good name for sales potential.

The Instant Gratification Society

In an instant gratification society, people want to see rapid results, and they like rewards. One of the benefits of the Internet is the ability to put a "try before you buy" version of a product into the users' hands. Such demos aren't limited to software products. We've seen cellular phones, real estate developments, and many other hard goods effectively demonstrated this way. Limited-time trials are particularly popular among information products and online, or "cloud," software. Similarly, subscription software usually allows you to cancel at any time.

REDEFINING ROLES: THE DATABASE

Many companies have been investing in software that turns their websites into automated database-driven websites.

For example, ordering and tracking software can help a company find out where in the supply chain a product they have ordered is, and how long it is going to take to get it. Being database-driven, the Web pages are created dynamically, as required. And of course, when new data is added to the database, the Web pages will automatically reflect the changes. As your company grows, its reliance on the data in your database grows with it. Perhaps the best known type of database-driven software is a Software as a Service (SaaS), or rental software. Salesforce.com or Highrise.com are typical SaaS suites used extensively by small businesses for sales and marketing. Web-based data stores can also provide access to colour photos or even video, which allows you to display hundreds or thousands of images of products on your site.

Real-time access to inventory data means a customer can see what's available, scan current promotional offers, browse pages describing manufacturers' latest products, place an order, and receive immediate confirmation. And retailers can track their shipments, too, thanks to live data feeds from Purolator, United Parcel Service Inc. (UPS Canada) and FedEx Canada.

ONLINE CREDIT CARD PROCESSING

The next step beyond this level of sophistication is to delve into electronic payments. In this case, your system—or the system of a secure transaction partner—holds financial data on customers and processes credit card purchases.

The system tracks outstanding invoices and credit status, yields reports, or exports data to accounting systems as needed. If all's okay, the system accepts the order and sends out an invoice via e-mail while the system forwards the paid order to the shipping department.

At the most basic level, you need what is known as a Merchant Services account to be able to accept credit card payments. There are different types of Merchant Service accounts available, ranging from the low-risk "card present" system that typically employs a card-swiping machine for sales at a retail location, through to the "card not present" systems used to process telephone orders, to the electronic ultimate: Internet-based e-commerce transactions. Unfortunately, the banks view "card not present," and especially e-commerce transactions, as high-risk activities and usually require a bond before such service can be provided. This amount varies, but can be as high as $10,000. Make an appointment with the Merchant Services representative at your local bank(s) to find out the details—and be sure to read the fine print. Aside from the Merchant Service bond costs, it should be obvious that developing a sophisticated Web-based database system can be costly.

Merchant Accounts and Transaction-Processing Systems

A number of companies act as transaction-processing systems, but do not provide merchant services accounts. To use one of these swiping machines, you still need to go to your bank(s) and set up merchant services accounts for Visa, MasterCard, and/or any other credit card services you wish to offer. This typically involves specifying that you want a "Telephone order/card-not-present" account, which in turn typically requires a security deposit.

An alternative to this process is to use the services of a company that provides merchant services and takes a per-transaction or flat fee. PayPal is probably the best known example, but there are many others, including Google and Amazon, offering these services.

In Canada, the largest online payment system service is the Interac system (interac.ca), which mirrors the offline banking system online. This service, which moves money from one financial institution to another online, is currently being used by some 24 million Canadians. Essentially, it offers online clients the same payment service they would have in a retail store. Another comprehensive Canadian service is Beanstream (beanstream.com/site/ca/index.html), which provides merchants with secure, flexible payment-processing tools to handle credit care, Interac online, visa debit, the American service Automated Clearing House (ACH), and direct/debit payment transactions for e-commerce, mail order/telephone order, and other card-not-present environments.

Potential Pitfalls

Consider the relative merits and drawbacks of dealing direct versus working with distributors. Considering how e-commerce can affect traditional vendor/customer relationships, dealing direct makes sense when the volume or dollar value justifies it. However, in lower volumes, the distributor's value is clear. Further, some manufacturers have been creating their own distribution networks, in a sense cutting the retailer out of the system. So the retailer must offer some value-add to compete.

Thus, when customers call, say, a hotel to make travel reservations, a clerk will ask if they would be interested in joining a discount club for the whole chain, offering $20 in free gas coupons as an incentive. This idea of pinpointing the exact times when consumers are most receptive to a certain pitch is one that anyone selling a product can leverage to improve sales opportunities.

Whether you are building e-commerce systems or reinforcing shopper loyalty using the equivalent of frequent flyer points, such questions are worth asking. Online databases have sprung up along with e-commerce opportunities, indicating the enabling facility of the Web as a ubiquitous business information access tool.

Here are some of the techniques to more efficiently solve customer support issues, while helping you to keep an eye on emerging technologies that could end up as profitable product lines.

Searching the Internet

One of the many valuable aspects of the Internet is the way that search engines, primarily Google, Yahoo, or Microsoft Bing (although there are many others that specialize in specific subject areas), allow users to mine for data on the Web. In fact, the vast majority of Web users find sites through search engines, while most of the remainder are referred by other websites.

However, if you or your employees are getting 12,000,000 matches when you search for something on the Net, you might want to brush up on your searching skills, perhaps by taking a night school course, or minimally by reading the Help pages that describe the advanced search functions of any search engine. Better still, train your employees on how to more effectively deal with support-intensive customers by using a search engine.

You can register your site for free with top search engines at submit-away.com/top-search-engines.htm or any one of dozens of search engine submission sites. For example, in Canada alone, a Google search for free search engine sites generates 19 million answers. Browse them and pick the top three or four that promise the best service that fits your needs. Recognize, of course, that free search engines are in the business of advertising and so, to generate traffic, may promise more than they offer. As with anything that is free on the Net, a dose of skepticism can be healthy.

Fishing for hits

Along with registering your website with search engines, it's important to ensure that the pages index well. You would do this with meta tags, or keywords encrypted to be picked up by a browser. Also, you will want to liberally sprinkle relevant keywords throughout your website copy to attract search engines. In fact, as the Web becomes the marketing platform of choice for millions of businesses, Search Engine Optimization, or SEO, as it's known, has become a multimillion-dollar segment of marketing. Some marketers predict that in the near future it will be the dominant form of marketing (it certainly is for smaller companies that can't afford the high-priced advertising favoured by the very large firms).

Meta tags embedded into the HTML code helps define the page. Some of today's more sophisticated Web-authoring tools are database-driven, and these tools can generate these lists of meta tags automatically. Even if you add the tags manually, you are increasing the likelihood that a customer looking for the product or service you offer will find your page near the top of the list of results displayed by a search engine.

Keywords are those words that are commonly searched for through the engines, and the number of times they appear in your website copy usually governs your site's ranking with the search engines.

Google's AdWords system, which sells keywords for its online advertisements, also offers for free the Google Keyword tool (googlekeywordtool.com), which suggests keywords around a subject area, and also reports which keywords garner the most views. However, there is a methodology to using the tool: don't simply pick the words that have the most views, such as dry cleaning (plus your city), because you'll be swamped by irrelevant results. Instead, drill down to very specific keywords that relate to your business or geographic niche, and use those in your copy. You may attract fewer searchers, but they will have a higher level of interest in your product or service.

A commercial system that offers similar but more robust services, as well as a great deal of education on SEO, is WordTracker at wordtracker.com. It also has a free version that is less robust.

Lastly, here's a tip for writing for the search engines. Research has shown that phrases usually return better results than single words: phrases of three to five words show the best results, because they tend to be very specific and return far more relevant results. For example, instead of writing in keywords such as "dry cleaning (your city)," use strings of ever-more-relevant words, such as "drycleaning silk blouses (your city, your neighborhood)," or "removing spaghetti sauce stains from silk blouses." This will attract a much more motivated customer.

Obviously, your website content will have to be more specific to allow for these kind of searches. This is why so many small businesses now write helpful "how-to" articles as well as basic information about the business. Generally known as "content marketing," this form of writing is produced specifically for search engines and is rapidly taking over online marketing.

CUSTOMER E-MAIL AND RESPONSE

The Fine Line between Promotion and Spam

Promotion is an evolving art and for those with something to sell, the Internet looms large as an area of ever-growing importance. With its increasingly dominant role as the e-commerce marketplace, we have work to do to set up our shops, unfurl our banners, and get the message out there.

E-Mail

One of the key ways Internet contacts can be established is, of course, via electronic mail. While this once dominant marketing format has been replaced somewhat by direct website marketing, it is still a formidable marketing method, because it plays an integral part in customer communication.

The real likelihood is that, sooner or later, you are going to need to improve your ability to efficiently respond to e-mailed information requests. As your company's Web presence grows, you are going to receive a lot of e-mail, so you had better have a plan in place to deal with this happy problem. Some of the methods you may find useful for managing requests for information include having "bots" which is like an e-mail form letter or automated direct response that provides information on certain topics. You, or your e-mail service provider, could, for example, set up a bot to automatically e-mail a price list or a product specification sheet in response to a request. For maximum efficiency, provide several e-mail addresses on your website, where visitors can categorize their response, depending on, for example, the relation to sales, information, technical help, or a problem with the website.

You can use a bot to thank people for writing, to let them know that their letter has been received and that it will be read. Or, after a sale, you can use this acknowledgment as a subtle follow-up marketing technique, suggesting other "you may also like" products or services. Remember, however, that an automated response is no substitute for a personal reply. Although the bot provides an immediate response to let people know their message made it through and that it is appreciated, such missives ring hollow unless you then follow up with a real human reply.

Automatically generated e-mail has its dangers, of course. Send too much, send it more than once, or send it to the wrong parties, and you may be accused—or guilty—of spamming. In general, we'd recommend providing a prechecked check-box on your request-for-information Web page. This option will allow the people who use it to decide whether they would like to receive future product information on updates or promotional offers from you. If they agree, their names can be added to a mailing list, electronic or otherwise. In any case, a privacy statement on your website, detailing your policies on the sale or loan of their e-mail address, is a must.

Internet usage has grown rapidly over the past two decades, with Canada among the world's top users According to Internet World Stats, in 2008 some 85% of Canadians, or 28 million people, used the Internet, placing us among the world's heaviest users. Since then, the Canadian Internet population has likely grown to more than 90%, which by all accounts means saturation usage. Interestingly, Canada is slightly ahead of the United States in Internet usage, with 77% connected. The country with highest number of Internet users is China, where nearly half a billion people are connected, but this does not translate to high usages in percentage terms. Compare this growth with radio, where it took 38 years to reach 50 million users, or the 25 years between 1920 and 1945 it took the telephone to reach the 50-million mark. Forester Research predicts that e-commerce retail sales in the United States will hit $249 billion in the next few years. When combined with "web-influenced" (i.e., purchases were researched online) retail sales, the projected total will be in the trillions of dollars.

One Percent Margin—Billion-Dollar Market

If you think the retail or wholesale business is tough, talk to purveyors of Web goods, whose margins are razor thin. As Asian companies flood the Internet with low-cost goods, margins have been shrinking faster than ice cubes in August. Let's face it, for anyone selling goods or services today, the Web is a tough place to compete. As the e-economy grows and the industrial economy declines, the Internet has become a disruptive force in many countries' economies, knocking over industries like tenpins. Every day you hear about some giant company in consumer electronics or media or publishing that is struggling as its customer base moves to the much cheaper Web. Certainly, there are business efficiencies which make this shift compelling. Consider how full-service brokerages that charged $150 for a stock trade suffered when online trading could be had for less than $10. Look at how newspapers have struggled to hold on to readers (and the advertisers who follow them) as they move to the Net, where information is more readily available and ultra–low cost, or free.

The initial hesitance of consumers fearful of security issues has long ago faded, as shoppers heard of the low prices to be had online. Couple this with an increasingly cooperative regulatory environment and a strong technology infrastructure in terms of bandwidth and processing power, and it adds up to a compelling business value. It should not be surprising that Canada's millions of Internet users spent more time online than anywhere on earth, an average of 43½ hours a month, according to the Web research firm comScore.

E-commerce offers the potential for revenue enhancement, cost reduction, and expansion in terms of product, customer base, and available channels. Just don't forget to take off the rose-coloured glasses.

How to Get Additional Revenue from Your Site

In addition to the customer e-mail response option discussed earlier, there are a number of other possibilities for generating additional revenue from your site, although it should be stressed that a website is best viewed as a strategic tool, not a mere profit centre. The value of the Net as an intelligence-gathering tool is undeniable, but not easily quantified in dollars and cents. But keep in mind the following sites when looking for new sources of cash:

- Use social media such as Facebook, LinkedIn, or Twitter to point users to your company's content and other offerings and to demonstrate expertise in a particular area. Some companies also use the "for sale" sites, such as Craigslist and Kijiji, to advertise inventory.
- Many entrepreneurs use an electronic newsletter to keep in touch with customers. If your e-newsletter displays extreme knowledge or insight into a specialty, you may be able to charge for it. This is rare, however, so most newsletters are free and aim to create a "community of interest" around a subject that also results in sales. Anyone with a website can get advertisers, although if you're new or small you may have to find advertisers, instead of expecting them to come to you. You can do this by joining an "affiliate" network of various sites, which is an agency or broker, such as thefreecountry.com, or in Canada, ConnexPlace (connexplace.com/en), where you can select from a variety of advertisers, or Amazon.ca or Chapters.ca. Of course the 800-pound gorilla in the online advertising space is Google's AdSense, which earns the company billions of dollars every year.
- Payment systems for online advertising usually follow three methods.

  CPM or pay-per-impression, pays you a nominal fee for every time the advertiser's banner is displayed on your site. The amount you earn is usually based on the number of thousand (the "M" is derived from the Latin word for 1000) "impressions" or banner displays. It is also low, such as $5 per thousand, so you need high traffic to earn with this method.

With PPC or pay-per-click, you are paid when visitors click on the advertisers' banner or ad on your site. PPC pays more than PPM because it has a higher "conversion" rate (a visitor clicking on the ad), which leads to more sales.

Pay-per-sale or pay-per-lead pays you if a visitor clicks through the ad and purchases or takes some other action the advertiser desires. This method has the lowest conversion rate but carries the highest payment rates.

- Link exchanges were once popular methods of advertising, but have faded because Google's search methods have effectively made them obsolete. You can still use a form of link exchange by linking to websites that are similar to yours in subject matter, primarily through blogs. If the site links back to you (or your blog), you have performed a legitimate exchange.

Load your site with keyword-optimized information. If your small business involves a common product or service, you can feature other articles or blog posts that talk about that subject (be sure to credit the authors/sources. It's theft not to!) This will add many keywords to your site, thus pleasing the search engines and elevating your ranking.

Chapter 20

Insuring Your Business's Future

There are worse things in life than death. Have you ever spent an evening with an insurance salesman?

—Woody Allen

You undoubtedly know you need insurance for your business and peace of mind. However, many people are confused as to what types of insurance to select. This chapter will discuss organizing your insurance program and types of business and personal insurance. How to select the right insurance broker for your business was discussed in Chapter 4, "Selecting Professional Advisors."

You may be unaware of the types of liability you could be exposed to in your business. Here are a few examples and the type of insurance coverage that would protect you:

Case 1. You provide a computer consulting service, and a client who relied on your advice subsequently suffers a $100,000 loss. You are being sued for negligence for the financial loss that your client suffered. (professional liability/malpractice insurance)

Case 2. You operate a day care business, and while you are transporting children, your car is accidentally hit by another car, and a child is injured. You are sued as the driver and car owner. (automobile insurance)

Case 3. You operate a catering business, and someone who eats one of your muffins cracks a tooth on a walnut shell. He sues you for dental expenses. (product liability insurance)

Case 4. You operate a tailoring business, and a client who comes to your house slips on the stairs, breaks her leg, and is off work for 2 months. You are sued for damages. (general liability insurance)

Case 5. You have expensive desktop publishing hardware and software in your basement. A fire breaks out, damages your equipment, and destroys all your clients' records. (fire/business property/business replacement cost insurance)

Case 6. You are a contractor, and while lifting a heavy object, you dislocate your back. You are immobilized for 3 months and cannot perform any work. You are the sole income earner and need income to meet your normal personal expenses. (disability insurance)

ORGANIZING YOUR INSURANCE PROGRAM

It is important to consider all criteria to determine the best type of insurance for you and your business. Your goal should be adequate coverage. That can be achieved by periodic review of the risk you are insuring for and by keeping your insurance representative informed of any changes in your business that could affect the adequacy or enforceability of your coverage. Such changes could include additional equipment purchases, extensions to your home, or the business use of your personal car.

The following advice will help you plan an insurance program:

- Assess your business and identify the likely risk exposure.
- Cover your largest risk(s) first.
- Determine the magnitude of loss that the business can bear without financial difficulty, and use your premium dollar where the protection need is greatest.
- Insure the correct risk.
- Decide which of these three kinds of protection will work best for each risk:
  - absorbing the risk (e.g., budgeting to cover any loss or expense without getting insurance)
  - minimizing the risk (e.g., reducing the factor that could contribute to the risks, rather than getting insurance)
  - insuring against the risk with commercial insurance.
- Use every means possible to reduce the cost of insurance.
  - Negotiate for lower premiums if your loss experience is low.
  - Increase deductibles as much as you can if you need the protection, but can't afford a low deductible premium.
  - Shop around for comparable rates and analyze insurance terms and provisions offered by different insurance companies.
  - Avoid duplication of insurance. Have one agent handle all your business insurance.
  - Incorporate if necessary to further reduce personal liability.

As your risk exposure changes, a periodic review will save you from insuring matters that are no longer exposed to the same degree of risk. Conversely, you may need to increase limits of liability. Reviews can help avoid overlaps and gaps in coverage and thereby keep your risk and premiums lower. This is especially important if the business is growing. Reviews can also help you keep current with inflation.

TYPES OF INSURANCE

The types of insurance coverages you might need will vary, of course, depending on the nature of your business operation. The following brief overview is intended to alert you to the main types of coverage you may wish to consider.

General Liability

This type of policy covers losses that you would be liable to pay for causing bodily injury to someone (e.g., in an accident) or damage to the property of others. Make sure that your policy covers all legal fees for your defence and all other, related costs incurred. This type of policy generally covers negligence on your part that accidentally causes injury to clients, customers, employees, or the general public.

Business Property

If you are operating out of your home, your current basic homeowners' or apartment owners' policy may void any coverage of business-related assets. Therefore, you should request that coverage be added to include the business assets, or purchase a separate policy. If you own a computer, you may wish to get a special "floater" policy covering risks unique to computer owners. This extra coverage should insure such factors as power-surge damage, as well as fire and theft of software and hardware.

Fire

This coverage enables you to replace or rebuild your office or home and replace inventory and equipment. Make sure your policy is a "replacement" policy and covers business use of the premiums.

Theft

This type of policy covers losses due to robbery and is generally part of a comprehensive general liability coverage plan.

Automobile

Automobile insurance protects against physical damage to the car and bodily injury to the passengers, as well as damage to other people's property, cars, or passengers. It also covers theft of your car. Make sure that your car is insured for business use. Otherwise, if the facts came out on a claim that it was being used for that purpose, your policy would normally be voided, and your claim would be disallowed.

Business Loan

Business loan insurance will cover the balance outstanding of a business bank loan and is usually arranged through the bank at the time of the loan. In the event of your death or disability, the loan is paid off completely. Depending on the amount of the loan or bank policy, you may be required to obtain this insurance as a condition of funding.

Malpractice

Malpractice insurance, also referred to as a professional liability insurance, protects you from claims for damages from your clients. This could arise out of negligence or failure on your part to exercise an acceptable degree of professional skill.

Business Interruption

Business interruption insurance compensates for lost earnings during a temporary cessation of business caused by fire, theft, flood, or other disaster. This policy covers you until you return to normal working conditions. Check to make sure the coverage includes the costs of temporarily renting other premises.

Business Continuation

Business continuation insurance provides for the transfer of a shareholder's or partner's interest in the event of that person's death.

Overhead Expense

Overhead expense insurance is purchased by professionals and business owners whose income would cease if they were temporarily disabled by illness or accident. In this event, the insurance would cover the cost of their fixed business overhead expenses. Other insurance would need to be obtained for loss of income.

Key Personnel

Key personnel life insurance provides protection for the business owner against the death of a key person that could seriously affect the earning power of the business. Normally, the company takes out the insurance.

Life

Life insurance coverage, if a term life policy, insures a person for a specific period of time or term, and then stops. Term life does not have a cash surrender value or loan value, such as is found with a whole life plan. Term premiums are less expensive than whole life premiums. If you have a bank loan or personal or business obligations, you should consider term life coverage. Whole life insurance costs more money, as it includes a "term" component plus an investment savings component. That is, you obtain interest on your investment part of your premium.

Home Office

Operating a business from your home presents areas of risk exposure. For example, your office equipment could be the cause of a fire or someone could break in and steal your office equipment. In addition, you could have a client or customer who is at your home for business purposes and trips, falls, and is seriously injured. It is important to recognize these potential risks and the types of insurance policies available for protection against them. If you don't have insurance protection, you could be personally liable for all financial losses. First of all, you should advise your insurance agent in writing that you are operating a business from your home. You will need to have extra coverage to protect you for any risk areas involved directly or indirectly with your business operation.

Because of the higher risk involved with operating a business from your home, the insurance company obviously will be charging you an increased premium on your current home insurance policies. It tends to be a fairly modest extra premium. Almost all homeowner policies exclude home businesses, as these policies they are designed for "personal use only."" However, it will still be a large savings compared with the higher insurance premium you would be required to pay if your business were located in commercial premises. Attempt to use the same insurance broker for all your policies, if possible, as you should be able to negotiate better rates, if any flexibility is available. Make sure you receive copies of the extra policy coverage for your file.

Employee

Employee insurance is usually taken out for employees by the employer as part of an employee group benefit package. Such group benefit insurance plans usually include life, medical, dental, and disability insurance.

Property

Property insurance covers destruction or damage to the insured property caused by a certain peril specified in the coverage, such as fire, flood, and burglary. Marine insurance protects goods during shipment. Boiler and machinery insurance covers damage and injury caused by explosion or other mishaps. Property insurance also covers property items, such as glass (from breakage) and automobiles (from collision, theft, fire, and vandalism).

Liability

Liability insurance covers any area in which the business, or the directors, officers, partners, employees, or agents might be held liable for negligence or some other act or omission. The most common type of liability insurance is general liability, which covers negligence causing injury to customers, employees, and the general public. Other examples include:

- product liability (purchased by manufacturers of a product)
- errors and omissions liability (purchased by lawyers, accountants, architects, insurance agents)
- tenants' liability (purchased by a tenant of leased space in a building)
- employers' liability (purchased by employers; relates to worker safety)
- officers' and directors' liability.

Disability

Good health is by far our greatest asset. With it, we can acquire other assets and improve our financial net worth. Without it, only liabilities.

The chances of becoming disabled are sobering. Statistics show that the chance of becoming disabled between 40 and 65 years of age for a minimum of 3 months is almost 40%. It is equally disturbing to know that almost one-half of those still disabled after 6 months will continue to be disabled at the end of 5 years.

Depending on the nature of the disability, you might be covered by Workers' Compensation benefits, Canada Pension Plan benefits, or Employment Insurance disability benefits. Possibly you have coverage under group disability plan insurance benefits or personal disability insurance plan coverage. Group and individual plans will only cover a portion of your gross earnings.

It is important to review exactly what protection you currently have, if any, and the nature of that protection. You can then make appropriate plans to increase your protection on your lifestyle and financial needs. Basically, disability is defined as the inability, due to illness or injury, to continue to work. Disability insurance is designed to compensate the insured for a portion of the income that is lost due to the disabling injury or illness.

Definitions of disability vary from insurance company contract to contract. Whether or not your policy will pay you benefits may well depend on how the company defines disability. Most contracts define disability according to one of four types. Carefully read the wording of your contract, as some are so restrictive that it might be almost impossible to be eligible for a claim. Here is an overview, from the least to the most restrictive:

1. **Own occupation.** Disability is defined as inability to work in your own occupation only. Prove that you are disabled from doing your own job and are under the care of a doctor, and you qualify for benefits. Even if you went to work in another occupation, you might still qualify for benefits. Individual insurance contracts may offer an "own occupation" clause to age 65.

2. **Regular occupation.** This type would provide coverage in the event that you are disabled and unable to work in your own occupation, provided that you choose not to work in an alternative occupation.
3. **Any occupation.** This would cover disability from any suitable occupation, based on your education, training, and/or experience. Most, but not all, group insurance contracts specify an "any occupation" disability after the first 2 years of disability.
4. **Total and permanent.** Some insurance contracts require that you not only be totally disabled from working, but also that your disability must be permanent. Naturally, this insurance is high-risk for you, due to the severe nature of disability required before coverage commences. The insurance premium is lower therefore, as the risk is lower to the insurance company.

Out-of-Country Emergency Medical

If you are travelling outside Canada for business or pleasure, you need to have out-of-country emergency medical insurance. The potential financial risk exists whether you leave the country for an hour, a day or a month. You could be travelling anywhere in the world, but the country with the most expensive medical system is the United States.

If you have a serious injury or illness in the United States and require emergency medical attention, you will be financially devastated unless you have out-of-country medical insurance. The need for this extra insurance protection is simple. Provincial health insurance plans vary by province, but each provides you with the necessary protection when travelling within Canada. Coverage by provincial plans for hospital care outside Canada is nominal, for example, $75 to $500 or more Canadian funds per day, depending on your province. This is very low compared with medical costs in the United States. It may only cover 5%, if that, of your total outlay.

The problem is that health care in the United States is very different from the health coverage we take for granted in Canada. We are not accustomed to being personally billed, so we don't fully appreciate the real cost of treatment. In the U.S. system, private hospitals and doctors operate in a profit-oriented environment, and costs are much greater. In the United States, the average hospital stay often exceeds US$1,500 per day, and can run as high as US$10,000 per day for intensive care. Certain emergency surgical operations can cost US$100,000 or more. For example, bypass surgery could cost $250,000 or more. So who pays the shortfall if you have a medical emergency in the United States? You do. Unless, of course, you have wisely purchased supplemental medical insurance before you left Canada, for the duration of your U.S. stay, be it 1 day or 6 months. Keep in mind this supplemental insurance covers emergency nonelective treatment for injury or illness only. It does not cover nonemergency treatment or services. It is not a substitute for Canadian health care.

You can get extended-stay coverage or a multitrip plan. This latter type of plan allows you to travel outside Canada for as many times as you like within the 1-year period of the plan up to a certain number of days at a time. You select the number of days, for example, 10, 20, 30 days, etc. Premium rates vary greatly between insurers, depending on factors such as the nature of coverage, your age and existing medical condition, policy exclusions and limitations, the deductible portion of the policy, whether you have a preferred (for healthy people) or standard rate plan, and the duration of your stay. Do not choose a plan based on price alone, but consider such factors as benefits, limitations, exclusions, and deductibles. Remember to claim your insurance premiums for a tax credit on your income tax return under "medical expenses."

Check out as many insurance programs as you can that offer the type of coverage you are seeking. A full range of comparisons to evaluate the relative strengths and weaknesses of the various plans will make your final decision much less stressful. To eliminate misunderstanding, get confirmation in writing of any representations or responses to requests made by you to your insurance company. You need to be very honest and accurate in your application about pre-existing illnesses or medical conditions and any change in your medications or condition before you depart. Otherwise, it will provide grounds for the insurance company to deny your claim. Insurance companies are strict about risk management and assessing risk. Premiums are commensurate with risk. Alternatively, they may decline to cover you, increase the premium, limit certain types of coverage, or ask for a large deductible in the event of a claim. Keep copies of all correspondence between you and your insurance company, as well as any receipts for items to be claimed for reimbursement.

Here is a brief overview of the three common types of out-of-country emergency insurance plan options.

Extended-Stay insurance

This coverage is intended to protect you for the whole duration of your travel or stay in the United States, Mexico, or elsewhere, for a continuous period. The premium is based on the duration of your stay, for example, up to 6 months. You pay for the exact number of days you need.

Multitrip insurance

This plan is designed to cover a shorter-term stay coverage outside Canada. You arrange coverage for a packaged number of days, for example, a maximum single-duration stay not exceeding 5, 10, 15, 30, 45, 90 days, etc. This means you can travel outside Canada as many times as you like within the length of your policy coverage, as long as any one trip does not exceed your maximum number of days per trip (e.g., 5–90, etc.). As soon as you return to Canada for at least 1 day, the cycle starts again.

These multitrip plans are usually based on an annual premium, for example, covering a calendar-year period or 12 months from the time you take it out. One of the key benefits of a multitrip plan is that it is available for spontaneous trips any time you cross the Canada-U.S. border or go to any other country. You can obtain multitrip plans through travel agents, banks, and some credit card companies or from insurers directly.

Top-Up insurance

This plan provides additional supplemental emergency medical coverage to top up an existing out-of-country medical plan. This existing plan could be covered as a retiree from a government, other employer, union or association plan, or credit card plan. Alternatively, you could pay for the top-up yourself. There are risks, however, with this top-up approach. Some plans don't permit top-ups. There can be great differences between different plan policies. There is a risk that there could be a lapse in time periods between coverage, or disputes between different insurers as to the issue of coverage. For example, if your basic medical plan coverage has a ceiling cap of $50,000 and lasts for a maximum number of days, and your top-up plan kicks in at the end of that time period, what happens if you have a catastrophic injury just before the first plan lapses? You are only covered for $50,000. Your expenses could be $200,000. You would be out the difference. Another problem could arise if the top-up company deems your illness was pre-existing, if you make a claim with your first insurer first. An alternative is to coordinate a basic plan and top-up plan from the same insurer.

It is generally less expensive and less risky to just have one plan cover everything. It certainty eliminates the uncertainty and saves the inconvenience and frustration of having to deal with two different claims procedures.

Workers' Compensation

If you have employees who, in the course of their daily work, may suffer personal injury, you should make certain that they are covered by Workers' Compensation insurance. This insurance covers all costs that may occur due to an injury to an employee. If you do not have coverage, and your type of business requires it, you could be personally liable for all medical and other disability losses incurred. Note: Some types of work, such as desk-type jobs, which have low injury risk, are exempt from Workers' Compensation regulations. Check with your provincial coverage and requirements.

Surety and Fidelity Bonds

Many people are confused by the terms surety or fidelity bonds. Bonding is a common requirement in business, depending on the nature of the business. A surety bond or guarantee bond is a contract between two parties and the bonding company relating to performance of a contractual obligation. Examples include following through on a bid, a performance of a construction contract, or supplying a product. The bonding company is called a surety and guarantees that the party obligated to do so meet its obligations. If the contractual obligations are not met, the bonding company pays out the amount of money in the bond agreement described. A fidelity bond is purchased by one who desires protection against the acts of others. An example would be protection against theft by a person cleaning a building under a maintenance contract.

Many insurance brokers also provide bonding services, although it is a specialized area. Look in the *Yellow Pages* print and online under "Bonds—Surety and Fidelity." Make sure you obtain competitive quotations from at least three advisors. This will provide you with an objective basis for comparison and selection. Refer to the section on "Selecting an Insurance Representative" in Chapter 4.

When starting a business, it is common for people to want to save on expenses whenever possible. This is a good attitude to have, but when it comes to insurance, it is important to be realistic and prudent. You have to weigh the risks and potential personal financial exposure if you have no insurance or inadequate coverage. Look upon insurance premiums as an additional cost of doing business, and budget accordingly.

Chapter 21

Time and Stress Management

Do not squander time, for that is the stuff life is made of.

—Ben Franklin

Time is a precious and limited resource. We are each given 24 hours in a day to spend whichever way we please. However, if we don't use our time wisely today, we cannot take it with us into tomorrow; whatever is wasted is lost forever. When managing a business, there are numerous demands placed on your time, and you will want to make the most efficient use of it. In your business plan, you have outlined a number of your goals and objectives, and you will need an action plan to keep you on track. Effective time management means organizing your day so that you accomplish your goals and objectives within the time frames you have established. You may not be able to complete all of your tasks; some will have to be deferred until the next day, and others will have to be delegated to others. To be a good manager, you must be able to set priorities and decide which tasks should be delegated and which ones should not.

When you become overburdened with a heavy workload and fatigue from working long hours, there is usually a buildup of negative stress. It is commonly viewed that stress is a bad thing and dangerous to our health. On the contrary, most people work most effectively while under a tolerable amount of stress. And the absence of any stress in one's life usually leads to severe depression and feelings of low self-worth. It is necessary, therefore, to distinguish between positive stress, which is a motivator, and negative stress, which endangers your personal and business health.

POSITIVE STRESS

Positive stress can be defined as the stress of pleasure, challenge, and fulfillment. All activities involve stress, from a game of tennis to writing a business proposal. In fact, the motivating factors that influence a person to start a business—risk, drive, challenge, fulfillment—can be viewed as positive stressors. A person with a high degree of self-confidence will usually have a correspondingly high degree of positive stress. A sense of being in control enables a person to handle minor setbacks within the scope of day-to-day activities. Stress is a very individual reaction. An activity such as making a presentation at a business meeting will affect people differently. One person will display confidence and enthusiasm, while another will become extremely nervous and perhaps nauseous. What we want is the right amount of stress for the right length of time—at a level that is best suited for us. To know what this level is, we should look at circumstances in which we have gone beyond this level and which led to distress.

NEGATIVE STRESS

When the activities that bring us positive stress are insufficient, excessive, or inappropriate, then frustration, discomfort, disease, or psychosomatic illness (negative stress) may result. Negative stress is typically referred to as a loss of control. By examining your own behaviour in previous circumstances in which you have been under a great deal of pressure, you may be able to identify characteristics of which you are not particularly proud. Think of a situation in which you have been impatient with staff, curt with your answers, or guilty of shouting. Often in hindsight, we can clearly see how the situation could have been handled quite differently if we had regained control before permitting an emotional response. Looking into the root of the situation, you may be able to attribute the cause of your negative behaviour to being late for a deadline or appointment, a missed opportunity, too heavy a workload, fatigue, feeling out of control, someone else's mistake, or being treated unfairly.

The purpose of delving into past experiences is not to relive them and burden ourselves with guilt, which is a type of self-induced stress. Rather, we should learn from these experiences the circumstances that typically lead to such negative stress. Then, when we see ourselves falling into the same trap, we can take measures to alter the outcome of the situation. For instance, a person who has an extremely heavy workload and is frustrated by always being behind schedule should practise effective time management techniques, delegate responsibilities to others or hire part-time staff, and reduce his or her expectations of what can be reasonably accomplished in a normal workday. Or the person who feels he or she is being treated unfairly may decide to take an assertiveness training course to build self-confidence and composure when faced with difficult situations. Staff errors could be reduced by providing additional training and outlining procedures carefully in writing and circulating them to all staff.

The person who feels out of control should recognize the danger of no one being at the helm of the ship. It is necessary to step back and look objectively at the situation and make a list of all your frustrations. This can sometimes best be done with another person who knows you and your business well: a partner, a senior staff person, a business advisor. You should refer back to your business plan and see if you are still on track, if you need to expand, or hold back for a future planned expansion. Possibly your business goals are no longer appropriate in light of current circumstances and have to be revised.

As individuals, we all react to stressful situations in different ways. Some people are able to conceal their expressions of negative emotions, but carry them inside and start to feel a mounting pressure. Often this type of individual will suffer from hypertension, insomnia, headaches, ulcers, and other physical signs of the negative stress. If your body starts to show symptoms of stress, it is necessary to take an honest and objective look at your personal and business life. It may also mean that you are neglecting your physical health. A healthy diet and regular exercise are necessary to keep your mind alert and your body fit to handle a challenging and longer workday. You must take action to reduce the negative stress.

TIME MANAGEMENT TECHNIQUES

Like any other valuable resource, time can be managed. The better it is managed, the more productive and profitable your business will be. All the other acquired skills you possess will lose much of their effectiveness if you are disorganized. As you probably will not have the time to attend to all the matters requiring your attention, you must ensure that the important tasks get done. Prioritize activities that generate continued profitability and future growth. By using some of the following proven techniques, you can considerably increase your efficiency, productivity, and satisfaction.

Set Priorities

Based on the goals you have established for your business, set your high, medium, and low priorities. Write them down. High-priority items are those that are vital to the business, have a deadline affixed to them, and usually need your personal attention. Medium-priority tasks are necessary to the business, but may not require your immediate attention; perhaps some of these tasks could be delegated. Low-priority items may be postponed to a more convenient time or not done at all.

It is not sufficient to know in your mind what has to be done. Making a list of your "to do" jobs enables you to plan your day effectively. A Day-Timer, computerized pocket organizer, or similar day calendar system is a useful tool. At the end of each day, list and classify the next day's jobs into A, B, and C priority. The A items are those you must accomplish today. B items may be accomplished today, or could be dealt with tomorrow as an A priority job. The C items may be used as filler jobs at the end of your day or at a time when your concentration is not sufficient to handle an A or B priority job. Examples of A priority jobs are writing paycheques, if it's the 15th day of the month; drafting a proposal for a bid on a large contract which closes in 3 days' time; telephoning the airlines to make a flight reservation on the last day of the discount rate period (may be a B priority if you can delegate it to someone else to do as their A priority). As each job is completed, cross it off your list. At the end of the day, those items not crossed off must be carried over to the next day, along with any new jobs that might have arisen. At the end of each week, list those items that need to be accomplished the following week.

Keeping a "to do" list provides a source of satisfaction and feeling of progress as items are crossed off. It can also alleviate the stress that results from trying to remember everything that has to be done.

Dealing with the high-priority items first is a particularly effective time management technique. By handling a critical task early in your day, you have the reward of feeling a sense of accomplishment. Often this provides additional motivation and drive to maintain the productivity momentum. If there are unexpected interruptions, or minor problems arise, you are able to devote attention to them, knowing that you have already dealt with your top-priority item. If on the other hand, you defer your high-priority item until the afternoon, chances are that problems will arise that prevent you from getting to that high-priority task. As there can be a daily stream of unexpected interruptions, some people operate day after day in this time trap, never getting to those critical tasks.

In order to accomplish your high-priority tasks, it will be necessary to have a block of uninterrupted time. Ask your staff to hold all calls for the first hour of each day, or have your calls answered by a professional answering service to present a positive business image, or have your calls go into voice mail and your cell phone and e-mail notify you of the voice mail message with a voice clip, who phoned, and when. Schedule other blocks of time necessary to fully complete a priority task.

Avoid procrastination. If one of your critical tasks doesn't have a built-in deadline, set one. In this way, you will ensure that it gets to the top of your priority list. Perhaps you are having trouble starting a major project because it appears to be massive and you don't know where to begin. It is helpful to divide the major project into manageable stages. For instance, when preparing a bank loan proposal, one day's task may be to make a list of all the items you will include in your proposal. The other stages will be preparing each of the items on your list: sales projection charts, net worth statement, marketing concept, and loan rationale. Handling a large project in this manner of bite-size pieces, it is conceivable that the task could be accomplished within a week.

Be Organized

If you make a habit of writing everything in your Day-Timer or diary, or Smartphone calendaras soon as you become aware of an event, you will avoid double-booking appointments or forgetting them. You may decide to schedule your appointments for the afternoon whenever possible, to allow your morning to be a free block of time during which you can accomplish items on your "to do" list. When scheduling your workday, allow yourself some flexibility and leeway, as things don't always go according to plan. Allow sufficient time so that each task can be carried out in a thorough, unhurried manner.

Having an up-to-date and efficient filing system will enable you to find your files quickly. On the other hand, keeping every piece of paper that comes across your desk in an escalating stack, or in overstuffed files, only creates frustration and delay when you are trying to locate a piece of information. Of course you will need to keep a copy of your important correspondence, proposals, and bookkeeping records. But filing space is expensive. Before filing a piece of paper you need to ask yourself, "Will I ever have to refer back to this? Can I get another copy of this if sometime in the future I need to refer to it?"

For example, keeping a copy of equipment suppliers' brochures and price lists is usually unnecessary. Chances are that when you decide to purchase that type of equipment, the brochure and price list will be out of date, and a newer model of equipment will be available. Another example may be copies of newsletters, agendas, and minutes of meetings of the professional association of which you are a member. Unless you are on the executive committee or have a specific need to refer to such dated material, it can consume a lot of file space and never be referred to after it has been filed. If you do need to refer back to an item, a master set will be available at the association office.

There is much to be said for the person who is able to keep a tidy work space. While many defend their cluttered desks by saying, "I know exactly where everything is," it is not known how much time is wasted shuffling papers. The hidden time waster is the distraction created by a cluttered work area. Instead of having a clear train of thought when working on the critical priority items, a casual glance at the clutter may trigger numerous reminders of things that must be done. This could create unnecessary delays in completing the immediate task, as well as cause extra stress and a feeling of being overwhelmed.

Being prepared for meetings and appointments saves time otherwise spent in prolonged discussions. Before the meeting, you should review your file, make notes, prepare an agenda and stick to it. Anticipating potential problems will enable you to have an action plan ready to implement, rather than merely reacting to events as they occur.

Delegate

As your staff increases and your company expands, it will be necessary for you to delegate some of your responsibilities to others. At times it will appear easier to do it yourself than to train, supervise, and check someone else's work. You are quite right—at least for the first time and perhaps the second time. However, once you have trained someone in how to handle the task, your time can be spent elsewhere. It is necessary that your employee, in addition to carrying out the task, has sufficient scope and authority to make decisions within the responsibility. Delegating the authority builds staff morale, competence, and motivation.

Learn to say no. You may receive a request, for example, to participate in a community activity that will require taking time from your business day. Knowing your daily workload and having the ability to say no is important to your time management.

Be Decisive

Preciseness in identifying problems and decisiveness in the actions to be taken will save time in your workday. Similar to the technique used with large or insurmountable tasks, by breaking a problem down into different parts you can see more clearly the root of the problem. To resolve it, then, list the various alternatives and rate the degree of effectiveness of each. Practising this technique will help you develop the ability to go through this process quickly in your mind. This will enhance your effectiveness in resolving small problems before they escalate into larger ones.

The art of speaking and writing concisely is a time saver for you and your associates. It will also foster improved communication between you and your staff and customers. The effective use of e-mail and voice mail messaging can greatly enhance your time management.

AVOID TIME WASTERS

Voice mail

Allows customers to send voice mail messages to you directly. It creates a better impression than a telephone answering machine and is far more versatile. A full 75% of all business calls are not completed on the first attempt. The effect is an incredible amount of wasted time and energy. Here are some prime examples of the benefits of office or personal voice mail:

- **Reduces "telephone tag."** Lets people communicate the complete message without regard for confidentiality or complexity of the information. More accurate and private than pink slips. Messages are in the caller's own voice, with all the original intonations and inflections.
- **Saves time and money on long-distance charges.** When messages are left on voice mail, calls are invariably shorter, as the caller gets right to

the point. Live communications encourage "chit-chat"—wasting time and money. When you are out of town, you can call in to the voice mail to receive your messages in the evening when the long distance rates are lower.

- **Eases the time zone/business hour dilemma.** No more waiting until noon (or rising at 6:00 a.m.) to call the other coast. This will save a lot of time and inconvenience.
- **Increases productivity of staff.** Instead of staff answering many phone calls and taking messages, staff can be more efficient and do additional tasks or provide more personal service to callers who wish to bypass the voice mail and speak directly to a receptionist or secretary.
- **Cuts down on paging and holding times.** Caller can go directly to voice mail rather than waiting on hold.
- **Voice mail/autoattendant works 365 days a year, 24 hours a day.** You can phone in anytime from anywhere to receive your messages with a confidential access number. The voice mail system can route callers to appropriate voice mailboxes, take messages, play customized greetings depending on the time of day or evening, offer other mailbox menu selections for specific information, and perform many other features, as noted below.
- **Automatic relaying of all voice mail messages.** Your voice mail can be programmed to call you as soon as messages are left on the service. You can leave or program instructions as to where calls should be directed (cellular, pager, home, or associate's number) as they are received. You can also have your e-mail or text messaging automatically notified that there is a message for you, who it is from, and the phone number and time, as well as a voice mail clip of the actual message.
- **Fax response option.** This means that a caller can phone a voice mailbox number, input his or her fax number, and your fax message is instantly transmitted to the caller's fax machine. You can store on the computer any number of pages to be transmitted automatically upon request.

E-mail

As you know, e-mail can be a great time saver when used effectively and efficiently. Conversely, it can be a great time waster. It all depends on how you control your e-mail communication protocols and triage priorities.

- Communicating with others in different time zones is greatly enhanced with e-mail. The business day virtually becomes 24 hours long. When an e-mail request is sent at 9:00 a.m. Toronto time, for instance, it awaits the Vancouver recipient's 9:00 a.m. arrival which is by then 12:00 noon in Toronto. If the response is completed by 5:00 p.m. Vancouver time (8:00 p.m. in Toronto), the business activity stretched 11 hours! Thus, a lot more can be accomplished within a week doing business in this manner. If these two individuals tried to rely on telephone conversations, their business communication time is reduced to 4 hours (subtracting 2 hours for their respective lunch breaks).

- Costs are considerably less, as there are no long distance telephone charges.
- Messages are briefer and to the point. The formalities typical of business letter writing are omitted and replaced by informal greetings and sign-offs. Formatting is simplified and expedient, with less time being spent making it "look nice" for the reader, as with business letters.
- When receiving an e-mail message, it is quick and easy to send a brief acknowledgement or reply by selecting the "reply to" option on the e-mail program menu. The recipient's address, as well as your own, is automatically inserted for you.
- It is easy to send a copy of the message to other parties for their information, action, or response by adding their e-mail addresses. In this way, you can receive group feedback on a proposal within a short time frame.

Strategies such as setting priorities, staying organized, delegating, being decisive and concise will help you to sharpen your time management skills and likewise respect the time of your business associates. However, you may find that external factors over which you have less control still rob your time. Following are some tips on being assertive, saying "no," and, in general, avoiding time wasters.

Too Many Telephone Calls

Ensure that written and verbal telephone messages are complete. Knowing not only the name and phone number of the person calling but also the purpose of the call enables you to deal with the response quickly and effectively, often delegating the response to someone else. Bunch your calls before lunch or towards the end of the day, when people are less likely to chat. Use e-mail or voice mail messages instead of a telephone call when one-way transfer of information is all that is required.

Overscheduling/Too Many Things to Do

Concentrate on important items and disregard trivia. Use your personal computer and smartphone or written diary to plan your day and prepare a priority list of tasks. Learn to say no. Delegate.

Too Much Paper

Deal with each piece of paper only once. If it is junk mail, throw it out. Request to be taken off the distribution list of unknown faxes and junk e-mail. If it is for the file, file it immediately. If it requires a response, a handwritten response or a telephone call may suffice. Or delegate routine matters to another staff member. By handling your morning mail in this manner, you will avoid tomorrow's task of dealing with the paperwork you set aside today.

Reading Reports/Trade Magazines

Have someone else highlight the important parts for you. Learn to skim or speed-read. Skip to the summary or recommendations. Review the table of contents of magazines and read only those articles of specific interest. Skip to the highlighted sections or main points; usually the essence is given in the first two paragraphs.

Unexpected Visitors

Keep the visit brief. Conduct stand-up meetings. Once someone is settled into a comfortable chair in your office with a coffee in hand, a good portion of your day could disappear. Arrange to meet the person for lunch or after work for an extended discussion.

Scheduled Meetings

Be certain they start and end on time, and follow the agenda. Keep on topic. Ensure that a summary is given, noting any action to be taken after the meeting and by whom.

Errors

Draw conclusions from errors made, and avoid repetition. Perhaps retraining of personnel is necessary or instructions need to be clarified. Have job procedures detailed in writing and included in your procedures manual for circulation and future reference. Ask the person in the position to draft the detailed job procedures for your later review. This also helps reinforce to the individual the step-by-step process involved.

Lack of Communication

State clearly what is expected when assigning work. If the work is submitted in an unfinished manner, rather than correcting it yourself (also known as upward delegation), return it in a tactful manner with an explanation of the finishing touches required. This will also help the employee's personal growth and understanding of the business. Encourage staff to ask questions if they are uncertain—remember, dumb questions are easier to handle than dumb mistakes!

Perfectionism

Striving for excellence is healthy, gratifying, and attainable. However, aiming for perfection is frustrating, neurotic, and a waste of time.

Fatigue

If you find you are unable to work productively owing to fatigue, take time to relax and refresh yourself. Stretch, take a break from what you are doing, take a short walk. You will find that when you return, so has your energy and concentration. Eat regularly but sparingly, and avoid alcohol.

KEEPING A TIME LOG

A helpful tool to demonstrate how effectively or poorly you are managing your time is to keep a daily time log for a random week. This in itself is a time-consuming task, as it means you need to record minute by minute how you spend your time. It will include the telephone calls you make, those you receive, the tasks you accomplish on your priority list, the interruptions you receive, what you read, what you write, and so on. A time log is shown in Sample 34. After completing a week of such logs, you need to review them and assess the portion of your day that is spent productively. The logs will also show the time wasters which repeatedly frustrate accomplishments. Once you have this information, you are better able to plan your day and to block out interruptions. For example, you may set aside an hour or two of uninterrupted time for your priority tasks. You may train your staff on the procedures for handling certain tasks, thereby delegating the responsibility to them.

From time to time you may choose to repeat the time log exercise to check back on your degree of success in time management. As situations change, new time wasters may appear. Deal with them. Sample 35 shows a weekly time analysis which may be helpful in summarizing your completed daily time logs. By rating yourself on your use of time management techniques, you will identify your strong and weak areas. Asking yourself questions such as, "What else could I delegate?" and "How can I reduce or eliminate specific time wasters?" will help you to focus on developing good habits. The weekly time-use analysis is an effective planning and management tool. Write it in your diary and do it! You can also maintain a log online or through business management computer software or smartphone software, of course.

Remember: time is money. And, while labour costs are high, as the owner-manager your time is worth the most. By ensuring your time is well spent managing and planning for growth of the business, you will enable your staff to learn useful techniques from you. They will become more productive in the day-to-day running of your business.

Conclusion

To get profit without risk, experience without danger, and reward without work is as impossible as it is to live without being born.

— A. P. Gouthey

Now that you have read this far, perhaps you should regard this book as just a beginning. Perhaps the time is right for you to consider the exciting, stimulating, and challenging world called entrepreneurship. Perhaps you have already made that commitment. If you have gone through all the chapters relevant to your business interest, and have completed the relevant checklists, you have certainly exhibited those precious qualities so essential to operating a successful business—qualities such as initiative, drive, resourcefulness, and the desire for knowledge.

But how is success really measured? Like beauty, it is often in the eyes of the beholder. It is difficult to apply an objective formula to a subjective test. If you decide to embark on an entrepreneurial career, and you feel a high degree of joy and satisfaction from accomplishing your goals, surmounting obstacles, doing your best, and receiving the respect of those important to you, then you have attained success.

Are monetary rewards a test of personal success? Although the money you make is necessary for basic comfort needs, it is generally just a yardstick for evaluating the results of your business efforts. Different people, of course, have different and changing needs. In a national survey, people listed their criteria for personal success from the most important to the least important in the following order: good health, enjoyable job, happy family, quality relationships, good education, peace of mind, good friends, intelligence, unlimited money, luxury car, and an expensive home.

If you have decided to satisfy the dream to be your own boss, take the first step and complete Sample 36, "Action Plan Checklist."

If you would like to know about our small business seminars and programs to help you achieve entrepreneurial success, or would like to provide us with your feedback, please refer to the last page of the book for our contact information. Our website is: smallbiz.ca.

We wish you success, good fortune, and happiness!

Samples and Checklists

SAMPLE 1
(See Chapter 2)

Personal Net Worth Statement
(Format Commonly Requested by Lenders)

Name	Date of Birth	Social Insurance Number

Street Address	City	Province	Postal Code

Home Phone _____   Residence   How long at address?

Office Phone _____   ____Own ____Rent   ____Years ____Months

Fax _____   ____Other

E-mail _____

Occupation   Currently employed with: How long with employer?

Employer's Phone   ____Years ____Months

____Married   ____Unmarried   ____Separated

Number of dependents ____

Your principal financial institution and address

Personal Data on Your Spouse

(Under the laws of Canada or the provinces your spouse may have a legal interest or obligation arising from your business dealings and may also have an interest in your personal assets.)

Spouse's Name   Spouse's Occupation

Spouse currently   How long with employer?   Spouse's work phone
employed by   ____Years ____Months

Financial Information

As at _____ (day) _____ , _____ (month) _____ , 20____

SAMPLE 1 Continued

Assets

(List and describe all assets)   **Value**

Total of chequing accounts	$ _____
Total of savings accounts	$ _____
Life insurance cash surrender value	$ _____
Automobile: Make _____ Year_____	$ _____
Stocks and bonds (See Schedule A attached)	$ _____
Accounts/Notes receivable (please itemize) _____	$ _____
_____	$ _____
_____	$ _____
Term deposits (cashable)	$ _____
Real estate (See Schedule B attached)	$ _____

Retirement plans

RRSP	_____	$ _____
Employment Pension Plan	_____	$ _____
Other	_____	$ _____

Other Assets (household goods, etc.)

Art	_____	$ _____
Jewelry	_____	$ _____
Antiques	_____	$ _____
Other	_____	$ _____

Total Assets (A) $ _____

Liabilities

(List credit cards, open lines of credit, and other liabilities—including alimony and child support)	Balance Owing	Monthly Payment
Bank loans	$ _____	$ _____
Mortgages on real estate owned	$ _____	$ _____
(see Schedule B attached)	$ _____	$ _____
	$ _____	$ _____

	Balance Owing	Monthly Payment
Monthly rent payment	$ _____	$ _____
Credit cards (please itemize) _____	$ _____	$ _____
_____	$ _____	$ _____
_____	$ _____	$ _____
_____	$ _____	$ _____
Money borrowed from life insurance policy	$ _____	$ _____
Margin accounts	$ _____	$ _____
Current income tax owing	$ _____	$ _____
Other obligations (please itemize) _____	$ _____	$ _____
_____	$ _____	$ _____
_____	$ _____	$ _____
Total monthly payments		$ _____
Total Liabilities (B)	$ _____	
Net Worth (A – B)	$ _____	

Income Sources

Income from alimony, child support, or separate maintenance does not have to be stated unless you want it considered.

Your gross monthly salary	$ _____
Your spouse's gross monthly salary	$ _____
Net monthly rental (from Schedule B attached)	$ _____
Other income (please itemize) _____	$ _____
_____	$ _____
_____	$ _____
Total	$ _____

Sundry Personal Obligations

Please provide details below if you answer Yes to the following question.

Are you providing your personal support for obligations not listed above (i.e., co-signer, endorser, guarantor, indemnifier)?___ Yes ___ No

Details of any of the above:

SAMPLE 1 Continued

Schedule A—Stocks, Bonds, and Other Investments

Quantity	Description	Where Quoted	Market Value	Pledged as Collateral Yes	No
		Total			

Schedule B—Real Estate Owned

Please provide information on your share only of real estate owned.

Property address (primary residence) Legal description

_____

Street   City   Province

Type of property   Present market value   Amount of mortgage liens

$ _____ 1st $ _____

                                    2nd $ _____

Gross monthly   Monthly mortgage payments

income rental   1st $ _____

$ _____ 2nd $ _____

Monthly taxes, insurance,   Net monthly rental income
maintenance, and miscellaneous

$ _____ $ _____

Name of   First mortgage   Second mortgage
mortgage
holder(s)

Percentage ownership   Month/Year acquired   Purchase price

                                           $
% _____

General Information

Please provide details if you answer Yes to any of the following questions.

Have you ever had an asset repossessed? ____Yes ____No

Are you party to any claims or lawsuits? ____Yes ____No

Have you ever declared bankruptcy? ____Yes ____No

Do you owe any taxes prior to the current year? ____Yes ____No
Details:

_____

The undersigned declare(s) that the statements made herein are for the purpose of obtaining business financing and are to the best of my/our knowledge true and correct. The applicant(s) consent(s) to the Bank making any inquiries it deems necessary to reach a decision on this application, and consent(s) to the disclosure at any time of any credit information about me/us to any credit- reporting agency or to anyone with whom I/we have financial relations.

Date	Signature of Applicant(s) Above

SAMPLE 2
(See Chapter 2)
Personal Cost-of-Living Budget

A. Income (Average monthly income—actual or estimate)

Salary, bonuses, and commissions $ _____

Dividends $ _____

Interest income $ _____

Pension income $ _____

Other _____ $ _____

_____ $ _____

Total Monthly Income $ _____

B. Expenses
Regular Monthly Payments

Rent or mortgage payments $ _____

Automobile(s) $ _____

Appliances/TV $ _____

Home improvement loan $ _____

SAMPLE 2 Continued

Credit card payments (not covered elsewhere) $ _____

Personal loan $ _____

Medical plan $ _____

Installment and other loans $ _____

Life insurance premiums $ _____

House insurance $ _____

Other insurance premiums (e.g., auto, extended medical, etc.) $ _____

RRSP deductions $ _____

Pension fund (employer) $ _____

Investment plan(s) $ _____

Other _____ $ _____

_____ $ _____

Miscellaneous $ _____

Total Regular Monthly Payments $ _____

Household Operating Expenses

Telephone $ _____

Gas and electricity $ _____

Heat $ _____

Water and garbage $ _____

Internet access charges (ISP) and cable/satellite $ _____

Other household expenses (repairs, maintenance, etc.) $ _____

Other _____ $ _____

_____ $ _____

Total Household Operating Expenses $ _____

Food Expenses

Food—at home $ _____

Food—away from home $ _____

Total Food Expenses $ _____

Personal Expenses

Clothing, cleaning, laundry $ _____

Drugs $ _____

Transportation (other than auto) $ _____

Medical/dental $ _____

Daycare $ _____

Education (self) $ _____

Education (children) $ _____

Dues $ _____

Gifts and donations $ _____

Travel $ _____

Recreation $ _____

Newspapers, magazines, books $ _____

Automobile maintenance, gas, and parking $ _____

Spending money, allowances $ _____

Other _____ $ _____

_____ $ _____

Total Personal Expenses $ _____

Tax Expenses

Federal and provincial income taxes $ _____

Home property taxes $ _____

Other _____ $ _____

_____ $ _____

Total Tax Expenses $ _____

C. **Summary of Expenses**

Regular monthly payments $ _____

Household operating expenses $ _____

Food expenses $ _____

Personal expenses $ _____

Tax expenses $ _____

Total Monthly Expenses $ _____

Total Monthly Disposable Income Available $ _____
(Subtract total monthly expenses from
total monthly income)

SAMPLE 3
(See Chapter 2)

Financial Needs for First 3 Months

		Expense	Date Due

A. Personal Living Expenses

From last paycheque to opening day of
business (shortfall in income) $ _____ _____

For 3 months after opening day (from
Sample 2, "Personal Cost-of-Living Budget") $ _____ _____

Other _____ $ _____ _____

_____ $ _____ _____

Total Personal Living Expenses $ _____

B. Deposits, Prepayments, Licences

First and last months' business rent $ _____ _____

Second and third months' business rent $ _____ _____

Telephone installation and utility deposits $ _____ _____

Sales tax deposit (if applicable) $ _____ _____

Business licences $ _____ _____

Insurance premiums for business, personal,
auto, travel, theft, fire, liability, disability, etc.
(State quarterly, semi-annual, or annual
payments) $ _____ _____

Other _____ $ _____ _____

_____ $ _____ _____

Total Deposits, Prepayments and Licences $ _____

C. Leasehold Improvements

Remodelling and redecorating $ _____ _____

Fixtures, equipment, displays $ _____ _____

Installation, labour $ _____ _____

Signs—outside and inside $ _____ _____

Other _____ $ _____ _____

_____ $ _____ _____

Total Leasehold Improvements $ _____

	Expense	Date Due

D. Extraordinary Start-Up Expenses
(Required primarily for first 3 months, rather than a regular ongoing expense)

Legal, accounting, consulting $ _____ _____

Supplies and stationery $ _____ _____

Fixtures, equipment $ _____ _____

Furniture $ _____ _____

Opening day announcements, advertising, pamphlets, etc. $ _____ _____

Other _____ $ _____ _____

_____ $ _____ _____

Total Extraordinary Start-Up Expenses $ _____

E. Inventory

Delivery of merchandise or inventory $ _____ _____

Merchandise (approximately two-thirds of this amount generally invested in opening stock) $ _____ _____

Other _____ $ _____ _____

_____ $ _____ _____

Total Inventory $ _____

Total operating expenses for first 3 months (from Sample 8 "Income Statement")—
projected, or multiply average month x 3 $ _____

Reserve to carry customers' accounts $ _____

Cash for petty cash, change, etc. $ _____

Contingency reserve for unexpected expenses $ _____

Other _____ $ _____ _____

_____ $ _____ _____

Total Financial Needs for First 3 Months $ _____

SAMPLE 4
(See Chapter 2)

Business Plan Outline

A. Table of Contents

B. Summary (1–2 pages)
   1. Business description (existing or proposed):
      - name
      - product or service
      - location and plant description (if applicable)
      - market and competition
      - management expertise
      - history of the company
   2. Business goals (short-term 0–2 years, medium-term 3–5 years, long-term over 5 years)
   3. Summary of financial needs and application of funds
   4. Summary of earnings projections and potential return to investors, if applicable
   5. Security you are prepared to pledge (if applicable)

C. Market Analysis and Strategy
   1. Description of total market
   2. Industry trends (past, present, and future)
   3. Target market
   4. Your competition
   5. Your marketing advantage/niche
   6. Risks
   7. Your past sales and future sales projections
   8. Your pricing policy
   9. Your selling terms (credit policy)
   10. Your distribution plan
   11. Your marketing plan/strategy
   12. Your promotion plans
   13. Your methods of selling
   14. Your product servicing plan

D. Products or Services
   1. Description of products and/or services, including an assessment of their strengths and weaknesses
   2. Proprietary position: patents, copyrights, trade secrets, and legal and technical considerations
   3. Technologies used
   4. Comparison to competitors' products

E. Land, Buildings, and Equipment
   1. Location:
      - give description
      - provide reason for locating where you have

2. Provide details as to the amount of land required, site plan, costs of land and buildings, including installation of services
3. List all machinery and equipment required:
   - indicate costs and installation charges
   - indicate from whom and where purchases are to be made
4. If leasing land, buildings, and equipment, describe the lease terms and costs

F. Operations
1. Workflow:
   - provide diagrams if applicable
   - type of quality control procedures
2. Inventory control
3. Supplies and materials: availability of supplies, costs, and terms
4. Employees:
   - include informal job descriptions along with organization chart
   - give salary or wage schedules
   - number of employees required (part-time and full-time)
5. Manufacturing costs
6. Operations schedule:
   - key events and decision points
   - time schedule

G. Management
1. Form of business organization
2. Board of directors composition (if corporation)
3. Officers: organization chart and responsibilities (if corporation)
4. List of owners/shareholders, addresses, and percent equity in business
5. Résumés of key personnel

H. Financial Data
1. Five-year financial projections with explanations (first year by quarters, remaining years annually):
   - first 3 months' financial needs
   - capital expenditure estimates
   - profit-and-loss statements
   - balance sheets
   - cash flow charts
   - break-even charts
2. Explanation of projections
3. Key business ratios applicable
4. Explanation of use of new funds
5. Potential return to investors: comparison to average return in the industry as a whole (if applicable)

I. Summary and Analysis of Major Risks and Significant Opportunities
II. 1. SWOT Analysis (Strengths, Weaknesses, Opportunities, Threats)

SAMPLE 4 Continued

J. References
1. Name of banks or other lenders with whom you have had financial dealings (outline types of loans, terms, etc., previously held)
2. Name and particulars of your accountant
3. Name and particulars of your lawyer
4. Name and particulars of your consultants

K. Appendices
(Not all these items will be applicable, necessary, or available)
1. Personal financial net worth statement
2. Detailed management biographies
3. List of assets with full description, identification numbers, etc.
4. List of inventory with designation
5. List of leasehold improvements and/or fixtures with description
6. Product or service literature, brochures, etc.
7. Letters of intent
8. Letters of reference
9. Patents, copyrights, and trademarks documentation
10. Major contracts
11. Lease documentation
12. Recent evaluation of assets
13. Market research, engineering, or other studies
14. Recent accountant's financial reports (if applicable)
15. Details of insurance coverage
16. Accounts receivable summary
17. Accounts payable summary
18. Copies of advertising and promotional material

SAMPLE 5
(See Chapter 2)

Business Regulations

Business Regulations/Legislation	Applies To Me	Does Not Apply To Me	Need Further Info	Further Info Obtained
A. Municipal				
• City Business Permit	_____	_____	_____	_____
• Zoning Bylaws (opening hours and location)	_____	_____	_____	_____
• Zoning Bylaws (noise, fumes, etc.)				
• Zoning Bylaws (home-based business)	_____	_____	_____	_____
• Health Regulations (preparation of food, removal of waste products, training of staff, etc.)	_____	_____	_____	_____
• Land Use Regulations	_____	_____	_____	_____

Business Regulations/Legislation	Applies To Me	Does Not Apply To Me	Need Further Info	Further Info Obtained
• Business Taxes	___	___	___	___
• Property Taxes	___	___	___	___
• School Taxes	___	___	___	___
• Water Taxes	___	___	___	___
• Building Permits (applicable to alteration also)	___	___	___	___
• Building Codes (plumbing, electrical, fire, and health hazards)	___	___	___	___
• Other: _____	___	___	___	___

B. Provincial

	Applies To Me	Does Not Apply To Me	Need Further Info	Further Info Obtained
• Business Registration (proprietorship, partnership, and/or trade style name)				
• Bulk Sales	___	___	___	___
• Director's liability to statutory creditors (that is, to provincial government departments with such legislation and claim rights, such as employment standards, Workers' Compensation Board, sales tax, environmental protection, human rights, etc.)	___	___	___	___
• Incorporation (provincial charter)	___	___	___	___
• Land Use Regulations (certain provinces)	___	___	___	___
• Environmental Protection Regulations	___	___	___	___
• Provincial Business Licence	___	___	___	___
• Provincial Income Tax (corporate or personal)	___	___	___	___
• Quebec Place of Business Tax (Quebec only)	___	___	___	___
• Provincial Sales Tax	___	___	___	___
• Provincial Building Codes (electrical apparatus and equipment, fire and health hazards)	___	___	___	___
• Minimum Age for Employment	___	___	___	___
• Minimum Wage for Employment	___	___	___	___
• Trade Practices	___	___	___	___
• Consumer Protection	___	___	___	___
• Sale of Goods	___	___	___	___
• Hours of Employment	___	___	___	___
• Annual Vacations and Public Holidays	___	___	___	___

SAMPLE 5 Continued

Business Regulations/Legislation	Applies To Me	Does Not Apply To Me	Need Further Info	Further Info Obtained
• Human Rights	_____	_____	_____	_____
• Pay Equity	_____	_____	_____	_____
• Workers' Compensation	_____	_____	_____	_____
• Quebec Pension Plan (Quebec only)	_____	_____	_____	_____
• Safety and Health	_____	_____	_____	_____
• Liquor Licence	_____	_____	_____	_____
• Provincial Health Insurance	_____	_____	_____	_____
• Maternity Leave	_____	_____	_____	_____
• Termination of Employment				
• Other: _____	_____	_____	_____	_____

C. Federal

	Applies To Me	Does Not Apply To Me	Need Further Info	Further Info Obtained
• Incorporation (federal charter)	_____	_____	_____	_____
• Federal Income Tax (corporate or personal)	_____	_____	_____	_____
• GST or HST	_____	_____	_____	_____
• Export/Import Permit	_____	_____	_____	_____
• Customs Duties	_____	_____	_____	_____
• Building Codes	_____	_____	_____	_____
• Directors liability to statutory creditors (that is, to federal government departments with such legislation and claim rights, such as employment standards, GST, income tax, environmental protection, human rights, etc.)	_____	_____	_____	_____
• Health and Safety Standards	_____	_____	_____	_____
• Employment Insurance	_____	_____	_____	_____
• Human Rights	_____	_____	_____	_____
• Pay Equity	_____	_____	_____	_____
• Canada Pension Plan (except Quebec)	_____	_____	_____	_____
• Payroll Tax Deductions (monthly remittances to government)	_____	_____	_____	_____
• Environmental Protection Legislation	_____	_____	_____	_____
• Trademarks	_____	_____	_____	_____
• Copyrights	_____	_____	_____	_____
• Industrial Designs	_____	_____	_____	_____
• Patents	_____	_____	_____	_____
• Product Safety	_____	_____	_____	_____
• Competition Act (includes false or misleading advertising)	_____	_____	_____	_____
• Other: _____	_____	_____	_____	_____

SAMPLE 6
(See Chapter 2)

Cash Flow Worksheet
(Explanation follows)

Month of:	January		February		March	
	Planned	Actual	Planned	Actual	Planned	Actual
Cash Receipts (Cash In)						
1. Cash sales						
2. Collection from A/R (credit sales payments)						
3. Term loan proceeds						
4. Sale of fixed assets						
5. Other cash received						
6. **Total Cash In**						
Cash Disbursements (Cash Out)						
7. Rent (for premises, equipment, etc.)						
8. Management salaries						
9. Other salaries and wages						
10. Legal and audit fees						
11. Utilities (heat, light, and water)						
12. Telephone						
13. Repairs and maintenance						
14. Licences and municipal taxes						
15. Insurance						
16. Other operating expenses						
17. Payments on purchase of fixed assets						
18. Interest paid on loans (short-term loans, lines of credit, overdrafts)						
19. Payments on mortgages/ Term loans						
20. Income tax payments						
21. Cash dividends paid						
22. Payments on A/P						
23. Other cash expenses						
24. **Total Cash Out**						
Reconciliation of Cash Flow						
25. Opening cash balance						
26. Add: Cash In (Line 6)						
27. Deduct: Cash Out (Line 24)						

SAMPLE 6 Continued

Month of:	January		February		March	
	Planned	Actual	Planned	Actual	Planned	Actual
28. Surplus or Deficit	___	___	___	___	___	___
29. Increase/Decrease operating bank loan	___	___	___	___	___	___
30. Closing cash balance	___	___	___	___	___	___
31. **Bank Loan Balance at Month End** (Operating loan or overdraft)	___	___	___	___	___	___

Explanation

Lines 1, 2, and 22 of the cash flow come from the information obtained from Samples 6A and 6B (which follow), and their totals should then be inserted on the worksheet.

Line 3   Loans: If you take possession of borrowed money during the month, list this cash receipt.

Line 4   Sale of fixed assets: If you sell a fixed asset, such as a piece of office furniture or a vehicle, list the cash income in the monthly column when payment is received.

Line 5   Other cash: List all other cash income such as interest.

Line 6   Total of lines 1–5.

Lines 7–16   Operating expenses: Enter the amount of cheques that you write for your monthly expenses. This is actual cash outlay for the month; for example, if you write a cheque in January for the full year's insurance, then the amount of the cheque would be put in the January column and nothing would be entered for the rest of the year.

Line 17   Payments on purchase of a fixed asset: If money is spent for the purchase of fixed assets, such as a vehicle or a filing cabinet, list the amount in the column for the month when the cheque is written.

Line 18   Interest paid on loans: This is the interest paid monthly on short-term loans, such as bank overdrafts or lines of credit. Since you are in the process of working out the amount of money you will need to borrow, this interest figure may be very difficult to estimate. Consequently, you may decide to leave the line blank for now. If it is likely to be a small amount, you may decide to omit it altogether.

Line 19   Payments on mortgages/loans: Indicate the monthly payment for the principal and interest on tong-term loans. For example, if you borrow $20,000 to purchase a half-ton truck and monthly payments are $550 with the first payment due in March, then $550 will be entered on line 19 for each month beginning in March.

Lines 20–21   Income tax payments and cash dividends paid: The amounts you expect to pay if any.

Lines 16 & 23 Other operating expenses and other cash expenses: The expense items listed in the format may not be applicable to your business; if this is the case, the headings should be changed so that they are appropriate for your situation.

Line 24   Total all possible cash payments for the month.

Line 25   Opening cash balance is the amount of money that you started out the month with.

Line 28	Surplus (or deficit): Cash in minus cash out.
Line 29	If line 28 is a deficit, the operating bank loan should be increased to cover the deficit. Sometimes a bank will require a minimum balance to remain in the account at all times. If line 28 is a surplus, excess funds should be applied to the operating loan.
Line 30	Closing cash balance is the amount of money you started out with plus (or minus) the amount of cash surplus in the month. The closing cash balance becomes next month's opening cash balance. This should normally indicate a surplus, even if you are operating on an overdraft. In these instances lines 28, 30, and 31 are the same. If adding lines 25 and 26 produces a negative amount, then that is the amount that will have to be borrowed in order to make planned payments.
Line 31	By adding the amount shown on line 29 to the previous month's balance, you will have the current loan balance. The highest amount shown on this line for the year will indicate the minimum operating loan required.

SAMPLE 6A

Projected Cash Sales and Accounts Receivable

Month: Projected sales Cash sales (Line 1)			
Collection of previous month's sales			
Collection of sales from 2 months previous			
Collection of sales from more than 2 months previous			
Collection from accounts receivable (Line 2)			

SAMPLE 6B
Projected Accounts Payable

Month:

Planned purchases

Payments on current month's
  purchases

Payments on purchases from
  2 months previous

Payments on purchases
  from more than
  2 months previous

Payments on accounts
  payable (Line 22)

SAMPLE 7
(See Chapter 3)

Balance Sheet or Statement of Financial Position
As of (Current Date/Year)

	20__ (Previous Year)	20__ (Current Year)
Assets		
Accounts receivable (attach aged list)	$_____	$_____
Less: Allowance for bad debts (net)	_____	_____
Cash and balance in bank accounts	_____	_____
Prepaid expenses (e.g., insurance, rent, etc.)	_____	_____
Inventory at lesser of cost or realizable value	_____	_____
Other current assets	_____	_____
Total Current Assets	$_____	$_____
Property and Equipment (net book value after depreciation)	$_____	$_____
Land and buildings		
Furniture, equipment, and fixtures	_____	_____
Motor vehicles	_____	_____
Total Property and Equipment	$_____	$_____
Other Non-Current Assets (e.g., lease payments)	$_____	$_____
Total Assets	$_____	$_____
Liabilities		
Current (due within 12 months)		
Accounts payable	$_____	$_____
Bank loans	_____	_____
Loans—Other	_____	_____
Employee deductions and sales taxes payable	_____	_____
Income taxes payable	_____	_____
Current portion of long-term debt	_____	_____
Other current liabilities	_____	_____
Total Current Liabilities	$_____	$_____
Long-Term (over 1 year)		
Mortgages payable	$_____	$_____
Less: Current portion noted above	_____	_____
Loans from shareholders and partners	_____	_____
Other loans of long-term nature	_____	_____
Total Long-Term Liabilities	$_____	$_____
Total Liabilities	$_____	$_____
Net Assets (Total Assets—Total Liabilities)	$_____	$_____

	20__ (Current Year)	____ (Previous Year)
Shareholders' Equity		
Share capital	$ _____	$ _____
Retained earnings		
Total Shareholders' Equity	$ _____	$ _____
Total Liabilities and Shareholders' Equity	$ _____	$ _____

SAMPLE 8
(See Chapter 3)

Income Statement
(Also referred to as statement of profit or loss,
P & L statement, or statement of operations)
For Month and Year-To-Date Ended _____ 20__

	Current Month		Year-to-Date	
	Amount	Relative To Total Income %	Amount	Relative To Total Income %
Sales				
Gross sales	$		$ _____	
Less returns and allowances (discounts)	$ _____		$ _____	
Net Sales	$ _____	100%	$ _____	100%
Cost of Goods Sold				
Beginning inventory			$ ___%	$ _____ ___%
Plus inventory purchases			$ ___%	$ _____ ___%
Plus plant and other manufacturing costs			$ ___%	$ _____ ___%
Less closing inventory			$ ___%	$ _____ ___%
Total Cost of Goods Sold	$ _____	___%	$ _____	___%
Gross Income (Subtract total cost of goods sold from net sales)	$ _____	___%	$ _____	___%
Operating Expenses				
Advertising and promotion			$ ___%	$ _____ ___%
Bad debts			$ ___%	$ _____ ___%
Bank service charges			$ ___%	$ _____ ___%
Depreciation (e.g., equipment)			$ ___%	$ _____ ___%
Employees' wages			$ ___%	$ _____ ___%
Insurance	$ _____	___%	$ _____	___%

SAMPLE 8 Continued

| | Current Month | | Year-to-Date | |
	Amount	Relative To Total Income %	Amount	Relative To Total Income %
Owner's salary	$ _____	___%	$ _____	___%
Repairs and maintenance	$ _____	___%	$ _____	___%
Supplies	$ _____	___%	$ _____	___%
Taxes and licences	$ _____	___%	$ _____	___%
Telephone and utilities	$ _____	___%	$ _____	___%
Miscellaneous expenses	$ _____	___%	$ _____	___%
Other (itemize)	$ _____	___%	$ _____	___%
Total Operating Expenses	$ _____	___%	$ _____	___%
Net Operating Income (Subtract Gross Expenses from Gross Profit)	$ _____	___%	$ _____	___%
Less: Income Taxes	$ _____	___%	$ _____	___%
Net Profit (Loss) after Taxes	$ _____	___%	$ _____	___%

SAMPLE 9

(See Chapter 3)

Summary of Ratio Analysis

(Ratios found in Chapter 3)

	Ratio Last Period	Ratio This Period	Published Ratio*

A. Working Capital Ratios:

1. Current ratio (#)   _____
2. Quick ratio-acid test (#)   _____
3. Receivables turnover (# of times)   _____
4. Average days receivables (days)   _____
5. Working capital turnover   _____
6. Payables turnover (days)   _____
7. Average days payable (days)   _____

B. Productivity and Debt Ratios:

1. Debt/equity ratio (#)   _____
2. Collection period (days)   _____
3. Inventory turnover (# of times)   _____
4. Inventory supply   _____
5. Operating expense/Net sales (%)   _____

	Ratio Last Period	Ratio This Period	Published Ratio*
C. Profitability Ratios:			
1. Gross profit margin (%)			
2. Net profit margin (%)			
3. Return on investment (%)			
4. Return on owner's investment (%)			
D. Equity Ratios:			
1. Debt capital ratio (#)			
2. Owner's equity ratio (#)			
E. Other Ratios (complete as required)			

*Dun & Bradstreet, Trade Association, Statistics Canada, and related publications

SAMPLE 10
(See Chapter 5)

Partnership Agreement Checklist

_____ 1. Date of agreement

_____ 2. Description of partners:
  (a) individuals have attained the age of majority
  (b) each partner is acquiring interest for own benefit

_____ 3. Firm name:
  (a) name search to ensure no conflict with existing trade, corporation or partnership name
  (b) registration of name as required by law
  (c) continued use of name after death or withdrawal of any partner or after reorganization
  (d) restriction on use of name in any other activity

_____ 4. Term of partnership:
  (a) commencement
  (b) termination at specified time or on specified events

_____ 5. Place of business:
  (a) specify geographical limits if desired

_____ 6. Business purpose of partnership:
  (a) description of authorized business activities
  (b) limitations on business activities
  (c) provisions for future changes in business activities

_____ 7. Capital contributions:
  (a) percentage contribution of each partner

SAMPLE I0 Continued

       (b) form of contribution (cash, assets, etc.)
       (c) when contribution to be made
       (d) valuation of non-cash contributions
       (e) interest on contributions
       (f) adjustments to contributions
       (g) loans to partnership
       (h) future capital contributions:
          i) circumstances when required
          ii) amount and form
          iii) apportionment of contribution among partners
          iv) redistribution of partnership interest for nonproportional contributions

_____ 8. Division of profits and losses:
       (a) proportion of division among partners
       (b) salaries and benefits as elements in profits for distribution
       (c) guarantee of minimum profits to certain partners
       (d) reserve fund for partnership expenses paid into prior to distribution
       (e) limitation on partner's share in profits or losses
       (f) distribution to partnership

_____ 9. Records of business:
       (a) nature of records
       (b) partners' access
       (c) statements to be given to partners

_____10. Appointment of accountant/auditor

_____11. Fiscal year

_____12. Accounting and valuation principles:
       (a) generally accepted accounting principles (specify if desired)
       (b) valuation principles (book value, multiple of earnings, etc.)

_____13. Banking arrangements:
       (a) bank and branch
       (b) kinds of accounts
       (c) signing authority
       (d) maximum loan amount without approval of all partners

_____14. Financial restrictions on partners:
       (a) prohibition against partner giving bonds or guarantees, charging his partnership interest for his separate debts or otherwise impairing his financial position to the detriment of partnership
       (b) prohibition against any one partner borrowing for partnership or releasing debt of partnership
       (c) indemnity by partner breaching these provisions

_____15. Attention to business:
       (a) partners to devote full time and attention to business
       (b) partners not to engage in competing business, or any other business
       (c) liability of partners to account for outside income (e.g., director's fees)
       (d) salary for full-time partners
       (e) specify responsibilities

_____16. Control of policy:
   (a) majority rule or unanimity
   (b) voting:
      i) one partner—one vote
      ii) votes proportional to interest
_____17. Management:
   (a) designation of responsible partners
   (b) division of functions (e.g., administration, sales)
   (c) provision for business meetings
   (d) records of decisions
   (e) establishment of policies
   (f) simple or special majority or unanimous approval
   (g) authority to enter contracts, negotiate loans, pledge credit, hire and fire employees
   (h) provision for review of decisions by all partners
_____18. Drawing arrangements and benefits:
   (a) frequency
   (b) maximum amount or percentage
   (c) vacations
   (d) other benefits
_____19. Powers of partners and limitations:
   (a) engaging in nonpartnership business
   (b) defining scope of partners' authority, collectively and individually
   (c) delegation of powers to management committee
   (d) acting outside scope of partnership committee
   (e) patents and trade secrets
_____20. Restrictive covenants (to prevent competition in the event of depature):
   (a) reasonable time, scope, and geographic area
_____21. Retirement or death:
   (a) provide for continuance notwithstanding retirement or death
   (b) purchase of retiring partner's interest —valuation criteria and method of payment
   (c) purchase of deceased partner's interest or provision for estate to act as partner
_____22. Sale of partnership interest:
   (a) prohibit
   (b) allow, with right of first refusal to remaining partners, compulsory buy–sell, etc.
   (c) restriction on who may purchase
   (d) terms of sale
   (e) right to sell or to compel purchase by partnership on reorganization, or on being outvoted on major decision
_____23. Expulsion of partner:
   (a) majority vote or unanimity of remaining partners
   (b) specify grounds:
      i) insolvency
      ii) fraud

SAMPLE I0 Continued

_____24. Dissolution:
        (a) specify grounds
        (b) specify events that are not to result in dissolution (e.g., death, insolvency)
        (c) dissolution on vote in case of major split among partners
        (d) tax effects

_____25. Admission of new partners:
        (a) special majority or unanimity on vote of partners
        (b) acceptance qualifications
        (c) new partner's capital contribution
        (d) allocation of new partner's interest from others
        (e) method of payment

_____26. Purchase of partner's interest:
        (a) obligation to purchase on death, retirement, expulsion, insolvency
        (b) option-to-purchase terms
        (c) right of first refusal
        (d) compulsory buy–sell

_____27. Partnership property:
        (a) identification of assets
        (b) valuation of assets including goodwill
        (c) title to assets
        (d) control of assets
        (e) maintenance, repair, and replacement
        (f) restrictions on personal use
        (g) distribution on termination

_____28. Insurance:
        (a) kinds, limits, and deductibles
        (b) fire, boiler, theft, automobile, tenant's liability, personal injury, products liability, errors and omissions
        (c) life insurance on other partners sufficient to fund purchase of other partner's share, and agreement of partners to facilitate obtaining such insurance (provision if a partner is uninsurable)

_____29. Partners' liability:
        (a) to one another
        (b) to third parties
        (c) partnership liability

_____30. Arbitration:
        (a) named individual (auditor for financial matters)
        (b) Arbitration Act

_____31. Registrations:
        (a) grant irrevocable power of attorney to other partners for purpose of effecting all necessary registrations

_____32. Amendment:
        (a) written
        (b) majority rule or unanimity

_____33. Applicable law (province)
_____34. No assignment of agreement
_____35. Addresses of partners
_____36. Partners' signatures on agreement

SAMPLE 11
(See Chapter 5)

Shareholders' Agreement Checklist

_____A. **Date**

_____B. **Parties**
   1. Shareholder names (Principals)

_____C. **Conduct of Company Affairs**
_____ 1. Board of directors
     (a) composition
     (b) quorum
     (c) matters requiring Board approval
        i) salaries
        ii) dividends
        iii) capital expenditures
        iv) contracts
        v) other
_____ 2. Officers
     (a) titles
     (b) appointments of
_____ 3. Shareholders
     (a) involvement in company affairs—both positive and negative clauses, i.e., obligation on a shareholder to perform certain tasks (being positive covenants) and requirements of shareholders not to interfere (being negative covenants)
     (b) matters requiring approval by resolutions of shareholders with a particular majority (or unanimous approval)
        i) sale or other disposition of a particular asset or of all or substantially all of the assets of the company
        ii) changes in the capital of the company
        iii) loans or guarantees by the company
     (c) casting vote
     (d) noncompetition clause—both during involvement with company and after termination of involvement, regardless of reason for departure
_____ 4. Articles
     (a) additions to; such as special rights and restrictions and casting vote provisions (i.e., voting or nonvoting shares, redeemable preferred shares, pro rata rights, or first refusal on share transfers or allotments, etc.)
     (b) amendment of articles to be consistent with provisions of Shareholders' Agreement

_____D. **Financial Matters**
_____ 1. Bank
     (a) signing officers

       (b) how many signatures required
       (c) borrowing authority

_____ 2. Capital subscriptions
       (a) amounts and timing
       (b) issuance of different classes of shares (e.g., "A," "B," "C")

_____ 3. Shareholders' loans and guarantees
       (a) amounts and timing
       (b) subordination of loans to other lenders
       (c) collateral security for guarantees, such as houses
       (d) repayment of shareholders' loans, such as when and in what amounts
       (e) interest on shareholders' loans
       (f) security from company to shareholders for shareholders' loans

_____ 4. Auditors—whether required or not
_____ 5. Accounting principles—such as how depreciation is to be taken and method of valuation of inventory

_____ **E.** **Restriction of Alienation of Shares and Shareholders' Loans**
_____ 1. General prohibition—except in accordance with terms of agreement and if shareholders not in default under agreement
_____ 2. Right of first refusal
       (a) pro rata offering just to same class or to all shareholders
       (b) only applicable if all shares purchased or will it apply to a portion of shareholders' shares
       (c) time offer to be left open to other shareholders
       (d) if refused, time within which to sell to third parties
       (e) third parties to sign agreement upon becoming a shareholder

_____ 3. Exempt alienations
       (a) transfers to controlled entities
       (b) other exemptions, such as conversions or redemptions

_____ 4. Only mortgage or pledge interest in shares and shareholders' loans if mortgagee or pledgee takes subject to terms of agreement and then questions whether or not consent of other share-holders required

_____ 5. Share certificates
       (a) endorsed and left in possession, or
       (b) escrow agreement

_____ **F.** **Buy/Sell Obligations**
_____ 1. Who buys?
       (a) other shareholders, pro rata, or otherwise
       (b) the company, or
       (c) a third party

_____ 2. What is bought and sold?
       (a) shares, all or a portion thereof
       (b) shareholders' loans
       (c) assets of the company

_____ 3. Buy/sell provisions
      (a) compulsory buy–sell
         i) death
         ii) mental or physical incapacity
         iii) bankruptcy
         iv) termination of employment
         v) default or agreement
      (b) voluntary buy–sell

_____ 4. Purchase price
      (a) termination
         i) annual determination by shareholders— unanimous or otherwise
         ii) independent third-party determination—triggered by sale or done annually or otherwise
         iii) formula to be applied
      (b) discount or premium depending upon whether compulsory or voluntary buy–sell
      (c) payment of purchase price
         i) cash, stock, debt, or assets
         ii) upon sale or by way of a pay-out

_____ 5. Funding of purchase price
      (a) insurance
      (b) other, such as company self-insurance

_____ 6. Election under Income Tax Act

_____ 7. Removal from guarantees of corporate indebtedness

_____ **G. Escrow Agent**
_____ 1. Directions to escrow agent
_____ 2. Rights of escrow agent

_____ **H. General Provisions**
_____ 1. Probate provisions
_____ 2. Insolvency restrictions where corporate repurchase
_____ 3. Waiver of pro rata repurchase requirement where corporate repurchase
_____ 4. Precedence over company articles
_____ 5. Termination of agreement
_____ 6. Notice provisions
_____ 7. Time of essence
_____ 8. Further assurances
_____ 9. Revocation of previous agreements
_____ 10. Interpretation
_____ 11. Restrictions on assignment
_____ 12. Enurement
_____ 13. Arbitration
_____ 14. Governing law (province)

SAMPLE 12
(See Chapter 5)

Sample Management Contract

THIS AGREEMENT made as of the _____day of _____20__.

BETWEEN: ABC LIMITED
(hereinafter called "the employer")

OF THE FIRST PART

AND: JOHN SMITH
(hereinafter called "the employee")

OF THE SECOND PART

WHEREAS the employer and the employee have agreed to enter into an employment relationship for their mutual benefit and are desirous of setting out terms and conditions thereof, this agreement witnesses that the parties agree as follows:

1. Employment
   (a) The employee represents to the employer that the employee has the required skills and experience to perform the duties and exercise the responsibilities required of the employee as a Marketing Manager. In particular the employee represents that he or she will be able to undertake a senior responsibility for sales and marketing training, supervision, planning, and budgeting. In carrying out these duties and responsibilities the employee shall comply with all lawful and reasonable instructions as may from time to time be given by superiors representing the employer.
   (b) In consideration for the employee's agreement hereto and the employee's performance in accordance herewith the employer employs the employee.
   (c) The effective performance of the employee's duties requires the highest level of integrity and the employer's complete confidence in the employee's relationship with other employees of the employer and with all persons dealt with by the employee in the course of employment.
   (d) It is understood and agreed to by the employee that the employer reserves the right to change the employee's assignments, duties, and reporting relationships. In particular it is understood and agreed to that the employer plans, in its discretion, to involve the employee in national sales matters with a view to his or her being able, if so directed, to assume full responsibility for national sales.

2. Exclusive Service
   (a) During the term of employment the employee shall well and faithfully serve the employer and shall not, during the term, be employed or engaged in any capacity in promoting, undertaking, or carrying on any other business.
   (b) The employee is employed on a full-time basis for the employer and it is understood that the hours of work involved will vary and be irregular and are those required to meet the objectives of the employment.

3. Confidential Information

(a) The employee acknowledges that as Marketing Manager, and in such other position as he or she may from time to time be appointed to, the employee will acquire information about certain matters and things which are confidential to the employer, and which information is the exclusive property of the employer, including:

  i) customer lists;
  ii) pricing policies;
  iii) list of suppliers.

(b) The employee acknowledges such information as referred to in clause 3(a) above could be used to the detriment of the employer. Accordingly, the employee undertakes to treat confidentially all such information and agrees not to disclose same to any third party either during or after the term of employment.

(c) The employee acknowledges that, without prejudice to any and all rights of the employer, an injunction is the only effective remedy to protect the employer's rights and property as set out in clauses 3 (a) and 3 (b).

4. Noncompetition

(a) The employee acknowledges that as Marketing Manager for the employer he or she will gain a knowledge of, and a close working relationship with, the employer's customers, which would injure the employer if made available to a competitor or if used for competitive purposes. The employee therefore agrees that, for a period of six (6) months from the termination of employment pursuant to this agreement for any reason or cause, the employee will not be employed by another employer directly or indirectly engaged in a business which is in competition with the employer, in a position where the duties are the same or similar to those duties performed for the employer pursuant to this agreement.

5. Remuneration and Benefits

(a) In consideration of the employee's undertaking and the performance of the obligations contained herein the employer shall pay and grant the following salary and benefits:

(1) A salary of $_____ per annum, payable in arrears in equal bi-weekly installments, subject to an annual review on or about January 1 of each year of this contract, the first such review to be on or about January 1, 20__.

(2) Such other benefit program as is made generally available by the employer from time to time pursuant to the provisions thereof.

(3) The reimbursement of any expenses authorized and incurred pursuant to the employee's employment in accordance with the employer's generally established practice as applied from time to time.

(4) An automobile allowance of $_____ per month plus reimbursement for gas and repair expenses generated by use of the automobile on behalf of the employer. The employee shall insure said automobile at his expense in an amount satisfactory to the employer and shall produce proof of same to the employer when requested to do so.

(5) An annual bonus in the absolute discretion of the employer which bonus may not be given at all in any year.

SAMPLE 12 Continued

6. Termination

(a) This agreement may be terminated in the following manner in the specified circumstances:

(1) By the employee upon the giving of not less than one (1) month's notice to the employer.

(2) By the employer upon the giving of not less than two (2) months' notice to the employee in which case the employee shall be free to seek other employment.

(3) By the employer, at its option, for cause including:

  i) a material breach of the provisions of this agreement, including the policies attached hereto;

  ii) conviction of the employee of a criminal offence punishable by indictment where such cause is not prohibited by law;

  iii) alcoholism or drug addiction of the employee;

  iv) the absence of the employee from the performance of his or her duties for any reason, other than for authorized vacation, for a period in excess of 40 working days total in any 6-month period.

(4) By the employee for cause including a material breach of this agreement.

(b) The giving of notice or the payment of severance pay by the employer to the employee upon termination shall not prevent the employer from alleging cause for said termination.

(c) The employee authorizes the employer to deduct from any payment due to the employee at any time, including from a termination payment, any amounts owed to the employer by reason of purchases, advances, or loans, or in recompense for damage to or loss of the employer's property save only that this provision shall be applied so as not to conflict with any applicable legislation.

7. Severability

(a) In the event that any provision herein or part thereof shall be deemed void or invalid by a court of competent jurisdiction, the remaining provisions, or parts thereof, shall be and remain in full force and effect.

8. Entire Agreement

(a) This agreement constitutes the entire agreement between the parties hereto with respect to the employment of the employee, and any and all previous agreements, written or oral, express or implied between the parties hereto or on their behalf relating to the employment of the employee by the employer are hereby terminated and cancelled and each of the parties hereto hereby releases and for- ever discharges the other of and from all manner of actions, causes of action, claims, demands whatsoever under or in respect of any such agreement.

9. Notices

(a) Any notice required or permitted to be given to the employee shall be sufficiently given if delivered to the employee personally or if mailed by registered mail to the employee's address last known to the employer.

(b) Any notice required or permitted to be given to the employer shall be sufficiently given if delivered to _____ personally or if mailed by registered mail to the employer's head office at its address last known to the employee.

(c) Any notice given by mail shall be deemed to have been given forty-eight (48) hours after the time it is posted.

IN WITNESS WHEREOF the parties have duly executed this agreement this _____day of _____, 20__, in the city of _____ in the province of _____

_____   _____
ABC Limited   John Smith
(Authorized Signatory)   (Signature)

CHECKLIST A
(See Chapter 7)

Buying a Business

Check when
answered to
your
satisfaction

Preliminary

1. What are your reasons for considering buying a business rather than starting from scratch or buying into a franchise?
2. Have you made a list of what you like and don't like about buying a business someone else has started?
3. Have you compared the cost of buying a business with the cost of starting a new business?
4. Have you talked with other business owners in the area to see what they think of the firm?
5. Have you fully explored the alternative types of businesses you might be interested in?
6. Have you selected the type of industry that would most interest you?
7. Have you expertise and experience in the type of business you are considering? Is it compatible with your personal goals, personality, and financial resources?
8. Have you established the criteria that you require in an existing business for your needs?
9. Are you comparing identical types of businesses for sale so that you can make a comparative value judgment?
10. Do you know the real reasons the business is for sale? How do you know they are accurate?
11. Have you checked out the firm's reputation with the Better Business Bureau, Credit Bureau, Dun & Bradstreet, suppliers, creditors, competitors?
12. Have you made sure that you have escape clause conditions in any offer to purchase contract (e.g., subject to satisfactory review by purchaser's lawyer and accountant, financing, inspection of records, receiving licences, rights, and other transfers)?

CHECKLIST A Continued

Costs

13. Is the inventory accurately shown at true current value for calculating actual cost of goods sold? _____
14. Did the seller prepay some expenses? Must you reimburse him or her for your share? _____
15. Are expenses all-inclusive? Will new ownership change them? _____
16. Is another business involved in the accumulation or payment of expenses? _____
17. Will some annual expenses be due soon? _____
18. Have some expenses been delayed (e.g., equipment maintenance)? _____
19. What new or increased expenses should you anticipate? _____
20. Was interest paid for money lent to the business? _____
21. Are wages as well as an attractive profit margin provided for working owners? _____
22. Must staff salaries be adjusted soon? _____
23. Does equipment value reflect reasonable annual depreciation? _____
24. Has your solicitor checked out the lease? _____
25. What expenses do similar businesses have? _____
26. How will sales fluctuations affect cost? _____
27. What costs are allocated to which product? How would a change in product mix affect costs? _____

Sales

28. What's the future of your product or service? Is it expanding? Becoming oversold? Obsolete? _____
29. Can sales increase with current resources? _____
30. Have you checked with the suppliers in terms of the history of the business for sale? _____
31. Is the location good, or is a poor location the reason for the sale? _____
32. Are bad debts deducted from records or are they still shown as receivables? _____
33. Have all sales been reliably recorded? Are the total sales broken down by product line, if applicable? _____
34. Are some goods on consignment and able to be returned for full credit? _____
35. Are some goods on warranty? If so, will financial allowance be made for possible warranty commitments? _____
36. What is the monthly and annual sales pattern? Is it consistent? Seasonal? Related to other cycles? _____
37. Are sales fluctuations due to one-shot promotions? _____
38. Is the seller's personal role critical to success? _____
39. Is there a salesperson who contributes significantly to success? _____
40. Will existing suppliers be available to you? _____

41. Is reported stock turnover in line with industry practice ratios? Does existing stock include items from another business?
42. Are sales figures solely from this business?
43. Are prices competitive? Who are the competitors and are their price strategies gaining them a larger market share?

Profits

44. Do you know minimum and maximum likely sales?
45. How will sales fluctuations affect profits?
46. What are the book values, market values, and replacement values of the fixed assets?
47. If inventory and/or work in progress are included, has a value been agreed upon at time of offer? Have you agreed on how it will be adjusted at time of closing, and within what limits?
48. Is there inventory sold but not shipped?
49. How will inflation affect sales and costs?
50. Are profits enough to take the risk?
51. Based on the history, have you projected future cash flow and profitability? Have you determined your break-even point?
52. Have records been well kept?
53. Have you and a qualified accountant analyzed the records thoroughly? Balance sheets? Profit-and-loss statements? Tax returns? Purchases and sales records? Bank statements? How far back have you gone?
54. Must you build up your own accounts receivable? How will this affect cash flow?
55. Is some equipment leased? At what cost?
56. Is equipment in good repair? Efficient? Up-to-date? Easy to service? Saleable?
57. Have you checked with comparable industry profit ratios and are they consistent with the business you are examining?

Liabilities

58. Is the seller cooperative in supplying financial information?
59. Are there any contingencies, such as warranties or guaranteed debts or accounts?
60. Are your assets free and clear of debts and liens? Do you have in writing the terms of debts you are assuming?
61. Will cash flow cover debts?
62. Are you assuming any risk of liability for the seller's actions (e.g., if you are buying shares of a limited company)? Will customers expect you to make refunds or honour warranties or risk losing goodwill, even though you are not legally obliged to do so?

63. How is the business's credit rating with suppliers?   _____

64. Are there advances or prepayments that should be turned
over to you?   _____

65. Are there goods that have been prepaid to the business but not
delivered by the business? Should these advance payments be
given to you?   _____

66. If buying part of a company or entering a partnership, what
limitations are there, and what authority will you have in the
management of the firm? Have you read the chapter that covers
shareholders' agreements and partnership agreements?   _____

The Purchase Agreement

67. Is the business a limited company? Are you buying assets or
shares? Have you consulted with your lawyer and accountant on
the pros and cons of this issue?   _____

68. Does the contract of sale cover assets to be purchased, liabilities
to be assumed, when business is to be taken over?   _____

69. Are you prepared to negotiate, remembering a business is only
worth what someone will pay and what a seller will accept?
Do you have the skills to negotiate directly yourself?   _____

70. Did you include escape clauses in the proposed offer to
purchase contract covering obtaining finance, inspection of
records, receiving licences, rights, and other transfers, and
satisfactory review by your lawyer and accountant?   _____

71. Have you discussed the proposed business with someone who
understands this type of business?   _____

72. Will the seller agree not to set up in competition with you for an
agreed time and within a specified geographic area?   _____

73. Will the seller train and assist you after the purchase?   _____

74. Have you selected a lawyer who is skilled in commercial law,
including buying a business? Are you going to discuss the
purchase terms with your lawyer before removing the escape
clauses or, better still, before formally submitting an offer?   _____

75. Have you selected an accountant who is skilled in the financial
evaluation and assessment aspects of buying a business? Are
you going to discuss the purchase terms with your accountant
before removing the escape clauses or, better still, before
formally submitting an offer?   _____

SAMPLE 13
(See Chapter 8)

Sample Franchise Agreement Format

1. Date of agreement.
2. Parties.
3. Grant of franchise and licence to use trademarks, logos, signs, symbols of franchisor.
4. Franchisor's obligations to:
   (a) financially assist franchisee (e.g., in obtaining line of credit, granting direct loans, etc.);
   (b) aid in the selection and leasing of the site for the business, and in construction of the facilities;
   (c) provide management assistance, including advice respecting the establishment of accounting and bookkeeping systems to ensure a proper flow of relevant financial information to both parties;
   (d) train franchisee and give advice regarding hiring and training of personnel;
   (e) aid in the selection of merchandise;
   (f) advise with respect to opening-day procedure;
   (g) carry out national and regional programs of advertising and publicity.
5. Franchisee's obligations to:
   (a) follow franchisor's specifications in constructing, decorating, and furnishing the facilities;
   (b) use products specified by franchisor;
   (c) purchase supplies from franchisor or from approved outlets;
   (d) conduct the business in accordance with franchisor policies;
   (e) conduct no other business on the franchised premises;
   (f) obtain amount and types of insurance specified by franchisor;
   (g) use prescribed accounting and bookkeeping system;
   (h) make books available to franchisor for inspection;
   (i) submit periodic financial statements and reports;
   (j) use prescribed employee uniforms;
   (k) participate in the advertising programs of franchisor and contribute to their cost;
   (l) submit all local advertising to franchisor for approval;
   (m) observe covenants on part of franchisor contained in its lease of franchised premises;
   (n) make withdrawals within limits specified by franchisor;
   (o) maintain working capital of the business at a specified level;
   (p) devote full time and attention to the business;
   (q) assume all liabilities for any claims arising out of the franchised business and indemnify franchisor.
6. Full disclosure of payments required by franchisor:
   (a) initial fee;
   (b) annual royalties;
   (c) fee for use of premises owned/leased by franchisor;
   (d) monthly consulting or management service fee;

SAMPLE 13 Continued

   (e) franchisee's proportionate share of franchisor's advertising and promotional programs;

   (f) payment for supplies or inventory purchased from the franchisor.

7. Termination of franchise:

   (a) grounds for termination:
   - i) notice by either party,
   - ii) default under the agreement,
   - iii) failure to meet minimum sales or earnings quotas,
   - iv) deviation from quality standards,
   - v) bankruptcy or death of franchisee,
   - vi) end of term;

   (b) winding- up of franchisee's business on termination:
   - i) return of franchisor's trademarks, all materials bearing its insignia, manuals, and so forth,
   - ii) purchase of fixtures, equipment, and inventory by franchisor,
   - iii) assignment of lease, or deed, of franchised premises, to franchisor,
   - iv) settlement of accounts.

8. Noncompetition covenants:

   (a) from franchisor:
   - i) not to cause or assist the invasion of the assigned business territory by other franchisees or any franchisor-controlled competitive business;

   (b) from franchisee:
   - i) to refrain from engaging directly or indirectly in any business similar to the franchised business during the term of the franchise and for a specified period thereafter,
   - ii) to take reasonable steps both during and after the term of the franchise to protect confidential know-how of the franchisor that was unknown to the franchisee prior to the contract,
   - iii) not to hire employees of the franchisor or other franchisees or induce such employees to leave their employment during the term of the franchise and for a specified period thereafter.

9. Prohibition against assignment of franchise by franchisee without prior approval of franchisor, agreement to be freely assignable by franchisor.

10. Guarantee by principals of franchisee.

11. General contract provisions:

   (a) franchisee an independent contractor and no agency relationship created;

   (b) all payments to be in Canadian currency;

   (c) arbitration provisions;

   (d) all representations, promises, or agreements embodied in agreement;

   (e) agreement to be construed in accordance with the laws of specified province;

   (f) severability of clauses;

   (g) time to be of the essence;

   (h) address for service of notice, and method of giving notice.

12. Signature of parties.

CHECKLIST B
(See Chapter 8)
Franchise Assessment Checklist

Check when answered to your satisfaction

The Franchisor

1. How long has the franchise been in business?
2. Is it a well-established company?
3. How long has it been offering franchises?
4. Does it have proven experience of operating a franchise chain?
5. If a new firm, how long has the concept been tested?
6. What are the results of the concept testing?
7. Is it the subsidiary of another company? If so, who is the parent company? Has that company ever franchised other products or services? What was their track record?
8. What business is the company really in? Is it more interested in selling franchises than in marketing a viable product or service?
9. How does the company make its money? From "upfront" fees or from continuing royalties? (Reputable franchisors are interested in the continuing success of their franchisees; money should come from successful franchises and products, not reselling unprofitable franchises).
10. How many franchised outlets are currently in operation? How many outlets are company-owned?
11. Have any outlets failed in the past? If so, why? What is the ratio of successful franchises to those which have failed?
12. Have you received the franchisor's recent audited financial statements? Is the company financially stable? Has your accountant analyzed the statements?
13. Who are the franchisor's directors and officers, and what is their business experience?
14. Are these management people employed full-time by the franchise company?
15. How long has the present management been with the company?
16. What is the depth and quality of the franchisor's management team and supervisory personnel?
17. Does the franchisor have a reputation for dealing honestly with its franchisees? With its customers?
18. What due diligence research have you done? What is the franchisor's standing with the Chamber of Commerce? The Better Business Bureau? Dun & Bradstreet? Its bank? Your bank? Canadian Franchise Association?
    Franchise Consultant feedback. Franchise lawyer feedback?
19. Have you discussed the franchisor's plans for future development and expansion or diversification?

CHECKLIST B Continued

Check when
answered to
your
satisfaction

20. What effect will development and expansion have on your dealings with the franchisor?   _____

21. What innovations has the franchisor introduced since first starting?   _____

22. Are there immediate plans for further expansion in your area? Will that affect your sales?   _____

23. Where will new franchises be located?   _____

24. Has the company shown a pattern of solid growth?   _____

25. How selective is the franchisor when choosing its franchisees? Have your qualifications and financial standing been reviewed?   _____

26. Has the franchise been registered in your province and is there franchise legislation in your province? Have you seen the prospectus or Statement of Material Facts and Disclosure Statement?   _____

27. Has the franchisor shown you any certified figures indicating exact net profits of one or more franchisee firms which you have personally checked yourself with the franchisee?   _____

28. Is the franchisor connected in any way with any other franchise company handling similar merchandise or services?   _____

29. If the answer to the last question is yes, what is your protection against this second franchisor organization?   _____

30. Are there any lawsuits pending against the franchisor or its key people? What is the nature of the claim? Has there been a history of dissatisfied franchisees litigating against the franchisor?   _____

The Product or Service

31. How is the firm's image in the community? How is the product regarded?   _____

32. Are you prepared to spend the rest of your business life with this product or service?   _____

33. Will this product/service sell all year round or will you be out of business for some months each year? Would you be prepared for such a slack period?   _____

34. Might this product/service just be a fad? Or will demand increase? Is it a luxury?   _____

35. Is it well packaged to promote sales?   _____

36. Where is the product/service now sold?   _____

37. What assurance do you have that the franchisor will be able to continue getting the product for you at a fair price?   _____

38. How many people in the area are potential customers?   _____

39. Is the product or service protected by a trademark or copyright? Is it patented?   _____

40. What makes the product or service unique, and does it satisfy a particular need in your market?   _____

41. Can the product or service be easily duplicated by your competitor? _____

42. How much of this product or service is presently sold, and have sales been increasing or decreasing? _____

43. Would you buy the product or service on its own merits? _____

44. How long has it been on the market in its present form? _____

45. Is the product or service marketable in your territory? How do you know? _____

46. Is the price competitive with similar products or services on the market? Do you have many competitors? _____

47. Have you reviewed the federal/provincial standards and regulations governing the product or service? _____

48. Are there product warranties or guarantees? Are they your responsibility or the franchisor's? _____

49. Are you allowed by the franchisor to carry other product lines? _____

The Location and Territory

50. How well-defined is the franchised sales area? Is it outlined on a map? In the contract? _____

51. Are there proposed changes in traffic patterns or redevelopment which could affect the business in the proposed location? (Check municipal offices about local bylaws.) _____

52. How expensive are taxes and insurance in the area? _____

53. Are your franchised rights exclusive for the area? What guarantee do you have? Can the company open its own outlets? _____

54. What competition is in the area? _____

55. Can you select your own location? _____

56. Do you lease or own the premises? What are the terms? _____

57. Will you receive assistance in selecting a location? Is there a fee for this? _____

58. Will the population in the territory given you increase, remain static, or decrease over the next 5 years? Does the franchisor have information on these matters? _____

59. Will the product or service you are considering be in greater demand, about the same, or less demand than today 5 years from now? _____

60. Can you, or the franchisor, change the size of your territory in the future? _____

61. Do you have a profile of the people in your area, including age, income, and occupation? _____

The Franchise Contract

62. Does the contract fully explain your rights and obligations under the franchise agreement, and those of the franchisor? _____

63. Does the contract benefit both parties—you and the franchisor? _____

CHECKLIST B Continued

64. Can you terminate the contract if, for some reason, you have to? _____

65. What is the cost or penalty if you do terminate the contract? _____

66. Will you have the privilege of selling or transferring the franchise and under what conditions or restrictions? Will you have the option of selling it yourself, or must it be handled as a resale by the franchisor? How is the resale price then set? _____

67. Does the contract give the franchisor the right of cancellation for almost any reason, or must there be good cause? Are the reasons for cancellation outlined? _____

68. If the franchisor can terminate, will you be compensated for goodwill? _____

69. Are the payments to the franchisor spelled out in detail? What do they include? _____

70. Must you purchase a minimum amount or all of the merchandise from the franchisor? _____

71. Can you use your own suppliers? _____

72. Must you purchase or lease equipment directly from the franchisor? _____

73. Are makes and/or sources of supply for equipment, furnishings, and fixtures specified? _____

74. Who is responsible for repairs to fixtures and equipment? Are warranties provided? _____

75. Do you fully understand the terms of any leasing agreement you sign? (Refer to Chapter 9 on location and leases). _____

76. Is there an annual sales quota? Is it realistic? Can the company terminate the contract if the quota is not met? _____

77. Does the contract prevent you from establishing, owning, or working in a competing business for a certain period after termination? _____

78. Before you sign the sales contract, are you sure that the franchise can do something for you that you cannot do for yourself? _____

79. Does the franchisor provide continuing assistance? Is this specified in the contract? _____

80. Is training-school attendance required? Is it of a calibre that you and your staff require? _____

81. Have you examined and seen in operation the company's franchise handbook, the accounting system, and all other systems and methods to which you will have to adhere? _____

82. Will the franchisor help with the financing arrangements? What will it cost you? _____

83. Are advertising and sales support adequate? What is the cost? _____

84. If a well-known personality is involved in the advertising, does he/she assist you directly? How? What happens if the celebrity quits or dies? _____

**Check when
answered to
your
satisfaction**

85. What controls does the franchisor specify in the following areas? _____
    - operational procedures _____
    - product/service quality _____
    - hiring staff _____
    - advertising _____
    - accounting _____
    - insurance _____
    - prices _____
    - reporting and records _____
    - other _____
86. Are you allowed to hire a manager, or must you run the
    franchise yourself? _____
87. Does the franchisor perform a market study for each potential
    franchise location? _____
88. Is the chosen franchise location right for your own needs? _____
89. What standards does the franchisor specify for the property? _____
90. If a lease is involved, are you leasing from the franchisor or
    from an independent landlord? _____
91. Can you sublease, assign the lease, or move the franchise if
    necessary? _____
92. Is the franchise contract for a specified number of years, at
    which time a new agreement must be negotiated? Or is the
    franchise term indefinite, with automatic renewal privileges,
    subject to certain mutually agreeable restrictions? _____
93. Does the franchise agreement provide for arbitration in the
    event of a dispute or default? _____
94. Are your payments to the franchisor clearly specified? Are the
    following shown?
    - the franchise fee _____
    - any fixed yearly payments the franchisor receives _____
    - royalty payments based on a percentage of gross sales _____
    - the monthly percentage of gross sales required for advertising _____
    - fees for continuing services provided by the franchisor _____
95. Are these costs realistic or overly burdensome to profitability? _____
96. What happens if supplies from the franchisor are interrupted?
    Can you purchase goods from alternative suppliers? _____
97. Have you the right to the franchisor's latest innovations? _____
98. Does the contract cover in detail all the franchisor's verbal
    promises made during the interview? _____
99. If leasing the location, will the lease be for the same term as the
    franchise agreement? Can the lease be renewed if you renew
    the franchise? _____
100. Are you responsible for the construction or improvement of the
    premises? If so, will the franchisor provide you with plans and
    specifications, and can these be changed? _____

CHECKLIST B Continued

101. If you default on the contract, how much time do you have to rectify the situation?

102. What happens to the business in the event of your prolonged illness or death? Have questions regarding succession been clearly addressed?

103. Before you sign the contract, are you sure that the franchise can do something for you that you cannot do for yourself?

104. Will the franchisor arrange financing?

105. Does the franchise call upon you to take any steps which are, according to your lawyer, unwise or illegal in your city or province (e.g., Sunday openings)?

106. Are you prepared to give up some independence of action to secure the advantages offered by the franchise?

107. Do you really believe you have the innate ability, training, and experience to work smoothly and profitably with the franchisor, your employees, and your customers?

108. Have you had your accountant and lawyer carefully check out the agreement, particularly those areas dealing with bankruptcy, termination, renewal, transfer, and sale of the franchise? What is their opinion?

The Experience of Current Franchisees

109. Was the profit projection by the franchisor accurate?

110. What reports to the company are necessary? Are they reasonable?

111. Is there a minimum quota of sales? Is it difficult to achieve?

112. Are the products and equipment supplied by the franchisor satisfactory and delivered promptly?

113. How reliable is delivery from the franchisor?

114. What problems have been encountered with the franchisor?

115. How did the franchisor's income projections compare with the results experienced by existing franchisees?

116. What was the total investment required by the franchisor?

117. Were there any hidden or unexpected costs?

118. Has the franchise been as profitable as expected?

119. How long was it before the operating expenses were covered by revenue?

120. How long was the franchise in operation before the business became profitable?

121. How long was it before the franchise was able to pay a reasonable management salary?

122. Does the franchisor respond promptly and helpfully to questions asked?

123. Has there ever been a serious disagreement with the franchisor? What about? Was it settled amicably?

124. What kind of management and staff training was provided? Did it meet expectations? Where was it held?

125. Is the marketing, promotional, and advertising assistance received from the franchisor satisfactory?

126. What steps have been taken to make the franchise location successful?

127. Do franchisees advise anyone else to start a franchise with this particular franchisor?

128. If the contract could be changed, what would be changed?

Note: Further franchise checklists can be obtained from the Canadian Franchise Association, the provincial government, accounting firms, and bank publications.

SAMPLE 14
(See Chapter 10)
Bank Loan Proposal Letter

From: XYZ Bank
To: ABC Limited

Term Sheet
(for discussion purposes only)

Confidential

Borrower ABC Limited

Lender XYZ Bank

Amount $70,000 Demand Operating Facility
3,000 Corporate VISA

Availment Operating facility may be availed of by way of overdraft.

Purpose To assist with general corporate financing and specifically to finance day-to-day operations and purchase of inventory.

Repayment Demand facility to fluctuate.

Interest Rates/ Fees, etc. Demand overdraft facility—Bank Prime + 1% payable monthly

Operating overdraft will be subject to an administration fee of $25 per month; Service Charge will be at the standard rate plus $10 per month; night deposit service will be at the standard rate of $1.10 per deposit bag.

SAMPLE 14 Continued

Security   General assignment of accounts receivable registered in (province).

Assignment of inventory under Section 42 of the Bank Act, with fire insurance over inventory, loss payable to the Bank firstly.

Covenants
1. Total debt to equity shall not exceed 1:1. Equity shall be defined as the sum of paid-up capital, retained earnings, shareholders' loans and deferred management salaries less advances made to shareholders or associated companies.
2. Operating overdrafts will not exceed 50% of total assigned inventories and eligible assigned accounts receivable.
3. There are to be no dividend payments, unusual withdrawals, or redemption of shares without the prior written consent of the Bank.
4. Capital expenditures in any one year shall not exceed $10,000 noncumulative without the prior written consent of the Bank, such consent not to be unreasonably withheld.
5. Monthly inventory declarations and receivable listings will be provided during those periods where an operating facility is in effect.
6. Annual financial statements prepared consistent with generally acceptable accounting principles by an accredited accounting firm shall be provided within 120 days of the borrower's fiscal year end.
7. Monthly profit-and-loss statement prepared internally shall be provided monthly.
8. The Bank may request any other financial information it considers necessary for the ongoing administration of the credit facility.
9. The Bank agrees to pay interest on credit balances in excess of $10,000 in your current account #0000 at the rate of the Bank's Prime Lending Rate less 3% per annum to be calculated on the average daily credit balance and payable monthly.

Events of Default   The usual events of default shall apply.

Review of Credit   The credit is subject to periodic review relative to the financial information to be provided, as well as an annual review by no later than May 30, 20__, in light of the annual statements.

This Term Sheet is for discussion purposes only, is not an offer and represents no commitment, express or implied, on the Bank's part. During our further analysis, information could come to our attention which would detract from the merits of the application and we reserve the right to discontinue the application at any time.

R. B. Jones
Manager

SAMPLE 15
(See Chapter 10)

Business Loan Application
(format commonly requested by lenders)

Please Check:

☐ Proprietorship   ☐ Corporation   ☐ General Partnership   ☐ Limited Partnership

Business Name:

Nature of Business:

Business Address: (Street, City, Postal Code)

Business Telephone   Year Business Established
(   )

E-mail Address:

How long under present ownership? Number of employees?

Amount of loan(s)	1. Please describe below how you plan to use your business loan(s)

$

2. What will be your primary source of repaying the loan(s)?	3. What are your usual terms of sale you offer your customers?

4. What are the usual terms of sale offered by your major suppliers?	5. Do you wish this loan(s) to be insured? ☐ Yes ☐ No

6. Please describe any seasonality or business cycle requirements related to your business.

SAMPLE 15 Continued

Principals/Owners

Full Name and Address	% Ownership	Title/Position

Historical/Projected Summary

- Existing businesses please provide financial information for the last 3 fiscal years.
- New business please provide projected financial information.

Financial Statements Prepared by	☐ Self ☐ Acct't ☐ Other	☐ Self ☐ Acct't ☐ Other	☐ Self ☐ Acct't ☐ Other
Year Ending (Date)	20__	20__	20__
Sales	$ _____	$ _____	$ _____
Gross Profit	$ _____	$ _____	$ _____
Net Profit after Tax	$ _____	$ _____	$ _____
Depreciation/Amortization	$ _____	$ _____	$ _____
Current Assets	$ _____	$ _____	$ _____
Total Assets	$ _____	$ _____	$ _____
Current Liabilities	$ _____	$ _____	$ _____
Total Liabilities	$ _____	$ _____	$ _____
Business Net Worth	$ _____	$ _____	$ _____

Credit Relationships

- Please provide details of your business credit relationships below.

Name of Creditor and Address	Purpose of Loan/Credit	Original Amount/ Limit	Amount Presently Owing	Repayment Terms	Maturity Date If Any
_____	_____	$ _____	$ _____	_____	
_____	_____	$ _____	$ _____	_____	
_____	_____	$ _____	$ _____	_____	
_____	_____	$ _____	$ _____	_____	

Sundry Obligations

- Please provide details below if you answer YES to any of the following questions.

Is the business providing support for obligations not listed on its financial statements (i.e., co-signer, endorser, guarantor, indemnifier, covenentor)? ☐ Yes ☐ No

If yes, please indicate total contingency liability $ _____

Is the business a party to any claim or lawsuit? ☐ Yes ☐ No

Has your business ever sought legal protection from its creditors (i.e., bankruptcy, receiver, receiver-manager)? ☐ Yes ☐ No

Does the business owe any taxes for years prior to the current year (i.e., sales tax, income tax, property tax, municipal business taxes or provincial corporation taxes)? ☐ Yes ☐ No

Amount $ _____ Owed to _____

Amount $ _____ Owed to _____

Amount $ _____ Owed to _____

Details of any of the above

_____

_____

Business References

- Trade creditor, personal, etc., in addition to those noted.

	Name	Address	Business Phone
Banker			
Lawyer			
Accountant			
Other			

SAMPLE 15 Continued

Insurance Coverage

- Existing businesses, please provide details of present coverage.
- New businesses, please state planned coverage.

Type of Coverage	Insurance Company	Amount of Coverage	Annual Premiums
_____	_____	$ _____	$ _____
_____	_____	$ _____	$ _____
_____	_____	$ _____	$ _____

The undersigned declare(s) that the statements made herein are for the purpose of obtaining business financing and are to the best of my/our knowledge true and correct. The applicant(s) consent(s) to the Bank making any inquiries it deems necessary to reach a decision on this application from a credit reporting agency or otherwise, and consent(s) to the disclosure at any time of any credit information about me/us to any credit reporting agency or to anyone with whom I/we have financial relations.

Per:_____   Per:_____
                Signature   Signature

_____   _____
                Date   Date

_____   _____
                Title   Title

SAMPLE 16
(See Chapter 10)

Loan/Financing Proposal Outline

A. Summary

1. Nature of business
2. Amount and purpose of loan
3. Repayment terms
4. Equity percentage of borrower (debt/equity ratio after loan)
5. Security or collateral (listed with market value estimates and quotes on cost of equipment to be purchased with the loan proceeds, if applicable)
6. If private investor, the amount of equity offered

B. Personal Information

(On all corporate officers, directors, and individuals owning any equity in the business)

1. Education, work history, and business experience
2. Credit references (if requested)
3. Financial net worth statements

C. Company Information

(Whichever is applicable below: 1 or 2)

1. New business:
   (a) Business plan (attach copy of your business plan)
   (b) Projections (this may have already been covered in your business plan):
     • profit-and-loss projection (monthly, for 1 year), explanation of projections and assumptions
     • cash flow projection (monthly, for 1 year), explanation of projections and assumptions
     • projected balance sheet (1 year after loan), explanation of projections and assumptions
2. Purchasing a business/Expanding an existing business:
   (a) Information on existing business or business to be acquired:
     • copy of offer to purchase agreement (if applicable)
     • business history (include seller's name, reasons for sale)
     • current profit-and-loss statements (preferably less than 60 days old) and previous 3 years
     • current balance sheet (not over 60 days old) and previous 3 years
     • cash flow statements for last year
     • business income tax returns as submitted to Revenue Canada (past 3 to 5 years)
     • copy of sales agreement with breakdown of inventory, fixtures, equipment, licences, goodwill and other costs
     • description and dates of permits or licences already existing
     • lease agreement
     • other relevant material
   (b) Business plan (attach copy of your business plan)
   (c) Insurance coverage
   (d) Partnership, corporation or franchise papers, if applicable

CHECKLIST C
(See Chapter 10)
Sources of Financing

Sources of Financing	Possible Source	Need Further Info	Further Info Obtained
Conventional Sources of Financing			
1. Banks			
(a) Short-term loans:			
• demand loans	___	___	___
• secured commercial loans	___	___	___
• unsecured commercial loans	___	___	___
• operating loans	___	___	___
• lines of credit	___	___	___
• accounts receivable loans	___	___	___
• warehouse receipt loans	___	___	___
• bridge financing	___	___	___
(b) Medium- and long-term loans:			
• term loans	___	___	___
• fixed charge debentures	___	___	___
• floating charge debentures	___	___	___
• conventional mortgages	___	___	___
• collateral mortgages	___	___	___
• business improvement loan	___	___	___
• chattel mortgages	___	___	___
• leasing	___	___	___
(c) Other financing services:			
• charge card for business expenses	___	___	___
• charge card for personal use	___	___	___
• factoring services	___	___	___
• leasing services	___	___	___
• letters of credit	___	___	___
• letters of guarantee	___	___	___
2. Business Development Bank of Canada (BDC)			
• term loans	___	___	___
• loan guarantees	___	___	___
• bridge financing	___	___	___
• equity financing	___	___	___
• leasing	___	___	___
• financial broker program (packaging loans to external lenders)	___	___	___
• joint ventures	___	___	___
• equity participation	___	___	___
3. Trust Companies			
• long-term loan	___	___	___
• mortgage financing	___	___	___

Sources of Financing	Possible Source	Need Further Info	Further Info Obtained
4. Credit Unions			
• term loans	_____	_____	_____
• working capital loans	_____	_____	_____
• mortgage financing	_____	_____	_____
• equity participation	_____	_____	_____
5. Insurance Companies			
• mortgage loans	_____	_____	_____
• loans based on insurance policy (cash surrender value)	_____	_____	_____
6. Investment Dealers			
• equity purchase	_____	_____	_____
• private placement	_____	_____	_____
• public issue of stock	_____	_____	_____
7. Commercial Finance Companies			
• equipment leasing	_____	_____	_____
• real estate loans	_____	_____	_____
• factoring	_____	_____	_____
• machinery and equipment loans	_____	_____	_____
• inventory financing	_____	_____	_____
• accounts or notes receivable financing	_____	_____	_____
8. Government Funding/Incentive/Purchasing Services			
(a) Federal government:			
• Foreign Affairs and International Trade Canada	_____	_____	_____
• Industry Canada	_____	_____	_____
• Canadian Commercial Corporation	_____	_____	_____
• Canadian International Development Agency (Crown corporation)	_____	_____	_____
• Export Development Canada (Crown corporation)	_____	_____	_____
• Public Works and Goods and Services Canada	_____	_____	_____
• Small Business Loans Act	_____	_____	_____
• Small business bond program	_____	_____	_____
• Business development centre	_____	_____	_____
• Human Resources and Skills Development Canada	_____		
• Business Development Bank of Canada	_____	_____	_____
• Community Futures Program	_____	_____	_____
• Other _____			
_____			
_____			
(b) Provincial government:			
• Small business ministries	_____	_____	_____
• Provincial development corporations (Crown corporations)	_____	_____	_____

CHECKLIST C Continued

Sources of Financing	Possible Source	Need Further Info	Further Info Obtained
• Provincial purchasing commissions	_____	_____	_____
• Other _____			
_____			
_____			
(c) Municipal/Regional governments:			
• Economic development commissions	_____	_____	_____
• Municipal government	_____	_____	_____
• Small business incubator start-up program	_____	_____	_____
• Other _____			
_____			
_____			

Creative Sources of Financing or Saving Money

1. Modifying Personal Lifestyle
   - reducing personal long-distance telephone calls — _____ _____ _____
   - minimizing entertainment expenses — _____ _____ _____
   - minimizing transportation costs (e.g., car pool, using more gas-efficient car) — _____ _____ _____
   - cutting down on tobacco and alcohol — _____ _____ _____
   - reducing number of restaurant meals by packing your own lunch — _____ _____ _____
   - combining personal and business travel — _____ _____ _____
   - taking on a part-time job — _____ _____ _____

2. Using Personal Assets
   - using credit cards — _____ _____ _____
   - using personal line of credit — _____ _____ _____
   - reducing premiums by reassessing insurance policy — _____ _____ _____
   - using funds in personal bank accounts — _____ _____ _____
   - renting out part of your home or garage — _____ _____ _____
   - selling stocks and bonds — _____ _____ _____
   - cashing in pension plans (e.g., RRSP) — _____ _____ _____
   - selling unnecessary personal possessions (e.g., second car) — _____ _____ _____
   - selling personal assets to the business — _____ _____ _____
   - remortgaging your home — _____ _____ _____

3. Using Private Investors Known to You
   - previous employers — _____ _____ _____
   - previous co-workers — _____ _____ _____
   - friends — _____ _____ _____
   - neighbours — _____ _____ _____
   - doctor — _____ _____ _____
   - lawyer — _____ _____ _____

Sources of Financing	Possible Source	Need Further Info	Further Info Obtained
• accountant	_____	_____	_____
• dentist	_____	_____	_____
• stockbroker	_____	_____	_____
4. Using Other Private Investors			
• through word-of-mouth contacts (various network groups)	_____	_____	_____
• answering ads online or in newspapers and magazines that read "investment capital available"	_____	_____	_____
• placing ads for a private investor in newspapers and magazines	_____	_____	_____
5. Family Assistance			
• loans from relatives	_____	_____	_____
• loans from immediate family members	_____	_____	_____
• equity financing from relatives	_____	_____	_____
• equity financing from immediate family	_____	_____	_____
• employing family members	_____	_____	_____
• sharing an office used by family members	_____	_____	_____
• using a family investment company	_____	_____	_____
6. Using Customers' Funds			
• having a cash-only policy	_____	_____	_____
• invoicing on an interim basis	_____	_____	_____
• asking for advance payments or deposits	_____	_____	_____
• providing discounts for prompt payments	_____	_____	_____
• charging purchases on customers' credit card accounts	_____	_____	_____
• getting signed purchase orders or contracts (collateral for bank)	_____	_____	_____
• third-party billing long-distance phone calls to customer's account	_____	_____	_____
7. Employees as Investors			
• asking staff to co-sign on loan guarantees	_____	_____	_____
• asking staff to invest in the business	_____	_____	_____
• direct loans from staff	_____	_____	_____
• paying partial salary in the form of stock	_____	_____	_____
8. Using Suppliers' Funds			
• supplier loans	_____	_____	_____
• establishing credit accounts with suppliers	_____	_____	_____
• buying goods on consignment	_____	_____	_____
• floor planning	_____	_____	_____
• equipment loans from manufacturer	_____	_____	_____
• rack jobbers	_____	_____	_____
• installment financing	_____	_____	_____
• conditional sales agreement	_____	_____	_____

CHECKLIST C Continued

Sources of Financing	Possible Source	Need Further Info	Further Info Obtained
• leasing equipment			
• co-op advertising			
9. Selling Ownership			
• incorporating and selling shares			
• taking on partners or shareholders			
10. Renting			
• sharing or subletting rental space, staff, and equipment costs with another business			
• renting a packaged office (office space, telephone answering, mailing address, secretarial services, equipment, etc.)			
• renting office space, furniture, and equipment			
11. Leasing			
• selling your assets and leasing them back through a commercial leasing company			
• leasing assets rather than purchasing			
12. Factoring Companies			
• factoring without recourse			
• factoring with recourse			
• company sets up its own factor			
• block discounting			
13. Volume Discounts			
• buying groups			
• agency discounts			
• co-op advertising			
• group rates on insurance			
14. Financial Matchmaking Services (lists of interested private investors)			
• federal government— entrepreneur immigrants under Immigration Act			
• provincial government small business departments			
• regional/municipal economic development commissions			
• Business Development Bank of Canada			
• chartered banks			
• Canadian Chamber of Commerce			
15. Other Creative Financing Techniques			
• advance royalty deals			
• licensing your product or service			
• franchisor financing			

Sources of Financing	Possible Source	Need Further Info	Further Info Obtained
• franchising your business			
• joint ventures			
• limited partnerships			
• business brokers			
• mortgage brokers			
• mortgage discounters			
• mutual fund companies			
• overseas lenders and investors			
• pension fund companies			
• small business stock savings plans (provincially regulated)			
• small business venture capital corporations (provincially regulated)			
• venture capital companies			
• local venture capital clubs			
• financial consultants			
• business consultants			
• obtaining services in exchange for equity			
• contra bartering (exchanging service/product for service/product)			
• RRSP (defer tax)			
• assigning exclusive rights to copyright or patent, etc.			
• proposal under Bankruptcy and Insolvency Act			
• informal proposal to creditors outside of Bankruptcy and Insolvency Act			

CHECKLIST D
(See Chapter 10)
Security Document Checklist

Name of Security	Already Understand Nature of Security	Need to Have Lawyer Explain	Lawyer Has Explained To My Satisfaction
1. S.427 Bank Act			
2. Debenture			
3. General Security Agreement			
4. Specific Security Agreement			
5. Assignment of life insurance policy			
6. Assignment of accounts receivable (book debts)			
7. Assignment of contract proceeds			
8. Assignment of lease			
9. Assignment of mortgage			
10. Assignment of rents (Hypothecation Agreement)			
11. Pledge of securities			
12. Chattel mortgage			
13. Conventional mortgage			
14. Collateral mortgage			
15. Conditional sales agreement			
16. Demand note			
17. Promissory note			
18. Indemnity agreement			
19. Personal guarantee—unlimited			
20. Personal guarantee—limited			
21. Personal guarantee—joint and several			
22. Postponement of claim			
23. Warehouse receipt			
24. Floor plan contract			
25. Other _____			

Note: Many of the security documents above are covered by a Specific Security Agreement or General Security Agreement under Provincial Personal Property Security legislation. Several of the descriptive names used above are therefore common or colloquial terms.

SAMPLE 17
(See Chapter 11)

Payroll Records

For Each Employee

Employee Name: _____ Position: _____

Address: _____

Home Telephone: _____ Salary: _____ Start Date: _____

Social Insurance No.: _____ Fed. Tax Exemption: _____

Pay Period	Hours Worked	Rate	Gross Pay	EI	CPP/QPP	Fed. Tax	Prov. Tax*	Med.	Other	Total Deductions	Net Pay	Cheque No.

* Quebec only.

SAMPLE 17 Continued

For Each Month

Payroll Summary

Employee Names	Gross Earnings	EI	CPP/QPP	Fed. Tax	Prov. Tax*	Med.	Other	Total Deductions	Net Earnings
Total									

* Quebec only.

SAMPLE 18
(See Chapter 11)

Policy Statements

Hours of Work

Detail here the number of hours to be worked per week, the number of days per week, evening and holiday work, and the time and method of payment for both regular and overtime work. Unnecessary payment of overtime at premium rates is a source of needless expense. By planning ahead, you may be able to organize your employees' work to keep overtime to a minimum. When peak periods do occur, you can often handle them by using part-time help paid at regular rates.

Wages

You may decide to pay employees the average of rates for similar work in the community; to comply with all applicable wage legislation, such as minimum wage and vacation pay legislation; and to review wages and individual performance at least once a year.

Fringe Benefits

You may consider offering your employees discounts on merchandise, free life insurance, health insurance, tuition payments at schools and colleges.

Vacations

How long will vacations be? Will you specify the time of the year they may be taken? With or without pay?

Time Off

Will you allow employees time off for personal needs, emergencies in the family, doctor and dental appointments? Up to a certain amount per month or per year?

Training

You must make sure that each employee is given adequate training for the job. Effective training techniques may be included in your procedures manual.

Personnel Review

Will you periodically review your employees' performance? What factors will you consider? Will you make salary adjustments, training recommendations? Will you increase responsibilities and change job titles?

Termination

The conditions warranting discharge, with or without warnings, severance pay, layoffs, seniority rights, etc., should be outlined.

SAMPLE 19
(See Chapter 11)

Job Description

Job Title: Administrative Assistant

Accountable to: Manager

Job Summary
To perform reception, telephone answering, and secretarial duties.

Duties and Responsibilities
To answer the telephone in a pleasant and courteous manner, answering whenever possible by the third ring; advise appropriate personnel; take messages when necessary.

To greet customers and visitors in a friendly manner, see that they are comfortably seated in reception area; advise appropriate company personnel promptly on visitor's arrival.

To word process efficiently and accurately correspondence, reports, statements, manual updates, mailing-list updates, etc., as requested.

To record invoice detail in sales journal log on a regular basis, and balance entries at end of month.

To compile information and prepare reports as requested from time to time.

To order and maintain inventory of supplies.

To assist and back up Senior Secretary as required.

Job Requirements

High school diploma or equivalent.

At least 2 years' experience in a similar job. Able

to type a minimum of 60 words per minute.

Proficiency in grammar, spelling, and punctuation skills; able to identify and correct such errors.

Able to operate: fax machine, computer (understanding of a wide range of software), postage meter, photocopier, 20-line switchboard.

Date Description Created/Revised: _____

SAMPLE 20
(See Chapter 11)

Employment Application Form

(Please print or write neatly.)   Date: _____

Application for Position as: _____

Seeking part-time or full-time _____   Date Available:_____

First Name: _____   Last Name: _____

Home Phone: _____   Work Phone:_____

Address:_____

Education:

1. Post-Secondary: Institution: _____ From/To: _____

                    Program:_____ Degree:

2. High School: School/City: _____ From/To: _____

                    Program:_____ Graduated: _____

3. Other: Institution: _____ From/To: _____

                    Program:_____ Diploma: _____

Previous Employment

1. Last Position: Company: _____ From/To: _____

                    Address: _____ Beg. Salary _____

                    Position: _____ End Salary _____

                    Duties: _____

                    Reason for Leaving: _____

2. 2nd-Last Position: Company: _____ From/To: _____

                    Address: _____ Beg. Salary _____

                    Position: _____ End Salary _____

                    Duties: _____

                    Reason for Leaving: _____

3. 3rd-Last Position: Company: _____ From/To: _____

                    Address: _____ Beg. Salary _____

                    Position: _____ End Salary _____

                    Duties: _____

                    Reason for Leaving: _____

(indicate by number which employers you do not wish us to contact:

☐ 1 ☐ 2 ☐ 3.)

Other Information _____

_____

SAMPLE 20 Continued

References
(Provide names of references who are not previous employers or relatives.)

1. Name: _____ Occupation: _____ Phone: _____

2. Name: _____ Occupation: _____ Phone: _____

3. Name: _____ Occupation: _____ Phone: _____

I hereby certify that all information in this application is correct and complete to the best of my knowledge and belief. I understand that intentional falsification of information could result in refusal of employment or immediate discharge. I authorize the schools, employers, or persons above-named to provide information regarding my education, employment, character, and qualifications.

Signature: _____ Date: _____

SAMPLE 21
(See Chapter 11)

Interview Form

Applicant's Name: _____ Date: _____

Abilities	Poor (1–2)	Fair (3)	Good (4–5)	Comments
• Education/Training				
• Experience				
• Job knowledge and skills				
• Intelligence/Alertness				
• Verbal communication skills				
• Organizational skills				
Characteristics				
• Maturity				
• Goals and ambition				
• Motivation and initiative				
• Confidence				
• Personal grooming and poise				
• Personality				
• Manner and attitude				
Salary requirement				
Additional training required				
Availability				
Total				

List applicant's strong and weak points for the position.

Strong_____   _____

Weak_____   _____

(Score on a scale of 1 to 5, with 5 being the highest score. Total all scores to give overall rating.)

SAMPLE 22
(See Chapter 11)

Telephone Reference Check Form

Applicant:_____

Person contacted: _____Title: _____

Company: _____Phone: _____

   "Hello, my name is _____ from <u>(company)</u>. We are considering hiring one of your former employees,<u>(applicant's name)</u>, and would like to verify some information with you."

1. What were the dates of his/her employment with you?
   From: To:

2. What were his/her earnings and positions held?

3. Why did he/she leave your company?

4. Would you re-employ? If no, why not?

5. On a scale of "excellent, average, poor," how would you rate his/her:

	Poor	Average	Excellent
• Attendance			
• Quality of work			
• Dependability			
• Personality			
• Degree of supervision needed			

6. Did he/she get along well with other people?

7. Did he/she accept supervision willingly?

8. While in your employ were there any questionable activities?

9. Remarks

SAMPLE 23
(See Chapter 11)

Employee Performance Review

For Period Ending _____

Employee _____ Time in Position _____

Position Title _____ Employment Date _____

Department _____

Instructions

Evaluate the employee on job now being performed. Consider each characteristic separately regardless of the rating for any other characteristic. Consider the row of nine boxes (three below each phrase) as a scale, the extreme right approaching perfection and the extreme left indicating inadequacy. Place a check in the most appropriate of the three boxes below the phrase that most accurately describes the employee's level of performance for each characteristic.

1. Knowledge of Job and Responsibilities

Consider knowledge of job and responsibilities gained through education, training, and experience.

Fair or little knowledge of specific job and related work	Satisfactory knowledge of job and related work	Thorough knowledge of job content and related responsibilities
_____ _____	_____ _____	_____ _____

2. Analytical Ability and Judgment

Consider ability to analyze situation or problem, sense of perception and judgment shown in work.

Difficulty in analyzing problems, judgment occasionally faulty	Average perception and judgment	Unusually perceptive, makes sound judgments
_____ _____	_____ _____	_____ _____

3. Initiative

Consider ability to originate or develop constructive ideas and to take necessary steps for accomplishment.

Follows precedent, contributes little beyond what is required	Exhibits average initiative, makes routine contributions	Resourceful, makes frequent constructive contributions
_____ _____ _____	_____ _____ _____	_____ _____ _____

4. Planning and Organization

Consider ability to plan and organize assigned work to make most effective use of personnel, materials, and equipment.

Lacks some ability to plan and organize	Effective under most conditions	Successful under most adverse conditions
____ ____	____ ____	____ ____

5. Dependability

Consider thoroughness, efficiency, and reliability of results.

Work lacks some thoroughness and dependability	Meets standard requirements, results usually dependable	Work thoroughly completed, results are consistently accurate
____ ____	____ ____	____ ____

6. Cooperation

Consider ability to work with other persons within the company towards best interests of all concerned.

Inclined to resist cooperation	Cooperates when necessary or when asked	Cooperates well, frequently provides constructive assistance
____ ____	____ ____	____ ____

7. Leadership

Consider ability to inspire willingness and desire towards given objectives and ability to develop aptitudes in others.

Difficulty in directing and/or developing aptitudes of others	Satisfactory direction and leadership of others	Effectively leads and develops capabilities of others
____ ____	____ ____	____

8. Willingness to Express Ideas

Consider courage to express and defend logical principles and convictions

Tends to agree with others against own judgment	Expresses honest convictions when asked to do so	Defends principles and opinions even under adverse conditions
____ ____	____ ____	____ ____

9. Ability to Communicate Effectively

Consider ability to express thoughts and ideas effectively in writing and orally.

Some difficulty expressing ideas orally and/or in writing	Normal ability to communicate orally and/or in writing	Superior ability to communicate effectively in writing and orally
____ ____	____ ____	____ ____

SAMPLE 23 Continued

Is employee properly placed? _____

Comments_____

_____

_____

Highlight strong and weak points of job performance_____

_____

_____

_____

_____

_____

_____

How can employee best improve his or her value to the company?_____

Other comments _____

_____

_____

_____

_____

Employee under my supervision for _____months

Prepared by _____Date _____

Approved by_____Date _____

I have read this performance review and discussed it with my supervisor. My signature indicates that I am aware of its content, but does not imply either agreement or disagreement.

Employee's Signature _____Date _____

Employee's Comments (Optional) _____

_____

_____

_____

_____

_____

_____

_____

SAMPLE 24
(See Chapter 12)

Equipment Comparison Chart

	#1	#2	#3	#4
Suppliers				
Company Name:				
Model Name and Number:				
Needed Features				
• Monthly volume:				
• Ease of operation				
• High quality				
•				
•				
•				
•				
•				
•				
Costs:				
• Equipment				
• Add-on features				
• Delivery and installation				
• Start-up kit of supplies				
• Training				
• Total cost				
• Total budget $ _____				
Service:				
• Cost				
• Warranty period				
• Cost of extended warranty				
• Response time—urgent				
• Response time— not urgent				
• Company stability				

CHECKLIST E
(See Chapter 13)

Media Mix Checklist

Media	Will Use	Will Not Use	Need Further Info	Further Info Obtained
1. Radio				
• commercials	____	____	____	____
• jingles	____	____	____	____
• live broadcasts	____	____	____	____
• news events	____	____	____	____
• sponsorships	____	____	____	____
2. Television				
• commercials	____	____	____	____
• live broadcasts	____	____	____	____
• sponsorships	____	____	____	____
3. Newspapers				
• community papers	____	____	____	____
• daily papers	____	____	____	____
• weekend papers	____	____	____	____
• weekly papers	____	____	____	____
4. Trade Publications				
• consumer magazines	____	____	____	____
• directories/catalogues	____	____	____	____
• magazines	____	____	____	____
• newsletters	____	____	____	____
• newspapers	____	____	____	____
• specialty publications	____	____	____	____
5. Advertising on the Internet				
• banner advertising, Google Ads	____	____	____	____
• own website	____	____	____	____
– Other				
6. Miscellaneous Publications				
• local and community publications	____	____	____	____
• mail tabloids	____	____	____	____
• religious publications	____	____	____	____
• theatre programs	____	____	____	____
• university and school publications	____	____	____	____
• foreign language or ethnic press	____	____	____	____

Media	Will Use	Will Not Use	Need Further Info	Further Info Obtained
7. Direct Mail				
• booklets, catalogues, brochures				
• circulars				
• envelope enclosures: stuffers, folders				
• letters				
• postcards and mailing cards				
• self-mailing folders				
8. Miscellaneous Direct Mail				
• flyers				
• gift novelties				
• handbills, circulars				
• merchandise labels				
• package inserts				
• prints of advertisements				
• special delivery letters				
• store publications				
• telegrams				
• wrapping supplies				
9. Telephone				
• sales phone call				
• automated/computer phone call				
10. Outdoor Signs				
• billboards				
• electric signs				
• posters				
11. Indoor Signs/Displays				
• bus station display advertising				
• train station display advertising				
• ferry terminal display advertising				
• elevator display advertising				
• product postcard service				
• shopping cart display advertising				
• supermarket advertising				
• stadium advertising				
• theatre screen advertising				
• point-of-purchase displays				
12. Cars				
• car signs				
• transit advertising (interior and exterior)				

CHECKLIST E Continued

Media	Will Use	Will Not Use	Need Further Info	Further Info Obtained
13. Trade Shows				
• demonstrations	___	___	___	___
• exhibits	___	___	___	___
• fashion/product shows	___	___	___	___
• industry shows	___	___	___	___
• local trade fairs	___	___	___	___
14. Miscellaneous				
• airplane banners	___	___	___	___
• airport display advertising	___	___	___	___
• bench signs	___	___	___	___
• kites and balloons	___	___	___	___
• promotional films	___	___	___	___
• skywriting	___	___	___	___
• slide presentations	___	___	___	___
• street banners	___	___	___	___
• taxicab signs	___	___	___	___
• truck signs and posters	___	___	___	___
• window signs	___	___	___	___
15. Promotional Aids				
• business cards	___	___	___	___
• calendars	___	___	___	___
• pens	___	___	___	___
• store bags	___	___	___	___

SAMPLE 25
(See Chapter 15)

Confidential Credit Application
(Please Complete In Full)

Company Name (Please complete in full):

Legal Name: _____

Trade Style—if other than above:_____

Business location: Street_____City _____

　　　　　　　　Province _____Postal Code_____

Mailing Address:_____

Company is a

☐ Proprietorship　☐ Partnership　☐ Limited Corporation　☐ Subsidiary

If a corporation, is it ☐ Federal　☐ Provincial

If subsidiary, parent company is:

Legal Name: _____

Business location: Street_____City _____

                       Province _____Postal Code_____

Officers/Directors:

Name: _____ Title: _____

Residence Address: _____ City: _____

Province:_____ Postal Code: _____

Telephone: _____ Years with Business: _____

Name: _____ Title: _____

Residence Address: _____ City: _____

Province:_____ Postal Code: _____

Telephone: _____ Years with Business: _____

Name: _____ Title: _____

Residence Address: _____ City: _____

Province:_____ Postal Code: _____

Telephone: _____ Years with Business: _____

Nature of business: ☐ Retail ☐ Service ☐ Wholesale ☐ Other

Please describe: _____

Length of time in business:_____ Average no. of employees: _____

Annual sales volume of business: _____

Business Property:

Owned _____ Name of mortgage holder:_____

Rented_____ Name of landlord: _____

Bank (if more than one, please list):

Bank: _____ Address: _____

Bank: _____ Address: _____

Trade References:

1. Name:_____

   Address: _____

2. Name:_____

   Address: _____

3. Name:_____

   Address: _____

SAMPLE 25 Continued

4. Name: _____

    Address: _____

5. Name: _____

    Address: _____

Authorized purchasing agent(s): _____

Credit limit requested: _____

Name of your Accounts Payable Manager: _____

The undersigned confirms and acknowledges that:

a) the seller's terms are set out fully (e.g., net due on receipt, 10 days, 30 days, or 50% prepayment on every order for first 6 months, discounts, etc.).

b) all freight and insurance charges are solely the buyer's responsibility.

c) a service charge shall be rendered on any overdue balances at an interest rate of (e.g., 1½%) per month.

d) the credit limit, payment terms and overdue interest rate may change from time to time depending on circumstances, and the applicant shall be notified of any changes in writing and shall be bound by these changes.

The undersigned further declares that the statements made herein are for the express purpose of obtaining a commercial credit account and are to the best of my/our knowledge and belief true and correct. The applicant understands that additional information, if required in support of this application, may be required before adequate consideration can be given to this application.

The undersigned officers/directors hereby confirm that they will personally benefit if credit is extended to the company (if corporation) and in consideration of credit being extended to the company, irrevocably guarantee and covenant to jointly and severally be responsible in their personal capacities for all outstanding debts owing by the company.

The undersigned company (if corporation) and its directors/officers signing on their own behalf, and on behalf of the company (if corporation), or owner (if proprietorship) or partners (if partnership) hereby authorize(s) the person or firm to whom this application is submitted to obtain such credit reports or other information as may be deemed necessary, from time to time, in connection with the establishment and maintenance of a credit account on the company and/or its officers/directors (or owner or partners).

Dated this _____day of _____, 20__.

_____   _____
Name of Applicant Business   Director

_____   _____
Authorized Signatory (State title)   Director

_____   _____
Authorized Signatory (State title)   Director

SAMPLE 26
(See Chapter 15)

Aged List of Accounts Receivable
As of _____, 20__

Names of Debtors	Total (Omit Cents)	Current	31–60 Days	61–90 Days	Over 90 Days and Holdbacks	Remarks
Total Dollars						
Total Number						
Percentage						

Trend Analysis ($ Percentage)

Age	J	F	M	A	M	J	J	A	S	O	N	D
Current												
31–60 days												
61–90 days												
91–120 days												
Over 120 days												

SAMPLE 27
(See Chapter 15)

Reminder Letter

Dear _____:

Re: Invoice # (Number), Balance $ (Amount)

Payment of the above-noted invoice in the amount of $ (Amount) does not yet appear to have been received. As you know, the terms that we agreed upon require payment within 30 days of the date of purchase, which made this amount due and payable on (Date).

Since you have established an excellent credit rating with us, possibly it is an oversight that we have not yet received your payment. If there is an error, or you are unable to pay the amount due immediately, please contact me to discuss this matter.

Thank you in advance for your cooperation and attention to this matter.

Yours very truly,

_____

P.S. If you have already paid this balance and it is in the mail, please disregard this letter and we apologize for any inconvenience.

SAMPLE 28
(See Chapter 15)

Payment Past Due Follow-up Letter

Dear _____:

Re: Invoice # (Number), Balance $ (Amount)

We are concerned that we have not received any response to our recent invoice, nor to our letter/telephone call of (Date). Your account is now (No.) days overdue. The total amount owing is $ (Balance owing).

If there is some reason why you are unable to pay immediately, please contact me personally as soon as you receive this letter. Only with your cooperation can we work out an arrangement mutually agreeable yet realistic for your present circumstances.

We regret that until we have resolved this matter, no new purchases may be credited to your account. We are sure you wish to preserve your past highly satisfactory credit standing with us, and we trust that you will appreciate our position in this regard.

Thank you.

Yours very truly,

_____

P.S. A stamped, self-addressed envelope has been enclosed for your convenience.

SAMPLE 29
(See Chapter 15)

Delinquent Payment Notice

Dear _____:

Re: Invoice # (Number), Balance $ (Amount)

In spite of repeated requests for payment, we still have not received your cheque, nor have you contacted us about mutually satisfactory repayment arrangements.

We have sincerely attempted to be fair, and have extended credit to you far beyond our usual terms and policy. We must insist on immediate payment or a satisfactory reason for nonpayment by return mail, to prevent serious collection measures against you.

Yours very truly,

_____

SAMPLE 30
(See Chapter 15)

Final Request

Dear _____:

Re: Invoice # (Number), Balance $ (Amount)

It is obvious that our efforts to settle the account on a mutually agreeable basis have been unsuccessful.

Unless we receive payment in full from you within seven (7) days from today's date, or alternatively a mutually satisfactory arrangement by that date, the account will be turned over immediately to our lawyers for further action.

Not only will this procedure create extra costs to you, it will also cause serious damage to your credit rating. We are sure you do not want that rating impaired, as it will show up in the Credit Bureau records and therefore be known by all your current or future creditors when an inquiry is made.

Please call, or visit my office immediately so that we can resolve the matter, without resorting to further actions.

Yours very truly,

_____

SAMPLE 31
(See Chapter 15)

Confirmation Letter

Dear _____:

Re: Invoice # (Number), Balance $ (Amount)

We refer to our telephone conversation of (today/yesterday), when we inquired as to the reason for nonpayment of this invoice for $ (Amount) dated (Date) . Because you have experienced some temporary difficulties that prevent payment immediately, we confirm that we accept your offer to make payment in full within the next two (2) weeks (or payments over time by postdated cheques, etc.).

We therefore look forward to receiving your cheque(s) by (Date). Thank you.

Yours very truly,

_____

CHECKLIST F
(See Chapter 15)
Credit and Collection Procedures

Credit Approval

	Yes	No	N/A
1. Is a written credit application required with every credit request?			
2. Do you have a standard form for credit applications?			
3. Did you have your lawyer prepare/review your credit application form?			
4. If extending credit to a corporation, do you make the principals personally guarantee the corporate data?			
5. Are you a member of your local Credit Bureau? Dun & Bradstreet?			
6. Are applicants (corporate and personal) automatically checked out with the credit bureau or credit agency (e.g., Dun & Bradstreet) before credit is extended?			
7. Does your evaluation procedure include automatically checking bank references?			
8. Do you confirm credit application acceptance in writing?			

Terms of Sale

	Yes	No	N/A
9. Do you offer a cash discount?			
10. Do you impose a late-payment penalty?			
11. Do you charge interest on overdue accounts?			
12. Are the payment terms and time limit for payment clearly stated on invoices, statements, and credit contracts?			

Invoices

	Yes	No	N/A
13. Are invoices prepared and mailed promptly or on a regular basis?			
14. Is the invoice preparation always accurate?			
15. Are payment terms clearly stated?			
16. Are customers' special instructions followed carefully?			

Statements

	Yes	No	N/A
17. Are monthly or bi-monthly statements mailed to all open accounts?			
18. Are statements prompt and accurate?			
19. Do you have an efficient, organized system for rendering statements?			

CHECKLIST F Continued

Identification of problems	Yes	No	N/A

20. Do you determine your average collection period on a regular basis? _____ _____ _____

21. Do you compare your collection period:
    • with industry averages? _____ _____ _____
    • with your previous experience? _____ _____ _____
    • with your payment terms? _____ _____ _____

22. Do you have a monthly aging of all outstanding accounts receivable? _____ _____ _____

23. Have you pledged your receivables to the bank as security for a line of credit? _____ _____ _____

24. Is your bank satisfied with the aging status of your accounts? _____ _____ _____

25. Do you allow any of your accounts to be beyond 60 days before handing it over to a lawyer or collection agency? _____ _____ _____

26. Do you calculate your monthly bad debt percentage and is this acceptable to you? _____ _____ _____

27. When a percentage problem is identified, is corrective action prompt and firm? _____ _____ _____

Collection

28. Do you have a systematic procedure to follow up slow accounts? _____ _____ _____

29. Do you use the telephone to contact delinquent accounts? _____ _____ _____

30. Is your telephone collection technique effective? _____ _____ _____

31. Do you write a confirmatory letter following all collection calls? _____ _____ _____

32. Do you accurately record on a client account details on the collection conversations? _____ _____ _____

33. Do you have special arrangements for collecting past-due accounts? _____ _____ _____

34. Do you try to retain the goodwill of your customers in your collection procedures? _____ _____ _____

35. Do you have a late-payment penalty or interest charge, and do you attempt to collect it? _____ _____ _____

36. Do you sell to delinquent accounts on COD terms? _____ _____ _____

37. Do you send all overdue accounts over 45 or 60 days to a collection agency (credit bureau or Dun & Bradstreet) or to your lawyer, or both? _____ _____ _____

Credit Policy

	Yes	No	N/A
38. Have you taken any seminars on credit and collection techniques from Dun & Bradstreet, BDC, or others?	___	___	___
39. Has your staff taken any seminars on credit and collections from Dun & Bradstreet, BDC, or others?	___	___	___
40. Do you use liberal credit terms to promote sales in certain situations, and do you believe this is risky?	___	___	___
41. Are your credit terms comparable to those of your principal competitors?	___	___	___
42. Do you accept cheques from unknown customers?	___	___	___
43. Have you contracted with a cheque verification service for unknown clients?	___	___	___
44. Do you have a stamp you place on the back of a cheque requesting details from the unknown customer?	___	___	___
45. Do you take credit cards for customer payment (Visa, MasterCard, American Express)?	___	___	___
46. Have you considered the merchant commission discount savings by being a member of the Retail Merchants Association of Canada branch in your province?	___	___	___
47. Have you thoroughly considered the advantages and disadvantages of extending credit in your business operation?	___	___	___
48. Do you use a computerized system for keeping track of accounts, rendering invoices and monitoring outstanding amounts?	___	___	___

SAMPLE 32
(See Chapter 18)

Confidentiality/Nondisclosure Agreement

ABC LIMITED
1234 Front Street
Toronto, Ontario
xxx xxx

June 1, 20__
David Jones
MPS INTERNATIONAL INC.
678 Main Street
Vancouver, B.C.
xxx xxx

Re: Confidentiality and Nondisclosure Agreement

Dear Mr. Jones:

I am writing to outline our understanding and agreement concerning the confidentiality of information likely to be made known to MPS International Inc. (referred to as "MPS") and ABC Limited (referred to as "ABC"), respectively, as a result of discussions concerning mutual business opportunities in Canada and/or a possible joint venture arrangement.

In general, I believe our understanding may be summarized as follows.

In consideration of the mutual willingness of ABC and MPS to furnish or disclose to each other certain confidential and proprietary information (i) in order to assist in the evaluation of ABC's products and services with a view towards purchasing, leasing, or otherwise using such products and services; and/or (ii) in connection with a contract or agreement between MPS and ABC for the use of ABC's services and products, the parties hereto, intending to be legally bound, agree for itself and any subsidiaries as follows:

1. Confidential Information shall include all information emanating from ABC or MPS or their agents and relating to MPS and its plants, processes and facilities, or ABC or any of its services or products including, but not limited to, trade secrets, technical information, designs, drawings, processes, systems, procedures, formulae, test data, know-how, improvements, price lists, financial data, supplies, vendors, sketches and plans (engineering, architectural or otherwise), or any other compilation of information whatsoever, in written form and marked confidential, secret, or the like, or if initially disclosed orally, subsequently reduced to writing, and so marked and provided by the disclosing party to the receiving party within thirty (30) days thereafter, except that Confidential and Proprietary Information shall not include information which:

   (a) prior to the receipt thereof: (i) was generally publicly available; or (ii) was in Recipient's possession free of any restrictions on its use or disclosure from a source other than the party divulging the information under terms of this Agreement; and

(b) after receipt thereof: (i) becomes publicly available without the fault of Recipient; or (ii) is acquired by Recipient from a third party, free of any restrictions as to its disclosure.

2. Any and all information claimed confidential under paragraph 1 by a claimant shall be reduced to writing so marked and forwarded by the claimant to the following representatives of each party, at the respective addresses set out below:

(a) ABC

Roberta White
ABC Limited
1234 Front Street
Toronto, Ontario
xxx xxx

(b) MPS

David Jones
MPS International Inc.
678 Main Street
Vancouver, B.C.
xxx xxx

It is understood, however, that Recipient nevertheless shall keep confidential the fact that any such disclosed information is similar or identical to any such exceptional information.

3. All Confidential and Proprietary Information which is furnished to or acquired by MPS or ABC or any officers, directors, employees, agents, or other representatives of MPS or ABC shall be held in the strictest confidence. Confidential and Proprietary Information shall be copied, duplicated, used, or disclosed solely for the purposes of evaluating or procuring ABC's products or services, and shall not be disclosed for such purposes except to such employees, agents, or representatives of the undersigned as are necessary to perform such evaluations or procure said products or services.

MPS and ABC agree that all of their employees, agents, and representatives who have any access for whatever reason to the Confidential and Proprietary Information shall have agreed similarly in writing to hold such in the strictest confidence and not permit its unauthorized copying, duplication, use, or disclosure.

4. Copies of any and all tangible Confidential and Proprietary Information furnished to or acquired by MPS or ABC, including all duplicates or copies thereof, shall be immediately returned at the owner's request.

5. The parties hereby acknowledge that MPS and ABC would be irreparably damaged in the event that any of the terms of this Agreement are violated and that such terms shall be enforceable through issuance of an injunction restraining the unauthorized copying, duplication, use, or disclosure of any Confidential and Proprietary Information furnished to or acquired by the parties or any employees, agents, or representatives, or through any other equitable remedies which shall be cumulative with and not exclusive of any other remedy available to the parties.

SAMPLE 32 Continued

6. This Agreement constitutes the entire agreement between MPS and ABC and supersedes all other communications, oral and written, relating to the subject matter hereof. This letter Agreement shall be governed and construed in accordance with the laws of the Province of _____, and shall inure to the benefit of and be binding upon the successors, assigns, heirs, administrators, trustees, and representatives of the undersigned and ABC.

7. The undersigned officers of ABC and MPS represent that they have the authority to execute this document to bind themselves, the corporation, and others in the corporation that might have access to the Confidential Information.

I believe that the foregoing accurately summarizes our understanding. If you agree, please signify your concurrence by executing this Agreement below and returning the original to me at your earliest convenience.

Agreed and accepted this_____day of _____, 20__.

ABC LIMITED

_____   _____

Witness   Roberta White
                                   President

MPS INTERNATIONAL INC.

_____   _____

Witness   David Jones
                                   President

SAMPLE 33
(See Chapter 18)
Employer-Employee Agreement

MEMORANDUM OF AGREEMENT made the _____day of _____, 20___ , between ABC Limited (herein called the employer), of the first part, and John Doe (herein called the employee), of the second part.

WHEREAS the employer is engaged in the manufacture or production of

_____,

and owns or controls patented and secret methods, processes, and formulae applicable thereto, and may from time to time become engaged in the manufacture or production of other and different products or commodities, and acquire or develop additional methods, processes, and formulae (all of which are hereinafter referred to as inventions), which constitute a very valuable part of the assets of the employer;

AND WHEREAS in connection with the study of the problems relating to such manufacture and production and the discovery, improvement, and perfection of inventions, many of the employees of the employer, even though not directly engaged in such manufacture or production, are by reason of the nature of their duties informed with respect to such inventions and are from time to time enabled to contribute new inventions or improvements on existing inventions;

AND WHEREAS the employee desires to enter (or continue as the case may be) in the employment of the employer and, to such extent as may be possible, to cooperate in the improvement of the employer's inventions:

NOW THEREFORE the employer and the employee, in consideration of the respective mutual promises and agreements hereinafter set forth, promise and agree each with the other as follows:

1. During the period of his said employment, the employee shall devote his or her entire time and best efforts to such duties as may be assigned to him or her by the employer, and will faithfully and diligently serve and endeavour to further the interests of the employer.

2. Any and all inventions and improvements thereon which the employee may conceive or make during the period of his or her said employment, relating or in any way appertaining to or connected with any of the matters which have been, are, or may become the subject of the employer's investigations, are to be the sole and exclusive property of the employer, and the employee will, whenever requested to do so by the employer, execute any and all applications, assignments and other instruments which the employer shall deem necessary in order to apply for and obtain Letters Patent of Canada or foreign countries for such inventions or improvements and in order to assign and convey to the employer the sole and exclusive right, title, and interest in and to such inventions, improvements, applications, and patents.

3. The employee shall not, directly or indirectly, disclose or use, at any time, either during or subsequent to his or her said employment, any secret or any confidential information concerning the employer's processes, methods, formulae, apparatus specifications, materials, and sources of supply thereof, customers, their identities and requirements, discoveries, inventions, patents (including applications and rights in either), contracts, finances, personnel, their duties and capabilities, research, plans, policies, and intentions, including matters, though not technically trade secrets, the dissemination of a knowledge whereof might prove prejudicial to employer.

4. The employer shall employ the employee (or continue the employee's employment as the case may be) at a wage or salary to be mutually agreed upon between them for such length of time as shall be mutually agreeable.

5. The employee's obligations to execute the papers referred to in paragraph 2 hereof shall continue beyond the termination of his employment with respect to any and all inventions or improvements conceived or made by him or her during his or her employment, and such obligations shall be binding on the assigns, executors, administrators, or other legal representatives of the employee.

6. The expense of applying for and obtaining the Letters Patent referred to in paragraph 2 hereof shall be borne entirely by the employer.

7. This agreement shall be binding upon and enure to the benefit of the employer, its successors, and assigns.

SAMPLE 33 Continued

IN WITNESS WHEREOF the parties have executed their signatures.

_____
ABC LIMITED

_____   _____
WITNESS   EMPLOYEE

SAMPLE 34
(See Chapter 21)

Time Log

To accomplish today: Date: _____

1. _____
2. _____
3. _____
4. _____
5. _____

Time	Activity	Total Min.	Priority Level A/B/C/	Comments
A.M.				
P.M.				

Priority Level:

High _____ hrs. _____ min. (_____ %)

Medium _____ hrs. _____ min. (_____ %)

Low _____ hrs. _____ min. (_____ %)

SAMPLE 35
(See Chapter 21)

Weekly Time-Use Analysis

A. Planning and Priorities

Rate on a scale 1-5 (one point for each day)

1. Did I plan my day (to do lists)? _____
2. Did I set priorities? _____
3. Did I stick with them? _____
4. High priorities: Number achieved _____

                    Number—some progress _____

                    Number—no action _____

5. Overall success score on priority setting _____
6. Problems encountered: _____
7. Possible solutions: _____
_____

	When?	What did I do?
8. Most productive time:	_____	_____
9. Discretionary time:	_____	_____
10. Did I set a quiet hour?	_____	_____

B. Time Management

1. Delegation:

   a) What did I delegate? _____

   b) How effective? _____

   c) What else could I delegate? _____

2. Paperwork:

   a) Handled papers once: how effective? _____

   b) Tidy, clear desk: how effective? _____

   c) How much paper shuffling? _____

   d) Ways to improve: _____

3. Meetings:

   a) Effectiveness of meetings I ran: _____

   b) Effectiveness of someone else's meetings: _____

   c) Problems: _____

   d) Solutions: _____

SAMPLE 35 Continued

C. Time Wasters

    1. Interruptions:

        a) Who? What purpose? How long? _____

        b) Ways to cut down or eliminate:_____

    2. Procrastination:

        a) What? Why?_____

        b) Possible solutions: _____

    3. Other time wasters:

        a) What? Who? How much? _____

        b) Causes: _____

        c) Solutions: _____

N.B. You may choose to highlight your solutions and build them into your plan for next week.

SAMPLE 36
(See Conclusion)

Action Plan Checklist

Step	Estimated Date of Completion	Actual Date of Completion	Comments
1. Preliminary research on business idea completed	_____		
2. Feedback on venture idea from family and friends obtained	_____		
3. Feedback from partners (if any) obtained	_____		
4. Advice from provincial and small business counsellors obtained	_____		
5. Advice from BDC counsellor obtained (if applicable)	_____		
6. Advice from lawyer and accountant obtained	_____		
7. Market survey completed	_____		
8. Personal commitment to business venture finalized	_____		
9. Market segment goal determined			
10. Market share goal determined			
11. Cash flow projection completed			
12. Operating forecast completed for Year 1			
13. Personal financial statement prepared			
14. Detailed business plan completed			
15. Feasibility study completed	_____		

Step	Estimated Date of Completion	Actual Date of Completion	Comments
16. Sources of financing identified	_____	_____	_____
17. Sources of financing explored	_____	_____	_____
18. Adequate financing arranged	_____	_____	_____
19. Suitable premises located	_____	_____	_____
20. Arrangements made to prepare location for occupancy	_____	_____	_____
21. Equipment and machinery ordered	_____	_____	_____
22. Fixtures, furnishings, supplies, and printing ordered	_____	_____	_____
23. Permits and licences obtained	_____	_____	_____
24. Insurance and security protection arranged	_____	_____	_____
25. Utilities and services arranged	_____	_____	_____
26. Employees selected and hired as of opening	_____	_____	_____
27. Accounting and record-keeping decisions in place	_____	_____	_____
28. Signs and advertising completed	_____	_____	_____
29. Equipment and machinery received	_____	_____	_____
30. Fixtures, furnishings, supplies, and printing received	_____	_____	_____
31. Inventory priced, marked, and placed	_____	_____	_____
32. Training of staff completed	_____	_____	_____
33. Review of business plan to ensure all steps on schedule	_____	_____	_____
34. Preopening meeting of partners, if applicable, for any last-minute changes	_____	_____	_____
35. Opening ceremony arranged	_____	_____	_____
36. Opening announcement made	_____	_____	_____
37. Employees ready	_____	_____	_____
38. Doors open for business	_____	_____	_____
39. Candid assessment of administrative effectiveness on a daily basis	_____	_____	_____
40. Actual to projected sales measured after:			
1 week	_____	_____	_____
1 month	_____	_____	_____
3 months	_____	_____	_____
41. Actual and projected cash flow measured after:			
Week 1	_____	_____	_____
Week 2	_____	_____	_____
Week 3	_____	_____	_____
Week 4	_____	_____	_____

SAMPLE 36 Continued

Step	Estimated Date of Completion	Actual Date of Completion	Comments
42. Operating forecast tested after:			
1 month	_____		
3 months	_____		
6 months	_____		
43. Customer survey to measure satisfaction and feedback completed at end of 1 month after opening	_____		
44. Candid assessment of overall business plan accuracy completed	_____		
45. Modifications made to business plan, if required	_____		
46. Changes to management decisions, if required	_____		

Appendix A

Master Checklist

The following questions will serve as a master checklist of things to do or consider during the initial planning and start-up phases of your business. What you have learned by reading the previous chapters will provide options, rationale, and advice for completing these. Therefore, this checklist is designed to be used as a guide after you have finished reading the book, as well as during the preparation of your business plan. Obviously, depending on your type of business activity, not all questions will apply.

As you work through the questions, be certain to mark in the two right-hand columns whether further information or study is required. This will vary from one person to the next, depending upon your background, qualifications, and previous business experience.

Topic	Yes	No	Don't Know	Need More Info or Study	Answered To My Satisfaction
	(Check one)			(Check one)	
Self-Assessment					
1. Have you determined your main motive(s) for going into your own business?					
2. Have you thoroughly discussed going into business with your family?					
3. Do you believe your family is fully supportive of you going into business?					
4. Is your personal situation right to start a business now? Your age? Your present job? Your future prospects? Your family responsibility? Your finances?					
5. Have you written down an honest assessment of your strengths and weaknesses?					
6. Have you rated yourself on the personal qualities necessary for success in your own business?					
7. Have you compared the advantages and disadvantages of running your own business?					
8. Do you like to take calculated risks?					
9. Are you in shape physically to withstand the stresses and long hours involved in starting a business?					
10. Are you a self-starter?					
11. Do you have a high energy level?					

12. Are you willing to work long hours? _____
13. Do you like to make your own decisions? _____
14. Do you enjoy competition? _____
15. Do you have willpower and self-discipline? _____
16. Can you control discouragement over obstacles? _____
17. Do you plan ahead? _____
18. Do you get things done on time? _____
19. Can you take advice from others? _____
20. Are you adaptable to changing conditions? _____
21. Do you have the emotional strength to withstand the strain of running a business? _____
22. Are you prepared to lower your standard of living for several months or years, if necessary, to start your own business? _____
23. Are you prepared to lose your savings or investment in the business? _____
24. Have you worked in a business like the one you want to start? _____
25. Do you know which skills and areas of expertise are critical to the success of your project? _____
26. Do you have these skills? _____
27. Does your idea effectively utilize your own skills and abilities? _____
28. Do you have the management skills needed? _____
29. Can you find personnel who have the expertise that you lack? _____
30. Have you ever hired or managed staff? _____
31. Do you have any sales experience? _____
32. Have you ever dealt with the public? _____

(Continued)

Topic	Yes	No	Don't Know	Need More Info or Study	Answered To My Satisfaction
33. Do you like to meet people?					
34. Do you know how to discover new business ideas and opportunities?					
35. Have you examined thoroughly the alternatives of starting from scratch, buying an existing business, or buying a franchise?					
36. Have you performed a feasibility study for your venture idea?					
Obtaining Advice					
37. Have you discussed your venture ideas with a provincial small business counsellor, BDC counsellor, local economic development officer or other advisor?					
38. Have you talked to a qualified accountant (CA or CGA) on the tax and accounting aspects of starting or buying a business?					
39. Have you spoken to qualified persons such as your colleagues or friends who are in business about the prospects of being your own boss?					
40. Have you talked to a business lawyer regarding the legal aspects involved?					
41. Have you talked to an insurance broker as to all the insurance considerations and costs involved?					
42. Have you talked to a banker?					

Business Structure

43. Have you decided on the business structure (proprietorship, corporation) of your venture?

44. Do you know what the advantages and disadvantages are of the structure you have selected?

45. Did you obtain legal and accounting advice before you chose the business structure?

Partners

46. Do you want to have one or more partners in your business?

47. Do you really need a partner?

48. Do you know where you are going to find potential partners?

49. Have you realistically determined the personality traits, qualities, and skills required for a partner to ensure compatibility with your personal and business needs?

50. Have you determined the strengths and weaknesses of your potential partners?

51. Have you determined what ownership portion of your business you are prepared to give up to a partner?

52. Have you determined in detail exactly what contribution you expect from your partner (e.g., money, time, contacts, expertise, etc.)?

53. Have you discussed signing a partnership or shareholders' agreement with your partner(s) setting out the full terms of your relationship?

54. Have you and your partners prepared an informal outline of all the key points you want in a partnership or shareholders' agreement?

(Continued)

Topic	Yes	No	Don't Know	Need More Info or Study	Answered To My Satisfaction
55. Have you had a lawyer draw up a final partnership agreement?					
56. Have you prepared a management contract?					
Government Regulations					
57. Are you aware of the government legislation or restrictions affecting your business operation?					
58. Do you have knowledge of, and have you complied with, any and all municipal, provincial, and federal legal requirements affecting your specific type of business?					
— business licence					
— liquor licence					
— building bylaws					
— fire bylaws					
— zoning and development bylaws					
— vehicle licensing bylaws					
— shop closing bylaws					
— sign bylaws					
— health regulations					
— employee labour regulations					
— Worker's Compensation Board regulations					
— sales tax regulations and tax number					
— business registration (proprietorship or partnership)					
— corporation registration (incorporated company)					

— Canada Revenue Agency deductions (income Tax, EI, CPP); GST/HST

— federal excise regulations and tax number (manufacturers)

— other regulations

— trade practice regulations

— consumer protection regulations

59. Have you complied with regulations governing the use of a firm or trade name, brand names, or trademarks?

60. Is a licence necessary to handle special commodities?

61. Have you determined whether or not your product(s) meets the government standards, where applicable?

62. If you intend to operate an import or export business, do you have the necessary permit?

63. If you are importing goods, do you have any information regarding the amount of customs duties levied?

64. For your raw material purchases, do you have a manufacturing licence for federal sales tax exemption?

65. Have you provided for an adequate system of record-keeping that will furnish essential information for provincial and federal taxation purposes?

66. Are there long-range regional economic development plans occurring that could impact on your business?

67. Will any competitive advantages you currently find at the location you're considering be diminished by zoning changes or changes in city or highway traffic?

(Continued)

Topic	Yes	No	Don't Know	Need More Info or Study	Answered To My Satisfaction
Employees					
68. Have you decided how many employees you will be hiring?					
69. Have you planned your staff organization chart?					
70. Have you analyzed the jobs that you will offer, and do you have a job description for them?					
71. Have you decided what special skill or training your employees should have?					
72. Is there an adequate labour force available?					
73. Do you know how to recruit and select applicants?					
74. Have you decided whether you will hire part-time, experienced or inexperienced people?					
75. Would it be an advantage or disadvantage to hire a friend or relative?					
76. Are you familiar with the provincial and federal regulations relating to employees?					
77. Will you offer training? If so, do you have a training plan?					
78. Are your proposed pay and salary scales competitive with similar businesses in your community?					
79. Have you determined what holidays, sickness leave, and overtime pay you will allow, outside what is required by law?					
80. Have you made decisions on employee benefits, including pensions, group insurance, profit-sharing, etc.?					
81. Have you considered how you will keep employees satisfied and motivated?					

82. Have you planned working conditions to be as desirable and
    practical as possible?

83. Do you intend to actively solicit employee feedback and
    suggestions to pre-empt problems and maintain morale?

84. Have you established a set of personnel files and records?

85. Do you know how to evaluate your employees' performance?

86. Do you have the skills to lead and motivate your employees?

Financial

87. Are you willing to risk uncertain or irregular income for the next
    few years?

88. Have you calculated how much income you desire or need for
    your personal living expenses during the start-up phase?

89. Have you estimated your financial requirements for working capital
    and operating expenses until the business is able to support itself?

— advertising and promotion

— employee benefits

— equipment

— furnishings

— insurance

— Internet access

— interest

— inventory

— licences

— professional fees

— rent

— supplies

— tax

(Continued)

Topic	Yes	No	Don't Know	Need More Info or Study	Answered To My Satisfaction
— telephone					
— transportation					
— utilities					
— wages and salaries					
— website maintenance					
90. Do you know which expenses are direct, indirect, or fixed?					
91. Have you been conservative in your estimates?					
92. Have you compared advantages and disadvantages of leasing or renting your premises, equipment, machinery and automobile rather than purchasing them?					
93. Have you compared the benefits of contracting out (subcontracting) certain activities of the business with what it would cost you to do the work yourself?					
94. Have you determined how much money of your own you can put into the business?					
95. Do you have other assets which you could, if necessary, sell or on which you could borrow to get additional funds?					
96. Have you determined your potential return on investment (ROI) in this business?					
97. Do you know where you can borrow the rest of the money you need to start your business and for the first year of operation?					
98. Have you considered the following options?					
— banks and near-banks					
— capital stock					

— factoring

— franchising

— friends and family

— house or chattel mortgage

— insurance policies

— trade credit

— venture capital

99. Have you investigated government assistance programs at the provincial and federal levels?

100. Have you established a credit rating?

101. Do you know how much credit you can get from your suppliers?

102. Have you considered the impact on your relationship with friends or relatives if the business venture does not succeed and they have invested in your business?

103. Have you completed a cash flow projection for the first year of operation?

104. Have you completed a pro forma balance sheet and income statement for the first year of operation?

105. Do you have a realistic sales forecast?

106. Do you have standard operating ratios to use as guidelines from your trade associations or Dun & Bradstreet to assist you in financing and managing your business?

107. Are you able to find out how your financial statements compare with similar businesses in terms of sales, cost of sales, expenses, inventory turnover?

108. Do you know how to analyze your financial statements?

109. Have you prepared a detailed financial business plan?

(Continued)

Topic	Yes	No	Don't Know	Need More Info or Study	Answered To My Satisfaction
110. Have you consulted a qualified accountant (CA or CGA) in setting up your systems, developing your projections, analyzing your statements and business plan and tax planning?					
111. Have you decided who will be responsible for keeping your records up-to-date and who will prepare your financial statements and budgets?					
112. Have you established a line of credit with your banker?					
Record-keeping					
113. Have you researched an effective computerized system of keeping records in all areas of your business?					
— payables					
— receivables					
— accounting					
— tax					
— employees					
— other					
114. Have you secured the necessary forms to enable you to start keeping adequate records from the first day of operation of the business? Have you discussed financial management software programs with your accountant for greater efficiency and data management?					
115. Can you use standardized forms available at most office supply outlets?					

116. Have you investigated the possibility of using simplified computerized record-keeping systems for some of your needs?

117. Do you intend to maintain separate records for both cash and credit sales?

118. Have you planned your record system so that appropriate use will be made of standard operating ratios?

119. Have you made plans for the safekeeping of essential records in addition to your accounting record, with computer backup systems

120. Do you have a computer with all the features you require?

121. Are you going to maintain the records yourself or hire staff or an offsite accountant or bookkeeper to do so?

Location and Leasing

122. Have you considered working out of your own home, and using a telephone answering service or business ID package from a packaged office service?

123. Have you considered a "packaged office" service?

124. Do you need premium downtown space?

125. If your employees use public transit, are there bus or subway stops nearby?

126. Is the business easily accessible and visible?

127. Is exterior lighting in the area adequate to attract evening shoppers and make them feel safe?

128. Are you near your suppliers?

129. Can you ship business products easily from your location via truck, train, air, or ship?

130. Have you chosen a location accessible to your target market?

(Continued)

Topic	Yes	No	Don't Know	Need More Info or Study	Answered To My Satisfaction
131. Is the trade area heavily dependent on seasonal business?					
132. Are there any competitors close to your location?					
133. Do local civic attitudes favour a business like yours?					
134. Have you checked whether the neighbourhood is improving or declining?					
135. Is security in your area handled by police and fire departments?					
136. Is the cost of your location affordable?					
137. Are property and business taxes in your location reasonable now and will they increase in the future?					
138. Do you know the present zoning and future zoning of your building?					
139. Do you plan to operate the business in your first location indefinitely?					
140. If the proposed building does not meet all of your important needs, are there any good reasons for deciding to use it?					
141. Have you projected your space requirements over the next few years?					
142. Have you included the cost of extras in your budget, such as utilities, maintenance, and taxes?					
143. Do your computers need special heating, lighting, or wiring systems, or a separate room with special ventilation?					
144. Can you renovate before you move in?					
145. Are there restrictions on what you can do to renovate your space?					

146. Is your rent fixed every month? _____

147. Are customer restroom facilities available/required? _____

148. Does the location have awnings or decks to provide shelter during bad weather? _____

149. Have you planned your proposed layout for the building to scale on paper? _____

150. Are there storage facilities available or nearby? _____

151. Has the lease and zoning been thoroughly checked by your lawyer? _____

152. Do you have to pay to have the lease drawn? _____

153. Are you aware of your responsibilities in the lease? _____

154. Will all government regulatory bodies approve your use of the building, i.e., zoning, health, fire marshal, transportation, environment, and labour? _____

155. Are there protective covenants that will limit your sales or other legal restrictions in your lease? _____

156. Is the term of the lease long enough to protect you? _____

157. Does the lease provide for reimbursement for alterations? _____

158. Are there restrictions regarding size and location of signs on the building? _____

159. Do you need a special card to gain access to the building after regular business hours? _____

160. Are you permitted to sublet? _____

161. Do you know under what conditions you can break your lease and how much it will cost? _____

(Continued)

Topic	Yes	No	Don't Know	Need More Info or Study	Answered To My Satisfaction
Insurance					
162. Have you made plans for protecting your store against thefts of all kinds—shoplifting, robbery, burglary, employee stealing?					
163. Have you purchased general comprehensive insurance coverage?					
164. Has insurance protecting against damage suits and public liability claims been purchased? Do you have home office insurance added to your regular home insurance coverage?					
165. Do you know what other risks should be insured against?					
166. Have you obtained sufficient personal insurance in excess of all your personal business guarantees to cover your liability in the event of your death? Disability, key personnel coverage?					
167. Have you obtained a minimum of three quotations from insurance brokers before making your decision, to satisfy yourself as to premiums and coverage?					
168. Have you obtained advice from your accountant regarding tax implications and the structure for your insurance policies?					
Equipment					
169. Do you know what furniture, fixtures, and equipment and computer systems you will need, and at what cost?					
170. Have you calculated how much money you have available for equipment and fixtures?					

171. Have you planned for expansion and future additions to your equipment?

172. Can you get quick service from your suppliers when something breaks down?

173. Have you held your purchase plans to the minimum without omitting any essential items?

174. Is your investment in fixtures and equipment in proper proportion to your financial structure?

175. Have you decided whether you are going to buy or lease the equipment?

176. Is buying secondhand equipment a viable option to buying new equipment?

177. Have you obtained advice from your professional accountant as to the nature and form of purchase in advance?

178. If buying fixtures and equipment is a part of the purchase of a going business, are they similar to the modern type you would select now?

Purchasing and Inventory Control

179. Have you made a list of every item of inventory and operating supplies needed?

180. Have you decided what goods to carry in relation to what your target customers want?

181. Are there any product lines which you can get the privilege of handling exclusively?

182. Have you estimated how much your total stock should be?

(Continued)

Topic	Yes	No	Don't Know	Need More Info or Study	Answered To My Satisfaction
183. Have you broken this estimate down into the major lines to be carried?					
184. Do you know the quantity, quality, technical specifications, and price ranges desired for each product?					
185. When considering each item of merchandise, ask yourself the following:					
— after markup is the selling price in line with similar merchandise?					
— does it compare with similar items in quality?					
— is it in style?					
— does it have special selling points or exclusive features?					
— will I be the sole distributor in my territory?					
— if the item sells rapidly, can it be replaced quickly?					
— will it spoil quickly?					
— does it meet a particular need?					
— are product claims honest? Exaggerated?					
186. Do you know the name and location of each potential source of supply?					
187. Have you given careful consideration to the choice of suppliers, basing your decision on location, delivery, service, trade terms, selection, experience, and financial stability?					
188. Are you aware of which supplies have an advantage relative to transportation costs?					

189. Is there a risk of shortage for any materials or merchandise? _____

190. Have you investigated advantages of affiliating with a voluntary or cooperative buying group for your business? _____

191. Have you made arrangements with wholesalers? _____

192. Have you decided what merchandise you will buy from manufacturers? _____

193. Have you set up a model stock assortment to follow in your buying? _____

194. Do you know how much stock to buy, when to buy it, and at what cost? _____

195. Do you have provisions to check the receiving and marking of goods? _____

196. Can you store your purchases securely? _____

197. Have you worked out any stock-control plans to avoid overstocks, understocks, and out-of-stocks? _____

198. Are you aware of procedures involved in taking physical inventory? _____

199. Have you listed the purposes and uses of information you plan to secure from your inventory or store's control system? _____

200. Have you established systems to measure and control theft and pilferage? _____

201. Have you decided on an insurance policy for your inventory? _____

Pricing

202. Have you determined what price "image" you want for your business? _____

203. Have you decided on the formula or method you will use in pricing each class of goods and services? _____

(Continued)

Topic	Yes	No	Don't Know	Need More Info or Study	Answered To My Satisfaction
204. Does your pricing allow for a comfortable profit margin after calculating your break-even point?					
205. Have you considered the probable reaction of competitors to your pricing practices?					
206. Have you decided how and to what extent you will meet probable price competition?					
207. Are you aware of the free or low-cost publications on pricing?					
Competition					
208. Do you know who your major competitors are?					
209. Do you know the major strengths and weaknesses of each of your competitors?					
210. Are you familiar with the following factors concerning your competitors?					
— price structure					
— product lines (quality, breadth, width)					
— location					
— promotional activities					
— sources of supply					
— image from a consumer's viewpoint					
211. Do you know of any competitor's plans for expansion?					
212. Do you know of any competitors who plan to enter your territory?					

213. Have any firms of your type gone out of business lately?

214. Do you know the sales and market share of each competitor, and whether it is increasing, decreasing, or stable?

215. Do you know if your competitors' profits are increasing, decreasing, or stable?

216. Do competitors leave an opening for you to enter business because they are not alert and aggressive?

217. Are competitors well established?

218. Do you know if your competition is strong and active, or weak and sluggish?

219. Are people in your community buying from outside your community because of poor or unavailable supplies or service?

Marketing

220. Have you defined the geographical areas from which you can realistically expect to draw customers?

221. Will your business product/service appeal to the entire market segment you have selected?

222. Have you decided on what basis (e.g., price, selection, quality, location) you will appeal to your potential customers?

223. Have you decided what business image to project?

224. Have you considered the characteristics of your market (potential customers) and methods to reach them with your advertising?

— age

— buying habits

— education

—family size

(Continued)

Topic	Yes	No	Don't Know	Need More Info or Study	Answered To My Satisfaction
— income					
— marital status					
— occupation					
— sex					
225. Do you know about the population growth trend in your marketing areas?					
226. Is your market segment large enough to support your business at start-up and over the long term?					
227. Do you know what the consumers' attitudes are towards a business like yours?					
228. Do you know about consumer shopping and spending patterns relative to your type of business?					
229. Does your product/service/business serve an existing market in which demand exceeds supply?					
230. Do you know what segment of the market your competitors are serving?					
231. Will your market be affected by demographic change in the future?					
232. Have you completed a marketing plan that includes your strategies to attain your objectives and means of evaluating the effectiveness of your efforts?					
233. Have you determined the best ways of distributing your product in this market?					

234. Have you researched all available media and evaluated them relative to your needs (e.g., print, radio, TV, direct mail)? _____

235. Is the market accessible through existing media at an affordable cost? _____

236. Have you developed a promotion strategy? _____

Advertising

237. Have you decided how you will advertise (newspapers, posters, handbills, radio, mail, online, website, e-commerce,other)? _____

238. Do you know where to get help preparing your advertisements? _____

239. Do your ads relay the benefits of your products or services from the customer's viewpoint? _____

240. Do your ads portray the image of your business/products/services that you want to project? _____

241. Have you considered using seasonal interests or trends to advertise your products or services? _____

242. Have you considered different features of your business that would be appropriate for special promotions timed to your customers' needs and interests? _____

243. Do your store signs, displays, and layout present the right image and entice the prospective customer to stay and shop? _____

244. Have you observed what other stores do to get people to buy? _____

245. Have you written down the pros and cons of the different types of advertising and promotion options? _____

246. Have you put in writing your own list of dos and don'ts to guide your advertising? _____

(Continued)

Topic	Yes	No	Don't Know	Need More Info or Study	Answered To My Satisfaction
247. Have you selected the most promising reasons for people to patronize your business and incorporated them in plans for your opening advertising?					
248. Have you decided how you can measure and record the degree of success achieved with each sales promotion so that you can repeat the hits and avoid the duds?					
249. Have you reviewed the additional resource material on advertising and promotion outlined in Appendix B?					
Sales					
250. Do you know how to motivate your customers to buy?					
251. Have you thought about why you like to buy from some sales clerks, while others frustrate you?					
252. Have you or your sales staff taken sales training courses?					
253. Do you or your sales staff participate in a sales networking group?					
254. Have you anticipated how you will handle customer objections?					
255. Have you clearly identified your customers' needs/wants and stressed these and the product benefits in your sales presentation?					
256. Usually the first person a customer speaks with is the receptionist. Is your receptionist aware of basic sales information and style in order to create a positive first impression?					
257. Are you aware of effective nonverbal selling techniques in terms of voice tone and modulation, posture, eye contact?					

258. Are you aware of sales closing techniques? _____

259. Do you have a method of recording your prospective customers for follow-up at a later date? _____

260. Do you have a record of all your customers for follow-up? _____

261. Do you know what percentage of these are repeat customers? _____

262. Did you base your sales forecast on concrete data? _____

263. Did you set realistic as well as optimistic sales objectives? _____

264. Are there conditions or trends that could change your forecast of total sales? _____

265. Have you calculated the gross profit you can make based on sales volume? _____

266. Will your sales records be broken down by type of merchandise and/or department? _____

Credit and Collection

267. Are you aware of the risks and administrative costs of extending credit? _____

268. Have you carefully investigated the need for and desirability of credit extension by your business? _____

269. Have you investigated the services, benefits, and costs associated with becoming a member of your local credit bureau? _____

270. Have you planned the basic procedures you or your staff will always follow before extending credit to any applicant? _____

271. Have you formulated plans to control and monitor all credit accounts? _____

(Continued)

Topic	Yes	No	Don't Know	Need More Info or Study	Answered To My Satisfaction
272. Have you obtained information on the benefits of obtaining a merchant number for accepting credit cards such as Visa, MasterCard, or American Express?					
273. Have you or your staff taken any courses or seminars on credit and collection?					
274. Are you aware of the numerous services and publications available through Dun & Bradstreet?					
275. Have you had your lawyer review your credit and collection policies, procedures, and documentation?					
276. Have you considered using one of the service companies that protect you from an NSF cheque loss?					
Taxes					
277. Does your proposed business structure (proprietorship, partnership, or corporation) minimize taxes, both now and in the future? Have you applied for a CRA business tax number, GST/HST, provincial payroll tax number, and provincial tax numbers if applicable?					
278. Are you identifying and taking advantage of available investment and other tax credits?					
279. Have you contacted any accounting firms to request they keep you on the mailing list for free tax information booklets?					

280. Did you explore the tax implications of anticipated business transactions with your professional accountant?

281. Do you have a plan for the succession of the business—at the lowest tax cost to your family members?

Will/Estate Planning

282. Do you have a will? Does your executor know where it is kept?

283. Have you revised your will since starting your business?

284. Did you have a lawyer draft your will after advising you?

285. Have you obtained advice from a qualified accountant in terms of planning the tax considerations of your estate in relation to your business?

286. Have you prepared a detailed list of all your personal and business affairs (including debtors and creditors) so that if you died suddenly, your executor would know your affairs?

287. Do you update your will annually? Do you have a health care and financial power of attorney?

Overall Management

288. Are you aware of how business plans can help you obtain financing and manage your business?

289. Does your business plan meet the expectations of your lenders, key investors, and associates?

290. Do you have formal short-term and long-term goals that you monitor regularly?

291. Do you know enough about your particular type of business to operate it effectively and profitably?

(Continued)

Topic	Yes	No	Don't Know	Need More Info or Study	Answered To My Satisfaction
292. Have you set out reporting procedures that enable you to monitor progress towards your business objectives?					
293. Have you assigned responsibilities for meeting your objectives to key personnel?					
294. Have you set objectives for the various parts of your business?					
295. Are you receiving timely answers to your "what if" planning questions?					
296. Are you making effective use of business and marketing planning an financial software in the planning and management process?					
297. Do you have the information needed to permit you to efficiently analyze the financial factors and trends affecting your business?					
298. Have you planned the way you will organize duties and responsibilities?					
299. Have you developed adequate management planning approaches before making commitments or important decisions covering future activities of the business?					
300. Have you made an honest, objective investigation of the probable success of your proposed policies?					
301. Have you written down the main provisions of your general and major policies?					
302. Do you have policies to deal with customer needs (servicing, complaints, etc.)?					

303. Have you developed a policy on maintenance and replacement of your fixed assets? _____

304. Have you discussed your proposed policies with competent advisors and are they in agreement? _____

305. Have you made adequate provisions to ensure that your policies will be understood and enforced, and that you will receive ample warning of the need for policy adjustments? _____

306. Do you have procedures and systems in place for your staff to implement and maintain effectively? _____

307. Have you established effective business and personal time management practices? _____

308. If you are a manufacturer, have you developed specifications and plans for your production process, including:
— scheduling _____
— materials requirements planning _____
— production methods _____
— quality control _____
— product distribution _____

309. Have you taken any business management programs through the Business Development Bank of Canada or college or school board night school? _____

Appendix B

Sources of Further Information

As a fledgling small business owner or a potential one, you may feel overwhelmed by the amount of information that you need to know. Many entrepreneurs don't know where to access the most current and practical information easily, effectively, and inexpensively. The next best thing to knowing something is knowing where to find it out.

The following information should assist you in that search. It contains the names of key business and trade publications, directories, handbooks, and magazines. It also lists Canadian publications which are primarily free of charge, although a few are sold at a nominal cost. Most of these publications are also available online. The main business and trade associations in Canada are described, as well as information on courses, seminars, and consulting and counselling services. A lack of knowledge is a frequent cause of business failure in Canada.

BUSINESS AND TRADE PUBLICATIONS

The best source of printed information, aside from the Internet, is the reference section of a large public library. Also consider in your search your local college or university library, which will have a large collection of journals and either electronic or physical subscriptions to those journals. The librarian will assist you in locating the sources of information that you require. There are newsletters or trade journals for every type of business. Some of the most common directories for business or trade publications include:

Gale Directory of Publications
Business Periodicals Index
Canadian Advertising Rates & Data (CARD)
Canadian Almanac & Directory
Canadian Business Periodicals Index
Gale's *Encyclopedia of Business Information Sources*
Gale's *Business Plans Handbook*
Standard Rates and Data Service (srds.com)
Ulrich's International Periodicals Directory

BUSINESS DIRECTORIES

There are directories covering every conceivable area of business information. Whether you are looking for suppliers, distributors, manufacturers, or wholesalers; trying to locate the names and addresses of associations; or looking for information about conventions, trade fairs, or government departments, there are publications to help you. Many directories are expensive but are available for reference in provincial government small business resource centres, Canada Business Network centres, and public libraries. Here is a partial listing of some of the more popular directories and topics:

Shows and Exhibitions

Printed directories of shows arranged by industry with a geographical and date index are often available in public libraries. Also includes a geographically arranged directory of convention facilities and services in Canada. There are numerous websites providing extensive directories of trade shows, including biztradeshow.com, tsnn.com, and expoabc.com.

Canadian Key Business Directory

A two-volume source of information on large- and medium-sized Canadian companies. Access is by company name, location, product classification, and by DUNS (Dun & Bradstreet) number. Yearly sales figures, number of employees, and the name of the chief operating manager are given.

Canadian Trade Index

A comprehensive list of Canadian manufacturers having more than a local distribution for their products. Products, brand names, plants, parent firms, subsidiaries, executive names, and number of employees are given.

Directory of Directors

Gives career-related information about Canadian company directors and executives living in Canada. This information is also available at an online database (fpinfomart.ca/help/topic/fp/dod) but requires a subscription, which some libraries may have.

Frasers Canadian Trade Directory

Very detailed listings of Canadian manufactured products by type of product. Also lists companies alphabetically and by trade name. This directory is now available exclusively online at frasers.com.

World Chambers Network

Complete list of U.S., regional Canadian, and foreign (principal cities) chambers of commerce. Complete online search available at chamberdirectory. worldchambers.com.

National List of Advertisers

An annual directory of advertisers in Canadian media, showing addresses, telephone numbers, personnel, products, agencies, ad budgets, and media used. Also lists client accounts of advertising agencies and direct-mail advertising agencies. The *National List of Advertisers* is now online at cardonline.ca, but has an annual subscription fee. Many libraries may offer access to this service to their patrons.

Principal International Businesses

World marketing directory to the world's leading enterprises. Gives addresses, sales volume, number of employees, and lines of businesses. This database is maintained by Dun & Bradstreet, and libraries may offer various forms of access.

Scott's Directories

Provides a list of manufacturers in Canada, classified by product and other company information. Scott's now offers an online subscription service at scottsinfo. com, to which many libraries may be able to provide access.

Thomas' Grocery Register

Three-volume directory of U.S. grocery chain stores, wholesalers, brokers, exporters, warehouses, products, services, brand names, and trademarks. Thomas also maintains an extensive online directory of various suppliers and manufacturers in a variety of specialties at thomasnet.com.

Thomas' Register of American Manufacturers

This multivolume set is a registry of U.S. manufacturers, products, services, and brand names. Includes pages from manufacturers' catalogues and names of some distributors.

Thomas, registers are also available online at thomasnet.com.

BUSINESS REFERENCE HANDBOOKS AND MANUALS

The following are some of the business reference handbooks and manuals available in many public libraries:

Blue Book of Canadian Business

Ranks major corporations in terms of sales, assets, net income, advertising expenditures, and stock performance. Includes profiles of leading Canadian companies and short descriptions of numerous others. An online subscription service is also available at cbr.ca.

Canadian Government Programs and Services

A definitive reference guide on the various federal government programs and services, including federal government assistance programs (looseleaf service from CCH Canadian Ltd.; cch.ca).

Canadian Labour Law Reporter

Federal and provincial laws on employer–employee relations, fair wages, vacations, statutory holidays, hours of work, industrial standards, fair employment practices, etc. Two update reports generated each month (in loose-leaf format from CCH Canadian Ltd.; cch.ca).

Tax Planning for Small Business Guide

A practical and informative desk reference manual for those concerned with financial and tax planning functions within a small business, and for their advisors, especially lawyers and accountants. Updated monthly (looseleaf service from CCH Canadian Ltd.; cch.ca).

Canadian Tax Reporter

Weekly reports on federal, corporate, and personal income tax laws, regulations, and rulings, with digests of board and court decisions. This multivolume looseleaf service contains all federal tax acts and regulations in full text, including Interpretation Bulletins, Information Circulars, and Advance Rulings (looseleaf service from CCH Canadian Ltd.; cch.ca.).

Europa World Year Book

Detailed factual information on every country in the world and on hundreds of international organizations. Includes statistical charts and addresses of principal transportation, media, and other companies and institutions, including universities. Government and constitution also described. An online subscription service is also available at europaworld.com.

O'Brien's Encyclopedia of Forms

A multivolume set of working nonlitigious forms covering every field of law for the average general legal practitioner. Includes corporate and commercial law; mortgages and conveyances; leases, wills, and trusts; forms of agreement; and contracts. (Published by Canada Law Book Inc. This series is designed for lawyers.) It is also now available online at obriensforms.com as a paid subscription service.

WorldBase—Who Owns Whom

Arranged alphabetically by name of parent company and by name of subsidiary for the United States and Canada. This is a database developed and maintained by Dun & Bradstreet, to which many libraries have access.

MAGAZINES

Magazines are still an important means of keeping current on trends, ideas, opportunities, and legislation. Many excellent print magazines and web-based publications tailored to the needs of small and medium-sized businesses can be found. There are also national, provincial, and local business publications in Canada that might interest you. In addition, there are many U.S. and international publications that provide fresh ideas, trends, and perspectives that can stimulate your imagination. Your subscription costs are tax deductible as a business expense. A partial listing of suggested national publications follows:

Canadian Business	Canadianbusiness.com
Entrepreneur	Entrepreneur.com
Small Business Computing	Smallbusinesscomputing.com
Inc.	Inc.com
Profit	profitguide.com
Small Business Opportunities	sbomag.com
Success	Success.com
BizTech	Biztechmagazine.com

FREE OR LOW-COST PUBLICATIONS

These publications are either free of charge or sold at a nominal cost. Many can be downloaded online as PDFs.

Federal Government

The following outline just highlights some of the many publications available. Ask for a current list. The contact addresses for further information are outlined in Appendix D, "Key Government and Other Contact Sources."

Industry Canada   Ic.gc.ca.

Trademarks, copyright, industrial design, and patents
Bankruptcy Consumer protection federal incorporation
Material on financial assistance programs and application procedures
Directory of courses and other informational material relating to recreation, tourism, and hospitality
Market surveys

Foreign Affairs and International Trade Canada   International.gc.ca.

Export information kit

Directory of Canadian foreign trade representatives and Canadian consulates abroad
Guide for Canadian exporters series (covers several countries in the world and various states or regions in the United States)
Numerous other excellent publications—see Chapter 14 on export/import

Business Development Bank of Canada   Bdc.ca

(See section on banks)

Canada Revenue Agency   Cra.gc.ca

Income tax and small business employer's kit
Goods and Services Tax (GST)/Harmonized Sales Tax (HST) interpretation bulletins Information circulars
Pamphlets, leaflets, guides, and forms
Thinking about Importing? What You Should Know and *Customs Commercial System: Questions and Answers*
Numerous other publications on importing and related taxes

Statistics Canada   Statcan.gc.ca

Catalogue of all publications

Public Works and Government Services Canada   Pwgsc.gc.ca

Merx.ca
Information kit
Supplier's guide

Series of pamphlets on subjects such as: tendering, buying government surplus, marketing your products and services, late or delayed bids, profit policy, unsolicited proposals, and payment on contracts
Numerous other publications

Provincial Governments

Many excellent publications are available, most free of charge. You can request publications from provinces in addition to your own. For contact addresses and phone numbers, refer to Appendix D.

Municipal Governments

Contact the city hall in your community to obtain information on licensing requirements and local bylaws. Also make inquiries from your local economic development commission and Chamber of Commerce for pamphlets and other assistance they can provide. Many communities have excellent information and support services for people considering starting up a small business, including incubator centres. Your community may also have a business development centre or Community Futures Program. These are frequently partly funded by the federal government to stimulate business enterprise. Do a Google search with keywords in your area.

Banks

For copies of small business publications, contact the commercial branch of any of the chartered banks listed below.

Canadian Bankers' Association

Contact: Box 348,
Commerce Court West,
199 Bay Street, 30th Floor,
Toronto, Ontario M5L 1G2 website: cba.ca

Bank of Montreal

Canadian Imperial Bank of Commerce Business Development
Bank of Canada Royal Bank of Canada
TD Canada Trust
Bank of Nova Scotia

Accounting Firms

The major accounting firms with branches across Canada have numerous publications that are helpful to your small business success. In most cases, they are free of charge and cover a wide range of subject areas. The primary national and international firms follow. Their websites are noted in Appendix C.

BDO Dunwoody
Deloitte

Ernst & Young
KPMG
PriceWaterhouseCoopers

Dial-A-Law

Several provinces throughout Canada have a free service providing taped information over the phone on small business law matters, as well as other areas of law. The program is normally sponsored by the Canadian Bar Association in conjunction with the provincial law society. The Dial-A-Law scripts and recordings are also available online at dialalaw.com and include translations into a number of languages.

The tapes are approximately 10 minutes in length and cover a wide range of topics. More information on the service is available at dialalaw.com.

Miscellaneous Publications

The following associations or organizations have various publications available. Most are available online.

Canadian Franchise Association (cfa.ca)
Canadian Chamber of Commerce (chamber.ca)
Canadian Credit Institute (creditedu.org)
Canadian Institute of Chartered Accountants(cica.ca)
Canadian Manufacturers and Exporters (cme-mec.ca)
Canadian Restaurant and Foodservices Association (crfa.ca)
Canadian Securities Institute (csi.ca)
Dun & Bradstreet of Canada (dnb.ca)
Investment Industry Regulatory Organization of Canada (iiroc.ca)
Montreal Board of Trade (btmm.qc.ca)

ASSOCIATIONS

Business and trade associations provide an excellent means of staying current on legislation, market factors, and trends affecting your industry. Other benefits of belonging to an association include access to free or nominal-cost publications, regular meetings, conferences, seminars, trade fairs, newsletters, contacts, and assistance to new business owners. There are usually national, provincial, and local associations or chapters. Associations can be found online, through a search engine, or the websites of national associations.print or online, and do Google searches under the appropriate keywords of interest to you.

Small Business Associations

Canadian Chamber of Commerce chamber.ca
Has offices in Ottawa, Toronto, and Montreal. Has a small business committee, an active body which lobbies the federal government level on various issues. Check with your local chamber of commerce or board of trade regarding membership benefits.

Canadian Council of Better Business Bureaus bbb.org/canada
Businesses may join national or local division; offices throughout Canada. Local divisions assist businesses with various services, including arbitration of customer complaints.

Canadian Federation of Independent Business (CFIB) cfib-fcei.ca
Has offices in major Canadian cities. The largest political action group for small and medium-sized businesses in Canada, with over 109,000 members nationally. Provides services and library access for members only.

Construction Industry

Canadian Construction Association cca-acc.com
Membership includes access to bid depository on upcoming projects. Services include seminars, newsletters, and publications. Branches in most provinces.

Consulting Industry

Canadian Association of Management Consultants cmc-canada.ca
Primarily represents the interests of Canada's large consulting firms. Various services to members including directory, newsletters, meetings, etc.

There are many other provincial and local associations in specialty areas of consulting.

Credit and Collection

Canadian Credit Institute credited.org
Provincial chapters in major Canadian cities. Offers a program for certification in credit management, as well as books, manuals, and regular chapter meetings.

Direct Marketing/Direct Selling

Canadian Marketing Association the-cma.org
Represents the marketing industry. Benefits include conferences, workshops, publications, newsletters, etc.

Direct Sellers Association   dsa.ca
No local chapters. Represents the direct-selling (but not direct-mail) industry in Canada. Benefits include conferences, seminars, newsletters, and publications.

Family Business

Canadian Association of Family Enterprise   cafecanada.ca
Association deals with the unique needs of a family business, including succession planning, etc.

Food and Beverage Industry

Canadian Restaurant and Foodservices Association   crfa.ca
This association caters to the needs of the food service industry. Branches in major cities of most provinces. Benefits include seminars, conferences, publications, newsletters, etc.

Franchising

Canadian Franchise Association   cfa.ca
Holds seminars and conferences. Provides services to member franchisors.

Investment

Canada's Venture Capital and Private Equity Association   cvca.ca
An association of over 1900 venture capital companies in Canada who together have over $88 billion invested and with full-time venture investment managers. Contact them to obtain a list of members in your area and their investment criteria.

Investment Industry Regulatory Organization of Canada   iiroc.ca
An association whose members handle more than 95% of all Canadian securities transactions (public companies on stock exchange). Contact them to obtain a list of their members and their investment criteria. Offices are located in Toronto, Montreal, Calgary, and Vancouver.

Manufacturing Industry

Canadian Manufacturers and Exporters   cme-mec.ca
This association operates nine regional divisions across Canada. Excellent resource services include newsletters, bulletins, courses, seminars, and trade fairs. In addition, it organizes trade missions.

Marketing/Sales/Advertising

American Marketing Association   marketingpower.com
Branches in major Canadian cities. Membership benefits include conferences, meetings, seminars, publications, and newsletters. Primary emphasis is on service and product marketing.

Association of Canadian Advertisers   acaweb.ca
This association primarily represents the major corporations that advertise in Canada. The association sets standards and ethics in advertising for its members to follow. Publications are also available for the general public.

Sales and Marketing Executives International   smei.org
Branches throughout Canada. Offers diploma courses in marketing and sales management, as well as sales training programs. Regular meetings, conferences, networking benefits, and newsletters.

Retail Industry

Retail Council of Canada   retailcouncil.org
The council represents the retail community to government. Affiliated with the retail merchant associations across Canada.

Retail Merchants Association of Canada   rmacanada.com
Provincial chapters in major Canadian cities. This is an organization for small independent retailers. Provides services such as seminars, workshops, books, manuals, hotline for assistance, monthly newsletter (Canadian Retailer), as well as provincial newsletter, statistical information, cost-saving services, pension plans, group insurance, and charge card discounts.

Standards

Canadian Standards Association   csa.ca
Has volunteer and corporate members. Provides Canadian standards, testing, certification, and related services for the benefit of the public, government, and business. Services available through offices located in major Canadian cities.

Trade Import and Export Industries

I E Canada: Canadian Association of Importers and Exporters   iecanada.ca
Services include seminars, publications, and newsletters.

Canadian Manufacturers and Exporters
Refer to previous list under "Manufacturing Industry."

Wholesale/Distributors

Purchasing Management Association of Canada   pmac.ca
Provincial chapters in major Canadian cities. Membership includes meetings, seminars, workshops, conferences, and publications.

Women

Business and Professional Women (BPW Canada)   bpwcanada.com
Has local chapters in many Canadian cities. Benefits include regular meetings, networking, seminars, etc.

Many cities also have other associations and networks for women in business, women business owners, and women in nontraditional businesses and trades. Look under "Associations" in your telephone directory or online using a search engine.

Youth

Junior Achievement of Canada   jacan.org
Promotes economic understanding of business and private enterprise among Canadian youth. Local chapters in major Canadian cities.

COURSES AND SEMINARS

There are numerous sources of information through courses and seminars. Contact the closest office of the following institutions or companies and request to be put on their mailing list for upcoming business offerings. Many courses and seminars are available through online and distance-education programs.

Business Development Bank of Canada (BDC)

Offers a wide range of small business seminars covering such topics as tax tips, understanding financial statements, conducting a market survey, retailing, credit and collection, raising financing, motivating employees, and time management.

Provincial Governments

Most provincial government small business ministries offer business seminars on an ongoing basis.

School Boards

Generally offer 10- to 12-week evening adult education courses and condensed 1-day Saturday programs on a range of small business management topics.

Community Colleges/Institutes of Technology

Have extensive course offerings of 1- and 2-day programs relating to small business management. Generally seminar leaders are experts from inside or outside the community with practical "real world" experience. Also have a full selection of daytime and evening business management courses leading to a Certificate in Business Administration. Some courses are transferable for credit toward a university degree. Some of these courses can be completed through online education.

Universities

Noncredit continuing education courses of 1- or 2-day duration on business start-up or specialized subject areas, such as marketing professional services, employee relations, etc.

Dun & Bradstreet Dnb.ca

Offers a wide selection of practical education programs relating to areas of small business management, such as sales, telemarketing, and credit and collection.

CONSULTING/COUNSELLING SERVICES

Many sources of free or low-cost counselling are available. To gain the most benefit from the assistance, be certain to prepare a list of specific questions in advance. Listed here are some sources to explore.

Business Development Bank of Canada (BDC)

BDC offers a variety of supports for counseling and consulting, including consulting services and seminars. Visit bdc.ca for details.

Provincial Government Small Business Ministries

All provincial governments have a free counselling program that provides small business assistance ranging from start-up to management and financing. You can obtain the advice in person, online, or over the telephone via the toll-free small business hotline. Many provinces also have an excellent business resource library, including database access and video recordings. For provincial contact addresses, phone numbers, and websites refer to Appendix D.

Local Economic Development Commission

Many communities have an economic development department or enterprise development centre that provides free advice and counselling to prospective and existing small business owners. They can also assist you in cutting through government bureaucracy and provide you with information on current government funding assistance procedures, local community initiatives or incentives, as well as statistical information and future growth trends in the community.

Community Colleges/Institutes of Technology

Many commerce or business management departments have clinics set up for the public to provide small business assistance, staffed by students with guidance from their instructors.

Universities

The students of business schools of many universities provide a low-cost or free consulting service to small business owners. The students benefit through practical "real world" business experience. Backup assistance is provided by their instructors to ensure that quality advice is given to the business owner. Assistance provided can include preparation of a business plan, market research study, feasibility study, and financial analysis.

Appendix C

Website Resources

Tax Information

Canada Revenue Agency	*cra-arc.gc.ca*
United States Internal Revenue Service (IRS)	*irs.gov*
Canadian Tax Information for Small Businesses	*sbinfocanada.about.com/od/taxinfo/*
Canadian Enterprise Institute	*smallbiz.ca*
PriceWaterhouseCoopers Accounting	*pwc.com/ca*
KPMG Accounting Firm	*kpmg.ca*
Deloitte Accounting Firm	*deloitte.ca*
Ernst & Young Accounting Firm	*ey.ca*
BDO Dunwoody	*bdo.ca*

Financial and Stock Market Information

Toronto Stock Exchange	*tmx.com*
Bloomberg Financial News	*bloomberg.com*
CNBC Financial News	*cnbc.com*
Google Finance	*google.ca/finance*
Financial Times Markets	*markets.ft.com*
Canadian Business	*canadianbusiness.com*
Yahoo! Finance	*ca.finance.yahoo.com*
Sedar (database information filed with regulatory agencies by public companies and mutual funds)	*sedar.com*
Stockwatch	*stockwatch.com*

Financial Institutions

BMO (Bank of Montreal)	*bmo.com*
Scotiabank (Bank of Nova Scotia)	*scotiabank.ca*
CIBC Canadian Imperial Bank of Commerce	*cibc.com*
Royal Bank of Canada	*rbcroyalbank.com*
TD Canada Trust	*tdcanadatrust.com*
HSBC Bank Canada	*hsbc.ca*
Credit Union Central of Canada	*cucentral.ca*

(Continued)

Federal Government

Canada Business Network	*canadabusiness.ca*
Business Development Bank of Canada	*bdc.ca*
Service Canada	*servicecanada.gc.ca*
Industry Canada	*ic.gc.ca*

Provincial Governments and Departments

Government of Alberta	*gov.ab.ca*
Government of Alberta Business Information Service	*canadabusiness.ab.ca*
Government of British Columbia	*gov.bc.ca*
Small Business BC	*smallbusinessbc.ca*
Government of Manitoba	*gov.mb.ca*
Manitoba Business Information	*gov.mb.ca/business*
Government of Ontario	*ontario.ca*
Ontario for Business	*ontario.ca/en/business*
Government of Prince Edward Island	*gov.pe.ca*
Prince Edward Island for Business	*gov.pe.ca/business*
Government of Quebec	*gouv.qc.ca*
Services Quebec-Entreprises	*www2.gouv.qc.ca/entreprises*
Government of New Brunswick	*gnb.ca*
Government of Newfoundland Labrador	*gov.nl.ca*
Government of Newfoundland and Labrador Department of Business	*business.gov.nl.ca*
Government of Nova Scotia	*novascotia.ca*
Business Nova Scotia	*business.novascotia.ca*
Government of Saskatchewan	*gov.sk.ca*
Enterprise Saskatchewan	*enterprisesaskatchewan.ca*
Government of Nunavut	*gov.nu.ca*
Nunavut Development Corporation	*ndcorp.nu.ca*
Government of Yukon	*gov.yk.ca*
Yukon Economic Development	*economicdevelopment.gov.yk.ca*
Government of Northwest Territories	*gov.nt.ca*
Canada Business Northwest Territories	*bdic.ca/canada-business-nwt*

News Publications

Financial Times	*ft.com*
National Post	*nationalpost.com*
The Globe and Mail	*globeandmail.ca*
Toronto Star	*torontostar.com*
Postmedia Network	*canada.com*
Canadian Press	*cp.com*

Travel Information (including Visa, Safety, and Health Tips)

Canadian Department of Foreign Affairs and International Trade	*international.gc.ca*
Travel Reports and Warnings	*travel.gc.ca*
Travel Health	*travelhealth.gc.ca*
CBSA Travel Abroad	*cbsa-asfc.gc.ca/*
Canadian Automobile Association	*caa.ca*
Cross Border Services	*crossborderservices.org*
NEXUS Border Clearance	*cbsa-asfc.gc.ca/prog/nexus*
The Weather Network	*theweathernetwork.com*
Google Maps and Directions	*maps.google.com*
Lonely Planet	*lonelyplanet.com*
TripAdvisor—Travel Reviews	*tripadvisor.com*
Flyertalk for Frequent Flyers	*flyertalk.com*

Financial Planning

Advocis: The Financial Advisors Association of Canada	*advocis.ca*
Canadian Estate Planning Institute Inc.	*estateplanning.ca*
Canadian Retirement Planning Institute	*retirementplanning.ca*
Canadian Snowbird Institute Inc.	*snowbird.ca*
Investor Education Fund	*getsmarteraboutmoney.ca*
Financial Planning Standards Council	*fpsc.ca*
About Financial Planning	*financialplan.about.com*

Estate Planning

Canadian Estate Planning Institute	*estateplanning.ca*
Canadian Retirement Planning Institute Inc.	*retirementplanning.ca*
Canadian Snowbird Institute Inc.	*snowbird.ca*

Life and Health Insurance

Canadian Life and Health Insurance Association	*clhia.ca*
OmbudService for Life and Health Insurance	*olhi.ca*
Financial Consumer Agency of Canada	*fcac-acfc.gc.ca*

Family Business

Canadian Association of Family Enterprise	*cafecanada.ca*
BDO Family Business Resources	*bdo.ca/markets/familybusiness*
Sauder School of Business UBC Business Families Centre	*sauder.ubc.ca/bfc*
Dalhousie Centre for Family Business	*familybusiness.dal.ca*

(Continued)

Business Families Foundation	*businessfamilies.org*
Alberta Business Family Institute	*business.ualberta.ca*
International Business Families Centre	*expertise.hec.ca/businessfamilies*
Family Firm Institute	*ffi.org*

Small Business Information

Canadian Enterprise Institute	*smallbiz.ca*
About Small Business	*sbinfocanada.about.com*
CanadaOne	*canadaone.com*
Canadian Bankers Association	*cba.ca/en/consumer-information*
Canada Revenue—New Businesses	*cra-arc.gc.ca*
Canada Small Business	*ic.gc.ca*
US Small Business Administration	*sba.gov*
Small Office Home Office	*soho.ca*

Aboriginal Businesses

Aboriginal Affairs and Northern Development Canada	*aadnc-aandc.gc.ca*
Canadian Council for Aboriginal Business	*ccab.com*
Industry Council for Aboriginal Business	*icab.ca*
Aboriginal Canada Portal	*aboriginalcanada.gc.ca*

Women in Business

Canadian Women's Business Network	*cdnbizwomen.com*
Business Women in International Trade	*dfait-maeci.gc.ca/businesswomen*
Canadian Association of Women Executives and Entrepreneurs	*cawee.net*
RBC: Women Entrepreneurs	*royalbank.com/sme/women*
WE Connect Canada	*weconnectcanada.org*
Young Women in Business	*ywib.ca*
Centre for Women in Business	*centreforwomeninbusiness.ca*
Women's Enterprise Centre	*womensenterprise.ca*

Home Based Business

Home-Based Business	*canadabusiness.ca*
Home-Based Working Moms	*hbwmcanada.com*
Manual for Home Based Business	*smallbusinessbc.ca*
About Home Based Business	*sbinfocanada.about.com/od/homebusiness*

Franchise Business

BeTheBoss	*betheboss.ca*
Canadian Franchise Association	*cfa.ca*
Canadian Enterprise Institute	*smallbiz.ca*

Young Entrepreneurs

Advancing Canadian Entrepreneurship	*acecanada.ca*
Canadian Youth Business Foundation	*cybf.ca*
JCI Canada	*jcicanada.com*

Entrepreneurship and Management

Canadian Enterprise Institute	*smallbiz.ca*
Canadian Federation of Independent Business	*cfib.ca*
Business Development Bank of Canada	*bdc.ca*
Entrepreneurship Institute of Canada	*entinst.ca*
The Next 36	*thenext36.ca*
Canadian Innovation Centre	*innovationcentre.ca*
Kauffman Foundation	*entrepreneurship.org*
Licensing Industry Merchant's Association	*licensing.org*
Profit Guide	*profitguide.com*

Business Planning

Business Planning	*canadabusiness.ca*
Sample Business Plans	*bplans.com*

Statistics and Research

Statistics Canada	*statcan.gc.ca*
International Center of Shopping Centers	*icsc.org*
Moody's Reports	*moodys.com*
Competitive Intelligence Guide	*fuld.com*

Patent Information

Canadian Patents Database	*patents1.ic.gc.ca*
Canadian Intellectual Property Office	*cipo.ic.gc.ca*

Canadian and International Product Standards

GS1: Product Codes	*gs1ca.org*
Standards Council of Canada	*scc.ca*
Canadian General Standards Board	*tpsgc-pwgsc.gc.ca/ongc-cgsb*

Appendix D

Key Government and Other Contact Sources

INTRODUCTION

The cliché that "knowledge is power" is a fundamental truism when dealing with the issue of financing. Thorough knowledge will greatly assist you in reaching your financing goals. It will show you are resourceful, enhance the quality of your decision-making, increase your confidence and decrease your stress. Knowledge is a function of research and the utilization of available resources. There are many resources to assist your learning curve. The following is a summary of key contact sources to facilitate your search.

Many of the following federal government departments and agencies have local or regional offices. Check Google, or the *Blue Pages* of your telephone directory. In many cases, government offices have toll-free phone numbers or they will accept collect calls or phone you back at their expense. This is helpful if you are making general or specific enquiries or want information sent to you but there is no local office.

The phone numbers, as well as the names given here relating to government departments, change from time to time. If this happens, the correct number can be obtained from directory assistance. You can also phone the Government of Canada toll-free to obtain current information on federal government programs, services, and contact addresses and phone numbers. The number is listed in the *Blue Pages* of your directory under "Government of Canada." The current toll-free number is 1-800-0-CANADA. The central Government of Canada website is canada.gc.ca.

A. FEDERAL GOVERNMENT

Canada Business Network
1-888-576-4444
Web: canadabusiness.ca

The Canada Business Network is a collaborative network of federal government departments and agencies, provincial and territorial departments, and non-profit agencies. It has an extensive website and provides extensive information on financing, start-ups, resources and links, government requirements, business registration, and business planning. It has physical service centres in all provinces and territories.

Industry Canada
235 Queen Street
Ottawa, Ontario K1A 0H5
(613) 954-5031
Web: ic.gc.ca
info@ic.gc.ca

Contact for information on matters relating to federal incorporation, trademarks, trade names, copyright, patent, industrial design, bankruptcy, and consumer protection legislation, federal government assistance and incentive programs for small business, and publications. District offices in major cities throughout Canada. Industry Canada has a superb website.

Foreign Affairs and International Trade Canada
125 Sussex Drive
Ottawa, Ontario K1A 0G2
(613) 994-4000
Toll-free: 1-800-267-8376
Web: international.gc.ca

An excellent and comprehensive information source of all federal government programs, services, assistance, and financial support for the novice or experienced exporter. Also contact for information relating to imports.

Business Development Bank of Canada (BDC)
800 Victoria Square
5 Place Ville Marie Suite 400
Montréal, Québec H3B 5E7
Toll-free: 1-877-329-9232
Web: bdc.ca

A federal Crown corporation with an extensive website, applications, and publications for use and reference by entrepreneurs. Contact for information on small business management seminars, clinics, CASE counselling, financing, financial matchmaking, do-it-yourself kits, publications, and government programs (federal, provincial, and municipal).

Statistics Canada
150 Tunney's Pasture Driveway
Ottawa, Ontario K1A 0T6
(613) 951-8116
Toll-free: 1-800-263-1136
Web: statcan.gc.ca

Contact for information and statistics on geographic, demographic, and other population characteristics for small business planning and decision-making. Publications and computer data access are available. Offices in major cities throughout Canada.

Public Works and Government Services Canada
11 Laurier Street, Phase III, Place du Portage
Ottawa, Ontario K1A 0S5
Toll-free: 1-800-0-CANADA
Web: pwgsc.gc.ca

Contact for information on how to sell products or services to federal government and Crown corporations, statistical information, and publications. Public Works operates the computerized "open bidding service" system accessible by potential suppliers. Offices in major cities throughout Canada.

Service Canada
Canada Enquiry Centre
Ottawa ON K1A 0J9
Employer Contact Centre: 1-800-367-5693
Web: servicecanada.gc.ca

Contact for information on being an employer, as well as business start-up resources, micro-loans, self-employment initiatives, and entrepreneurship resources for aboriginal businesses and businesses owned by people with disabilities.

B. PROVINCIAL AND FEDERAL GOVERNMENTS—SMALL BUSINESS

For information on provincial and federal small business financial assistance and matchmaking programs, free counselling, seminars, publications, small business reference material, selling goods or services to provincial governments, and management assistance programs.

Refer to the Canada Business Network website (*canadabusiness.ca*). It will list all the provincial and territorial offices that are part of the Canada Business Network. Websites for all provinces' business and economic investment departments are available in Appendix C.

C. NETWORKING ORGANIZATIONS

Many major cities have venture or enterprise clubs or forums. The purpose of such groups is to provide networking, business opportunities, and education programs in an informal setting, designed for investors and those looking for investment.

Two major resources specifically for business networking groups are:

Business Networking International—Canada (*bnicanada.ca*) and Networking Today (*networkingtoday.ca*). Meetup.com also lists many business networking groups in cities and towns across Canada.

D. EDUCATIONAL ORGANIZATIONS

This organization provides research, consulting and education programs on a national basis, on all aspects of business development. This includes business start-up, expansion, diversification, purchase, sale, management, franchising and financing.

Canadian Enterprise Institute Inc.
#300-3665 Kingsway
Vancouver, British Columbia V5R 5W2
Web: smallbiz.ca

Glossary

Accountant   One who is skilled at keeping business records. Usually the name *accountant* refers to a highly trained professional, such as a *chartered accountant*, *certified general accountant*, or *certified management accountant*, rather than one who keeps books.

Accounting   The principles and practices for recording and analyzing financial information.

Accounts payable   The outstanding bills of a firm; money that a firm owes to its suppliers for goods and services purchased for the operation of the business. Accounts payable are included on the balance sheet under current liabilities.

Accounts receivable   The money that is owed to a firm by its customers for goods or services they have purchased from it. Accounts receivable are included on the balance sheet under current assets.

Accounts receivable aging   A scheduling of accounts receivable according to the length of time they have been outstanding. This shows which accounts are not paid in a timely manner and may reveal any difficulty in collecting long overdue receivables. This may also be an important indicator of mounting cash flow problems.

Accrual accounting   The accounting of expenses, such as wages, taxes, insurance and interest, prior to their payment, on a periodical basis.

Acid test ratio   Current cash and "near" cash assets (e.g., government bonds, current receivables, but excluding inventory) compared with current debts (bank loans, payables). The acid test shows how much and how quickly cash can be found if a company gets into trouble. Also referred to as *quick ratio*.

Advertising   Techniques and activities involved in conveying information about a product or service in order to persuade people to buy it.

Agent   Someone who legally represents someone else, and can act in that person's or company's name.

Aging   Measurement of the length of time in days that an account (payable or receivable) has been outstanding. Accounts are usually grouped into 30-, 60-, and 90-plus-days categories. Not only can aged accounts be compared with the original terms, but they can quickly show whether a situation is improving or deteriorating.

Amortization   A long-term expense calculated on a monthly or periodic cost basis.

Annual report   A report made at the end of a fiscal year, presenting the financial transactions of the past year and their results.

Appreciate   To increase in value.

Arbitration   The resolution of a dispute between two parties by an impartial third party. Used in commercial disputes when direct negotiations fail. The arbitrator's decision may or may not be final, depending on previous agreements. Each province has an Arbitration Act setting out procedures.

Arm's length   Refers to a transaction between two or more unrelated companies or individuals.

Arrears   Payments that are in arrears are overdue.

Articles of incorporation   A legal document filed with the province and/or federally that sets forth the purposes and/or regulations for a corporation. These papers must be approved by the province and/or federally before a corporation legally exists and is allowed to do business.

Assessment   The valuation of land and buildings, or any asset, for tax purposes.

Assets   The valuable resources or property rights owned by an individual or business enterprise. Tangible assets include cash, inventory, land, and buildings, and intangible assets include patents and goodwill.

Audit   A check of an organization's financial statements by someone whose independence of the organization and professional qualifications create faith in his or her judgment. An audit testifies to the honesty and accuracy of the organization's records. It is performed by professionally qualified accountants.

Authorized capital   The number of shares a corporation may sell and their par value.

Bad debts   Money owed to you that you can't collect.

Bad faith   An unspoken attitude on the part of one or more parties to a negotiation that there is no need to negotiate seriously or to live up to any agreement made.

Bait and switch   An illegal selling technique. A "special" is advertised, but "sold out" when the customer appears. The advertiser hopes the customer will buy something else.

Balance   The amount of money remaining in an account. The total of your money in the bank after accounting for all transactions (deposits and withdrawals) is the balance.

Balance sheet   An itemized statement which lists the total assets and total liabilities of a given business to portray the business's net worth at a given moment in time.

Bank of Canada   The agency of the federal government through which it implements and manages its money policies. It lends money only to the chartered banks and to a few recognized dealers in government securities.

Bank rate   The rate of interest charged by the Bank of Canada to chartered banks, thus generally passed on to all financial institutions. Referred to as the *prime rate*.

Bankruptcy   The financial and legal position of a person or corporation unable to pay debts. A legal bankrupt must transfer control of any remaining assets to a trustee in bankruptcy. Governed by the federal Bankruptcy and Insolvency Act.

Bargaining unit   Any group of employees recognized as an acceptable party to labour-management negotiation under federal or provincial labour law.

BDC   See Business Development Bank of Canada.

Board of directors   Representatives elected by the shareholders to direct the affairs of a company.

Bonded area   An area (warehouse, etc.) on the soil of any nation within which goods may be kept without payment of duty, sales, or excise tax. Taxes are payable only when the goods are moved from the bonded area.

Bonded carrier   A commercial shipper, such as a truck or airline, that may bring goods into the country with import requirements being met at the final destination rather than at a border crossing.

Book debts   A banking term for trade debts or receivables. Frequently assigned to the bank as security for an operating line of credit.

Book value   See Net worth.

Bookkeeping system   A way of organizing and recording all the financial transactions of a business to ensure that everything is properly accounted for.

Breakup value   The estimated value of a business after its operations are stopped and the assets are sold and the liabilities are paid off. Usually less than the "going concern" value.

Bridge loan   A short-term loan to cover the purchase or construction of an asset until permanent financing, frequently a previously arranged mortgage loan, can be placed against the completed asset.

Broker   Anyone who brings a potential buyer and a potential seller together in return for a fee or commission charged to one, the other, or both (e.g., business, franchise, insurance).

Budgeting   A basic tool of financial planning that shows revenues and/or expenses that are planned for the coming period.

Business   The production of goods or services for profit. Such activity can be carried out by an individual, a family, a partnership, or an incorporated company.

Business Development Bank of Canada (BDC)   A federal government Crown corporation providing a full range of services to encourage successful small and medium-sized business management in Canada.

Business expense   An expense of producing and/or selling a product, which can be deducted from gross income to arrive at net income for taxation purposes.

Business GNP   The segment of Gross National Product (the dollar value of total goods and services a country produces) produced by business corporations, excluding the segments produced by government and chartered banks.

Business plan   The overall map of what you intend to do in your business, how you intend to do it, and how you will measure the results.

Buy-sell agreement   See Shotgun agreement.

Caisse populaire   See Credit union.

Canada Revenue Agency (CRA)   Federal government department that collects personal and corporate income taxes, GST and HST taxes, employee deductions, etc.

Capital   The amount of money owner(s) have invested in the business (including profits that are not taken out). Also called *equity, owners' equity,* or *shareholders' equity.*

Capital asset   A possession, such as a machine, which can be used to make money and has a reasonably long life, usually several years.

Capital costs   Cost involved in the acquisition of fixed assets. Hence, they are "capitalized," showing up on the balance sheet and depreciated (expensed) over their useful life.

Capital equipment   Equipment which you use to manufacture a product, provide a service, or use to sell, store, and deliver merchandise. Such equipment will not be sold in the normal course of business, but will be used and worn out or be consumed over time as you do business.

Capital gain   Increase in the value of an asset that produces a profit if the asset is sold.

Capital requirement   The amount of money needed to establish a business.

Capital stock   The money invested in a business through founders' equity and shares bought by stockholders.

Cash-based accounting   The opposite of accrual accounting. Income and expenditures are recorded at the time they are received and paid. Not commonly used.

Cash discount   An incentive provided by vendors of merchandise and services to speed up collection of accounts receivable. The common discount is 2% on payment within 10 days versus the total payment in 30 days.

Cash flow   The flow of cash in and out of a company. Its timing is usually projected month by month to show the net cash requirement during each period.

Cash flow forecast   A schedule of expected cash receipts and disbursements (payments). It highlights expected shortages and surpluses and is essential to good cash management. Important also in negotiating loans.

Cash poor   A situation in which a profitable business runs out of cash, usually because it is growing at a rate that cannot be supported by profit alone.

Casualty insurance   Insurance other than accident and life insurance: fire, theft, general liability.

Certificate of origin   A certification from the country where the product was made.

Certified cheque   A cheque bearing a guarantee from the signer's bank that funds have been reserved to cover it.

Channel of distribution   The physical means of conveying goods from producer to wholesaler to retailer to final consumer. See Distribution network.

Chartered bank   In Canada, a bank created by its own Act of Parliament. The federal government defines and regulates its activities. Other financial institutions (such as credit unions and trust companies) may provide banking services, but only chartered banks may borrow from the Bank of Canada.

Chattel mortgage   A charge over goods or equipment of a movable nature as opposed to real estate. This document must be registered with the provincial government.

CIF (Cost, Insurance, Freight)   The exporter pays the cost of the goods, cargo insurance, and all transportation charges to the named point of destination.

Codicil   A change or addition to a will.

Collateral   Assets placed by a borrower as security on a loan.

Collection period   The average number of days it takes a company to collect receivables. See also Aging.

Collective agreement   A contract between employees (through their union) and employer that states the rights and obligations of both sides.

Commercial invoice   Prepared by the exporter or the forwarder. It is needed by the buyer to show ownership and arrange for payment to the exporter.

Common carrier   A shipping or transport business whose service is by law available to all customers at the same price.

Common law   The precedents established by previous court decisions, which have all the force of written statutes unless Parliament passes a law to the contrary.

Competition   A market in which rival sellers are trying to gain extra business at one another's expense and thus are forced both to be as efficient as possible in their service and to hold their prices down as much as possible.

Computer virus   A dangerous program that can delete or scramble data or shut down your computer.

Conditional sale   A sale made but not final until certain acts or events take place.

Consignment   Sale of goods through a third party, whereby ownership of the goods remains in the name of the supplier until the goods have been sold, at which time the seller is indebted to the supplier.

Consortium   A group of companies involved in a joint venture to the benefit of all. Controlled by law in domestic ventures, encouraged for export schemes.

Consular invoice   May be required by certain foreign governments to have tighter control over their imports. A consular invoice requires approval of that country's consulate in Canada and frequently involves a fee.

Consumer sovereignty   The free-market assumption that it is consumers who, through their power to choose how to spend their money, determine what shall be produced and in what quantity.

Contingencies   A reserve for unforeseen costs or circumstances. All financial projections should provide an allowance for contingencies.

Contract   An agreement regarding mutual responsibilities between two or more parties. In business law, a contract exists when there has been a meeting of minds, whether the contract is written or oral. However, a contract should be clear and in written form to protect your interests.

Controllable expenses   Those expenses that can be controlled or restrained by the business person. Some of the costs of doing business can be postponed or spread out over a longer period of time.

Copyright   The legal registration and ownership of the product of a writer, painter, singer, musician, choreographer, photographer, or other original creator. The owner of a copyright owns all rights to use the copyrighted material. Copyright laws are subject to international treaties.

Corporation   A business comprising one or more individuals treated by the law as a separate legal entity. Liability is limited to the assets of the corporation. See Limited company.

Co-signers   Joint signers of a loan agreement, pledging to meet the obligations in case of default. When you ask someone to co-sign a note, you are asking them to fully assume a debt with you if you can't pay it back. They guarantee the loan will be paid back, and the lender can take legal action against them if they refuse to pay.

Cost of goods sold   The direct costs of acquiring and/or producing an item for sale. Excludes any overhead or other indirect expenses.

Cost of merchandise inventory   Cost of purchase plus ordering/receiving costs plus holding costs.

Costing (or cost accounting)   The procedure concerned with attributing appropriate cost elements to an activity or a product.

Cost-plus agreement   An agreement or contract to provide goods or services at a price consisting of the total cost of providing it plus an agreed additional amount. The full sales price is thus unknown to both parties when the agreement is made.

Countertrade   A generic term encompassing export transactions in which a sale to the purchaser is conditional upon a reciprocal purchase or undertaking by the exporter. Forms of these may include counterpurchase, barter, compensation, or offsets.

Countervailing duties   Duties imposed to cancel the effect of subsidies by foreign governments on the prices of imported goods.

Credit   Credits and debits are used in bookkeeping to record transactions. To credit is to plan an entry on the right side of an account. A credit in an asset account makes it smaller. A credit in a liability account makes it larger. Another definition: The business owner's reputation for prompt payment of obligations, as in "a good credit rating."

Credit bureau   A business whose product is information, which it sells, on the credit transactions and relevant personal information of individual people, as well as companies.

Credit union   A cooperative bank. Takes deposits and makes loans in the usual way, but is owned by and run for the benefit of its members.

Creditor   One to whom money is owed.

Current assets   Cash or other items that will normally be turned into cash within 1 year (accounts receivable, inventory and short-term notes), and assets that will be used up in the operation of a firm within 1 year.

Current debt   A debt or liability payable within a given accounting cycle. Interest on loans and suppliers' bills are current debt.

Current liabilities   Amounts owed that will ordinarily be paid by a firm within 1 year. Such items include accounts payable, wages payable, taxes payable, the current portion of a long-term debt and interest, and dividends payable.

Current ratio   Current assets compared with current liabilities. Used as an indication of liquidity. It is the measure of the cash or near-cash available for the running of a business. See Working capital.

Customer profile   A description of the key characteristics of the people who buy your products or services.

Customs documentation charges   Special documents required by some countries to identify the origin and/or value of the shipment.

Customs invoice   Prepared by exporter or forwarder, this is a copy of the seller's commercial invoice, describing the goods bought. Customs invoices are used for import clearances and, occasionally, vary from commercial invoices.

Damages   Money that must be paid to someone who has suffered financial losses or personal injury.

Debenture   A formal legal document provided as security for a loan. It has the practical effect of being a "mortgage" on the corporation. Only a corporation can issue a debenture.

Debit   An entry on the left side of a balance sheet, indicating an asset or prepaid expense.

Debt   Money that must be paid back to someone else, sometimes with interest.

Debt capital   Capital invested in a company which does not belong to the company's owners. Usually consists of long-term loans and preferred shares.

Debt financing   Money provided to the business in the form of a loan. Normally repaid with interest.

Debt-to-equity ratio   The ratio of long-term debt to owner's equity. Measures overall profitability.

Debtor   One who owes money to someone else.

Deductible   1. In an insurance contract, the amount of the damage insured against that the insured person must pay. 2. In income tax, an amount that can be subtracted from total income in calculating taxable income.

Deductions at source   The salary deductions that the employer is required to take out of employees' paycheques for remittance to Canada Revenue Agency.

Deemed realization   A transfer of assets which is considered by Canada Revenue Agency a sale, though no cash or other consideration may be involved.

Default   Failure to pay a debt or meet an obligation in accord with the agreed terms.

Delegation   Assigning responsibility and authority to someone else; empowering someone else to do a job.

Demand   The combined desire, ability, and willingness on the part of consumers to buy goods or services. Demand is determined by income and by price, which is, in part, determined by supply.

Demand loan   A loan that must be repaid whenever the lender chooses.

Demand pull promotion   Advertising a product to its final consumers to create a demand that will encourage wholesalers and retailers to supply it.

Demand push promotion   Advertising a product to wholesalers and retailers to encourage them to sell it to the consumer market.

Demographics   Statistics based on population-related factors (e.g., density, gender, age, education, etc.).

Depreciation   A method of calculating and writing off the costs to a firm of fixed assets, such as machinery, buildings, trucks, and equipment. Investment in such fixed assets, which wear out or become obsolete over time, is a nominal expense of business.

Direct sales   Sales made directly to the consumer without any intermediary such as a retail merchant. Door-to-door or mail-order sales are direct sales.

Direct tax   A tax paid to the government by the person on whom it is levied. Personal and corporate income tax is a direct tax.

Discharged bankrupt   One who has been declared legally bankrupt, and thus has no liability to debtors.

Discounting   Lowering a price in return for buying a large volume of goods, paying promptly, etc.

Discretionary income   The amount of money people have available to spend after they have purchased the basic necessities of food, shelter, and clothing.

Disposable income   The amount of money people have available to spend after paying taxes.

Distribution network   The chain of businesses involved in getting goods from producers to consumers. Includes manufacturers, wholesalers, agents, jobbers, and retailers. Also known as *channels of distribution*.

Dividend   Money paid by a corporation to its shareholders. The shareholders' return on investment.

Dock and warehouse receipt   Domestic bill of lading needed for contracting with a trucking firm or railroad to ship goods from the exporter's loading dock to the destination port.

Domain name   The name assigned to an organization or individual that is linked to the Internet.

Double-entry bookkeeping   A method of keeping track of the financial state of an organization which works through recording every transaction twice when posting to a general ledger: as a debit (an asset given up) and as a balancing credit (an asset acquired). When the books are properly kept, they balance; total credits equal total debits.

Drop-shipper   An agent wholesaler who takes orders for a manufacturer. The manufacturer invoices the drop-shipper but delivers to the final customer.

Dumping   The selling of goods on the international market for less than their price on the domestic market.

Durable goods   Goods expected to last more than 3 years.

Earnings statement   A financial statement, usually part of an annual report, showing money taken in, its sources, and how it has been spent. The bottom line is the net profit.

Efficiency   The most effective use or allocation of resources to yield the maximum benefits. Efficiency in one sense—the effective use of resources—is often applied to individual firms in comparing how well they organize the productive process (labour, management, machinery, new technology) to achieve the lowest possible production cost for their products. In a broader sense, it refers to the way in which all of the various factors of production are used to achieve maximum output throughout the economy at the lowest cost, or to achieve a distribution of the output of society that results in the greatest degree of satisfaction.

Employment standards   The provincial or federal labour laws which establish minimum wages, hours, overtime pay, parental leave, paid vacation, etc.

Entrepreneur   An initiator or owner of a business enterprise who recognizes opportunities to introduce a new product or service, a new production process, or an improved organization, and who raises the necessary money, assembles the factors of production, and organizes an operation to exploit the opportunity or manage the enterprise. Another definition is simply a small business owner-operator.

Equity   The difference between the assets and liabilities of a company, often referred to as net worth.

Equity capital   The capital in a firm that represents ownership. The owners of the equity share capital in the firm and are entitled to all the assets and income of the firm after all the claims of creditors have been paid.

Equity capital/financing   All money invested in a business in exchange for ownership (shares). Venture capital is equity provided by outside investors (i.e., not the owner-manager). Equity does not have to be repaid on a specific date, and there are no interest charges (although dividends are normally paid from time to time).

Escrow The deferment of an obligation to pay or right of ownership for a stated time or until stated conditions are met.

Excise tax A tax on specific goods or service, such as alcohol or tobacco.

Executor A person appointed in a will to see that its terms are carried out.

Ex-factory The price of goods at the exporter's loading dock (i.e., the buyer owns the goods at that point and bears all the risks and costs for subsequent delivery).

Export declaration Prepared by exporter or freight forwarder for shipments valued in excess of a specified amount.

Export licence May be required for some export shipments (e.g., strategic goods).

Export management company (EMC) An independent firm which acts as the exclusive sales department for noncompeting manufacturers. There is usually a formal agreement to manage the manufacturer's exports. Some act as an agent for the manufacturer and, in such cases, are paid a commission on the export sales. Others operate on a buy–sell basis (i.e., EMCs buy from their manufacturers at a set price and resell to foreign customers).

Ex-works price This price normally includes export credit insurance, financing charges, and the profit margin. It excludes any costs that relate specifically to the home sales operation.

Factoring The selling of a company's accounts receivable at less than their full paper value. The purchasing firm is called a *factor*, and makes its profits by collecting at full value.

Failure Going out of business because the business cannot be run at a profit. Not always equivalent to bankruptcy.

Fair market value The price a commodity can command on a free market, one in which there is no compulsion on buyer or seller to accept or reject a certain amount.

FAQ A website document summarizing frequently asked questions.

FAS (free alongside) The price of goods to delivery on the docks during loading. The buyer becomes responsible for the goods once they are on the docks alongside the ship.

Feasibility study The study of a project to see if it is technically possible and commercially profitable.

FIFO (first in, first out) A method of valuing inventory in which the merchandise acquired earliest is assumed to be first and the stock acquired more recently is assumed to be still on hand in inventory (see also Last in, first out).

Financial analysis The interpretation of financial statements and knowing how to prepare and understand comparative and percentage analysis and the use of ratios and break-even analysis.

Financial planning The analysis of the future and the preparation of forecasts. Pro forma statements and cash forecasts are important tools for this planning and should be prepared before starting any new venture or expansion. See Pro forma.

Financial statements Documents that show your financial situation. Two major statements are needed to cover the information necessary to run a business and get financing (income statement and balance sheet).

Financing Obtaining money resources. Businesses usually have to obtain financing at some time, either to go into business or to expand operations.

Firefighting Dealing with the day-to-day problems and crises of running a business. Can get in the way of planning and control.

First refusal The right of a party to have the first option to buy shares or property. The right usually has a specific time period attached to it.

Fiscal year An accounting cycle of 12 months that could start at any point during a calendar year. The government uses April 1 to March 31.

Fixed assets Those things that a firm owns and uses in its business and that it keeps for more than 1 year (including machinery, equipment, fixtures, vehicles, etc.).

Fixed costs or expenses Those costs that don't vary from one period to the next and usually are not affected by the volume of business (e.g., rent, salaries, telephone, etc.).

Fixed interest Interest payments that remain constant despite changes in the profitability of the invested capital or in the official prime interest rate.

Floating rate A floating rate in currency exchange or interest set in response to changing external forces in the market, such as prime rate, risk, demand, etc. The vendor or creditor is not bound to any particular rate.

FOB (free on board) The prices of goods on board a vessel at a port of shipment. From this point all transportation, insurance, and other charges are payable by the customer. If you have quoted FOB prices, you are responsible for the shipment until it is loaded on board.

Forecast income statement A financial document that estimates income and expenses for a future period of time.

Foreclose To sell or cause to be sold a property when the owner fails to meet mortgage, tax, or other debt payment on it. Must be approved by the courts.

Form of business organization The legal structure that is established and registered at the appropriate level(s) of government in order to carry on a business. The three most common forms are proprietorships, partnerships, and limited companies.

Franchisee   The person (or firm) who has purchased a franchise and is responsible for managing the business.

Franchising   A way of starting a business whereby an already established firm supplies the product, trademark, techniques, materials, and expertise, and sets standards in exchange for purchase price and ongoing benefit.

Franchisor   The person (or firm) granting a franchise.

Fraudulent conveyance   An illegal transfer of ownership from one person to another for the purpose of cheating creditors.

Freeware   A computer program that has been created for free distribution and can be used with no remuneration paid to the program creator.

Freight forwarder   An export agent who moves goods through customs.

Fringe benefits   Benefits, other than salary, that employees get from their employer (e.g., medical, dental or group insurance plans, bonuses, etc.).

Frozen assets   An asset that cannot be used or sold (usually by court or government decision), pending outcome of a dispute over ownership or indebtedness.

Garnishee   To deduct money from a debtor's wages or receivables to pay a creditor. The creditor obtains a court order directing the person, company, or bank to make the deduction and pay it into court.

Going public   The action of a private corporation in offering its shares for general sale to the public through the stock exchange.

Good faith   An unspoken attitude of honesty and serious intention between two or more parties.

Goodwill   The value of customer lists, trade reputation, etc., which is assumed to go with a company and its name, particularly when trying to arrive at the sale price for the company. In accounting terms, it is the amount a purchaser pays over the book value.

Gross revenue   The total amount before deductions.

Gross profit   Profit after the deduction of all costs of material or merchandise, labour, and overhead, but before selling and administrative costs.

Guarantor   A person or company that guarantees to pay the financial obligations of a business or contract. Used frequently relating to leases or loans. Similar term include *indemnitor* or *indemnifier*.

Hardware   Computer machinery.

Hiring process   A systematic procedure for finding the right person for the right job. Involves five steps: job analysis, recruiting, selection, training, and analysis.

Holding company   A company which exists to buy and own a majority of shares in other companies, thus to control them.

Human resources   The people who work in the business of hiring staff.

Hypothecate   To pledge a security without transferring title to the creditor, as in a mortgage.

Income   Money coming in; the total revenue or sales.

Income-splitting   A tax-planning device frequently available to business owners in which total tax paid by the company and the shareholders can be minimized. Splitting can refer to splitting between salaries and dividends, husband and wife salaries, etc.

Income statement   A financial document that shows how much money (revenues) came in and how much money (expenses) was paid out. Subtracting the expenses from the revenues gives the net profit; all three are shown on the income statement. Also called *profit-and-loss statement.*

Indemnifier or Idemnitor.   See Guarantor.

Industry ratios   Financial ratios established by many companies in an industry in an attempt to establish a norm against which to measure and compare the effectiveness of a company's management.

Innovation   The use of a new idea, material, or technology by an industry to change either the goods or services produced or the way in which the goods or services are produced or distributed.

Intangible asset   Assets such as trade names or patent rights which are not physical objects or sums of money.

Intellectual property   Knowledge and information which can be legally owned, as defined by laws governing copyright, trademarks, patents, royalty obligations, etc.

International competitiveness   A term used to describe how competitive a country's products or services sold abroad are in relation to other countries' producers. Because of Canada's small market of 36 million people, the ability to sell competitively abroad is especially important to many small businesses.

Invention   The creation of a new technology or process, as opposed to its application.

Inventory   A list of assets being held for sale or use. If you are in a retail business, the stock you have on the shelves is inventory, but then so are your available supplies, goods received or stored, and any expendable items on hand.

Inventory control   The process of supervising inventory from the moment of purchase to the moment of sale. It includes knowledge of what goods are on hand, in what quantities, and at what cost.

Inventory turnover   The number of times the value of inventory at cost (either based on an average level or at year end) divides into the cost of goods sold in a year. Both are a measure of your efficiency and effectiveness in selling your product.

Investment   Pay-out of money for any purpose for which a profit is expected. One way to evaluate whether an investment in a business is worthwhile is to consider what you would receive on that same amount of money put into a low-risk investment, such as a bank account or Canada Savings Bonds.

Investment capital   The money set aside for starting a business. Usually this would cover such costs as inventory, equipment, preopening expenses, and leasehold improvements.

Jobber   A small wholesaler, one who buys from producers and large wholesalers and sells to small retailers.

Joint and several liability   A legal term meaning that each (general) partner is fully liable for all the debts of the partnership and his or her personal assets may be required to pay off debts incurred by another partner.

Joint venture   A business partnership formed for the sake of a specific project. Joint ventures may be undertaken by two or more companies or individuals, or by the government and private companies.

Key personnel insurance   Special insurance available on the lives of the principal active shareholders in a company. Can be used to fund buy–sell agreements, as well as to provide funds to continue the company in the event of one manager's death. The name the policies are registered in, as well as who pays the premiums, can have important tax implications. Therefore, obtain tax advice in advance.

Labour-intensive   An industry that requires large numbers of employees and relatively fewer capital funds and equipment.

Lead time   The time it normally takes to receive an order (i.e., from the moment the order is placed until the goods are received).

Lease   A contract in which the owner of a piece of property gives the exclusive use of it to someone else, in exchange for a stated sum of money, for the duration of a specific time.

Leasehold improvement   Renovation and other improvements made to the business premises. These become the property of the landlord.

Letter of credit (L/C)   An arrangement whereby an importer arranges with his or her bank to transfer the amount of the transaction to a Canadian bank for payment to the Canadian exporter. This amount is available to the exporter provided the requirements of the letter of credit are met. When the exporter presents the invoices and shipping documents to the bank, he or she receives immediate payment.

Letters patent   Charter or documents issued by the government making a new corporation legitimate.

Leverage   The ratio by which debt exceeds equity. A healthy ratio is usually not more than 2 to 1, ideally 1 to 1. Too high a leverage can make a company highly vulnerable in times of economic downturn or reduced profit.

Leveraged buy-out   To complete the financing in the purchase of a company, the purchaser borrows against its unused borrowing capacity (usually based on the company's market value of its assets rather than the book value).

Liabilities   All the debts of a business. Liabilities include short-term or current liabilities, such as accounts payable, income taxes due, the amount of long-term debt that must be paid within 12 months; and long-term liabilities, such as long-term debts and deferred income taxes. On a balance sheet, liabilities are subtracted from assets; what remains is the shareholder's equity or ownership in the business.

Lien   A charge placed over an asset by such parties as (1) the seller of that asset or (2) in the case of construction or repairs, by the person (contractor) who carries out the work. The lien holder may take possession until the asset/work is paid for in full. Liens must be registered under the various provincial laws in order to be protected and enforceable.

LIFO (last in, first out)   A method of valuing inventory in which the merchandise acquired latest is assumed to be used immediately and what was acquired earliest is assumed still to be in inventory. LIFO attempts to match the current cost of materials against current sales. Compared with First in, first out (see separate definition), the LIFO method usually results in the reporting of less income when prices are rising, and more income when prices are falling. Under LIFO, current purchase prices immediately affect operating results. It allows adjustment of selling prices to reflect current costs and therefore the maintenance of gross margins.

Limited company   A separate legal entity that is owned by shareholders for the purpose of carrying on business. Assets and liabilities of owners (shareholders) are separate from the company. Can be private or public, as well as provincial or federal. Also called *incorporated company* or *corporation*.

Limited liability   The legal protection accorded shareholders of an incorporated company, whereby the owner's financial liability is limited to the amount of his or her share ownership, except where he or she owes money to the company or has assumed additional liabilities (e.g., personally guaranteeing its debts).

Limited partnership   A legal partnership in which certain owners assume responsibility only up to the amount of their investment. Investors who put up money for a business venture without being directly involved in its operation are not held responsible for the debts of the other partners beyond the possible loss of the money they have invested.

Line of credit   A negotiated agreement with a bank, subject to periodic review, whereby the borrower is permitted to draw upon additional funds up to a specified limit at a certain rate of interest (e.g., prime rate plus 2%).

Lines of communication   The ways in which people pass information within an organization. Note that there are both formal and informal (grapevine) lines of communication in all organizations.

Liquid assets   Cash on hand and anything that can easily and quickly be turned into cash.

Liquidate   To settle a debt or to convert to cash.

Liquidity   A term used to describe the solvency of a business and which has special reference to the degree of readiness in which assets can be converted into cash without a loss. Also called *cash position*. If a firm's current assets cannot be converted into cash to meet current liabilities, the firm is said to be *illiquid*. A frequent measurement of liquidity is the quick or acid test ratio (see Acid test ratio).

Long-term liabilities   Debts that will not be paid off within 1 year.

Loss leader   An item sold at a loss in order to attract buyers who will then buy other items as well. The capacity of certain large retail chains such as supermarkets to sell at a loss for the sake of eventual profit gives them an advantage over small independent retailers.

Management style   The approach, attitude, and manner of giving orders, and directing and controlling others.

Market   The population sector that is most likely to purchase your product or service. The demand, actual or potential, for a product or service.

Market economy   An economy in which the setting of prices and allocating of resources are determined largely by the forces of supply and demand.

Market niche   The special advantage in the marketplace where a business positions itself as unique in its offering of products or services. Should be based on some competitive advantage (e.g., location, patent, intimate knowledge of area, etc.). Maximizing effectiveness of the niche requires identification of customers (target market), clear understanding of customer benefits, ability to communicate the benefits of the offering to the right customers, and an overall plan to coordinate efforts and measure results.

Market research The systematic gathering, recording, and analyzing of data relating to the marketing of goods and services.

Market segment A group of potential customers who are similar in some important way. Can be demographic, geographic, psychographic, or based on other consumer characteristics.

Market share The amount of a company's sales for a particular product as a percentage of total industry sales for that product.

Marketing All those activities involved in creating an interest or desire for your product or service.

Marketing board In Canada, a group given power by the government to regulate production, distribution, and prices of any one product.

Marketing mix The particular combination of design, price, distribution, and advertising strategies chosen to profit from a given product.

Marketing plan The marketing program that outlines what you want to accomplish (objectives) and how you propose to achieve these goals (strategy).

Marketing strategy An outline of methods to reach marketing goals. Marketing strategy starts with market research, in which consumer needs and attitudes and competitors' products are assessed, and continues through into advertising, promotion, distribution, and, where applicable, customer servicing and repair, packaging, and sales and distribution.

Markup The amount a vendor adds to the purchase price of a product to take into account the vendor's expenses plus profit. Not the same as net profit, since a small markup on a large quantity of goods sold may produce more profit than a large markup on a small quantity of goods sold.

Maximum–minimum control A method for deciding how much to buy and when to buy based on the maximum that can be on hand and the minimum that must always be available.

Medium-term financing Loans or other credit on which the principal does not have to be repaid for 3 to 5 years.

Merchandise Goods bought and sold in a business. Merchandise or stock is a part of inventory.

Merchant bank A bank that exists to finance and invest in business ventures and does not deal with the general public.

Middle management Those managers between first-line supervisors (foremen, etc.) and the executives at the top. Middle management includes the specialized support staff who assist executives in analyzing decisions and getting the job done.

Minimum turnover method   A technique for deciding on how much to buy based on maintaining a certain level of inventory turnover for a certain item.

Misleading advertising   Advertising that lies, implicitly or explicitly, about the price, quality, or use of a product. Illegal.

Money market   The sources of short-term credit and securities. An organized, distinct industry, whose members are banks and other financial institutions, governments, and the Bank of Canada.

Money supply   The sum of money available for investment within an entire economy at any one time.

Monopoly   The domination of the entire market by a product or service from one supplier.

Near bank   A credit union, caisse populaire, or trust company. These institutions may not borrow from the Bank of Canada, although they perform the usual financial services of all banks.

Negative covenant   An undertaking not to do certain things. It is frequently argued that negative covenants are preferable to positive covenants, because it is easier to establish whether something which was not to have been done has in fact been done, rather than vice versa. The breaking of a covenant usually constitutes a default, which in turn gives rise to certain specified remedies which can be taken by the security holder.

Negotiating   The act of reaching an agreement through bargaining.

Net   The amount that is left of a gross amount after deduction of expenses or debts. For example, the net working capital is the total current assets after deductions of the total current liabilities.

Net lease   Signifies a property lease where a lessee/tenant is responsible for all costs such as taxes, heat, light, power, insurance, and maintenance.

Net worth   The value of a business represented by the excess of the total assets over the total amounts owing to outside creditors (total liabilities) at a given moment in time. Also referred to as book value. Also, the net worth of an individual as determined by deducting the amount of all personal liabilities from the total value of personal assets.

Objectives   Goals or targets. The basic essential starting point for any planning process.

Ocean (or airway) bill of lading   Prepared by the carrier or freight forwarder as a contract between the owner of the goods and the carrier. It is needed by the buyer in order to take possession of the goods.

Open-to-buy method   A way of deciding how much to order based on the difference between the total required and the amount presently on hand and on order.

Operating costs Expenditures arising out of current business activities. In other words, your operating costs for any period of time are what it costs you to do business—the salaries, electricity, rental, deliveries, etc., that are involved in performing the business dealings.

Operating ratios See Industry ratios.

Option The right to buy a property, business, or other asset or right within a certain time. The potential buyer must pay for this right, but the owner of the property may not sell to anyone else until the agreed-upon time has passed.

Organization structure The titles and responsibilities of staff showing the relations between people and jobs. A chart that ranks the hierarchy of each person within the business and indicates their major responsibility or department and position.

Overdraft A debt to the bank incurred by withdrawing more money from an account than it holds.

Overhead Expenses such as rent, heat, property tax, etc. (e.g., monthly, fixed, or variable) expended to keep a business open.

Owner-manager One who owns and operates a business.

Par value The stated face value of a share shown on the certificate. It rarely has any relationship to the traded or book value of the stock. *Non par value stock* (NPV) is stock for which there is no stated face value.

Pareto's law The law of the vital few and the trivial many; e.g., 20% of items account for 80% of sales and profits. Based on this, key inventory items can be isolated for more careful control.

Pari passu Side by side at an equal rate or in equal installments or, in terms of security, ranking equally.

Partnership A legal business relationship of two or more people or companies who share responsibilities, resources, profits, and liabilities. An agreement in writing is essential, detailing the nature of the relationship. Each province has a Partnership Act which governs this type of business structure.

Patent The legal right to ownership of an invention issued in Canada under the Patent Act. By granting this right to inventors, society hopes to encourage invention and innovation, and thus to benefit from increased economic efficiency and growth. The benefit to the inventor is that, for a limited period, the inventor can charge a royalty for the use and application of the invention or sell such rights to another person.

Payables Trade or other liabilities that are due. One of the basic records kept by a bookkeeper is accounts payable.

Penetration pricing Deliberately setting the selling price of a new item low, so that it will be able to enter a market dominated by better-known brands.

Perpetual inventory control A method of keeping up-to-date records on all inventory items by recording every time an item enters or leaves inventory.

Personnel management All that's involved in developing and keeping productive staff. Among other things, this includes: knowing what your organization structure is so that job descriptions show people how they fit in; knowing who to look for and where to find them; knowing how to select, train, and evaluate staff; knowing how to keep staff satisfied (pay scales, benefits, working conditions, etc.) and motivated (challenging jobs, increasing responsibility, personal relations, etc.); and, finally, keeping clear records to satisfy both internal management needs and government filing requirements.

Physical inventory control (periodic) A physical count of all stock to record what is on hand.

Piecework Money paid based on the quantity of work produced, rather than by the hours worked.

Port charges Charges for unloading or storing goods and for dock space before loading on a ship.

Posting The act of making an entry in an account. Literally, post means to give a position to something, so when you post figures in a ledger, you are assigning them their right position in the firm's account books.

Preferred creditor A creditor who must be paid after secured creditors and before unsecured creditors in the event of a business failure under the Bankruptcy and Insolvency Act. Usually certain provincial and federal government departments.

Price fixing Collusion among competitive businesses to keep prices up. Illegal.

Price skimming Charging a high price for a new product for which there is no competition, to take advantage of a demand which cannot be met elsewhere.

Price spread The difference between selling price and cost of production.

Pricing Setting the selling price. One of the most difficult jobs in business is selecting the right price. You have to consider how much profit you need, what your competition is charging, and how much your customers are willing to pay.

Prime rate The interest charged by chartered banks on corporate loans. Ultimately determined through the Bank of Canada.

Principal Property or capital assets, as opposed to income; also, one who is directly concerned in a business enterprise.

Product differentiation   Details of design, promotion, and pricing planned to distinguish competing products in the minds of consumers.

Product life cycle   The curve of profit in relation to costs and sales described by every product in the time between entering and leaving the market.

Production-oriented   The focus is on what can be produced rather than on what can be sold.

Productivity   The output of goods and services from the effective use of various inputs, such as skilled workers, capital equipment, managerial know-how, technological innovation, and entrepreneurial activity.

Pro forma   A projection or estimate of what may result in the future from actions in the present. A pro forma financial statement is one that shows how the actual operations of the business will turn out if certain assumptions are realized.

Profit   The excess of the selling price over all costs and expenses incurred in making the sale. Gross profit is the profit before corporate income taxes. Net profit is the final profit of the firm after all deductions have been made.

Profit-and-loss statement   Listing of revenue and expenses showing the profit (or loss) for a certain period of time. Also called an *income statement*.

Profit margin   The difference between your selling price and your costs. Many factors affect profit margin both inside and outside the business.

Promotion   All messages about a business that are communicated to potential customers. Promotion tools or vehicles include advertising, personal selling, sales promotions, and publicity (public relations).

Promotion message   What you tell people about how your business and products or services can satisfy their needs.

Promotion mix   The combination of types of advertising, advertising media, and means of selling chosen for a particular product.

Proprietorship   Sole ownership of a business. Personal and business assets and liabilities are not considered separate legal entities. Also called *sole proprietorship*.

Public relations   The various activities of an organization that are undertaken to make the organization known to its public in a favourable fashion.

Publicity   Any news or activity that makes a product or service and the company making or selling it generally known. Usually free of cost or of minimal cost.

Purchasing and inventory control   The systems involved in knowing what to buy, when and how much to buy, and controlling stocks once they are received. The overall goal is to provide the right goods at minimum cost.

Purchasing system   The policies and procedures for getting the necessary goods into the business. Includes deciding on the kind of goods and their assortment, choosing suppliers, processing and follow-up on orders (when to order and how much), and keeping up to date with market changes.

Quick ratio   See Acid test ratio.

Rack jobber   A wholesaler who sells discounted goods on consignment to a retailer.

Recapture   A case where the amount of sale of an item is greater than the depreciated amount of that item, and the difference is taken back into income after the sale of the asset.

Receivership   The control of a business and its assets by a receiver (usually a chartered accountant). This person is appointed by the creditor under the term of a debenture and remains in control until the debts are paid or the business and/or assets are sold.

Retained earnings   The accumulated earnings after taxes. Retained earnings can in fact be a negative figure, if a company has net accumulated losses.

Return on investment (ROI)   The determination of the profit to be accrued from a capital investment. Where the investment risk is high, the expected profit from the investment (ROI) should also be high, in relation to other forms of investment, such as Canada Savings Bonds, real estate, or savings accounts. The higher the risk, the higher the return you would expect.

Sale and leaseback   A process by which a firm sells assets, such as land, buildings, or equipment to another firm (or institution) and leases the assets back for a specific period of time.

Secured   Protected or guaranteed. A secured loan makes the lender better protected, by having the debtor place something of value as collateral as a guarantee of repayment (e.g., a chattel mortgage, debenture, etc).

Shotgun agreement   An agreement between partners that gives either party the right to offer to buy all of the other's shares in the event of a disagreement. The offer states a price, which can be accepted or rejected. If the other party refuses the bid, he or she must buy the offerer's shares at the offerer's offering price.

Small business   A firm with 20 or fewer employees. This is the definition used in Statistics Canada's monthly employment survey. According to the federal or various provincial governments, a small business is any manufacturing firm with fewer than 100 employees or, in any other sector, a firm with fewer than 50 employees. Using either definition, small business accounts for 80% to 90% of all businesses in Canada.

Spread   Expression used among financial sources to describe the difference between the interest rate they pay on money and the interest rate received (e.g., cost is 12%, rate charged is 14%, spread is 2%).

Subject clauses   Conditions that have to be met or escape options in an offer to purchase and sell, allowing the potential buyer or seller to back out if the deal starts to look unsatisfactory.

Subordinated debt   An obligation in which one lender has agreed in writing to rank behind another in claiming against an asset. The lender will receive his or her capital back only after the other has been fully paid out. A bank will often insist that shareholder loans be subordinated to the obligations to the bank. This is also known as *subrogation*.

Supervising   Directing, coordinating, motivating, and controlling staff in getting things done.

Supplier discounts   Price reductions given by suppliers based on the kind of customer (trade discounts) or the size of orders (quantity discounts) or to encourage prompt payment (cash discount).

T-account   The basic device of double-entry bookkeeping and modern accounting. All debits are listed on one side, all credits on the other. They equal one another if the books are properly kept.

Tangible   Something that is real. Literally, tangible means that the thing is such that you can touch it, but the meaning for business is something that can be seen and evaluated. Does not therefore include goodwill.

Target market   The specific individuals, distinguished by socioeconomic, demographic, and/or interest characteristics, who are the most likely potential customers for the goods and/or services of a business.

Tariffs   Foreign government taxes levied on exports.

Term (debt) loan   A loan, generally obtained from a financial institution, which matures within a specified period beyond 1 year.

Terms of sale   The conditions concerning payment for a purchase.

Trade credit   The credit terms offered by suppliers (no interest is charged until after the due date).

Trademark   A name, symbol, or other mark that identifies a product to customers and is legally owned by its manufacturer or inventor.

Trading houses   Companies specializing in the exporting, importing, and third-country trading in goods and services produced by others and which provide related export services. They may act on a merchant or agent basis.

Trend analysis   Analysis of a business's financial ratios over a period of time, in order to determine whether its financial situation has improved or deteriorated.

Trial balance   The result of adding all credits and all debits to see if the two sums are equal. A device used to check the accuracy of a company's books.

Turnkey operation   A project such as setting up a business or an office in which all work is done by a contractor and handed over in working order to the owner.

Turnover   The number of times a year that a product is sold and reordered.

Unlimited liability   Fully responsible for all the debts of the business (i.e., personal assets can be required to pay off the business debt).

Variable costs   Those costs that vary depending on the volume of production or business activity, as opposed to fixed costs, which do not vary.

Venture capital   Investment capital made available to new businesses. More expensive than bank loans, since the higher risk requires higher rates of return.

Visual inventory control   Personal examination of stocks to verify that the proper items and amounts are on hand.

Warranty   A promise to the buyer that the product sold is of good quality and that, if not, certain repairs and replacements will be made.

Wholesale business   Selling for resale. Wholesalers distribute manufacturers' products to retailers and to other distributors in different regions. Usually, they are not permitted to sell to the end-user.

Winding up   The legal procedures of closing down a limited company.

Word-of-mouth advertising   The positive things that people tell their friends or associates about a product or a business. The most powerful type of promotion, because it is accompanied by a credible testimonial. Best stimulated by high satisfaction.

Work environment   All those factors that are part of the workplace (e.g., noise, space, lighting, heat, safety, etc.).

Working capital   The funds available for carrying on day-to-day operation of a business after an allowance is made for bills that have to be paid within the year. Working capital is the excess after deduction of the current liabilities from the current assets of a firm, and indicates a company's ability to pay its short-term debts.

Write down   To reduce the value of an asset, old inventory for instance, in the company's books to reflect the real loss in value on the market.

Write-off   The removal of a worthless asset from a company's books.

Zone pricing   Setting the price of an item according to where it is sold, to allow for extra shipping charges or other costs that vary from region to region.

About the Authors

Douglas Gray, LL.B., is Canada's authority on small business law and entrepreneurial development. He has given seminars for more than 250,000 people in Canada and throughout the world in his various areas of expertise – small business, real estate, personal finance, and retirement planning. He is frequently interviewed by the media throughout Canada as an expert on entrepreneurship. Over 2,000 interviews have been given. He has founded 12 successful businesses.

Formerly a practicing business and real estate lawyer in Vancouver, he morphed into a consultant, speaker, and author of 25 bestselling books, In addition, he has written numerous articles on a variety of topics, and has been a nationally syndicated real estate columnist. Douglas is the founder and president of the Canadian Enterprise Institute Inc. in Vancouver. His website is: smallbiz.ca.

Diana Gray is an author, entrepreneur and business centre consultant. Diana opened her first business centre in 1981 in Vancouver. Since that time she has started two additional business centres in Vancouver.

In addition, as a business centre consultant, Diana established 4 centres from the business plan stage through to initial operations. This included developing and implementing all telecommunications and computer systems, producing operational manuals, and hiring and training the initial staff from receptionist to manager.

Diana coauthored *Home Inc.: The Canadian Home-Based Business Guide*. She has also written numerous articles on small business for various small business organizations and publications.

She is a founding member of the Elite Group of Business Centres, and past-president of the Collingwood Business Improvement Association, and the Association of Women Business Owners.

Reader Input, Seminars, and Consulting Services

If you have thoughts or candid suggestions that you believe would be helpful for future editions of this book, are interested in having a seminar or presentation given to your group or association, or would like further information on consulting services, please contact the Institute at smallbiz.ca.

Index

Praise from Book Reviewers

(All books authored or co-authored by Douglas Gray)

THE COMPLETE CANADIAN SMALL BUSINESS GUIDE

(WITH DIANA GRAY)

"This guide is truly a gold mine ... an admirable job ... taps into the author's expertise."

— *Profit Magazine*

"I can say with absolute certainty that this guide is the best .... It is well organized, written in an informative way and at the right level of detail.... The samples, checklists, glossary and sources of information can best be described as exemplary. Just a great piece of work ... recommended to everyone I deal with."

— *Steve Guerin,*
Former Project Manager,
Office of Research and Innovation,
Ryerson Polytechnic University, Toronto

"The ultimate in small-biz aid – if I ever quit my day job, this is one of the first books I'd rush out and buy"

— *Linda A. Fox, The Toronto Sun*

"Excellent ... geared especially to Canadians, unlike most small business guides"

— *Financial Times*

"If you're thinking of launching your own business, or if you want to pick up invaluable tips on running the one you already own, this Canadian book on small business is a terrific resource tool."

— *This Week in Business, Montreal*

"Contains a wealth of information to help you maximize your chances of success .... If you can't be bothered reading an excellent book like this, you probably shouldn't bother going into business for yourself."

— *Mike Grenby,*
National Syndicated Financial Columnist

"The strength of the book is its attention to the practical needs of small business ... provides a broad overview of 18 major topic areas ... full of numerous 'street-smart' tips on how to successfully open and operate a business ... contains a plethora of 'how-to' features and useful resource information."

— *Ottawa Citizen*

"Written in an easy-to-read, matter-of-fact manner which helps take much of the mystique out of starting and developing a business ... provides a signpost guide through the key areas of small business development ... a wealth of practical information ... this book is a must for every Economic Development Officer's library"

— *Christopher Bryant,*
Past Director,
Economic Development Program,
University of Waterloo

"The most informative and comprehensive guide on this subject matter."

— *The Toronto Star*

HOME INC: THE CANADIAN HOME-BASED BUSINESS GUIDE
(WITH DIANA GRAY)

"Should be required reading for all potential home-basers ... authoritative, current and comprehensive."

— *Edmonton Journal*

"An absolute necessity for your bookshelf ... crammed with useful information."

— *Victoria Times-Colonist*

THE COMPLETE CANADIAN FRANCHISE GUIDE
(WITH NORM FRIEND)

"....This book tells it like it is, a realistic look at franchising and what it takes to be successful. The information provided is clear, concise, practical, and easy to apply ..."

— *Richard B. Cunningham,*
President, Canadian Franchise Association and Co-Chair,
World Franchise Council

"Down to earth, comprehensive, easy to read and packed with practical information. A superb guide to buying a franchise. Invaluable samples and checklists. Highly recommended."

— *Terry and Fran Banting, Franchisees*

RAISING MONEY: THE CANADIAN GUIDE TO SUCCESSFUL BUSINESS FINANCING
(WITH BRIAN NATTRASS)

"..... The authors have combined their formidable talents to produce what may be the definitive work on raising money in the Canadian marketplace . . . . written in plain language, with a user-friendly question and answer format, and contains invaluable checklists, appendices, and information sources . . . . a definite keeper for potential and practicing entrepreneurs alike . . ."

— *Canadian Business Franchise*

MAKING MONEY IN REAL ESTATE

"Gray delivers the goods. It is all-Canadian, and not a retread book full of tips that are worthless north of the U.S. border. It's chock-full of practical streetsmart strategies and advice, pitfalls to avoid, samples, what-to-look-out-for, checklists and information . . . . The information that Gray passes along is invaluable, thorough and eminently usable . . . the book has an easy style to it that is almost conversational."

— *Business in Vancouver*

"The prolific output of real estate and financial books establishes Gray as a Canadian voice . . . provides consumer insights into securing the best deal and avoiding the pitfalls . . . Gray's legal background has given him valuable insights."

— *Edmonton Journal*

"Author knows what he is talking about . . . full of street-smarts and practical advice."

— *Halifax Chronicle-Herald*

"Thorough and wide-ranging . . . bursts with practical tips and explanations"

— *Vancouver Sun*

"Detailed, very informative, scrupulously objective as well as being written in a style that is refreshingly clear of jargon . . . this one is a 'must' buy"

— *B.C. Business*